Making Europe

VOLUME I: TO 1790

Making Europe

PEOPLE, POLITICS, AND CULTURE

Frank L. Kidner
San Francisco State University

Maria Bucur
Indiana University

Ralph Mathisen
University of Illinois at Urbana-Champaign

Sally McKee
University of California, Davis

Theodore R. Weeks
Southern Illinois University, Carbondale

Houghton Mifflin Company
Boston   New York

Publisher: *Suzanne Jeans*
Senior Sponsoring Editor: *Nancy Blaine*
Senior Marketing Manager: *Katherine Bates*
Senior Developmental Editor: *Jeffrey Greene*
Senior Project Editor: *Jane Lee*
Art and Design Manager: *Jill Haber*
Cover Design Director: *Tony Saizon*
Senior Photo Editor: *Jennifer Meyer Dare*
Composition Buyer: *Chuck Dutton*
New Title Project Manager: *James Lonergan*
Editorial Associate: *Adrienne Zicht*
Marketing Associate: *Lauren Bussard*
Editorial Assistant: *Anne Finley*

Cover image: *Empress Theodora*, detail from crown of Byzantine Emperor Constantine IX Momomachos, 11th century. Hungarian National Museum, Budapest, Hungary/Erich Lessing/Art Resource, NY

Printed in the U.S.A.

Library of Congress Catalog Number: 2007938069

ISBN 13: 978-0-618-00480-5
ISBN 10: 0-618-00480-7

2 3 4 5 6 7 8 9-CRK-11 10 09 08

Brief Contents

Contents

Maps

Features

Echo

Preface

For years we five professors from across the country have taught Western Civilization courses without the textbook we really wanted to have—a textbook with a coherent strategy for helping students to study and learn. In 1999 we commenced to develop such a text. This book is the result.

The five of us bring to this book a variety of backgrounds, interests, and historical approaches, as well as a combined total of nearly one hundred years of teaching history. Two of us completed graduate degrees in literature before turning to history. We have all studied, worked, or lived on three continents; we are all American citizens, but not all of us were born in the United States. Although we come from different parts of the country and have different historical specializations, all of us teach in large state university systems. We have a strong commitment to the kinds of students who enroll in our schools and in community colleges—young people and nontraditional students from richly diverse cultural and ethnic backgrounds who are enthusiastic and prepared to work but have little knowledge of history and few formal skills in historical analysis. We were gratified to be developing a new kind of textbook that met their needs.

We conceived of a textbook that would be lively and absolutely up-to-date but did not presume a great deal of prior knowledge of western civilization. We also wanted to include new types of learning aids that were fully integrated into the text itself. Our greatest hope is that students who use this book will come to understand how the West has developed and, at the same time, to see the importance of the past for the present. In other words, we want to help them value the past as well as understand it and thus to think historically.

Approaches and Themes

This textbook introduces the cultural unit we call "the West" from its beginnings in the ancient Near East to the present. It is focused around five themes: politics, religion, social history, biography and personality, and individual and collective identity.

Politics: Our book's first theme centers on western politics, states, and the state system from the emergence of civilization in Mesopotamia and Egypt down to our own century. Politics provides the underlying chronological backbone of the text. Our experience has taught us that a politically centered chronology is the most effective way to help inexperienced students get a sense of what came before and what came after and why. Political chronology helps them perceive trends and recognize the forces for historical continuity and change.

If there are sensible reasons for organizing the text around a political chronology, there are pitfalls as well. The chief one is the disaffection many students may have felt in the past with a history that seems little more than a list of persons, reigns, and wars ("Kings and Things") needing to be memorized. To avoid this pitfall we have adopted an approach that centers on dynamic exchanges between states and political elites on the one hand and citizens or subjects on the other. In this textbook students will read and think about the ways taxation, the need for armies, and judicial protection affect ordinary people and vice versa—how the marginal and unrepresented affect the politically powerful. Our approach focuses both on what states and their political elites want from the people who live in them and on what benefits they provide to those people. In turn, we also consider what ordinary people do or do not want from the state, and what kinds of people benefit and do not benefit from the state's policies. When relevant, we also treat the state's lack of impact.

Religion: Our second theme takes up the history of western religion. We have aimed for an expansive treatment of religious activity that includes its institutions and beliefs but is not confined to them. Our textbook ranges widely over issues of polytheism, monotheism, civic religion, philosophically inspired religion, normative religion, orthodoxy and heresy, popular practices, ultimate spiritual values, and systematically articulated agnosticism or atheism. Since from beginning to end we emphasize religious issues, this book is set apart from most Western Civilization texts that treat religious matters fairly consistently up through the sixteenth century but then drop them.

Our distinctive post–1600 emphasis on religion arises from our sense that religious beliefs, values, and affiliations have continued to play a central role in European life up to and including the twenty-first century. Although in part compartmentalized or privatized in the last several centuries as states pursued various secularizing agendas, religious sensibilities still have had considerable impact on economic behavior, social values, and political action, while simultaneously adjusting to or resisting changes in other aspects of life. In addition, of course, they regularly influenced European activity in colonies and empires.

In our treatment of religion we do not focus simply on the dominant religion of any time or place. Judaism, for example, is discussed throughout the text, while Islam, introduced in Chapter 8, is discussed again in connection with such issues as the Moriscos of Spain, the Habsburg re-conquest of Hungary, tension in Russian Central Asia and the Balkans before World War I, Soviet campaigns against religion, the arrival of Muslim immigrants in post–World War II Europe, and the dissolution of Yugoslavia. In addition, an emphasis on religious pluralism in European life leads to discussions of the variety of subcultures found in the West, many of which believe that their religious and ethnic identity is integral to their other values and practices. Indeed, our belief that religion continues to play an important role in modern European history rests in large part on the abundant evidence showing it to be a core component of life for subcultures within the larger western context. Catholic and Protestant Irish, Protestant northern Germans and Catholic southern Germans, Orthodox Russians, and Bosnian Muslims stand as examples of communities whose values and actions have been significantly shaped by ongoing religious allegiances and whose interactions with those practicing other religions have had lasting repercussions. Our intention is to present the religious past of the West in all its complex, multifold voices to students who are more and more self-consciously aware of racial, cultural, and ethnic diversity in their own world.

We also believe that attention to religion reflects the current public debate over values, using students' experience of this contested territory to stimulate their interest. Their awareness of current values-based programs can serve as a springboard for a study of the past. Does one choose aggression, persuasion, or passive resistance and nonaggression?

Social History: The theme of social history is integrated into the text as consideration is given to the way politics and religion affect people and societies. Discussions of daily lives and family structures are illuminated through occasional spotlights on the experience of a single, typical individual. We also pay close attention to issues of gender norms and roles in the past, drawing on the work of a generation of historians concerned with the history of ordinary men, women, and children. We see many possibilities for engaging the interest of students in this approach. We hope our book will stimulate productive class discussions of what it meant to live as a woman or a (male) citizen in the Athenian city-state, as a peasant or a landlord in the relatively stateless world of the early Western Middle Ages, as a man or woman during the French Revolution, and as a soldier or nurse in the trenches of World War I.

Biography and Personality: To give focus and immediacy to the themes we emphasize, we have chosen to highlight the biographies of important or representative figures in the past and, when possible, to give students a sense of their personalities. We want key figures to live for students through their choices and actions and pronouncements. Biography and personality are the focus of chapter openings and are integrated into the chapter narratives. Portraits of cities occasionally stand in for biographies by providing a picture of the places and spaces that have been important in a particular era or have continuing significance across centuries.

Identity: An emphasis on individual and collective identity is another distinctive feature of our book. By addressing matters of identity for each era, we believe that we can help students see themselves in—or as against—the experiences of those who preceded them. To this end, the relationship between the individual and the group is examined as well as changing categories of identity, such as religion, class, gender, ethnicity, nationality, citizenship, occupation or profession, generation, and race. In a real sense, this emphasis flows from the preceding four themes. It means that the political narrative is personalized, that history is not only an account of states, institutions, and policies, but also of people.

The West and the World

In addition to emphasizing the themes outlined above, we have adopted a view about the West that shapes this volume. It derives from our rejection of the tendency to treat the West as a monolithic entity or to imply that the West is "really" western Europe after 500 and, after 1500, specifically northwestern Europe. We define the West more broadly. Throughout the book, students remain informed about developments in eastern Europe, western Asia, and Africa. We show that, far from being homogeneous, the West represents a diversity of cultures. By taking this approach we hope to be able to engage students in a way that will lead them to understanding the causes, effects, and significance of the cultural diversity that exists in the modern world.

We also address the issue of cultural diversity by looking at the impact of the non-western world on the West from antiquity to the present. We discuss both western knowledge and western fantasies about non-western peoples, the actual contact or lack of contact with non-western societies, and the growing global impact of Europe and Europeans during the last five hundred years. The emphasis is always on the West—on how the West did or did not make contact with other societies and, in the case of contacts, on their consequences for everyone involved—but the effect is to place the West in its larger global context as one of humanity's many cultural units.

Pedagogy and Features

One of the most common questions our students ask is: "What's important?" This textbook aims to help them answer that question for themselves. We have found that students can profit from a text that takes less for granted, provides a consistent and clear structure for each chapter, and incorporates primary documents. For both teachers and students, "Western Civ" is often the most difficult history course in the curriculum. With this textbook, we hope to change its reputation. We have developed a strong pedagogy realized through a series of innovative features that will assist students in understanding the book's content and help them master it. We also kept instructors in mind, because we believe that carefully constructed chapters that convey basic information are the best support for teaching. Instructors may then build on the text or modify it to meet specific needs.

Chapter Opening Feature: "Choice": Each chapter opens with an account of an individual making a crucial choice that mattered, that had important consequences, and that can be used to introduce the chapter's central concerns. Our intention in this feature is to foreground human agency, to spark the interest of students, and to guide them on into the chapter. Thus, Chapter 5, which introduces students to the rise of Rome, opens with Spartacus' revolt in 73 B.C.E. to help them understand the role of slavery in Roman political and social history. Chapter 22, which discusses the "triumph" of the nation-state in the late nineteenth century, opens with an account of Theodor Herzl's endorsement of Zionism as a way to discuss the impact of nationalist ideology and to carry out the book's emphasis on religious diversity in the West.

Primary Source Feature: "Voice": Each chapter has a document from an individual who lived during the era of the chapter, sometimes from the same individual featured at the beginning of the chapter in "Choice." An explanatory headnote sets the context for the document. Students are then helped to analyze it historically through a series of marginal notes called "Exploration Points." The points are also designed to aid instructors seeking to integrate primary sources into their classrooms.

End-of-Chapter Feature: "Echo": This feature is a brief exploration of an interesting and often fun connection between the chapter's era and the student's life today. Topics often relate to material culture, identity and memory, and technology. For example, Chapter 14, which deals with sixteenth-century reform movements in the western church, picks up on the important role of the new technology of the printing press in reformers' programs to discuss "Media Revolutions" down to the present. Chapter 28 takes us on a journey in the post–World War II Volkswagen Transporter minibus as it caught on with Europeans on both sides of the "Iron Curtain," then with American hippies of the 1960s, and finally morphed into the suburban minivan of today.

In addition, we have built into each chapter a strong framework of pedagogical aids to help students navigate the text. Each chapter opens with a **map** that provides a geographical orientation to political content. A **timeline** highlights seven to nine landmark events that define the time frame. Each chapter opening also has an **outline** of chapter topics and subtopics, listed together with chapter features. A chapter **introduction** provides an overview of chapter topics and themes. Chapter openings also include a **chronology** that lists events and serves as a guide to the text and as a study aid. Each major chapter division begins with two **focus questions** that direct students' attention to the central concerns and issues about to be examined. Where events follow thick and fast, **brief boxed chronologies** outline their sequence. At the end of the chapter is a **summary,** preceded by three synthetic **review questions** that prompt students to draw connections among the chapter's focus questions. One review question in every chapter highlights the identity theme. Basic answers to these questions can be found in the summary, which reinforces what the students have read, but instructors will find that the review and focus questions prompt students to do more than regurgitate pat answers. Their aim has been to prompt critical thinking. At the end of the summary is a **thinking back, thinking ahead question** that asks students to extend their thinking to previous eras or into the eras to come. At the end of each chapter is a short list of **suggested readings,** classic or important publications that students can easily locate as well as three especially good **websites** that they might find helpful. Additional sources for each chapter will be listed on the book's website. The most distinctive feature of our text is the **glossary**—a system whereby boldfaced names, terms, organizations, concepts, and events are explained or defined on the same page where they are introduced. These definitions support students whose vocabulary and knowledge of history are weak, enhance the background a better-prepared student may have, and serve as a convenient review and study aid. In the printed book each chapter will have a rich array of maps and illustrations that will expand the chapter contents through informative captions.

Flexible Format

Western Civilization courses differ widely in chronological structure from one campus to another. To accommodate the differing divisions of historical time into intervals for various academic year divisions, *Making Europe: People, Politics, and Culture* is published in three print versions, two of which embrace the complete work, and two electronic versions:

- One-volume hardcover edition: *Making Europe: People, Politics, and Culture*
- Two-volume paperback: *Making Europe: People, Politics, and Culture, Volume I: To 1790* (Chapters 1–17); *Volume II: Since 1550* (Chapters 15–30)
- *Making Europe: People, Politics, and Culture, Since 1300* (Chapters 12–30), for courses on Europe since the Renaissance
- An ebook of the complete one-volume edition
- A two-volume ebook of volumes one and two

Ancillaries

A wide array of supplements accompany this text to help students better master the material and to help instructors in teaching from the book:

- Student Website
- Instructor Website
- *HM Testing* CD-ROM (powered by *Diploma*)
- Online *Instructor's Resource Manual*
- Online *Study Guide* (powered by eCommerce)
- *PowerPoint* maps, images, and lecture outlines
- *PowerPoint* questions for personal response systems
- *Blackboard*™ and *WebCT*™ course cartridges
- *Eduspace*™ (powered by *Blackboard*™)

- Interactive ebook
- *HistoryFinder*

The student website, HM HistorySPACE™, which is accessible by visiting **college.hmco.com/pic/ kidner1e,** is a companion website for students that features a wide array of resources to help students master the subject matter. The website, prepared by Craig Pilant of the County College of Morris, and Mark Seidl, is divided into three major sections:

- "Prepare for Class" includes material such as learning objectives, chapter outlines, and preclass quizzes for a student to consult before going to class.
- "Improve Your Grade" includes practice review materials such as interactive flashcards, chronological ordering exercises, primary sources, and interactive map exercises.
- "ACE the Test" features our successful ACE brand of practice tests as well as other self-testing materials.

Students can also find additional text resources such as an online glossary, audio mp3 files of chapter summaries, and material on how to study more effectively in the "General Resources" section.

The instructor website, HM HistorySPACE™, also accessible by visiting **college.hmco.com/pic/ kidner1e,** is a companion website for instructors. It features all of the material on the student website plus additional password-protected resources that help instructors teach the course, such as an electronic version of the *Instructor's Resource Manual* and *PowerPoint* slides.

The *Instructor's Resource Manual*, prepared by Doug McGetchin of Florida Atlantic University, contains instructional objectives, chapter outlines, lecture suggestions, suggestions on using primary sources, activities for the Choice feature, activities for the Voice feature, activities for the Echo feature, map activities, audiovisual bibliographies, and internet resources.

HM Testing (powered by *Diploma*) offers instructors a flexible and powerful tool for test generation and test management. Now supported by the Brownstone Research Group's market-leading *Diploma* software, this new version of *HM Testing* significantly improves on functionality and ease of use by offering all the tools needed to create, author, deliver, and customize multiple types of tests. Diploma is currently in use at thousands of college and university campuses throughout the United States and Canada. The *HM Testing* content for this text was developed by Kathleen Addison of California State University at Northridge and offers key term identification, essay questions (with guidelines for how to effectively write the essay), and multiple-choice questions (with page references to the correct response).

The *Online Study Guide* (powered by eCommerce) offers students additional materials to aid their study and mastery of the text. The *Study Guide* content was developed by Robert Shannon Sumner of the University of West Georgia and offers learning objectives, chapter key points, topics for essay and discussion, fill-in-the-blank activities, matching activities, multiple-choice questions, chronology exercises, literary analysis, geography questions, and map activities.

We are pleased to offer a collection of Western Civilization *PowerPoint* lecture outlines, maps, and images for use in classroom presentations. Detailed lecture outlines correspond to the book's chapters and make it easier for instructors to cover the major topics in class. The art collection includes all of the photos and maps in the text, as well as numerous other images from our Western Civilization titles. *PowerPoint* questions and answers for use with personal response system software are also offered to adopters free of charge.

A variety of assignable homework and testing material has been developed to work with the *Blackboard*™ and *WebCT*™ course management systems, as well as with *Eduspace*™: Houghton Mifflin's Online Learning Tool (Powered by **Blackboard**™). *Eduspace*™ is a web-based online learning environment that provides instructors with a gradebook and communication capabilities, such as synchronous and asynchronous chats and announcement postings. It offers access to assignments such as over six hundred and fifty gradable homework exercises, writing assignments, interactive maps with questions, primary sources, discussion questions for online discussion boards, and tests, which all come ready-to-use. Instructors can choose to use the content as is, modify it, or even add their own. *Eduspace*™ also contains an interactive ebook, which contains in-text links to interactive maps, primary sources, and audio pronunciation files, as well as review and self-testing material for students.

HistoryFinder, a new Houghton Mifflin technology initiative, helps instructors create rich and exciting classroom presentations. This online tool offers thousands of online resources, including art, photographs, maps, primary sources, multimedia content, Associated Press interactive modules, and ready-made PowerPoint slides. HistoryFinder's assets can easily be searched by keyword, or browsed from pull-down menus of topic, media type, or by textbook. Instructors can then browse, preview, and download resources straight from the website.

Acknowledgments

It is a pleasure to thank the many instructors who read and critiqued the manuscript through its development:

Patricia E. Behre, Fairfield University
Robert J. Brennan, Cape Fear Community College
Dorothy L. Brown, Columbia College
Peter Buhler, Boise State University
Christine Caldwell, St. Louis University
Susan Carrafiello, Wright State University
Maryanne Cline Horowitz, Occidental College
Luanne Dagley, Pellissippi State Technical Community College
A. Dudley Gardner, Western Wyoming College
Kathryn A. Edwards, University of South Carolina
Carla C. Falkner, Northeast Mississippi Community College
Joanne M. Ferraro, San Diego State
Carlos R. Galvao-Sobrinho, University of Wisconsin, Milwaukee
Paul S. George, Ph.D., Miami-Dade Community College
Eva Giloi, Rutgers University, Newark
Jay Harmon, Catholic High School
Robert Henry, Skyline College
John Howe, Texas Technical University
Paul J. L. Hughes, Ph.D., Sussex County Community College
Theodore M. Kluz, Troy State University
Craig Koslofsky, University of Illinois, Urbana
Michael Kulikowski, University of Tennessee
Tom Lansburg, Front Range Community College
F. Thomas Luongo, Tulane University
Molly McClain, University of San Diego
Andrew McMichael, Western Kentucky University
T. Mills Kelly, George Mason University
Prudence Moylan, Loyola University
Charlotte Newman Goldy, Miami University
Patricia O. O'Neill, Central Oregon Community College
William A. Paquette, Tidewater Community College
Ricky E. Parrish, Brevard Community College
Brian A. Pavlac, King's College
Ty M. Reese, University of North Dakota
Paula M. Rieder, University of Nebraska, Kearney

James B. Robinson, University of Northern Iowa

Jim Roderick, Truckee Meadows Community College

Ian Rush, Washtenaw Community College

Philip Schaeffer, Olympic College

Stuart Smyth, State University of New York, Albany

David R. Stone, Kansas State University

Dale R. Streeter, Southwest Missouri State University

Laura Trauth, Community College of Baltimore County, Essex

Alice N. Walters, University of Massachusetts, Lowell

Andrea Wilford, Muscatine High School

In addition, we would like to thank the History 205A and 205B classes at Southern Illinois University at Carbondale who used this text, in preliminary form, during Fall 2006 and Spring 2007. Thanks to all the students, and in particular, thanks to:

Matt Adelman
Stephanie Borrelli
James Bradley
Jeffrey M. Cap
Kyrus Daugherty
Jill L. Genovese
Jacob Heath
Ashley Jones
Sheri Keller
Viridiana Ortega
Daniel Polivka
Craig Rose

Joseph Schmelter
Savannah Short
Jaron Smith
Anran Wang

Frank Kidner wishes to thank his colleagues Bob Cherney, Trevor Getz, Pi-Ching Hsu, Julyana Peard, and Jarbel Rodriguez for their help at various points in *Making Europe*'s development.

Maria Bucur wishes to thank her husband, Daniel Deckard, for continued support and inspiration in matters intellectual and musical, and her children Dylan and Elvin, for putting up with the many hours mommy had to be away from them and reinvigorating her in the hours she was lucky to be with them.

Ralph Mathisen wishes to thank Frank Kidner for getting this project going and keeping it on track. He would also like to thank his two children, Katherine and David Mathisen, for putting up with piles of civ texts, notes, and drafts spread all over for these past eight years.

Sally McKee wishes to thank her fellow authors for their mutual support, epicurean disposition, and good cheer over the years.

All of us wish to express our deepest thanks to our development editor, Ann Hofstra Grogg, who worked with us throughout the writing of this book. A thousand thanks, Ann!

F. L. K.
M. B.
R. M.
S. M.
T. R. W.

About the Authors

Frank L. Kidner is Professor of History Emeritus at San Francisco State University, where he taught from 1968 until his retirement in 2006. He has also taught in the Western Civilization program at Stanford University and at Amherst College. His courses include Western Civilization, undergraduate and graduate courses in Early Modern Europe, and the history of the Christian Church as well as a graduate course in historical methodology. He has authored articles on topics in Late Antiquity and co-edited *Travel, Communication and Geography in Late Antiquity*.

Maria Bucur is Associate Professor and John V. Hill Chair in East European History at Indiana University, where she teaches an undergraduate course on "The Idea of Europe" and other topics in nineteenth- and twentieth-century eastern Europe. Her research focus is on social and cultural developments in eastern Europe, with a special interest in Romania (geographically) and gender (thematically). Her publications include *Eugenics and Modernization in Interwar Romania* and the co-edited volumes *Staging the Past: The Politics of Commemoration in Habsburg Central Europe, 1848 to the Present* and *Gender and War in Twentieth-Century Eastern Europe*.

Ralph Mathisen is Professor of History, Classics, and Medieval Studies at the University of Illinois at Urbana-Champaign. He is a specialist in the ancient world with a particular interest in the society, culture, and religion of Late Antiquity. His teaching experience includes Western Civilization and topics in the Ancient Near East, Greece, Rome, Byzantium, coinage, and Roman law. He has written more than seventy scholarly articles and written or edited ten books, the most recent of which is *People, Personal Expression, and Social Relations in Late Antiquity*. He is also the editor of the *Journal of Late Antiquity*.

Sally McKee is Associate Professor of History at the University of California at Davis, where she teaches courses on Western Civilization and medieval history. Her research focus has been Venice and its colonies and Mediterranean slavery, but her new project centers on nineteenth-century France. She is the author of articles that have won prizes and been anthologized, and she has also published a three-volume edition of Venetian-Cretan wills and a monograph, *Uncommon Dominion: Venetian Crete and the Myth of Ethnic Purity*.

Theodore R. Weeks is Professor of History at Southern Illinois University at Carbondale, where he teaches Western Civilization and world and European history. His research centers on nationality, inter-ethnic relations, and antisemitism in eastern Europe. He is the author of *Nation and State in Late Imperial Russia* and *From Assimilation to Antisemitism: The "Jewish Question" in Poland, 1850–1914*, and his articles have appeared in several languages, including Lithuanian and Belarusian.

Making Europe

The Origins of Western Civilization in the Ancient Near East, 3000–1200 B.C.E.

CHAPTER OUTLINE

10,000 B.C.E.	9000 B.C.E.	8000 B.C.E.	7000 B.C.E.	6000 B.C.E.	5000 B.C.E.

8000 B.C.E.
Neolithic Age begins

3000 B.C.E.
Beginning of Bronze Age
civilization in Sumeria and Egypt

2700 B.C.E.
Old Kingdom
in Egypt begins

8000	3000	2500

Note: B.C.E. means "before common era."

The Near Eastern World, ca. 1500 B.C.E.

In 1500 B.C.E., the most important ancient western civilizations were located in Egypt in the Nile River valley, in Mesopotamia in the Tigris and Euphrates River valleys, and in Crete and Greece bordering on the Mediterranean Sea. Why do you think these ancient civilizations developed along rivers and seas?

Black Sea

Caspian Sea

ANATOLIA

HITTITES

TAURUS MTS.

Tigris R.

Euphrates R.

ZAGROS MTS.

ELAM

Knossos

Rhodes

Phaistos

Crete

Cyprus

Ugarit

SYRIA

Mediterranean Sea

Byblos

Sidon

Tyre

PALESTINE

LEVANT

Babylon

KASSITES

Uruk

BABYLONIA

Ur

Persian Gulf

LOWER EGYPT

Memphis

Nile R.

UPPER EGYPT

Thebes

ᴀRABIA

NUBIA

Red Sea

Egyptian civilization

Old Kingdom (2700–2200 B.C.E.) and Middle Kingdom (1250–1786 B.C.E.)

Expansion of Egyptian Empire during New Kingdom (1570–1070 B.C.E.)

Other civilizations, ca. 1400 B.C.E.

Mycenaean civilization

Kassite Kingdom

Hittite Kingdom

0 100 200 Km.

0 100 200 Mi.

4000 B.C.E. 3000 B.C.E. 2000 B.C.E. 1000 B.C.E. 1 B.C.E./1 C.E. 1000 C.E.

2050 B.C.E.
Middle Kingdom in Egypt begins

1760 B.C.E.
Old Babylonian Empire begins

2350 B.C.E.
Akkadian Empire begins

2000 B.C.E.
Minoan palace complexes appear in Crete

1600 B.C.E.
Mycenaean civilization begins in Greece

1200 B.C.E.
Bronze Age ends, Iron Age begins

1570 B.C.E.
New Kingdom in Egypt begins

2000 1500 1000

Choice

Akhenaton and Nefertiti

A relief, ca. 1350 B.C.E., shows Akhenaton and Nefertiti playing with their daughters as they bask in the rays of the sun god Aton. Aton was depicted as a disc whose descending rays terminated in human hands that oversaw the welfare of Egypt. Akhenaton was devoted to the worship of Aton, and determined to make him the main god of Egypt. (Bildarchiv Preussischer Kulturbesitz/Art Resource, NY)

Akhenaton Decides to Make Aton the Main God of Egypt

In the fourteenth century B.C.E., the Egyptian Empire was at its height, and its ruler, the pharaoh Amenhotep IV, was considered to be a living god. The Egyptians worshiped many other gods besides Amenhotep, such as the chief sun god Ra, the bull god Amon, and Osiris, the god of the dead. All these gods played important roles in the everyday life of an Egyptian society that had been remarkably stable for sixteen centuries. But then Amenhotep, who had complete authority over Egyptian government and religion, decided to make a revolutionary change in Egyptian religious practices by declaring there was only one god worth worshiping and forbidding the worship of all other gods.

For reasons that remain unclear, Amenhotep, a man of strong beliefs, had become completely committed to the worship of an obscure sun god named Aton, whom he made the single most important god in Egypt. To demonstrate his devotion to Aton, Amenhotep changed his own name to Akhenaton ("Glory of Aton") and established a new capital city in honor of Aton, calling it Akhetaton ("The Horizon of Aton"), on the site of today's El-Amarna. Akhenaton forbade the worship of all other gods, but at the same time he decreed that only the royal family would be allowed to worship Aton. Artworks were created that showed only Akhenaton and his family, no one else, receiving the beneficial rays of Aton. To ensure that no other gods would be worshiped, Akhenaton closed and defaced their temples.

Akhenaton's religious reforms deeply affected the Egyptian people. The priests who oversaw the worship of all the other gods lost their livelihood. And ordinary Egyptians could no longer worship Osiris, the god who, they believed, gave them their afterlife. Civil unrest arose, and the Egyptian army had to be called out to maintain order. Over time, the army became so occupied with controlling internal strife that it could no longer defend the Egyptian Empire and ultimately turned against Akhenaton. His name and the name of Aton were erased from the monuments; the temples of Aton were destroyed, Akhetaton was abandoned, and Akhenaton disappeared from history. It may be that the army decided to get rid of this unpopular pharaoh.

It remains a mystery why Akhenaton introduced measures that had such disastrous consequences. One school of thought sees his reforms as a calculated effort to undercut the power of the priests and increase the power of the pharaoh. If so, Akhenaton seriously miscalculated, and the plan went badly wrong. So perhaps a more likely suggestion is that Akhenaton was a true religious reformer. He was determined to make his god the primary god in Egypt regardless of what kinds of misery and disasters doing so brought upon the Egyptian people and nation.

Akhenaton's favoring of Aton in spite of the consequences can be viewed as a clash between Akhenaton's personal beliefs about the nature of God and his responsibilities as a ruler. And the reaction of the Egyptian people can be seen as an example of how attempts to change deeply felt religious beliefs and rituals can inspire resistance to political authority. Both of these themes recur often in western history.

Introduction

The effect of Akhenaton's religious reforms on the Egyptian people is but one of many examples of the power of religion in early human societies. Religion arose because people felt there was something greater than themselves that controlled their environment, something they could interact with and influence. For more than a million years, humans have been struggling to define the role of religion in their lives, but it is only over the past 5,000 years, with the beginning of history and of civilization, that human religious experiences—and other developments in human society, culture, politics, and thought—can be traced in increasingly greater detail.

Western civilization as defined by modern historians arose around 3000 B.C.E. in the ancient Near East—Mesopotamia (modern Iraq) and Egypt—and then spread westward to Europe. The origins of human culture and society, however, go back over a million years to central and southern Africa, where early humans used stone tools and were primarily concerned with acquiring sufficient food—by hunting wild animals, gathering naturally growing foodstuffs, or scavenging—to meet their basic needs. It was not until 8000 B.C.E. that people in some parts of the world gained greater control over their food supply by herding animals and planting their own crops. The adoption of agriculture brought great changes in human society and culture. Populations increased. People could remain in the same place, build cities, and specialize in specific occupations. Metal technology advanced with the introduction of bronze weapons. The invention of writing brought the origin of written history. Taken together, these cultural advances created the first phase of civilization, known as the Bronze Age, around 3000 B.C.E.

Geography played a major role in the rise of the first Near Eastern civilizations, which developed in fertile river valleys that offered rich soil and a dependable water supply. The most representative Bronze Age civilizations were based on the extensive exploitation of agriculture. In Mesopotamia, the Sume-rians created a civilization in the Tigris and Euphrates River valleys. Because Mesopotamia had no natural barriers, Semitic and Indo-European peoples invaded, established the first empires, and absorbed the culture of the people they had conquered. In the Nile River valley, on the other hand, the civilization of Egypt grew largely in isolation, for it was protected by surrounding deserts. Outside the large river valleys, in Syria, Crete, and Greece, Bronze Age civilizations took advantage of their location on lines of communication and compensated for their lack of rich soil by creating economies based more heavily on trade. The end of the Bronze Age, around 1200 B.C.E., was marked by disruptions caused by Indo-European invaders known as the Sea Peoples.

Before History, 2,000,000–3000 B.C.E.

↓ How did methods of acquiring food change during the course of the Stone Age?

↓ What social and economic factors influenced the rise of civilization?

For the earliest humans, life was a constant struggle just to eat. People obtained food by hunting animals and gathering wild plant products, but food often ran short. Around 8000 B.C.E., people in a few places in the world learned how to grow plants for food. Thereafter food supplies were more dependable. The result was increasing populations and more organized societies. Humans gained a greater self-consciousness about how they related to the world around them, recognizing forces that seemed to control their fate and searching for ways to interact with these forces or even control them.

The Old Stone Age

The first, and by far the longest, period of human existence is known as the Old Stone Age, a name derived from the material used for making the most

Chronology

2,000,000 B.C.E. Homo habilis uses crude stone choppers to butcher animals	**1790 B.C.E.** Hammurabi becomes king of Babylon
1,000,000 B.C.E. Homo erectus learns the use of fire.	**1730 B.C.E.** Hyksos invade Egypt
40,000 B.C.E. Homo sapiens create cave paintings	**1600 B.C.E.** Beginning of Mycenaean civilization in Greece
8000 B.C.E. Neolithic Age begins	**1570 B.C.E.** New Kingdom in Egypt begins
4000 B.C.E. Sumerians drain Tigris and Euphrates River valleys for agriculture	**1500 B.C.E.** Kassites settle in Mesopotamia
3000 B.C.E. Beginning of Bronze Age civilization Narmer unifies Egypt	**1498 B.C.E.** Hatshepsut becomes pharaoh of Egypt
2700 B.C.E. Old Kingdom in Egypt begins	**1483 B.C.E.** Thutmose III becomes pharaoh of Egypt
2600 B.C.E. Building of the largest Egyptian pyramids	**1400 B.C.E.** Mycenaeans destroy Minoan civilization
2500 B.C.E. Ebla becomes a commercial center	**1350 B.C.E.** Akhenaton institutes religious reforms in Egypt
2350 B.C.E. Sargon creates Akkadian Empire	**1200 B.C.E.** Invasion of the Sea Peoples End of the Bronze Age
2050 B.C.E. Middle Kingdom in Egypt begins	**1180 B.C.E.** Ramses III defeats the Sea Peoples
2000 B.C.E. Amorites settle in Mesopotamia Indo-Europeans settle in Iran, Anatolia, and the Balkans Minoan palace complexes appear in Crete	*Note:* B.C.E means "before the Common Era."

durable tools. People of the Old Stone Age left no written records, so their lives are known only from the study of the physical remains they left behind. These remains, known as **material culture,** consist primarily of stone tools and the bones of slaughtered animals. The material culture of past human societies is recovered and analyzed by the field of study known as **archaeology.** Using archaeological evidence, historians see that during the Old Stone Age, human society gradually became increasingly complex as a result of biological evolution, technological development, and climate variation.

The earliest human population, called Homo habilis ("skillful human"), evolved in central and southern Africa some two million years ago. These people were smaller than modern humans and used crude stone choppers to butcher animal carcasses. They banded together for protection and found shelter under overhanging cliffs. Beginning about a million years ago, a more advanced population, known as Homo erectus ("upright human"), about the same size as modern people, learned how to use fire. Flint, a very hard and easily worked stone, became the preferred material for making tools, which included weapons used to hunt big game, such as elephants.

Homo sapiens ("thinking human") appeared in Africa about 400,000 B.C.E., and by 150,000 B.C.E. a Eu-

material culture Physical remains left by past human societies.

archaeology Scientific study of the remains of past human societies.

ropean subspecies known as the Neanderthals was making more advanced implements, such as axes, scrapers, and projectile points, from stone flakes chipped from larger pieces of flint. For shelter, the Neanderthals often made use of caves (hence the derogatory term *cave men*), which offered security from wild animals, protection from the weather, and storage space.

Initially, all human societies acquired food by hunting wild animals and gathering naturally growing plant products. Most food consisted of wild fruits, nuts, berries, roots, seeds, and grains. Early peoples supplemented this diet by hunting, fishing, or scavenging animal carcasses. Observing that some areas were better for hunting and gathering, humans traveled long distances, following migrating animals and seeking wild crops. But a change in animal migration routes or a drought could lead to starvation.

Stone Age life can be reconstructed from the archaeological remains and by making anthropological comparisons with modern populations with similar lifestyles. Males would have hunted and engaged in activities that took them far from their residences, whereas women would have gathered plant foods and overseen child care. In addition, the manufacture of stone tools, necessary during hunting expeditions, would have been primarily a male activity, and women would have concentrated on tasks that could be performed in camp or at home, such as scraping and curing hides and preparing food or preserving it by drying or storing in pits.

About 100,000 years ago, a human subspecies known as Homo sapiens sapiens ("wise-thinking human")—essentially like modern humans—appeared in Africa and began to spread throughout the world. For unknown reasons, the other humans, including the Neanderthals, then gradually disappeared. About 40,000 years ago, new technologies helped people exploit the natural food-producing environment more effectively. For example, tree resin was used to bind tiny stone blades to wood or bone shafts in order to make sickles for harvesting wild grains.

At the same time, humans gave increasing attention to religion. Archaeological remains provide evidence for a belief in supernatural powers that governed the universe and controlled important aspects of life, such as food production, fertility, and death. Humans came to believe that they could influence these powers by means of religious rituals. For example, paintings found deep in caves in Spain and southern France show animals pierced by spears, suggesting that the painters hoped to bring about the same result in the real world. A cave painting from Spain show-

A cave painting called *The Sorcerer*, dating to about 13,000 B.C.E. from southern France, depicts a man with a bearded face, an owl's eyes, a horse's tail, and a lion's claws. It might represent a shaman, a spiritual leader believed to be able to communicate with the supernatural world of animals and gods. *(Visual Connection Archive)*

ing nine women in knee-length skirts dancing around a small naked man probably represents a fertility ritual intended to promote the production of human offspring. The many large-breasted broad-hipped female figurines found on Stone Age sites also demonstrate the power attributed to female fertility in Stone Age societies, which may have been matriarchal— that is, governed by women. Elaborate burial rituals

Neanderthals   Human subspecies that originated as early as 350,000 B.C.E. and became extinct soon after 40,000 B.C.E., discovered in Germany's Neanderthal ("Neander Valley") in 1856.

anthropology   Scientific study of modern human cultures and societies.

matriarchal society   (from Greek for "rule by mothers") Society in which women have the primary authority.

arose. The dead were buried sprinkled with red ocher (a mixture of clay and iron oxide) and accompanied by clothing, shells, beads, and tools, suggesting a belief in an afterlife.

The Neolithic Revolution

Soon after the end of the last ice age, about 10,000 B.C.E., great changes occurred in human lifestyles, in part because of the warming climate but also because of continuing human social and technological evolution. The **Neolithic Age,** which began in the **Near East** about 8000 B.C.E., marked the final stage in stone tool technology. Finely crafted stone tools filled every kind of need. Obsidian, a volcanic glass, provided razor-sharp edges for sickles. Bowls and other items were made from ground as opposed to chipped stone. Long-distance trade brought ocher from Africa, flint from England, and obsidian from the islands of the Aegean Sea to markets in the Near East and elsewhere. Technologically, however, stone tools had reached their limits in durability and functionality, and people began to experiment with the use of metals, such as copper, for making weapons and jewelry.

More significantly, the Neolithic Age brought two revolutions in food supply methods. One was the **domestication** of animals that could be used as a source of both food and raw materials. Sheep, goats, pigs, and cattle—which were nonaggressive toward humans, had a natural herd instinct, matured quickly, and had an easily satisfied diet—were best suited for domestication. These qualities help to explain why animal domestication arose in Asia and the Near East, where these particular animals were found, rather than in Africa, where the native animals, such as buffalo, gazelles, and large carnivores, were less suited for domestication. Domesticated animals kept in flocks and herds gave people a dependable food supply in the form of milk products as well as clothing made from the animals' wool and hides. Only in times of need, or for ceremonial purposes, or when an animal died, were the livestock—which were also a form of wealth—actually eaten. Other animals, such as the dog and cat, also were domesticated. People who kept domestic animals are called **pastoralists** because they were constantly searching for new pastures. Their diet was supplemented by hunting and gathering, but they still were subject to climatic changes. Prolonged periods of drought, for example, could have disastrous consequences. Nevertheless, pastoralism offered greater security than a purely hunting-and-gathering economy, and it quickly spread over nearly all of Europe, Asia, and Africa.

An even more revolutionary development of the New Stone Age was the domestication of certain kinds of plants, which led to **agriculture,** or farming. As early as 10,000 B.C.E., hunter-gatherers were experimenting with cultivating wild grains, such as rice in China and rye in Syria. Recent studies of ancient climate variations suggest that droughts also may have encouraged people to take greater control over their food supply. Around 8000 B.C.E., several Near Eastern populations began to cultivate grains including wheat, barley, and emmer. These grains evolved into greater usefulness both through natural selection (in which plants naturally mutate into more useful varieties) and selective breeding (in which humans select seeds for their desirable qualities). Other crops such as peas, beans, and figs supplemented the grain-based diet, and domestic animals provided meat and milk products.

Agriculture also arose in Africa, India, China, and Central and South America, sometimes independently and sometimes by the process of **cultural assimilation,** in which people who did not practice agriculture learned it from those who did. Gradually, the knowledge of agriculture spread throughout the world and brought increased economic productivity. In western Europe, social organizations based on agricultural economies mobilized great amounts of manpower. Beginning around 4000 B.C.E., massive standing stones called megaliths were erected, as at Stonehenge in England, a feat that requiring hundreds or thousands of participants. Beyond the physical achievement of their erection, the stones demonstrate an elementary knowledge of astronomy, for they were aligned with the heavens and permitted people to predict the seasons based on the alignment of certain stars, such as Sirius, in relation to the stones.

Neolithic Age   (from Greek for "new stone") Period between 8000 and 4000 B.C.E., during which people gained greater control over their food supply.

Near East   In antiquity, Egypt, the Levant, Mesopotamia, Anatolia, and Iran; in the modern day sometimes also known as the Middle East.

domestication   Practice of adapting wild animals to live with humans or wild plants for cultivation.

pastoralism   Mobile lifestyle based on keeping flocks and herds.

agriculture   Sedentary style of life based on the cultivation of crops.

cultural assimilation   Acquisition by one group of people of the cultural traits of another people.

The practice of agriculture brought two main changes to human existence: it required people to remain in the same place year after year, and it created a dependable food supply that yielded a surplus, which created wealth. The food surplus also meant that a larger population could be supported. People settled together in villages—permanent settlements with several hundred residents and houses made from local materials such as reeds, mud brick, or timber. Agricultural productivity was limited only by the amount of land placed under cultivation and the availability of water. A larger population meant that more land could be brought into cultivation and that even more food could be produced. A settled lifestyle opened up the opportunity for individuals to pursue specialized occupations, such as pottery making, carpentry, and home building. Some farmers and craftworkers were more successful than others, which led to social differentiation—that is, the division of society into rich and poor. By 7000 B.C.E., villages such as Jericho, near the Jordan River in Palestine, were home to several thousand persons and were protected by thick walls.

Life in permanent settlements also brought problems. Too much emphasis on grain could result in an unbalanced diet and greater susceptibility to disease. Larger populations living close together and surrounded by their own waste increased the possibility of the spread of communicable diseases such as tuberculosis, smallpox, malaria, and plague. Villages with food surpluses could be targets for raids by pastoralists who were short of food. In addition, farmers sometimes destroyed their own environment. As land was deforested for agriculture or overgrazed by domestic animals, the soil could be eroded by being washed or blown away. And the watering and fertilization of cropland could result in a buildup of salt that reduced soil fertility. Hunter-gatherers or pastoralists could always move when living conditions deteriorated in one location, but once farmers had committed themselves to an agricultural economy, they were compelled to make do with the agricultural economy as best as they could.

Religious practices also continued to evolve during the Neolithic period. Maleness was seen as the source of the rain that brought fertility to the land and was represented by phallic imagery. Great Mother cults, evidenced by female statuettes, suggest that femaleness was associated with the earth as the provider of the bounty of herds and crops. Clay-covered skulls found at Jericho suggest a form of ancestor worship in which deceased loved ones remained with the living.

The Emergence of Near Eastern Civilization

The most extensive exploitation of agriculture occurred in river valleys, where there were both good soil and a dependable water supply regardless of the amount of rainfall. In the Near East, this happened in the **Fertile Crescent**, a region extending up the Nile River valley in Egypt, north through the **Levant** (Palestine, Lebanon, and Syria), and then southeast into the Tigris and Euphrates River valleys of **Mesopotamia.** The richest soil was located in the deltas at the mouths of the rivers, but the deltas were swampy and subject to flooding. Before they could be farmed, they needed to be drained and irrigated and flood control systems had to be constructed. These activities required administrative organization and the ability to mobilize large pools of labor. In Mesopotamia, perhaps as a consequence of a period of drought, massive land reclamation projects were undertaken after 4000 B.C.E. to cultivate the rich delta soils of the Tigris and Euphrates Rivers. The land was so productive of crops that many more people could be fed, and a great population explosion resulted. Villages grew into cities of tens of thousands of persons.

These large cities needed some form of centralized administration. Archaeological evidence indicates that the organization initially was provided by religion, for the largest building in each city was a massive temple honoring one of the many Mesopotamian gods. In Uruk, for example, a sixty-foot-long temple known as the White House was built before 3000 B.C.E. There were no other large public buildings, suggesting that the priests who were in charge of the temples also were responsible for governing the city and organizing people to work in the fields and on irrigation projects building and maintaining systems of ditches and dams.

The great concentration of wealth and resources in the river valleys brought with it further technological advances, such as wheeled vehicles, multicolored

Fertile Crescent   Arc of fertile land running through Egypt, the Levant, and Mesopotamia, in which early agriculture was practiced.

Levant   Lands between the eastern coast of the Mediterranean and Mesopotamia, including Palestine, Lebanon, and Syria.

Mesopotamia   (Greek for "between the rivers") Lands surrounding the Tigris and Euphrates Rivers and the site of a Bronze Age civilization; modern Iraq.

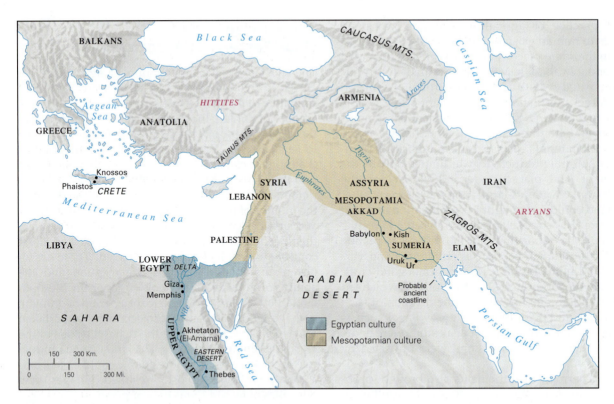

MAP 1.1   **The Fertile Crescent** During the Bronze Age, river valley civilizations based on the extensive exploitation of agriculture arose in a "Fertile Crescent" extending from the Nile valley in Egypt up through the Tigris and Euphrates valleys in Mesopotamia.

pottery and the pottery wheel, and the weaving of wool garments. Advances in metal technology just before 3000 B.C.E. resulted in the creation of bronze, a durable alloy (or mixture) of about 90 percent copper and 10 percent tin that provided a sharp cutting edge for weapons.

By 3000 B.C.E., the economies and administrations of Mesopotamia and Egypt had become so complex that some form of record keeping was needed. As a result, writing was invented. Once a society became literate, it passed from the period known as prehistory into the historic period, leaving written records that can be used along with archaeology to learn more about the life of its people. In fact, the word **history** comes from a Greek word meaning "narrative": people could not provide a detailed permanent account of their past until they were able to write.

The totality of these developments resulted in the appearance, around 3000 B.C.E., of a new form of culture called civilization. The first civilizations had several defining characteristics. They had economies based on agriculture. They had cities that functioned as administrative centers and usually had large pop-

ulations. They had different social classes, such as free persons and slaves. They had specialization of labor, that is, different people serving, for example, as rulers, priests, craftworkers, merchants, soldiers, and farmers. And they had metal technology and a system of writing. As of 3000 B.C.E., civilization in these terms existed in Mesopotamia, Egypt, India, and China.

This first phase of civilization is called the **Bronze Age** because of the importance of metal technology. In the Near East, the most characteristic Bronze Age civilizations, those of Mesopotamia and Egypt, were located in river valleys, were based on the extensive

history   (from Greek for "narrative") Accounts of the human past that use written records.

Bronze Age   In the Near East, the period from 3000 to 1200 B.C.E., when bronze was used for weapon making and when the most characteristic civilizations were located in river valleys, based on extensive agriculture, and had large populations.

exploitation of agriculture, and supported large populations. Bronze was a valuable commodity; the copper and tin needed for its manufacture did not exist in river valleys and had to be imported—tin from as far away as Britain. Bronze therefore was used mainly for luxury items, such as jewelry or weapons, but not for everyday domestic items, which were made from pottery, animal products, wood, and stone. In particular, bronze was not used for farming tools. Thus, civilizations based on large-scale agriculture, such as those of Mesopotamia and Egypt, were feasible only in soils that could be worked by wooden scratch-plows pulled by people or draft animals such as oxen. Other Bronze Age civilizations, however, such as those that arose in the Levant and the eastern Mediterranean, took advantage of their location on communication routes to pursue economies based on trade.

Mesopotamian Civilization, 3000–1200 B.C.E.

> ↓ How did geography influence Mesopotamian civilization?
>
> ↓ How did Mesopotamians seek to gain control of their world?

Mesopotamian civilization was greatly influenced by geography. The Tigris and Euphrates River valleys were subject to unexpected floods and open to invasion, and the resulting uncertainties in their lives gave the Mesopotamians a pessimistic outlook on the world. Every Mesopotamian city had one chief god. At first, priests ruled each city in the name of its god, but later military leaders also arose. Because the Mesopotamians did not trust the gods to impose order on the world, they sought to do so themselves, often by issuing elaborate law codes. Over time, the Mesopotamians came into contact with neighboring Semitic and Indo-European peoples, who invaded Mesopotamia and adopted Mesopotamian culture.

Sumerian Gods and Legends

Mesopotamian civilization began around 3000 B.C.E. in Sumeria, the rich agricultural delta where the Tigris and Euphrates Rivers empty into the Persian Gulf. Sumerian civilization was built on cities. Twenty principal cities such as Uruk, Kish, and Ur had populations of over 50,000 each and occupied all of the good farmland close to the rivers. What is known about Sumerian civilization comes from both archaeological remains and written records. The Sumerian writing material was clay, and the writing instrument

was a stylus, or pointed stick, that made wedge-shaped indentations in the clay. The writing system, called cuneiform, began as a multitude of pictograms, signs that looked like what they represent, such as a star. By 3000 B.C.E., about a hundred of the signs had come to stand for syllabic sounds—that is, a consonant plus a vowel (*ba, be, bi, bo,* and so on)—and could be used to spell any word. Significant numbers of texts, however, do not appear until about four hundred years later. Sumerian accounts of their earlier history, such as their lists of kings, are therefore often based on myths and legends—stories passed down orally about gods and heroes—that often seem fantastic but usually are based on a core of truth.

Sumerian ideas about their place in the world stemmed largely from their geography. Mountains rise to the north of Mesopotamia, and to the south and west lies the Syrian-Arabian Desert, a semiarid area that supported substantial pastoralist populations. Sumeria proper received less than ten inches of rainfall a year, but the upper reaches of the rivers in the mountains of Anatolia (modern Turkey) often received heavy rainfalls that surged downriver. These inundations were useful for agriculture, but they also sometimes flooded the cities without any warning and Mesopotamians lived in constant fear of floods. They also feared raids by mountain peoples from the north and desert dwellers from the south. Life in Sumeria thus was full of uncertainties, which gave the Sumerians a pessimistic outlook on life and a great concern for organizing their world to make it as safe as possible.

The Sumerians were polytheists who believed that the world was controlled by many gods, who had created people to do the gods' work. The gods were conceived of as being anthropomorphic—that is, looking like people. Making the world secure meant being able to influence the gods. Because life was uncertain, the gods also were considered to be

---

cuneiform (from Latin for "wedge-shaped") Mesopotamian writing system that put wedge-shaped indentations on clay tablets.

myths Stories, often about gods, explaining things that people did not understand.

legends Accounts of people and events in the distant past that have been passed on orally.

Anatolia Modern-day Turkey, also known as Asia Minor.

polytheism Belief in the existence of many gods.

anthropomorphic (from Greek for "human-shaped") Looking and behaving like people.

unpredictable and not to be trusted to look out for the people's best interests. The Sumerians therefore tried to assert some control over the gods. People placed small statues of themselves in temples to ensure that the gods would be watching over them. They attempted to learn what the gods intended by looking for signs in dreams, animal entrails, and even wisps of smoke—a practice known as **divination.** The most important gods were assigned numbers proportional to their relative status. An, the father of all the gods, was the god of the universe. He dwelt somewhere among the stars and was rarely concerned with what happened on earth. An was assigned the number 60, the basis of the Sumerian number system. Enlil (50), a sky god who controlled lightning and thunder, was the god most directly concerned with life on earth. Enki (40), the water god, was thought to have brought civilization to humanity. Other important gods included the moon god, Nanna (30); the sun god, Shamash (20); and Ishtar (15), the goddess of fertility. Ranking the gods by numbers gave the Sumerians an additional feeling of having control over them.

Sumerian pessimism is reflected in their perceptions of the afterlife. They believed that the underworld, or "Land of No Return," was ruled by Ereshkigal, the sister of Ishtar, and her partner, the war god Nergal. The dead were buried with offerings that were believed to be stolen by demons as the spirits of the dead traveled to the underworld. The dead then ate clay and dust and spent eternity weeping over their fate. The dream of every Sumerian was to become immortal and escape being sent to the underworld. The most famous Sumerian legend tells how the hero Gilgamesh, the king of Uruk, became upset by the death of his friend Enkidu and attempted to escape his own death. He traveled the world searching for the tree of life, which bore a magic fruit that kept one eternally young. Gilgamesh eventually found the fruit, only to have it stolen by a serpent. Not even a great hero could escape his fate.

Another legend involving Gilgamesh exemplifies Sumerian relations with their unpredictable gods. During his travels, Gilgamesh met Ut-Napishtim, who told Gilgamesh that long ago the sky god Enlil had decided to destroy humanity. Ut-Napishtim was advised by the god Enki to build an ark and to fill it with every species of animal. They all survived the flood, and Ut-Napishtim became the only man ever to become immortal. According to Sumerian lists of their kings, this great flood occurred around 2600 B.C.E. and separated a period when legendary kings ruled for thousands of years from a period of kings with normal life spans. It is quite likely that the legend recollects an actual flood, such as one that left an eleven-foot layer of silt found at Ur. Legends like these, used in conjunction with archaeology, offer the opportunity to reconstruct the history of periods for which no written records survive.

Sumerian Government and Society

The Sumerian cities were **city-states,** independent nations, and were rarely united politically. In fact, disunity was a defining characteristic of Mesopotamian politics. Nevertheless, the cities all shared the same culture—the same religious practices, the same kinds of government, and the same traditions. Each city had one primary god. At Ur, for example, the main god was Nanna, the moon god. The god's temple, called a **ziggurat,** was a massive step-pyramid, 150 feet on a side and over 100 feet high, built of fired brick laid over a mud-brick core. Looking like a staircase rising to heaven, it was the most visible building in the city. There also were numerous smaller temples of other gods.

The Sumerians believed that the true ruler of each city was its god but that the god delegated the work of ruling on earth to priests. The earliest rulers were priest-kings who, along with being religious leaders, also were responsible for organizing the agricultural and irrigation work of the city. By around 2600 B.C.E., conflicts had arisen between cities over access to river water, bringing further uncertainties to Sumerian life. For defense, cities constructed massive walls several miles long, and a class of professional soldiers arose. Because of a need for effective military leaders, some cities replaced the priest-kings with generals as rulers. But all rulers continued to act as representatives of the city's god.

Sumerian society had a **hierarchical structure**—that is, people were ranked according to their social, economic, and legal status. This hierarchy is apparent in art, for example, where more important people, such as the king, appear larger than less important people. Ranking below the king were the nobles, who served as administrators and generals and owned large

divination   Religious practice in which people looked for signs to determine future events and the will of the gods.

city-state   City that is also an independent nation.

ziggurat   Step-shaped pyramid serving as the main temple in Mesopotamian cities.

hierarchical structure   Social structure organized according to rank, status, and privilege.

One side of the Standard of Ur, ca. 2600 B.C.E., shows Sumeria at war, with troops marching on foot and riding on carts and with bodies of slain enemies lying at the bottom. The other side shows the land at peace, with the king holding court at the top and farmers and merchants doing their work below. *(Courtesy of the Trustees of the British Museum)*

tracts of land, and the priests, who oversaw the temples and the property of the gods. Next in status were civil servants and soldiers. Ranking below them, in a sort of middle class, were artisans and specialized laborers, including potters, artists, metal and leather workers, weavers, bricklayers, stonemasons, teachers, scribes, fishers, sailors, and merchants. The majority of the population, however, was occupied in farming. A few small farmers owned their own land, but most worked plots belonging to nobles or priests and paid rents of about one-seventh of their produce. Lowest in status were the slaves, who included war captives, persons born as slaves, and those who had been sold into slavery for debt. Slaves usually performed household tasks. Even slaves were full-fledged members of the community, for they, too, were believed to be doing the work of the gods, and it was understood that after performing enough work, they deserved to be set free.

Economic activity was largely controlled by the government. There was no coined money. Economic transactions took place by **barter,** the exchange of goods and services. The government collected taxes in produce and in labor. Landowners paid a percentage of their crops, which were stored in government warehouses and redistributed to pay the salaries of government employees, who included soldiers, shepherds, fishermen, craftworkers, and even snake charmers. The annual salary of a typical government worker was thirty bushels of barley and one ounce of silver. Labor taxes were paid with work on public works projects ranging from temple building to digging and cleaning irrigation ditches. Government bureaucrats kept detailed records of every tax payment, distribution of rations, and bit of labor.

The lack of any local resources besides water, mud, and plant materials created a need for raw materials, which could be acquired only through trade—often under government supervision. Sumerian exports

> **barter**   Form of exchange using goods and services rather than coined money.

included woolen textiles, grain, and worked-metal items. Imports were primarily raw materials, such as copper, tin, timber from the mountains to the north, and gemstones and spices from as far away as India, Arabia, and Africa. Imports were used to manufacture products such as jewelry and weapons. In the course of their manufacturing activities, the Sumerians invented the dyeing and bleaching of fabrics, the art of engraving, and accounting.

Sumerian society also was **patriarchal,** a form of hierarchical social organization in which customs and laws generally favor men. For example, in cases of adultery, a guilty man was forgiven, but a woman was sentenced to death. Married women were expected to provide children, and infertile women could be divorced. A husband could even sell his wife and children into slavery to pay off debts. Women whose fathers could not support them or find husbands for them could be devoted to a god as sacred prostitutes, known as "sisters" of the god. But women did have some rights. A wife kept control over her **dowry**—the money provided by her father when she married to support her and her children—and had equal authority with her husband over their children. Family property was usually managed by the husband or a grown son, but if they were lacking the wife was in charge. Women also could engage in business in their own name. Children, however, had no legal rights and could be disowned by their parents and expelled from the city at any time.

In the countryside, Sumerians lived in houses made of bundles of reeds that had beaten-earth floors and were plastered on the outside with **adobe,** a mixture of clay and straw. Farm animals lived with the family. City houses, made of sun-dried mud brick, were small—just a few hundred square feet—and packed together on narrow streets that sometimes were only four feet wide in order to make maximum use of the protected space within the city walls. Their thick walls and lack of windows helped keep them cool, and their flat roofs were used for cooking and for sleeping in hot weather. Furniture was minimal. Food and water were stored in large clay pots. A rudimentary sewage system conducted waste to the river but did little to keep down the stench. The Sumerian diet consisted primarily of grain products, lentils, onions, lettuce, fish, and beer. Clothing was made from woven wool. The usual garment was a rectangular piece of cloth that women draped around themselves from the left shoulder and men wrapped around their waist. Sumerians wore sandals and protected their heads from the hot sun with caps. Women adorned themselves with bracelets, necklaces, anklets, and rings for their fingers and ears.

Semitic and Indo-European Peoples

The Sumerians occupied only a tiny geographical area of the Near East and were surrounded by non-Sumerian peoples with whom they regularly came into contact. Over the course of centuries, many of the economic, technological, and religious practices that arose in Mesopotamia spread outward and were assimilated by other peoples. The first people to assimilate Mesopotamian civilization were the **Semitic peoples**—pastoralists who lived in the semiarid regions of Syria and northern Arabia to the south and east of Mesopotamia and whose similar Semitic languages gave them a sense of shared identity. The Semitic peoples had a long history of contact with the Sumerians, whom they knew had the ability to grow and store large food surpluses. Soon after 3000 B.C.E., the **Akkadians,** one of the Semitic peoples, moved into the river valleys themselves, just upstream from the Sumerians. They created an agricultural civilization of their own that assimilated the culture of the Sumerians. Subsequently, in what became a regular pattern of invasion and assimilation, other peoples likewise moved into the river valleys and adopted the civilized style of life.

Around 2350 B.C.E., the Akkadian leader Sargon embarked on a career of conquest. By his own account, the infant Sargon had been set adrift in a basket in the Euphrates River by his mother, perhaps because he was of illegitimate birth. He was rescued by a gardener, entered the service of the king of Kish, and even claimed to be the lover of the goddess Ishtar. Sargon seized power and defeated Uruk, Ur, and the other Sumerian cities. Claiming to have conquered territory all the way to the Mediterranean Sea, he called himself King of Sumer and Akkad and established the Akkadian Empire, the first Near Eastern empire.

Sargon had to administer an **empire** made up of

---

patriarchal society   (from Greek for "rule by fathers") Society in which men have the primary authority.

dowry   Financial contribution provided to a bride by her family.

adobe   Mixture of clay and straw dried in the sun, used to make plaster or bricks.

Semitic peoples   Pastoral peoples living in semiarid regions of Syria and northern Arabia who spoke versions of the same language.

Akkadians   Semitic people who established the first Near Eastern empire, the Akkadian Empire, in 2350 B.C.E. under their king, Sargon.

empire   Political unit incorporating different peoples and nations under a single government.

tore down the walls of Sumerian cities, and installed Akkadian governors. He even made his daughter Enheduanna priestess of Nanna at Ur, where she wrote several surviving poems in Sumerian, including one called "Praise of Ishtar." After his death, Sargon's empire crumbled. His successors confronted revolts by the conquered peoples and raiders from the northern mountains and the kingdom of **Elam** in eastern Iran. Mesopotamia soon returned to its customary disunited condition. The empire's most lasting legacy was the establishment of the Akkadian language, written in Sumerian cuneiform characters, as an international language that was used throughout the Near East for centuries.

Once Sumeria was free of the Akkadians, the city of Ur attempted to establish its authority over Sumeria. But Mesopotamia soon faced further invasions. Around 2000 B.C.E., Semitic peoples known collectively as the **Amorites** moved into Mesopotamia from the west. They included the **Assyrians,** who settled in the upper reaches of the Tigris River valley, and the **Babylonians,** who occupied central Mesopotamia. Like earlier pastoralists who had settled in Mesopotamia, the Babylonians assimilated Sumerian culture. They used cuneiform to write their language, and they adopted many Sumerian gods, although they did retain their own supreme god, Marduk, a storm god whom they equated with Enlil. They also gave their name to Babylonia and established a capital city at Babylon.

In 1790 B.C.E., **Hammurabi** (r. 1790–1750 B.C.E.) became king of the Babylonians. Using a shrewd mixture of diplomacy and military might, by 1760 B.C.E. he brought all of Mesopotamia under his control and created the Old Babylonian Empire, the second Near Eastern empire. He introduced measures intended to unify the many different peoples of his empire. For example, in the marketplaces he required the use of

This bronze bust depicts Sargon of Akkad, founder of the Akkadian Empire, ca. 2350 B.C.E. The eyes originally were inlaid with semiprecious stones that were dug out by grave robbers in antiquity. Beards like Sargon's were worn by warriors; priests had shaven heads and cheeks. The bust was preserved in the National Museum of Iraq in Baghdad until 2003, when it was stolen during the looting of the museum after the American occupation of Iraq. *(Claus Hansmann/ Interfoto)*

cities that did not get along with one another. In some ways he tried to be conciliatory. For example, even though he favored Ishtar, he respected Enlil, the most important Sumerian god, by calling himself the Great King of Enlil. In other ways, however, Sargon was excessively domineering. He humiliated defeated rulers,

Elam   Ancient kingdom located in modern-day Iran.

Amorites   Western Semitic peoples, including the Assyrians and Babylonians, who moved into Mesopotamia around 2000 B.C.E.

Assyrians   Semitic people who settled in the upper Tigris River valley around 2000 B.C.E.

Babylonians   Semitic people who settled in central Mesopotamia around 2000 B.C.E and established the Old Babylonian Empire in 1760 B.C.E.

Hammurabi   (r. 1790–1750 B.C.E.) Mesopotamian ruler who created the Old Babylonian Empire and issued a famous law code around 1760 B.C.E.

standard weights based on the **talent,** which weighed about fifty-six pounds. There were sixty minas in a talent and sixty shekels in a mina. Around 1760 B.C.E. Hammurabi issued a standard legal code that placed everyone under the same laws.

The Babylonians also advanced the study of mathematics and astronomy. Using the cumbersome 60-based number system, Babylonian mathematicians dealt with concepts such as square roots and algebraic unknowns (which they called a false value). Lacking a symbol for zero, Babylonians substituted a blank space. These innovations had practical applications, such as calculating compound interest or the amount of building material needed for a ziggurat. Babylonian astronomers divided the year into 360 days (6 times 60), the day into 6 parts, and the hour into 60 minutes. By keeping detailed records of the movements of the sun, moon, and planets, they were able to predict the phases of the moon. They also believed that the positions of astronomical bodies had a predictable effect on what happened on earth, giving rise to **astrology.**

In spite of Hammurabi's best efforts to create unity, his empire disintegrated soon after his death around 1750 B.C.E. A new group of invaders then appeared, the **Indo-European peoples.** Like the Semitic peoples, the Indo-Europeans consisted of different groups of pastoralist peoples speaking versions of the same language. Their homeland lay in the grassy **steppes** of Central Asia north of the Black and Caspian Seas. Every so often, groups of Indo-Europeans left to seek new homes because of overpopulation or food shortages. The earliest known Indo-European migration occurred around 2000 B.C.E. One group, the **Aryans,** settled in modern-day Iran. Another, the **Hittites,** moved into Anatolia, and yet others migrated into the **Balkans.** The first Indo-Europeans to invade Mesopotamia were the Hittites, who raided Babylonia in 1595 B.C.E. Shortly thereafter, around 1500 B.C.E., one group of Aryans invaded India, destroying the Bronze Age civilization there. Another Aryan group, the **Kassites,** occupied Mesopotamia, making use of new military technology, the horse and chariot. They assimilated Mesopotamian culture—including religion, dress, and language—so thoroughly that nearly the only element of their native Indo-European culture they preserved was their names. The Kassites continued to rule much of Mesopotamia until about 1200 B.C.E.

The Code of Hammurabi

The most important document to survive from ancient Mesopotamia is the law code of Hammurabi, which placed everyone in the Old Babylonian Empire under a single legal system. The code was a compilation of existing laws and customs relating to civil and criminal procedures. It recognized three classes of people: nobles, free persons, and slaves. Many laws dealt with business and property, setting prices for manufactured items and wages for laborers such as sailors, barbers, physicians, veterinarians, home-builders, artisans, and farm workers. Other laws dealt with agriculture. For example, someone whose dam broke and caused flooding was to be sold as a slave to pay for the damages.

Of the 282 laws in the code, 49 dealt with marriage. First marriages usually were arranged by a girl's family. Men were permitted to have two wives, but women were allowed only one husband. The code acknowledged that marriages did not always work out. If a wife was childless, her husband could pay her a mina (about a pound) of gold for a divorce or take a second wife, who would rank beneath the first wife. If a wife became incapacitated by disease, a husband could marry a second wife but had to support the first wife as long as she lived. A man who divorced a wife who had borne him children had to support her until the children were raised; she then received part of his property so she "could marry the man of her heart." A woman who "ruined her house, neglected her husband, and was judicially convicted" could be divorced but would be forced to remain with her ex-husband as a servant even if he remarried. A woman whose husband left her received a divorce, but a woman who left her husband was thrown into the river (and presumably drowned).

---

talent Mesopotamian unit of weight, about 56 pounds, comprised of 60 minas, with each mina being composed of 60 shekels.

astrology (from Greek for "knowledge of the stars") Branch of learning based on the belief that the future was ordained by the gods and can be read in the motions of the stars and planets.

Indo-European peoples Pastoral peoples of central Asia who settled in areas from India to Europe and spoke versions of the same language.

steppe Flat treeless plain covered by short grass.

Aryans Indo-European peoples who settled in Iran around 2000 B.C.E.

Hittites Indo-European people who settled in Anatolia around 2000 B.C.E.

Balkans Southeastern Europe, including modern Greece, Bulgaria, and Romania.

Kassites Indo-European people who invaded Mesopotamia around 1500 B.C.E.

A six-foot tall black basalt obelisk created ca. 1760 B.C.E. bears the Code of Hammurabi. Hammurabi, standing at the left, is shown receiving the code from the sun god Shamash. Hammurabi said, "The gods called me, Hammurabi, who feared God, to bring about the rule of righteousness and to destroy the wicked and the evil-doers, so that the strong would not harm the weak." Copies of the law code were posted throughout the empire. *(Hirmer Verlag München)*

In the case of criminal law, many crimes—such as making false accusations, stealing temple property, receiving stolen property, kidnapping, stealing or harboring escaped slaves, breaking and entering, robbery, rape, and shoddy construction—were punished by death. Some death sentences were quite gruesome. Sons and mothers guilty of incest and looters who burned houses were burned alive. Male and female lovers who killed their spouses were **impaled.** Other punishments involved physical mutilation.

Cutting off the hands was the penalty for physicians who bungled operations, for farm workers who stole grain, and for sons who struck their fathers. Men who slandered women were branded on the forehead. Punishments also could vary according to a person's social status. A free person who struck a noble received sixty blows from an ox-whip, but if he struck someone of equal rank, he merely paid a fine. A slave who struck a free person lost an ear. A noble who put out the eye of another noble was subject to the law of retaliation and had his own eye put out. But if a noble put out the eye of a free person, he paid a fine of one mina of gold.

In other regards, the code attempted to provide fair treatment for everyone. Judges who rendered bad decisions were removed from office, and victims of crimes were reimbursed by the community. Even slaves had legal rights. Male slaves were allowed to marry free women. The children of such unions were free, but when the slave died, the marital property was divided between the wife and the slave's owner. If a free man had children by a slave woman, they and the woman were freed at his death. If a man sold his children, his wife, or himself into slavery to pay off a debt, they were set free after three years of labor. The Code of Hammurabi not only reflected contemporary Mesopotamian standards of justice but also provided a model for future lawmaking.

Egyptian Civilization, 3000–1200 B.C.E.

↓ How did geography influence Egyptians' views of themselves, the world, and the afterlife?
↓ How and why did the role and status of the pharaoh change during the course of Egyptian history?

Generally speaking, civilization developed in Egypt in much the same way as in Mesopotamia. In more detailed regards, the two civilizations were very different. Unlike the Mesopotamians, the Egyptians were geographically isolated, and for more than a thousand years they experienced no foreign invasions. Their country was usually unified. The Egyptians trusted their gods to look after them, had an optimistic outlook on life, and believed that they would enjoy a delightful afterlife. Each of the three

impalement Form of execution in which a victim was skewered on a sharpened stake.

periods of Egyptian history—the Old, Middle, and New Kingdoms—had particular identifying characteristics. During the Old Kingdom, the pharaohs had absolute authority. Only the pharaohs were believed to have afterlives, and they constructed gigantic pyramids as their tombs. During the Middle Kingdom, the pharaohs had less authority, and Egyptians believed that all had access to the afterlife. The New Kingdom saw the rise of the Egyptian army and the Egyptian Empire.

The Gift of the Nile

As in Mesopotamia, civilization in Egypt arose around 3000 B.C.E. in a fertile river valley, with extensive exploitation of agriculture and the use of bronze for weapons and jewelry. Unlike the Tigris and Euphrates Rivers, however, the flooding of the Nile was predictable. Every summer, heavy rains in central Africa fed water into the Nile, causing it to overflow its banks in mid-August. By November, the river had returned to its banks, leaving behind a layer of fertile soil. Irrigation ditches were dug, and the land was planted. Agricultural life was organized according to three seasons: Inundation of the Nile, Emergence (planting), and Deficiency (low water and harvest). To forecast the seasons and the Nile floods, the Egyptians created a calendar based on the moon. It had twelve months of 30 days each. Five feast days added at the end made a 365-day year that serves as the basis of our own calendar. Egypt was the richest agricultural land in the Mediterranean world, and Egyptian life was focused on the Nile. The Egyptians' own word for their land was Kemet, the "black land," a reference to the rich, dark soil that was the gift of the Nile. Because people were never far from the river, they traveled by boat and at first had no need for wheeled carts or horses to pull them.

Geography also isolated Egypt from the rest of the world. The Nile Valley was a thin strip of agricultural land six hundred miles long but only four to twenty miles wide, surrounded on the east and west by the inhospitable and sparsely populated Sahara Desert. If the approaches to Egypt in the north and south were protected, as they were until the eighteenth century B.C.E., the country was safe from invasion. The predictable renewal of the soil and the lack of concern about invasion or floods gave the Egyptians an optimistic outlook on life. They were convinced they had the best life of anyone on earth and thought themselves superior to the black peoples of Africa to the south and to the Semitic and other peoples of the Levant and Mesopotamia to the north. Geographical iso-

lation also meant that influence from outside was restricted. Change came slowly.

The Egyptians divided the Nile valley into two sections, Lower Egypt (the Nile Delta) and Upper Egypt (the rest of the river valley south to **Nubia**). These designations are used because water flows from higher to lower ground. Before 3000 B.C.E., Upper and Lower Egypt were separate kingdoms, but around 3000 B.C.E., the two kingdoms were united by a ruler named Narmer and political unity became the normal condition of Egypt. To unify Egypt further, Narmer founded a new capital city at Memphis, where Upper and Lower Egypt met. This unity further contributed to the Egyptians' sense of optimism. Narmer was the first of a multitude of rulers known as **pharaohs.** Subsequently, pharaohs belonging to the same family were organized into **dynasties.**

During the first two dynasties of pharaohs (3000–2700 B.C.E.), all the fundamental aspects of Egyptian culture, religion, and government evolved. Egyptian writing, known as **hieroglyphics,** had more than seven hundred symbols that represented different words, thoughts, or meanings. Only highly educated scribes could write. The usual writing materials were stone, for large monuments, or papyrus (the source of our word *paper*), for record keeping. Hollow papyrus reeds were split down the middle, flattened, and glued together in a two-layer crosshatched pattern to form sheets about fifteen inches square. Writing was done with a pen and ink.

Egypt was divided into forty-two smaller territories called **nomes,** each administered from a city center. As in Mesopotamia, cities served as centers for administration and for the storage and distribution of food supplies. Each Egyptian city—again, as in Mesopotamia—had its own main god. Egyptian cities were not large population centers, however, and they were not walled. Most of the people lived securely in the countryside, close to their fields.

The Egyptians had a multitude of gods, many of whom were depicted as animals, such as Anubis, the

Nubia   Region of Africa located in the Nile valley just south of Egypt.

pharaoh   (in Egyptian, "great house") Ruler of ancient Egypt.

dynasty   Group of rulers belonging to the same family.

hieroglyphics   (from Greek for "sacred writing") Earliest form of Egyptian writing.

nomes   Smaller geographical and administrative regions of ancient Egypt, governed by nomarchs.

jackal god. Several important gods were connected to the sun. In the time of Narmer, Ra, the god of the noonday sun, became the most important god of Egypt. In addition, rather than just being representatives of the gods, as in Mesopotamia, Egyptian pharaohs were considered to be gods in their own right. Pharaohs also took on the personality of other gods, such as Ra. The Egyptians were confident that their pharaohs, and their other gods, would take care of them. The goddess **Ma'at,** for example, provided order, stability, and justice. Even the pharaoh was expected to rule according to Ma'at.

Egyptian Government and Society

The pharaoh stood at the peak of Egyptian government and society. The pharaoh was assisted in governing by an increasingly large bureaucracy. His main assistant was the vizier, a chief executive officer in charge of administrative details. Upper and Lower Egypt each had governors, and nomarchs managed the nomes. The government oversaw tax collection and the administration of justice. As in Mesopotamia, taxes were paid in kind—in produce (a percentage of crops) or in labor, including work on irrigation projects and the upkeep of temples and palaces. All free persons were equal under the law. Criminal law was based on getting a confession from the accused party, often by torture, which included whipping and mutilation. Persons who refused to confess could be set free. Many crimes carried physical punishment. The penalty for extortion, for example, was one hundred blows and five open wounds; the penalty for interfering with traffic on the Nile was cutting off the nose and exile. The death sentence, in forms including impalement, burning, drowning, or decapitation, was exacted for crimes such as treason, sacrilege, murder, and tax evasion. In contrast to Mesopotamia, however, Egypt had no professional soldiers at this time, for there was no fear of invasion. If the pharaoh needed a military force to raid a neighboring region, a band of farmers and artisans would be armed and then disbanded when the campaign was over.

Like Mesopotamian society, Egyptian society was hierarchical. The pharaoh had the highest rank. Next came the pharaoh's family, which consisted of a chief wife, who often was also the pharaoh's sister (by this means, pharaohs behaved like gods and kept power in the family); additional wives and **concubines**; and the pharaoh's children. The pharaoh's successor usually was a son, although female pharaohs were not prohibited. Pharaohs advertised their divine status with large stone sculptures of themselves—such as

the Great Sphinx, which showed the pharaoh as a man-headed lion.

Ranking after the royal family were nobles and priests. Nobles held high state offices and owned large amounts of land. Priests administered the lands belonging to the temple. Next in status were specialized workers such as scribes, acrobats, singers, dancers, musicians, artists, stonemasons, perfume makers, and professional mourners at funerals. Most of these positions were open to both men and women. Lower in status was the majority of the population, which labored in farming or on public works projects such as digging and cleaning irrigation ditches. Lowest in status were slaves, who were either Egyptians who had been sold for debt or captives acquired by occasional raids into Nubia to the south or Asia to the north. Some slaves were set free and even became governmental officials. Most, however, were employed in domestic and farm work.

Egyptians treasured their family life. Many scenes in Egyptian art depict affection between husbands and wives or of parents for their children. Egyptians usually married in their teens. An Egyptian proverb advised men, "Take a wife while you are young." Even though marriages were usually arranged by families, young people still composed love poems. One young woman wrote, "He torments my heart with his voice, he makes sickness take hold of me." Marriage contracts specified the rights of the husband and wife to their own possessions, the amount of the allowance that the husband would provide to his wife, and how the property would be divided in case of a divorce. The marriage ceremony consisted of the bride moving her possessions to her husband's house. Either party could initiate a divorce, and divorced wives were entitled to continued support from their ex-husbands. Male and female children inherited the family property equally. In general, women had parity with men when it came to having careers, owning property, and pursuing cases in court.

Egyptian homes were made of adobe brick, and doors and windows were covered with mats to keep out insects. A room on the upper storey with an open wall could be used for sleeping on hot nights. Furniture consisted of stools, mats for sleeping, and large and small jars for storing food and personal items. The diet was primarily bread, along with fruit, fish,

Ma'at Egyptian goddess who represented order, justice, and stability.

concubine Female sexual partner ranking below a wife.

The three largest pyramids were constructed at Giza beginning ca. 2600 B.C.E. The "Great Pyramid" of the pharaoh Khufu, in the center, is 781 feet at the base, 481 feet tall, and contains 2.3 million stone blocks weighing from two to fifteen tons each. The smaller pyramids in the foreground were for other members of the royal family. *(TIPS Images)*

and beer made from barley. Household sewage flowed directly into the Nile. Clothing was made from linen. At work, men wore loincloths and women, short skirts. For special occasions, women wore dresses held up by straps and men wore kilts. Both men and women wore jewelry made from copper, gold, and semiprecious stones, including anklets, rings, bracelets, earrings, and beaded necklaces. The use of cosmetics, such as black and green eye shadow and red cheek and lip gloss, was also common.

The Age of the Pyramids

Historians divide Egyptian history into three chronological periods during which Egypt was united: the Old, Middle, and New Kingdoms. These periods were separated by "intermediate periods" during which Egyptian unity broke down. Each period had its own distinctive traits. Even though Egyptian civilization began around 3000 B.C.E., it is not until the Old Kingdom (2700–2200 B.C.E.), from which written records survive in significant numbers, that the history of ancient Egypt begins to be clearly known. The Old Kingdom was characterized by all-powerful pharaohs who built gigantic stone pyramids that

served as their tombs. The largest pyramids were built during the Fourth Dynasty, beginning around 2600 B.C.E. The pharaoh's burial chamber was hidden deep inside the pyramid—safe, it was hoped, from grave robbers. It contained all the wealth, jewelry, and domestic objects that the pharaoh would need in the afterlife. It even contained clay figures of servants to take care of the pharaoh's future needs. The tomb chamber also contained pyramid texts, magical spells written on the walls to ensure that the pharaoh's transition to the afterlife would go smoothly. At the beginning of the Old Kingdom, only the pharaohs were thought to have an afterlife. Therefore, nobles hoping to share the pharaoh's afterlife placed their tombs next to a pyramid.

Building a pyramid required a vast supply of material and workers that only a pharaoh, who had the authority of a god, could mobilize. Stone quarried from the cliffs next to the Nile was ferried during the flood season to the royal burial ground just west of Memphis. Tens of thousands of Egyptian workers were fed and housed at the pharaoh's expense while they dragged the massive stone blocks up earthen ramps to the top of the new pyramid. A large pyramid took fifteen years or more to complete.

Pharaohs did all they could to ensure that work proceeded as quickly as possible, and here lay the seeds of future problems. Pharaohs gave private estates, tax exemptions, and special privileges to nomarchs who fulfilled their labor and supply quotas, and the sons of nomarchs were allowed to succeed them, thus strengthening the noble class. These policies helped individual pharaohs in the short term but made fewer resources available to their successors. Pyramids became smaller and smaller, reflecting a decline in the pharaohs' resources. At the same time, nobles gained a greater sense of self-importance and began to build tombs for themselves with pyramid texts in their own nomes, a sign that they believed they now had their own afterlife without needing to share the pharaoh's. Powerful nobles began to challenge the pharaoh's authority and compete with one another for power. The last pharaoh of the Sixth Dynasty (2350–2200 B.C.E.) was Nitocris, the first woman to rule Egypt. After her death, revolts among nobles broke out, and Egypt lost its customary unity and stability.

The Age of Osiris

The loss of unity during the First Intermediate Period (2200–2050 B.C.E.) caused a breakdown in irrigation, and famines occurred. Not until 2050 B.C.E. was the nomarch of Thebes able to reunify Egypt, beginning the Middle Kingdom (2050–1786 B.C.E.). As a symbol of the change of rule, the bull god Amon, the chief god of Thebes, became the most important god of Egypt. Ra, Egypt's previous main god, was often linked with Amon, creating a composite second chief god, Amon-Ra. Moreover, pharaohs of the Middle Kingdom were weaker than those of the Old Kingdom. They still were seen as living gods and buried in small pyramids, but their authority was threatened by ambitious nobles and priests who controlled more and more of Egypt's land and produce.

For most of the population, the biggest change during the Middle Kingdom was that the afterlife now was available to everyone. The result was a great increase in reverence for the Osiris, the god of the underworld. Egyptians believed that Osiris, who had brought civilization to Egypt, had been killed and chopped up by his envious brother Set. Isis, the wife of Osiris, put the pieces back together and breathed life back into him, whereupon Osiris became the judge who decided whether the dead would receive a good afterlife. Osiris's son Horus, the falcon god, defeated Set and became the defender of the dead when they were judged.

The Egyptians believed that if Osiris could live happily after death, so could they. They anticipated continued enjoyment of all the best spiritual and material things they had enjoyed during life—providing their bodies were preserved by **mummification.** All the internal organs except the heart were removed and mummified separately. The brain was scrambled, sucked out through the nose, and discarded, and the remaining skin, bones, and muscle were soaked in natron, a salt solution that removed moisture. The dried corpse then was wrapped with linen bandages and buried underground in an elaborately decorated coffin, accompanied by grave goods such as food, jewelry, and domestic items. Those who could not afford this expensive process made do with a simpler burial in the desert sand, which often resulted in natural mummification.

Egyptians believed that before receiving a good afterlife they would be questioned by Osiris to determine whether they had lived according to Ma'at. Those who failed the test were devoured by the Eater of the Dead, a demon that was part crocodile, part hippopotamus, and part lion. To ensure that they passed, Egyptians wrapped mummies with a collection of answers to Osiris's questions known as the **Book of the Dead,** which contained advice such as, "Say 'No' when asked if you ever stole anything." Thus, even in death, Egyptian optimism prevailed; everyone was believed to pass the test and receive a good afterlife.

About 1730 B.C.E., the Middle Kingdom came to an end when Egypt was invaded by a Semitic people known as the **Hyksos.** Using the latest military technology, including the horse and chariot and the compound bow—a bow made from laminated layers of wood and animal horn for extra strength—the Hyksos easily overcame the undefended cities and untrained armies of the Egyptians, and Egypt again entered a period of disunity, the Second Intermediate Period (1730–1570 B.C.E.). The Hyksos became pharaohs in northern Egypt but allowed the rest of Egypt to be governed by Egyptian subordinate rulers called **vassals,** who were left alone as long as they acknowledged Hyksos authority.

mummification   Drying process by which bodies are preserved after death.

Book of the Dead   Catalogue of magical spells that was buried with mummies to ensure that Egyptians received a good afterlife.

Hyksos   (from Semitic for "rulers of foreign lands") Semitic people who conquered Egypt in 1730 B.C.E.

vassals   Subordinate rulers who declare loyalty to a higher-ranking ruler.

The "Papyrus of Nany" shows a dead woman, on the left, holding her mouth and eyes in her hand, being judged by Osiris, sitting on the right. In the center, the jackal god Anubis weighs Nany's heart against Maat to see whether she had led a just life. Anubis keeps his hand on the weighing pan to ensure that her heart does not fail the test. In the Egyptian view, the gods ensured that everyone would receive an afterlife. *(Metropolitan Museum of Art, Rogers Fund, 1930 [30.3.31]. Image © The Metropolitan Museum of Art.)*

The Hyksos enthusiastically assimilated Egyptian culture and even preserved documents from the Old Kingdom that otherwise would have been lost. The Egyptians, however, could not tolerate being ruled by foreigners. They mastered the use of the chariot and compound bow and created professional armies. In 1570 B.C.E., led by the ruler of Thebes, they counterattacked. The Hyksos were expelled and pursued up the coast of Palestine, where they were completely destroyed. The Egyptians then obliterated nearly every trace of the Hyksos and were determined never again to let foreigners invade Egypt.

The New Kingdom

The reunification of Egypt after the expulsion of the Hyksos marked the beginning of the New Kingdom (1570–1070 B.C.E.), an era characterized by strong pharaohs, a standing army, and the creation of an **Egyptian Empire.** Pharaohs became military leaders. Their armies included both native Egyptians, who often were rewarded with land, and paid foreign soldiers called **mercenaries,** many from Nubia. Support from the army gave pharaohs the means to reassert their dominance over unruly nobles and priests. In Egyptian art, the pharaoh now was customarily shown shooting a bow from a war chariot, a forceful

reminder to everyone of the source of his power. At the same time, the pharaoh's chief wife was promoted to the status of god's wife. By these measures, the royal family was able to regain much of the authority that it had lost during the Middle Kingdom.

The pharaohs' first task was to ensure the security of Egypt, by defending the borders and by establishing a military presence beyond them. Pharaoh Thutmose I (r. 1527–1515 B.C.E.) campaigned into Nubia in the south and all the way to the Euphrates River in the north, thus impressing Egypt's neighbors with his military might. His daughter **Hatshepsut** (r. 1498–1483 B.C.E.) was crowned pharaoh, and to enhance her stature, she claimed she was the daughter of the bull god Amon. She wore male royal clothing and a false royal beard and as commander in chief of the army led an attack into Nubia. Hatshepsut also constructed border fortifications and a huge terraced temple in honor of Amon, considered to be one of the

> **Egyptian Empire**   Egyptian conquests in Palestine and Syria that served to protect Egypt from invasion, created by Thutmose III (r. 1483–1450 B.C.E.)
>
> **mercenaries**   Hired soldiers who fight for pay.
>
> **Hatshepsut**   (r. 1498–1483 B.C.E.) Female pharaoh who fortified Egypt.

most beautiful buildings of the ancient world. The building activities of other pharaohs, too, were focused on temples, which often advertised their military achievements. Pharaohs no longer built pyramids but were buried in underground stone tombs.

Hatshepsut's son, Thutmose III (r. 1483–1450 B.C.E.), subdued the peoples of Palestine and Syria and created an empire that served as a buffer between Egypt and potential enemies, thus increasing Egypt's security. Rather than making conquered lands part of Egypt, Thutmose followed the Hyksos' model of making defeated rulers into vassals and allowing them to remain in power as long as they remained loyal, paid tribute, and sent hostages to Egypt to guarantee their good behavior. Every year or so, the pharaoh assembled the Egyptian army, marched north, and reminded the vassals—who were always ready to revolt—of his overwhelming power. These demonstrations reinforced the pharaoh's position as military commander and renewed the army's loyalty to him.

The empire remained stable for about a hundred years, until Amenhotep IV (r. 1350–1334 B.C.E.) ascended the throne. Even though Egypt had the most conservative culture of all the ancient Near Eastern peoples, Amenhotep departed from Egyptian tradition by ruling that **Aton,** a minor sun god, was the only god who could be worshiped (see Choice). He even changed his own name to Akhenaton to honor the god. The move so distressed the Egyptians that the army was compelled to remain in Egypt to maintain order, which gave the Hittites an opportunity to occupy parts of the Egyptian Empire. Akhenaton then disappeared from history, perhaps a victim of the unrest that his reforms had caused.

> **Aton**   Sun god whom the pharaoh Akhenaton (r. 1350–1334 B.C.E.) attempted to make the supreme god of Egypt.

VoiceVoiceVoiceVoice

Akhenaton, "Great Hymn to Aton"

The pharaoh Akhenaton's "Great Hymn to Aton," found engraved on the tomb of the pharaoh Ay at El-Armana, expresses Akhenaton's personal devotion to the god Aton in formal and ceremonial language. The hymn begins with praises of Akhenaton and his wife, Nefertiti, and Akhenaton also is referred to by his coronation name, Nefer-kheperu-Ra Wa-en-Ra ("Sole-One-of-Ra"). The text has similarities to the scriptures of other world religions.

Praise of the King of Upper and Lower Egypt, who lives on truth, the Lord of the Two Lands: Nefer-kheperu-Ra Wa-en-Ra, the Son of Ra, who lives on truth, the Lord of Diadems, Akhenaton, long in his lifetime; and praise of the Chief Wife of the King, his beloved, the Lady of the Two Lands: Neferneferu-Aton Nefertiti, living, healthy, and youthful forever and ever.

Akhenaton says:
➡ Thou appearest beautifully on the horizon of heaven,
Thou living Aton, the beginning of life!
Thou art gracious, great, glistening, and high over every land;
Thy rays encompass the lands to the limit of all that thou hast made.
As thou art Ra, thou reachest to the end of the lands;
➡ Thou subduest them for thy beloved son.
➡ When thou settest in the western horizon,
The land is in darkness, in the manner of death.
Darkness is a shroud, and the earth is in stillness.

➡ Why does Akhenaton think Aton is important?

➡ What is the significance of the transition from darkness to light?

➡ Who is this son?

At daybreak, when thou arisest on the horizon,
When thou shinest as the Aton by day,
Thou drivest away the darkness and givest thy rays.

➡ **Who benefits from the blessings of Aton?**

➡ The Two Lands are in festivity every day,
Their arms are raised in praise at thy appearance.
All beasts are content with their pasturage;
Trees and plants are flourishing.
The birds that fly from their nests,
Their wings are stretched out in praise to thy ka [soul].

➡ Creator of seed in women,
Thou who makest fluid into man,
Thou who maintainest the son in the womb of his mother . . .
O sole god, like whom there is no other!
Thou didst create the world according to thy desire:
The countries of Syria and Nubia, the land of Egypt,
Thou settest every man in his place,
Thou suppliest their necessities:
Everyone has his food, and his time of life is reckoned.

➡ **How does Akhenaton portray Aton's relation to the other gods? What similarities are there between Akhenaton's hymn and the scriptures of other world religions?**

➡ Their tongues are separate in speech,
And their natures as well;
Their skins are distinguished,
As thou distinguishest the foreign peoples.
Thou makest a Nile in the underworld,
Thou bringest forth water as thou desirest
To maintain the people of Egypt.
All distant foreign countries, thou makest their life also,
For thou hast set a Nile in heaven,
That it may descend for them and make waves upon the mountains,
To water their fields in their towns.
How effective they are, thy plans, O lord of eternity!

➡ **How did the Egyptians feel about foreign peoples?**

➡ The Nile in heaven, it is for the foreign peoples,
While the true Nile comes from the underworld for Egypt.

➡ **Why does Akhenaton speak of two Niles?**

➡ Thou are in my heart,
And there is no other that knows thee
Save thy son Nefer-kheperu-Ra Wa-en-Ra,
For thou hast made him well-versed in thy plans and in thy strength.

➡ **How does Akhenaton emphasize his special relationship with Aton?**

Source: Pritchard, James, *Ancient Near Eastern Texts Relating to the Old Testament—Third Edition with supplement.* © 1950, 1955, 1969, renewed 1978 by Princeton University Press. Reprinted by permission of Princeton University Press.

Akhenaton was followed by several short-lived boy pharaohs. One of them, Tut-ankh-aton, soon changed his name to **Tut-ankh-amon** (r. 1334–1325 B.C.E.), a sign that the god Amon had returned to favor. When Tut-ankh-amon died, he was buried so secretly that his was the only pharaoh's tomb not to be robbed in antiquity. After its discovery in 1922 C.E., the boy king was nicknamed King Tut.

The next pharaohs were army generals, suggesting that the army had taken over. The pharaohs of the Nineteenth and Twentieth Dynasties (1293–1070 B.C.E.), most of whom were named Ramses, struggled to restore and maintain the Egyptian Empire. **Ramses II**

(r. 1279–1212 B.C.E.), the greatest of the warrior pharaohs, fought the Hittites for twenty years before the two empires made peace in 1259 B.C.E., establishing fixed boundaries and agreeing to defend each

Tut-ankh-amon (r. 1334–1325 B.C.E.) Also known as King Tut; the only Egyptian pharaoh whose tomb was not robbed in antiquity.

Ramses II (r. 1279–1212 B.C.E.) Egyptian pharaoh who made peace with the Hittites and constructed many temples.

other against outside aggressors. To seal the bargain, each ruler married a daughter of the other. Ramses spent the remainder of his reign engaged in massive building projects. He not only constructed many temples in his own name; he also put his name on monuments of his predecessors. By the time of his death in 1212 B.C.E., Ramses II was over ninety years old, and great changes were soon to occur. The Bronze Age was drawing to a close and, with it, the days of Egypt's greatest glory.

Lost Civilizations of the Bronze Age, 2500–1200 B.C.E.

↓ What factors encouraged the development of trading economies during the Bronze Age?

↓ What factors helped bring about the decline of Bronze Age civilization?

The Bronze Age was the great age of river valley civilizations based on the extensive exploitation of agriculture. At the same, however, other peoples living outside large river valleys in the Levant, on the island of Crete, and in Greece created civilizations of their own. These peoples focused on trade as a means of expanding their economies. Around 1200 B.C.E., Bronze Age civilization came to an end as the result of disruptions caused by the arrival of Indo-European invaders known as the Sea Peoples.

Ebla and Canaan

The assumption by historians that Egypt and Mesopotamia were the only important civilizations of the Near Eastern Bronze Age was stunningly disproven in 1968 when Italian archaeologists discovered **Ebla,** a Syrian city mentioned in Akkadian and Egyptian records but whose location had previously been unknown. Excavations revealed eighteen thousand cuneiform tablets showing that as early as 2500 B.C.E., Ebla was a thriving commercial center. The city walls enclosed about 125 acres and housed some thirty thousand persons. Ebla was a cultural crossroad, as demonstrated by the many languages used in the tablets, including Assyrian, Akkadian, Sumerian, Hittite, and the previously unknown language of the Eblaites. Some tablets listed the meanings of Eblaite words in Sumerian and other known languages, making Ebla's Semitic language easy for scholars to decipher. The tablets tell us much about the people who lived there.

Controlling territory from southern Anatolia to the Euphrates River, Ebla was able to oversee trade south to Egypt, east to Mesopotamia, north to Anatolia, and west into the Mediterranean. Like all ancient peoples, the Eblaites had an agricultural economy, but their farmland did not produce a large surplus. To expand their economy, they traded manufactured products, such as linen and wool textiles and fine inlaid wooden furniture, and raw materials, such as timber, copper, and silver. In the course of their commercial activities, the Eblaites assimilated religious practices from neighboring cultures, worshiping the western Semitic god **Ba'al** and the Mesopotamian Shamash and Ishtar. The tablets also contained names like U-ru-sa-li-ma (Jerusalem), Ab-ra-mu (Abraham), and Da-u-dum (David), which would reappear centuries later in Jewish scripture. In about 2250 B.C.E., Ebla was sacked and burned by the Akkadians. The fires baked the clay tablets in the palace archives, thus preserving them.

The Levant continued to be a center of commercial activities after 2000 B.C.E. The Assyrians on the upper Tigris sent caravans of woven textiles to Anatolia, where the Hittites attempted to gain control of the lucrative metal trade. Trading cities such as Byblos, Sidon, Tyre, and Ugarit arose around 1500 B.C.E. on the coast of **Canaan,** sometimes independent and sometimes under the domination of **imperialist** states such as Egypt or the Hittite kingdom. The Canaanite cities experimented with writing systems using symbols that represented not ideas, words, or syllables but consonants. These vastly simplified systems were the forerunners of the **alphabet** and made writing more accessible to the general population, especially to merchants, and less the monopoly of priests and scribes.

The Minoans of Crete

Another Bronze Age civilization based on trade, the **Minoan civilization,** arose on Crete, a Mediterranean island south of Greece. It is named after King Minos,

Ebla Syrian city that established a civilization with a trading economy around 2500 B.C.E.

Ba'al (from Semitic for "master") Name given to several western Semitic gods.

Canaan Area of the Levant bordering the Mediterranean coast (modern Lebanon and Palestine).

imperialist Having to do with building empires.

alphabet (in Greek, "alpha beta") System of writing in which symbols represent individual consonants.

Minoan civilization Bronze Age civilization that developed on the island of Crete soon after 3000 B.C.E.

The Minoan activity known now as bull leaping may reflect either sport or religious ritual, and is one of many examples of the importance of bulls in ancient societies. This comic-strip-like portrayal from the Minoan palace at Knossos shows a long-horned bull charging a young man or woman who grasps the horns, flips over the bull, and lands with arms outstretched—much like a modern gymnast—behind the bull. *(Scala/Art Resource, NY)*

a legendary Cretan king. Soon after 3000 B.C.E., an advanced culture centered on coastal towns appeared, and by 2000 B.C.E., several small urban centers known as "palace complexes" had been built near the coast, including Knossos in the north and Phaistos in the south. Minoan palaces complexes had rooms of roughly equal size organized around a central plaza. As the complex expanded, additional rooms were added on the periphery. The palace complexes were administrative centers overseeing the manufacture, storage, and distribution of goods rather than population centers. They seem to have been independent of each other, and their lack of walls indicates that they were at peace with one another and not threatened by foreign attack. Most people lived in the palace suburbs or in the countryside, in houses that had doors, windows, and even indoor plumbing.

Crete did not have fertile river valleys that could be used for large-scale grain production. For economic expansion, the island location encouraged trade by sea, and Minoan ships traveled the Mediterranean. Most were merchant vessels propelled by

sails, but some were oar-driven warships whose purpose was to protect the Minoan trading fleet. The Minoans imported metal from the Aegean islands and Italy, as well as amber that had reached the Mediterranean from the Baltic Sea. Their exports included olive oil, made from olive trees grown on sunny hillsides, and manufactured goods such as fine pottery, stoneware, carved gemstones, and intricate metal jewelry, which they shipped to Greece, Anatolia, the Levant, and Egypt. Egyptian wall paintings record a people called the Keftiu who came from "the islands in the great green sea," generally thought to be a reference to Minoan traders. The Minoans also established trading colonies on islands, such as Thera, in the Aegean Sea, and even on the coast of Anatolia. From about 2000 to 1400 B.C.E., the Minoans had a virtual monopoly on Mediterranean trade.

The Minoans created their own writing system, known as Linear A, which is unlike that of Mesopotamia or Egypt. Characters were scratched on clay with a pointed wooden stylus. Linear A has not yet been deciphered, but the purpose of Minoan documents is clear. Most are lists of words followed by a number and clearly represent inventories and accounts.

In other ways, too, Minoan civilization was different from its Near Eastern counterparts. The Minoans had no high-profile gods worshiped in elaborate temples. Minoan religion was personal rather than public, practiced in caves and small shrines in the countryside. Worshipers demonstrated their devotion by depositing **cult objects,** such as small golden double-axes, in the shrines. Many deities represented the forces of nature. One was a goddess known later to the Greeks as the Lady of the Wild Things. Small statuettes depict her wearing an open-breasted, flounced dress and holding two snakes in her upraised hands. Artistic portrayals, in which men and women are represented equally, suggest that Minoan worshipers dressed like the deity they were worshiping and worked themselves into a religious ecstasy in which they believed they could see the god or goddess.

Also unlike other Near Eastern civilizations, the Minoans did not have self-conscious kings who erected monuments commemorating their great deeds. In fact, there are few representations of rulers in Minoan artwork. The so-called throne room at Knossos is a modest chamber with an unpretentious stone chair that may have been used by a low-key administrator.

Minoan art focused on nature. Typical pottery decorations include geometric designs (such as lines and circles), leaves and other vegetation, and animals such as octopuses and bulls. Some of the rare Minoan artworks portraying people depict what seem to be sporting events, such as boxing.

The impression of peaceful, unassuming nature worshipers that emerges from the archaeological evidence is very different, however, from the picture of the Minoans provided by the ancient Greeks. According to Greek historians writing nearly a thousand years later, Minos, king of Knossos, created a sea-based power that dominated the Mediterranean Sea. It was said that Minos's wife Pasiphë mated with a sacred bull and produced the Minotaur, a bull-headed man. Minos compelled the Greeks to provide seven maidens and seven youths annually to feed the Minotaur. Like most ancient legends, this one had a basis in truth. It correctly recalled Minoan skill at seafaring and interest in bulls, and the Minotaur's cannibalism might be somehow related to a recent archaeological discovery of infants who were butchered and eaten at Knossos.

Around 1400 B.C.E., the major Minoan cities were destroyed, and the Minoan civilization collapsed. It once was thought that a cataclysmic volcanic explosion on the island of Thera created huge tidal waves that overwhelmed Crete. More recent studies indicate, however, not only that the eruption—which did destroy the Minoan colony on Thera—had relatively little impact on Crete but also that it occurred two hundred years earlier. It now is thought that the fall of the Minoan civilization was caused by an aggressor people. As of 1400 B.C.E., the Minoan Linear A script was replaced in Crete by Linear B script, which used the Minoan symbols to write a different language. Linear B tablets also were found on the Greek mainland, and in 1953, Linear B was deciphered and discovered to be an early form of Greek. The presence of Linear B on Crete suggests, therefore, that mainland Greeks destroyed the Minoan civilization and even occupied some of the Cretan cities.

The Mycenaeans of Greece

The Linear B tablets proved that Greek civilization began much earlier than once believed. The Greeks who occupied Crete were the descendants of Indo-Europeans who had settled in the Balkans beginning around 2000 B.C.E. and are called **Mycenaeans,** after the Bronze Age fortress of Mycenae in central Greece. The Mycenaeans had much in common with the Minoans. Greece, like Crete, lacked big river valleys, but its hills and sunny, dry climate were ideal for cultivating olives and grapes. The early Mycenaeans came into contact with Minoan traders and assimilated much of Minoan culture, often adapting it to their own needs. They mimicked Minoan pottery manufacture and copied Minoan art. The Mycenaeans built their own palaces to serve as centers for the accumulation and distribution of resources. As their economy expanded, a means of keeping records was needed. The Mycenaeans therefore developed their own Linear B writing system by adapting Minoan Linear A to the Greek language. By 1600 B.C.E., the Mycenaeans had created the first civilization on the European mainland.

Mycenaean cities, such as Mycenae in central Greece, Pylos in the west, and Athens in the east, were built on defendable hills, not right on the coast, and were surrounded by massive walls built from huge roughly hewn blocks. These fortified sites suggest that the Mycenaeans were more security minded than the Minoans and felt vulnerable to attack. Later Greek legends suggest that the cities were independent and

cult object Any object associated with the performing of religious rituals.

Mycenaeans Indo-European people who settled in Greece and established the first Greek civilization around 1600 B.C.E.

Massive Mycenaean fortifications like the Lion Gate of Mycenae, ca. 1250 B.C.E., indicate a need for defense against attack. The later Greeks believed that these walls had been built by the Cyclops, the one-eyed giants of Greek myths *(Benaki Museum)*

that there was no unified Mycenaean nation. City government consisted of an obsessively bureaucratic administration headed by a king. The possessions of each citizen were minutely catalogued each year, presumably for the purposes of tax assessment. Every bit of palace income or disbursement was likewise recorded. Manufacturing, ranging from weaving to the crafting of gold ornaments, was controlled from the palace.

Mycenaean art is full of unpeaceful activities, such as hunting and warfare. Lions, boars, and bulls were the favorite prey of Mycenaean hunters. Men's graves contained bronze swords, daggers, armor, and headgear made of boars' tusks. Women as well as men are depicted driving chariots. These images suggest that violence was an everyday aspect of Mycenaean culture.

From the Minoans, the Mycenaeans learned that trade was an effective means of economic expansion. They took to the sea and began to trade in the same markets as the Minoans. Competition arose, and the Mycenaeans made good use of their warlike ways:

by 1400 B.C.E., they had invaded Crete and defeated the Minoans. For the next two hundred years, the Mycenaeans controlled trade in the Mediterranean. They established trading colonies in Crete, Syria, Anatolia, and Cyprus. Their trading income made them wealthy, and Mycenaean kings were buried in massive stone-lined underground tombs capped by beehive-shaped ceilings more than forty feet high and containing gold ornaments such as elaborate death masks.

The Sea Peoples and the End of the Bronze Age

By 1200 B.C.E., the Bronze Age was ending in Mesopotamia and Egypt. For a long time, there had been no major technological, economic, cultural, or intellectual advances in the river valleys; most innovations had been occurring in places like Syria, Crete, and Greece. Archaeological evidence from around 1200 B.C.E. shows massive population movements that began with an invasion of several groups of Indo-Europeans from the Central Asian steppes. Collectively, the Egyptians called the invaders the **Sea Peoples,** and the disruption they caused was remembered in both contemporary documents and later legends.

Evidence for the first appearance of the Sea Peoples can be found in the Greek legend of a Mycenaean attack on **Troy,** a rich and powerful trading city in northwestern Anatolia. Centuries later, the Greek poet **Homer** wrote in a poem called the *Iliad* that King Agamemnon of Mycenae led a Greek coalition of a thousand ships (each carrying about fifty men) against Troy. The city was captured, sacked, and burned after a ten-year siege. For centuries it was thought that Homer's account was just a legend and that Troy could not have existed at that place and time. In the late nineteenth century, however, archaeologists discovered Troy, which was just as Homer had described. In addition, the legendary date of the Trojan War, 1184 B.C.E., is consistent with the movements of the Sea Peoples just after 1200 B.C.E. So, too, are the Egyptian accounts of groups of Sea Peoples called the Danuna and Akawasha, names strikingly similar to the Danaans and Achaeans, as Homer's

Sea Peoples Large group of Indo-European peoples who attacked Mediterranean lands shortly after 1200 B.C.E.

Troy City of northwestern Anatolia destroyed by the Mycenaeans shortly after 1200 B.C.E.

Homer Blind Greek poet of about 800 B.C.E. whose *Iliad* and *Odyssey* told of the Trojan War and its aftermath.

Greeks were called. It is possible, therefore, that groups of Mycenaeans were caught up in the southward movement of the Sea Peoples and that Troy was one of the first places to be attacked.

The Sea Peoples threatened the entire eastern Mediterranean. Surviving correspondence among local kings shows concern about impending attacks. The Hittite king wrote to Ammurapi, king of Ugarit, to warn about invaders "who live on boats." Ammurapi reported the sighting of enemy ships to the king of Cyprus, who replied, "If this is true, then make yourself very strong. Be on the lookout for the enemy." Ammurapi's answer depicts a dire situation: "Enemy ships have come and set my ships ablaze, and have done wicked things to the country." In the end, the Hittite kingdom was destroyed and Ugarit was sacked and burned.

The Sea Peoples then advanced on the rich land in Egypt. Around 1180 B.C.E. they smashed into the Nile Delta, where they were met by pharaoh **Ramses III** (r. 1182–1151 B.C.E.). The Egyptian account of the battle is the longest surviving hieroglyphic inscription, attesting the importance the Egyptians ascribed to their heroic resistance. It began, "The foreign countries made a conspiracy in their islands. No land could stand before their arms. They were coming toward Egypt and thinking, 'Our plans will succeed!'" Ramses was ready. He said, "I had the river mouths prepared like a strong wall with fully equipped warships. On land, the charioteers consisted of picked men, prepared to crush the foreign countries." The battle ended in an overwhelming Egyptian victory. Ramses boasted, "Those who reached my frontier, their heart and their soul are finished forever. Those who entered the river mouths were like birds ensnared in a net. They were enclosed and prostrated on the beach, killed and made into heaps." Those Sea Peoples who escaped scattered about the Mediterranean, creating further destruction. Egypt, after this great victory, sank into obscurity.

In Greece, disorder continued. The Mycenaean trading economy fell into a severe depression as a consequence of the devastation in the eastern Mediterranean. About 1150 B.C.E., Indo-Europeans known as the **Dorians** took advantage of Mycenaean weakness and made their way from northern to southern Greece. Documents from the city of Pylos tell of the approaching peril. One mentions "watchers on the coasts" and lists the disposition of hundreds of rowers for warships. Another reports, "The enemy grabbed all the priests and murdered them by drowning. The northern strangers continued their attack, terrorizing and plundering." In spite of Mycenaean efforts, Pylos, too, was sacked and burned. By 1100 B.C.E., all the Mycenaean centers except the stronghold of Athens had fallen to the invaders. The Dorians enslaved many of the local people they conquered. Some Mycenaeans fled to **Ionia,** on the western coast of Anatolia, and founded new cities. Additional disruption occurred at roughly the same time in Mesopotamia, where shortly after 1200 B.C.E., the Kassite kingdom was destroyed by the Elamites of Iran. Throughout the Near East, the Bronze Age ended in chaos.

> **Ramses III** (r. 1182–1151 B.C.E.) Egyptian pharaoh who defeated the Sea Peoples around 1180 B.C.E.
>
> **Dorians** Indo-Europeans who began to settle in southern Greece about 1150 B.C.E.
>
> **Ionia** Western coastal region of Anatolia, the site of Greek colonies founded by the Mycenaeans.

Summary

Review Questions

↑ What factors resulted in the creation of Near Eastern civilization?

↑ In what ways were the civilizations of Mesopotamia, Egypt, and the eastern Mediterranean similar to and different from one another?

↑ How did geography influence the way Near Eastern peoples saw their place in the world?

Of the million-plus years of the human past described in this chapter, only 1800 years, from 3000 to 1200 B.C.E., cover periods of human civilization. Almost all of the entire human past took place in the prehistoric period, before the invention of writing. People lived a wandering existence focused on finding food and shelter. Beginning around 8000 B.C.E., however, humans gained greater control over their food supply through the domestication of animals and plants. Expanded agriculture brought increased food supplies, larger populations, and, ultimately, the creation of cities. Around 3000 B.C.E., the first phase of civilization—a form of culture defined by the presence of agriculture, cities, writing, metal technology, social differentiation, and specialization of labor—arose in the river valleys of Egypt, Mesopotamia, India, and China. In this period, known as the Bronze Age, the most representative civilizations were located in fertile river valleys, produced vast food surpluses through the extensive exploitation of agriculture, and supported large populations. The use of writing marked the beginning of history, for people now could create permanent narrative accounts of their past. Over time, pastoral peoples such as the Semitic and Indo-European peoples interacted with the river valley peoples and assimilated their culture, and civilization spread out of the river valleys.

Western civilization began with the civilizations of Egypt and Mesopotamia. Although these two civilizations were similar in their general outlines, they had very different specific traits. The Mesopotamians were geographically exposed, politically disunited, and generally pessimistic. The Egyptians were geographically protected, usually united into a single kingdom, and extraordinarily optimistic. The Mesopotamians had little faith that their gods would take care of them; the Egyptians had complete confidence in their gods. Both peoples made fundamental contributions to western civilization in the areas of government and law, economic development, technology, religious belief, and literary and artistic expression.

Both the strength and the weakness of river valley civilizations was that they were based very heavily on agriculture, with few opportunities for economic expansion through trade. At the same time, however, experiments in economic activity that focused more heavily on trade were occurring elsewhere in the Levant, Crete, and Greece. By 1200 B.C.E., the initial phase of civilization, based on the extensive exploitation of agriculture in river valleys, was over. Destructive attacks by the Sea Peoples brought the Bronze Age to an end.

← **Thinking Back, Thinking Ahead** →

In Bronze Age civilizations, religion played an important role in helping people to understand the world and their place in it. How do you think religion might continue to shape the way people defined their place in the world?

ECHO ECHO ECHO ECHO ECHO

The Return of the Mummy

Ever since antiquity, people have been fascinated by the civilization of ancient Egypt. Modern interest in Egypt received a boost in the nineteenth century, when hieroglyphic writing was deciphered, and was revived in 1922, when the tomb of Tut-ankh-amon, popularly known as King Tut, was unearthed. In the 1970s a dance called the "King Tut" even enjoyed a brief vogue. Egyptian settings are particularly common in the movies, ranging from *Cleopatra* to *Stargate* to *The Scorpion King*. The most popular Egyptian-based movies involve bringing a mummy back from dead. Nearly a hundred mummy films have been made. The most famous one, "The Mummy," was released in 1932 and starred Boris Karloff as Imhotep, an Egyptian priest who was mummified alive. It was remade in 1999 under the same title. After archaeologists bring Imhotep back to life by reading a spell from the "Scroll of Thoth," he then desires to revive his lost love, Ankhsenamun. He briefly does so, but both soon die a second death.

Why are we so interested in mummies? Why does Egyptian civilization fascinate us? Does it still have something to tell us? People certainly do not watch mummy movies to learn history. Along with pyramids, palm trees, and loincloths, mummy movies contain just enough factual information to provide a background for the plot. For example, there really was an Imhotep, but he was an architect, not a priest. There also was a book of spells that gave life after death, but it was the Book of the Dead, not the "Scroll of Thoth." And although the Egyptians certainly did create mummies, they did not believe that they would rise from the dead.

Mummy movies do, however, deal with issues of great interest in the present day, such as the relationship between bodily death and perpetual life. In any mummy movie, the mummy is revivified and then attempts once again to enjoy earthly pleasures. In addition, unlike historical dramas that take place in the past, mummy movies bring the past into the present and portray the contrasts between past and present cultures and value systems. Even though the mummies are often villains, we nevertheless can feel sympathy for their desire to recover their lost lives and lost loves. But their attempts to do so, which sometimes involve human sacrifice, bring them into conflict with modern-day ethics and morality, and as a result the revived mummies almost always are compelled to return to the grave.

Suggested Readings

Breasted, James H. *The Ancient Records of Egypt.* 5 vols. Urbana: University of Illinois Press, 2001. A thorough look at the kinds of documents produced by the Egyptians.

Hallo, William W., and William K. Simpson. *The Ancient Near East: A History.* 2nd ed. New York: Holt Rinehart Winston, 1997. A general survey of ancient Near Eastern history.

Jackson, Danny P., Robert D. Biggs, and James G. Keenan. *The Epic of Gilgamesh.* Wauconda, Ill.: Bolchazy-Carducci, 1997. A translation of the adventures of the Sumerian hero Gilgamesh.

Knapp, A. Bernard. *The History and Culture of Western Asia and Egypt.* Chicago: Dorsey, 1988. A survey of the history of Mesopotamia, Egypt, and the Levant to the fourth century B.C.E.

Palmer, L. R. *Mycenaeans and Minoans: Aegean Prehistory in Light of the Linear B Tablets.* 2nd ed. New York: Knopf, 1965. A discussion of Bronze Age Minoan and Mycenaean history based on translations of early Greek Linear B tablets.

Roux, Georges. *Ancient Iraq.* 3rd ed. Harmondsworth, UK: Penguin, 1992. A classic summary of the evolution of ancient Mesopotamian civilization.

Sandars, N. K. *The Sea Peoples: Warriors of the Ancient Mediterranean, 1250–1150 B.C.* London: Thames and Hudson, 1985. A study of the causes and effects of the invasion of the Sea Peoples.

Websites

Sources on ancient civilizations, including prehistory and archaeology, **The History of the Ancient Near East Electronic Compendium,** at http://ancientneareast.tripod.com

For Sumerian literature, **The Electronic Text Corpus of Sumerian Literature,** at http://etcsl.orinst.ox.ac.uk/index.html

On Ancient Egypt, **Tour Egypt!,** at www.touregypt.net/ancientegypt

Iron Age Civilizations, 1200–500 B.C.E.

CHAPTER OUTLINE

1500 B.C.E.	1000 B.C.E.	500 B.C.E.	1 B.C.E./1 C.E.

1200 B.C.E. Bronze Age ends, Iron Age begins	1100 B.C.E. Dorians settle southern Greece	970 B.C.E. Solomon becomes Hebrew king	900 B.C.E. Rise of the Assyrian Empire

1200	1150	1100	1050	1000	950	900	850

The Assyrian and Persian Empires, 900–500 B.C.E.

The Assyrian and Persian Empires were the greatest Iron Age Empires. The Assyrian Empire was the first to incorporate both Egypt and Mesopotamia under the same rule, and the even vaster Persian Empire contained parts of India and Europe. How do you think the Assyrians and Persians managed to administer such large empires?

Assyrian homeland
Growth of the Assyrian Empire to 570 B.C.E.
Persian homeland
Growth of the Persian Empire to 500 B.C.E.

GREECE
IONIA
Ephesus
LYDIA
Sardis
CARIA
Crete
Rhodes
Aegean Sea
CILICIA
TAURUS MTS.
ANATOLIA
PERSIAN ROYAL ROAD
CAUCASUS MTS.
ARMENIA
Caspian Sea
Aral Sea
Jaxartes
SOGDIANA
Oxus
BACTRIA
HINDU KUSH
Nineveh
Nimrud
ASSYRIA
Ashur
SYRIA
Aradus
Byblos
Sidon
Tyre
Damascus
PHOENICIA
ARAMEANS
Euphrates
Tigris
Behistun
Ecbatana
ELBURZ MTS.
MEDIA
PARTHIA
ZAGROS MTS.
PLATEAU OF IRAN
INDIA
Mediterranean Sea
LIBYA
CYPRUS
Samaria
Jerusalem
ISRAEL
JUDAEA
Babylon
BABYLONIA
Susa
ELAM
Pasargadae
Persepolis
PERSIA
GEDROSIA
Indus
Memphis
EGYPT
Red Sea
Nile
Persian Gulf
SAHARA
ARABIAN DESERT
Thebes
Arabian Sea
INDIAN OCEAN

0   200   400 Km.
0   200   400 Mi.

500 C.E.   1000 C.E.   1500 C.E.   2000 C.E.

612 B.C.E.
Assyrian Empire ends

814 B.C.E.
Phoenicians found Carthage

753 B.C.E.
Rome is founded in Italy

721 B.C.E.
Assyrians conquer Israel

650 B.C.E.
Lydians invent coinage

587 B.C.E.
Chaldeans capture Jerusalem and send Jews into exile

550 B.C.E.
Persian Empire begins

800   750   700   650   600   550   500

Choice Choice

Deborah

Women usually were kept in the background in Hebrew political life. In times of stress, however, able women such as Deborah took leadership roles. In this illustration from a manuscript in the Bodleian Library in Oxford, England, Deborah is shown, sword in hand, leading the Hebrew army against the Canaanites. The accompanying text reads, "Therefore came Deborah and Barak son of Abynoam against the enemies of Israel in battle and routed them." (Bodleian Library, Oxford/The Art Archive)

Deborah Leads the Hebrew People Against the Canaanites

The biblical book of Judges reports that not long after the Hebrews settled in Canaan they faced an attack by the Canaanite king Jabin and his general Sisera. The male Hebrew leaders were reluctant to act, so it was a woman, Deborah, who led the Hebrew resistance. Deborah must have been a woman of great character, for at this time political leadership was almost always exercised by men. Deborah overcame convention and served as one of the Hebrew judges, leaders who arose to help the Hebrews overcome spiritual or military troubles. Deborah may have been able to take charge of the Hebrew resistance because she also was called a prophetess, meaning that she was thought to be in direct communication with God.

When Deborah's story begins, she is holding court under a palm tree where Hebrews come to have their disputes settled. The Hebrew people call out to God for help against the Canaanites, and when the Hebrew men do nothing, it is Deborah who acts. Summoning the Hebrew general Barak, she reminds him that God had commanded him to assemble ten thousand men to fight the Canaanites. Barak timidly responds, "If you will go with me, I will go; but if you will not go with me, I will not go." It was unusual for women to accompany armies into battle, but Deborah replies, "I will go with you, but you will not gain any honor, for God will surrender Sisera into the hands of a woman." The Hebrews were especially afraid because Sisera's army included 900 iron chariots. Iron had only recently begun to be used for weapons and was thought to bestow a great military advantage. Deborah again encourages Barak to take action, saying, "Get up, for this is the day that God has delivered Sisera into your hands."

Then Barak led his ten thousand men to face the Canaanites, and Deborah went with him. Sisera called out his chariots, but a fierce storm turned the ground into mud and Sisera's chariots were unable to maneuver. The Hebrew army charged and put the Canaanites to flight.

Sisera fled and took refuge in the tent of Jael, a distant female relative of Moses. She cunningly welcomed him, tucking him into bed with a bottle of milk. But when he was fast asleep, she hammered a tent peg into his head and killed him. Barak arrived in pursuit to discover that Deborah's prophecy had been fulfilled—Sisera had been surrendered into the hands of a woman.

Deborah then sang a victory song, which may well be the oldest original composition to survive in Hebrew scripture. Her story provides a brief insight into a world dominated by men where one woman serving as God's spokesperson took a leadership role in the Hebrew resistance and another woman slew an enemy general. One has to wonder whether there were other occasions when women also provided leadership—occasions that were not preserved in the historical sources, almost all of which were written by and about men.

Introduction

The iron chariots used by Sisera's army illustrate a significant change that occurred in western civilization around 1200 B.C.E. By this time, the river valley civilizations of the Bronze Age had expanded to their limits. Future technological, economic, and political developments would occur outside the river valleys, facilitated by the growing use of a new metal, iron, which was much less expensive to manufacture than bronze. If bronze was the metal of society's elite, iron was the common person's metal, and it gave its name to the Iron Age. Iron could be used for tools such as plows, which permitted agriculture to spread to areas with tougher soils outside the river valleys. Another important characteristic of the Iron Age was the vastly increased use of trade as a means of economic and political expansion by peoples of the eastern Mediterranean coast.

Eventually the Iron Age also saw the creation of empires much larger than those of the Bronze Age, first in Assyria and then in Persia. These empires were more concerned than Bronze Age empires with economic expansion, the encouragement of trade, and the accumulation of wealth. They also were characterized by powerful rulers overseeing vast administrative systems.

At the same time, the Hebrews, a people descended from the Semitic groups that inhabited the fringes of Mesopotamia, created a religious culture incorporating not only belief in a single god but also concepts of morality and ethics that would have great influence on the subsequent evolution of western civilization. The story of the Hebrews' struggle to preserve their cultural and religious identity continues to resonate in the modern day.

Merchants and Traders of the Eastern Mediterranean, 1200–650 B.C.E.

⬇ Why did the importance of trade increase during the Iron Age?

⬇ What was the role of iron in the Iron Age?

The new patterns of Iron Age civilization first appeared about 1200 B.C.E. in the lands bordering the eastern coast of the Mediterranean Sea. Here peoples who previously had existed in the shadows of the civilizations and empires of Mesopotamia and Egypt were able to achieve a greater degree of political, economic, and religious self-expression. They made tools and weapons of iron, engaged in widespread trade, and, outside of the major river valleys, built small, fortified cities that were lively centers of commerce. Over time, the Iron Age way of life diffused out of western Asia and westward into Europe.

From Bronze to Iron

Even though the Iron Age began in the Near East around 1200 B.C.E., the use of iron actually had begun in the Bronze Age, when it was a luxury item. In the nineteenth century B.C.E., for example, Assyrian merchants valued iron at forty times its weight in silver. King Tut was buried with a rare iron dagger, still unrusted when the tomb was opened in 1922. But for a long time, iron did not enter into widespread use. It was much more difficult to mine and work than bronze. Unlike the copper and tin used in making bronze, iron in its metallic form was extremely rare, found mainly in meteorites. Most iron occurred in combination with other elements, such as sulfur and oxygen, in ores that had to be smelted to release the iron. The relatively low melting point of bronze, 950 degrees Celsius (1,742 degrees Fahrenheit), made it an easy alloy to work in ordinary pottery kilns. The smelting of iron ore, however, required a much higher temperature, 1,538 degrees Celsius (2,800 degrees Fahrenheit).

The early production of iron often is associated with the Hittites, but they produced only limited quantities of iron implements before their empire collapsed around 1200 B.C.E. Not until then—at the same time as and perhaps even because of the disruptive movements of peoples that ended the Bronze Age—did the knowledge of iron-working technology spread throughout western Asia (Iran, Mesopotamia, Anatolia, and the Levant). By 1100 B.C.E., iron-working technology had diffused into southwestern Europe, reaching all the way to Britain by about 700 B.C.E. The Egyptians, however, clung to the old ways. Iron did not become widely used in Egypt until the seventh century B.C.E.

Once iron-making became widespread and economical, the transition from bronze to iron occurred quickly. Iron could be used for manufacturing commonplace items, such as tools and household utensils, that would have been prohibitively expensive if made from bronze. Metal implements now became available to everyone, not just the rich. Only in weapons manufacture did the transition to iron take longer, for early **cast iron** was soft and brittle and did

cast iron   Raw molten iron that is poured into molds and allowed to cool.

Chronology

1270 B.C.E.	Hebrew Exodus from Egypt	**671 B.C.E.**	Assyrians conquer Egypt
1230 B.C.E.	Hebrews settle in Canaan	**650 B.C.E.**	Lydians invent coinage
1200 B.C.E.	Beginning of Iron Age in the Near East	**612 B.C.E.**	Chaldeans and Medes capture Nineveh
1150 B.C.E.	Deborah serves as Hebrew judge	**587 B.C.E.**	Chaldeans capture Jerusalem; Babylonian Captivity begins
1050 B.C.E.	Saul becomes first Hebrew king	**550 B.C.E.**	Persian Empire begins
1010 B.C.E.	David becomes Hebrew king	**547 B.C.E.**	Persians conquer Lydia
970 B.C.E.	Solomon becomes Hebrew king	**539 B.C.E.**	Persians conquer Babylon
814 B.C.E.	Carthage founded by the Phoenicians	**535 B.C.E.**	Babylonian Jews return to Judah
800 B.C.E.	Semiramis becomes queen of Assyria	**525 B.C.E.**	Persians conquer Egypt
750 B.C.E.	Zoroaster formalizes teachings of Persian religion	**513 B.C.E.**	Darius attacks the Scythians
721 B.C.E.	Assyrians conquer Israel		
701 B.C.E.	Assyrians besiege Jerusalem		
700 B.C.E.	Persian kingdom is founded		

not keep a sharp edge. Initially, therefore, bronze remained the best metal for weapons, which had to hold up in battle. Only over time did processes such as carburizing (alloying iron with about 1 percent carbon), quenching (sudden immersion of heated iron in water), tempering (reheating quenched iron and allowing it to cool slowly), and hammering come into use for creating hard, nonbrittle, and sharp iron weapons.

The use of iron brought great economic changes. Iron plows could work tough soils, such as those in the Danube and Rhine valleys in Europe, that wooden scratch-plows could not, and large-scale agriculture thus expanded out of the Near Eastern river valleys. But Iron Age societies could never be as completely dependent on agriculture as the river valley civilizations of the Bronze Age, for their soils were not nearly as rich. Thus, in the Iron Age, people had to find other ways of expanding their economies, and they did so by focusing much more heavily on manufacturing and trade, which became another of the distinguishing characteristics of the Iron Age.

During the Iron Age, peoples living outside river valleys gained a greater opportunity to expand their political and economic influence. The centers of civilization, culture, and economic development moved out of the river valleys and, in general, toward the west, first to the Levant, then to Anatolia and the Balkans, and then to western Europe. The Iron Age was a period of smaller, fortified cities, located either in uplands for protection or near seacoasts for access to water transportation, with economies based largely on commerce. Artisans no longer concentrated on luxury goods, as in the Bronze Age, but on mass-produced pottery and textiles. Merchants grew wealthy transporting goods from one trading center to another. Typical Iron Age culture arose first on the eastern coast of the Mediterranean, represented by the Phoenicians, Arameans, and Philistines. It then spread to the Lydians in western Anatolia.

The Phoenicians

Many of the seacoast cities of Phoenicia (modern Lebanon) recovered following the attacks of the Sea Peoples. The hilly and forested coastal land was unsuitable for extensive agriculture, so the **Phoenicians,**

Phoenicians   Semitic people engaged in sea trade who inhabited modern-day Lebanon.

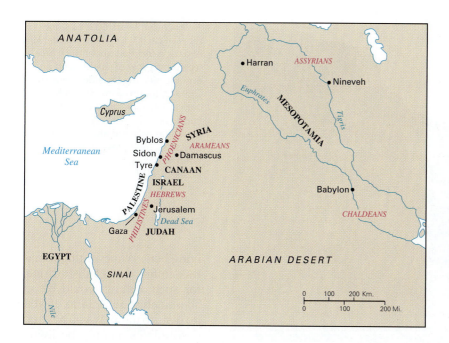

such as ivory, gemstones, and peacocks from Africa and India; papyrus from Egypt; spices such as myrrh and frankincense from Arabia; and metals such as gold, silver, tin, and copper from Cyprus, Spain, Britain, and Africa. These raw materials were either reexported or used in local manufacturing. The city of Byblos exported so much papyrus that the Greek word for "book," *biblion*, and hence the word *Bible*, come from the city name. Fine furniture was made from the extensive cedar and hardwood forests. Phoenician glassblowing, including the creation of transparent glass, began a tradition that lasted for centuries. Other local products such as timber, salted fish, and wine also were exported. But the Phoenicians were best known for "Tyrian purple," a dye made from a local shellfish that was used for coloring royal garments.

As an aid in keeping business records, the Phoenicians perfected the alphabet. The Phoenician alphabet had twenty-two consonants beginning with the letters *aleph* (originally a consonant), *beth*, and *gimel*. This alphabet was later borrowed by the Greeks, from whom it made its way to the Romans and then to us. And as another means of assisting in their commercial enterprises, the Phoenicians established colonies along their trade routes. **Carthage,** founded on the coast of modern Tunisia in 814 B.C.E. by Princess Elissa of Tyre, later became a major power in its own right. Cadiz, on the Atlantic coast of Spain just beyond the **Strait of Gibraltar,** was a port for ships that traded all the way to the British Isles.

another of the Semitic peoples, turned to trade as a means of economic expansion. The great trading city of Ugarit was never rebuilt, but other cities, such as Tyre, Sidon, and Byblos, became centers of a reinvigorated seaborne commerce. Each Phoenician city was an independent city-state, governed by a king who was advised by a council of nobles.

Borrowing nautical technology from the Sea Peoples, the Phoenicians built ships with keels for improved strength and maneuverability. They traveled the Mediterranean and beyond, navigating by the sun and the stars. Because rowers were expensive and took up valuable deck space, Phoenician merchant ships were driven by sails. Ancient sailing ships were unable to sail against the wind effectively, so trading ships could be stuck in port for weeks waiting for a favorable wind. Like all ancient sailors, the Phoenicians hugged the coast rather than striking out for the open sea, and they headed for shore at the first sign of bad weather. Each Phoenician city also maintained a navy to protect its trade. Warships had to be maneuverable and ready to go at a moment's notice, regardless of the wind, so they were propelled by oarsmen. With two banks of oars, rows of shields, a bronze ram, and an armed body of marines, a Phoenician galley (an oar-driven ship) would have been a fearsome sight to any pirate.

Phoenician merchants became legendary. The Bible describes the Phoenicians of Tyre as those "whose merchants are princes, whose traders are honored in the world." The Phoenicians imported luxury goods

Carthage   Phoenician trading colony founded on the coast of modern Tunisia in 814 B.C.E. by the city of Tyre.

Strait of Gibraltar   Strait between Spain and North Africa that connects the Mediterranean Sea with the Atlantic Ocean.

A Phoenician warship on a stone relief of ca. 800 B.C.E. has two banks of oars, a fortified upper deck protected by a row of shields, and a ram for piercing the side of enemy ships. Warships were driven by oars rather than sails because they had to be able to travel even when there was no wind and to go in any direction, regardless of where the wind was coming from. *(HIP/Art Resource, NY)*

The Phoenicians worshiped a **triad** of three primary gods, who were reflected in the architecture of Phoenician temples, which had three chambers. The creator god was El, a word that meant simply "god." El, who was called the "father of the gods" and "the creator of the creators," was often worshiped at an altar in a "high place." The son of El was Ba'al, a storm god who was viewed as the most important god on earth. Ba'al eventually eclipsed El, much as the god Enlil had overshadowed his father An in Sumeria. Ba'al had many forms: in Tyre; he became Melqart and under that name was exported to Carthage. The third primary deity was **Astarte,** a goddess representing fertility, sexuality, and war. Astarte was known under different names to many different peoples: she was called Ishtar in Mesopotamia, Ashtoret in the Bible, and Aphrodite in Greece. A surviving **cult statue** of Astarte has holes punctured in her breasts that could be stopped up with wax. When the wax was subtly melted during a ceremony, milk (stored in the statue's hollow head) flowed from her breasts. Early Phoenician worship also included human sacrifice, a practice that continued in Carthage even after it had been abandoned in the Phoenician homeland.

Like the Egyptians, the Phoenicians believed in an afterlife and attempted to preserve their dead in elaborate tombs and coffins, even though Phoenician mummies soon decomposed in the damp seacoast climate. A Phoenician king inscribed on his coffin these words: "I, Tabnit, priest of Astarte, King of Sidon, am

lying here. Whoever might find this coffin, do not disturb me, for such a thing would be an abomination to Astarte. If you do disturb me, may you have no descendants among the living and no rest among the dead." Tabnit's tomb, unlike the thousands of others that were plundered in antiquity, lay undisturbed until its discovery in the 1800s.

Other Eastern Mediterranean Traders

Along the eastern Mediterranean, other peoples also assimilated Iron Age culture. The **Arameans,** a Semitic people from northern Arabia, established city-kingdoms such as Damascus to the east of the Phoenicians just before 1200 B.C.E. and gained a virtual monopoly on trade by land. Aramean caravans carried goods ranging from agricultural products to textiles south to Egypt and Arabia, north to Turkey and Central Asia, and east all the way to India. Because Arameans traveled everywhere, their language, Aramaic, replaced Akkadian as a common language that allowed people from different countries to communicate.

triad Group of three.
Astarte Goddess of fertility, sexuality, and war worshiped by many Near Eastern peoples.
cult statue Statue serving as a stand-in for a deity in a temple.
Arameans Semitic people living in Syria who engaged in trade by land.

A crude gold coin, known as a skekel, issued by the Lydian king Croesus ca. 550 B.C.E. bears the facing heads of a lion and a bull on one side and two punch marks on the other. The symbols identify who had issued the coin and guaranteed its weight and purity. Croesus was so wealthy that he still serves as the basis for the saying to be "rich as Croesus." *(Courtesy of the Trustees of the British Museum)*

To the south of the Phoenicians, on the seacoast of modern-day Palestine, lived the **Philistines,** an Indo-European people descended from the warlike Sea People known to the Egyptians as the Peleset, who had settled there just after 1200 B.C.E. The Philistines established their own city-states, such as Ashkelon and Gaza, each ruled by its own lord. They left no written records and so are known only from writings of their enemies and from a few archaeological remains, such as a furnace used for making iron swords. They appear in the Bible as warriors known for their iron weapons who threatened the peoples around them. In spite of their military reputation, however, the Philistines were primarily farmers, for they had productive agricultural land. Lacking good seaports, they never became sailors, but they did become wealthy by controlling the land and sea traffic passing north and south between Egypt and Phoenicia. They adopted the worship of the Canaanite deity Dagon, a crop and fertility god who was also called on for help in battle, and also worshiped Dagon's wife Astarte.

Iron Age civilization soon spread to the western seacoast of Anatolia, where the kingdom of **Lydia** arose after the destruction of the Hittite kingdom around 1200 B.C.E. Their coastal cities on the Aegean Sea gave the Lydians access to the trading markets of the Mediterranean. The Lydians also controlled gold-bearing streams, giving rise to the legend of King Midas, who was said to turn everything he touched into gold. The Lydians thus grew rich through gold mining and trade. They also made one of the most important economic advances of all time by inventing coinage. Previously, gold and silver had been recognized by traders as having great value but had been traded by weight. Around 650 B.C.E., the Lydians began using lumps of gold and silver that all had the same weight, and thus the same value, as a means of exchange in business transactions. These lumps were the first coins. They were so useful that other trading peoples soon adopted them, and the use of coinage rapidly spread throughout the Mediterranean and Near Eastern worlds.

The Hebrews and Monotheism, 1800–900 B.C.E.

- ↓ What made the Hebrew people distinctive?
- ↓ How did the Hebrews relate to their God?

The Hebrews originated as Semitic pastoralists living on the fringes of the civilized world and went on to form a powerful Iron Age kingdom. But their primary importance was religious rather than political, for they created a religious culture that would have great influence on later western civilization. The Hebrews' intensely personal relationship with a single God made their religion different from every other religion of pre-Christian antiquity. In addition, written teachings gave the Hebrews their sense of identity, and the Hebrew Bible became one of the most influential documents of western history.

Philistines Indo-European people who gave their name to Palestine, where they settled just after 1200 B.C.E.

Lydia Trading kingdom in northwestern Anatolia that invented coinage.

Hebrew Origins

The Hebrews, later known to history as the Jews, played a major role in the history of the early Iron Age. They were the first **People of the Book,** that is, people who, like the Christians and Muslims after them, based their beliefs on teachings that were preserved in written form, known as **scripture,** and that were thus resistant to change over the centuries. Hebrew scripture, known to Jews as the **Tanakh** and to Christians as the Hebrew Bible or the Old Testament, describes not only the relations of the Hebrews with their God but also the history of the Hebrew people. It begins with five books called the **Torah,** and also contains nineteen books of Prophets and eleven books known as Writings. For the ancient Hebrews, scripture provided an accurate portrayal of their ancient history. Today, a comparison of Hebrew scripture with other evidence, such as archaeology or contemporary Near Eastern records, shows that the Bible is no more or less accurate than any other historical sources surviving from the early Iron Age. In many instances, archaeological evidence strikingly confirms the outlines of what is reported in scripture, but in other cases, such as the dates of the creation of the world and the Hebrew Exodus, startling inconsistencies have produced debates among theologians and historians. The following discussion is based primarily on the Hebrews' view of their history as preserved in the Tanakh.

In Hebrew scripture, the human past began with God's creation of the world and the first two humans, Adam and Eve, over 6,000 years ago. The Hebrews believed that their special relationship with their God began about 1800 B.C.E., when God, at that time known as **El Shaddai** (God Almighty), made a **covenant**—a binding agreement—with Abraham, the **patriarch,** or head, of a group of Semitic pastoralists. In the book of Genesis, God said to Abraham, "I will establish My covenant as an everlasting covenant between Me and you and your descendants after you for the generations to come, to be your God and the God of your descendants after you. The whole land of Canaan, where you are now an alien, I will give as an everlasting possession to you and your descendants after you; and I will be their God." As for the Hebrews, God said, "You are to undergo circumcision, and it will be the sign of the covenant between Me and you." By keeping this covenant, the Hebrews became the "chosen people" of God.

Previously, like other peoples of that time, the Hebrews had believed in many gods, but God's covenant with Abraham set them on the path to **monotheism,** the belief that there is only one god.

The Hebrew God was incorporeal, having no shape or form that could be represented in physical form, and was everywhere. God also had humanlike emotions and could be loving, jealous, angry, and demanding. The Hebrew relationship with God was very personal. God was a real presence and spoke directly to the Hebrews through **prophets,** of whom Abraham was the first. Prophets did not have to be priests but could be anyone, regardless of social status or gender—such as Deborah (see Choice). Prophets were able to converse and even negotiate with God, and they exercised leadership over the Hebrew people as a consequence of their direct contact with God.

The period of Hebrew history that began with Abraham is known as the age of the patriarchs, when the Hebrews were one of many **clans** of wandering Semitic pastoralists who lived on the semiarid fringes of the Mesopotamian river valley civilizations. An elderly male patriarch led each clan. The people kept sheep and cattle, lived in tents, and traveled about in search of pasturelands. Sometimes they stayed long enough in one place to plant a crop of grain, but they never settled for long. In this male-dominated society, women had an inferior status. Property belonged to the clan and was controlled by the men. Men had both wives and concubines. Men could divorce their wives for several reasons, such as infertility, and could take second wives to provide children. Even though they rejected urban life, the ancestors of the

People of the Book   People who base their beliefs on teachings that are preserved in written form.

scripture   Sacred or religious writings of a religion.

Tanakh   Jewish scriptures, consisting of the Torah, the Prophets, and the Writings.

Torah   First five books of Jewish scripture.

El Shaddai   Original name of the Hebrew god, meaning "God Almighty."

covenant   Agreement by which God agreed to make the Hebrews His chosen people and the Hebrews agreed to follow God's law.

patriarch   (from Greek for "father") In early Hebrew history, the male leader of an extended family group; later, the spiritual leader of the Jews, and in the later Roman Empire, the bishops of the most important Christian cities.

monotheism   (from Greek for "one god") Belief in the existence of only one god.

prophets   Persons through whom God communicated to the Hebrews.

clan   Extended family group of people descended from a common ancestor.

Hebrews assimilated much of Mesopotamian culture, including its legal concepts, the Sumerian word *edin* (a flat plain), stories of a great flood, descriptions of ziggurats, and tales of heroes who were cast adrift as infants. These elements reappeared a thousand years later in Hebrew scripture in the judicial concept of "an eye for an eye," and in stories of the garden of Eden, Noah's flood, the tower of Babel, and the infant Moses being cast adrift in the Nile.

The Hebrew people expanded. According to scripture, the twelve sons of the patriarch Jacob, the grandson of Abraham, gave rise to twelve **tribes,** or extended clans. The tribes were later known as the children of **Israel,** because Jacob also was known as Israel. During a period of famine, Jacob's son Joseph moved his family to northern Egypt—possibly between 1700 and 1600 B.C.E., during the Hyksos period, when Egypt's northern frontiers were open to outsiders—and the Hebrews became agricultural laborers or slaves working on building projects. Their stay in Egypt thus turned the Hebrews from wandering pastoralists into settled farmers and artisans. Aside from scripture, however, there is little record of the Hebrews' stay in Egypt. Near Eastern documents of the thirteenth century B.C.E. and later make generic, often derogatory, references to the Ha-bi-ru, a word meaning "the dusty people." They appear as slaves, laborers, bandits, and mercenaries. Egyptian records, for example, speak of "the Ha-bi-ru who drag stone for the great building of Ramses II." Eventually, the word Ha-bi-ru came to be applied to the Hebrews alone. It has also been suggested, but with little justification, that Hebrew monotheism influenced Akhenaton's belief that Aton was the one primary god.

The Exodus and the Age of Judges

One of the greatest events in Hebrew history was the **Exodus,** in which the prophet **Moses** led several thousand Hebrew slaves out of captivity in Egypt. According to scripture, the infant Moses was placed in a basket and set adrift in the Nile River by his mother because the pharaoh had ordered all male Hebrew children to be killed. Moses was rescued downstream by an Egyptian princess and then raised in the Egyptian royal household. This scriptural account is consistent with the Egyptian origin of Moses's name, which is similar to that of the pharaoh Thutmose. The biblical book of Exodus goes on to report that after killing an Egyptian overseer, Moses took refuge in the Sinai Desert, where God addressed him from a burning bush and revealed His true name: "I appeared to Abraham, to Isaac, and to Jacob by the name of El Shaddai, but my name YHWH was not known to

them." In Hebrew scripture, the name of God was never completely spelled out but was represented by the Hebrew letters for YHWH (in English, Yahweh, the Christian Jehovah), which means something like "the one who is." God then ordered Moses to free the Hebrews from bondage in Egypt; after several confrontations with the pharaoh, Moses successfully guided the refugee Hebrews across the Red Sea and into the Sinai Desert, where Moses received the **Ten Commandments** of Hebrew law from God.

The biblical account then states that after forty years in the wilderness, the Hebrews entered Canaan. Led by Joshua, the Hebrews successfully occupied some territory, often in the uplands, but they were constantly threatened by neighboring peoples. There were atrocities on both sides, and the Hebrews sometimes massacred Canaanite populations to protect Hebrew religious practices from foreign influence.

The dating of the Exodus and the settlement in Canaan is one of the great controversies of biblical studies. The Bible states that the Hebrews departed "from the city of Ramses," thus placing the Exodus during the reign of one of the eleven pharaohs named Ramses, whose rule began around 1300 B.C.E. The biblical references to massive building projects at this time fit the known activities of Ramses II (r. 1279–1212 B.C.E.). In addition, the earliest nonbiblical evidence for the Palestinian Hebrews—a monument erected in 1208 B.C.E. by the pharaoh Merneptah, who bragged after a campaign in Canaan that "Israel lies desolate"—indicates that a Hebrew nation existed in Palestine by that time. A similar date is provided by Palestinian archaeological finds showing destruction in the thirteenth century B.C.E., attributed to the campaigns of Joshua. This evidence would put the Exodus around 1270 B.C.E. and the settlement in Canaan forty years later, around 1230 B.C.E. The book of Kings, however, states that the Hebrew king Solomon's temple, constructed around the year 966 B.C.E., was built in the 480th year after the Exodus, thereby dating the Exodus to around 1446 B.C.E. The controversy over

tribes   Descendants of the twelve sons of the Hebrew patriarch Jacob, who also was known as Israel.

Israel   Another name for the patriarch Jacob; it became the name for the Hebrew people in general and also for the northern Hebrew kingdom.

Exodus   (from Greek for "departure") Departure of the Hebrews from Egypt, led by Moses.

Moses   Hebrew prophet who led the Hebrews out of Egypt and received the Ten Commandments from God.

Ten Commandments   Laws that the Hebrews received from God in the Sinai Desert after the Exodus.

the date of the Exodus is still unresolved, but at present, the later date—that is, 1270 B.C.E.—is generally thought to be more consistent with the evidence. The Hebrew invasion of Canaan thus provides one more example of the movement of peoples that occurred toward the end of the Bronze Age.

After the settlement in Canaan, the Hebrew tribes were united religiously by a shared shrine at Shiloh, where a sacred container known as the **Ark of the Covenant** preserved the Ten Commandments. But the Hebrews lacked any political unity, which made them easy prey to enemies such as the Canaanites to the north and the Philistines on the coastal plain to the west. The most important Hebrew leaders now were called **judges.** Believing themselves to be acting under Yahweh's authority, judges led short-lived coalitions of tribes against foreign threats, especially the Philistines. The unsettled times gave persons who ordinarily were lacking in privilege the opportunity to assume significant leadership roles, as when Deborah served as a judge around 1150 B.C.E. and led an army to victory against the Canaanites. Another Hebrew judge, Samson, was a warrior of very great strength. According to Hebrew scripture, he killed many Philistines in single combat and did great damage to Philistine crops, but he then was captured, blinded, and enslaved. The Philistines continued to dominate the Hebrews, even capturing the Ark of the Covenant and forbidding the Hebrews to make use of iron technology.

> **Ark of the Covenant**   Sacred container that held the stone tablets inscribed with the Ten Commandments.
>
> **judges**   Leaders of the Hebrews after the settlement in Canaan.

Voice

The Song of Deborah

The account in the biblical book of Judges of the Hebrew victory over the Canaanite general Sisera is followed by "Deborah's victory song," in which the Hebrew judge Deborah expresses her thanks to Yahweh for bringing victory to the Hebrews. It is generally considered to be one of the oldest texts in Jewish scripture, having been composed in the late twelfth century B.C.E., and is one of the rare instances in which a primary source was inserted directly into the text of the Bible. The song recapitulates much of the story told in the previous chapter of Judges. Even though the song begins with the names of both Deborah and her general Barak, the text clearly shows that it is Deborah who is speaking, and it provides a rare portrayal of a woman's point of view.

➡ *Why might Deborah have been called a "mother" here and not a judge or prophetess as she is called elsewhere?*

➡ *How many of the Hebrew tribes actually resisted the Canaanite army?*

1 Then sang Deborah and Barak the son of Abinoam on that day: 2 "That the leaders took the lead in Israel, that the people offered themselves willingly, bless Yahweh! 3 Hear, O kings; give ear, O princes; to Yahweh I will sing, I will make melody to Yahweh, the God of Israel. . . . 6 In the days of Shamgar, son of Anath, in the days of Jael, caravans ceased and travelers kept to the byways. ➡ 7 The peasantry ceased in Israel, they ceased until you arose, Deborah, arose as a mother in Israel. . . . 12 Awake, awake, Deborah! Awake, awake, utter a song! Arise, Barak, lead away your captives, O son of Abinoam. ➡ 13 . . . The people of Yahweh marched down for Him against the mighty. 14 From Ephraim they set out thither into the valley, following you, Benjamin, with your kinsmen; and from Zebulun those who bear the marshals staff; 15 the princes of Issachar came with Deborah, and Issachar faithful to Barak; into the valley they rushed forth at his heels. Among the clans of Reuben there were great searchings of heart. 16 Why

did you tarry among the sheepfolds, to hear the piping for the flocks? Among the clans of Reuben there were great searchings of heart. **17** Gilead stayed beyond the Jordan; and Dan, why did he abide with the ships? Asher sat still at the coast of the sea, settling down by his landings. . . . **19** The kings came, they fought; then the kings of Canaan fought, at Taanach, by the waters of Megiddo [a great Canaanite city]; they got no spoils of silver. **20** From heaven fought the stars, from their courses they fought against Sisera. **21** The torrent Kishon [a flash flood] swept them away. . . . **22** Then loud beat the horses hoofs with the galloping, galloping of his steeds. **23** Curse Meroz [a village that let the Canaanite fugitives escape], says the angel of Yahweh, curse bitterly its inhabitants, because they came not to the help of Yahweh. . . . ➡ **24** Most blessed of women be Jael, the wife of Heber, of tent-dwelling women most blessed. **25** Sisera asked water and she gave him milk, she brought him curds in a lordly bowl. **26** She put her hand to the tent peg and her right hand to the workmen's mallet; she struck Sisera a blow, she crushed his head, she shattered and pierced his temple. **27** He sank, he fell, he lay still at her feet; at her feet he sank, he fell; where he sank, there he fell dead. **28** Out of the window she peered, the mother of Sisera gazed through the lattice: 'Why is his chariot so long in coming? Why tarry the hoofbeats of his chariots?' **29** Her wisest ladies make answer, 'Nay.' She gives answer to herself, **30** 'Are they not finding and dividing the spoil? A maiden or two for every man; spoil of dyed stuffs for Sisera, spoil of dyed stuffs embroidered, two pieces of dyed work embroidered for my neck as spoil?' **31** So perish all thine enemies, O Yahweh! But thy friends be like the sun as he rises in his might"

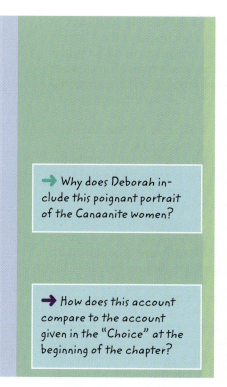

➡ *Why does Deborah include this poignant portrait of the Canaanite women?*

➡ *How does this account compare to the account given in the "Choice" at the beginning of the chapter?*

The Evolution of Hebrew Identity

The Exodus was understood as a sign that Yahweh was performing His part in the covenant with the Hebrews. Those who had escaped from Egypt came to be called the children of Israel. During the forty years of wandering in the wilderness, Moses finalized the Hebrews' covenant with God when he received the Ten Commandments. God renewed his promise to make the Hebrews His chosen people and to lead them into Canaan, the promised land of good fortune, and the Hebrews, in turn, agreed to obey God's laws as set forth in the Ten Commandments and to recognize Yahweh as their only god, to the exclusion of all others. Over the centuries, many other regulations written in the Torah and elsewhere specified the Hebrews' religious duties toward God and their moral conduct toward other people. Under the guidance of the prophets, Hebrew laws and traditions emphasized ethical behavior, personal morality, and social justice involving both governments and individuals. The prophets taught that all people were equal before God, and the rich and powerful were reminded to protect the poor and weak. Rulers were expected to rule justly and to obey God's law. If they did not do so, then the prophets were justified in rebuking them. As individuals, the Hebrews learned to value righteousness, justice, kindness, and compassion.

Hebrew laws were in many ways much more comprehensive than the laws of other Near Eastern peoples, for they dealt not only with religious, civil, and criminal law but also with intimate aspects of personal behavior, such as personal hygiene and food preparation. Laws often were expressed as prohibitions that began with the words "Thou shalt not" and were addressed not to society in general, as were the laws of most other nations, but to individuals. Four of the Ten Commandments had to do with honoring Yahweh, including not worshiping any other gods and respecting the **Sabbath,** the day of worship. The remaining six commandments regulated human society and prohibited behaviors such as adultery, theft, murder, false testimony, and covetousness. These briefly stated regulations did not specify punishments for guilty parties, but other sections of Hebrew law did. In many cases, violations of the law, such as not respecting the sanctity of the Sabbath, were punishable by death. But most Hebrew adherence to the law was self-imposed. It was the individual responsibility of every Hebrew to live an upright life.

In some ways, Hebrew law, religion, and society were similar to those of other Near Eastern peoples.

Sabbath Jewish holy day, modern Saturday.

For personal injuries, Hebrew law specified the same "eye for an eye" law of retaliation found in the Babylonian Code of Hammurabi. As in many other Near Eastern societies, women were disadvantaged and could not own or sell property or initiate lawsuits or divorces. Initially, women participated in some religious rituals, but, over time, they lost this right. Just as Mesopotamian gods were believed to be the true rulers of Mesopotamian cities and kingdoms, Yahweh was believed to be the true ruler of the Hebrews, and individual Hebrew leaders acted on His authority. In other Near Eastern societies only a small royal or priestly segment of the population was thought to be in communication with the god, whereas any Hebrew could potentially serve as Yahweh's spokesperson. In addition, other Near Eastern societies acknowledged the existence of some form of afterlife, but, on this point, Hebrew scripture was divided. The book of Isaiah, for example, stated, "The dead shall live, their bodies shall rise," but the book of Psalms said, "The dead cannot praise the Lord."

Their belief that a single god had made them God's chosen people, along with their following of Yahweh's laws and their pursuit of a life based on moral and ethical behavior, united the Hebrews, gave them a unique identity, and kept them separate from other peoples. But meeting all of Yahweh's expectations was not always easy. The Bible reports numerous occasions on which Hebrews were caught engaging in the worship of other gods, making Yahweh angry and causing Him to punish them. Nevertheless, the Hebrews persevered and never abandoned their devotion to their God no matter what tribulations they faced. The Hebrew God continues to be worshiped in the present day, whereas the worship of nearly all the other Near Eastern gods ended thousands of years ago. The Hebrew code for living a moral and ethical life likewise provided a model that was later assimilated by Christianity and Islam.

The Hebrew Kingdom

Eventually, scripture relates, the Hebrews realized that their disunity was a weakness, and they asked the prophet Samuel, the last Hebrew judge, to give them a king. Samuel attempted to dissuade them, but the people insisted, saying, "No! We will have a king over us, so we may be like all the nations, and so our king may govern us and go out before us and fight our battles." Samuel therefore **anointed** two kings in succession, consecrating them with holy oil, first **Saul** (r. 1050–1010 B.C.E.) and then **David** (r. 1010–970 B.C.E.). Under their leadership, the Hebrews defeated and expelled the Philistines from Canaan. In

the process, David captured the heavily fortified Canaanite city of Jerusalem and made it the Hebrew capital. He also expanded the borders of the kingdom all the way to the Mediterranean coast. The creation of this expanded Hebrew kingdom was seen as the fulfillment of Yahweh's promise to Abraham to provide a land for His chosen people.

David was succeeded as king by his son **Solomon** (r. 970–930 B.C.E.), who centralized Hebrew worship by constructing in Jerusalem a temple to contain the Ark of the Covenant. The Temple was designed by architects from Tyre and built, over seven years, at great cost, with 70,000 haulers, 80,000 quarryers, and 3,300 foremen taking part in its construction. It became the focus of Hebrew religious rituals, and once a year, a high priest entered the Holy of Holies, the sanctuary of the Temple, to pray and sacrifice on behalf of the people.

Like other Near Eastern rulers, Hebrew kings had great authority. Solomon ruled wisely and was famous for his fair settlements of lawsuits and quarrels. But Hebrew kings also sometimes abused their power. David, for example, connived to take the woman Bathsheba from Uriah the Hittite, a foreign mercenary serving in Israel's army, by sending Uriah into the front line of battle, where he was soon killed. David, however, did not go unpunished. The prophet Nathan rebuked him, saying, "Because you have utterly scorned the Lord, the child that is born to you shall die." Other prophets, also acting under Yahweh's authority, approached other Hebrew kings to advise and censure them and to ensure that they ruled according to the law.

By the time of Solomon, the Hebrews had changed from a loosely organized group of pastoral peoples bound together by a shared religion into an urbanized and politically centralized kingdom that was a full participant in the political and economic life of the early Iron Age. The Hebrew kingdom now extended from the Euphrates River to the Sinai Peninsula. The Hebrews controlled the trade routes between the Mediterranean and Red Seas, and they taxed caravans traveling from the east. Trade brought a profitable return on goods such as gold, silver, ivory, and exotic animals, and tribute and gifts came

anoint To consecrate by applying holy oil.

Saul (r. 1050–1010 B.C.E.) First king of the Hebrews

David (r. 1010–970 B.C.E.) Hebrew king who made Jerusalem the Hebrew capital city.

Solomon (r. 970–930 B.C.E.) Hebrew king who built the Hebrew Temple in Jerusalem.

JERUSALEM

THE TEMPLE MOUNT during
THE SECON TEMPLE PERIOD

A RECONSTRUCTION BASED ON HISTORICAL AND ARCHAEOLOGICAL EVIDENCE

L. RITMEYER
© RAD 2001

This reconstruction of the temple built in Jerusalem by King Solomon ca. 966 B.C.E. shows its three-part plan, with two side sections and a larger central section. The style is similar to the three-chambered temples of the Phoenicians and may be attributed to Solomon's use of Phoenician architects and artisans. The Temple provided a centralized site for the performance of Hebrew religious rituals and gave the Hebrew kings great religious authority. *(Ritmeyer Archaeological Design)*

from foreign rulers. Solomon's international relations extended to Phoenicia in the northwest and to Arabia in the south. Using Phoenician expertise, Solomon constructed a fleet of trading ships and engaged in joint trading expeditions with the Phoenicians. Camel caravans from Sheba, an Arabian kingdom on the Red Sea, provided gold, as well as the frankincense and myrrh needed for Hebrew religious rituals. During a famous visit, the queen of Sheba brought camels, spices, gold, and gems. These mercantile and diplomatic initiatives brought great wealth into the Hebrew kingdom. The Bible declares, "King Solomon exceeded all the kings of the earth for riches" and "Solomon made gold and silver as plentiful as stones in Jerusalem." Solomon's army had more than ten thousand cavalry and a thousand chariots, and his international reputation was so great that he was able to marry a daughter of the Egyptian pharaoh.

After Solomon's death, popular unrest over high taxes caused the kingdom to split in two. In the south, the tribes of Judah and Benjamin became the kingdom of **Judah,** with its capital at Jerusalem, and its inhabitants became known as "Judaeans," or Jews. The remaining ten tribes were incorporated into the northern kingdom of Israel, with its capital at Samaria, and became known as Samaritans. Having lost its unity, the Hebrew kingdom also lost its economic and political importance, and the Hebrews once again suffered attacks by their more powerful

neighbors. They also came under foreign religious influence. The Bible tells of prophets rebuking Hebrews who worshiped foreign gods. Prophets were uncompromising. Their fearlessness in criticizing even the policies of kings provided models for later Christian holy men and women who challenged kings and emperors.

The northern kingdom of Israel continued to evolve along typical Iron Age lines, with much trade and exchange of ideas with foreign peoples. The Bible shows the northern Hebrews adopting elements of Phoenician culture, such as the worship of the god Ba'al, who was portrayed as the primary competitor of Yahweh. King Ahab reportedly lived in an ivory palace and married a Phoenician princess named Jezebel. After Ahab built a temple to Ba'al for Jezebel, the two were said to have been punished by Yahweh for their sins: Ahab bled to death in battle, and Jezebel was thrown from a building and eaten by dogs. The southern kingdom of Judah, however, remained more conservative and less affected by foreign influences. The kings of Judah supported the monotheistic movement and consolidated the position of the Temple in Jerusalem as the religious center of Jewish worship

Judah One of the twelve Hebrew tribes; also the name for the southern Hebrew kingdom.

At the same time, Hebrew oral traditions of their past history and their relations with Yahweh began to be committed to writing, using the alphabet borrowed from the Phoenicians.

The Assyrians and Their Successors, 900–550 B.C.E.

↓ What effect did the growth of the Assyrian Empire have on the Assyrian economy?

↓ What methods did the Assyrians use for gaining and retaining their empire?

The age of small nations that characterized the beginning of the Iron Age came to an end with the creation of the first Iron Age empire by the Assyrians. The Assyrian Empire was the first Near Eastern empire to incorporate both the Nile and the Mesopotamian river valleys. The Assyrians reflected Iron Age patterns by showing great concern for economic expansion and the accumulation of wealth. They also created a model of an empire based on military might, and their economic exploitation of the peoples they conquered led to their fall.

The Rise of the Assyrian Empire

The Assyrians were a Semitic people who had settled along the upper reaches of the Tigris River around 2000 B.C.E. They assimilated Mesopotamian culture and in language, culture, and religion were very similar to the Babylonians. From the beginning, the Assyrians were confronted by economic challenges. Because the soil in Assyria was not as rich as that farther downstream, the Assyrians could not exploit agriculture to the same extent as the people of lower Mesopotamia. They therefore took advantage of their access to profitable trade routes on all sides and turned to commerce as a means of expanding their economy. As early as 1900 B.C.E., the Assyrians maintained a trading colony in Anatolia.

For a thousand years, the Assyrians engaged in a struggle for survival. The Assyrian kingdom had no natural defenses and also was situated squarely on the routes used by armies going back and forth across Mesopotamia. This left the Assyrians exposed to attack from Arameans to the west, wild mountain peoples from the north, and ambitious empire builders downriver in Mesopotamia. In response, the Assyrians created the most effective military machine the world had yet seen.

The Assyrian army consisted of the Assyrian people under arms. Indeed, the Assyrians originated the concept of a standing army—that is, an army al-

ways on call. Native Assyrian farmers made up the backbone of the army. The Assyrians assimilated the most up-to-date military tactics from the steppe **nomads** to the north. Cavalry mounted on horseback replaced old-fashioned chariots. Cavalrymen had no saddles or stirrups but sat on a blanket and held a set of reins. A lance was useless—a warrior would slide off the back of his horse if he were to impale someone with this weapon—but swords and short spears could be used to hack or jab downward at a foe. Mounted archers were particularly effective as mobile shock forces. Specialist troops included engineers skilled in siege warfare, which involved battering rams, tunnels to undermine walls, scaling ladders, and movable towers. The Assyrians also created the first military based on the new iron weapon-making technology. Nearly 150 tons of unworked iron bars found in the palace of one Assyrian king probably were meant to be used for making weapons. The Assyrian kingdom became focused on institutionalized warfare. Even Assyrian religion was militaristic. The Assyrian people were named after Assur, their god of war, and Ishtar was imported from Babylon as the goddess not only of fertility but also of war. For the Assyrians, conquest became a mission from the gods.

Around 900 B.C.E., the Assyrians began to expand. King Shalmaneser III (r. 858–824 B.C.E.) repeatedly defeated the Arameans and Babylonians. A monument recording his victory over the Arameans of Damascus bragged: "They marched against me to offer battle. The king of Damascus sent 1,200 chariots, 1,200 horsemen, and 20,000 men. . . . Ahab of Israel sent 10,000 men. With the noble might granted by the lord Assur, I fought with them. I slew 14,000 of their soldiers. I desolated and destroyed the city, I burnt it." Shalmaneser later forced Jehu, king of Israel, to pay tribute, as recorded on the famous Black Stele: "I received the tribute of the Tyrians, Sidonians, and Jehu." Later, the Assyrian queen Sammuramat, who ruled around 800 B.C.E. and was known in later Greek legend as Semiramis, was said to have fought many successful wars. She was so famous as a builder that many Near Eastern monuments, including huge levees that kept the Euphrates River from flooding, were later attributed to her.

The greatest Assyrian king was **Tiglath-Pilezer III** (r. 745–727 B.C.E.). Said to have begun life as a gar-

nomad　Pastoralists who travel on horesback rather than on foot.

Tiglath-Pilezer III　(r. 745 to 727 B.C.E.) Assyrian king who annexed Phoenicia, the Arameans, and Babylonia.

The Black Stele, an inscribed stone pillar of the Assyrian king Shalmaneser, shows King Jehu of Judah humbly paying tribute to the Assyrians ca. 830 B.C.E. Shalmaneser had been unable to defeat Jehu completely, but realizing that he could not resist an all-out Assyrian attack, Jehu chose to submit and become an Assyrian vassal. The palace attendants standing behind Jehu announce to the king the amount that Jehu has paid. (*Courtesy of the Trustees of the British Museum*)

dener, he later became a soldier and was made king by the army because of his great military ability. Tiglath-Pilezer made the territorial acquisitions that created the final phase of the Assyrian Empire. He conquered the Arameans and Phoenicians, thereby giving the Assyrians access to the timber of Lebanon and the ports of the Mediterranean Sea. He also seized Babylonia, where a Semitic people known as the **Chaldeans** had recently settled, and claimed to have **annexed** the **Medes,** an Indo-European people of western Iran.

Subsequent kings continued to expand the empire. In 721 B.C.E., Samaria, capital of the northern Hebrew kingdom of Israel, fell to Sargon II (r. 721–705 B.C.E.). Soon afterward, the Philistines were annexed, giving the Assyrians control of the entire eastern Mediterranean coast. Under **Sennacherib** (r. 704–681 B.C.E.), the Assyrians invaded the southern Hebrew kingdom of Judah, as attested not only by Hebrew and Assyrian documents but also by archaeology. In preparation for his defense, the Jewish king Hezekiah built a tunnel, which still exists, 1,750 feet long that led to wells outside the walls and gave Jerusalem a dependable water supply. The Assyrians besieged Jerusalem in 701 B.C.E., and Sennacherib boasted: "Hezekiah the Jew did not submit. I besieged his cities, and conquered them with earthen ramps, battering rams, and tunnels. I drove away 200,150 people, young and old, male and female, and considered them booty. Himself I shut up in Jerusalem, like a bird in a cage." Nevertheless, the city held out. According to Hebrew scripture, Hezekiah, guided by the prophet Isaiah, sought the help of Yahweh, and 186,000 Assyrian besiegers died in a single night by divine intervention. By listening to a prophet, Heze-

kiah became a model of a good king. Eventually, he persuaded the Assyrians to leave by agreeing to pay tribute to Sennacherib. In 671 B.C.E., the Assyrian king **Esarhaddon** (r. 681–668 B.C.E.) invaded Egypt, where a southern dynasty from Nubia had assumed power. Esarhaddon occupied Lower Egypt and declared himself king not only of Upper and Lower Egypt but of Ethiopia as well. For the first time in history, both major river valleys of the Near East were controlled by the same power.

Assyrian Economy and Government

In the Assyrian Empire, warfare was a way of life. The Assyrians went to war for three reasons: defense, territorial expansion, and economic growth. Peoples who had attacked the Assyrians in the past, such as the Arameans or Babylonians, were defeated. Conquered territories also created a defensive buffer zone, as they had for the Egyptians. The Assyrians consolidated their military gains by placing army garrisons in the hills and on trade routes and by granting land to Assyrian settlers. Important conquered territories

Chaldeans Semitic people who settled in Babylonia in the eighth century B.C.E.

annex To incorporate a conquered territory into an empire or kingdom.

Medes Indo-European people occupying western Iran.

Sennacherib (r. 704–681 B.C.E.) Assyrian king who attacked Jerusalem in 701 B.C.E.

Esarhaddon (r. 681–668 B.C.E.) Assyrian king who conquered Egypt in 671 B.C.E.

This relief from the Assyrian palace at Nimrud shows Tiglath Pilezer III and the Assyrian army besieging a city with scaling ladders and a battering ram. Impaled bodies at the bottom show the results of the siege. The Assyrians' ability to capture heavily fortified cities was a primary factor in their army's, and their empire's, success. (*Courtesy of the Trustees of the British Museum*)

were annexed, made into **provinces,** and directly governed by Assyrian administrators. More distant or marginal defeated peoples were made into vassals and permitted to govern themselves as long as they followed Assyrian orders.

The empire was a moneymaking enterprise. Foreign trade benefited the state, and luxury goods were funneled into the royal court. Warfare created income in several ways. Tribute was assessed on defeated peoples, and additional contributions also were extorted from them. Raiding parties plundered beyond the empire's frontiers. Wherever they went, the Assyrians siphoned off as much wealth as possible. In general, they had no concern for the economic well-being of subject peoples and did not incorporate them into Assyrian society or give them a share in the benefits of empire. Trading peoples such as the Phoenicians and Arameans, who helped meet the insatiable Assyrian demand for luxury goods, did have a privileged legal status, but their resources were drained for the benefit of the Assyrians. These short-sighted policies resulted in constant unrest, resistance, and revolt in the conquered territories.

The Assyrians used terror tactics to maintain control of their subject populations. Opposition was punished by enslavement, expulsion, and harsh treatment. For example, Assyrian records report that when some Phoenicians resisted paying their taxes, Assyrian soldiers "made the people jump around" with the points of their spears. When a Syrian leader revolted, he was captured and skinned alive. In order to demoralize newly conquered peoples, the Assyrians often **deported** large numbers of them, especially the well-to-do, to other conquered territories far

across the empire, where, as newcomers, they would be unlikely to cause trouble. For example, after the conquest of Israel in 721, thousands of Hebrews were deported to Iran, and conquered peoples from other areas were settled in Israel. These Hebrew exiles were later known as the **ten lost tribes of Israel.** King Sargon II proclaimed, "In the first year of my reign I besieged and conquered Samaria. I deported 27,290 inhabitants. I settled prisoners there, people from all lands. I set up my officials over them as governors. I laid tribute upon them." These relocations also promoted economic expansion, as the Assyrians moved persons with skilled trades, such as artisans and merchants, into economically underdeveloped regions, thus creating new sources of income for the empire. Most of the deported peoples became integrated into the populations among whom they were settled and lost their previous cultural identity. Yet even these extreme measures could not extinguish unrest, and Assyrian kings were constantly suppressing revolts.

To administer their growing empire, the Assyrians created the first unified system of **imperial** government. Past empires, such as those of the Akkadians,

provinces   Foreign territories annexed and administered by another nation.

deportation   Removal of people from their home country.

ten lost tribes of Israel   Ten Hebrew tribes of the kingdom of Israel that were deported by Sennacherib in 721 B.C.E.

imperial   Relating to an empire.

Table 2.1

Assyrian Rulers

Shalmaneser III (r. 858–824 B.C.E.)
Sammuramat (r. 800 B.C.E.)
Tiglath-Pilezer III (r. 745–727 B.C.E.)
Sargon II (r. 721–705 B.C.E.)
Sennacherib (r. 704–681 B.C.E.)
Esarhaddon (r. 681–668 B.C.E.)
Assurbanipal (r. 671–627)

Babylonians, and Egyptians, had dealt with conquered peoples individually. In contrast, the Assyrians created a centralized administrative system that applied equally to all conquered territories. At the top of the Assyrian administrative and social structure was the king, who, like all Mesopotamian kings, was seen as the representative of the primary god, in this case Assur. Assyrian art, however, often depicts the king as even more prominent than the god. The king was the supreme political, military, judicial, and religious leader. In short, he was the state, and, in a very personal way, it was the king who unified the otherwise diverse empire. As ruler of an empire perpetually at war, he was primarily a military leader.

Each year the army visited conquered and neighboring peoples, extorting financial contributions along the way. Grandiose monuments catalogued the peoples the king had defeated and the plunder he had accumulated. In fact, one of the reasons so much is known about the Assyrians is that Assyrian rulers recorded so many of their achievements. After several campaigns, for example, King Shalmaneser III gloated, "I carried away their possessions, burned their cities with fire, demanded from them hostages, tribute, and contributions, and laid on them the heavy yoke of my rule." As warrior kings, Assyrian rulers are often depicted in artwork participating in a pastime considered appropriate for a military monarch: hunting—and hunting the most dangerous quarry of all, lions, which still lived wild in the Near East. The king would hunt with bow and arrow, either on foot or on horseback. Units of the Assyrian army would accompany him and serve as beaters, driving the lions into the center of a circle, where the king awaited. One king claimed that on a single hunt he killed 10 elephants, plus 120 lions on foot and 800 from his chariot.

The king was at the heart of the centralized administrative web. All imperial officials were servants of the king and responsible directly to him, as were the nobles and priests. The king kept close watch on government officials through a system of royal messengers who reported personally to him. A class of scribes, using standard Mesopotamian cuneiform writing, kept yearly chronicles of events such as military campaigns and eclipses, thus permitting modern historians to establish Assyrian chronology with a great degree of accuracy. State control even extended to traders and craftsmen, who were organized into government-run associations. And multitudes of slaves, many of whom were war captives, performed a wide range of duties. Slaves were protected from harsh treatment by their owners and had the rights to own property, make binding contracts, and testify in court.

Assyrian kings built magnificent palaces that served as the administrative and social centers of the empire. Sennacherib established Nineveh as the primary Assyrian capital, where he built what he called "the palace without a rival," 600 by 630 feet in size. Later kings added additional palaces there, along with temples to Ishtar, Nergal, Nanna, and other deities. The palaces housed the king's family, which included multiple wives and many children. It was expected that a king would be succeeded by a son, and male children plotted to be named as the next king. Also living in the palaces were rulers and nobles of conquered and vassal peoples, who were kept in honorable captivity to ensure the good behavior of their people.

The Assyrians, who considered books and learning to be another form of plunder, originated the concept of libraries. **Assurbanipal** (r. 671–627 B.C.E.), for example, assembled at Nineveh an extensive collection of texts dealing with history, mythology, religion, law, mathematics, astronomy, grammar, and, in particular, magic. Some twenty thousand clay tablets from Assurbanipal's library have been discovered during excavations of the ruins of Nineveh, and it is thanks to him that many of the literary works of ancient Mesopotamia have survived to the present day.

The Successors of the Assyrians

Eventually the Assyrian method of governing resulted in the fall of their empire. Because the king and his court enjoyed most of the profits of empire, free peasant farmers, who made up the bulk of the army, and rural nobles often went unrewarded, causing internal unrest; on one occasion, the entire royal family was assassinated. In addition, Assyrian rule was so

Assurbanipal (r. 671–627 B.C.E.) Assyrian king who created a magnificent library at Nineveh.

oppressive that only Assyrians could be trusted to serve in the army. As the empire expanded, the army was spread more and more thinly. Moreover, because they always were on campaign, Assyrian farmers who also served as soldiers were unable to work the land back home, and the Assyrian agricultural economy fell into decline. Tiglath-Pilezer attempted to confront the recruitment problem by raising troops in the provinces, allowing some subject peoples to serve in the army instead of paying taxes. Troops were also recruited from vassals, such as the Medes. These measures provided a larger but inferior army, which became less homogeneous, less dependable, and less Assyrian.

Even though the empire appeared to be enjoying its greatest success during the reign of Assurbanipal, there were signs of trouble. The Medes and Chaldeans continued to resist Assyrian rule, and a new threat appeared from the north in the form of the **Scythians,** Indo-European steppe nomads from Central Asia. The best that the Assyrians could do was to enlist the Scythians as mercenaries. In the 650s B.C.E., the Assyrians were expelled from Egypt and soon thereafter faced revolts in Babylon and Phoenicia. The final swift decline began in the 620s B.C.E., when the Chaldeans and Medes revolted and formed an alliance against the Assyrians. The Assyrians initially were able to hold them off by using Scythian mercenaries, but the conclusive blow came in 612 B.C.E., when the Scythians changed sides and a joint army of Medes and Chaldeans defeated the Assyrian army and captured, sacked, and destroyed Nineveh. The Assyrian Empire had been held together by the Assyrian army. With the destruction of the army, the empire was no more. In the future, the Assyrians would provide an example of how not to run an empire.

The Assyrian Empire was succeeded by four smaller, regional powers: Egypt, the Medes, Lydia, and the New Babylonians. Egypt experienced a momentary revival of influence. The Egyptians finally entered the commercial spirit of the Iron Age by establishing a trading colony in the Nile Delta, where they received silver in exchange for wheat, papyrus, and linen textiles. They also began to construct a canal linking the Mediterranean and Red Seas, and they sent an expedition all the way around Africa. The Medes created a long, thin kingdom that extended north of Mesopotamia from Iran to central Anatolia. In the west, the kingdom of the Medes bordered on the rich and powerful trading kingdom of Lydia.

The strongest of the Assyrian successor states was the **New Babylonian Empire,** established in Mesopotamia by the Chaldeans. It extended from the Persian Gulf to the Mediterranean and incorporated what was left of the Assyrian people. The most effective Chaldean king was **Nebuchadrezzar** (Nebuchadnezzar in the Bible) (r. 605–562 B.C.E.), who strengthened the walls of Babylon, making the city virtually impregnable, and built an elaborately decorated gate dedicated to the goddess Ishtar. For his queen he built the famous hanging gardens of Babylon, one of the Seven Wonders of the Ancient World. No designs for the gardens survive, but they probably incorporated some kind of terraced arrangement, perhaps associated with the ziggurat of Marduk, who continued as the national Babylonian god.

The New Babylonian Empire was a center of scientific learning. Chaldean priests were famous for their knowledge of astronomy—the study of the positions and motions of stars, moon, and planets—and astrology, the belief that these heavenly bodies contained messages from the gods. The Chaldeans devised the **zodiac,** an astronomical map that divided the heavens up into twelve constellations, and they learned to calculate the movements of the sun, moon, and planets. By compiling and studying lists of eclipses, they also were able to calculate future eclipses. Chaldean astronomical learning had much influence on later Greek and Roman science.

Nebuchadrezzar proposed to conquer the southern Hebrew kingdom of Judah, something the Assyrians had never done. The prophet Jeremiah had already predicted that, because of the Jews' failure to follow the law, Jerusalem would be destroyed and the Jews would be scattered and persecuted. Jeremiah also foretold: "'The days are coming,' declares the Lord, 'when I will raise up a king who will reign wisely and do what is just and right in the land.'" Such prophecies by Jeremiah and other prophets gave rise to a belief in a **messiah,** or "anointed one," a descendant of King David who would be sent by Yahweh to restore the Jews' political independence and bring peace to the world. In 587 B.C.E., Nebuchadrezzar attacked Judah. According to Jewish tradition,

Scythians   Indo-European nomads from Central Asia.

New Babylonian Empire   Empire established by the Chaldeans that succeeded the Assyrian Empire in Mesopotamia.

Nebuchadrezzar   (r. 605–562 B.C.E.) Chaldean king of the New Babylonian Empire who captured Jerusalem in 587 B.C.E.

zodiac   Astronomical map used in astrology that divides the heavens up into twelve constellations.

messiah   (from Hebrew for "the anointed one") The person the Jews believed would be sent by Yahweh to restore their independence and bring peace.

The Ishtar Gate, built under King Nebuchadnezzar, provided a massive ceremonial entrance for Babylon during the Chaldean period. Wealthy and powerful cities needed protection from possible attackers. The entrance to Babylon was protected on three sides, making it virtually impossible for enemies to approach the gate. *(Bildarchiv Preussischer Kulturbesitz/Art Resource, NY)*

the heroine Judith charmed the Babylonian general Holofernes, got him drunk, and then cut off his head. In spite of Jewish resistance, however, Nebuchadrezzar captured Jerusalem, destroying its walls and Solomon's Temple. Following the Assyrian model, Nebuchadrezzar deported large numbers of influential Jews to Mesopotamia in what later became known as the **Babylonian Captivity.** Some of the exiles prospered. They were permitted religious freedom, and worship at the Temple was replaced by the study of scripture in **synagogues,** as Jewish places of worship came to be known. The exile caused the Jews to renew their commitment to maintaining a separate identity in the midst of foreign influences, and Jewish law forbade marrying non-Jews and working on the Sabbath. For almost all the rest of their history, up to

the year 1948, Jews would be under the domination of foreign rulers. But Jewish history has been one of resilience, of being able to survive terrible oppression because of their conviction that they were the chosen people of God.

The Persian Empire, 550–500 B.C.E.

> ↓ How did King Darius try to unify the Persian Empire?
> ↓ How were Persian policies toward subject peoples different from those of the Assyrians?

A little more than fifty years after the end of the Assyrian Empire, an even greater Iron Age empire arose—that of the Persians. The Persian homeland was in southern Iran, marking the first time that a major Near Eastern empire had not originated in a large river valley. The Persian Empire was similar to the Assyrian Empire in that the Persians also were interested in economic expansion and the accumulation of wealth. It was very different, however, in that the Persians were much more successful in convincing their subject peoples that they had a share in the benefits of the empire.

Cyrus and the Rise of the Persian Empire

Like the Medes, the **Persians** were descended from Indo-European Aryan peoples who had settled in Iran beginning around 2000 B.C.E. The Persians occupied the southern part of Iran and the Medes, the western part. The Persian kingdom was established around 700 B.C.E., but for the next century and a half the Persian kings were vassals of the Medes. The founder of the Persian Empire was the Persian king Cyrus. As in the case of Sargon of Akkad, Moses, and other ancient leaders, popular legends arose regarding Cyrus's childhood. It was said that Astyages, the king of the Medes, had a dream that a giant vine grew from the womb of his daughter Mandane, who was married to

Babylonian Captivity Deportation of thousands of Jews to Babylon after the capture of Jerusalem by the New Babylonians in 587 B.C.E.

synagogue (from Greek for "assembly") Jewish place of worship, prayer, and study.

Persians Indo-European people who settled in southern Iran.

the king of Persia, and covered the entire world. Astyages's priests, called **Magi,** interpreted this as meaning that Mandane's son would overthrow him. He therefore ordered the nobleman Harpagus to kill the baby. But the shepherd that Harpagus ordered to carry out this deed substituted his wife's stillborn infant, and they raised baby Cyrus themselves. Eventually, Cyrus's royal character was revealed, and when Astyages discovered what had happened, he slaughtered Harpagus's own son, invited Harpagus to dinner, and served him the head of his son on a platter. Harpagus took revenge by encouraging Cyrus to revolt. In 550 B.C.E., **Cyrus** (r. 550–531 B.C.E.), defeated the Medes and became king of the Medes and Persians, marking the beginning of the Persian Empire.

Like the Assyrians, the Persians had a great interest in economic development and expanded commercial activity. An outlet to the Mediterranean was essential. Thus, in 547 B.C.E., Cyrus attacked the seacoast kingdom of Lydia. In the climactic battle, the Lydian horses caught the scent of the camels in the Persian baggage train and fled, resulting in a total Persian victory. The Persians thereby gained control not only of Lydia but also of the Greek cities of Ionia, on the western seacoast of Anatolia.

Cyrus then turned to Mesopotamia, where Nebuchadrezzar's successors were facing local unrest because of conflicts with the influential Chaldean priests. In particular, the Chaldean king had attempted to favor the moon god Sin over the Babylonian national god Marduk, thereby arousing great popular opposition led by the powerful priests of Marduk. When Cyrus invaded Babylonia in 539 B.C.E., the people welcomed him as their savior, and Cyrus captured Babylon without striking a blow. Instead of imposing himself as a conqueror, Cyrus showed respect for local traditions by claiming the support of Marduk and taking the ancient Mesopotamian title of King of Sumer and Akkad. As a result of this spirit of conciliation, the cities of Syria and Palestine also acknowledged Cyrus's authority. Under Cyrus, the Persians gained a reputation for lenient and accommodating treatment of their subject peoples. Recognizing that they could not hope to rule such a large empire without local cooperation, the Persians often made native leaders officials in the Persian administration.

In 535 B.C.E., Cyrus demonstrated additional consideration for his subjects by allowing the deported Jews of Babylon to return home to Judah. Cyrus therefore was praised in the Hebrew Bible, which reported: "Thus says Cyrus, king of Persia: The Lord has given me all the kingdoms of the earth. Whoever is among you of his people, let him go up to Jerusalem and rebuild the house of the Lord." The Temple

was completed in 515 B.C.E., beginning the Second Temple period of Jewish history. Some Jews chose to remain in Babylon, and Jewish communities also arose in other places, such as Egypt. Thus began the Jewish **Diaspora,** the dispersion of Jews throughout the world. Because the Jews of the Diaspora were considered just as much a part of the Jewish world as the Jews of Palestine, the Jewish people came to define themselves not by place of residence but by belief and cultural identity. Some Jews prospered under Persian rule. For example, Jewish scripture relates that Esther, a Babylonian Jew, was raised in the household of a Persian king and eventually married him. After the king had been tricked into authorizing a plan to destroy the Jews, she persuaded him to change his mind. In 445 B.C.E., Nehemiah, another Babylonian Jew, was made governor of Judah by the Persians and was permitted to rebuild the walls of Jerusalem. At same time, the Torah assumed its final official form under the prophet and scribe Ezra. As a consequence of this written scripture, many Jewish concepts and practices were transmitted to the two subsequent great "religions of the book," Christianity and Islam.

Cyrus expanded the Persian Empire to the frontiers of India. In 530 B.C.E., he attacked the Scythians, who had been raiding Persian territory and disrupting Persian trade routes to the east. After Cyrus captured the son of the Scythian queen Tomyris, she sent a message to him saying, "If you return my son to me, you may leave my land unharmed, but if you refuse, I swear by the sun, the lord of the Scythians, that I will give you your fill of blood." Cyrus refused this request and was killed in the ensuing battle. Tomyris then was said to have filled an animal skin with blood and dipped Cyrus's head into it, saying, "Thus I make good my promise," and the Scythians continued to threaten the Persian northern frontier. Cyrus was succeeded by his son **Cambyses** (r. 530–522 B.C.E.), who continued to expand the empire by invading Egypt in 525 B.C.E. The Persians were victorious, and Cambyses was installed as pharaoh, once again demonstrating Persian respect for native cus-

Magi   Priests of the Medes, they gave their name to the modern word *magic.*

Cyrus   (r. 550–531 B.C.E.) Persian king who established the Persian Empire.

Diaspora   (from Greek for "dispersion") Spread of the Jews throughout the Near Eastern and Mediterranean worlds.

Cambyses   (r. 530–522 B.C.E.) Persian king, the successor of Cyrus, who conquered Egypt in 525 B.C.E.

The remains of the Persian capital city of Persepolis illustrate the mountainous geography of Iran. Persian cities were not population centers and consisted of little more than the king's palace. Persian kings had several such palaces, and traveled among them during the course of the year. *(Robert Harding World Imagery)*

toms. In 522 B.C.E., Cambyses was on his way home when he died under curious circumstances, reportedly falling on his sword while getting off his horse.

Darius and the Consolidation of the Empire

The successor of Cambyses was **Darius** (r. 521–486 B.C.E.), a distant relative of the royal family. Darius's primary achievement was the establishment of an administrative system that tied the empire together and ensured its long-term survival, even under undistinguished rulers. At the head of the Persian administration was the king. Like other Mesopotamian monarchs, Persian kings saw themselves not as gods but as the earthly representatives of their primary god, **Ahura Mazda,** the god of light. Nevertheless, their subjects treated them as if they were gods. Everyone living in the Persian Empire was considered a slave of the king, and the Persian king was known as "the Great King, the King of Kings." He wore elaborate gold and purple robes, sat on a golden throne, and was attended by a court of worshipers. Those introduced into his presence prostrated themselves face down on the floor. To publicize their great deeds, Persian rulers had huge **reliefs** carved on the sides of cliffs—one, for instance, depicts how Darius became king by suppressing a revolt by the Medes. As absolute monarchs, Persian kings could act on their whims—and often cruelly: those who had particularly angered the king were impaled. The king's

court was centered on palaces located in several capital cities, such as Susa and Persepolis. In fact, Persian cities often consisted of little more than the palace, for most of the population lived in the countryside. The palaces were staffed by **eunuchs** because only castrated men were allowed into the personal chambers of the royal women. Reliefs lining the walls of Darius's palace at Persepolis display the Persian court in operation: rows of humble rulers bring offerings, and Darius's bodyguard still keeps watch.

Darius's plan for administering the empire's subject peoples was based on respect for their traditions and a willingness to give them a share in the responsibilities and the benefits of empire. The Persians expected three things from their subject peoples: loyalty, taxes, and troops. Taxes were moderate, and, to keep costs down, troops were called up only as they were needed. The only standing professional army was the king's personal bodyguard, ten thousand elite Persian soldiers known as the Immortals. The remainder of the army was recruited from the subject peoples, who provided contingents based on local specialties: Medes provided cavalry, Mesopotamians infantry, Phoenicians warships, and so on. That most of the Persian army was composed of subject peoples demonstrates how much the Persians trusted their loyalty. This system put immense military forces, about a quarter of a million soldiers, at the Persians' disposal. The army's most effective branch was its

Darius (r. 521–486 B.C.E.) Persian king who established the administrative procedures of the Persian Empire.

Ahura Mazda God of light who was the chief Persian deity.

relief Image carved in relief (raised form) on a stone surface.

eunuch Male who has been castrated.

archers, both mounted and on foot, for the infantrymen were lightly armored, often protected only by wicker shields. The Persians usually defeated their enemies not by fighting skill but by sheer numbers. A built-in weakness of the Persian recruitment system was the length of time necessary—up to two years—to mobilize the army, thus leaving the Persians vulnerable to sudden attacks.

Like the Assyrians, the Persians organized their subject peoples into annexed territories and vassals. Vassals remained under native rulers as long as they stayed loyal. The annexed territories—most of the empire—were divided up into twenty very large units called **satrapies.** Egypt, Lydia, and Babylonia were each separate satrapies. A satrap appointed by the king governed each satrapy. Sometimes the satraps were local people, but usually they came from an elite group of Persian noble families known as The Seven. Satraps were very powerful, almost like petty kings, and it took a strong-willed king to control them. When a king died, the next king was chosen from the royal family by The Seven. Sometimes they chose a weak king so that they would have more freedom of action. The Persian Empire was therefore much more loosely organized than the Assyrian Empire. Local officials, thousands of miles from the court, had much **autonomy.** Darius did what he could to keep officials under his authority and sent out spies, known as "the eyes and ears of the king," who reported back to him regarding what was going on in the satrapies. There was no direct oversight, however, of a satrap's day-to-day activities, and a prudent king always had to be prepared to deal with satraps who abused their authority.

Darius and later kings introduced policies intended to unify their huge empire, to facilitate trade, and to increase economic productivity. Standardized law codes reduced confusion about which laws applied to whom. A simplified cuneiform system reduced the number of signs from several hundred to forty-two alphabetic symbols, thus making record keeping much easier. Aramaic was used as a universal language of commerce and diplomacy. Good communications were crucial, and Darius introduced the first large-scale road system in antiquity. The Royal Road, which extended 1,600 miles from Susa in Persia to Sardis in Lydia, was used by merchants and imperial couriers; the latter could carry a message its full length in a week by changing horses at regular stops. A nautical trade route from India to Egypt was opened, and the canal connecting the Mediterranean and Red Seas was completed, permitting merchant ships to sail from Spain to India. Economic exchange and productivity were facilitated by Darius's introduction of a standardized coinage system, and the

gold daric and silver siglos were accepted throughout the Near Eastern world. Persian kings amassed incredible wealth, with huge gold and silver reserves stored in palace treasuries, and were often more concerned with hoarding their money than with using it for necessary expenditures.

Persian Society and Religion

Persian society was organized around the family. Members of the seven noble families led a privileged existence. According to a Greek historian, young Persian nobles were taught only "horse-riding, archery, and speaking the truth." An elderly male headed each Persian clan, and fathers had absolute authority over their children. It was important to have legitimate heirs, and men could therefore have several wives. The most prosperous Persians were landowners, for Persian soldiers were granted land by the king in exchange for their military service. The Persians were not known as artisans; for this kind of work, they generally made use of the skills of their subject peoples. Among skilled workers, scribes were particularly favored for their importance in keeping royal records relating to matters such as tax payments and military recruitment. Most of the remaining Persian people were herders and small farmers. Much menial labor was performed by a large population of slaves, many of whom who were seized in the regular wars in which the Persian king engaged. Slaves served on the vast imperial properties, in the mines, on building projects, and in the imperial palaces.

Persian religion was dualistic; that is, it viewed the universe in terms of a perpetual conflict between good and evil. It had two kinds of deities: daevas, skygods who were bad, and ahuras, abstract moral qualities that were good. The chief deity was Ahura Mazda, a god of light who represented truth and justice and who was worshiped at fire altars, for fire represented purity. Ahriman, a daeva, represented darkness and evil. Around 750 B.C.E., the Persian prophet Zarathustra, called **Zoroaster** in Greek and known now chiefly by that name, formalized the teachings of Persian religion. In the Gathas, poems believed to have been writ-

satrapy Large administrative unit of the Persian Empire, governed by a satrap.

autonomy (from Greek for "self rule") A degree of independence or self-government of a territory or people within a larger political unit.

Zoroaster Persian prophet (in Persian, Zarathustra) who established the Persian religion known as Zoroastrianism.

A huge rock carving at Behistun in Iran shows the Persian king Darius receiving captives—he is trampling on one of them—as the Immortals, armed with bows and spears, stand behind him and the god Ahura Mazda looks down from above. *(Robert Harding World Imagery)*

ten by Zoroaster himself, Zoroaster declared, "There is one God, the Wise Lord, he called Ahura Mazda." Zoroaster taught that the universe was a battle between the forces of good and evil. Spiritual things represented good and material things, evil. At the end of time the good would triumph.

The essential teaching of Zoroaster was to "be like God." People did so by making it their personal responsibility to follow the path of good rather than the path of evil and thus to assist in the triumph of good. Good was equated with order, law, justice, and truth, and evil with disorder and lies. It was believed that, at the end of time, everyone would be judged in the fire by Ahura Mazda and that, after death, the soul came to the Bridge of the Separator, where all one's actions, words, and thoughts would be evaluated in terms of good and evil. The good would be allowed to cross the bridge into the heavenly world, but the evil would fall down below. These concepts of the end of the world and salvation through a savior god are consistent with—and influenced similar beliefs in—other world religions, such as Christianity.

Zoroaster's teachings, which later bore the name Zoroastrianism, were preserved by Magi in scriptures known as the **Zend Avesta.** Zoroastrianism became the Persian state religion, with the Persian king at its head. For example, a huge rock carving proclaimed: "King Darius says: By the grace of Ahura Mazda I became king; Ahura Mazda granted me the empire. I always acted by the grace of Ahura Mazda. Ahura Mazda brought me help because I was not wicked, nor was I a liar, nor was I a tyrant. I have ruled according to righteousness. Neither to the weak nor to the powerful did I do wrong. Whoever helped my house, him I favored; he who was hostile, him I

destroyed. You who shall be king hereafter, protect yourself vigorously from lies; punish the liars well." Persian kings saw their rule as reflecting the eternal conflict between good and evil and viewed the expansion of the empire as part of their religious responsibility to further the ultimate victory of Ahura Mazda. Their expressed desire to rule justly is one of the reasons the Persian Empire was administered more effectively than earlier empires. Zoroastrianism still survives in small pockets of the Middle East and in India, where it is known as Parsiism.

Persia, the West, and the Future

Like his predecessors, Darius expanded the Persian Empire. He conquered the Indus River valley in India, marking the first time that three of the major river valleys of the ancient world had been brought under one rule. Confronted by problems on the northern frontier, where the Scythians continued to raid Persian territory, Darius also mounted a massive invasion of Central Asia in 513 B.C.E. Like other invaders of the area, however, Darius soon learned that Central Asia was bigger than he had thought. The Scythians refused to be drawn into battle and lured the Persian army farther and farther into the steppes. Running low on supplies, Darius finally had no choice but to return home. In an exercise of good generalship, he got his army out intact, but just barely. Darius's invasion was, however, in some ways a success. Even though his army had not defeated the

Zend Avesta   Scriptures of the Zoroastrians.

Scythians, they were sufficiently demoralized that they no longer posed a serious menace. In addition, the Persians gained Thrace (modern-day Bulgaria), a new satrapy south of the Danube River.

The Persian occupation of Thrace marked the first time that a Near Eastern empire had occupied territory in Europe, and it brought the Persians into direct contact with the first European civilization, that of the mainland Greeks. The confrontation between these two civilizations became one of the most important focal points of the future history of western civilization.

Thrace   Persian satrapy in modern Bulgaria.

Summary

Review Questions

↑ How did the new styles of Iron Age life affect the development of cities and empires?

↑ How did the Hebrews establish their identity in the Near Eastern world?

↑ Describe the similarities and differences between the Assyrian and Persian Empires.

The Iron Age built on the Bronze Age to mark the next progressive step in the evolution of western civilization. The Bronze Age civilizations of Egypt and Mesopotamia had exhausted the possibilities for the expansion of a river-valley economy based almost exclusively on agriculture using wooden farm implements. The Iron Age gave increased importance to trade as a means of economic expansion and an economic advantage to peoples who had ready access to raw materials and were located on transportation routes. In addition, the widespread availability of cheap iron implements made it possible to work the tougher soils outside of the Near Eastern river valleys. Most of the world now could be effectively farmed, and during the Iron Age, the centers of new political, economic, and cultural developments moved out of the river valleys.

The first examples of Iron Age economies are found on the east coast of the Mediterranean, where peoples like the Phoenicians, Arameans, Philistines, and Hebrews all benefited in their own ways from the opportunities to expand their economies through mercantile activities. Eventually, empires arose based on the Iron Age economic model. The Assyrian Empire focused on short-term economic gains by exploiting the economic resources of the peoples it conquered and by making no effort to give its subject peoples a share in the empire. The Assyrians thus aroused distrust and resentment that often flared up into open resistance and resulted in the destruction of the Assyrian Empire at the end of the seventh century B.C.E.

The most successful Near Eastern empire was that of the Persians. The Persian Empire succeeded because of its ability to recruit a large and loyal army, its good treatment of its subject peoples, its effective system of administration, and its Zoroastrian religion, which advocated ethics and morality. On the other hand, the empire also had two weaknesses: an administrative structure that put great power in the hands of the satraps and required an effective king to keep them under control, and a cumbersome army recruitment system that took up two years to assemble the empire's full military strength.

The aspect of the Iron Age having the greatest future impact was the evolution of the religious beliefs and practices of the Hebrews. The Hebrews' belief that they were the chosen people of a single God, coupled with their moral and ethical teachings, made their religion different from all of the other Near Eastern religions. The Hebrews' creation of written scripture was especially important in preserving their beliefs and identity in the course of many centuries during which they had lost their political independence. Their struggle to preserve their religious identity and cultural heritage would result in the creation of a great world religion that in the future also would have an enormous influence on the birth and development of Christianity and Islam. The Hebrews thus laid the religious foundations for the subsequent religious history of western civilization.

In many ways, we still are in the Iron Age. Our cities still are focused on economic expansion through manufacturing and trade. Wide-ranging commercial and political powers still search for unifying factors that can bring people together and give them common ground. Lastly, religions still are based on written scriptures, moral and ethical teachings, and the belief in a single God.

← Thinking Back, Thinking Ahead →

In what ways are the policies and practices of Iron Age cities and empires similar to those of peoples, countries, and governments in the present day?

ECHO ECHO ECHO ECHO ECHO

From the Lydian Shekel to the Silver Dollar

Ever since the Bronze Age and before, gold and silver, two rare and valuable metals, have been used to store wealth and as a medium of exchange. In the Bronze and early Iron Age, they were just commodities, like copper or fish, that had to be laboriously weighed out with every transaction. Not until about 650 B.C.E. did merchants from Lydia begin to create lumps of gold and silver that all had the same standard weight. These became the first coins. They took their name, the shekel, from a unit of weight, about 2 1/2 ounces.

Coins must have a reliable weight and metal content to be trusted by the people using them. The merchants who created the first coins were not always dependable. They could go out of business or be difficult to hold accountable. The right to issue coins was therefore taken over by the Lydian government, which guaranteed that the coins had the proper metal content by placing a symbol of a lion or bull on them. It was in the government's interest to control the coinage because good coinage facilitated trade, which increased the tax income. The government also severely punished counterfeiting, which undermined popular trust in the coins, with the chopping off of hands and even death.

Coinage spread quickly. Gold and silver coins issued by the Persians became the standard means of exchange throughout their vast empire. Other commercial peoples, such the Greeks, Phoenicians, and even the Celts of western Europe, also issued coins. Ever since then, world economies have been based on the use of money that has a standard value. In the United States, the monetary system initially was based on gold and silver coins, such as the twenty-dollar gold piece and the silver dollar. As the U.S. economy expanded, however, metal coins became cumbersome and paper money came into use. At first, U.S. paper money was backed up by gold and silver, but in 1933, the United States went off the gold standard, and, as of 1964, paper money no longer could be exchanged for silver. As a result, the dollar became "worth just the paper it was printed on," resulting in growing inflation. The value of the dollar now is determined by economic forces such as "purchasing power" and the "money supply," and gold and silver have returned to the status they had in the Bronze Age—just one more commodity.

Suggested Readings

Boyce, Mary. *Zoroastrians: Their Religious Beliefs and Practices.* 2nd ed. London: Routledge, 2001. A detailed discussion of the Persian national religion.

Briant, Pierre. *From Cyrus to Alexander: A History of the Persian Empire.* Winona Lake, Ind.: Eisenbrouns, 2002. The history of the Persian Empire from its foundation by Cyrus until its conquest by Alexander the Great.

Harden, Donald. *The Phoenicians.* 2nd ed. London: Penguin, 1980. A study of the great seafaring traders of the early Iron Age.

Matthews, Victor H. *A Brief History of Ancient Israel.* Louisville, Ky.: Westminster John Knox Press, 2002. A history of the ancient Hebrews from their origins until the fourth century B.C.E.

Olmstead, Albert T. *History of the Persian Empire.* 2nd ed. Chicago: University of Chicago Press, 1959. The standard in-depth discussion of the Persian Empire.

Roux, Georges. *Ancient Iraq.* 3rd ed. London: Penguin, 1992. A classic summary of the evolution of Assyrian civilization.

Thompson, Thomas L. *Early History of the Israelite People: From the Written and Archaeological Sources.* Leiden, The Netherlands: Brill, 1992. A discussion of Hebrew history focusing on geography, anthropology, and sociology.

Websites

Collection of sources related to early Jewish history, **Internet Jewish History Sourcebook,** at http://www.fordham.edu/halsall/jewish/jewishsbook.html

History, religion, and culture of the Assyrian Empire, **Assyria,** at www.crystalinks.com/assyrian.html

History, religion, and culture of the Persian Empire, **Persia,** at www.livius.org/persia.html

CHAPTER 3

The Rise of Greek Civilization, 1100–387 B.C.E.

CHAPTER OUTLINE

1500 B.C.E.	1000 B.C.E.	500 B.C.E.	1 B.C.E./1 C.E.

1100 B.C.E.
Dorians settle southern Greece
First wave of Greek colonization begins
Greek Dark Ages begin

776 B.C.E.
First recorded Olympic games
Archaic Age begins

1200	1100	1000	900	800

The Greater Greek World During the Peloponnesian War, 431–404 B.C.E.

The Peloponnesian War was the ancient equivalent of a world war, as it involved not only Sparta and Athens but also other cities and powers ranging from Syracuse (Sicily) in the west to the Persian Empire in the east. Why would so many different regions have become involved in a war between these Greek cities?

Legend:
- Athens and allies
- Sparta and allies
- Neutral Greek states
- Persian Empire
- ✕ Major battle

Black Sea

THRACE

Sea of Marmara

ILLYRIA

• Epidamnus

ITALY

Pella •
Amphipolis
422 B.C.E.

THASOS

Aegospotami
405 B.C.E.

Cyzicus 410 B.C.E.

MACEDONIA

CHALCIDICE

Hellespont

ANATOLIA

Potidaea
432–430 B.C.E.

LEMNOS

PERSIAN
EMPIRE

CORCYRA
Corcyra 427 B.C.E.

EPIRUS

THESSALY

*Aegean
Sea*

Mytilene 428–427 B.C.E.

Arginusae Islands
406 B.C.E.

LESBOS

• Sardis

*Ionian
Sea*

PINDUS MTS.

ACARNANIA
AETOLIA

Delphi

EUBOEA

CHIOS

Naupactus
429 B.C.E.

BOEOTIA
Thebes
Delium 424 B.C.E.

Plataea 429–427 B.C.E.

ATTICA

Megara
Athens

IONIA

Ephesus

SAMOS

• Miletus

ACHAEA
ARCADIA

Corinth

Mantinea
418 B.C.E.

Olympia •

• Argos

AEGINA

DELOS

Halicarnassus

PELOPONNESUS

MESSENIA

• Sparta

Melos
416 B.C.E.

SICILY

Pylos
425 B.C.E.

LACONIA

MELOS

RHODES

• Syracuse

CRETE

M e d i t e r r a n e a n   S e a

0   100   200 Km.
0   100   200 Mi.

Timeline:

500 C.E.   1000 C.E.   1500 C.E.   2000 C.E.

753 B.C.E.
Rome is founded in Italy

750 B.C.E.
Second wave of Greek colonization begins

508 B.C.E.
Cleisthenes creates the Athenian democracy

500 B.C.E.
Classical Age begins

480 B.C.E.
Greeks fight Persians at Thermopylae and Salamis

431 B.C.E.
Peloponnesian War begins

399 B.C.E.
Death of Socrates

387 B.C.E.
King's Peace ends warfare between Sparta and Athens

700   600   500   400   300

Choice Choice Choice

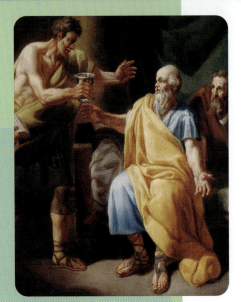

Socrates

After the Athenian philosopher Socrates was sentenced to death on trumped-up charges of "corrupting the youth," he had several opportunities to escape execution, but instead he chose to demonstrate his convictions by carrying out the sentence on himself. Socrates' suicide has been portrayed in many modern artworks, as in this 1780 painting by the French painter Jean-Antoine Watteau depicting Socrates taking the cup of hemlock while surrounded by grieving students and friends. (Réunion des Musées Nationaux/Art Resource, NY)

Socrates Chooses Death

In 399 B.C.E., the Athenian philosopher Socrates was put on trial on false charges and sentenced to death. He was given the chance to go into exile, but to show his commitment to his beliefs, he chose to abide by the sentence and died by drinking poison. At this time, Athens was in turmoil. Five years earlier, the Athenians had lost a hard-fought war with Sparta and they were looking for people to blame for the political instability that followed.

In his early life, Socrates seemed much like an average Athenian. He was the son of a sculptor and a midwife and fought heroically in the lengthy war against Sparta. After the war, however, rather than taking part in public life by attending meetings of the assembly or holding public office, he chose to become a philosopher—in Greek, a "lover of wisdom." Socrates was interested in concepts of right and wrong, justice, virtue, and love. He believed that vice came from ignorance and that people had a natural tendency to be good if they could only be taught what good was. Feeling that he could serve Athens best by teaching the Athenians to look into their souls, he spent his time in the marketplace, questioning people about their beliefs and guiding them by his questions to a greater understanding of goodness. What is the nature of the gods, he asked; what is the role of government? Is striving for wealth, office, and status more important than seeking wisdom, morality, goodness, and the health of one's soul?

By challenging some of the Greeks' most fundamental beliefs, Socrates made enemies. Raising such questions was dangerous at a time when Athens was having political difficulties, and in a democracy where any citizen could bring a legal charge against anyone else. Socrates was well aware that he was taking risks. But when asked whether his choice to challenge conventional values concerned him, he replied, "You are wrong, sir, if you think that a man who is any good at all should take into account the risk of life or death; he should look to this only in his actions, whether what he does is right or wrong, whether he is acting like a good or a bad man."

Eventually Socrates was accused of neglecting the gods and corrupting the youth by teaching that the gods did not exist. He was put on trial before a jury of five hundred Athenian citizens. Instead of respectfully defending himself against the charges, he used the occasion to present his teachings, thereby insulting the jury, which convicted him and sentenced him to death. Socrates declined to make an appeal, which might well have been granted, and asserted not only that Athens could kill his physical body but never his soul, but also that by killing him, his judges were harming their own souls.

The Athenians had a tradition that those sentenced to death could escape the penalty by going into exile, and many of those who voted to convict Socrates may have done so simply to get him out of town. However, when his friends urged Socrates to flee, he refused, claiming that he must respect the law: if he were to flee, it would seem that he was arguing that the laws should be disobeyed, which is the last thing he wanted to do. Rather than being executed by the state, Socrates was given the opportunity to commit suicide. On the designated day, surrounded by his friends, Socrates told them that his soul soon would be in the realm of the blessed and that only his body would be left behind for burial. He then drank a cup of hemlock, a common poison used for suicide in those days, and a fatal numbness crept up from his legs to his vital organs.

To maintain his self-respect, as a Greek and as a philosopher, Socrates chose death. As a Greek, he was expected to display his virtue publicly, and once he had taken his stand, he was committed to following through. As a philosopher, he had to remain true to his beliefs, even at the cost of his life.

Introduction

The Greek cultural concepts that Socrates challenged had been evolving ever since the end of the Bronze Age, when Greece lost the complex civilization of the Mycenaeans and entered a period called the Dark Ages. During this dimly known period, Greek city-states began to take shape and the Greeks grew intensely competitive. It took hundreds of years for Greek civilization to revive. During the subsequent Archaic Age, the pressure of overpopulation brought great changes, including a revival of trade, the founding of foreign colonies, and the rise of recurrent warfare. The governance of most Greek cities progressed through a series of stages, from rule by a king to rule by aristocrats to rule by the wealthy. Subsequently, the city of Athens achieved democracy—rule by the people.

Greek culture also recovered during the Archaic Age as a consequence of contacts with the civilizations of the Near East. In spite of their political differences, the Greeks were culturally united and created a spectacular civilization in which all Greeks took pride. During the following Classical Age, Greek artistic, architectural, and literary achievements were at their height. Greek architecture, sculpture, and pottery were circulated throughout the Mediterranean by Greek traders and colonists, as was Greek philosophy, poetry, drama, and history. The Greek culture of the Archaic and Classical Ages left a legacy that significantly shaped western civilization.

During the sixth century B.C.E., the two largest Greek cities, Sparta and Athens, also became politically the strongest. In many ways they were opposites. Sparta was politically conservative; Athens was liberal. Sparta retained its kings, whereas Athens introduced democracy. Sparta's economy was depended on agriculture; that of Athens, on trade.

Sparta's military power was based on its army; that of Athens, on its navy. When Greece was invaded by the mighty Persian Empire in the early fifth century B.C.E., Sparta and Athens joined with other city-states to defeat the invaders. But Greek rivalry soon reasserted itself. Sparta and Athens resumed their competition for power and influence. At the end of the fifth century a lengthy war between them led to the defeat of Athens and a collective weakening of the Greeks that soon brought about their political downfall.

The Development of Greek Identity, 1100–776 B.C.E.

↓ How did Greek political organization evolve during the Dark Ages?
↓ What role did competition play in the creation of Greek identity?

During the Dark Ages, the Greeks lost the civilization that had been created by the Mycenaeans. Long-distance commerce disappeared, and the Greek economy became purely agricultural. No historical records survive from this period, and thus only the most general changes can be identified, including the evolution from monarchy to aristocracy as the main form of government, the development of the city-state, and the expansion of competition as a characteristic of the Greek way of life.

The Greek Dark Ages

Unlike the Near East, Greece did not recover quickly from the disruptions that ended the Bronze Age. After the Dorian settlement and the final collapse of the Mycenaean Bronze Age civilization around 1100 B.C.E.,

Chronology

1100 B.C.E. Dorians settle in southern Greece; Greek Dark Ages begin; First wave of Greek colonization begins	**490 B.C.E.** Athenians defeat Persians at Battle of Marathon
776 B.C.E. First recorded Olympic Games Archaic Age begins	**480 B.C.E.** Persians defeat Spartans at Battle of Thermopylae; Greeks defeat Persians at Battle of Salamis
ca. 750 B.C.E. Homer's *Iliad* and *Odyssey* are committed to writing	**479 B.C.E.** Greeks defeat Persians at Battle of Plataea
750–550 B.C.E. Second wave of Greek colonization occurs	**440s B.C.E.** Herodotus writes *The Histories*
ca. 700 B.C.E. Lycurgus establishes Spartan Good Rule	**431–404 B.C.E.** Peloponnesian War
650–500 B.C.E. Age of the Tyrants	**430–427 B.C.E.** Plague devastates Athens
621 B.C.E. Draco composes Athenian law code	**410 B.C.E.** Aristophanes writes the *Lysistrata*
592 B.C.E. Solon creates the Athenian oligarchy	**404 B.C.E.** Sparta occupies Athens
546 B.C.E. Peisistratus becomes tyrant of Athens	**401 B.C.E.** Xenophon's March of the 10,000
508 B.C.E. Cleisthenes creates the Athenian democracy	**399 B.C.E.** Socrates dies
500 B.C.E. Classical Age begins	**387 B.C.E.** King's Peace ends warfare between the Spartans and Athenians

Greece entered the Iron Age with a period of cultural reversion known as the **Greek Dark Ages** because so much of the period is hidden from history. The complex administrative and economic systems of the Mycenaeans vanished, taking with them urbanization, large-scale political organization, massive stone architecture, a trading economy, writing, and the manufacture of fine pottery, sculpture, and metalwork. As a result, little is known of post-Mycenaean Greece.

There was no written literature in the Dark Ages, but folk memories were preserved in myths and legends passed orally from generation to generation. Collections of myths described how the gods had created and continued to control the world, and cycles of legends described the deeds of Greek heroes. These tales were put into verse and memorized by wandering bards who were welcomed wherever they went, for they provided a rare kind of entertainment. The Greeks considered these stories to be their ancient history, and because the myths and legends were so well known, they provided material for later Greek art and literature that any Greek would at once understand.

Two epic poems composed around 800 B.C.E. by the blind poet Homer and then passed on orally deal with the most famous Greek legend, the story of the massive Greek attack on the city of Troy in northwestern Anatolia. The *Iliad* tells of the events leading up to the capture of Troy, including the arrival of a thousand Greek ships (each carrying about fifty men) and the quarrel between king Agamemnon of Mycenae and the Greek hero Achilles, son of a goddess and a mortal man. And the *Odyssey* describes the ten-year struggle of the Greek hero Odysseus to return home from Troy and the stratagems used by his wife Penelope to fend off a crowd of suitors. Homer's poems became two masterpieces of Greek poetry and mark the beginning of European literature. Although Homer's stories are based on fact, they also contain a vast amount of exaggeration that makes it difficult to

Greek Dark Ages   Period from 1100 to 776 B.C.E. in which the Greeks lost the culture developed during the Mycenaean Bronze Age civilization.

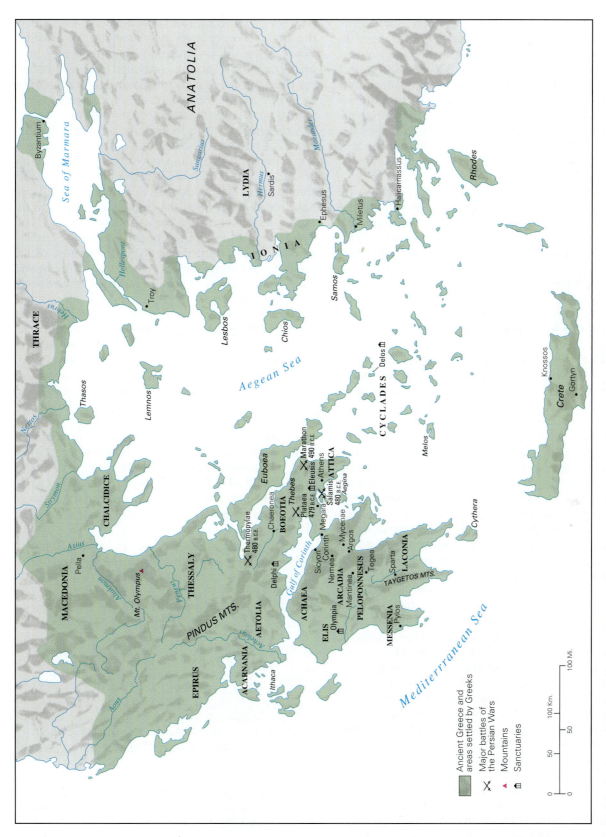

MAP 3.1 **Ancient Greece, ca. 1050** B.C.E. During the Dark Ages, the Greeks inhabited both the Greek mainland and Ionia, the western coast of Anatolia. City life developed in Ionia and in the southern part of Greece to a much greater extent than in Macedonia and in the north.

separate fact from fiction. For example, the poems contain some recollections of the Bronze Age, as when king Agamemnon is described as "glorious in his armor of gleaming bronze." But they also reflect the later life of the Iron Age, as when Agamemnon proposes to give Achilles "twenty iron cauldrons." Aside from these general impressions, the written remains are of little help in compiling a narrative of the Dark Ages. Nor does archaeology help much in this regard, for only very meager material remains survive.

Several general developments can, however, be identified for this era. One was the settlement of the Dorian Greeks, who destroyed the Mycenaean culture. Although it is difficult to find archaeological evidence for the Dorian occupation, the distribution patterns of Greek dialects show that by the end of the Dark Ages, the most fertile agricultural lands of southern Greece were inhabited by people speaking Dorian Greek. The Mycenaean versions of Greek virtually disappeared from the Greek mainland, being preserved only by Greeks who held out on the **Acropolis,** a fortified rocky bluff, at Athens and who settled in Ionia on the coast of Anatolia, where, around 1100 B.C.E., some Mycenaeans fled to avoid the Dorians. This migration was the first wave of Greek colonization.

During the Dark Ages people lived in isolated rural villages, where agriculture was virtually the sole basis of economic life. They were supported by a **subsistence economy** in which all resources, ranging from grain (wheat, barley, oats) and animals (sheep, goats, pigs, cattle) to home-smelted iron, were locally produced. Social organization was based on the family. It was the family's responsibility, for example, to retaliate against another family for wrongs done to a family member, and such retaliations could lead to long-term cycles of blood feuds. The smallest family unit was the household, and several households made up an extended family. Extended families were organized into larger units, the clan and the tribe. People's status in society was determined largely by which family, clan, and tribe they belonged to.

Villages were independent political units administered by petty kings whose original function was to serve as war leaders. Most Greek governments, therefore, began as **monarchies,** ruled by kings. Gradually, economic and political power gravitated into the hands of those who acquired the most and best land. These people came to identify themselves as aristocrats, a word meaning "the best people." Eventually, the only way to become an aristocrat was to be born one. The eldest aristocrats were members of a council that advised the king. During the more peaceful times after the initial Dorian settlement, the need for kings

who served as war leaders declined, and nearly all of the kings were replaced by a new kind of **constitutional,** or legal, government called an **aristocracy.** In an aristocracy, the aristocrats continued to be members of the chief legislative body, the council, and shared the most important offices, as generals, city priests, and annual presiding officials known as **archons.**

Other free members of Dark Ages communities included a few craftworkers and traders as well as a larger number of commoners who owned small plots of land, rented land from an aristocrat, or worked as shepherds or farmworkers. Commoners could not hold office or serve on the council, but they did attend a citizen assembly. The assembly, however, had little authority except to approve decisions already reached by the council. Finally, at the bottom of the social ladder were slaves, owned mostly by aristocrats. Slaves were not always well treated and were often ready to revolt.

Another development during the Dark Ages was the rise of the **polis,** or city-state. City-states were created when several villages coalesced for the purpose of physical security and economic and political consolidation. A polis usually was centered on a fortified acropolis that provided a place of refuge and overlooked an **agora,** or marketplace. The city of Athens had formed by about 1000 B.C.E. Not long afterward, five villages joined to form Sparta, and eight villages combined to create Corinth. By about 800 B.C.E., more than a hundred other cities had formed in a similar manner, and all of Greece south of Macedonia was divided into city-states. The polis became the focus of Greek political life.

acropolis (Greek for "high point of the city") Fortified high point that provided a refuge for people living in a Greek city.

subsistence economy Economy in which necessary products are produced locally and there is no surplus food supply.

monarchy (Greek for "rule by one person") Constitutional form of government based on rule by a king.

constitution Written or unwritten legal basis for the government of a city.

aristocracy (Greek, for "rule by the best people") Constitutional form of government based on rule by aristocrats who own the best land and are related by blood.

archons (Greek for "leaders") Chief officials in Greek aristocracies and oligarchies.

polis (Greek for "city") Greek city-state and source of the English word *politics,* which means "life in a city."

agora (Greek for "marketplace") Central market and gathering place of a Greek city.

Greek cities introduced new concepts in government. Unlike Near Eastern kingdoms and cities, which were ruled by kings or gods, Greek cities, to a greater or lesser degree, were ruled collectively by their citizens. Someone was a citizen if one of his or her parents was one. Slaves and resident foreigners, therefore, were not citizens. A city could make a foreigner a citizen, but this did not happen very often. Citizens were equal under the law, and all adult male citizens had some degree of participation in the government, even if only to vote in the assembly. This degree of popular rule was unheard of in the Near East, and it gave citizens a special sense of identity with and ownership of their cities. Civic loyalty could be just as important as family loyalty. Even though some cities were very small, just a few thousand people and covering less than a hundred square miles, each Greek thought that his or her polis was the best one in Greece.

Competition and Conflict

During the Dark Ages competition and conflict became characteristic aspects of the Greek way of life. Individuals competed with individuals for status, power, wealth, and influence. Social classes clashed with each other as the privileged tried to protect their interests against the unprivileged, and cities competed for resources. In fact, the Greeks saw all of human activity as a competition. Even the gods were worshiped through athletic competitions, which also were held at funerals to honor the dead. Nor was it enough simply to win. The Greeks believed that the joy of victory was magnified if a defeated rival was humiliated. In Greek unconditional warfare, it was customary for the victors to extend no mercy to the losers, and it was acceptable, even if it did not often happen, for the men to be killed and the women and children to be sold into slavery. The Greeks had no good losers and no moral victories. At the Olympic games, for example, there was no prize for second place. Competitors prayed for "either the wreath of victory or death."

Greek competitiveness grew out of a desire to demonstrate *aretē,* or personal excellence. In the epics of Homer, aristocrats were expected to embrace a warrior code that valued honor above all else. *Aretē* had to be displayed in some outward form. External appearances were what mattered, not intentions. Most of all, bravery in war was glorified, whereas cowardice, such as throwing away one's shield and running away from a battle, carried the greatest disgrace. *Aretē* was also demonstrated by excelling in a competitive endeavor, such as politics, speechmaking, warfare, or athletic competition, as well as by openly caring for one's parents, showing hospitality to strangers, and honoring the gods. Successful pursuit of excellence brought fame and public recognition. Failure to demonstrate *aretē* led to dishonor, loss of reputation, and shame.

For male aristocrats, military glory was what counted most. When the Greek hero Achilles was given the choice between a short, glorious life and a long, colorless one, his choice was obvious. These attitudes could create conflicts between the desire for glory in warfare and devotion to family at home. Homer sympathetically portrayed this tension in his account of the Trojan hero Hector's farewell to his wife Andromache and son Astyanax:

> *Andromache spoke to him, "My dear husband, your warlike spirit will be your death. You have no compassion for your infant child, for me, your sad wife, who before long will be your widow. For soon the Greeks will attack you and cut you down." Great Hector answered her: "Wife, all this concerns me, too. However, I'd be disgraced, dreadfully shamed if I should slink away from war like a coward." With that, Hector reached toward his son, who shrank back, terrified by the horse-hair plume on his father's helmet. Laughing, glorious Hector pulled the glittering helmet off. Then he kissed his dear son, holding him in his arms.*

No matter how dear his family was to him, Hector had to demonstrate his bravery publicly, even if that meant putting himself into a situation in which he would almost surely be killed.

The Greek competitive spirit was both a blessing and a curse. It encouraged the Greeks to great achievements in literature, art, and architecture, but it also produced constant conflict and warfare that weakened the Greeks so much that they eventually succumbed to invaders.

Gender Roles

Another way that Greek men demonstrated their superiority was by controlling Greek women. In nearly every Greek city, women were an underclass in both public and private life, a subordinate position that began at birth. Male children were preferred, and it was not uncommon for families to abandon unwanted infants, females in particular. Abandoned infants could

aretē   (Greek for "excellence") Greek sense of personal excellence.

In ancient Greek society, a woman's place was in the home, where she oversaw the domestic economy, which included making clothing for the family. This scene of the everyday life of women, from an Athenian vase painting of ca. 540 B.C.E., showing women weaving cloth on a loom. *(Image copyright © The Metropolitan Museum of Art/Art Resource, NY. The Metropolitan Museum of Art, New York, NY, U.S.A.)*

time with other women, very close friendships, including sexual ones, were common between them. Less privileged women, on the other hand, and in particular slaves, appeared regularly in public and often were badly treated. Many poor women engaged in prostitution. Two things in particular worried Greek women. Childbearing was filled with risk, for medical care was minimal, and it was not uncommon for women to die in childbirth. And Greek women also feared violence at the hands of their husbands. There was no defense against battering, which was prevalent because of the competitive nature of Greek public life. If a man was not doing well outside the home, he might take out his frustrations on his wife.

be taken by anyone, and many were raised as slaves. Male children of citizens gained full citizenship rights after they reached adulthood. Citizen women were protected by the city's laws and passed citizenship on to their children, but they could never exercise any public citizenship rights. They could not attend assembly meetings, could not hold office, and did not serve in the military. Their public activities were limited to participation in religious ceremonies restricted to women. Women could not inherit property, which passed to sons or, if there were none, to the eldest male member of the family. Married women often were prohibited from controlling any more money than could be used to buy a bushel of grain.

A woman's primary duties were to keep house and bear and raise children. Women were married as young as fourteen years of age, often to a man forty or fifty years old. Well-to-do women did not appear in public unless accompanied by a male, even if only a boy. Because respectable women spent most of their

Greek men were equally segregated and were rarely in the company of women who were not mothers, wives, or prostitutes. Male citizens spent most of their time with each other out of the house, exercising nude in the gymnasium, participating in politics, and serving together in the military. Male homosocialization was fostered by a system in which a man around thirty years of age mentored a fourteen- or fifteen-year-old youth, instructing him in what it meant to be a citizen. This bond usually involved sexual activity, although actual penetration was forbidden, as this disqualified a man from citizenship. A favorite male activity was the symposium, or drinking party. Female company was provided by high-class prostitutes, known as companions, who were often well educated and trained in such activities as music, dance,

In Greek mythology, after Zeus received a prophecy that Metis, the goddess of wisdom, would bear a son stronger than he, he swallowed her when she became pregnant. When Zeus began to have terrible headaches, the god Hephaestus chopped open his head to see what was wrong. This Athenian black-figure ointment container of ca. 570 B.C.E. shows Athena springing fully armed from the head of Zeus, shown with his thunderbolt. Zeus is flanked by two birth goddesses with their arms raised, accompanied by Hephaestus with his ax and Poseidon with his trident. *(Erich Lessing/Art Resource, NY)*

and sex play—things that men did not expect from their wives.

Greek Religion and Culture

Although they were politically and socially disunited, the Greeks were culturally united. Collectively, they thought of themselves as **Hellenes**—that is, those who came from Hellas, or Greece. Anyone who spoke Greek was a Hellene. The Greeks believed they were culturally superior to all other peoples and called those who did not speak Greek **barbarians,** because to the Greeks, their speech sounded like *bar-bar-bar.*

Greeks shared the same gods and religious practices. In Greek mythology, the most important twelve deities were called the **Olympian gods** because they were believed to meet on Mount Olympus, in northern Greece. The chief Olympian god was Zeus, the god of lightning and thunder, and the others were his siblings and children. The siblings were his wife Hera, the goddess of marriage and childbirth;

Hellenes   (from Greek *Hellas,* for "Greece") Collective name of the ancient Greeks for themselves.

barbarians   (Greek for "a person who speaks bar-bar-bar") Greek term for anyone who did not speak Greek and therefore was not Greek.

Olympian gods   Important Greek gods and goddesses who were said to meet on Mount Olympus in northern Greece

Poseidon, who ruled the sea and caused earthquakes; Aphrodite, the goddess of love and sex; and Demeter, the goddess of the harvest. Zeus's Olympian children included Ares, the god of war; Athena, the goddess of wisdom; Artemis, the goddess of hunting; her brother Apollo, god of the sun, prophecy, medicine, and music; Hephaestus, the craftsman; Hermes, the messenger of the gods; and Dionysus, the god of wine. Other important gods were Zeus's sister Hestia, in charge of hearth and home, and Zeus's brother Hades, who ruled the underworld. Each Greek city identified one god who was believed to take special care of that city: Athena, for example, was the patron goddess of Athens, and Artemis, of Sparta.

Greek gods were anthropomorphic, and the Greeks believed that their gods had the same kinds of quarrels, friendships, and personal relationships as humans. In Greek mythology, mortals often interacted with gods in a way that most Near Eastern people never did. Zeus, for example, fathered many sons by mortal women and, like Greek men, was fond of boys. There also were half-gods, such as Hercules and Perseus, whose parents were a human and a god. Humans who accomplished great deeds, such as the winners of athletic contests or victorious generals, were thought to share in the divinity of the gods. In most regards, however, the gods had a less pervasive presence in Greece than in the Near East. The Greeks did not have a large class of publicly supported priests and did not believe that gods actually ruled their cities. For the Greeks, the gods put order into the world but then left people to carry on their own business. The gods were fundamentally just and would punish evildoers, especially those who did not pay respect to the gods, and therefore the Greeks performed rituals designed to maintain the goodwill of the gods.

In each city, public religious rituals were carried out at temples by local officials who also served as state priests. The priests offered sacrifices, usually a slaughtered animal, intended to ensure that the god would look favorably on the city. Bones wrapped in fat were burned as offerings to the god, and the meat was cooked and served to the people. Temples usually were not frequented for personal religious purposes, although they could provide asylum for those whose personal safety was at risk. In general, the worship of a city's patron deity aroused little emotional enthusiasm but was considered necessary to keep the god well disposed toward the city.

In order to receive personal attention from the gods, individual Greeks left offerings in temples for favors received, such as being cured of a disease; for help in the future, as on an upcoming sea voyage; or as amends for a terrible crime, such as killing a relative or disrespecting the gods. At shrines in the countryside, people could receive **oracles,** messages from the gods about the outcomes of future events. Oracles could be received in many forms, such as through the interpretation of dreams or the sounds in a brook. The shrines of gods who provided oracles were some of the few places in Greece where there were permanent staffs of priests and priestesses.

By the eighth century B.C.E., Greek cities were in more frequent contact. The fame of the oracle of Apollo at Delphi, in northern Greece, for example, spread, and even foreigners came to seek advice on matters ranging from settling quarrels to undertaking wars. A priestess inhaled volcanic fumes and then recited a cryptic answer that could often be interpreted in several ways. Consulting the oracle provided a means whereby local disputes, such as crimes involving bloodguilt that followed from the killing of a relative, could be resolved once the oracle's advice had been given.

In 776 B.C.E., the first firmly attested date in Greek history, the Greeks began to record the meetings of a **pan-Hellenic** festival in honor of the god Zeus held at Olympia in southern Greece. Zeus was honored with athletic contests known as the Olympic games, which subsequently were held every four years. The names of the victors were preserved with great care, and the four-year periods, known as **Olympiads,** became a standard means of dating. The great statue of Zeus at Olympia, designed by **Phidias,** the most distinguished sculptor of Greek antiquity, became one of the Seven Wonders of the Ancient World. In theory, warfare was supposed to cease during the games so that athletes and spectators could attend with relative personal security. Customs such as these gave the Greeks an even stronger sense of being Greek.

oracle Message about future events believed to come from the gods; also used for the priest or priestess who delivered the message.

pan-Hellenic Relating to or including all the Greeks.

Olympiad Four-year period that separated each holding of the Olympic games.

Phidias Greek sculptor of the fifth century B.C.E. who designed the statue of Zeus at Olympia and the statue of Athena at Athens.

The Archaic Age, 776–500 B.C.E.

↓ How did foreign contacts influence the revival of Greek culture?

↓ How did the growth of Greek trade affect political evolution?

By the eighth century B.C.E., the people of Greece were emerging from the isolation and cultural regression of the Dark Ages. Population growth brought a need for larger food supplies, which was met by trade, by establishing colonies, and by warfare to seize another city's land. These activities brought increased contacts among the peoples of the Mediterranean world, resulting in cultural interchanges that stimulated a revival of Greek culture. At the same time, a handful of Greek cities gained exceptional economic and political importance. By the end of the Archaic Age, Sparta and Athens had become the most powerful cities in Greece, and Greece had become a major economic and political force in the Mediterranean world.

The Revival of Trade and Culture

The year 776 B.C.E., when the winners of the Olympic games were first recorded, also marks the beginning of a new period of Greek history, the **Archaic Age,** which brought a revival of culture, the economy, and political significance to Greece. During the relatively peaceful Dark Ages, populations had gradually increased to the point where Greece's rocky and hilly soil could not produce enough agricultural staples. Methods for dealing with larger populations had to be found. One solution was to import additional foodstuffs. As a consequence, Greek commerce and production of trade goods expanded. In exchange for grain imported from Egypt and the lands around the Black Sea, the Greeks traded olive oil, fine pottery, and silver. This explosion of commerce brought the Greeks into direct conflict with the existing Mediterranean trading power, the Phoenicians. The warlike Greeks constructed fleets of maneuverable iron-beaked fifty-oared galleys, for which the unwieldy Phoenician two-decked warships were no match. The Greeks soon wrested control of important Mediterranean trade routes from the Phoenicians.

A second solution to the overpopulation problem was to seek new farmland elsewhere. In a second wave of colonization, lasting roughly from 750 to 550 B.C.E., Greek cities established colonies on the shores of the Black Sea, the Adriatic Sea, and the Mediterranean Sea in North Africa, France, and Spain. Because colonists wanted access to the sea for trade, they occupied only coastal sites. Corinth, for example, founded the great city of Syracuse in Sicily. The most extensive immigration was into southern Italy and western Sicily, which became known as Great Greece.

Colonies had the same culture, social structure, and government as the cities that founded them. Although they maintained sentimental ties to their mother city, they were completely independent. Because the colonists were mostly male, they found wives, and slaves, among the local populations whose land they also had taken. A consequence of this intermingling was the spread of Greek culture, which became a common culture throughout the Mediterranean world and diffused into central Europe through the colony of Marseilles in southern France and into southern Russia via the Black Sea colonies.

The revival of Greek trade also brought Near Eastern culture into Greece. From the Phoenicians the Greeks borrowed the alphabet, for they now had a need to keep records. From the Lydians, they picked up coinage, and the silver coins of Corinth and Athens became standard currency throughout the Mediterranean world. The Greeks also assimilated artistic ideas. The simple geometric patterns of the Dark Ages gave way to eastern influences. Greek sculpture assumed a very Egyptian look, and Greek pottery depicted many eastern designs, such as sphinxes, lions, and bulls. Almost always, however, the Greeks modified what they borrowed to suit their own preferences. For example, they were the first people to put designs on both sides of coins. They changed some letters of the Phoenician alphabet from consonants into vowels. And Greek potters and sculptors soon used designs from their own myths and legends.

Greek pottery was a particularly important trade good. Some pots, such as large urns used as grave monuments, were made for ceremonial purposes, but most were utilitarian. Four-foot-tall jars called amphorae stored wine, olives, and other edibles. Many kinds of bowls, plates, and cups served as tableware. Greek potters soon were the acknowledged Mediterranean masters of pottery making. All Greek cities produced pottery for local use, and the pottery of important trading cities was valued throughout the ancient world. During the sixth century B.C.E., Corinth was famous for pottery featuring black figures on a lighter background, but by 500 B.C.E.,

Archaic Age (based on Greek *archaios,* "ancient") Period of Greek history from 776 to 500 B.C.E., during which Greek culture and civilization revived.

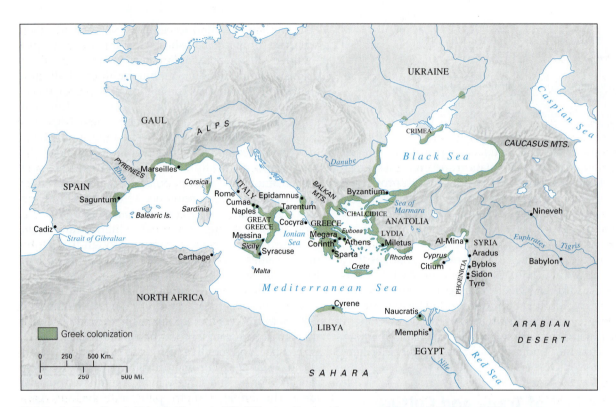

M A P 3 . 2 **Greek Colonization, ca. 750–550 B.C.E.** During the second wave of Greek colonization, Greek colonies were established along the shores of the Black, Adriatic and western Mediterranean seas and carried Greek culture far beyond the Greek mainland.

Athenian pottery with red figures on a black background had become the preferred style.

During the Archaic Age the Greeks also began to build stone temples as focal points of civic pride as well as to honor their primary gods. Temples usually were constructed in simple rectangular form, with a tile roof supported by external rows of stone columns. The **column style** evolved from the simple grooved fluted Doric style; to the Ionic style, with spiral rolls on the capital (the piece on top of the column); to the Corinthian style, with elaborate floral capitals. Temples often housed a statue of the god and an altar and were also places where offerings made to the god by individuals or cities were put on display.

The Evolution of Greek Literature and Thought

The Archaic Age also brought the creation of Greek literary culture. Rather than using writing primarily to keep business records, the Greeks also used it to create literature. As early as 750 B.C.E., the *Iliad* and the *Odyssey* were committed to writing. Fifty years later,

the poet **Hesiod** composed poems such as the *Theogony*, a catalogue of the gods, and the *Works and Days*, practical advice about farming. Soon afterward, Greeks began to express personal feelings in **lyric poetry**, which displayed a growing sense of individualism and provides the first examples of the modern concept of heterosexual and homosexual love. The poet Anacreon, for example, wrote, "Boy with a maiden's looks, I love you but you heed me not." And **Sappho** of Lesbos said of a young man she fancied: "The youth who sits next to you seems to me to be the equal of

> **column style** Doric, Ionian, and Corinthian artistic styles used in designing columns for temples and other public buildings.
>
> **Hesiod** Greek poet, ca. 700 B.C.E., who wrote the *Theogony* and *Works and Days*.
>
> **lyric poems** Poems expressing personal feelings, called "lyric" because they were meant to be accompanied by the lyre.
>
> **Sappho** Female Greek lyric poet from the island of Lesbos who wrote ca. 600 B.C.E.

the gods. My tongue grows numb; a subtle fire runs through my body. I sweat, I tremble, I turn pale, I faint." The poems of **Pindar,** the greatest lyric poet, glorified Olympic victors and traditional Greek *aretē*. Poems of other authors praised warfare as a means of demonstrating excellence. A Spartan poet wrote, "A man does not prove himself good in war unless he can endure the bloodshed of battle and take his stand against the enemy with eagerness. It is a noble thing for a brave man to die falling in the front ranks struggling for his own land." Poems also extolled the city, as when **Solon** of Athens wrote, "Our polis is destined never to perish." But there also was a contrary trend toward realism. The poet Archilochus violated conventional aristocratic standards when he admitted to his own cowardice by writing, "Some Thracian now enjoys the shield I left in the bushes. I didn't want to lose it, but I got away alive."

Greek scientific thought, also known as **philosophy,** also arose. Influenced by Babylonian astronomy and mathematics, Ionian Greeks speculated on cosmology—the nature of the universe. Rather than attributing everything to the activities of gods, as in mythology, they looked for rational explanations that usually did not directly involve any gods. **Thales,** for example, proposed in the early sixth century B.C.E. that the world had originated from water, but in the fifth century B.C.E. **Democritus** taught that all matter was made up of "atoms," tiny particles that could not be divided, providing the origin of our atomic theory. **Pythagoras,** an Ionian who migrated to southern Italy in the sixth century B.C.E., believed the universe could be understood in terms of mathematical harmony and devised a formula for calculating the lengths of the sides of a right triangle, known as the Pythagorean theorem. Heraclitus rejected the concept of underlying harmony and saw the world as perpetually in conflict. His famous phrase, "Everything flows," illustrates his view that nothing is constant. Heraclitus did, however, believe in an overall rational governing force, the **Logos,** behind the universe. The search to understand the Logos would challenge philosophers well into the Christian period. The approach of early Greek philosophers was to propose a theory and then make rational arguments in its favor; they did not perform experiments that would have actually proved or disproved their theories.

The Rise of Militarism

A third means by which a city could deal with overpopulation was to seize additional land in Greece. During the Archaic Age warfare between the city-states increased. Sparta, for example, conquered the fertile plains of the southern half of the **Peloponnesus.** Conflict also developed over the control of trade routes. After Corinth seized control of the shortest passage across the narrow isthmus connecting northern and southern Greece, it became the wealthiest Greek trading city.

The growth of trade and warfare had important consequences for Greek society and government. The expansion of trade led to the rise of a new moneyed class whose wealth came from trade rather than land. No matter how wealthy or influential these newly rich people became, however, they could never become aristocrats, for aristocratic status by now was based on birth. Wealthy merchants therefore could not hold office or serve on the council, duties that were limited to aristocrats. They grew discontented about having no voice in decisions that affected their ability to do business. The increase in warfare brought them opportunities to gain greater rights. In the past, fighting had been limited to aristocrats because only they could afford the necessary arms and armor. This situation changed when merchants grew rich. Trading cities that feared they would lose the next battle began to permit all those who could afford arms and armor to perform military service. As a result, many rich merchants and well-to-do but nonaristocratic farmers became full-fledged citizen soldiers. There was no way that a city with a small aristocratic army could hope to compete with a city fielding an army of

Pindar Greek lyric poet who wrote in the first half of the fifth century B.C.E.

Solon Politician and poet of Athens in the early sixth century B.C.E. who created the oligarchy at Athens in 592 B.C.E.

philosophy (Greek for "love of wisdom") Greek system of scientific thought that looked for rational explanations of the workings of the universe and human society.

Thales Greek philosopher of the early sixth century B.C.E. who taught that the universe had originated from water.

Democritus Greek philosopher of the fifth century B.C.E. who taught that matter was composed of tiny atoms that could not be divided.

Pythagoras Greek philosopher of the sixth century B.C.E. who devised a formula for calculating the length of the sides of a right triangle, known as the Pythagorean theorem.

Logos (Greek for "speech," "word," or "reason") The rational force that Greek philosophers such as Heraclitus believed governed the universe.

Peloponnesus Southern section of Greece.

A Corinthian vase shows a phalanx of Greek hoplites advancing in formation to the tune of flute player, whose music helps them to keep in step. Another phalanx attacks from the right. As long as the hoplites maintained their discipline, there would be a great shoving match. But eventually, the soldiers in one phalanx would lose their discipline, drop their shields, and flee for their lives. *(Scala/Art Resource, NY)*

all who could afford to serve. As a result, by 650 B.C.E., all the Greek cities had adopted the larger armies.

The wealthiest citizens, who could afford a horse, served in the cavalry, but most of the army consisted of heavily armed infantrymen called **hoplites.** A hoplite carried weapons and protective gear made from bronze or iron, including a helmet, cuirass (chest protector), shield, sword, spear, and greaves (shin guards). The primary weapon was not the sword but the spear. These larger armies fought in a packed mass called a **phalanx** that was four or more rows deep. Hoplites in the front few ranks pointed their eight-foot spears forward. Those in the rear ranks held their spears upward to keep them out of the way. A hoplite's left side was protected by his own shield, but his right side, where he held his spear, was protected by the shield of the man next to him. In battle it therefore was crucially important for hoplites to stay in formation. Battles began with enemy phalanxes shoving against each other. Nothing much happened as long as each phalanx maintained its discipline. Invariably, however, one phalanx would begin to break down and, as the other made its way into the breach, disintegrate. When a hoplite's phalanx crumbled, his only thought was to survive the battle. He would discard his heavy shield and run away.

That was when the slaughter started, as pursuing hoplites and cavalrymen cut down fleeing enemies from behind. The Greeks gained well-deserved reputations as excellent soldiers, giving rise to another way for dealing with overpopulation. Many adventurous Greeks went overseas to serve as mercenaries. As early as 650 B.C.E., Greek mercenaries, called "men of bronze," were serving in Egypt.

New Forms of Government

The rise of hoplite armies led to the decline of aristocratic governments. Once well-to-do merchants had gained a place in the army and had, on the basis of ability, gained military leadership positions, they demanded greater political rights. When aristocrats resisted, merchants joined with other disadvantaged social and economic groups, including poor farmers and resident foreigners. In most Greek cities, discon-

hoplite   (based on Greek *hoplon*, "large shield") Heavily armed Greek infantryman.

phalanx   Closely packed and well-organized body of Greek infantryman.

tent reached the point that the aristocrats had to make concessions.

One complaint of the nonaristocrats was that they did not know the laws, which were known only to aristocratic "law rememberers," whom the nonaristocrats did not always trust to remember the law correctly. Thus, in an effort to head off discontent, aristocrats in many cities appointed aristocratic **lawgivers** to write down the laws. Many of the written laws, however, were designed to protect aristocratic interests, especially their control of land, and to keep them in power. The law codes, therefore, did little to lessen the discontent of nonaristocrats.

In some cities, aristocrats made common cause with the most wealthy nonaristocrats and changed their constitutions to create a new form of government called **oligarchy,** in which the ability to participate in government was determined by wealth. All the old aristocrats plus the richest nonaristocrats became oligarchs, who could serve as archons or on a council that had the right to introduce laws. Citizens who did not qualify as oligarchs still belonged to the assembly, which could only vote yes or no on measures introduced by the council. Oligarchies were more stable than aristocracies because oligarchies could incorporate new members, thus providing some insurance against rebellion. Oligarchy became the standard form of Greek government, and once a city acquired an oligarchy, it usually kept it.

In some cities, the aristocrats resisted making any changes. In these cases, discontented groups, such as rich merchants, ruined farmers, and the urban poor, eventually overthrew the aristocracy and replaced it with an illegal ruler with absolute power called a **tyrant.** Not all tyrants were bad, as the modern sense of the word would suggest. Some governed responsibly, some not, but all were illegal rulers who could remain in power only as long as they kept their supporters happy. They did this by distributing free seed grain to small farmers, sponsoring grandiose building projects that kept the urban poor employed, and giving tax breaks to merchants to encourage economic expansion. These shows of favoritism gave previously disadvantaged groups a feeling of empowerment.

The period 650–500 B.C.E. is known as the Age of Tyrants because so many Greek cities replaced aristocracies with tyrannies. Big commercial cities, which had the most newly rich people, were the ones most likely to have tyrants. At Corinth, for example, Cypselus, the son of an aristocratic woman and a commoner, became commander of the army and seized power, exiling the aristocrats and establishing a hereditary tyranny. His son **Periander** gained a reputation as the most wicked of tyrants. He murdered his wife and sent three hundred boys from a rival city to Lydia to be made into eunuchs. But he also initiated many popular programs. He built a stone ramp across the Isthmus of Corinth and charged tolls for dragging ships between the Aegean Sea and the Gulf of Corinth, thus eliminating the dangerous coastal voyage around southern Greece. Corinth became so rich that Periander was able to eliminate taxes. He also increased the city's status by creating a powerful navy and establishing the Isthmian Games, which were held every four years (in between the Olympics). In spite of his evil reputation, Periander later was known as one of the "seven wise men of Greece" for his motto, "Forethought in all things."

Tyranny, because it was illegal, was fundamentally unstable. No matter how effective or popular a tyrant was, he always faced the threat of assassination. Eventually, all the Greek cities replaced tyrannies with much more stable oligarchies.

Sparta and Athens

↓ What were the reasons for and consequences of Sparta's adoption of a militaristic life?

↓ How did the Athenian democracy function?

During the Archaic Age, two cities in particular, Sparta and Athens, increased in strength, and by 500 B.C.E., they had become the two most powerful cities in Greece. They were similar in that they controlled large amounts of territory, but in many other ways they were opposites. They were also different from most other Greek cities.

The Spartan Way

Sparta was one of the many Dorian city-states that arose in the Peloponnesus. Unlike other important Greek cities, however, it was located inland, far from the sea. Sparta therefore always retained a purely

lawgivers Aristocrats who were appointed to write down the laws of a city.

oligarchy (Greek for "rule by the few") Constitutional form of government based on rule by the wealthy.

tyrant Illegal, unconstitutional Greek ruler who opposed the aristocrats.

Periander Tyrant of Corinth in the seventh century B.C.E. who made Corinth into a major commercial center.

agricultural economy, remaining poor at the time when coastal cities were becoming wealthy through commerce. The Spartans were so unsophisticated economically that they never issued coins; their money consisted of cumbersome iron rods. Sparta's military was its army, for Sparta did not need (and could not afford) an expensive navy. The only way the Spartans could expand their economic resources was by seizing the land of their neighbors, and by about 700 B.C.E., they had conquered the southern half of the Peloponnesus. Like many agricultural communities, the Spartans had a very conservative outlook on the world, always wary of foreigners and new ideas. They were the only Greek polis not to get rid of its kings, although they did move in the direction of aristocracy by devising a dual monarchy in which two kings were chosen from the two leading aristocratic families. The kings were advised, and supervised, by a Council of Elders comprised of twenty-eight men over sixty years old. An assembly of all male Spartan citizens over thirty approved measures submitted by the Council of Elders. The power of the kings was limited by five annually elected ephors, who presided over meetings of the council and assembly.

According to Spartan tradition, about 700 B.C.E., the Spartan lawgiver **Lycurgus** established the Spartan system of life known as the Good Rule, which was intended to unify the Spartan people, to make all male citizens equal, and to focus everyone's loyalty on the polis. Lycurgus established a militaristic society designed to do only one thing: raise good soldiers. Whereas the soldiers of other Greek cities were amateurs, a citizen militia, the Spartans were professional career soldiers. The Spartans had so much confidence in their army that they refused to build a wall around the city, trusting to their army for defense.

A child's participation in the Good Rule began at birth, when infants were inspected by a group of elders. If they seemed unhealthy, they were exposed on a mountainside and left to die. Children's military training began early. Boys went off to live in the military barracks when they were seven years old. They learned what it meant to be Spartan: to fight under all sorts of conditions, to live off the land by stealing food, and not to complain about bad weather or bad food. When they reached the age of twenty, young men would be elected into a military dining club of about fifteen men and become one of the Equals, the full citizens of Sparta. A single negative vote prevented a man from becoming a citizen: he would still live in Sparta, but it would be as if he did not exist. All the Equals were given a land grant that made them economically independent and thus able to concen-trate on their military training. Because of the need to produce offspring to supply the army, men were encouraged to marry by the age of thirty. Marriage ceremonies were militaristic. The bride dressed up as an enemy soldier, and the groom had to fight his way into her house and carry her off as a prisoner. Men then lived in the barracks until they were sixty years old, when they finally could return home.

Spartan women also were part of this militaristic system. Girls remained at home, but they learned to be just as tough as the men. According to the Greek historian **Plutarch,** Lycurgus "ordered the young women to exercise themselves with wrestling, running, and throwing the javelin, so that they would conceive their offspring in strong and healthy bodies. To toughen them, he ordered that they should go naked in the processions. Nor was there anything shameful in this nakedness. It taught them simplicity and a care for good health." Instead of wearing the enveloping clothing typical of other Greek women, Spartan women wore a single tunic slit down the side, which led other Greeks to call them "thigh flaunters". And whereas other Greek women often were married by the age of fourteen, Spartan women usually did not marry until eighteen, when they were considered more suitable for childbearing.

Spartan women also had a reputation for fearlessness. Once, when a Spartan woman was being sold as a slave, her buyer asked her what she knew how to do. "To be free," she replied. When he ordered her to do menial tasks not fitting for a free woman, she committed suicide. Spartan women even undertook military duties, something unheard of in other Greek cities. Another time, when the Spartan army was away at war, a Greek general attacked the city and was defeated by the Spartan women. Spartan mothers perpetuated the Spartan dislike of defeat. When a mother handed her son his shield before he went off to war, she told him, "Come back with this or on top of it." Being brought back dead was deemed better than abandoning one's shield to escape alive.

Spartan women were less restricted than other Greek women. Although they could not hold office, they appeared in public and had a voice in politics. Once when an Athenian woman asked a Spartan woman why "the women of Sparta were the only

Lycurgus   Spartan lawgiver of ca. 700 B.C.E. who established the Spartan way of life known as the Good Rule.

Plutarch   Greek writer of biographies and history of the second century C.E.

This bronze statuette of about 500 B.C.E., now in the British Museum in London, shows a Spartan girl running in the women's race at Olympia. Spartan girls received training in dance and gymnastics, and took part in public performances in the nude just like the boys. The entire Spartan population had to be well trained in order to defend the Spartan way of life. *(Archaeological Receipts Fund)*

women in the world who could rule men," she arrogantly replied, "Because we are the only women who are the mothers of men." While the men were away on campaign, Spartan women oversaw the household economies. They were responsible for providing each Equal's contribution to his army dining club. And they were the only women in Greece who were permitted to inherit property. In fact, it was said that nearly half of the land in Sparta eventually belonged to women.

The Spartans needed to maintain this military lifestyle because Sparta's agricultural land was worked by **helots,** agricultural slaves whose ancestors had been enslaved when Sparta conquered their territory. The Spartans were greatly outnumbered: only about 5 percent of the total population, never more than 8,000 soldiers, was Spartan; about 15 percent were free noncitizens; and the remaining 80 percent were helots. Plutarch also commented that in

Sparta, "those who were free were the most free anywhere, and those who were slaves were the most enslaved." The primary goal of the Spartans was to preserve their system and to keep the helots in their place. The helots were always ready to revolt. To make this point, Spartan men in their late teens were sent to spy on the helots and authorized to kill any who appeared disloyal. This duty impressed on young Spartans how greatly outnumbered they were and helped to justify the sacrifices they had to make in the service of the city. To protect themselves further against the helots, the Spartans also organized a mutual-defense alliance of Greek cities in the Peloponnesus, called the **Peloponnesian League.** Any member who was attacked could call on the help of any other member. The Spartans thus had a core of local allies to help them whenever the helots revolted. The constant fear of a helot uprising meant that the Spartans were very reluctant to send their army very far away from home.

The Evolution of the Athenian Government

The territory of Athens, known as Attica, extended over a thousand square miles and had a population of around six hundred thousand. It was second in size only to Sparta but in other regards the two cities were very different. The Athenians, descendants of the Mycenaeans, spoke the Ionian version of Greek, whereas the Spartans spoke the Dorian dialect. Unlike Sparta, Athens was located on the coast and developed an economy focused on trade. Whereas Sparta was poor, Athens was rich. Athens's military might lay not in its army but in its navy, which was funded by its mercantile profits. And whereas Sparta was exceptionally conservative, Athens had the most liberal political ideology of all the Greek cities and was open to ideas about new kinds of government.

Politically, Athens initially followed the standard Greek pattern. By 800 B.C.E., the monarchy had been replaced by an aristocracy. Each year, nine archons were chosen from among the aristocrats to run the government. Ex-archons became members of a council that initiated legislation, served as a supreme court, and chose the archons, always other aristocrats. The remaining male citizens were members of

helots Agricultural slaves of Sparta.
Peloponnesian League Allies of Sparta in the Peloponnesus.

the assembly, but all the assembly could do was to vote yes or no on measures introduced by the council. During the 600s B.C.E., increasing involvement in trade, based largely on the production of olive oil, brought great wealth to Athens, and a new moneyed class arose whose wealth was based on commerce. By 650 B.C.E., nonaristocrats who could afford their own weapons were eligible to serve in the army, but this service did not gain them any additional political rights.

By the late seventh century B.C.E., several Athenian groups had cause to be discontented. Rich merchants could never become aristocrats and therefore could not be part of the government. Newcomers, in particular merchants and craftworkers who had immigrated from other Greek cities, could not become citizens. Small farmers could be sold into slavery if they fell into debt to aristocrats who were eager to gain possession of their land. The urban poor often had no jobs. Dissatisfaction with aristocratic rule became so great that in 621 B.C.E. the aristocrats appointed a lawgiver named **Draco** to write down the laws. From a positive perspective, the law code attempted to end blood feuds by taking away from families the right to punish murder and creating instead a state-run court to try homicide. But Draco's code also was legendary for its harshness. It preserved the right of aristocrats to enslave debtors, and the punishment for even minor crimes was death. Draco's code thus created even greater dissatisfaction among nonaristocrats.

In response to the heightened unrest, in 594 B.C.E., the aristocrats appointed the aristocrat Solon to deal with social and economic complaints. Solon introduced a program known as the Lifting of Burdens, which abolished all of Draco's laws except for the murder court, forbade debt slavery and freed those who had been enslaved for debt, allowed foreign artisans who settled in Athens with their families to become citizens, and even established uniform weights and measures to stimulate the economy.

Solon's reforms not only helped end the economic unrest but also made Athens into a major commercial center. Their success led to Solon's reappointment in 592 B.C.E., as Reformer of the Constitution, to deal with political discontent. Solon then did what many other Greek cities were doing at the same time—changed the form of government from an aristocracy to an oligarchy. Solon divided the Athenian male citizen body into four groups based on wealth and made the ability to participate in the government dependent on one's contribution to the city's economic productivity. Archons were chosen from the most wealthy two groups. The right to initiate new legislation was given to a Council of 400, drawn from the top three groups. As before, all citizens were members of the assembly, and their only right continued to be to vote yes or no on measures already passed by the council. To compensate the poor for their lack of privileges, only the top three classes were taxed.

In most Greek cities, the establishment of an oligarchy brought political stability, but not in Athens. Its large territory created regional differences. Three groups competed for influence: wealthy, aristocratic, and conservative inhabitants of the coastal plain; poor farmers living in the hills; and liberal artisans, merchants, and sailors living on the coast. Each group had its own agenda. Those living on the plain wanted an aristocratic constitution, those in the hills wanted jobs, and those on the coast wanted increased foreign trade. In 546 B.C.E., the war hero **Peisistratus** seized power as tyrant. His policy for staying in power was to keep the support of the coastal and hill dwellers at any cost. He provided seed grain and jobs for the poor and loans to merchants. To ensure that there were no unemployed troublemakers, he sponsored massive building projects. His measures were largely successful. Under his rule, Athens overtook Corinth in the vase market. Moreover, he instilled pride in the city by creating an annual festival in honor of the god Dionysus at which plays were performed, with the Athenians voting afterward on which plays were the best.

The Athenian Democracy

Peisistratus was succeeded as tyrant by his two sons. One was assassinated, and the other was expelled in 508 B.C.E. The aristocrat **Cleisthenes** then gained the support of the people and was given the authority to reform the constitution in order to end factional fighting and create stability. To break down regional loyalties, Cleisthenes first divided the Athenian citizen body into three groups: the city (craftworkers and merchants), the coast (sailors and fisherman), and the plain (farmers). He then created ten new tribes, each of which had members from all three groups, so none would have obvious familial or regional affiliations.

Draco   Athenian lawgiver whose legal code issued in 621 B.C.E. was known for its harshness.

Peisistratus   (d. 527 B.C.E.) Athenian tyrant of the sixth century B.C.E. who created the festival of Dionysus.

Cleisthenes   Athenian leader who established Athenian democracy in 508 B.C.E.

Cleisthenes' new form of government was called **democracy,** or "rule by the people." All male citizens over thirty years old had an equal chance to participate in the government. The old Council of 400 was replaced by a Council of 500, to which each tribe contributed 50 members. Members of the council were chosen randomly by lot to serve for one year, and each day a member of one of the tribes was chosen by lot to serve as the chief official of the Athenian state. The archons likewise were chosen by lot. The assembly, which all male citizens over age twenty could attend, became the primary legislative body of Athens, and any member could propose legislation. This kind of democracy, in which all citizens are equally responsible for participating in governing, is known as radical democracy and is different from American representative democracy, in which people elect representatives to participate in government on their behalf. Athenian democracy also was different from modern democracies in another way. It was much less democratic in that only a small percentage of the Athenian population actually had full citizenship rights. About 40 percent of the population were slaves, and another 20 percent were noncitizen foreigners. Citizens thus made up 40 percent of the population, and half of these, the females, had no voting rights. Of the remaining 20 percent, the male citizens, about half would have been under the age of twenty and so did not have voting rights. Thus, only about 10 percent of the Athenian population, about sixty thousand persons at most, could actually participate in government. This level of participation was still much greater than in any nondemocratic Greek city, and far greater than in any Near Eastern state. In Greek oligarchies, for example, only about 1 percent of the population had full participation rights.

The Athenian democracy was cumbersome to operate. Meetings of the assembly could have six thousand or more members present, all with equal rights to speak and to introduce legislation. Discussion of a topic would begin with a herald asking, "Who wishes to speak?" Men over fifty were allowed to speak first, and no one under thirty could speak at all. In addition, any man convicted of not supporting his parents, throwing away his shield in battle, or being a prostitute also was barred from speaking. Those advocating unpopular opinions ran the risk of simply being shouted down. Voting was by a show of hands and thus was called "arm stretching." The majority of the assembly was made up of **thetes,** landless poor who often would vote for any measure that would improve their economic circumstances. Good speakers with glib tongues, called demagogues, could sway the assembly by introducing moneymaking measures. To restrict frivolous legislation, those whose bills did not pass were fined. And to keep bickering from getting out of hand, the Athenians introduced the practice of **ostracism.** Each year there was a vote for the "most unpopular man in Athens." If anyone received more that one-tenth of the vote of the entire citizen body, or about six thousand votes, he was compelled to leave Athens for ten years—a good way for ambitious politicians to get rid of their enemies.

Choosing officials by lot may have been democratic, but it was not a good method for filling jobs that required special talents. The Athenians therefore chose one important official by vote: each of the ten tribes elected a general known as a **strategos.** This arrangement made sense, for a city would at least want experienced generals. But because *strategos* was the most powerful elective office, ambitious politicians with no military abilities campaigned to be chosen, and Athens often was burdened with bad generals.

It soon became clear that only the well-to-do had the liberty to participate in government on a regular basis. To increase participation by Athenians who had to work for a living, citizens were paid for their services, a practice that made the Athenian democracy very expensive to operate. Poor Athenians such as the *thetes* looked on the government as a source of income, and Athens was continually looking for ways to raise money to pay for its democracy. The expensive nature of Athenian democracy helps to explain why it was so rarely adopted by other Greek city-states. Only an economic powerhouse like Athens could afford it.

The Classical Age, 500–387 B.C.E.

↓ What were the reasons for the Persian successes and failures in their conflicts with the Greeks?

↓ What were the causes of Athens's rapid rise and fall?

The fifth century B.C.E. is known as the Classical Age, the period when Greece was at its height both politically and culturally. By 500 B.C.E., the Greeks had

democracy   (Greek for "rule by the people") Constitutional form of government based on rule by the people.

thetes   Athenian citizens who did not own any land.

ostracism   Ten-year exile imposed on one man each year by vote of the Athenians.

strategos   (Greek for "general") Only elective office in the Athenian democracy.

established a unified culture and had become a great economic force in the Mediterranean world. Politically, however, they were divided. Hitherto, the Greeks had not faced any foreign threats. But soon after 500 B.C.E., they were drawn into a conflict with the greatest power the world had yet known, the Persian Empire. The Greeks later looked back on their victory over the Persians as their defining moment. Subsequently, however, they again fell to fighting among themselves, conflicts that culminated in the ruinous Peloponnesian War between Sparta and Athens. Yet this period of warfare also saw major achievements in sculpture, architecture, literature, and thought that had a permanent influence on western civilization.

The Persian Wars

Because the Greeks considered all foreigners to be barbarians, no Greek could tolerate being ruled by a non-Greek. As the Persian Empire expanded westward, it incorporated more and more Greeks, who chafed under Persian rule, resulting in a series of conflicts between the Greeks and the Persians. The first began in 498 B.C.E., when the Ionian Greek cities, led by the city of Miletus, revolted against the Persian king Darius. The Ionians, realizing they could not hold out for long, appealed for help to the European Greeks. The Athenians sent twenty ships and helped to burn the Persian provincial capital but then lost interest and went home. It took Darius a few years to raise an army to retaliate, but once he had done so, he burned Miletus and deported its inhabitants to the frontiers of India.

To prevent future Greek interference in the Persian Empire, Darius decided to attack the mainland Greeks. Before his invasion, Darius sent ambassadors to the Greek cities demanding earth and water, the Persian sign of surrender. Several Greek cities saw an alliance with the Persians as a way to gain an advantage over Greek rivals and allied themselves with the Persians. Athens refused to surrender, and when the Persian ambassadors arrived at Sparta, the Spartans threw them into a well and told them to get the earth and water themselves. The ambassadors died in the fall.

The first Persian attack on Greece came in 490 B.C.E. Two hundred ships carrying 25,000 soldiers sailed across the Aegean Sea and landed on the plain at Marathon, about twenty-six miles from Athens. The Athenians sent a messenger to Sparta asking for help, but the Spartans replied that they were performing a religious ceremony and could not leave for several days. The Athenian army of 10,000 heavily armed hoplites thus advanced almost alone to meet the 25,000 Persians. In the ensuing Battle of **Marathon,** the

lightly armed and inexperienced Persian infantrymen proved no match for the Greek hoplites. The Athenians posted most of their troops on the Persian flanks and allowed the Persians to push back the center of their line. The Athenian wings then closed behind the Persians, who fled for their ships and escaped as best as they could. The final toll was 6,400 Persian dead to 192 Athenians. A runner was sent to Athens with the news, the first running of the marathon. He fell dying in the marketplace, gasping, "Nenikekamen" ("We have won!"). The Spartans arrived the next day and could only congratulate the Athenians and lament that they had not been there to share in the glory.

The Battle of Marathon had shown that the Persians could be beaten. But it was by no means the end of Persian attempts to defeat the Greeks. The Greeks realized that the Persians would be back. When a huge silver mine was discovered near Athens, the *strategos* **Themistocles** convinced the Athenians to invest the money in a new fleet of 200 triremes, warships driven by three banks of oars. The thetes backed this measure because each ship required 180 rowers, who were recruited from thetes too poor to serve in the army and were handsomely paid. In the future, any proposals that would use the navy would be supported by the thetes.

Darius died in 486 B.C.E. His son Xerxes soon prepared a massive attack on Greece by land and sea. In 481 B.C.E., the Greek cities met at Corinth to plan their defense but immediately fell to quarreling over who would be in charge. Meanwhile, hoping to split up the Greeks, the Persians sent ambassadors to all the Greek cities except Sparta and Athens, demanding earth and water and promising them good treatment. About one-third of the Greek cities went over to the Persians. Another third decided to wait and see who was going to win. Only Sparta and Athens, and their trustworthy allies, resolved to resist the Persians. The situation looked bleak for the Greeks. Even the Delphic oracle foresaw failure, telling the Spartans that "they must lose their city or one of their kings" and recommending to the Athenians that they "flee to the world's end." When the Athenians asked for another oracle, they were told to "trust to their wooden walls," which many interpreted as meaning the wooden wall around the city.

> **Marathon** Battle in 490 B.C.E. in which the Athenians defeated the Persians.
> **Themistocles** Athenian leader who organized the resistance against the Persians in the 480s B.C.E.

The Olympias, a reconstructed Greek trireme, is shown being propelled by oars. The effective use of a trireme's three banks of oars, manned by 180 rowers, required extensive training and coordination. A trireme had a top speed of over 11 miles per hour and was maneuvered so that its iron ram could punch a hole in the side of an enemy ship. *(Paul Lipke/Trireme Trust USA)*

In 480 B.C.E. a Persian force numbering about 250,000 soldiers and 1,200 warships advanced out of Anatolia toward Greece by land and sea. The primary Persian advantage lay in numbers; Xerxes hoped simply to overwhelm the Greeks. The Greeks realized that to neutralize the Persian numerical superiority they would have to fight in confined quarters. Therefore, as a first line of defense they chose a narrow mountain pass in northern Greece at **Thermopylae.** A force of 7,000 Greeks led by 300 Spartans under King Leonidas was sent to delay the Persian advance. As the Spartans prepared to meet the Persian attack, a local farmer attempted to frighten a Spartan soldier by saying that the sky would go black when the Persian archers shot their arrows. The Spartan bravely replied, "Well, then we'll get to fight in the shade." The initial Persian attacks on the pass failed. Finally, Xerxes sent in his elite force, the Immortals, but they, too, were defeated by the well-trained Spartans. As Xerxes began to despair, a Greek traitor showed the Persians a narrow mountain path around behind the Spartans. Betrayed, the Spartans, who by that time had sent away their allies, were surrounded. But even then the Persians could not defeat them. Eventually, Xerxes ordered his archers to send volleys of arrows down on the Spartans until they all were dead. King

Leonidas was killed, and the oracle's prophecy thus was fulfilled. The Greeks later put up an epitaph to the 300 Spartans, reading: "Stranger, go tell the Spartans that we lie here, obeying their orders."

The Persians then marched south, capturing and burning Athens without a fight, for the Athenians had withdrawn to the island of **Salamis,** just off the coast. A great naval battle ensued when the Persian navy attempted to occupy Salamis, which was defended by a Greek fleet comprised mainly of the Athenian navy. The well-drilled Greeks won a spectacular victory. It now became clear what the oracle had meant by "wooden walls"—not the walls around Athens but the wooden hulls of the ships. Having lost the better part of his navy, and fearing for his safety, Xerxes returned to Persia by land, leaving his army in Greece. The following year, in 479 B.C.E., the Persian

Thermopylae   (Greek for "hot gates") Battle at a narrow pass in northern Greece where 300 Spartans were annihilated by the Persians in 480 B.C.E.

Salamis   Naval battle in 480 B.C.E. at an island off the coast of Athens where the Greeks defeated the Persians.

During the fifth century B.C.E. the large Athenian silver coin called a tetradrachm (or four-drachm piece—1 drachm weighed about 4 grams) became one of the standard coins of the Mediterranean world. Its images guaranteed its Athenian origin, for it had the head of Athena, the patron goddess of Athens, on one side and an owl, Athena's bird, on the other, with an olive branch, a symbol of Athens' primary manufactured product, to the upper right. *(Numismatica Art Classica)*

army was defeated at **Plataea.** The Spartans performed heroically, standing stoically under Persian arrow fire until it was their turn to charge. On the same day, it was said, the Athenians destroyed what was left of the Persian fleet in Ionia, and the Ionian cities again revolted from the Persians.

The Rise and Fall of Athens

The Persians' defeat marked their last attempt to conquer the Greek mainland. Later in their history, the Greeks looked back at the defeat of the Persians as their finest hour. Sparta and Athens now were the most powerful cities in Greece. Many Greeks wanted to continue the war against Persia. Athens was the natural leader, for it had a large navy, and the Spartans were reluctant to have their army away from home. In 478 B.C.E., Athens organized an anti-Persian league of Greek cities called the **Delian League** because it was headquartered on the Aegean island of Delos. Its goal was to set free the Ionian Greeks. League members contributed either ships or money. Under the leadership of Athens, the Greeks repeatedly defeated the Persians. As Athens grew in prestige, the Athenians tried to turn what had begun as a voluntary alliance into an empire, treating members of the league as if they were Athenian subjects. League membership became mandatory. Cities that attempted to resign were attacked and forced to accept Athenian-style democracies and to continue their payments, which now could be called **tribute,** as they were diverted directly into the Athenian treasury. In 448 B.C.E., the Persians made peace with Athens, giving up their claim to the Ionian cities. Once the war was over, many cities of the Delian League stopped making their contributions. But Athens forced them to con-

tinue paying, and the transition from Delian League to Athenian empire was complete.

The *strategos* **Pericles** was the most effective Athenian leader of this period, in good part because he focused his attentions on domestic matters rather than on costly foreign wars. His mother was the niece of Cleisthenes, and his father had been ostracized but had returned to Athens to become a distinguished general. As a young man he had studied with philosophers, from whom he learned to remain calm in the face of adversity. In the 460s B.C.E., Pericles began a political career based on an antiaristocratic, pro-people platform. He was an effective speaker able to manipulate the otherwise unruly electorate. He gave the people everything they wanted, including full employment and free entertainment. In 451 B.C.E., he sought to protect the privileges of poor citizens with a law limiting Athenian citizenship to those whose mother and father were both Athenian citizens. Doing so maximized the amount of benefits available to each thete. Pericles was greatly influenced by his mistress Aspasia, a courtesan from Miletus who, unlike most Athenian women, appeared regularly in public and spoke her mind. She was greatly envied

Plataea Battle in 479 B.C.E. in which the Greeks defeated the Persians.

Delian League Anti-Persian alliance of Greek cities organized by Athens in 478 B.C.E.

tribute A form of taxation paid as a fixed annual amount by a subject territory or people to a central government.

Pericles (d. 429 B.C.E.) Athenian leader during the Golden Age of Athens in the fifth century B.C.E. who sponsored many building projects.

This bust depicts Pericles, the leader of Athens, ca. 461–429 B.C.E. As the only Athenian politician who was able to control the Athenian voters, Pericles did his best to keep the Athenians out of disastrous wars and to focus their attentions on beautifying the city. *(Michael Holford)*

for her political influence. It was said that Pericles was so fond of her that he kissed her every morning when he left the house and every evening when he returned—a display of affection very unusual among the Greeks.

When Athens began to interfere in the affairs of Spartan allies on the Greek mainland, these cities appealed for help to the Spartans, who were duty bound to support them. The result was the **Peloponnesian War,** which lasted from 431 until 404 B.C.E. On one side were Sparta and its allies, including not only most of the Peloponnesian cities but also much of northern Greece and the powerful Sicilian city of Syracuse. Sparta could raise an army of 50,000 hoplites, but only about 100 ships. Athens was sup-

ported by its empire of some 300 cities, which could muster about 30,000 hoplites and more than 400 ships. A third interested party was Persia, which was ready to use its huge financial resources to gain any benefit it could from the conflict.

In the first phase of the war, the Athenians ravaged the Spartan coast with their navy, and the Spartans marched their army into Attica each year, destroying the crops. The Athenians withdrew behind their walls and refused to fight, supplying themselves by sea. A result of so much crowding was a terrible plague in Athens, graphically described by the historian **Thucydides**: "Many who were in perfect health were suddenly seized with illness. The disease brought on vomiting of bile and the body broke out in ulcers. The internal fever was intense; sufferers were tormented by unceasing thirst and could not sleep. Either they died on the seventh or ninth day, or the disease then descended into the bowels and produced violent diarrhea. Severe exhaustion then usually carried them off." One of the victims was Pericles himself.

At first, neither Athens nor Sparta gained an advantage. Eventually, however, the Spartans devised a strategy to win the war. They realized that to defeat Athens, they needed a navy, but navies were expensive and Sparta was poor. So the Spartans made an alliance with Persia, agreeing that in exchange for Persian money they would permit Persia to reoccupy Ionia if the Spartans won the war. Yet even with Persian money the Spartans were unable to defeat the Athenians at sea.

Finally, in 405 B.C.E., the Spartans surprised the Athenian fleet, which was pulled up on shore in Anatolia, destroying it and executing three thousand Athenians. Athens was financially drained and could not continue to fight, and the following year the Spartans occupied Athens. Given the hard-fought nature of the war, the Spartans were remarkably lenient and did not kill the men and enslave the women and children. Instead, they compelled the Athenians to abandon their empire and their fleet, to dismantle their city walls, and to obey Spartan foreign policy. The Spartans also forced the Athenians to abandon their democracy and accept an oligarchic government. They then went home. The following year, the Athenians restored their democracy, but the Spartans,

Peloponnesian War War between Athens and Sparta lasting from 431 to 404 B.C.E.

Thucydides Greek historian of the late fifth century B.C.E. known for his account of the Peloponnesian War.

The Athenian Acropolis was the most famous complex of temples in the ancient world. Most of the monuments were either begun or built during the time of Pericles, including the Parthenon, the great temple of Athena that was 101 feet wide and 228 feet long; the temple of Nike, the goddess of Victory; and the Erechtheum, with its distinctive caryatids, female statues that serve as columns. A grand entrance called the Propylaeum led up to the sacred area on top. These very expensive building projects were paid for with tribute brought in by the Athenian Empire. *(Sotiris Toumbis Editions)*

believing that Athens had been suitably weakened, made no response.

Sparta now was the strongest city in Greece, but the Persian reoccupation of Ionia put it in an awkward position. The Ionians appealed to Sparta, and to maintain their reputation, the Spartans felt obliged to abandon their agreement with Persia and send an army to Ionia. The Persians then threw their support to Athens. Using Persian money, the Athenians rebuilt their walls and their fleet, and the war with Sparta was renewed. Both sides were exhausted, but neither would allow the other to dictate terms of peace. The two sides finally asked the king of Persia to arbitrate. The **King's Peace** of 387 B.C.E. declared that the fighting would stop, that all the Greek cities were free, and that the Persian king would receive the cities of Ionia. Thus, after over forty years of warfare, the Greeks had succeeded only in weakening themselves. The only people to gain from the conflict were the Persians. The previous hundred years of conflict had demonstrated the fundamental inability of the Greeks to get along with each other.

The Golden Age of Greek Culture

At the same time that the Greeks were fighting self-destructive wars, they also were engaged in a great outpouring of artistic and literary production known as the **Classical Age.** Many of these cultural endeavors took place in Athens, which enjoyed its own Golden Age. The Athenians undertook monumental building projects, paid for by tribute from their empire. These projects were popular with the Athenian people because they gave work to the urban poor. In 449 B.C.E., Pericles passed a law allocating 9,000 talents (about 500,000 pounds) of silver for temple con-

King's Peace   Peace treaty arbitrated by the Persian king that ended the war between Sparta and Athens in 387 B.C.E.

Classical Age   The height of Greek artistic and literary endeavor, lasting from 500 until 323 B.C.E., which included the Golden Age of Athens.

struction work and began a large-scale rebuilding of the temple of Athena on the Acropolis known as the **Parthenon,** now recognized as the most beautiful temple of the ancient world. Except for its terra-cotta roof, the Parthenon was made entirely of marble. It contained a gold-plated statue of Athena designed by the sculptor Phidias, whose pupils created the many marble sculptures that decorated the temple. In the 430s B.C.E., a monumental gateway to the Acropolis known as the Propylaea was built, and during the 420s B.C.E., two more temples were added on the Acropolis–one, the Erechtheum, in honor of Poseidon and Erechtheus (a legendary early king of Athens), and the other dedicated to Nike, the goddess of victory. Taken together, these monuments made the Acropolis the most renowned temple complex of the ancient world.

The Golden Age of Athens also was the Golden Age of Greek drama. Every year, at the festival of Dionysus, the city financed dramatic productions. There were two kinds of drama, tragedy and comedy. Both dealt with important matters, but tragedies did so seriously and had sad endings, whereas comedies did so light-heartedly and had happy endings. The underlying theme of tragedies was that whoever failed to obey the will of the gods suffered greatly. The plots of tragedies were drawn from well-known myths and legends, meaning that the audience already knew the ending. But the characters in the play did not, and dramatic tension resulted from the manner in which the charac-ters were inexorably drawn to discover their awful fate. **Aeschylus** dramatized the betrayal and murder of the Greek high king Agamemnon by his wife and her lover. **Sophocles** told how Oedipus unknowingly married his mother and, when the truth was discovered, blinded himself. And **Euripides** described how Medea took revenge on her husband, Jason, by killing their own children. Comedies, on the other hand, were risqué and full of sexual innuendo. Because they allegedly were not meant to be taken seriously, they could deal with issues from current events. A comedy of **Aristophanes** called the *Lysistrata,* for example, responded to a pervasive desire to end the war with Sparta without sounding unpatriotic. No public figure was safe from ridicule. In another play of Aristophanes, the philosopher Socrates was depicted as living in "cloud cuckoo-land." Because Greek tragedies dealt with timeless themes of human emotion, faith, and morality, they continue to be meaningful today, while the many references to fifth-century events means that Greek comedies now seem less relevant.

Parthenon   Athenian temple on the Acropolis built in honor of Athena.

Aeschylus, Sophocles, and **Euripides**   Athenian writers of tragedy during the fifth century B.C.E.

Aristophanes   Athenian writer of comedies in the late fifth century B.C.E., author of the *Lysistrata.*

Voice

Aristophanes Suggests How to End the War

When dissent was expressed in Athens, it had to be done in a roundabout manner if its author hoped to avoid criminal charges. Comic plays permitted politically dangerous ideas to be raised in an ostensibly nonserious way. In Aristophanes' play Lysistrata, *presented ca. 410 B.C.E., the women of Greece come up with a plan for how to end the Peloponnesian War, which had been devastating Greece for nearly twenty years. The Athenians would have found this concept humorous because in all Greek cities except Sparta, women were expected to remain at home and not participate in politics. The selection begins when Lysistrata, who had summoned women from various Greek cities to a meeting, meets her friend Cleonice in the street in Athens. She is worried because the women she is expecting have not arrived.*

➡ What does this tell us about the role of Athenian women?

➡ What does Greece need to be saved from during this period?

➡ What does this exchange tell us about views of Spartan women?

➡ What was the role of the shield in Greek society?

➡ How does Lysistrata suggest the women can coerce the men into ending the fighting?

➡ How does Aristophanes intend the relations among these women to serve as a model for the men?

➡ Cleonice: Oh! They will come, my dear; but it's not easy, you know, for women to leave the house. One is busy pottering about her husband; another is getting the servant up; a third is putting her child to sleep or feeding the brat.

Lysistrata: But I tell you, the business that calls them here is far more urgent.

Cleonice: And why do you summon us, dear Lysistrata?

Lysistrata: It means just this, Greece saved by the women! Our country's fortunes depend on us. ➡ If the Boeotian and Peloponnesian women join us, Greece is saved.

Cleonice: But look! Here are some arrivals.

Myrrhine: Are we late, Lysistrata? Tell us, pray. What, not a word?

Cleonice: No, let's wait until the women of Boeotia arrive and those from the Peloponnesus.

Lysistrata: Yes, that is best. . . . Ah! Here comes Lampito. [*Lampito, a husky Spartan woman, enters with two women from Boeotia and one from Corinth.*] ➡ Good day, Lampito, dear friend from Sparta. How handsome you look! What a rosy complexion! And how strong you seem. Why, you surely could strangle a bull!

Lampito: Yes, indeed, I really think I could. It's because I do gymnastics and practice the bottom-kicking dance. But who has called together this council of women, pray?

Lysistrata: I have.

Lampito: Well then, tell us what you want of us.

Lysistrata: First answer me one question. Don't you feel sad because the fathers of your children are far away with the army?

Cleonice: Mine has been the last five months in Thrace.

Myrrhine: It's seven since mine left.

➡ Lampito: If mine ever does return, he's no sooner home than he takes down his shield again and flies back to the wars.

Lysistrata: And not so much as the shadow of a lover! Now tell me, if I have discovered a means of ending the war, will you all second me?

Cleonice: Yes, verily, by all the goddesses.

Lampito: Why, to secure peace I would climb to the top of Mount Taygetus [a mountain outside Sparta].

➡ Lysistrata: Then I will out with it at last, my mighty secret! Oh! Sister women, if we would compel our husbands to make peace, we must refrain . . .

Cleonice: Refrain from what?

Lysistrata: We must refrain from the male altogether. . . . Nay, why do you turn your backs on me? So, you bite your lips, and shake your heads, eh? Why these pale, sad looks? Why these tears? Come, will you do it—yes or no?

Cleonice: I will not do it, let the war go on. Anything, anything but that! To rob us of the sweetest thing in all the world, Lysistrata, darling!

Lysistrata: You, my dear, you from hardy Sparta, if you join me, all may yet be well. Help me, I beg you.

➡ Lampito: 'Tis a hard thing, by the two goddesses [Demeter and Persephone], it is! For a woman to sleep alone without ever a strong male in her bed. But there, peace must come first.

Lysistrata: Oh, my darling best friend, you are the only one deserving the name of woman!

Cleonice: Very well, if you must have it so, we agree.

The Classical Age also was the great age of historical writing. The Greeks were the first people to believe that one can learn from studying the past and thus not only avoid making the same mistakes over again but also anticipate how to behave in similar circumstances in the future. The three most influential early Greek historians all worked in Athens. During the 440s B.C.E., **Herodotus,** who has been called the father of history, composed a massive study intended to explain how the Greeks and Persians had become involved in the greatest war the world had yet known. Even though Herodotus portrayed the war as a conflict between civilization and barbarism, he was sympathetic to Near Eastern culture. He was the first historian to use the historical method, the system by which historians gather evidence, form hypotheses, test the validity of their evidence, and come to conclusions based on the most reliable evidence. Much of Herodotus' evidence was drawn from myth and legend, and, like the writers of tragedy, he adopted a moral approach to human behavior in which the gods rewarded the good and punished the wicked. For Herodotus, there were fundamental rights and wrongs, with no middle ground.

Thucydides, an Athenian general who had lost a battle and been sent into exile, wrote a history of the Peloponnesian War up to the year 411 B.C.E. In his view, the gods were not involved in the making of history. People were, and they were responsible for their own actions. For Thucydides, the most fundamental human motivation was a struggle for power. He observed, "The strong do what they can and the weak suffer what they must." Thucydides relied on written documents and first-person evidence for his conclusions and argued that there were two sides to every quarrel, without any absolute right or wrong. He believed it was possible to detect underlying patterns in events. He wrote for "those who wish to have a clear view of events that likely will occur again" and hoped that a critical study of the factors leading up to the Peloponnesian War could help to prevent ruinous wars in the future.

Xenophon, another Athenian general, continued the history of Greece from 411 to 362 B.C.E. Unlike Herodotus and Thucydides, however, Xenophon wrote his history mostly as narrative—first this happened, then this, then this—without any attempt to make events fit a particular model. His *March of the 10,000*—an account of how a band of trapped Greek mercenaries fought their way out of the Persian Empire in 401 B.C.E.—is one of the great adventure stories of all time. Most subsequent historians followed Xenophon's narrative style.

The Greeks also continued their study of philosophy. Philosophers turned from explaining the nature of the universe to examining the nature of human interactions. Educators known as **sophists,** who sometimes passed as philosophers, taught how to make effective arguments using debate and rhetoric, a useful skill to have in Athenian politics. Sophists often taught how to argue both sides of a question, for to them there was no absolute truth: everything was relative to the side of the argument one decided to support. Some Greeks thus viewed the sophists as immoral. The relativism of the sophists was opposed by the Athenian philosopher **Socrates** (see Choice), who taught during the latter part of the Peloponnesian War. He believed that truth could be discovered by question and answer, an approach still known as the Socratic method. Because he questioned some fundamental Athenian values, Socrates was sentenced to death in 399 B.C.E.

Socrates left no writings of his own, and his teachings have come down to us in the books of his pupil **Plato.** Plato established his own school of philosophy in Athens, known as the Academy. His written works investigate abstract questions such as, What is justice? Plato assumed the existence of a divinely established perfection that humans should strive to copy. The world we live in, he taught, is a very imperfect copy of the perfect forms and ideas that exist in the perfect static universe, and he was particularly disillusioned with the democracy that had condemned Socrates to death. Plato's most influential book, *The Republic,* presented a model for a perfect human society that was lacking the strife and contention so characteristic of the Greeks. Everyone living in Plato's republic was under the control of the state and had his or her fixed place. Some people were soldiers, and others were workers. The rulers, of course, were the philosophers, who could be either women or men.

Herodotus   Author, during the 440s B.C.E., of a history of the Persian Wars, known as the father of history.

Xenophon   Historian of the period after 411 B.C.E., author of the "March of the 10,000."

sophists   Greek teachers who taught the art of making effective arguments using debate and rhetoric.

Socrates   (d. 399 B.C.E.) Athenian philosopher of the late fifth century B.C.E. who used a question-and-answer method of teaching, now known as the Socratic method.

Plato   Athenian philosopher of the early fourth century B.C.E. who wrote *The Republic* and established a school called the Academy.

Summary

Review Questions

↑ What was the significance of the polis in defining the Greeks' personal identity?

↑ What was the nature of the conflict between Sparta and Athens?

↑ What were the causes and consequences of the Greeks' inability to unite?

Between 1100 and 387 B.C.E., the Greeks evolved from a backward agricultural society to the most important cultural and political presence in the Mediterranean world. Their development was fueled by a great sense of competition among individuals, social classes, and cities, as every Greek strove to gain some advantage over every other Greek. Competition extended to every aspect of Greek life, including politics, warfare, religion, athletics, literature, and art.

Greek life revolved around the polis, or city-state. Most Greek cities followed a sequence of political evolution from monarchy, rule by a king; to aristocracy, rule by the aristocrats; to oligarchy, rule by the wealthy. An intermediate stage, tyranny, often intervened between aristocracy and oligarchy. Curiously, the two most important Greek cities during this period, Sparta and Athens, were political exceptions—and very different from each other. Sparta scarcely got past monarchy, whereas Athens went one step beyond oligarchy to democracy, rule by the entire male citizen body. Sparta's need to control a large enslaved population resulted in its creation of a militaristic society, whereas Athens became the wealthiest trading city of the Greek world. At first, the great differences between the two cities meant that they had nothing to compete over, and together they led the Greeks in their resistance against the Persians between 490 and 480 B.C.E.

The Greek victory over Persia, however, was followed by a contest between Sparta and Athens over which would be the leader of the Greeks. To fund their expensive democracy, the Athenians created an empire of hundreds of other Greek cities, which paid tribute to Athens. This income funded the marvelous Athenian architecture and literature still admired today. But Athenian interference in other Greek cities eventually resulted in the ruinous Peloponnesian War, in which Sparta and Athens engaged in mutual destruction. At the end of the conflict, all Greek cities were weakened. The most lasting legacies of the Archaic and Classical Greeks were intellectual rather than political. The Greeks invented drama, history, and philosophy. In particular, the Greeks were the first people of antiquity to believe that they could understand the universe through speculative thought or through observation, without the need to attribute everything to the activities of the gods.

← Thinking Back, Thinking Ahead →

In what ways was Greek civilization similar to or different from the Near Eastern civilizations of the Bronze and Iron Ages?

ECHO

The Olympic Games

In both antiquity and the modern day, the value of athletic competition for both participants and spectators has been widely acknowledged. For the Greeks, the most important athletic games were the Olympics. The ancient Olympics had only a small number of events, such as footraces, the discus and javelin throws, the long jump, boxing, wrestling, horse racing, chariot races, and the pentathlon. All athletes participated in the nude. The winners received no medals, but simply an olive wreath, and there were no prizes for second or third place. Winning brought great acclaim from one's city. Victors were granted tax exemptions, front-row seats at all local athletic events, and the right to dine free in the town hall for the rest of their lives. Losing, on the other hand, was an unbearable disgrace. The poet Pindar described Olympic losers "sneaking home to their mothers by the back roads."

The holding of the ancient Olympics was outlawed in 393 C.E. by the Christian emperor Theodosius I because it was un-Christian. The Olympics were not held again until 1896, when they were revived by Pierre de Coubertin, a French historian, and held in Athens. The games of the modern Olympics are less violent than some of the ancient versions. In the ancient games, Greek boxers were allowed to wear weighted leather gloves, and in the pancration, a combination of boxing and wrestling, the contestants fought until one admitted defeat. Some competitors preferred death to giving up. The modern Olympics also have many more events than the ancient ones, and they admit any person designated as a representative of a country, whereas the ancient Olympics admitted only Greeks.

The most noticeable difference is that half of the competitors in the modern version are women. The ancient Olympics did not allow women at all, although in 396 B.C.E., horses trained by the Spartan woman Cynisca won the Olympic chariot race. Unmarried Greek women did participate at Olympia in their own games called the Heraia, in honor of Hera, queen of the gods and the wife of Zeus. The only event was a footrace in which the younger women were allowed to start first. They ran on the same track as the men and received the same olive wreath prize. Unlike the men, the women were permitted to wear clothing, a short tunic that hung loose from one shoulder.

Suggested Readings

Andrewes, Antony. *The Greek Tyrants.* London: Hutchinson's University Library, 1956. A classic discussion of the rise and role of Greek tyrants.

Boardman, John. *The Greeks Overseas: Their Early Colonies and Trade.* 4th ed. London: Thames & Hudson, 1989. A good overview of the role played by commerce in Greek civilization.

Dover, Kenneth J. *Greek Homosexuality.* 2nd ed. Cambridge, Mass.: Harvard University Press, 1989. A discussion of a controversial aspect of Greek society.

Guthrie, William K. C. *The Greek Philosophers from Thales to Aristotle.* London/New York: Routledge, 1989. An overview of Greek philosophy from the sixth through the fourth centuries B.C.E., including a discussion of the role played by Socrates.

Hammond, Nicholas G. L. *A History of Greece to 322 B.C.* 3rd ed. Oxford: Oxford University Press, 1986. A standard survey of the history of ancient Greece through the reign of Alexander the Great.

Just, Roger. *Women in Athenian Law and Life.* London: Routledge, 1989. A discussion of the legal and social status of women in ancient Athens.

Pomeroy, Sarah, Stanley Burstein, Walter Donlan, and Jennifer Roberts. *Ancient Greece: A Political, Social, and Cultural History.* Oxford: Oxford University Press, 1998. A briefer survey of ancient Greek history.

Websites

Professional site with several sections on ancient Greece, including Homer and ancient Athens, **Ancient Greece,** at www.stoa.org

Comprehensive collection of websites dealing with the ancient Greeks, **Ancient Greece,** at www.teacheroz.com/greeks.html

Greek site covering all the periods of ancient Greek history, **Hellenic History on the Internet,** at www.fhw.gr/chronos/en

CHAPTER 4

From Polis to Cosmopolis: The Hellenistic World, 387–30 B.C.E.

CHAPTER OUTLINE

1500 B.C.E.	1000 B.C.E.	500 B.C.E.	1 B.C.E./1 C.E.

336 B.C.E.
Alexander becomes
king of Macedonia

331 B.C.E.
Battle of
Guagamela

300 B.C.E.
Ptolemy I founds Alexandria Museum
Euclid publishes theorems of geometry
Zeno begins teaching Stoicism

338 B.C.E.
Macedonians
defeat the Greeks

330 B.C.E.
Third wave of Greek
colonization begins

280 B.C.E.
Final partition of
Alexander's empire

380	360	340	320	300	280	260	240	220	200

The Hellenistic Kingdoms in 280 B.C.E.

After Alexander's death in 323 B.C.E., his empire broke up into three large kingdoms, ruled by the Antigonid family in Macedonia, the Ptolemies in Egypt, and the Seleucids in Asia. Smaller powers included the kingdom of Pergamum and the island city of Rhodes. Which of these states might have been the most difficult to keep together?

0   200   400 Km.
0   200   400 Mi.

MACEDONIA
Pella
EPIRUS
THRACE
AETOLIAN LEAGUE
PERGAMUM
Pergamum
ACHAEAN LEAGUE
Athens
Sardis
Sparta
IONIA
CRETE
RHODES
CYPRUS

Black Sea
Aegean Sea
Mediterranean Sea
Caspian Sea
Aral Sea

GALATIA
ANATOLIA
PONTUS
CAPPADOCIA
COLCHIS
ARMENIA

CAUCASUS MTS.
Volga
Jaxartes

Furthest Alexandria
BACTRIAN KINGDOM
Bactra
HINDU KUSH
Alexandria in the Caucasus
Khyber Pass
Taxila
Sagala
Oxus

PARTHIA
Ecbatana
Babylon
Susa
Persepolis
PERSIA

INDO-GREEK KINGDOM
ARACHOSIA
Alexandria in Arachosia
GEDROSIA
Hyphasis (Beas)
Indus
INDIA
Pattala

Tarsus
Antioch
SYRIA
Damascus
Tyre
JUDAEA
Jerusalem
Euphrates
Tigris

Cyrene
Alexandria
Memphis
EGYPT
Siwa Oasis
Ptolemais
Nile
SAHARA
Red Sea
ARABIA

Persian Gulf
Arabian Sea

INDIAN OCEAN

The Hellenistic Kingdoms and Parthia, ca. 240 B.C.E.

- Seleucid dynasty
- Ptolemaic dynasty
- Antigonid dynasty
- Other independent kingdoms, leagues, and city-states
- Bactrian kingdom
- Parthian homeland, ca. 240 B.C.E.
- Parthian Empire, ca. 140 B.C.E.
- Indo-Greek kingdom, ca. 80 B.C.E.

| 500 C.E. | 1000 C.E. | 1500 C.E. | 2000 C.E. |

165 B.C.E.
Judas Maccabee defeats the Seleucids

30 B.C.E.
Cleopatra, last of the Ptolemies, commits suicide

| 180 | 160 | 140 | 120 | 100 | 80 | 60 | 40 | 20 | 0 |

Choice Choice Choice

Judas Maccabee

Sometimes making a choice was not just a personal issue but involved the survival of an entire people. Such was the case in the second century B.C.E. when the Hellenistic Jews had to choose between obeying the orders of a king or preserving their ancestral beliefs. The Jewish priest Mattathias and his sons, known as the Maccabees, rose in revolt against the powerful Seleucid Empire. In the decisive battle, depicted here in an engraving by the nineteenth-century French artist Gustav Doré, Judas Maccabee leads the Jewish army against the Seleucid war elephants. (Bettmann/Corbis)

The Maccabees Decide to Revolt

In the 160s B.C.E., the faith of the elderly Jewish priest Mattathias was put to the test. He could remain true to his religious convictions, or he could follow the orders of a Greek king and sacrifice to non-Jewish gods. Mattathias was in this position because ever since the fall of Jerusalem in 587 B.C.E., the Jews of Judaea had been under foreign domination. Their rulers—first the Chaldeans, then the Persians, then Alexander the Great—usually had allowed them religious freedom, and the Jews were confident that they would be able to continue to practice their religion without outside interference. But in 167 B.C.E., the Greek ruler of Judaea, King Antiochus IV, attempted to impose Greek culture on the Jews. As described in the book of the Maccabees in the Hebrew Bible, when the king's men attempted to force Mattathias to sacrifice a pig, an animal considered unclean by the Jews, Mattathias and his sons were horrified: they "tore their clothes, put on sackcloth, and mourned greatly." A royal official addressed old Mattathias: "You are a leader, honored and great in this town. Now be the first to come and do what the king commands, as all the Gentiles and the people of Judah and those that are left in Jerusalem have done. Then you and your sons will be numbered among the Friends of the king." Mattathias, however, knew where his duty lay and fearlessly replied, "I and my sons and my brothers will continue to live by the covenant of our ancestors. We will not obey the king's words by turning aside from our religion." He then killed both the official, who was about to make a sacrifice on a Jewish altar, and the king's officer. Crying, "Let every one who is zealous for the law and supports the covenant come out with me!" Mattathias fled into the hills with his five sons and was soon joined by many other Jews.

Mattathias's decision to resist the king's orders must have looked like certain suicide to most observers. The Jews were outnumbered and were facing an army that included professional mercenary soldiers. But the Jews were fighting for their religious freedom and were willing to die, whereas mercenary soldiers generally were used in battles in which both sides strove to limit their losses.

At first, the Greek army had an unfair advantage, for many Jews refused to fight on the Sabbath, the holy Jewish day of rest. On one occasion, thousands of Jewish men, women, and children were slaughtered when they refused to fight. Mattathias and his army, therefore, had another crucial choice to make: Would they abide by their law and be slaughtered, or put the law aside to be able to defend themselves? They said to each other, "If we do as our kindred did and refuse to fight with the Gentiles on the Sabbath, they will quickly destroy us." Thus they decided, "Let us fight against anyone who comes to attack us on the Sabbath day; let us not all die as our kindred died in their hiding places."

Mattathias soon died, and his son Judas took his place as the leader of the Jewish revolt. He, too, chose to continue the fight against all odds. When Antiochus's huge army approached, the Jewish rebels began to lose heart, saying "How can we, few as we are, fight against so great and so strong a multitude?" But Judas gave them courage by replying, "It is not on the size of the army that victory in battle depends, but strength comes from Heaven. They come against us in great insolence and lawlessness to destroy us and our wives and our children, and to despoil us; but we fight for our lives and our laws. God himself will crush them before us; as for you, do not be afraid of them." Judas then led the attack, and the enemy was routed. By refusing to adopt Greek culture and by choosing to fight for their beliefs, even if it meant doing so on the Sabbath, the Jews were not only able to preserve their way of life but even to overcome what, at the outset, appeared to be insurmountable odds.

Introduction

The revolt of the Maccabees took place at a time when Greeks and Greek culture were spreading throughout the Mediterranean and Near Eastern world. During the Archaic and Classical Ages, the history of Greece had been focused on the Greek mainland and on great cities such as Athens and Sparta. Believing that their culture was superior to that of all other peoples, the Greeks considered non-Greeks to be barbarians. But wars among themselves during the fifth century B.C.E. weakened the southern Greeks to the point that the Macedonian Greeks to the north, under King Philip II, were able to defeat them.

Led by Philip's son, Alexander the Great, the Greeks conquered the Persians and created a great empire that extended from Greece to western India. After the death of Alexander, however, his empire broke apart. Families of his generals gained control of large parts of it, and smaller powers took over the rest. Wherever the Greeks went, they brought their culture with them, especially by founding colonies. At the same time, they also absorbed much of eastern culture. The result was a hybrid Hellenistic culture that extended from the Strait of Gibraltar all the way to the Indus River valley.

The Hellenistic Age was a period of exploration, scholarship, and scientific investigation. Merchants and explorers wrote accounts of their travels to distant places, including India, Africa, and Britain. Hellenistic science, based on observation and experimentation, resulted in discoveries in astronomy and mathematics. Practical applications of scientific findings included the development of water clocks, steam engines, and even primitive computers.

But the opening up of a wider world also created an identity crisis for many Greeks, for whom the old Greek polis no longer provided the same sense of belonging. People now were part of the much larger world of the cosmopolis, or world-city, and had to learn how to relate to the new world around them. Many looked for meaning in religion. Some found comfort in mystery religions that promised an afterlife; others used philosophical beliefs to give them a model for their lives.

Alexander the Great, 387–323 B.C.E.

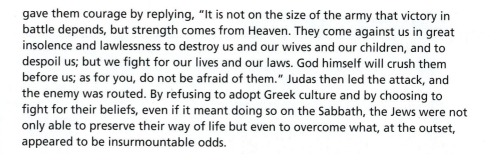

↓ Why was Alexander able to conquer such a large empire?
↓ What methods did Alexander use to make his empire secure?

After the King's Peace of 387 B.C.E., the Greek cities continued to be non-unified, and consequently the northern Greek kingdom of Macedonia imposed its authority over Greece. Led by the Macedonian kings Philip II and Alexander III, the Macedonians then attacked the Persian Empire. Young Alexander, later called the Great, went on to create the greatest empire the world had yet seen.

The Rise of Macedonia

For over six hundred years, from 1100 B.C.E. until 490 B.C.E., the Greeks had been able to develop their culture with little to fear from foreign invaders. One of the reasons they could do so was that the **Macedonians,** who inhabited Macedonia in northeasternmost Greece, had served as a buffer zone between the southern Greeks and any hostile peoples farther

Macedonians   Northern Greeks who lived in the kingdom of Macedonia.

Chronology

387 B.C.E.	King's Peace ends warfare between the Spartans and Athenians
359 B.C.E.	Philip II becomes king of Macedonia
338 B.C.E.	Philip II defeats the Greeks at Chaeronea
336 B.C.E.	Alexander III becomes king of Macedonia
335 B.C.E.	Aristotle founds the Lyceum
334 B.C.E.	Alexander invades Persian Empire
332 B.C.E.	Third wave of Greek colonization begins
331 B.C.E.	Alexander defeats Persians at Battle of Gaugamela
327 B.C.E.	Alexander invades India
323 B.C.E.	Alexander dies
c.300 B.C.E.	Ptolemy I founds Alexandria Museum; Euclid publishes geometry theorems; Epicurus teaches Epicureanism; Zeno teaches Stoicism; Pytheas of Marseilles explores Atlantic coast of Europe
280 B.C.E.	Final partition of Alexander's empire
250 B.C.E.	Parthians invade Seleucid kingdom; Aristarchus proposes heliocentric universe; Ctesibius uses air and water pressure in inventions
225 B.C.E.	Archimedes develops theories of physics
220 B.C.E.	Eratosthenes creates a map of the world
175 B.C.E.	Antiochus IV becomes Seleucid king
165 B.C.E.	Judas Maccabee defeats Seleucids
140 B.C.E.	Hipparchus creates first western star catalogue and defends geocentric universe
80 B.C.E.	Anticythera device is first known mechanical computing machine
50 B.C.E.	Greek rulers in India are defeated by Central Asian invaders
30 B.C.E.	Cleopatra commits suicide after defeat by Romans

north. The Macedonians pursued a life of hunting, drinking, and blood feuds. Even though they were Greeks, because of their difficult-to-understand northern Greek dialect and their rude manners, many southern Greeks were reluctant to accept them as being Greek. In 496 B.C.E., for example, when the Macedonian king Alexander I attempted to participate in the Olympic games, his Greekness was challenged. Only after proving that he was a direct descendant of the Greek hero Hercules was he permitted to compete, and he tied for first in the footrace. Some Macedonian aristocrats, and especially Macedonian royalty, were much attracted to southern Greek culture and served as patrons for Greek poets and teachers. Socrates was invited to Macedonia, but declined. The poet Euripides accepted an invitation and wrote a play about a Macedonian king before being attacked and torn to pieces by savage Macedonian hunting dogs.

The Macedonians were open to almost constant attack, and, like the Assyrians, in order to survive they eventually developed a powerful army. Because of their constant need for military leaders, the Macedonians, unlike the Greeks to the south, always kept their kings, who were chosen by a warrior assembly comprised of the Macedonian army. Rich silver mines gave the kings a dependable source of income. The Macedonian aristocrats, known as the king's companions, held their land from the king. They made up the Macedonian cavalry, which initially was the only effective part of the Macedonian military.

When the Persians invaded Greece in 480 B.C.E., the Macedonians were unable to resist and became Persian vassals, but they secretly supported the Greeks. They supplied the Athenians with ship timber and ambushed the retreating Persians after the Battle of Plataea. The Macedonians took advantage of the Persian defeat to expand their kingdom. Conquered territory known as spear land was distributed by the king to Macedonian peasants in exchange for their service in an untrained infantry that became known as the king's foot companions.

Macedonia became a major power during the 350s B.C.E. under the leadership of king **Philip II** (r. 359–338 B.C.E.). Philip molded the infantry into an effective fighting force by rigorously drilling it and arming it with sixteen-foot-long spears. The spears of the men in the front ranks were pointed forward, whereas those of the men in the rear were pointed upward to keep them out of the way and to deflect incoming arrow fire. The tightly packed Macedonian phalanx looked like a porcupine. It could go only in one direction—forward—and it cut through anything in its path. With its heavy cavalry protecting its flanks, the Macedonian army became the most formidable fighting force in the ancient world.

The Unification of Greece

During the fourth century B.C.E., the Greeks continued quarreling. Greek intellectuals suggested that the discord could be ended if the Greeks united politically in the same way that they were united culturally. Doing so would allow them to demonstrate their superiority over the Persians, for the one thing that all Greeks could agree on was dislike for the Persians. The philosopher **Aristotle,** for example, suggested that non-Greeks, like the Persians, were only fit to be slaves. Greeks also believed that an attack on the Persian Empire could help solve a recurrence of overpopulation by providing land for settlement. But Greek thinkers were unsure about how this unity could be created. The Athenian orator Isocrates thought that Philip of Macedon, whom he described as "a Greek, but a leader of barbarians," was the kind of person who could unite the Greeks.

Ultimately, Philip was drawn into factional conflicts in Greece. In 338 B.C.E., at **Chaeronea** in central Greece, he defeated a Greek coalition led by Athens. The decisive Macedonian cavalry charge was led by his impetuous eighteen-year-old son, Alexander. For the first time, Greece had been conquered. Declining the impossible task of actually ruling Greece directly, Philip formed the **League of Corinth,** a coalition of Greek cities, with himself at its head, whose ostensible purpose was to attack the Persian Empire. Philip hoped to seize Anatolia from the Persians and place Greece's excess population there. But two years later, before he could pursue his plans, Philip was assassinated by a disgruntled Macedonian.

Young Alexander (r. 338–323 B.C.E.) was proclaimed king, and many wondered whether he, only twenty years old, would be able to manage the kingdom, let alone put his father's plans into effect. Several Greek cities revolted. Alexander responded by attacking the ancient city of Thebes. The historian

Plutarch not only describes what happened but also provides insight into Alexander's personality: "The city was stormed and sacked. Only one house, that of the poet Pindar, was left standing. Alexander hoped that a severe example might terrify the rest of Greece into obedience. Thirty thousand Thebans were sold as slaves and upward of six thousand were put to the sword." When he felt it was necessary, Alexander could be brutal, and his show of force brought the Greek cities back into line. But Alexander also could be merciful, as Plutarch demonstrates in the story of Timoclea, a respectable Theban matron who was raped and robbed by a Thracian mercenary. When she was asked if she had any other valuables, she said they were hidden in a well, and "when the greedy Thracian stooped to look in the well, she pushed him in, and then flung great stones on him, until she had killed him." Alexander was so taken by her bravery that he let her and her children go free.

Alexander's Wars

Alexander proved any remaining doubters wrong. Believing himself the son of Zeus, he planned to conquer not just Anatolia but the whole world, all the way to the great eastern ocean that geographers believed lay on the far side of India. In 334 B.C.E., Alexander led his army into Anatolia. He had only 35,000 men, whereas against him the Persians could raise 250,000. But Alexander took the Persians by surprise, before they had time to assemble their entire army. Anatolia was defended only by an army of Greek mercenaries, who put up a very stiff resistance. At the Battle of the **Granicus River,** as in every battle, Alexander was in the thick of the fighting. According to Plutarch, one of the opposing mercenaries "gave Alexander such a blow with his battle-axe on the

Philip II   (r. 359–338 B.C.E.) King of Macedonia who defeated the Greeks in 338 B.C.E.; father of Alexander the Great.

Aristotle   (384–322 B.C.E.) Greek philosopher who established scientific classification methods and the school known as the Lyceum.

Chaeronea   Battle in which Philip II of Macedon defeated the Greeks in 338 B.C.E.

League of Corinth   Organization of Greek cities led by the king of Macedonia for the purpose of attacking Persia.

Granicus River   Battle in northern Anatolia in which Alexander the Great defeated the Persians' Greek mercenaries in 334 B.C.E.

Mosaic of the first century C.E. from the buried Roman city of Pompeii shows Alexander, at the far left, charging Darius III, standing in his chariot, at the Battle of Gaugamela in 331 B.C.E. This was the crucial moment of the battle, for when Darius fled, his army then followed and Alexander won a great victory. *(Scala/Art Resource, NY)*

helmet that he cut off its crest and the edge of the weapon touched the hair of his head." Only after a desperate fight were the mercenaries defeated.

By 333 B.C.E., the Persian king **Darius III** (r. 338–331) had been able to mobilize only the western half of his empire. Alexander met the Persian army at **Issus** in northern Syria. The sight of the advancing Macedonian phalanx sent Darius fleeing, and his army fled with him. Taken captive were Darius' mother, wife, and daughters, who were fearful of what would befall them at Alexander's hands. Alexander gained much credit for receiving them kindly. Before pursuing Darius, Alexander thought it prudent to occupy Egypt and the eastern Mediterranean coast so as not to leave any enemies in his rear. Most cities surrendered peacefully and were well treated, but the island city of Tyre held out, emboldened by Alexander's lack of a navy. Alexander used eight valuable months building an earth and stone jetty out to the city, which he then stormed and sacked. In Egypt, Alexander was welcomed as the pharaoh and as the son of Ra and the son of Zeus. At this point, Darius offered to turn over to Alexander all of the Persian Empire west of the Euphrates, but Alexander declined, for he had much more ambitious goals.

Alexander advanced into Mesopotamia in 331 B.C.E. By then, Darius had been able to assemble the full Persian army. The armies met on a flat plain at **Gaugamela.** The Macedonians were greatly outnumbered, and the battle began badly for them. Their cavalry was driven off by the Persian cavalry, leaving the flanks and rear of the phalanx open to attack. But at this point, thinking the battle was won, the Persian cavalry rode off to loot the Macedonian camp. Alexander then led a cavalry charge directly at Darius, who once again fled from the battlefield. His army followed, and the Persians had lost their last chance for organized resistance. Alexander now laid claim to the throne of the Persian Empire. Like foreign conquerors of the past, he assumed all the titles of Near Eastern monarchs, becoming the Great King of Persia and the King of Sumer and Akkad. When he occupied the Per-

Darius III   (r. 338–331) Last ruler of the Persian Empire.

Issus   Battle in northwestern Syria in which Alexander the Great defeated Darius III in 333 B.C.E.

Gaugamela   Battle in Mesopotamia in which Alexander the Great defeated the full Persian army in 331 B.C.E.

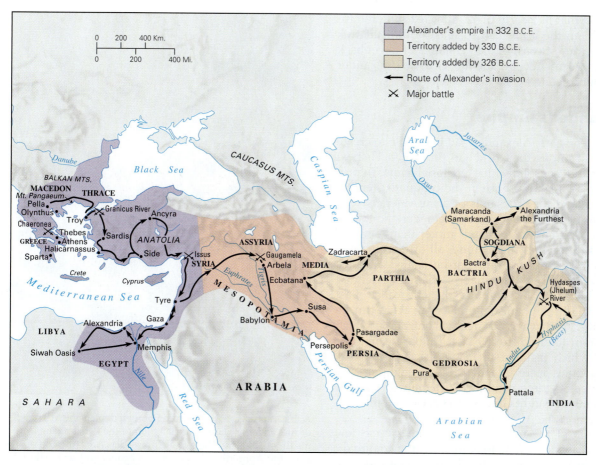

MAP 4.1   **The Empire of Alexander, 323** B.C.E.   Alexander's empire, created in just ten years, extended from Greece in the west into India in the east, and was the largest empire ever created in the western world.

sian capital of Persepolis, he discovered 180,000 talents (over 10,000 tons) of silver hoarded in the Persian treasury, which he used to pay his own mounting expenses. Indeed, Alexander issued so many silver coins that the price of silver plummeted throughout the Mediterranean world. When Persepolis burned soon afterward, some claimed it was in retribution for the Persians' burning of Athens in 480 B.C.E.; but others said it was an accident.

It took Alexander four more years to conquer the rest of the Persian Empire. **Bactria,** modern Afghanistan, proved especially difficult, but Alexander eventually won the allegiance of the natives by his bravery and magnanimity as well as by his marriage to a local princess named Roxanne. In 327 B.C.E., not content with having conquered the Persian Empire, Alexander invaded India. The Indians resisted desperately, village by village. Alexander himself was wounded many times. In one hard-fought battle, the

Macedonians defeated Porus, an Indian king whose army included war elephants. Alexander always emerged victorious, but the Macedonian army had been away from home for eight years, many soldiers had died, and the survivors were tired of fighting. With every hill they crossed, they expected to see the eastern ocean, but all they found were more hostile Indians. Exhausted, the army finally refused to take one step farther east. Alexander sulked in his tent for three days and then agreed to return home, but not the way they had come, for that would look too much like a retreat. The Macedonians, therefore, advanced down the Indus River valley, fighting every step of the way. In one encounter, Alexander was so badly

Bactria   Modern Afghanistan, a center of Greek civilization in the east.

wounded that he nearly died. After reaching the Indian Ocean, the army had to make a difficult trek along the desert coast of the Persian Gulf to get back to Persia. Many never made it back at all. Alexander finally returned to Persia in 324 B.C.E.

Alexander's Empire

In only ten years, Alexander had been able to create the largest empire the world had yet known. He next attempted to consolidate his territorial gains. To provide some Greek presence in the conquered territories, and land for thousands of army veterans who were disabled, ill, or whose services were no longer needed, Alexander founded more than seventy colonies throughout the empire, all of them named **Alexandria** except for one that he named after his horse, Bucephalus. Alexander's colonies extended from Alexandria in Egypt to the one called Last Alexandria in Afghanistan and began what can be called the third wave of Greek colonization, which lasted from about 332 to 250 B.C.E. Unlike the first two waves, which resulted in many seacoast colonies, these colonies were inland. After the fighting was over, Greek settlers continued to emigrate to Asia. The colonies brought Greeks and Greek culture to the far corners of the Asian world.

In spite of the colonies, there were far too few Macedonians to be able to administer the empire directly. Alexander realized that he would need the cooperation of the conquered peoples and therefore adopted the Persian model of showing respect for native customs. He copied the Persian method of administration by dividing his empire up into satrapies, and he integrated native peoples into his government. Furthermore, Alexander developed a vision for unifying the Greek and Persian peoples. He already had recruited 30,000 Bactrians into his army and trained them in Macedonian fighting styles. He also adopted Persian dress and customs and attempted to introduce the Persians to the Macedonians by having 5,000 Macedonians marry 5,000 Persian women. He himself took a second wife, Statira, the daughter of Darius.

Many conservative Macedonians objected to Alexander's adoption of so many Persian customs, and when Alexander suggested he would like his subjects to prostrate themselves before him, in the Persian manner, the Macedonians simply refused. But they could not resist the effects of their exposure to eastern culture. Most chose to remain in the east, and those who did return home brought eastern culture and customs with them. In one way or another, therefore, many Greeks were assimilating the ancient culture of the Near Eastern world.

A first-century C.E. fresco from Pompeii depicts the marriage of Alexander to Statira, the daughter of the Persian king Darius III, in 324 B.C.E. The two are dressed as Ares (the god of war) and Aphrodite (the goddess of beauty and sex), reflecting the idea that powerful monarchs shared some of the divinity and the qualities of the gods. (*Archaeological Museum Naples/ Dagli Orti/The Art Archive*)

In 323 B.C.E., Alexander established his capital at Babylon, on the borderland between the eastern and western halves of his empire. Ambassadors came from far and wide to congratulate him on his victories and to establish good relations. There were representatives not only from the powerful trading city of Carthage in North Africa but also from Rome, a city in central Italy that was just beginning to expand. Meanwhile, Alexander's plans to conquer the world continued. He intended first to attack the Arabs of Arabia and then to expand west into the Mediterranean, all the way to the Strait of Gibraltar. But Alexander's Babylonian astrologers had received bad omens and were concerned

Alexandria Name given to Greek colonies established by Alexander the Great, the most famous of which was in Egypt.

Voice VoiceVoiceVoice
Voice VoiceVoice

Plutarch and Arrian Describe Alexander's Mass Marriages

One of Alexander's goals was to integrate the Macedonian and Persian populations. Given past incompatibilities between Greeks and Persians, this would not have been an easy task. He decided that intermarriage would be a good way for the two peoples to get to know each other. He himself married two eastern women, and in 324 B.C.E. he supported the marriages of 5,000 Greek men to 5,000 Persian women. The following accounts are from two Greek historians who wrote in the second century C.E., during the Roman Empire. Plutarch, in his Life of Alexander, *describes the events associated with Alexander's marriage to Roxanne in 327 B.C.E. Arrian of Nicomedia, in* Campaigns of Alexander, *reports Alexander's marriage to the daughter of the Persian king Darius III in early 324 B.C.E., after he had returned from India.*

Plutarch

➡ Now, also, he more and more accommodated himself in his way of living to that of the natives, wisely considering that it would be wiser to depend on the good-will which might arise from intermixture and association as a means of maintaining tranquility, than on force and compulsion. As for his marriage with Roxanne, whose youthfulness and beauty had charmed him at a drinking entertainment, where he first happened to see her taking part in a dance, it was, indeed a love affair, yet it seemed at the same time to be conducive to the object he had in hand. ➡ For it gratified the conquered people to see him choose a wife from among themselves, and it made them feel the most lively affection for him, to find that in the only passion that he was overcome he yet restrained himself until he could obtain her in a lawful and honorable way.

Arrian of Nicomedia

➡ Then Alexander also celebrated weddings in Persia, both his own and those of his Companions. He himself married Statira, the eldest of Darius' daughters. He had already married previously Roxanne, the daughter of Oxyartes of Bactria. He gave Drypetis to Hephaestion, she too a daughter of Darius—his intention was that the children of Hephaestion should be cousins to his own children. . . . To Ptolemy the bodyguard and to Eumenes the royal secretary he gave the daughters of Artabazus, Artacama to one and Artonis to the other. To Nearchus he gave the daughter of Barsine and Mentor, and to Seleucus he gave Apame, the daughter of Spitamenes of Bactria.

➡ Similarly he gave to the other Companions the noblest daughters of the Persians and Medes, some 80 in all. The marriages were celebrated according to Persian custom. Chairs were placed for the bridegrooms, and the brides came in and sat down, each by the side of her groom. They took them by the hand and kissed them. ➡ The king began the ceremony, for all the weddings took place together. More than any action of Alexander this seemed to show a popular and comradely spirit. After receiving their brides, the bridegrooms led them away, and to all Alexander gave a dowry. And as for all the Macedonians who had already married Asian women, Alexander ordered a list of their names to be drawn up; they numbered over 10,000, and Alexander offered them gifts for the wedding.

Source: Reprinted by permission of the publishers and the Trustees of the Loeb Classical Library from *Arrian: Volume II,* Loeb Classical Library® Volume 269, translated by P. A Brunt on the basis of E. Iliff Robson's edition, Cambridge, Mass.: Harvard University Press, Copyright © 1929, 1976 by the President and Fellows of Harvard College. The Loeb Classical Library® is a registered trademark of the President and Fellows of Harvard College.

➡ Was this a sensible strategy?

➡ How did Alexander display his respect for native customs?

➡ Why are these particular women being married to Alexander's most important generals?

➡ Why did Alexander follow Persian rather than Greek custom?

➡ Do you think that performing these marriages would have been an effective way of uniting the Macedonian and Persian peoples?

for his safety. They even seated a commoner on Alexander's throne to absorb the bad luck they saw coming for him. In spite of this precaution, after a typical Macedonian drinking party, Alexander became very ill and died a few days later. Suggested causes of his death have ranged from the cumulative effects of past war wounds to malaria to poison. Almost immediately, Alexander passed into legend, remembered as Alexander the Great. Many believed that he became a god. Exotic tales of his adventures known as the **Alexander Romance** were widely circulated and still popular more than a thousand years later.

The Hellenistic World, 323–30 B.C.E.

> ↓ What happened to Alexander's empire after his death?
> ↓ How did Greek views of the non-Greek world change during the Hellenistic period?

After the death of Alexander, his empire was divided among the families of three of his generals, the Antigonids, the Ptolemies, and the Seleucids. The expansion of the Greek world into Africa and Asia brought Greeks into contact with many non-Greek cultures, and there was a growing popular interest in foreign places. Greek explorers and merchants wrote accounts of the peoples they encountered. The resulting awareness and appreciation of other cultures gave rise to an amalgamation of cultures known as Hellenistic civilization.

The Hellenistic Kingdoms

Alexander did not name an heir. As he was dying, he was asked who should inherit his kingdom. Some thought that he answered, "The strongest man." Alexander's only legitimate son, Alexander IV, was not born to Roxanne until after his death. The infant was hardly able to rule, and Alexander's generals began to carve out pieces of the empire for themselves. By 280 B.C.E., after years of civil war, the empire had been divided into three main kingdoms ruled by the families of three of Alexander's generals. The period between the death of Alexander and the end of the last of these kingdoms, from 323 until 30 B.C.E., is known as the **Hellenistic Age.**

The Macedonian homeland fell to the **Antigonids,** the descendants of Alexander's general Antigonus. But Macedonia was no longer a world power. The constant departure of soldiers had left the land depopulated, and the wars also had drained the economy. The best that the Antigonid kings could hope for was to remain the strongest power in Greece, and they did this by establishing strategic fortresses that kept the Greeks under control. Another Antigonid concern was the growing power of Rome, just across the Adriatic Sea.

Alexander's general Ptolemy seized control of Egypt, the wealthiest and most geographically secure satrapy of Alexander's empire. His family, the **Ptolemies,** was confronted by the need to rule over two populations, one Greek and one Egyptian. To their Greek subjects, the Ptolemaic kings were Macedonian kings and successors to Alexander. But to the Egyptians, they were a new dynasty of pharaohs. Like pharaohs of the past, Ptolemaic kings married their sisters and were worshiped as if they were gods. Ptolemy II, for example, took an Egyptian name meaning "Loved by Amon, Chosen by Ra." He married his sister Arsinoë and was known after his death as Ptolemy the Sister-Lover. Ptolemaic queens with names like Berenice, Arsinoë, and **Cleopatra** often were virtual rulers of the kingdom. According to one source, Arsinoë accompanied her troops and rallied them when a battle was going badly: "She went to the soldiers with wailing and tears, and exhorted them to defend themselves and their children and wives bravely, promising to give them each two minas [about two pounds] of gold if they won the battle. And so it came about that the enemy was routed, and many captives were taken."

The Ptolemaic administration of Egypt was very centralized. The top officials were Greeks, but lower-level bureaucrats, such as scribes, often were Egyptians. The economy was closely supervised by an extensive bureaucracy to ensure maximum income for the government. The kings sponsored irrigation, drainage, and land reclamation projects. To attract Greek settlers, the Ptolemies offered them land grants on the condition that they also provide military service. These Greek farmers were scattered throughout Egypt and, as a result, there was growing integration between the Greek and Egyptian populations.

Alexander Romance Legends about Alexander the Great circulated after his death.

Hellenistic Age (based on Greek for "Greek-like") Period from 323 until 30 B.C.E. that resulted in a mixing of Greek and eastern culture.

Antigonids Family that ruled Macedonia after the death of Alexander the Great.

Ptolemies Family that ruled Egypt after the death of Alexander the Great.

Cleopatra (69–30 B.C.E.) Queen and pharaoh of Egypt, last of the Ptolemies; committed suicide in 30 B.C.E.

A relief from Tanis in Egypt shows king Ptolemy II with his wife-sister Arsinoe II dressed as Egyptian pharaohs, thus illustrating the efforts of the Macedonian rulers of Egypt to demonstrate their respect for Egyptian customs. For their Greek subjects, they would have been kings and queens in the Greek tradition. *(Visual Connection Archive)*

The Asian parts of Alexander's empire fell into the hands of the **Seleucids,** the family of Alexander's general Seleucus. The Seleucid kingdom was the least unified and the most difficult to hold together, for it extended from Anatolia all the way to India. It contained a huge non-Greek population, and Seleucid kings found it hard to attract additional Greek settlers. More than any of Alexander's successors, the Seleucids knew they had to conciliate their subjects. Thus, after Alexander died, Seleucus was one of the few Macedonians who did not divorce his Persian wife. Understanding that he could not hope to hold India, Seleucus traded his Indian territories to an Indian king in exchange for five hundred war elephants. Other Seleucid territories were controlled by making alliances with powerful local leaders. For example, in Mesopotamia, the Seleucids allied themselves with priests who were afraid of a renewed Persian takeover. Elsewhere, native rulers were allowed local rule as long as they provided tribute and military aid. The Seleucid army was composed not of Greeks, as in Macedonia and Egypt, but mostly of contingents recruited from the subject peoples, as the Persians had done. In spite of Seleucid efforts, parts of their kingdom slipped away. Beginning about 250 B.C.E., for example, an Indo-European people known as the **Parthians** occupied Iran and split the Seleucid kingdom in half, leaving the Bactrian Greek colonies in complete isolation.

During the Hellenistic period, concepts of rule changed. Greek city-states, including Greek colonies, continued to be administered by oligarchies and democracies as in the past, but nearly all were incorporated into, or under the influence of, a Hellenistic kingdom ruled by an absolute monarch. As a consequence of their great authority, Hellenistic kings and queens, like Alexander before them, were believed to have godlike qualities, a concept previously foreign to the Greeks but consistent with Near Eastern thought. Kings and queens were often granted divine honors not only after their deaths but even while they were living. One Seleucid king, for example, took the title God Made Manifest.

Hellenistic economic life also functioned on a grand scale. The great infusion of Persian gold and silver into the Mediterranean world brought with it not only **inflation,** caused by the pouring of millions of silver coins into the economy, but also an increased prosperity, caused by the greater availability of money to more people. Many Greeks, not just rulers, became wealthy. Goods were manufactured and foodstuffs grown not just for local consumption but also for export, creating a **market economy.** Huge estates in Anatolia and Sicily, worked by hundreds or thousands of slaves, produced grain for cities throughout the Hellenistic world.

Eventually, all the Hellenistic kingdoms fell to Rome. The last was Ptolemaic Egypt. In 30 B.C.E., the Macedonian queen and pharaoh Cleopatra admitted defeat and committed suicide, ending not only the Hellenistic Age but also a line of pharaohs that stretched back three thousand years.

Seleucids   Family that ruled Asia after the death of Alexander the Great.

Parthians   Indo-European people that invaded Iran beginning in 250 B.C.E.

inflation   Process by which the cost of goods and services increases and the value of money declines.

market economy   Economy in which goods and services are exchanged between buyers and sellers.

Hellenistic Cities

Hellenistic civilization, like the civilization of the Archaic and Classical Ages, was built around cities that served as commercial centers. But Hellenistic cities outside Greece proper were different in that almost all were ruled by kings and no longer were centers of independent political life. They also were the places where Greeks settled, preserved their learning and culture, and retained their identity. Hellenistic monarchs were also great supporters of scholarly studies, and some major Hellenistic cities became famous centers of learning.

The Seleucids, for example, realized that their Greek population was far too small to disperse throughout the countryside, so they continued Alexander's policy of establishing colonies that could be centers of Seleucid rule. Greek colonies could be found across the length and breadth of the vast Seleucid territories. The most important Seleucid city was the great city of Antioch in Syria, named after the Seleucid king Antiochus I. It became the core of the Seleucid kingdom, with a reputation as a center for literature and the arts. By the first century B.C.E., it had a population of five hundred thousand.

The Hellenistic colonies left a curious legacy in the easternmost part of the Seleucid kingdom. After 250 B.C.E., the Greek cities of Bactria were cut off from the rest of the Greek world by the Parthians and forgotten by the western Greeks. Against all the odds, however, they maintained their Greek way of life as best as they could, although they also enlisted native help and incorporated native customs much more extensively than any other Greeks. For example, their coins carried lettering in both the Greek and Indian languages. And when the Bactrian king Menander invaded India, not only was he supported by the local Buddhists but, according to legend, he even became a Buddhist himself. He was later considered one of the four great Buddhist rulers of India. The last Greek rulers in India finally succumbed to invaders from central Asia about 50 B.C.E. The Greek kings of Bactria and India are known primarily through their coins and the archaeological remains of their cities.

In Egypt, the greater number of Greek settlers allowed the Ptolemies to continue the ancient Egyptian custom of having farmers live in villages rather than in cities. The exception was the capital city of the Ptolemaic kingdom, Alexandria, founded by Alexander in 332 B.C.E. on the Mediterranean coast at the mouth of the Nile and the only Macedonian colony in Egypt. The harbor entrance to the city was marked by a gigantic 384-foot-tall lighthouse that became one of the Seven Wonders of the Ancient World. Its mirror used sunlight or light from a fire to cast a beam of light that could be seen for more than thirty-five miles. Within a hundred years, Alexandria was the largest city in the world, with well over half a million inhabitants, including many Jews of the Diaspora. It became the cultural capital of the Greek world. There the Ptolemies founded the **Museum,** a university named after the Muses, the goddesses of learning, where a community of scholars pursued literary and scientific studies. Associated with the Museum was the great library of Alexandria, where books were deposited from throughout a Greek world that now extended from Spain to India.

Smaller powers also established important Hellenistic cities. The small kingdom of **Pergamum** in western Anatolia broke away from the Seleucids and was centered on a city of the same name. The kings of Pergamum saw themselves as the inheritors of the cultural traditions of Athens and built a massive acropolis modeled on the Athenian one. The huge marble Altar of Pergamum depicted in sculpture the origin of the gods and later appeared in the Christian book of Revelation, where it was described as "Satan's Throne." Pergamum also became a center of learning, with a library second only to the one in Alexandria and a famous school of medicine. One of the goods exported from Pergamum was *pergamene*, modern **parchment,** a writing material developed from stretched sheepskins at a time when there was a shortage of papyrus from Egypt.

South of Pergamum, the city of **Rhodes** controlled an island of the same name located off the southwestern coast of Anatolia. As the primary stopping point for commercial traffic traveling along the Anatolian coast, Rhodes became rich on harbor tolls. Its coins, which depicted a rose (*Rhodos* means "rose" in Greek), circulated throughout the Mediterranean world. In the early third century B.C.E., to commemorate a military victory, the city constructed a 110-foot-tall statue of the sun god known as the Colossus of Rhodes, another of the Seven Wonders of the Ancient World. To ensure the safety of the cargoes that passed through

Museum (from Greek for "home of the Muses") University established in Alexandria by the Ptolemies.

Pergamum Small Hellenistic city-kingdom in western Anatolia.

parchment (based on Greek *pergamene*, "from Pergamum") Writing material made from cured and stretched animal skins.

Rhodes (from Greek *rhodos*, "rose") Island city-state located off the southwestern coast of Anatolia.

The Bactrian city of Alexandria on the Oxus, modern Ai-Khanum, in mountainous Afghanistan, was on the very fringes of the Greek world. It included temples, colonnaded walks, a theater, gymnasium, and the other amenities of a Greek polis to make Greek colonists feel at home. The site recently was destroyed by the Taliban. *(Courtesy of Paul Bernard)*

the city and to suppress pirates, Rhodes maintained a powerful navy. Like other Hellenistic cities, Rhodes became a center of learning, providing instruction in philosophy, rhetoric, literature, and science.

Voyages of Exploration

Greek expansion during the Hellenistic period brought the Greeks into direct contact with a multitude of foreign cultures, stimulating a great interest in geographical exploration. A popular genre of travel literature known as the *periplus* described the strange places and peoples that travelers encountered in the course of their journeys. These literary works were often of a practical nature, having been commissioned by rulers interested in the nature of the territories to which they had laid claim or authored by merchants seeking the best places to trade and the safest routes for getting there. In contrast to earlier geographical accounts, which had been based on myth and legend, these were based on firsthand observations. Much of the impetus for these works came from the campaigns of Alexander the Great, especially his travels in India.

In 325 B.C.E., Alexander's admiral, **Nearchus**, was ordered to survey the coast between India and Persia. He did so in great detail, and after his return, around 310 B.C.E., he wrote a book about India. He told of trees so large that one of them could shade ten thousand people and he discussed the habits of elephants,

which Mediterranean peoples found fascinating: "If there is an intelligent animal, it is the elephant. I myself saw an elephant clanging the cymbals while other elephants danced; two cymbals were fastened to the player's forelegs and one on his trunk. As he rhythmically beat the cymbal on either leg in turn the dancers danced in a circle, raising and bending their forelegs." During the voyage in the Indian Ocean, Nearchus traveled so far south, he reported, that at noon the sun cast no shadow at all and at night some of the familiar stars could not be seen. According to another writer, Nearchus once encountered a pod of spouting whales, and when the rowers of the warships became distressed at the sight of these huge beasts, "Nearchus went and encouraged and cheered them. He signaled them to turn the ships' bows toward the whales as if to give battle and to raise their battle cry and make a great deal of noise. When they neared the monsters, they shouted with all the power of their throats, and the bugles blared, and the rowers made the greatest splashings with their oars. So the whales were frightened and dove into the depths, and much praise was showered on Nearchus for his courage."

periplus (Greek for "sailing around") Hellenistic genre of travel literature.

Nearchus Admiral of Alexander the Great who in the fourth century B.C.E. wrote a book about India.

A report of a voyage along the coast of the Red Sea (which extended all the way to India in this version) was written in the first century B.C.E. by an anonymous merchant who catalogued market towns and the kinds of goods that could be traded. He reported that, after leaving Egypt, a traveler encountered along the east coast of Africa the fish-eaters, the Berbers (a variation on the word *barbarians*), the flesh-eaters, and the calf-eaters. Farther along were trading cities with good harbors: "There are exported from these places ivory, and tortoise-shell and rhinoceros-horn, but practically the whole number of elephants and rhinoceros that are killed live in the places inland, although at rare intervals they are hunted on the seacoast." The merchant traveled no farther, however, than the Horn of Africa (modern Somalia), writing, "Beyond these places the unexplored ocean curves around toward the west, and running to the south of Africa it mingles with the western sea." A voyage down the coast of Arabia, on the other side of the Red Sea, was rather more dangerous. According to the merchant, "The country inland is peopled by rascally men who plunder those who approach the coast and enslave those who survive shipwrecks. Navigation is dangerous along this whole coast of Arabia, which is without harbors, with bad anchorages, foul, inaccessible because of breakers and rocks, and terrible in every way." But beyond this lay the "frankincense country." The business of producing frankincense, one of the most sought-after spices of antiquity, was controlled by the local king: "The frankincense is gathered by the king's slaves and those who are sent to this service for punishment. These places are very unhealthy, and almost always fatal to those working there." From there, the merchant sailed past Arabia toward India, reaching the Indus River. In India, the merchant obtained turquoise, lapis lazuli, silk, and indigo in exchange for frankincense, gold, and silver. Finally, this account makes the first known western mention of China, which the author called Thinae: "Silk, silk yarn, and silk cloth are brought on foot through Bactria, and are also exported by way of the river Ganges. But this land is not easy of access; few men come from there, and seldom."

Other merchants traveled west, out of the Mediterranean and into the Atlantic. One voyage story told of a fifth-century B.C.E. expedition by the Carthaginian sailor **Hanno** down the west coast of Africa, as far as the equator or beyond. Sailing up one river, Hanno encountered crocodiles and what he called hippopotamuses, a word meaning "water horses." At a later landing point, he wrote, "We could see nothing but forest by day, but at night many fires were seen and we heard the sound of flutes and the beating of drums and tambourines, which made a great noise.

We were struck with terror and our fortune-tellers advised us leave the island." Farther along, he reported encountering an "island full of savages. They had hairy bodies and the interpreters called them gorillas." If this account is true, Hanno must have gone as far as the Congo River. According to one account, Hanno eventually turned back because of a lack of supplies, but another version has him sailing around Africa and eventually arriving in Arabia.

Finally, a Greek sailor from Marseilles named **Pytheas** described a voyage he made up the Atlantic coast of Europe around 300 B.C.E. looking for a sea route to sources of tin and amber. He traveled to Britain, which he called Albion, and then continued even farther north to a place called Thule, six days' sail north of Britain, which has been identified as the Shetland Islands or even Iceland, places previously unknown to the Greeks. Pytheas noted that on June 21, the sun never set, suggesting that he even reached the Arctic Circle. He described sailing conditions in which there was no distinction between the earth, air, and sea, perhaps a reference to a very thick fog. He also was the first Greek to report on the tides and to connect them with the motion of the moon.

Hellenistic Culture and Science

> ↓ In what ways did Hellenistic scientists use methods different from those of earlier philosophers?
> ↓ What was the nature of Hellenistic scientific discoveries?

The incorporation of the Persian and even the Indian worlds into the Greek experience brought a new form of Greek culture called Hellenistic culture, through which the Greeks lost the Greek-centered view of the world of the Classical Age and learned to value other peoples and cultures. The old distinction between Hellenes and barbarians became less clear as populations and cultures from Greece to the Indus River valley became mixed. As during the Archaic Age, eastern influences in art, government, and thought flowed into Greece. Greek culture became a hybrid, an amalgamation of western and eastern culture that gave western and eastern people new common ground.

Hanno   Fifth-century B.C.E. Carthaginian explorer who wrote of a voyage down the west coast of Africa.

Pytheas   Greek sailor from Marseilles who wrote about his voyage to Britain around 300 B.C.E.

Art and Literature

Whereas classical Greek culture was marked by general agreement among the Greeks about what constituted excellence, Hellenistic culture was characterized by variety and **syncretism,** a melding of elements of different cultures. The cultural assimilation that came with the Hellenistic Age was affirmed by the Roman historian **Livy,** who commented, "The Macedonians, who have colonies in Egypt and Babylon and elsewhere in the world, have become Syrians, Parthians, and Egyptians." In the world of art, the simplicity and clean lines of classical art were overwhelmed by ornate Hellenistic extravagance. In architecture, for example, by the mid-fourth century B.C.E. the floral Corinthian column capital replaced the simple Doric and Ionic capitals as the preferred style for columns. In the eastern Greek colonies, eastern and western artistic traditions merged. Religious syncretism occurred in Egypt, where, to provide common ground between Greeks and Egyptians, the Ptolemies created a composite god, **Serapis,** who had attributes of the Greek Zeus and the Egyptian Osiris.

Hellenistic literature, on the other hand, could not rival the literature of the Archaic and Classical Ages. Form became more important than content, quantity more important than quality, and writers were more concerned with appealing to a larger audience. Comedies no longer dealt with current events but were concerned with everyday domestic life and were full of slapstick. Tales of the absurd multiplied, such as an account of a country where it was so cold that words spoken in the winter immediately froze and were not heard until they thawed out in the spring. Stories that combined love and adventure resulted in an early form of the novel. The primary literary contribution of the Hellenistic Age, however, was the genre of biography. This was an age of great personalities, and accounts of the lives of great men and women were very popular..

In academic circles, creative literature gave way to scholarship. Many authors became more interested in collecting and cataloguing the learning of the past than in dealing with grand, timeless issues of meaning and morality. Hellenistic scholars collected and edited the literature of Greek antiquity, such as the *Iliad* and *Odyssey,* creating editions that, by and large, are still in use. Likewise, the grammars and dictionaries created in Hellenistic times became the models for all later ones. In general, Hellenistic literature is best known for its attention to practical applications. Geographical treatises, scientific thought, school handbooks, and philosophical systems all would have great influence on western civilization. At the same time, a

A head of the god Serapis, who was a combination of the Egyptian Osiris and Greek Zeus, demonstrates the attempts of the Ptolemies to create a meeting ground between Greek and Egyptian culture. The hairstyle and beard are reflective of Zeus, but the kindly facial expression reminds one of Osiris. It was found in the harbor of Alexandria during recent underwater excavations. *(Sandro Vannini/Corbis)*

form of Greek known as *koinē* Greek became the standard language of both commerce and intellectual discourse throughout the Mediterranean and Near Eastern worlds. These regions became culturally

syncretism (from Greek for "bringing together") The mixing of elements of different cultures or religions.

Livy (59 B.C.E.–7 C.E.) Roman historian who wrote the history of Rome.

Serapis Composite Egyptian god with aspects of the Greek god Zeus and the Egyptian god Osiris.

koinē (Greek for "common") Common version of Greek in the Hellenistic Age.

united in a way they had never been before and never would be again.

Aristotle and the Rise of Practical Philosophy

During the Hellenistic period, Greek scientific thought turned from theory based on speculation and convincing argument to theory based on observation and experimentation. The first practical scientific thinker was Aristotle, a native of northern Greece whose father had been the personal physician and friend of King Philip II of Macedonia. After studying medicine with his father, the young Aristotle pursued his studies at Plato's Academy in Athens. He taught for a while at the Academy and then moved to Ionia, where he turned his attention to biology and began his practice of collecting observations. He then returned to Macedonia, where he is said to have tutored Alexander the Great. Eventually, in 335 B.C.E., Aristotle returned to Athens and founded his own school, called the Lyceum.

As Plato's most influential pupil, Aristotle reacted against the view that scientific problems could be solved simply by contemplation. Aristotle's method of understanding the universe and human behavior was to collect evidence, analyze it, and then come to conclusions based on observation. Rather than focusing purely on theory, as did the Academy, the Lyceum undertook broad scientific study of the real world of nature. Whereas Plato's Academy looked for a unified system that would explain everything in the world, Aristotle's interests were much more eclectic. He and his pupils believed in categorizing and subdividing all the fields of study and looking at each one individually. His work on animals and plants, for example, resulted in the categorization of different kinds of species. Aristotle published books on biology and zoology, astronomy, chemistry, poetry, rhetoric, mathematics, logic (a field he virtually invented), ethics, politics, sociology, and economics. His book *The Politics* formulated his own idea of an ideal society that was not theoretical, like Plato's, but fixed firmly in the real world and based on a collection of the constitutions of many different governments, including even those of barbarians like the Carthaginians. Aristotle believed that people could govern themselves, but only if they were virtuous.

Plato had denied the importance of change by arguing that the transitory things of this world are just imperfect reflections of the world of perfect unchanging forms. In contrast, Aristotle thought that the world was defined by the manner in which things do change. Every change, he believed, occurs for a reason, by means of some material cause and for some purpose. There was little room for gods in Aristotle's universe. He acknowledged that some kind of divinity had originally set the universe in motion, but it then became self-perpetuating. He created a method for understanding the world based on observation, logic, and common sense that could also be replicated—that is, proved by someone else—thus making Aristotle's model very different from the methods of earlier philosophers. Aristotle laid down many of the rules for what later would be known as the scientific method, in which evidence is collected, studied, classified, and analyzed, with conclusions based on the evidence, not on who can make the best argument. His approach was adopted by other Hellenistic scientists, whose experiments, observations, and conclusions in fields such as mathematics, medicine, physics, and astronomy were not superseded until the seventeenth century or later.

Hellenistic Science

Alexander the Great himself was a believer in scientific investigation, and his armies included a staff of scientists who observed and recorded discoveries in fields ranging from geography to botany. The works of his botanist Theophrastus, for example, served as the foundation for modern botany. Alexandria was especially famous as a center of science and mathematics, and the most influential of the Alexandrian scientists was the mathematician Euclid, who wrote a textbook on plane geometry around 300 B.C.E. that is said to be, after the Bible, the most influential book ever published. Euclid's textbook presented five axioms that were obviously true, such as that only one line parallel to another line can be drawn through a given point, and then combined them to prove more complex propositions, called theorems, which then could be used to prove other theorems. Modern

Lyceum School of philosophy established in Athens by Aristotle.

Theophrastus Third-century B.C.E. Greek philosopher and naturalist.

Euclid Hellenistic mathematician who around 300 B.C.E. wrote a textbook on geometry.

axioms and **theorems** In geometry, axioms, statements that are assumed to be true without needing to be proved, are used to prove theorems, hypotheses that must be proved by using axioms and previously proved theorems.

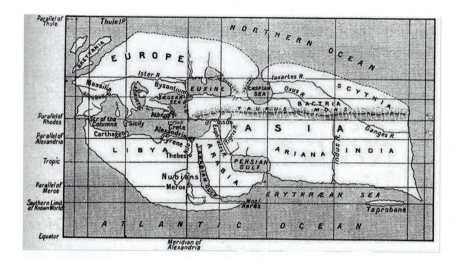

A reconstruction of Eratosthenes' map of the world from the third century B.C.E. In Eratosthenes' model, the world had three continents, Europe, Asia, and Libya (Africa), and was surrounded by a single large ocean. *(Visual Connection Archive)*

geometry textbooks do little more than reproduce Euclid's theorems.

Alexandria also was home to many famous astronomers. One topic of investigation was the place of the earth in the universe. Aristotle and other Greek scientists had assumed that the sun, moon, and planets revolved around the earth. Contrary to this view, **Aristarchus,** around 250 B.C.E., proposed a heliocentric universe, with the sun at the center and the earth rotating on its own axis. Shortly thereafter, Eratosthenes devised a method for computing prime numbers—numbers that cannot be divided by any other number—and estimated the circumference of the earth by comparing the difference in length between shadows cast at noon at two different places in Egypt. His figure of 24,887 miles was almost exactly correct (the actual circumference is 24,902 miles). Eratosthenes also made a map of the world and predicted that there were other continents in the Southern Hemisphere and that one could reach India by sailing west from Spain.

The most notable Hellenistic astronomer was **Hipparchus,** who around 140 B.C.E. established the field of observational astronomy by creating the first western star catalogue. He measured the exact positions of some five hundred stars with an astrolabe, a device using a long thin tube to pinpoint a star's location. To create his catalogue, Hipparchus had to devise a standard reference system, using lines of latitude and longitude that could be used to define positions both on the earth and in the sky. Hipparchus rejected Aristarchus's heliocentric model because it could not be proven observationally and returned to the traditional geocentric system, with the earth in the center of the universe. To explain the occasional looping motion of the planets against the stars, Hipparchus proposed a system whereby the planets moved not in perfect circles but in a complex pattern of circles within circles.

Hellenistic scientists also made advances in medical science, which had begun at the very end of the Classical Age with the work of **Hippocrates.** Known as the father of medicine, Hippocrates was the first Greek physician to reject the idea that illness was caused by the gods. He believed that sickness was caused by diet and environment and that an important point in an illness was the crisis, after which the patient would either recover or die. Because he believed that the body was largely capable of healing itself, through rest, he was reluctant to administer medicines. Hippocrates also taught the importance of observing symptoms so that similar illnesses could receive similar treatments. He established a school of medicine that included many later Greek doctors, and the medical ethics he developed are preserved in the modern Hippocratic Oath. During the Hellenistic period, medical science was expanded by an Alexandrian school of medicine that studied human anatomy and physiology by dissecting the bodies of condemned criminals. By this means, Alexandrian physicians discovered the function of nerves and the flow of blood through vessels.

Aristarchus Alexandrian astronomer who about 250 B.C.E. proposed a heliocentric (from Greek for "sun-centered") universe.

Hipparchus Alexandrian astronomer who believed in a geocentric (from Greek for "earth-centered") universe and about 140 B.C.E. created the first western star catalogue.

Hippocrates Greek physician of the early fourth century B.C.E who established Greek medicine and whose ethical model provides the oath taken by modern physicians.

Hellenistic Technology

During antiquity, technology generally evolved slowly, and antiquity is not generally thought of as a great age of invention. The Hellenistic Age, however, stimulated by the intellectual interaction of eastern and western thought, was a period of great technological advancement. Machines were invented both for practical purposes and as curiosities; some prefigured modern technological developments. The first great Hellenistic inventor, **Ctesibius of Alexandria,** was the son of a barber. His first invention was a counterweighted mirror that could be adjusted to the height of a customer's head. His realization that air was a substance that could be manipulated led to the invention of a number of devices based on the use of water pressure and compressed air. He created a water clock in which a system of valves turned the supply of water on and off, a high-pressure pump used to shoot streams of water at fires, and an organ that used water pressure to create airflow through sets of pipes—the first keyboard instrument.

Hero of Alexandria, nicknamed "the machine man," likewise devised machines based on air and water pressure. He invented the first steam engine, which transformed steam into circular motion by means of jets placed on the sides of a hollow sphere. The same principle is used in the modern jet engine. Instead of being put to practical use, Hero's engine was used only as a toy, to make puppets dance. Other curiosities invented by Hero included automatic door openers for temples. More practical were his hydraulic devices to force the oil out of olives. He also invented an odometer, a system of gears connected to a wheel that could be used to measure distances. During the Roman Empire, Hero's odometer was used to place the mile markers on the famous Roman road system.

The most famous Hellenistic inventor was **Archimedes,** a native of Syracuse in Sicily, who had been a pupil of Aristarchus at Alexandria. Around 225 B.C.E., Archimedes invented the field of mathematical physics. According to one story, Archimedes was once sitting in a bath when he observed that his body had displaced its own volume of water. On this basis, he was able to calculate specific gravity of any object, the ratio of the object's weight to the weight of the same volume of water. He also invented the Archimedes screw, a device for boosting water out of rivers and canals for irrigation.

Hellenistic inventions also could be used for warfare, as happened in 212 B.C.E., when Syracuse was attacked by the Romans. According to Plutarch, Archimedes used his engineering knowledge to attack the Roman navy: "huge poles thrust out from the

The octagonal Tower of the Four Winds in Athens was designed by the Hellenistic scientist Andronicus of Cyrrhus around 150 B.C.E. to be used on the outside as a sundial and weathervane and on the inside as a waterclock. The name comes from the depictions of the eight winds carved on the eight sides: Boreas, for example, represented the north wind. *(Ancient Art & Architecture Collection)*

walls over the ships sunk some by the great weights that they dropped down upon them; others they lifted up into the air by an iron hook and whirled about until the sailors were all thrown out, when at length they were dashed against the rocks below."

Ctesibius of Alexandria   Alexandrian Greek inventor of the water clock, after 250 B.C.E.

Hero of Alexandria   Inventor of an ancient steam engine.

Archimedes   Greek scientist from Syracuse who about 225 B.C.E. invented mathematical physics and developed the concept of specific gravity.

Archimedes also was said to have built a gigantic lens that set Roman ships afire by focusing sunlight on them. When the Romans finally took the city, Archimedes was in the midst of diagramming a problem in the sand. Plutarch reports, "He never noticed that the city was taken. A soldier, unexpectedly coming up to him, commanded him to follow him, which he declined to do before he had completed working out his problem. The soldier, enraged, drew his sword and ran him through."

Other machines were equally complex. The ability to predict the motions of the sun, moon, and planets had practical significance for astrologers, for it permitted them to cast **horoscopes** for any date in the past, present, or future. Elaborate geared mechanical devices were constructed that allowed the user to portray the position of the heavenly bodies at any time. One such device, the first known mechanical computing machine, was discovered by a Greek sponge diver in 1900 off the coast of Crete near the island of Anticythera, hence the name "the Anticythera device." Built around 80 B.C.E., it is the most complicated machine to be preserved from antiquity. The surviving section alone (part of it is missing) contains thirty-two gears. The device is based on the theories of Hipparchus and can predict the position of the sun, moon, and planets in the zodiac, along with the phases of the moon, with an accuracy of one part in 86,000.

Identity in a Cosmopolitan Society

> ⬇ How did religion give people a sense of identity?
> ⬇ How and why did the Jews resist Hellenistic culture?

For many Greeks, the Hellenistic period created a crisis of identity. The city-states that had been major participants in world politics had been superseded by Hellenistic kingdoms and no longer provided the same focal points for loyalty and personal identity. The importance of Greece itself had declined to the point that even being a Greek no longer created the same sense of self-satisfaction as before. Both Greeks and non-Greeks felt adrift in the new Hellenistic multicultural world. To hold on to their old identity or find a new sense of identity, many people turned to philosophy and religion.

An Age of Anxiety

During the Hellenistic period, there was no opportunity for a Greek polis to play an important role in world politics. This was a time of kings and kingdoms in which cities were shuffled around from one kingdom to another. As cities lost their political independence, Greeks lost part of their personal identity. Being a subject of a king simply could not replace the sense of belonging that came from being a citizen of an independent polis. The feeling now arose that one was a citizen of the **cosmopolis,** or world-city. People encountered the wider world every day—in the street, in literature, and in the schoolroom. In the marketplace, they heard not only Greek but also Persian, Aramaic, and Egyptian. Because they were constantly exposed to foreign cultures, the Greeks could no longer be supremely confident that their culture was the best in the world, and they felt that their sense of cultural identity was threatened. In fact, foreign cultures had many attractions for the Greeks, and they no longer felt that all foreign things were barbarian. Greek culture now was Hellenistic culture, which meant the assimilation of the cultures of many foreign peoples.

These changes made the Greeks uncomfortable. They were used to being in control, to being able to understand and feel integrated in their world. Now they felt lost. Life seemed unpredictably governed by **Tyche,** a goddess who represented blind chance, who could bring either good fortune or complete ruin. To try to regain a sense of control, many Greeks turned to personal religion. Some sought supernatural guidance, adopting some of the very same Near Eastern ideas that had made them uncomfortable in the first place. Babylonian astrology, which taught that the future had been ordained by the gods and could be read in the motions of the stars and planets, gained a great following. The famous Babylonian astrologer Berossus even moved to Greece around 290 B.C.E. and opened up a school. The use of magical spells also gave average people a sense of empowerment. An Egyptian charm was used to command a god to do one's bidding: "Hear me, because I am going to say the great name, Aoth, before whom every god prostrates himself and every demon shudders. Your divine name is Aeeioyo Iayoe Eaooyeeoia. I have spoken the glorious name, the name for all needs." In this case, it was believed a god could be controlled by speaking the god's secret name.

> **horoscope** (from Greek for "looking at the hours") Diagram of the positions of heavenly bodies used to forecast future events in a person's life.
>
> **cosmopolis** (Greek for "world-city") Universal city that people in the Hellenistic Age believed they belonged to; the origin of the modern word *cosmopolitan.*
>
> **Tyche** Greek goddess representing blind chance.

Magical charms also were used for self-medication, for then, as now, people were very concerned about their health. An ancient pregnancy test suggested, "You should make the woman urinate on the Great-Nile plant. When morning comes, if you find the plant scorched, she will not conceive. If you find it green, she will conceive." Incubation—that is, sleeping in the sanctuary of a healing god such as Asclepius—was thought to be a means of curing maladies ranging from psoriasis to lameness to cancer. Temple walls were hung with plaques attesting to various cures. One, regarding a wounded soldier, read, "As he was sleeping in the Temple the god extracted the spearhead. When day came he departed, cured." People also believed that they could receive help from the gods in dreams received while they slept in temples. According to one report, "Arata, a woman of Sparta, was dropsical. While she remained at home, her mother slept in the temple and saw a dream. It seemed that the god cut off her daughter's head and hung her body upside-down. Out came a huge quantity of fluid matter. Then he fitted the head back on the neck. Afterward she went home and found her daughter in good health."

The Hellenistic Mystery Cults

Another way people attempted to gain greater control over their lives was by attempting to find happiness after death. Many believed this could be done by participating in **mystery cults,** which promised a blissful afterlife gained by participating in secret rituals. Mystery cults taught that people could obtain **salvation** from the cares of this world by following the model of a god who had endured terrible suffering or death on earth and then had been either restored or reborn. If the god could triumph over the troubles of this world, people believed that they could, too. But participants in mystery cults could not obtain salvation by their own efforts. They needed help, in the form of going through the proper rituals, to understand the mystery of how the god they were worshiping had obtained salvation. Unlike modern religions of redemption, moreover, mystery religions were not intended to help someone obtain forgiveness and avoid punishment for past sins, but simply to ensure that a participant received an afterlife. There was no concept of guilt, repentance, or regret for past sins. Indeed, mystery cults had no concept of sin at all.

A participant in a mystery cult was thought to obtain salvation by participating in an initiation ceremony that allowed one to share the identity of the god and thus the god's immortality. Different cults created this mystical union in different ways, al-

though there were several general similarities. Initiates were sworn to secrecy, but enough information slipped out to give a general picture of the rites. The ceremony often began with a purification ritual that made the initiate fit to come into contact with the deity. The initiate then sat through, or participated in, an elaborate performance that explained the cycle of life and death.

To be initiated into most mystery cults, all one had to do was attend the ceremony, although some cults had more demanding initiations than others. The **Eleusinian mysteries** at Athens honored the grain goddess Demeter. In Greek mythology, Demeter's daughter Persephone had been carried off to the underworld by the god Hades but was allowed to return to earth six months of the year. The initiation began with a ritual purification in which initiates carried a piglet into the sea. Then the piglet was sacrificed, and the initiates were baptized by being sprinkled with its blood. They then took part in a torchlight procession to holy places in the Athenian countryside that appeared in the myth of Demeter and Persephone, thus sharing in the goddesses' experiences. The climax of the ceremony occurred in the Hall of Initiation, where a religious drama depicting the return of Persephone from the underworld was presented. Sacred objects, such as ancient wooden statues of the goddesses and wheat stalks, also were displayed. The poet Pindar wrote about these mysteries, "Blessed are those who have seen these things for they understand the end of mortal life and the beginning of a new life given by god."

Initiation into the Eleusinian mysteries took place only in Athens, but initiation into most other cults could occur anywhere. During the Hellenistic period, the ancient Egyptian cult of Isis, whose brother Osiris had been brought back from the dead after being torn to pieces, was revived. This cult was similar to the Eleusinian mysteries, but it also made greater demands. Initiates were expected to purify themselves by living in the temple with the priests and attending worship services, even if only for a day. Participants then viewed sacred books and were baptized in wa-

mystery cult   (based on Greek *mysterion,* "secret") Form of worship modeled on the experiences of a god and promising a happy afterlife through secret initiation rituals.

salvation   Process by which people believed they were saved from the suffering and troubles of this world and gained eternal life; also known as redemption.

Eleusinian mysteries   Mystery cult at Athens that honored the grain goddess Demeter.

A fresco from the buried Italian city of Hercunaleum shows a ceremony at a temple of Isis. In the center, at the top of the steps, a priest holds a covered urn. The priestess to his right shakes a rattle, and to his left a black priest holds a staff. The worshipers gather below, where another black priest watches over a priestess sacrificing ducks, joined by one musician playing a flute and others shaking rattles. *(Ediciones Dolmen)*

ter representing the life-giving Nile River. For the next ten days, initiates abstained from eating meat, drinking wine, and having sex. These requirements were a form of death, in which participants assumed the role of Osiris. The actual initiation began at sunset on the tenth day, when the candidate was taken into the innermost sanctuary of the temple of Isis, where there was a performance of a ritual death and resurrection, with the initiate, as Osiris, being reborn with the rising of the sun. At this point the initiates returned to the temple to be viewed as living gods. In one account, Isis herself addressed the initiate, "When you descend to the underworld, there you will see me shining and you will worship me as the one who has favored you."

The most demanding cult of all was that of the Asian Great Mother goddess, **Cybele.** She had caused her lover Attis, a vegetation god, to go mad and castrate and kill himself with a sharp stone so that no other woman could have him. Like vegetation, Attis was reborn every year in the spring. Initiation into the cult of Cybele occurred during a spring festival that began with the cutting of a pine tree to represent Attis. Participants were expected to fast for one day by not eating fruits and vegetables, although eating meat was permitted. The rites came to a head on "the day of blood," in which participants worked themselves into a frenzy dancing to the sounds of horns, drums, and cymbals. The slashed their bodies with knives, sprinkling blood on the sacred tree as a means

of calling Attis back to life. The Greek satirist Lucian described what happened next: "Frenzy comes on many who have come simply to watch and they subsequently perform this act on themselves. The initiate throws off his clothes, rushes to the center with a great shout, takes up a sword, and immediately castrates himself. Then he runs through the city holding the parts he has cut off. He takes female clothing and women's adornment from whatever house he throws the parts into." Having taken this irrevocable step, the initiate—if he survived—then became one of the wandering priests of Cybele.

The mystery cults required no faith. Salvation was gained by one's personal, albeit brief, devotion to the mystery deities. There was no need to engage in any continuing ritual. Nor were the cults exclusive. People could be initiated into as many mystery cults as they wished. These were the first religions offering personal salvation that were open to all, and they were extremely popular.

The Intellectual Approach to Identity

Greeks with intellectual inclinations sought to find their place in the universe through philosophical beliefs. The old philosophical schools of Plato and Aristotle usually had speculated about the nature of the universe and humanity in a broad sense, rarely on the level of the individual. For many, the teachings of these schools seemed out of date, and in the

Cybele   Asian mother goddess, the lover of Attis, whose worship included ritual castration.

Hellenistic period, before and after 300 B.C.E., new philosophical teachings aimed to fulfill the needs of individuals. In the mid fourth century B.C.E., the philosopher Diogenes, for example, taught that people could find their proper place in the world, and also become invulnerable to the unpredictability of Tyche, by discarding all human social conventions and "living according to nature." His followers gained the name Cynics, from the Greek word for "dog," because they lived like dogs, performing all of their natural functions—eating, sleeping, defecating, and having sex—in the street. Cynics were self-sufficient and indifferent to suffering. Their lack of respect for social conventions also meant they were outspoken social critics and took no account of rank or status. In a famous story, one day Alexander the Great visited Diogenes, who lay naked sunning himself. When Alexander asked Diogenes what he could do for him, Diogenes replied, "You could move to the side a bit and stop blocking the sun."

The philosopher Epicurus, from the Aegean island of Samos, took a materialistic approach to life. Beginning just before 300 B.C.E., in the philosophy known as Epicureanism, he taught that the universe was comprised of atoms randomly falling through space. There was no guiding principle and no underlying structure. There were no gods, no chance, no good or bad fortune, just falling atoms. Sometimes these atoms would swerve, clump together, and create the material world. The swerve also gave people free will by introducing an element of variation into the falling atoms. A person's only goal should be to pursue a form of pleasure that Epicurus defined as preventing one's atoms from being disturbed, and this meant avoiding pain. Thus, any pleasure that later caused pain, such as drunkenness or overeating, was to be avoided. To avoid pain, one also needed peace of mind and the ability not to be affected by circumstances. Epicurus thus advocated withdrawal from public life in favor of a calm life of seclusion spent with like-minded friends. But the focus on pleasure led to misunderstanding of Epicurus's teachings; today, the term *Epicurean* refers to someone who overdoes pleasure seeking, exactly the opposite of what Epicurus meant. Epicurus's school was unusual in that he admitted women.

Just after 300 B.C.E., Zeno, a native of Cyprus, presented a different view in the philosophy known as Stoicism. He also taught that the universe was materialistic, but for him it was highly structured and had an unalterable pattern established by a divine governing force called the Logos. The universe was like a finely organized machine, full of wheels and gears, that repeated the same cycle about every twenty-six

thousand years. Just as every part of the machine played its part in the smooth functioning of the mechanism, it was everyone's duty to perform his or her individual role in the pattern established by the Logos. Zeno, therefore, also taught that one should live by nature, but his point was that all must accept the role that they had been assigned in nature. The Stoic prayer was, "Lead me, O Zeus, wherever you will, and I will follow willingly, and if I do not, you will drag me." The only choice a person had was either to accept what already had been determined or to fight against it and inevitably be destroyed as a consequence. The importance given to performing one's duty made Stoicism attractive to individuals who were committed to political service.

Hellenistic Judaism

At the same time that mystery cults and new philosophies were emerging, a very significant religion of antiquity was once again facing challenges from outside. Under Persian rule, the Jews of Judaea, as the Jewish homeland was now called, had been permitted, and even encouraged, to pursue their worship with little or no interference from the government. When Judaea was absorbed into the empire of Alexander, the Jews continued to enjoy the same religious freedom. Following the disintegration of Alexander's empire, Judaea lay in the disputed border area between the Ptolemaic and Seleucid kingdoms and thus was often drawn into a long series of border wars. Eventually the Seleucids prevailed, and the Seleucid kings initially maintained the Jews' freedom to worship as they saw fit.

The situation changed with the Seleucid king Antiochus IV Epiphanes, who, desiring to unify his still vast and very disparate kingdom, sought to implant Greek culture in Judaea much more actively than had his predecessors. Many Jews, mostly from among the well-to-do, already had become Hellenized by learn-

---

Diogenes   Mid-fourth century B.C.E. Greek Cynic philosopher.

Epicureanism   Philosophy founded by Epicurus (341–270 B.C.E.) that advocated the avoidance of pain.

Stoicism   Greek philosophy founded by Zeno just after 300 B.C.E. that advocated doing one's duty in the universe.

Antiochus IV Epiphanes   (r. 175–164 B.C.E.; his name means "God Made Manifest") Seleucid king who attempted to Hellenize the Jews.

Hellenization   Process of implanting Greek culture.

ing Greek, studying Greek literature, and adopting Greek religious and philosophical practices and beliefs. Because Greeks, who exercised in the nude, believed that circumcision was a gross deformity, some Jews even underwent surgical processes to undo circumcision. The enthusiasm of these Hellenized Jews may have led Antiochus to believe that the rest of the Jews also were ready to adopt Greek culture.

Many conservative Jews, however, opposed Hellenization. The book of Maccabees in the Hebrew Bible reported, "In those days certain renegades came out from Israel and misled many, saying, 'Let us go and make a covenant with the **Gentiles** around us.' So they built a gymnasium in Jerusalem, according to Gentile custom, and removed the marks of circumcision, and abandoned the holy covenant." The greatest opposition to Antiochus's policies arose among less privileged Jews, led by the **Hasidim,** who feared that any adoption of Greek culture not only violated Jewish beliefs but also would lead to their destruction. Nevertheless, Antiochus pursued his policy of Hellenization by actively attempting to undermine Jewish practices. He issued laws forbidding circumcision, study of the Torah, and the observance of the Sabbath. The book of Maccabees continued, "They put to death the women who had their children circumcised, and they hung the infants from their mothers' necks." Antiochus Hellenized the Jewish Temple in Jerusalem by instituting ritual prostitution and placing in the Temple a statue and altar to Zeus on which pigs, which the Jews believed to be unclean, were sacrificed. The Jews referred to this affront to the Jewish religion as the "abomination of desolation." Antiochus even demanded that he himself be worshiped as a god.

In 167 B.C.E., rebellion broke out, led by the elderly Jewish priest Mattathias and his son Judas, nicknamed Maccabee ("The Hammer"). The rebels, joined by the Hasidim and other discontented Jews, became known as the **Maccabees.** Their goal was political independence, which they now believed was necessary for true religious freedom. Against all odds, Judas defeated Antiochus in 165 B.C.E. and liberated Jerusalem (see Choice). In the following year, the Temple was cleansed and reopened to the regular Jewish sacrifices, an event that is still commemorated each year in the Jewish festival of **Hanukkah.** The Seleucids, however, did not concede defeat easily. Fighting continued, and Judas and several of his brothers were killed. Ultimately, the revolt of the Maccabees resulted in the creation of an independent Jewish state, ruled by members of Judas's family, that would last for another hundred years.

Jewish independence did not mean an end to unrest and disagreements among the Jews themselves. There were conflicts over how Jewish law was to be interpreted and over the assimilation of non-Jewish culture. A group called the **Sadducees,** who represented the wealthy and were in charge of overseeing the temple in Jerusalem, embraced many Hellenistic beliefs and formed a secular-oriented group that cooperated with foreign rulers. They took a narrow interpretation of Jewish law, relying on written scripture only. Sadducees usually controlled the supreme legal and legislative body of the Jews, the **Sanhedrin,** which met in the Temple in Jerusalem and had seventy-one members, including the High Priest. On the other hand, the **Pharisees,** the successors of the Hasidim, who tended to come from well-to-do but not rich backgrounds, opposed Hellenization and supported a rigorous enforcement of Jewish religious law. They studied and interpreted scripture in synagogues and created a more religiously oriented party. During the reign of Queen Salome Alexandra (r. 76–67 B.C.E.), the Pharisees gained control of the Sanhedrin and were able to impose many elements of religious law. Their oral interpretations of the laws of Moses increased the number of prohibitions and regulations necessary for living a life acceptable to Yahweh. For example, biblical law identified 39 kinds of work prohibited on the Sabbath, a number eventually raised to 1,521 by oral interpretations. Even some Pharisees, however, were influenced by foreign religious beliefs to the extent that they adopted a belief in an afterlife that included the resurrection of the body.

At the same time, the Jewish Diaspora continued as Jews settled throughout the Mediterranean world. There continued to be a large Jewish population in Mesopotamia, and a large colony of Jews comprised of exiles, merchants, and mercenaries arose in Alexandria in Egypt, eventually outnumbering the Jews

---

Gentiles   (Latin for "peoples") Non-Jews.

Hasidim   (Hebrew for "pious ones") Jews who resisted the adoption of Greek culture.

Maccabees   Jewish rebels against the Seleucids in the 160s B.C.E.

Hanukkah   (Hebrew for "dedication") Jewish festival commemorating the defeat of the Seleucids by the Maccabees and the reopening of the Temple in Jerusalem.

Sadducees   Class of wealthy Jews who were in charge of the Temple in Jerusalem.

Sanhedrin   Supreme legal and legislative body of the Jews.

Pharisees   Class of Jews who supported a rigorous interpretation of Jewish law.

in Palestine. These foreign Jews were remarkably successful at preserving the fundamental aspects of their culture, such as adhering to dietary regulations, building synagogues, and keeping the Sabbath, in the midst of foreign cultures. But in other respects, especially language, foreign Jews were compelled to accommodate themselves to local conditions. The Jews of Alexandria eventually spoke Greek rather than Hebrew, and to make scripture available to these Greek-speaking Jews, a translation was needed. Ac-

cording to tradition, seventy Jewish translators went to work on their own translations into *koinē* Greek, each of which turned out to be exactly the same. This Greek version of the Old Testament was known as the **Septuagint.**

> **Septuagint** (based on Latin for "seventy") Greek translation of Jewish scripture by seventy translators.

Summary

Review Questions

↑ How did Alexander and his successors attempt to maintain control of the Macedonian conquests?

↑ What made the Hellenistic period different from preceding periods of Greek history?

↑ How did Hellenistic people try to find a sense of personal identity?

At the beginning of the Hellenistic period the conflicts between the Greeks and the Persians came to an end. Led by Alexander the Great, Macedonian Greek armies repeatedly defeated the Persians, resulting in the creation of an empire that extended from the Adriatic Sea to the Indus River. Before his death in 323 B.C.E., Alexander attempted to unify his empire by planting colonies of Greeks throughout the empire and by respecting the customs of conquered peoples. After Alexander's death, however, his empire disintegrated into three large pieces, ruled by the families of three of his powerful generals: the Antigonids, Ptolemies, and Seleucids. The Macedonian rulers of Egypt and western Asia were remarkably successful in creating a composite society that continued to respect the customs of their very culturally and ethnically diverse populations. Cities such as Alexandria and Antioch served not only as royal capitals but also as centers of learning. Smaller powers, based in the cities of Pergamum and Rhodes, also became centers of learning and economic wealth.

The conquests of Alexander had unforeseen cultural consequences for the Greeks, who were forced to reckon with the non-Greek world. Greeks no longer could hold the view that they were the best people in the world and that all non-Greeks were bar-

barians. Geographers brought accounts of the cultures of peoples living as far away as India, central Africa, and Britain. Foreign influences affected every aspect of Greek art and thought, creating a composite Hellenistic culture that extended from India across the Mediterranean. Never at any time in history has the western world, broadly defined, been so culturally united.

The study of science and technology emerged during the Hellenistic period. Most large cities were centers of some branch of learning. In Athens, the philosopher Aristotle introduced scientific classification. At the Museum of Alexandria, mathematicians created standard concepts of geometry, astronomers and geographers mapped both the heavens and the earth, physicians studied human anatomy, and inventors experimented with the uses of water and steam pressure.

The Hellenistic world also brought a sense of personal crisis to many Greeks, who felt lost now that the polis was no longer the focus of their lives. Many Greeks even lost the feeling of being Greek. Foreign languages and culture were everywhere. In an effort to discover a sense of identity and find their place in the world, many people turned to mystery religions, which promised an afterlife and to philosophies that provided guidelines for life. And in Judaea, the Jews strengthened their hold on their own identity by establishing their political independence for the first time in more than 400 years.

← **Thinking Back, Thinking Ahead** →

In what ways do you think that religious and cultural developments of the Hellenistic Age laid the groundwork for the rise of Christianity?

ECHO ECHO ECHO ECHO ECHO

The Seven Wonders of the Ancient World

Antiquity was a time of massive construction as rulers attempted to immortalize themselves, their nations, and their people with pyramids, temples, fortifications, palaces, and tombs. All the peoples of antiquity, from Mesopotamians to Egyptians to Persians to Greeks, placed great importance on architecture. But whereas the Near Eastern peoples such as the Egyptians are remembered for quantity, as represented in the size of their monuments, the Greeks are remembered for quality. Most Greek temples were in fact quite small but were so exquisitely designed that they have never been surpassed.

During the Hellenistic period, the competitive Greeks compiled a list of the seven most famous construction projects of antiquity. The Egyptians were represented by the pyramids, the Babylonians by their hanging gardens, and the Lydians by the temple of Artemis at Ephesus in Ionia. The remaining four entries were Greek. The classical period of Greek art was represented by the statue of Zeus at Olympia, the site of the Olympics (curiously, the Parthenon did not make the list). The Hellenistic period had three representatives: the mausoleum built ca. 350 B.C.E. at Halicarnassus in Ionia by King Mausoleus for his wife, Artemisia; the lighthouse built at Alexandria ca. 290 B.C.E.; and the giant statue of the sun god Helios built at the entrance to the harbor on the island of Rhodes circa 280 B.C.E. Of these wonders, only the pyramids survive.

Ever since antiquity, other rulers and other peoples have likewise attempted to make a lasting mark on history by constructing huge monuments—during the Roman Empire, amphitheaters; in the Middle Ages, cathedrals; today, massive museums, churches, libraries, and government buildings. And ever since antiquity, Greek styles of architecture have been used for monumental buildings. The architectural and artistic styles of Greek temples, with their rectangular format and rows of Doric, Ionic, or Corinthian columns and sculptural decoration, are as common today as in antiquity. Modern buildings often use the form of a Greek temple or other ancient model to create a sense of majesty, and even private homeowners wishing to create an air of elegance and permanence will put a row of Greek columns outside, or even inside, their homes.

Suggested Readings

Green, Peter. *Alexander to Actium: The Historical Evolution of the Hellenistic Age.* Berkeley and Los Angeles: University of California Press, 1990. A historical survey of the Hellenistic period from 336 to 30 B.C.E.

Hammond, Nicholas G. L. *Alexander the Great: King, Commander, and Statesman.* Bristol, England: University of Bristol Press, 1989. An excellent biography of Alexander by a leading classical historian.

Rihll, Tracy E. *Greek Science.* Oxford: Oxford University Press, 1999. An overview of Greek science with excellent coverage of Hellenistic scientific thought.

Roisman, Joseph. *Alexander the Great: Ancient and Modern Perspectives.* Lexington, Mass.: D. C. Heath, 1995. A survey of the historical importance of Alexander as seen from antiquity to the modern day.

Tarn, William W. *Hellenistic Civilization.* London: Arnold, 1927. The standard study of the history and culture of the Hellenistic world.

Tcherikover, Victor. *Hellenistic Civilization and the Jews.* Translated by S. Applebaum. New York: Atheneum, 1977. A study of the significance of the Jews in the context of the Hellenistic world, including the significance of the Maccabees.

Welles, C. Bradford. *Alexander and the Hellenistic World.* Toronto: Hakkert, 1970. The importance of Alexander the Great for the evolution of Hellenistic culture.

Websites

Resource site with links to more than 200 other sites relating to the Hellenistic world, **The Hellenistic World on the Web,** at www.isidore-of-seville.com/hellenistic

Well-illustrated site detailing the life and achievements of Alexander the Great, **Alexander the Great,** at http://1stmuse.com/frames/index.html

Technically oriented site with thorough coverage of Hellenistic inventions such as the Anticythera device, **The Science and Technology of Ancient Greece,** at www.mlahanas.de/Greeks/Greeks.htm

The Rise of Rome, 753–27 B.C.E.

1500 B.C.E.	1000 B.C.E.	500 B.C.E.	1 B.C.E./1 C.E.

753 B.C.E.
Rome is founded
by Romulus and Remus

509 B.C.E.
Roman Republic
is established

800	750	700	650	600	550	500	450	400

Roman Expansion to 44 B.C.E.

Between 227 and 44 B.C.E., Rome gained control of provinces extending from Spain in the west to Syria in the east. Even though historians call this period the Roman Republic, the Romans were in fact creating an empire. What kinds of problems could arise when a city gains control of so much foreign territory but refuses to take complete responsibility for governing it?

Roman territory

- ca. 500 B.C.E.
- added by 264 B.C.E.
- added by 241 B.C.E.
- added by 201 B.C.E.
- added by 120 B.C.E.
- added by 44 B.C.E.
- Parthian Empire in 44 B.C.E.
- ✕ Major battle

ATLANTIC OCEAN

Baltic Sea

GERMANY

BELGICA

GAUL
Lyons
Alesia 52 B.C.E.
ALPS
RAETIA
NORICUM
PANNONIA
DACIA
NARBONESE GAUL
Narbonne
Marseilles
CISALPINE GAUL
Trebia River 218 B.C.E.
Arretium
Lake Trasimene 217 B.C.E.
ILLYRICUM
MOESIA
THRACE
Byzantium
Philippi

FARTHER SPAIN
Numantia

NEARER SPAIN
Saguntum
Córdoba
Cadiz
New Carthage

Corsica
ITALY
Rome
Cannae 216 B.C.E.
Capua
Tarentum
Brundisium
Sardinia
Drepana 249 B.C.E.
SICILY
Messina
Syracuse
Carthage
Zama 202 B.C.E.
MACEDONIA
Pydna 168 B.C.E.
Cynoscephalae
Pergamum 197 B.C.E.
EPIRUS
Actium 31 B.C.E.
Pharsalus 48 B.C.E.
Corinth
ACHAEA
Athens
ASIA
Ephesus
PHRYGIA
GALATIA
ANATOLIA
CAPPADOCIA
Tarsus
Carrhae 53 B.C.E.
PAMPHYLIA
LYCIA
CILICIA
Antioch

Balearic Is.
Mediterranean Sea
Malta
Rhodes
Crete
Cyprus

MAURETANIA
NUMIDIA
AFRICA PROCONSULARIS
NORTH AFRICA
CYRENAICA
Cyrene
Alexandria
EGYPT

BOSPORAN KINGDOM
Black Sea
Caspian Sea
CAUCASUS MTS.
ARMENIA
PARTHIA
Ctesiphon
Seleucia
SYRIA
Damascus
JUDAEA
Jerusalem
Petra
ARABIAN DESERT
SINAI
Red Sea
Nile

SAHARA

0 200 400 Km.
0 200 400 Mi.

---

500 C.E.   1000 C.E.   1500 C.E.   2000 C.E.

390 B.C.E.
Rome is sacked by Gauls

218 B.C.E.
Hannibal invades Italy

202 B.C.E.
Romans defeat the Carthaginians at Battle of Zama

44 B.C.E.
Caesar is assassinated

108 B.C.E.
Marius creates the volunteer army

30 B.C.E.
Cleopatra, last of the Ptolemies, commits suicide

27 B.C.E.
Roman Republic ends, Roman Empire begins

350   300   250   200   150   100   50   0

Choice

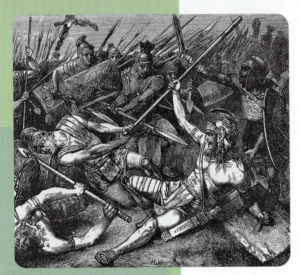

Spartacus

During the Roman Republic, most Roman slaves had no right to make meaningful decisions about their lives and could do nothing about their condition, no matter how badly they were treated. But Spartacus, a Thracian slave, chose to revolt and, by so doing, gave hope to the other slaves in Italy. Spartacus' example has intrigued people for centuries, and his story has been told in art and literature. This nineteenth-century engraving shows Spartacus and his fellow slaves being overwhelmed by Roman soldiers at the end of their revolt. (Bettmann/Corbis)

Spartacus Decides to Revolt

By the early first century B.C.E., the Romans had enslaved hundreds of thousands of non-Italian foreigners. Many of these slaves were very badly treated. One was Spartacus, a native of Thrace, a mountainous region north of Greece. According to the Greek historian Plutarch, "He was a Thracian belonging to one of the nomad peoples, and a man not only brave and of high spirit, but also rich in understanding. He was unexpectedly gentle, and more of a Greek than the people of his country usually are." It was said that when Spartacus was first sold as a slave in Rome, a snake coiled itself on his face and his wife, a prophetess and worshiper of the god Bacchus, saw the snake as a sign of future greatness but also of a bad end.

Spartacus was forced to become a gladiator at Capua, a city on the Bay of Naples. Gladiators performed at public spectacles, either individually or in groups, fighting in an arena until their opponents were either wounded or killed. Spartacus and his fellow gladiators realized that they would probably die in the arena, but they had no choice. Revolt would have seemed out of the question, for no slave revolt had ever succeeded, and slaves who tried to rebel were savagely punished.

Even though Spartacus knew the odds against him, he decided to fight for his freedom and, in 73 B.C.E., he led his fellow slaves in revolt. Breaking out of their cells, they grabbed knives in the kitchen, overpowered their guards, and seized weapons in Capua. Many of the rebels had formerly been soldiers, and under Spartacus's leadership, they defeated several units of Roman soldiers sent against them and even captured a Roman army camp. Their numbers were constantly increased by additional slaves who escaped from neighboring estates, and Spartacus soon had more than seventy thousand soldiers. They could be as brutal as the Romans they were fighting against, looting the countryside and dividing the spoils equally among themselves. When a friend was killed in combat, Spartacus sacrificed three hundred Roman prisoners to his dead friend's ghost. In the conflict between the rebels and the Romans, no mercy was expected, or given, on either side.

In spite of his successes, Spartacus realized that the rebels could not resist the Romans indefinitely. He therefore made another important decision: to lead his people out of Italy. He first planned to go north across the Alps, where the rebels could scatter and attempt to return to their homes, but the rebels preferred to continue their looting in Italy. Spartacus then planned to hire pirates to ferry the slaves across to Sicily, where he thought the large slave population also would be ready to revolt, but the pirates ran off with the payment, leaving Spartacus trapped in Italy.

In 71 B.C.E., the Roman general Crassus led eight legions (more than forty thousand soldiers) against Spartacus. When one of his armies was defeated by the rebels, Crassus showed that he was as tough as Spartacus by imposing the punishment called decimation: one of every ten of his disgraced soldiers was executed.

By doing so, he demonstrated that he would not tolerate failure. Crassus finally cornered Spartacus in southern Italy, and Spartacus had no choice but to fight the large, well-trained Roman army. In the ensuing battle, Spartacus and many of his followers were surrounded and slaughtered. Rebels who tried to escape were killed or captured, and six thousand captives were crucified along the road leading south from Rome. The great slave revolt was over, but if the example of Spartacus taught Italian slaves the futility of revolt, it also taught the Romans something, too. To prevent future slave revolts, they improved the conditions in which slaves were forced to live.

Introduction

By the time of Spartacus's revolt, Rome had become the greatest power the ancient world had yet known. But when Rome was founded around 750 B.C.E., it was just one of thousands of small agricultural villages around the Mediterranean. Nothing marked it for future greatness. Rome's location at a crossroads between northern and southern Italy brought the Romans into contact with other peoples, including the Etruscans, Greeks, and Celts, all of whom would influence the future development of Roman culture. Over time, the Romans learned not only to survive but to prosper by assimilating the culture and customs of the peoples around them.

The early Romans were hardy farmers who valued their traditions. They had a strong work ethic based on duty to their gods, to their families, and to Rome. Their religious and family values made them close-knit, willing to resolve disputes without resorting to violence and able to settle internal conflicts peaceably. The Romans' perseverance and ability to work together were major factors in their future success.

After first being ruled by kings, the Romans in 509 B.C.E. created a form of government called the Republic, in which the members of a governing body called the Senate shared power among themselves. Early in its history, the Republic was engaged in a struggle for existence against hostile neighbors. Beginning in the fourth century B.C.E., for reasons ranging from a fear of strong neighbors to a desire by senators for military glory, the Romans became involved in a series of wars first in Italy and then in the western and eastern Mediterranean. By 146 B.C.E. they had emerged victorious in all their wars and had become the strongest Mediterranean power. Nevertheless, the Romans resisted becoming an empire and taking full responsibility for governing their conquered territories.

The acquisition of great power had enormous consequences for Roman life. Some of the foreign customs and concepts that the Romans assimilated, especially from the Greeks, conflicted with traditional Roman values. During the first century B.C.E., the government of the Roman Republic collapsed as a result of its unwillingness or inability to deal with problems such as poorly administered foreign territories, armies that could no longer be controlled, and senators who put personal ambitions ahead of the best interests of Rome.

The Development of Roman Identity, 753–509 B.C.E.

↓ What values were important to the Romans?
↓ In what ways did Rome assimilate foreign peoples and customs?

At the time of its founding, Rome was a small agricultural village. Romans had a strong sense of duty that subordinated individuals to the greater goods of family, nation, and religion. They adopted what they believed were the best elements of foreign cultures and even accepted foreign peoples into their midst while at the same time preserving their own unique identity. The Romans' social and religious values gave them a strong sense of being able to work together and to overcome adversity.

A City on Seven Hills

The early Romans had no written history. The beliefs of later Romans about how Rome was founded were based on oral legends that had been passed down for centuries. Eventually—by around 200 B.C.E.—Greek and Roman historians created a standardized account of early Roman history that was drawn from many sources. One story started with Aeneas, a Trojan who

Chronology

1184 B.C.E. Aeneas escapes from Troy and later settles in Italy	**186 B.C.E.** Romans investigate Bacchus worshipers
753 B.C.E. Traditional date of the foundation of Rome by Romulus and Remus	**133–122 B.C.E.** Reforms of Tiberius and Gaius Gracchus
ca. 600 B.C.E. Etruscans bring civilization to Rome	**108 B.C.E.** Marius creates the volunteer army
509 B.C.E. Etruscan kings are expelled from Rome; Roman Republic is established	**90 B.C.E.** Italian allies revolt against Rome
500–287 B.C.E. Conflict of the Orders	**88 B.C.E.** Sulla uses his army to seize Rome.
451–450 B.C.E. Twelve Tables of Roman law are issued	**73–71 B.C.E.** Spartacus leads a slave revolt
390 B.C.E. Rome is sacked by Gauls	**63 B.C.E.** Cicero suppresses Catiline's conspiracy to overthrow Roman government
343–290 B.C.E. Romans fight Samnite Wars	**60 B.C.E.** Crassus, Pompey, and Caesar form First Triumvirate
264–146 B.C.E. Romans fight Punic Wars against the Carthaginians	**44 B.C.E.** Caesar is assassinated on Ides of March
227 B.C.E. Sicily becomes first Roman province	**43 B.C.E.** Lepidus, Mark Antony, and Octavian form Second Triumvirate
216 B.C.E. Hannibal defeats Romans at Battle of Cannae	**31 B.C.E.** Octavian wins Battle of Actium against Antony and Cleopatra, who commit suicide the next year.
212 B.C.E. Denarius is introduced	**27 B.C.E.** Roman Republic ends; Roman Empire begins
202 B.C.E. Scipio defeats Hannibal at Battle of Zama	

had escaped from the burning city of Troy around 1184 B.C.E. and fled to Italy. There he established a city not far from the future site of Rome that was populated by his Trojan followers and local people known as **Latins.** One of Aeneas's distant descendants was a woman named Sylvia, who gave birth to twin sons, **Romulus and Remus,** claiming that the god Mars was their father. Their uncle, who had stolen the throne, ordered the twins to be put to death, fearing that they would replace him. But the executioner did not have the heart to kill the boys, so he set them adrift in a basket in the Tiber River. Downstream, a shepherd found them being suckled by a wolf and raised them as shepherds. Subsequently, the legend continues, the two boys discovered their true identity and decided to establish their own city on a site with seven hills on the south bank of the lower Tiber River. In the course of an argument, Remus was killed by Romulus, and the new city was named Rome, after him. The date was April 21, 753 B.C.E.

According to legend, Romulus' city was first populated by Latin men who needed wives. They therefore kidnapped women from the Sabines, a nearby Italian people who spoke a slightly different dialect. Romulus established a monarchy and became the first of seven kings of Rome. Later Romans believed that these kings had established many of Rome's most ancient traditions and customs, such as that the kings had two powers: the **imperium,** which gave

Latins   Peoples living in Latium in central Italy, distinguished from the neighboring Italian peoples by their dialect; they gave their name to the Latin language.

Romulus and Remus   Twin brothers, the legendary founders of Rome in 753 B.C.E.

imperium   Power of Roman kings and consuls to govern Rome and command armies.

Terra cotta urns in the shape of the huts in which people lived were used for burying the ashes of the dead in early Rome. These urns can be used in conjunction with surviving post-holes that held the support posts of early Roman huts on the Palatine Hill to reconstruct the homes of the early Romans. *(Scala/Art Resource, NY)*

them the authority to lead armies, and the **auspicium,** the right to consult the gods.

These foundation legends played an important role in defining Roman identity. They exemplified the Roman willingness to integrate newcomers into their society. They also connected Rome to Greek antiquity and to Greek gods and revealed that the Romans wanted to be part of the broader, civilized Mediterranean world and to show the Greeks that they, too, had a distinguished history and were not barbarians.

Even though the legends are based on a core of truth, they also include many elaborations. Archaeological excavations offer more concrete information about the early history of Rome and demonstrate that the first settlement of the hills of Rome did in fact take place around 750 B.C.E. The presence of two populations is attested by the use of two different burial techniques, cremation, in which bodies were burned, and inhumation, in which bodies were buried without being burned. At first, Rome was just a small farming village of straw huts perched on some of the hills. The southern part of Italy was inhabited by Greeks in the coastal areas and Italian peoples in the uplands. Just north of Rome lived the **Etruscans,** a people who may have emigrated from the coastal region of Anatolia about 800 B.C.E. In several ways the Etruscans were like the Greeks. They were not unified, and they lived in twelve independent cities

ruled by warrior aristocracies. They had a highly developed economy based on trade and manufacturing, and they were especially expert at metalworking. Much Etruscan trade was with the Greeks; in fact, some of the best-preserved Greek pottery comes from graves in Etruria. The Etruscans used an alphabet adapted from Greek to write a language that is still undeciphered.

Around 600 B.C.E., the Etruscans began expanding south and occupied Rome. The site attracted them because it was strategically positioned at the best crossing of the lower Tiber River, providing a means of good communications between northern and southern Italy. The Etruscans brought urbanization and civilization to Rome. They drained the swampy land between the hills and constructed the first paved roads, the first stone buildings, and the **Forum,** or central meeting place. They introduced new occupations, such as trading and pottery manufacturing, and made Rome a commercial center. Their religious practices and version of the Greek alphabet also were adapted by the Romans. Under Etruscan influence, Rome developed from a village into a city.

The Etruscans also provided the last three kings of Rome. Patriotic legends told how the wicked son of the autocratic Etruscan king Tarquin the Proud raped the virtuous Roman matron Lucretia, who then committed suicide for having disgraced her family. An uprising of enraged native Roman aristocrats expelled Tarquin in 509 B.C.E., and the Romans resolved never again to have a king. To do so, in the same year they created the Roman **Republic.**

What It Meant to Be Roman

During the era of the kings the defining elements of Roman character and identity took shape. The Romans were fundamentally conservative and resistant to change. Reverence for the past guided their behavior, which was based on the concept of *mos maiorum,* "the ways of the ancestors." When faced with a problem,

auspicium   Power of Roman kings and consuls to determine the will of the gods.

Etruscans   Inhabitants of northwestern Italy whose culture greatly influenced early Rome.

Forum   The center of public life in Rome, with markets, temples, law courts, and the Senate house.

Republic   (in Latin, "the public thing") System of government introduced by the Romans after the expulsion of kings in 509 B.C.E., based on collegiate rule and rule by law.

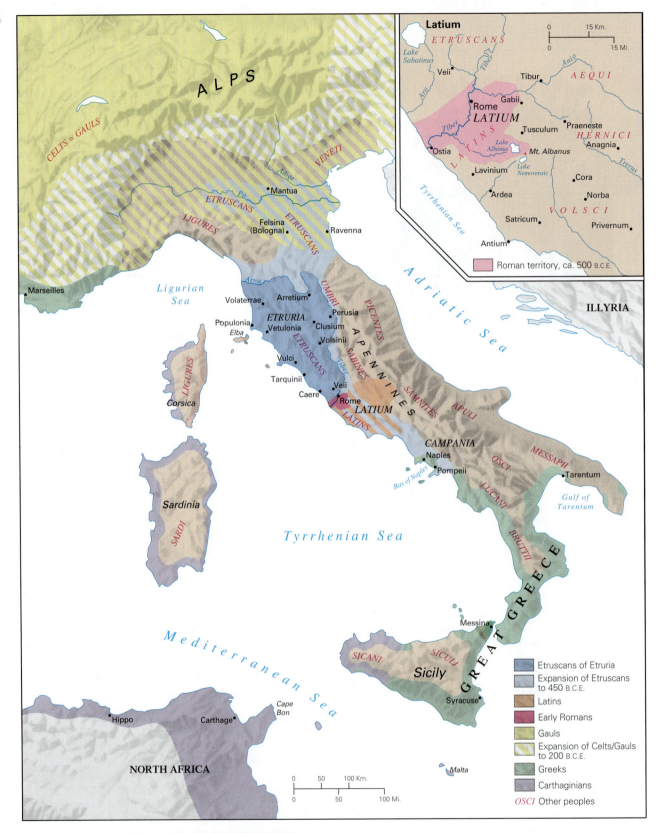

MAP 5.1 **Early Italy, ca. 760–500 B.C.E.** When Rome was founded ca. 750 B.C.E., Italy was occupied by three groups of peoples: Greeks on the southern coast, Etruscans in the northwest, and Italian peoples in the uplands. By 400 B.C.E., the Po Valley in northern Italy had been occupied by Celts (also known as Gauls) from Gaul. All these peoples influenced the development of Roman culture.

they first would ask, What would our ancestors have done? But the Romans were not blindly conservative. They also were very sensible and willing to adapt to changing conditions if circumstances required it. The Romans valued moral qualities such as responsibility, discipline, industry, frugality, temperance, fortitude, and modesty. Except on a very few occasions, such as after a great military victory, they refrained from self-promotion. The greatest Roman virtue was *pietas*, the sense of duty toward gods, family, friends, and country. Romans did their duty because of *religio* (from which our word *religion* is derived), a sense of subordination to external forces that included the gods, state officials, and family members. Everyone in Rome was subordinate to some greater authority and thus knew how he or she related to everyone else. Even when Romans pursued their personal ambitions, they always expressed themselves in terms of these traditional Roman values.

Early Roman society was composed mostly of free citizens belonging to three tribes believed to be the descendants of original populations of Latins, Italians, and Etruscans. Citizens enjoyed both private rights, which allowed them to marry, inherit property, and carry on business under Roman law, and public rights, which permitted male citizens to vote and run for public office. At this time, the population of foreigners and slaves was small because Rome was not yet very prosperous. Unlike in other ancient societies, the slaves of Roman citizens who were set free gained full Roman citizenship rights, providing another example of how the Romans were willing to integrate newcomers into their society.

Even as a city, Rome remained a primarily agrarian society. As some farmers grew more successful than others, two social orders evolved: the **patricians** and the **plebeians** (or plebs). The patricians were the equivalent of the Greek aristocrats; the only way to become a patrician was by being born one. The patricians owned the best land, and the heads of the patrician families were members of the **Senate,** a hereditary body of about one hundred that originally advised the king. The senators were the most powerful persons in Rome. They saw themselves as preservers of Roman tradition and as models of Roman virtue, which they believed was best exemplified through military service. The plebeians, on the other hand, were mostly farmers, working either their own small plots or land that belonged to the patricians. As a result of the expansion in commerce and manufacturing under the Etruscans, some plebeians became very wealthy, but even so they could not enter the hereditary patrician class. At the other extreme, plebeians who defaulted on loans could be sold into slavery.

Roman social relations revolved around the idea of bilateral (two-way) duty that was viewed in terms of contractual commitments. If someone did a Roman a favor, the Roman was obligated to that person until the favor had been repaid. This practice lay behind one of Rome's most important social institutions, the **patron-client relationship,** in which persons owed services to each other and were bound together in an almost religious union. At this time, the patrons were usually patricians, who would have many plebeians as their clients. A patrician patron provided physical protection, civil and criminal legal services, and economic support, including foodstuffs, seed grain, and even land to rent when times were tough. In return, the plebeian client accompanied the patrician in time of war (the patricians did most of the actual fighting), helped to raise a ransom if he should be captured, and contributed to a dowry when a patrician's daughter was married. This system of reciprocal responsibility knit Roman society together in a way that Greek society was not, with the result that Romans were much less likely to resort to violence against each other when disputes arose. The system also was designed to preserve the position and privileges of the patricians.

Early Roman Religion

Religious beliefs and practices were deeply embedded in early Roman society, culture, and politics. Much of the Romans' sense of subordination to a greater power derived from their religion. The Romans believed that their most ancient religious institutions had been established by Numa, the second king of Rome. But the Romans also adopted other religious practices from the Etruscans and the Greeks. Roman religion was polytheistic, with many gods who took many forms. Some gods looked after the welfare of the state as a whole, and others were concerned with Roman private life. The earliest Roman gods were *numina*, vague and shapeless forces of

patricians   The most privileged of the early Roman citizens, equivalent to aristocrats.

plebeians   (or plebs) The less privileged of the early Roman citizens; later, the generic term for Roman citizens.

Senate   Primary governing body of the Roman Republic; its members were senators.

patron-client relationship   The rendering of mutual services between a senior party (a patron) and a junior party (the client).

numina (sing. *numen*)   Formless forces of nature that controlled the natural environment.

Etruscan fears about the afterlife are reflected in this scene from an Etruscan tomb of ca. 300 B.C.E. depicting the execution of Trojan captives during the Trojan War to placate the ghosts of the dead. The underworld demons Charu (Greek Charon), who will hit the deceased with his hammer, and his winged female companion Vanth wait to escort the dead man to the underworld *(From Massimo Pallottino,* The Great Centuries of Painting: Etruscan Painting *[Milan: Skira Editore]. Courtesy, Princely House of Torlonia, Rome)*

nature that controlled the environment. The numen Janus, for example, who could be visualized with two faces pointing in opposite directions, was in charge of comings and goings and beginnings and endings. Each family had its own household gods, known as *Lares,* who looked after the well-being of the family, and *Penates,* who ensured that the storeroom was never empty. The *Manes* were spirits of beloved ancestors. The *Lemures,* on the other hand, were restless spirits of the dead who had to be placated every May with an offering of black beans. It was said that Romulus had begun this festival to pacify the spirit of Remus.

The Romans' social values were mirrored in their religious convictions. They believed that deities, too, had duties to perform, and they attempted to force the gods to do their duties by making ritualized contracts with them. Thus, each year a red dog was sacrificed at a crossroads to ensure that the *numen* Robigus did his duty and kept the red leaf blight from infect-

ing the crops. Religious rituals were marked by compulsive attention to detail. The slightest deviation from a ritual, such as a sneeze or whisper, would neutralize its effectiveness. The greatest personal sacrifice that an individual Roman could make was the ritual called devotion. When a Roman battle was going badly, a Roman commander sometimes devoted himself to the gods and then committed suicide by charging into the enemy ranks. His men then regained confidence in the belief that the gods would fulfill their part of the bargain by granting victory.

As a consequence of their contacts with the Etruscans and Greeks, the Romans also began to worship anthropomorphic gods and goddesses in permanent stone temples. Thus, Jupiter, along with being the formless *numen* of lightning and thunder, also could be visualized as a bearded man throwing a lightning bolt. In the course of creating Rome as a city, the Etruscans built several temples in the area of the Forum.

The most important was a three-chambered temple on top of the **Capitoline Hill,** the highest hill in Rome, where it could be seen from far out in the countryside. This was the temple of the gods who looked after the welfare of the Roman state: **Jupiter the Best and Greatest;** his wife, Juno; and Minerva, a war goddess—the Roman equivalents of the Greek Zeus, Hera, and Athena. The temple served as an important symbol of Roman power and authority. Sacrifices of oxen and other animals were made in exchange for the gods' support of the well-being of the Roman people.

State priests saw to it that the government functioned according to religious law and that the *pax deorum* ("peace of the gods") was maintained between the gods and the Roman people. The most important Roman priest was the *pontifex maximus,* who was in charge of other state priests and priestesses, including the vestal virgins, who kept the sacred hearth fire of the goddess Vesta burning in the Forum. The *pontifex maximus* also kept official lists of government officials and of important events and controlled the calendar, every so often adding an extra month after February to keep the months synchronized with the seasons because the year as established by King Numa was 10 days short of a 365-day solar year.

Many Roman religious rituals were borrowed from the Etruscans, who used divination to discover the will of the gods. Etruscan priests observed flights of birds and examined sheep livers, looking for good or bad omens. Roman state priests used the same rituals to discover whether the decisions of the Roman government had the support of the gods. If the priests found bad omens, government business could not proceed. Etruscan religious practices also found their way into Roman private life. Etruscan funeral ceremonies, which included wrestling matches, combats to the death, and human sacrifices intended to placate the demons of the underworld, evolved into Roman **gladiatorial** matches.

Roman Family Life

Roman society was very family oriented. In early Rome, every Roman citizen belonged to a gens, or clan, and bore a clan name ending in *-ius* or *-ia,* such as Julius for men or Julia for women. Shortly after birth, Roman infants also received a first name. The first names of boys came from a standard list of twenty-two names, such as Marcus or Gaius. Certain first names ran in the family, so someone named Marcus Tullius probably had a father and grandfather also named Marcus Tullius. Female children, on the other hand, were simply identified by sequence numbers. Thus the second daughter of a Marcus Julius would be Julia Secunda. Romans also had a third name identifying their family, a subset of a clan. Family names often referred to a physical characteristic of a distant ancestor, such as Caesar ("hairy"). Thus, a Roman citizen had three names, for example, Gaius Julius Caesar. Senators were extremely proud of their heritage. The foyers of their houses contained wax portraits of ancestors that were paraded during funerals. Roman fathers expected to have a son to carry on the family name and inherit the family property. If a man had no natural sons, a son could be brought into the family by adoption.

The concept of subordination to a greater authority carried over into Roman family life. The chief authority within each nuclear family (a father and all of his dependents) was the *paterfamilias,* who had life-and-death power over the household. A newborn baby was placed at the feet of its father; if he refused to pick it up, the infant was exposed and left to die. The father had the legal authority to execute any of those in his power as long as the cause (such as a violation of family or national honor) warranted doing so. In one legendary case, a Roman general executed his son, who had just won a battle, for disobeying orders; he was praised for putting loyalty to Rome before loyalty to his family. It was possible for a young man to become a *paterfamilias* in his own right if his father pretended to sell him as a slave three times and then set him free. Most men, however, simply waited for their fathers to die before becoming free of paternal authority.

Girls were permitted to marry young, and some were wed as young as age twelve, often to much older men. Men generally waited until a later age, around thirty. For a Roman marriage to be legally valid, the two parties both had to be Roman citizens. Marriages between Romans and foreigners or Romans and slaves did not convey any legal rights to

Capitoline Hill The tallest hill in Rome, site of the Capitoline temple of Jupiter, Juno, and Minerva.

Jupiter the Best and Greatest Most important Roman state god.

pontifex maximus (Latin for "the greatest bridge builder") An ancient title for the chief priest of Rome.

gladiator (Latin for "sword bearer," from Latin *gladius,* "sword") A person, usually a slave, who fought in an arena against animals or other gladiators for the entertainment of the audience.

paterfamilias (Latin for "father of the family") Head of a Roman family, with life-and-death power over family members.

Roman senators were extremely proud of their ancestors, who provided models of how good Romans should behave. In this statue of the first century C.E., a senator carries busts of his ancestors that would have been displayed in the foyer of his house and paraded during funerals of family members. (*Scala/Art Resource, NY*)

offspring, whereas children of married Roman citizens also were citizens. Marriage was a private matter between two consenting persons who agreed to treat a relationship as a marriage. No legal or religious ceremonies were required, although a wedding feast often was held as a means of publicizing the union, and the parents of girls usually provided a dowry. In a type of marriage common at the beginning of the Republic, called purchase, a father fictitiously sold his daughter to her husband, who then assumed authority over her. But as time went on, another type of marriage, called usage, became more popular. The wife remained under her father's authority as long as she spent three nights away from

her husband's house each year. In this kind of marriage, a woman came under her own authority when her father died, although even then she needed a cooperative male guardian to carry out any business, such as buying property or making a will, on her behalf. Either party in a marriage could obtain a divorce simply by declaring "I divorce you" three times before a witness. It was only in the matter of the disposition of property that fault was considered. For example, if a divorce occurred by mutual consent or if a husband declared a divorce without cause, the husband was required to return the entire dowry—a consideration that inhibited men from seeking divorce. But if the wife was guilty of adultery, the husband could keep one-sixth of the dowry. Any children went to the father, and a divorced mother had no right even to see them again.

Children in early Rome were educated mainly in the home by mothers and fathers, who shared the responsibility equally. Boys were instructed in law and history and engaged in physical training that would prepare them for military life. Girls learned household economy and were taught to perform the most virtuous feminine activity of all: spinning wool to make the family's clothing. Mothers instilled Roman virtues, such as reverence for the gods and respect for authority. Fathers took their sons along on their daily round of business activities and public life. In senatorial families, mothers and fathers both were responsible for forwarding the careers of their sons and for securing good marriages for their daughters.

Roman women were expected to be modest, obedient, and loyal. The primary duty of a married woman was to bear children. Poor women in particular were expected to have as many children as possible—often ten or more—to ensure that at least some of them, given the high infant mortality rate, survived to maturity. Many women died in childbirth. A Roman gravestone, for example, tells of a woman named Veturia, who was married at eleven, bore six children (only one lived), and died at twenty-seven. Women's duties also included supervising any household slaves and overseeing domestic activities such as cooking, clothing production, and child care. Plebeian women who were not fully occupied at home could help support themselves and their families by working in a senatorial household; in the clothing industry; in service positions, such as hairdressers, masseuses, midwives, maids, and wet nurses; or as entertainers, such as dancers and prostitutes. In several regards, Roman women had greater liberties and responsibilities than their Greek counterparts. Roman women regularly appeared outside the home, with or without their husbands, engaging in such activities as visiting the public baths and attending religious ceremonies and dinner parties.

The most honored Roman women were the six vestal virgins, who also were the only women completely free of male legal authority. They were permitted to manage their own property and make wills in their own names. Girls became vestals before the age of ten and served for thirty years. After they retired, they were permitted to marry, but many continued to serve the goddess and to keep their legal independence. Because the welfare of the state was tied to the vestals' purity, those convicted of being unchaste were sentenced to the horrible fate of being buried alive.

The Evolution of the Roman Republic, 509–146 B.C.E.

↓ How was the collective will of the Roman people expressed in Roman government?

↓ Why were the Romans initially reluctant to create an empire?

After the expulsion of the kings, the Romans created the Roman Republic, a system of government based on the sharing of power among several magistrates (officials). The Roman people were governed by the rule of law, which represented the collective will of the people. During the early Republic, a nonviolent conflict arose between the patricians, who monopolized economic and political influence, and the plebeians, who wished to gain greater self-expression. By the early third century B.C.E., the Senate, the primary governing body of Rome, included both patricians and influential plebeians. The Senate guided Rome through many wars, first in Italy and then throughout the Mediterranean world. At first, the only goal of these wars was to weaken potential enemies, and the Romans were reluctant to assume responsibility for administering foreign territory. But during the second century B.C.E., the Romans took direct control over foreign territories, known as provinces. By 146 B.C.E. Rome had become the strongest power in the Mediterranean world.

Roman Republican Government

The Roman monarchy was superseded by the Republic, a government based on the concept of **collegiality,** in which offices and responsibilities were shared by the members of the Senate, which now became the most important governing body in Rome. The king, for example, was replaced by two **consuls,** who were elected by the people every year. Like the king, the

consuls had the powers of imperium and auspicium. They had the right to introduce laws, oversee the administration of justice, and name new senators. But the primary duty of the consuls was to lead the Roman **legions** in war. The greatest honor that a senator could receive was to be granted a ceremony called a **triumph** after a military victory during his term as consul. The consul, with his face painted red like the god Jupiter, led a procession of cheering soldiers and pitiful captives through the streets of Rome and up to the temple of Jupiter on the Capitoline Hill. Only in grave emergencies did the Romans return to a very restricted form of one-man rule. In such cases the consuls would appoint a dictator, the highest ranking of all magistrates. But there were severe limitations on the dictator's authority: he could serve only until the crisis was over and never for more than six months.

Over time, other lower-ranking officials, elected by the people, also were introduced. These included, in descending rank, two praetors, who were the chief legal officials; four aediles, who managed the markets, streets, and public buildings; and six quaestors, who oversaw state finances. In addition, every five years, two censors, who ranked even higher than the consuls, were elected. They served for eighteen months, and their duties included assessing property for taxation purposes (the **census**) and appointing new members to the Senate. Because all Roman magistrates except the dictators served in groups of two or more, it was crucially important for the smooth operation of the government that they get along with each other. Table 5.1 provides a listing of the most important officials in the Roman Republic.

The Republican government operated according to a constitution that was a combination of customary practices and unwritten law. Supreme authority lay with the people, whose will was expressed by the votes of assemblies to which all male citizens belonged. The assemblies elected all officials except the dictators and voted on declarations of war, trials involving the death penalty, and laws regulating everyday Roman

collegiality   Shared responsibility for the same office.

consul   Highest-ranking annual Roman official, whose primary duty was to lead the army.

legion   Largest unit of the Roman army, roughly 5,000 men.

triumph   Victory ceremony given to a Roman general who had won a great victory.

census   Assessment of property carried out by the censors for taxation purposes.

Table 5.1

Officials of the Roman Republic (by 146 B.C.E.)

Title	Number	Duties	Term
Annually Elected Officials (in rank order)			
Consul	2	Leads Roman army, presides over assemblies	1 year
Praetor	6	Oversees law courts, governs some provinces	1 year
Aedile	4	Oversees buildings and markets in Rome	1 year
Quaestor	6	Oversees financial matters	1 year
Tribune	10	Presides over Council of the Plebs	1 year
Nonannual Officials			
Dictator	1	Replaces consuls during emergencies	6 months maximum
Censor	2	Assesses property, appoints senators	18 months
Proconsul	varies	Governs provinces	1–3 years
Legate	varies	Governor's assistant	Will of the governor

life. But the assemblies did not have the right to introduce laws. Instead, they could vote only on measures presented to them by the consuls, and the consuls were expected to have consulted with the Senate before they introduced any laws. The Senate thus was the primary governing body of Rome, and the patricians controlled the government because all three hundred or so members of the Senate were patricians and could instruct their plebeian clients how to vote in the assemblies. The patricians controlled the elections in the same way, and given that new senators were appointed by the censors, there was no chance that a plebeian would be chosen. In addition, only the patricians knew the laws, which were passed down by word of mouth from one generation to the next. At the beginning of the Republic, therefore, the patricians held virtually all the political, legal, social, and economic authority.

Voice

Polybius Describes the Roman Constitution

During the 130s B.C.E., the Greek historian Polybius, a Roman hostage who became a good friend of Scipio Aemilianus and other leading Roman senators, described the constitution of the Roman Republic as an evenly balanced combination of monarchy, aristocracy, and democracy. He equated the consuls with monarchy, the Senate with aristocracy, and the Roman people with democracy. By explaining Roman government in terms of various forms of Greek government, Polybius demonstrated both that Greeks were trying to understand Rome in terms of their own experiences and that Romans wanted their own traditions to be understood in terms of the more ancient Greek past.

➡ *How did these three forms of government function?*

Three kinds of government shared in the control of the Roman state with such fairness that it was impossible even for a native to pronounce with certainty whether the system was aristocratic, democratic, or monarchical. ➡ For if one

➜ How is Polybius putting Roman government into a Greek context?

➜ What is the relationship between the consuls and the Senate?

➜ How would the Senate expect its "friendly advice" to be received?

➜ How does Polybius's description of the role of the Senate compare with the description given in the chapter text?

➜ In what ways do the people not have as much power as Polybius suggests?

fixed one's eyes on the consuls, the constitution seemed completely monarchical; if on that of the Senate, it seemed again to be aristocratic; and when one looked at the power of the masses, it seemed clearly to be a democracy. The parts of the state falling under the control of each element are as follows. ➜

The consuls, before leading out their legions, exercise authority in Rome over all public affairs. Besides this, they consult the Senate on matters of urgency, they carry out in detail the provisions of its decrees. ➜ It is their duty to summon assemblies, to introduce legislation, and to preside over the enforcement of the popular decrees. As for warfare, their power is almost uncontrolled, for they are empowered to make whatever demands they choose. They also have the right of inflicting punishment on anyone under their command, and they are authorized to spend any sum from the public funds. So that if one looks at this part of the administration alone, one may reasonably pronounce the constitution to be a pure monarchy.

To pass to the Senate. It has the control of the treasury, all revenue and expenditure being regulated by it. In addition, crimes committed in Italy, such as treason, conspiracy, poisoning, and assassination, are under the jurisdiction of the Senate. It also occupies itself with the sending of all embassies to countries outside of Italy for the purpose either of settling differences, or of offering friendly advice, ➜ or indeed of imposing demands, or receiving submission, or of declaring war; and in like manner with respect to embassies arriving in Rome it decides answer should be given to them. All these matters are in the hands of the Senate, so that without the consuls the constitution appears to be entirely aristocratic. ➜

After this we might ask what part in the constitution is left for the people, considering that the Senate controls all the particular matters I mentioned, and that the consuls have uncontrolled authority as regards armaments and military operations. But nevertheless there is a very important part left for the people. The people alone have the right to confer honors and inflict punishment. They are the only court that may try capital charges. The people bestow office on the deserving, the noblest reward of virtue in a state. The people have the power of approving or rejecting laws, and they deliberate on the question of war and peace. Further, in the case of alliances, terms of peace, and treaties, it is the people who ratify all these or the reverse. Thus, here again one might plausibly say that the people's share in the government is the greatest, and that the constitution is a democratic one. ➜

A People Ruled by Law

Beginning around 500 B.C.E., a period of domestic unrest known as the Conflict of the Orders disturbed the Republic as plebeians attempted to gain social, economic, legal, and political power. The patricians were determined to maintain their privileged status and resisted plebeian calls for change. Two factors permitted the plebeians to pursue their goals. First, Rome could not be defended adequately from foreign enemies without plebeian military assistance. Therefore, soon after 500 B.C.E., the Senate sponsored reforms allowing wealthy plebeians who could afford their own weapons to fight in the army. Through their military service, these plebeians gained personal authority and found common ground with the patricians. The plebeians also found strength in numbers by creating their own assembly, the Council of the Plebs, which only plebeians could attend. It issued rulings that were binding on the plebeians. Each year the plebeians also elected ten tribunes of the plebs, who had the responsibility of defending the plebeians against patrician oppression. The plebeians swore to kill any patrician who ever harmed a tribune. The tribunes appropriated the right to say "Veto" ("I forbid") if the patricians did anything against plebeian interests. On such occasions, the plebeians went on strike until the tribune had been satisfied. In extreme cases, the plebeians threatened to secede and to establish their own nation.

The plebeians' earliest demand was to know the laws. Therefore, in 451 B.C.E., to avoid a secession of the plebeians, the Senate appointed a board of ten men, the decemvirs, to write down the existing laws. The result was the **Twelve Tables,** issued in 450 B.C.E., which became the basis for all later Roman law. One of Rome's most important contributions to western civilization is the concept of **rule of law,** the idea that governments and officials are subordinate to the law. Roman law represented not the will of the gods or the whims of godlike rulers, as in the Near East, but the collective will and wisdom of the people. Once the law was written down, the plebeians became more confident that it would be fairly enforced, and what was already a stable society became even more stable.

The Twelve Tables reveal much about how Roman society functioned. They dealt with trial procedures, inheritances, property ownership and transfer, lawsuits, and religious law. They reflect both the harsh nature of early Roman life and the Roman virtues of responsibility, discipline, fortitude, and frugality. Romans were expected to maintain proper decorum in times of stress, and it was decreed that "women shall not weep on account of a funeral." There was no place for nonproductive persons: another regulation stated, "A dreadfully deformed child shall be quickly killed." Serious crimes such as treason, arson, and perjury were punished by death. Some laws did appear to benefit less privileged persons. For example, a patron who "devised any deceit against his client" could be legally killed. But overall, the laws were designed to maintain the favored position of the patricians. One law specified that plebeian debtors could be loaded down with chains and sold as slaves, and another prohibited marriages between patricians and plebeians, blocking the one means by which members of a plebeian family could enter the aristocracy. The plebeians became so angered by such laws that they seceded. The patricians responded with laws that recognized the existence of the Council of the Plebs and guaranteed the personal safety of the tribunes of the plebs. At the same time, a new assembly, the Council of the People, was created, modeled on the Council of the Plebs but also including patricians.

Continued agitation by the most wealthy and influential plebeians soon brought the repeal of the ban on intermarriage. Plebeians married into patrician families, and the children of a plebeian woman who married a patrician were patricians. Plebeians also were permitted to hold military offices that gained them entry into the Senate and participation in its decision making. The patricians eventually acknowledged that to avoid future unrest they would have to give at least some plebeians a share in government, and they did so by allying themselves with the most wealthy and influential plebeians. A law of 367 B.C.E. declared that from then on, one consul had to be a plebeian. Subsequently, all other government offices also were opened up to plebeians. The Conflict of the Orders finally came to an end in 287 B.C.E., when the Hortensian Law gave the Council of the Plebs the right to pass laws binding on all the Roman people. These laws were introduced by the tribunes of the plebs, who, like the consuls, were expected to consult with the Senate before proposing any legislation. The result of the Conflict of the Orders was an evolution, just as had occurred in Greece, from an aristocracy, in which Rome was effectively governed by the patricians alone, to an oligarchy, in which both patricians and important plebeians served in the Senate and held high office.

The key to the success of Roman republican government lay in the willingness of the senators to share rule among themselves. But sharing rule was not always easy, for senators constantly competed with each other for status. Every five years, the censors drew up a list of senators in rank order, and every senator's ambition was to be the **princeps,** the "first man" on the list. Senators whose ancestors had been consuls became an inside group, called the nobles, who jealously monopolized access to this office. Only the most able non-nobles could be elected consuls, and someone who did so was called a **new man.** Though rare, the election of a new man demonstrated that an ambitious Roman man did have a chance to rise to the very top of Roman politics and society.

Going to War

The early years of the Republic were a struggle for survival as the Romans fought off Etruscan attempts to recapture the city and competed with neighboring Latins and Italians for control of the rich agricultural plain of Latium. The combined army of patricians and plebeians was able to defend Rome until 390 B.C.E., when a raiding party of Gauls from northern Italy attacked. The Gauls, more generally known as the

Twelve Tables   First written collection of Roman law, created by the decemvirs in 451–450 B.C.E.

rule of law   The idea that the law has higher authority than governments and officials.

princeps   (Latin for "first") The first man on the list of senators drawn up by the censors.

new man   A consul who did not have an ancestor who had been a consul.

A Roman copy of a Hellenistic statue shows a Gaul wearing a torque killing himself and wife so they would not be taken captive and enslaved. Many Greek and Roman statues of Celts show them dead or dying, reflecting the fear that the Celts created. Like many Gallic warriors, this one is portrayed in the nude, protected by the magical power of the torque that he wears around his neck. *(Erich Lessing/ Art Resource, NY)*

with naked six-foot-tall warriors wildly swinging their yard-long swords. At first, no Mediterranean people were able to resist them.

The Romans were completely dumbfounded by the wild and undisciplined charge of the howling Gauls. The Romans' tightly packed phalanx, a military formation they had adopted from the Greeks of southern Italy, collapsed, and the Romans fled. The Gauls then sacked and burned the city of Rome, departing only after they had exacted a large ransom. The Romans were determined that such a disaster would never happen again. It took them about fifty years to recover from the Gallic sack, after which they initiated a long series of military actions that ultimately resulted in Rome's becoming the most powerful nation in the Mediterranean world.

Rome's development as a world power has interested historians because the Romans got involved in so many wars and yet at first seemed uninterested in building an empire. The Romans could decide to go to war for several reasons. One was fear. Following the sack by the Gauls, the Romans were frightened by strong neighbors and sometimes made preemptive strikes against peoples they believed were becoming too powerful. In addition, to gain social and political status, Roman consuls often felt that they needed military glory and almost always voted for war if the opportunity arose. The Romans also took their treaty responsibilities seriously, and a Roman ally that was attacked could usually count on Rome to come to its

Celts, were an Indo-European people who inhabited the British Isles, **Gaul** (modern France), and the rest of Europe except for Greece and Italy. There were many independent Celtic groups, each governed either by a king or by a council of warrior aristocrats. Although the Celtic economy was based primarily on farming, the Celts also had a highly developed trading network, and Celtic metalwork was particularly prized. But it was for their fighting style that the Celts were best known. Celtic warriors wore an ornate metal ring called a torque, often of gold or silver, forged around their necks. Believing that their torques' magical powers would protect them from harm, the most enthusiastic warriors fought in the nude. Before a battle, Celtic warriors smeared wet lime into their hair to make it stand straight back when it dried and give them a more terrifying appearance. Celtic battles began with warriors leaping about and shouting insults at their enemy as they worked themselves up into the famous Celtic fury. Then came their terrifying charge,

Celts The people of inland Europe, also known as Gauls.

Gaul Modern France, homeland of the Gauls.

assistance. Occasionally, the Romans went to war to gain land for distribution to poor plebeians. Finally, of course, there were genuine threats, for the Romans had to resist when they were attacked by a foreign power.

Even though the Romans defeated a great many peoples in Italy and throughout the Mediterranean world, they at first were reluctant to take over, administer, or exploit the territory of the peoples they defeated. This policy was different from that of the Near Eastern and Greek peoples of the past, for several reasons. First, the Roman justifications for going to war, explained above, did not support empire building. In addition, the Romans had no tradition of conquest for economic or political gain. They did not believe that gaining territory contributed to the greater glory of Rome. Moreover, they recognized that building and keeping an empire would require a large professional army, something the Senate neither wanted nor could afford. The Roman government had very little tax revenue—taxes were very low, and there was no regular tax collection system—and the Roman economy was so undeveloped that the Republic did not issue coinage for more than two centuries after it began. Because there was no money to support a standing army, Rome's army was a citizen **militia.** Soldiers were recruited from among farmers and artisans only when a consul was assigned a war. They had to be able to supply their own weapons and largely to pay their own way as part of their civic duty. Thus, poor people were unable to serve in the army. When the war was over, the soldiers returned to civilian life, and the Senate did not have any responsibility for them. A citizen militia was not the kind of army that empire building required, and the Senate had no desire to expand Rome's government to administer an empire.

The Expansion of Rome

Shortly after 350 B.C.E., the Samnites, an Italian mountain people, began expanding west toward the Bay of Naples. Fearful of a threat to their security, the Romans fought three wars between 343 and 290 B.C.E. against the Samnites and their allies. After losing several battles, the Romans finally defeated a combined force of Samnites, Etruscans, and Gauls in 295 B.C.E., and the Samnites soon capitulated. Soon afterward, the Greeks of the southern Italian city of Tarentum, fearing Rome's growing power, summoned the able Greek general, King **Pyrrhus of Epirus,** to help them. Pyrrhus invaded Italy in 280 B.C.E. and won three hard-fought battles, but his losses were very heavy. His comment after one battle, "Another victory like this and I will be totally ruined," gave rise to the term Pyrrhic victory, meaning a victory so costly that one

might as well have lost. The losses of the Romans were even greater, but they simply refused to give up, and in 275 B.C.E., Pyrrhus withdrew and returned to Greece. The Greeks of southern Italy then made peace on Roman terms. In these campaigns, the Romans prevailed primarily because of their persistence and their willingness to take greater losses than their opponents. They lost more battles than they won, often because the consuls who led their armies were in office for only one year and not experienced generals.

Even though the Romans had defeated all the peoples of Italy by 268 B.C.E., they showed little interest in imposing direct control over them. Primarily, they wanted to keep their neighbors from posing a threat, and they did so in several ways. To be able to concentrate their forces quickly, they created a network of all-weather military roads. The first, the Appian Way, was begun in 312 B.C.E. and went from Rome to southern Italy. The Romans also occupied enough land to establish military colonies at strategic points such as mountain passes or river fords. These colonies also allowed the Romans to give land there to poor plebeians and thus make them wealthy enough for military service. The keystone of Roman foreign policy was to impose treaties on defeated enemies in which Rome was the patron and the enemy was the client. The former enemy remained independent but became a Roman ally. Whenever Rome went to war, its allies were expected to provide military units to assist the Roman legions, which were manned only by Roman citizens. This **Italian alliance** gave Rome access to a manpower reserve of close to a million men.

Rome soon became engaged in even bigger wars outside Italy. The first were with the powerful North African trading city of Carthage. The Carthaginians worshiped the goddess Tanit, who commanded that the first-born sons of Carthaginian families be sacrificed to her. Excavations of Carthaginian infant cemeteries testify that many devout Carthaginians observed this practice. During the third century B.C.E., Carthage attempted to gain control of the island of Sicily. The prospect of such a powerful neighbor only a few miles offshore from Italy worried the Romans. When Sicilian Greeks asked for Roman protection, a consul who was

militia   Military force of nonprofessional citizen soldiers.

Pyrrhus of Epirus   (318–272 B.C.E.) Greek king who fought the Romans between 280 and 275 B.C.E.

Italian alliance   Defeated cities and peoples of Italy who were required to follow Roman foreign policy and supply Rome with soldiers.

eager to win personal glory convinced the people to vote for war. Rome thus became committed to its first overseas conflict, the First **Punic War** (264–241 B.C.E.).

To get to Sicily, the Romans, who had little seafaring tradition, were compelled to create a navy. They won their first battle by simply running their ships alongside the Carthaginian ships, boarding them with soldiers, and effectively changing a sea battle into a land battle. The Carthaginians were not fooled again, but this unexpectedly easy victory only strengthened the Roman commitment to fight on until they had won. After a long war, the Carthaginians made peace in 241 B.C.E., agreeing to evacuate Sicily and to pay an **indemnity** of 3,200 talents of silver, for the Romans expected the defeated party to pay the cost of the war. The Romans then had to decide what to do about the territory Carthage had abandoned. Fearful of having the rich island of Sicily become another source of trouble, in 227 B.C.E., the Romans made it their first province, a foreign territory over which Rome assumed direct control. Two years later, Sardinia and Corsica, which in the past had been Carthaginian bases, became Rome's second province. Having no method for governing foreign territories, the Romans created two new praetors to serve as provincial governors. Otherwise, they did little with the new provinces, content simply to keep them from Carthaginian control.

Meanwhile, the fortunes of the Carthaginians revived under the leadership of **Hannibal**, one of the ablest generals of all time. After losing the First Punic War, the Carthaginians rebuilt their army using silver and Celtic mercenaries from Spain. In 218 B.C.E., after the Romans had attempted to interfere in Carthaginian-controlled Spain, Hannibal led an army of Celtic infantry, **Numidian** cavalry, and thirty-seven war elephants out of Spain, through the Alps, and into Italy, thus beginning the Second Punic War (218–201 B.C.E.), the most difficult war the Romans ever fought. Hannibal's goal was to break up Rome's Italian alliance. He quickly won three spectacular victories. At Cannae, in 216 B.C.E., a Roman army of more than 50,000 men was surrounded and virtually annihilated by Hannibal's smaller 30,000-man army. Subsequently, for fear of losing another battle, the Romans simply refused to fight Hannibal in Italy, and he marched about unopposed for another thirteen years.

Hannibal finally met his match in the Roman general **Scipio**. Scipio's father and uncle both had been killed fighting Hannibal, but Scipio was determined never to surrender. As a young man, he was placed in command of the Roman armies in Spain, where he gained a reputation for fair treatment of prisoners. By 206 B.C.E., Scipio had defeated three veteran Carthaginian armies and forced the Carthaginians to evacuate Spain. Chosen consul for the year 205 B.C.E., Scipio began training an army to invade Africa, which he did the next year. He convinced many Numidians to change sides, thus gaining some excellent cavalry. Scipio defeated the Carthaginians, who then recalled Hannibal from Italy. The final confrontation came in 202 B.C.E. at the Battle of Zama, where the Roman cavalry was able to slip behind the Carthaginian army and attack from the rear. Hannibal was defeated, and Scipio received the nickname "Africanus" ("the conqueror of Africa") in recognition of his victory. The next year, Carthage surrendered. The Romans did not take over any territory in Africa, but they did compel Carthage to give up Spain (which was made into two new Roman provinces), destroy its navy, and pay an indemnity of 20,000 talents. Scipio generously permitted Hannibal to live, but Carthage never again would be a strong military power.

The Romans looked back to the Second Punic War as their defining moment. They had never considered surrendering. All of Rome pulled together: Roman women donated their jewelry to the war effort, and contractors provided war supplies on credit. The war also demonstrated the strength of Rome's Italian alliance, for nearly all Rome's allies had stayed loyal. Rome now was the only power in the western Mediterranean.

The war also left Rome completely exhausted. Tens of thousands of soldiers had been killed, Italian property losses were staggering, and the Roman government was deep in debt. Nevertheless, Rome immediately was drawn into conflicts with two of the three great Hellenistic kingdoms to the east: Antigonid Macedonia, Seleucid Syria, and Ptolemaic Egypt. In 200 B.C.E., the Romans declared war on Macedonia because the Macedonians had made an alliance with Hannibal. Three years later, they soundly defeated the Macedonians and compelled them to pay a war indemnity, give up their navy, and evacuate their

---

Punic Wars   (from the Latin *Poenus,* "Phoenician") Series of three wars (264–241, 218–201, and 149–146 B.C.E.) that Rome fought against Carthage in North Africa.

indemnity   Monetary penalty imposed by the Romans on a defeated enemy.

Hannibal   (ca. 247–183 B.C.E.) Carthaginian general who invaded Italy in 218 B.C.E., beginning the Second Punic War.

Numidia   Region of western North Africa famous for horsemanship.

Scipio Africanus   (ca. 236–183 B.C.E.) Roman general who defeated Hannibal at the Battle of Zama in 202 B.C.E.

territory in Greece. Shortly thereafter, the Romans also defeated the Seleucids of Syria, who had frightened the Romans by invading Greece. The Seleucids were compelled to pay a large indemnity, give up their war elephants, and abandon their territories in Anatolia. In both cases, the Romans had the opportunity to take over foreign territory but chose not to do so. Their goal was simply to keep potential enemies weak. Then, in 171 B.C.E., it was rumored that the Macedonians planned to hire Celts to invade Italy. War again was declared, and the Macedonians were defeated in 168 B.C.E. This time the Romans took stronger measures to weaken Macedonia, dividing it into four independent countries. The Romans then went home, confident that the Macedonian threat finally had been eliminated.

But the wars still were not over. Carthage had rebuilt itself as an economic, although not as a military, power, creating jealousy in Rome. The hawkish senator **Cato the Elder,** an ambitious new man, ended each of his speeches in the Senate by declaring, "And I also think that Carthage must be destroyed." He got his wish in 149 B.C.E., when the Romans again attacked Carthage. The war dragged on until 146 B.C.E., when **Scipio Aemilianus,** the grandson by adoption of Scipio Africanus, captured the city in desperate house-to-house fighting. Many Carthaginians committed suicide by leaping into the burning temple of Tanit. In the same year, the Romans were victorious in yet another Macedonian war. At this point, the Roman attitude to foreign territories changed. Recognizing that allowing defeated enemies to remain independent caused problems later, the Romans changed their response in two ways. First, they taught a lesson to any people contemplating resistance by destroying two of the most famous cities of the Mediterranean world, Carthage in North Africa and Corinth in Greece. In addition, they annexed North Africa and Macedonia as new provinces and shortly after added the province of Asia in western Anatolia, and the southern part of Gaul. The building of what would become the Roman Empire now was well underway.

The denarius, first issued in 212 B.C.E., became the standard Roman silver coin. It was used by senators to glorify their families. This denarius, issued in 43 B.C.E. by the Brutus who assassinated Julius Caesar, commemorates the Brutus who was one of the first two Roman consuls in 509 B.C.E. The consul is accompanied by two lictors who bear the rods and axes symbolizing the consul's authority *(Snark/Art Resource, NY)*

their society and economy. They also were confronted by an influx of foreign cultural ideas, especially from Greece. Some Romans welcomed new cultural concepts; others saw them as a challenge to old Roman values. Administering the provinces effectively was difficult because the Senate was reluctant to make changes in the Roman system of government. Recruiting soldiers for the Roman army also became difficult. Efforts to deal with some of these problems met stiff resistance and flared into the first violence ever experienced in Roman politics.

The Transformation of Rome

By 120 B.C.E., Rome controlled territory extending from Spain to Anatolia. Its expansion had far-reaching

The Effects of Roman Expansion, 146–88 B.C.E.

⬇ How did Roman expansion create problems for the Romans?

⬇ What were the consequences of changes in Roman military recruiting policies?

The growth of Roman power had many consequences for Roman life. To cope with the acquisition of far-flung provinces, the Romans had to restructure

Cato the Elder (ca. 234–149 B.C.E.) Conservative Roman senator who represented old Roman values and opposed the assimilation of Greek culture.

Scipio Aemilianus (185–129 B.C.E.) Roman senator who defeated Carthage and favored the assimilation of Greek culture.

The Roman Forum was the center of Roman public life and contained temples and other public buildings. This view of the forum as it appears in the modern day shows several monuments initially built during the Republic. The remains of the house of the Vestal Virgins appear on the left. Three surviving columns of the ancient temple of Castor and Pollux, stand in front of the site of the basilica Julia, dedicated by Julius Caesar in 46 B.C.E., where the praetors heard legal cases. On the slopes of the Capitoline Hill in the background is the *tabularium*, the official records' hall. And on the far right stands the Senate house. *(Scala/Art Resource, NY)*

social, cultural, and economic effects. The influx of wealth from overseas brought the most noticeable changes. So many riches were seized from Macedonia in 168 B.C.E. that taxes on Roman citizens were eliminated. The Romans realized that provincial resources, such as the silver mines of Spain, could be made into a permanent source of income. Because of the financial opportunities created by Roman expansion, a new social class arose, the **equestrians,** who ranked just below the senators. They made fortunes in trade, manufacturing, moneylending, tax collecting, and selling supplies to the army. Senators, who preferred to invest in land, became even more wealthy than before through their service as provincial governors. Expansion also created the need for money to pay for it. A Roman silver coin, the **denarius,** was finally introduced in 212 B.C.E. when tremendous amounts of coinage were needed to meet the expenses of the Second Punic War. The denarius soon became the standard currency of the Mediterranean world.

The old Roman virtues of frugality and modesty gave way to taking pleasure in luxury and display. On one occasion, women protested against a law that no woman should own more than a half-ounce of gold, or wear multicolored clothing, or ride in a carriage in Rome. They blockaded the Forum and confronted the senators, engaging in an unprecedented form of political activism. The conservative consul Cato the Elder complained, "Our freedom is conquered by female fury, we even now let them meddle in the Forum," but the offensive law was repealed nonetheless.

equestrians (from Latin *eques,* a person wealthy enough to own a horse) Roman social class ranking just below the senators.

denarius Silver coin introduced by the Romans in 212 B.C.E.; it became the standard coin of the Mediterranean world.

New construction adorned the city of Rome. New temples were built, and old ones, such as the temple of Jupiter on the Capitoline Hill, were rebuilt on a grander scale. The first **basilica**, a large rectangular public building used for hearing legal cases, was built in the Forum. New aqueducts brought fresh water into Rome. For their building projects, the Romans used stone blocks, bricks, and concrete made from *pozzolana*, a fine, wear-resistant volcanic sand. They also made extensive use of the arch, the vault, and the dome, pioneering building types that would continue to be characteristic of western architecture in the Middle Ages, the Renaissance, and the modern day.

The Roman people came to expect expensive entertainments, which were held in honor of religious festivals or of military victories. One popular festival was the Saturnalia, a period of merriment held December 17–23 in honor of the god Saturn. People exchanged gifts, and slaves traded places with their masters. Chariot racing, borrowed from the Greeks and the Etruscans, attracted ever-larger crowds. Beginning in 211 B.C.E., an annual festival in honor of Apollo included two days of chariot racing. Races were held on racecourses known as **circuses,** and in the 170s B.C.E. the Circus Maximus, or "Greatest Circus," was rebuilt. Gladiatorial contests, which had been borrowed from the Etruscans, became increasingly popular. At first, gladiators fought only at the funerals of important persons. In 174 B.C.E., for example, the senator Flamininus, who had defeated Macedonia, celebrated his father's funeral by matching seventy-four gladiators against each other. Eventually, however, gladiatorial combats were put on purely for entertainment.

The Assimilation of Greek Culture

Roman expansion also exposed the Romans to foreign cultural influences, especially from Greece. Many Romans enthusiastically embraced Greek thought, literature, language, and culture. They patterned their educational system on the Greek model. Well-to-do Romans often hired or purchased a Greek schoolmaster for their children. Rich and poor boys and girls also attended private schools for a small fee. Grammar schools, for children aged twelve through sixteen, taught grammar and literature. Rhetoric schools, for children aged sixteen and up, taught public speaking, an important skill for a young man who wanted a career in public life. Corporeal punishment, such as hitting with a wooden switch, was regularly administered in the belief that it made students more attentive. Educated Roman youngsters grew up to be bilingual, often learning to read Greek before they

Some of the most important Roman laws were inscribed on stone or bronze tablets and posted where people could see them, either in Rome itself or in cities under Roman control. The Decree of the Senate on the Baccanalians, issued in 186 B.C.E., forbade the organized worship of the wine-god Bacchus and was inscribed on a bronze tablet that still exists. (*Kunsthistorisches Museum, Vienna*)

learned Latin. Many went on to pursue their studies in Greece.

Greek literature provided a model for Roman literature, which first developed in the second century B.C.E. Roman playwrights such as Plautus and the ex-slave Terence wrote Latin comedies based on Greek originals. The first histories of Rome, written in the years after 200 B.C.E., were written in Greek, not only by Romans but also by Greeks such as **Polybius,** a Greek hostage who was an eyewitness to the fall of Carthage. And the Stoic philosophy, which taught that doing one's duty was the highest virtue, found many followers in Rome. These undertakings were supported by influential Roman senators, such as Scipio Aemilianus.

basilica   A large rectangular public building with a large middle aisle and two side aisles.

circus   Long oval racecourse for chariot races and other forms of entertainment.

Polybius   (ca. 203–120 B.C.E.) Greek who was held as a hostage in Rome and wrote a history of Rome's rise to world power.

Not all Romans, however, thought that the acceptance of Greek culture was a good thing. Some conservative senators, such as Cato the Elder, feared that old Roman values would be destroyed by what he perceived as Greek luxury, extravagance, and immorality. He advised his son, "Take this as a prophecy: when those Greeks give us their writings, they will corrupt everything." As censor, Cato expelled from the Senate any senator who did not meet his moral standards. When Greek Epicurean philosophers, who Romans thought advocated a life of self-indulgence, visited Rome, Cato saw to it that they were deported. And in a personal protest against Greek literature, Cato wrote his own history of Rome in Latin. Later Roman authors followed his example, and by the end of the second century B.C.E., Latin had become an established literary language in its own right. The Romans even developed their own literary genre, satire, which used parody, obscenity, and abuse to project a critical but humorous view of society, morality, and personal behavior.

Romans' concerns about their values also surfaced with regard to foreign religious practices, which Rome also assimilated. At the end of the third century B.C.E., for example, the worship of the eastern mother goddess Cybele was introduced into Rome. The uninhibited practices associated with these religions caused anxiety in some conservative senators. In 186 B.C.E., a Roman consul received a report that worshipers of the wine god Bacchus were holding secret orgies. The Senate not only saw such behavior as a threat to conventional morality but also feared that the covert gatherings might lead to conspiracies against the government. According to the Roman historian Livy, many Romans were sentenced to death, with women being turned over to their families "so they could inflict the punishment in private." In spite of Roman resistance, however, Greek culture continued to infiltrate Rome.

Problems in the Provinces

The most significant consequence of Rome's wars was the acquisition of an increasing number of foreign provinces. By 146 B.C.E., these provinces had made Rome into an empire in everything but name. It soon became clear, however, that Rome was unable to cope with the administration of its foreign territories. Even though the Romans had the best intentions of fulfilling their responsibilities in the provinces, they lacked the institutions for doing so, and the conservative Senate saw no reason to alter Rome's form of government to accommodate the provinces. As a result, direct Roman administration was minimal. When a new province was created, a senatorial commission created a Law of the Province that established general administrative guidelines, but otherwise local customs were respected and native laws remained in effect. Roman governors held the office of either praetor or **proconsul** (a senator who in the past had held the office of consul). Governors served for two or three years and had very small staffs, consisting only of a quaestor to handle the finances and a few legates, deputies to whom their authority could be delegated.

The governors' primary responsibilities were to provide military defense, oversee the administration of justice, and collect taxes. Every effort was made to minimize expenses. Roman taxes were not excessive, but the Romans did expect the provinces to pay for themselves. To keep costs down, armies were sent to provinces only when needed. Because the governor did not have the staff to govern the province directly, local government was left in the hands of city governments. If a province did not already have cities, as in the case of much of Europe, the Romans created them. In Spain, for example, Romans redefined the territory of a Celtic people as belonging to a city created to serve as an administrative center. This process eventually would foster the urbanization of western Europe. Governors made a regular circuit of provincial cities to resolve legal disputes that could not be settled locally.

The rudimentary Roman provincial administration led to several problems. Provincial people had no rights in Rome, and the governor was the highest court of appeal. Corrupt governors therefore could enrich themselves by selling legal decisions to the highest bidder or by confiscating property, and there was nothing the provincials could do about it. Nor was there any established procedure by which provincials could become Roman citizens. But the provincials' greatest complaint involved tax collection. In some provinces tribute, a fixed annual sum, was collected and in others the **tithe,** a tenth of the crops. Because the Roman governor did not have staff to collect the taxes, the right to do so was auctioned off. Tax collection companies paid the Roman government a lump sum for tax-collection rights and then went out into the countryside and extorted as much

proconsul A senator who in the past had held the office of consul and later served as a provincial governer with the power of imperium.

tithe Form of taxation, one-tenth of everyone's crops, imposed on some Roman provinces; other provinces paid tribute, a fixed annual amount.

as they could. In provinces with the tithe, tax collectors known as publicans had a reputation for seizing large quantities of crops and calling it a tenth. Even if a governor protested against this practice, as many did, he did not have the workforce to prevent it.

At best, the Roman attitude toward the provinces could be called benign neglect. The Romans did not intend to exploit the provinces, and they did not make much money from them. Any corruption that arose benefited individual governors or profiteers, not the Roman government. The government simply did not have any centralized procedures for policing the provinces. One of the primary failures of the Republic was that it was unable to integrate the provinces, and their inhabitants, into the mainstream of Roman government and society.

The Gracchi and the Military Recruitment Crisis

Fighting wars and acquiring provinces created a need for armies, which led to another serious problem. Ever since the Samnite Wars, Roman armies had been fighting farther and farther from home for longer and longer periods. Because military recruiting policies required soldiers to be property owners, thousands of property-owning farmers were fighting far from home instead of farming, and Rome's agricultural economy suffered as a consequence. Moreover, many farmer-soldiers did not come back, and those who did often chose not to return to a life of drudgery on the farm and sold their land to senators, who always were looking to expand their landholdings. As a result, many landless plebeians settled in Rome, and senators acquired huge farms known as **latifundia.** These developments created a military recruitment crisis because there were fewer and fewer landowners eligible to serve in the army. The Senate could have addressed the crisis either by abandoning the property requirement for military service or by distributing state-owned public land to landless plebeians and thus making them eligible for military service. In typical fashion, however, the conservative Senate chose to do nothing.

Two brothers, Tiberius and Gaius Gracchus, attempted to deal with the recruitment problem. The **Gracchi,** as they were known, were related to the noblest Roman senatorial families. Their mother, Cornelia, was the daughter of Scipio Africanus, and after the death of her husband, she raised the two boys herself. She became the model Roman mother. According to one story, when a friend was showing off

her jewelry and asked to see Cornelia's jewelry, Cornelia called in her two sons and said, "These are my jewels." It came as a great surprise to many when these two distinguished senators attempted to reform the Roman landholding system

As a tribune of the plebs in 133 B.C.E., Tiberius Gracchus introduced legislation to distribute public land to poor plebeians in order to make them prosperous enough for military service. His proposal met great resistance from senators who had been renting public land and saw it as their personal property. Suspecting that the Senate would not pass his legislation, Tiberius took it directly to the Council of the Plebs, where it was passed and put into effect without first being discussed by the Senate. His ignoring of traditional procedures threatened the authority of conservative senators, who organized an armed mob that confronted Tiberius in the Forum. In the ensuing riot, Tiberius and several hundreds of his supporters were killed. Tiberius's younger brother Gaius then was elected as tribune in 123 B.C.E. and proposed additional reforms, including a law to confiscate land from senators and give it to poor plebeians. A year later, conservative senators organized another mob, and Gaius committed suicide rather than be captured alive. Over a thousand of his supporters reportedly were killed.

The deaths of the Gracchi and their supporters marked not only the first appearance of serious violence in republican politics but also the breakdown of the carefully cultivated cooperation among senators that had made the Republic work. Increasingly, senators looked out for their own self-interest as they competed to gain political influence and high office. Instead of working with the Senate, many ambitious senators now took their legislation directly to the assemblies, appealing to the urban poor by offering jobs, entertainment, subsidized food, free land, and reduced army service.

Marius and the Volunteer Army

The new land distribution policy did not meet the need for army recruits. The old recruitment system was sufficient as long as there were no large demands on it, but it broke down completely beginning around

---

latifundia   (in Latin, "wide-spread estates") Large estates belonging to Roman senators.

Gracchi   Tiberius (163–133 B.C.E.) and Gaius (154–122 B.C.E.) Gracchus, Roman reformers, ca. 133–122 B.C.E.

113 B.C.E. The first crisis came when two large groups of northern European Celts, the **Cimbri** and **Teutones,** arrived in southern Gaul looking for land and defeated one Roman army after another. At the same time, Rome went to war against the Numidian chieftain Jugurtha, whose army had massacred some Italian merchants, but Roman armies had little success against Jugurtha's hit-and-run tactics. In addition, there was a massive slave revolt in Sicily in 104 B.C.E. It was simply impossible to recruit enough soldiers to handle these emergencies.

The recruitment problem was solved by **Marius,** a member of a previously undistinguished equestrian family. After gaining a military reputation in Spain, Marius pursued a political career. As a newcomer, he had a difficult time and lost several elections, but he persevered. He also married Julia, a member of the distinguished Julius Caesar family. In 108 B.C.E., Marius was elected consul and thus became a new man. He was appointed to take command in Africa, and to raise an army he enlisted men who had no property at all. Other generals soon did the same, thereby creating a **volunteer army** of professional soldiers whose livelihood was based on their military service. Soldiers no longer fought to protect their homes, but for pay and any other kinds of personal profit. When the Senate refused to pay for these new armies or to reward the soldiers with land grants after the war was over, these responsibilities were left to the generals. The armies, therefore, began to feel more loyalty toward their generals than toward the state. Using this new army, Marius soon was able to defeat Jugurtha, the Cimbri and Teutones, and the Sicilian slaves. By 101 B.C.E., the military threats to Rome had been averted, and the military recruitment crisis was over. But Rome was now left with an even more serious problem—armies whose loyalty to the state was dependent on the goodwill of the senatorial generals who commanded them.

Military recruitment policies also created another problem for the Republic. Over time, Rome's Italian allies had provided an ever greater percentage of Rome's armies, increasing from half in the third century B.C.E. to two-thirds by the early first century B.C.E. The allies believed they were bearing more of the burden for Rome's wars but sharing less in the benefits. These concerns grew into Italian demands to be granted Roman citizenship. The Senate repeatedly refused, resulting in a massive revolt of the Italian allies in 90 B.C.E. The Romans could not hope to win such a war and once again showed that they could change if they had to. Citizenship was quickly granted to the Italians, and the fighting soon stopped. Nearly all of the free people living in Italy thus became Roman citizens. This unification of Italy, even though it was long in coming, provides another example of the long Roman tradition of being able to make outsiders into insiders.

The End of the Republic, 90–27 B.C.E.

↓ In what ways did senators put their own interests ahead of those of the Republic?

↓ What caused the fall of the Roman Republic?

By 90 B.C.E., the Republic faced grave problems that the Senate had been both unwilling and unable to deal with. The most serious problem was ambitious and powerful senators who controlled large armies. Although these senators tried to maintain their duty to Rome, too often their conflicts erupted into civil war. In the end, contests among ambitious senators led to the collapse of Roman republican government and Rome was left under the control of a single powerful general.

Sulla's Example

Following the Italian revolt, the Roman Republic confronted three overwhelming problems: ineffective administration of the provinces, lack of control over the volunteer army, and ambitious senators who put their personal interests ahead of the best interests of Rome. Dissatisfaction with provincial administration was especially widespread in prosperous provinces such as Sicily and Asia in Anatolia, where there was more opportunity for corruption. In 88 B.C.E., resentment of tax collection methods boiled over into open revolt in the province of Asia, providing an opening for Mithridates, the ambitious king of Pontus on the southeastern coast of the Black Sea, to invade the Roman province. Eighty thousand Romans were said to have been murdered on a single day, and a Roman general was executed by having molten gold poured down his throat while being told, "And now let the Roman thirst for gold be satisfied."

Cimbri and **Teutones** Celtic peoples who attacked Roman territory beginning in 113 B.C.E.; finally defeated by Marius in 101 B.C.E.

Marius (157–86 B.C.E.) Roman general who created the volunteer army ca.108 B.C.E.

volunteer army Professional Roman army comprised of men without any property.

Back in Rome, the Senate assigned the war against Mithridates to the consul **Sulla,** a shrewd member of a penniless patrician family who was hoping to restore his family's fortunes. Marius, however, who had hoped to get the command for himself, convinced the Council of the Plebs to transfer the command to him. Rather than accepting this disappointment, Sulla appealed to his army for support. His soldiers seized Rome, and Sulla forced the Senate to reconfirm his command. Sulla then sailed off to the east, where he eventually defeated Mithridates. Five years later, in 83 B.C.E., Sulla returned and again seized Rome. To retain absolute power, he had himself appointed dictator, but without the customary six-month limitation. In order to raise the money to pay off his army, he issued the **proscriptions,** a list of fifteen hundred enemies condemned to execution and the loss of their property. Before his death in 78 B.C.E., Sulla attempted to strengthen the authority of the Senate to prevent anyone else from doing what he had done, but it was his example of using an army to take control of the government that was his most important legacy.

Other ambitious senators also discovered uses for an army. Away from Rome, military victories allowed a general to gain clients in the provinces, to acquire wealth, and to win glory, and by doing so to fulfill Roman ideals of virtue. In Rome, soldiers could be used to manipulate votes in the Senate and assemblies. The only way to get authorization to recruit an army was to be assigned a war somewhere in the provinces. Ambitious senators therefore became even more eager for military commands.

Late Republican Politics

After Sulla's death, three ambitious senators struggled for power: **Crassus,** the richest man in Rome; **Pompey,** a young supporter of Sulla; and **Julius Caesar,** a member of an old patrician family. The next crisis for the Republic was another consequence of Roman expansion. Hundreds of thousands of war captives had been sold in Italy as slaves. Those with useful skills could look forward to a comfortable urban life and eventual freedom, but unskilled slaves were considered no more than "speaking tools," and large numbers were put to work, and often badly treated, in the fields of senatorial *latifundia*. Cato the Elder recommended that agricultural slaves be bought cheaply, often as war captives, fed little, worked to death, and then replaced with additional cheap slaves. Occasionally, slaves revolted and were brutally punished. This was the case in the slave revolt begun by **Spartacus** in 73 B.C.E. (see

Choice). Crassus was assigned the war against the slaves, raised his own volunteer army, and suppressed the revolt with great severity. This victory made Crassus one of the most powerful senators in Rome, but it also made the Senate reluctant to grant him another military command that would enable him to become even more powerful.

Pompey had gained a military reputation as a supporter of Sulla; for his enthusiastic execution of Sulla's enemies he was nicknamed "the Teenage Butcher." In 67 B.C.E., he was assigned to wipe out the pirates who infested the Mediterranean. He swept from Gibraltar to Anatolia, clearing out the pirates as he went. In the following year, he undertook and won another war against Mithridates. He then abolished the Seleucid kingdom and made Syria into a Roman province. He also annexed part of the Jewish kingdom, leaving the rest in the hands of a Jewish **client king,** who owed his position to Rome. When he returned home, Pompey discovered that the Senate was so jealous of his successes that it refused to approve his organization of Syria and Judaea and to grant land to his army veterans.

An ambitious senator who made his reputation not in the army but with his legal and oratorical talents was **Cicero,** who came from a previously undistinguished equestrian family. After a string of successful court cases, he was elected consul as a new man for the year 63 B.C.E. The senatorial conservatives had supported Cicero because they preferred him to his opponent Catiline, who was appealing to the poor by proposing to cancel all their debts. The disappointed Catiline then formed a conspiracy to overthrow the government. The conspirators raised

Sulla   (ca.138–78 B.C.E.) Roman senator who used his army to overthrow the government in 88 B.C.E.

proscriptions   List of enemies published by Sulla.

Crassus   (ca.115–53 B.C.E.) Very rich senator, member of the First Triumvirate.

Pompey   (106–48 B.C.E.) Excellent general, member of the First Triumvirate.

Julius Caesar   (100–44 B.C.E.) Member of the First Triumvirate who conquered Gaul and seized control of Rome after a civil war.

Spartacus   (d. 71 B.C.E.) Thracian slave who led a revolt of slaves against Rome in 73 B.C.E.

client king   Foreign ruler named by and dependent on the Romans.

Cicero   (106–43 B.C.E.) Roman senator known as an excellent speaker who was consul in 63 B.C.E. and suppressed the conspiracy of Catiline.

an army, and Cicero himself narrowly escaped being assassinated. In a series of famous speeches, Cicero warned the Senate about Catiline's plans, and Catiline fled. Cicero had Catiline's supporters in Rome arrested and illegally executed without a trial, and Catiline himself then was defeated and killed. This incident demonstrates that Roman politics had reached the point where any ambitious senator was willing to act illegally.

The third powerful general of this period was Julius Caesar, a member of a patrician family supposedly descended from the goddess Venus. Caesar was the nephew of Sulla's enemy Marius and had barely escaped after his name appeared on Sulla's proscription list. His political career therefore started slowly, but he still had great ambitions. Once, in his early thirties, he burst into tears when reading about Alexander the Great. When asked what was wrong, he replied that at his age Alexander had conquered the world, whereas he, Caesar, had not yet done anything memorable. Caesar was popular with the people, and in 60 B.C.E. he was elected consul for the next year. Like any ambitious senator, he wanted to be assigned a province where he would be able to recruit a large army and gain military glory. The Senate, however, insultingly assigned him "the cattle trails of Italy" as his province.

The Triumvirates

Crassus, Pompey, and Caesar all had been disrespected by the Senate. In 60 B.C.E., therefore, they formed an unofficial alliance known as the First **Triumvirate,** whereby they agreed to use their influence on one another's behalf. As consul, Caesar saw to it that Pompey's legislation was passed and that land was given to his soldiers. Caesar himself was reassigned two provinces in Gaul, giving him an opening for military adventures to the north. And Crassus, who desired to refurbish his own military standing, eventually was granted a military command against the Parthians in the east. The triumvirs thus controlled affairs in Rome by cooperating and avoiding competition with one another. Conservative senators were troubled by this arrangement but could do nothing about it.

In 58 B.C.E., Caesar took his army to Gaul, where he remained for nine years. One of the best generals of antiquity, Caesar played off one Celtic people against another and ultimately defeated them all. His reports of his campaigns, the *Gallic Wars,* are one of the best historical works of antiquity. By 50 B.C.E., Caesar had annexed all of Gaul up to the Rhine River, gained

great wealth, and created a battle-hardened army. Meanwhile, Crassus waged a disastrous war against the Parthians in 54 B.C.E. His army became trapped in the sands of Mesopotamia, Crassus himself was killed in a skirmish, and thirty thousand of his troops were killed or enslaved. Crassus's head ended up being used as a stage prop in a production of a Greek play in the Parthian capital.

In Rome, Cicero and other senators turned Pompey against Caesar by playing on his vanity. In 50 B.C.E., with Pompey's support, the Senate ordered Caesar to disband his army and return to Rome as a private citizen. Caesar realized that if he did so, he probably would be killed by his enemies. He therefore decided to bring his army back to Rome with him. In 49 B.C.E. he led his army across the shallow Rubicon River, the boundary between Gaul and Italy, an act that automatically put him in rebellion against the Roman state. Pompey and his supporters fled to Greece to prepare their own army. Caesar soon followed, and at the Battle of Pharsalus in 48 B.C.E. Pompey was defeated. Pompey fled to Egypt, the last independent Hellenistic kingdom, where King Ptolemy XIII, thinking to do Caesar a favor, beheaded him. But when Caesar arrived, he was not pleased that an Egyptian king had murdered a distinguished Roman senator. He therefore deposed Ptolemy in favor of Ptolemy's sister (and wife) Cleopatra. After his return to Rome, Caesar, like Sulla before him, had to decide what his official position would be. He attempted to make his one-man rule look legal by regularly serving as consul and by holding the position of dictator for life. But his unconstitutional policies and monopolization of high offices aroused hostility and jealousy in several senators, who conspired against him. At a meeting of the Senate on the Ides of March (March 15), 44 B.C.E., Caesar was stabbed to death.

Caesar's assassins presumed that after he was gone, the old Republic would be restored, but they were mistaken. Two of Caesar's generals, **Lepidus** and Marcus Antonius (known to us as **Mark Antony**),

---

triumvirate   A group of three men; the First Triumvirate (Caesar, Crassus, and Pompey) was formed in 60 B.C.E., and the Second Triumvirate (Antony, Lepidus, and Octavian) in 43 B.C.E.

Lepidus   (d. 13 B.C.E.) One of Caesar's generals and a member of the Second Triumvirate.

Mark Antony   (ca. 80–30 B.C.E.) One of Caesar's generals and a member of the Second Triumvirate; defeated by Octavian, committed suicide in 30 B.C.E.

The life and death of Cleopatra, the last queen and pharaoh of Egypt, fascinated the people of the Roman world, and she often appeared in artwork. This fresco from the Via Latina catacombs in Rome shows Cleopatra committing suicide as she holds a poisonous asp to her breast. Thus, even Christians were fascinated by the career of Cleopatra. *(Photo © Held Collection/The Bridgeman Art Library)*

made an alliance against the assassins with **Octavian,** Caesar's eighteen-year-old grandnephew, whom Caesar had adopted in his will. The three divided up Caesar's armies and in 43 B.C.E. formed the Second Triumvirate. To honor Caesar's memory, they had him **deified,** or declared to be a god, by the Senate. Initially, Roman politicians thought little of young Octavian, but he soon showed that he possessed a political shrewdness well beyond his years. The triumvirs seized control of the government, and Cicero, who had delivered a series of speeches against Antony, was murdered. In 42 B.C.E., the assassins were defeated at the Battle of Philippi in Macedonia. Another struggle then began among the triumvirs to see who would gain sole control of the state.

Lepidus soon was forced to retire, and Antony and Octavian divided up the Roman world, Octavian re-

ceiving Italy and the west, and Antony obtaining Syria and the east. Antony spent most of his time in Egypt, where Queen Cleopatra helped him to build up his forces. In 31 B.C.E., Octavian and Antony attacked each other, and their armies met at the Battle of Actium on the western coast of Greece. Antony and Cleopatra were defeated and fled back to Egypt. The following year, 30 B.C.E.., Octavian and his massive army arrived in Egypt. Antony and Cleopatra,

Octavian (63 B.C.E.–14 C.E.) Adopted son of Caesar and a member of the Second Triumvirate who gained control of the Roman world in 30 B.C.E.

deification An act whereby the Senate declared that a deceased Roman was a god.

not wishing to be disgraced by being displayed in Octavian's triumphal procession, committed suicide, and Octavian annexed Egypt as a new province. Once again, a powerful senatorial general had been able to use his army to eliminate all his rivals and to take control of the entire Roman world. The civil wars had demonstrated that the Republic could no longer work, and by 27 B.C.E., it had been replaced by the Roman Empire.

Society and Culture at the End of the Republic

By the end of the Republic, Rome had experienced many social and cultural changes. Roman women now enjoyed a freedom that would have been unthinkable in the past, and high-ranking women were even more visible in public life. In one famous case, the Second Triumvirate attempted to tax the wealthiest women of Rome, whereupon the women assembled in the Forum. There, Hortensia, the daughter of the orator Hortensius, delivered a speech in which she argued, "If we have no share in government or army commands or public office, why should we pay taxes?" The triumvirs responded by reducing the tax on women and raising that on wealthy men.

Latin literary culture experienced its **Golden Age,** and some Latin writers made their reputations solely on the basis of their literary accomplishments. These included the poets **Catullus,** known for his love poetry, and **Lucretius,** who gained fame with a lengthy poem called *On the Nature of Things,* which described the Epicurean view of the universe. But many late Roman writers also were active in public life because the senatorial ideal included the expectation that a senator would engage in literary activities. Politicians such as Caesar and Cicero also were well-known authors. Cicero, in fact, was later considered by many to be Rome's greatest writer, publishing not only speeches and letters but also works on oratory and philosophy. Roman politicians and generals thus also saw themselves as the representatives of Roman culture and values.

> **Golden Age**   Period of Latin literature beginning around 75 B.C.E. and represented by writers such as Cicero and Caesar.
> **Catullus**   (ca. 84–54 B.C.E.) Writer of Latin love poetry.
> **Lucretius**   (ca. 94–49 B.C.E.) Epicurean philosopher who wrote the poem *On the Nature of Things.*

Summary

Review Questions

↑ What kinds of beliefs and practices identified a person as being Roman?

↑ How did Rome grow from a small village to be the strongest power in the Mediterranean?

↑ What were some of the reasons for the failure of the Republic?

After its founding as a small farming village on the banks of the Tiber River in the eighth century B.C.E., Rome slowly grew to become the ruler of the entire Mediterranean world. Early in their history, the Romans learned to assimilate the cultures of other peoples, such as the Etruscans to the north and the Greeks to the south. Their shared values and sense of social responsibility gave the Romans a sense of community that permitted them to solve internal disputes peacefully, without resorting to violence. Their

concept of rule by law is one of their most important contributions to western civilization.

Under constant threat of attack, the early Romans also developed an army that was used not only for defense but also to attack peoples who were seen as threats. Eventually, the Romans defeated all the peoples in Italy and the Mediterranean world. Although they initially were reluctant to take over direct administration of the peoples they had defeated, by 30 B.C.E. they had annexed nearly all the lands surrounding the Mediterranean Sea.

Numerous foreign wars and the acquisition of overseas provinces had profound effects on Roman society and institutions. The Romans were exposed to many new cultural influences, especially from Greece and the east. Roman expansion created problems of military recruitment and provincial administration that the conservative Senate was unable to deal with. The old Roman virtues of duty and modesty were superseded by military ambition, as powerful senators put their personal interests ahead of the best interests of the state as a whole. Nevertheless, even in pursuit of personal glory, Roman senators always attempted to adhere to standards of Roman virtue and strove to show that they were good Romans. Generals such as Sulla and Julius Caesar saw themselves as Roman senators, not as kings or autocrats.

Contests between these powerful senators with their large armies brought strife and civil war to the Republic. Sulla, Caesar, and Octavian all used their armies to gain sole control of the Roman government, and all confronted the question of what their role in the government would be. By 27 B.C.E. the Roman republic was at an end. Governing the Roman world had become the responsibility of Octavian, the adopted son of Julius Caesar and the final victor in the civil wars.

← **Thinking Back, Thinking Ahead** →

How did the opportunities for the Roman people to participate in government compare with such opportunities for Greek and Near Eastern peoples?

ECHO

From Appian Way to Interstate Highway

The marvels of Roman engineering are most spectacularly evident in Rome's roads and bridges. In the past, Mediterranean peoples had used the sea for transportation and communication. But the Romans realized that to concentrate military resources quickly, it also was necessary to have a road system. The first military road was the Appian Way, begun in 312 B.C.E., which connected Rome to southern Italy. Eventually a network of roads radiating from Rome reached northern Italy, Gaul, Spain, and the rest of the Roman world. Roman roads were well-drained, with foundations of crushed stone several feet deep topped with cut-stone pavements. They were built largely by Roman soldiers.

More than twenty centuries later, the United States also discovered a need for a military road system. In 1956, construction of a National Defense Highway System was authorized by President Dwight D. Eisenhower to provide for the speedy concentration of military resources and the rapid evacuation of cities in case of nuclear attack. Plans called for the creation of some forty-two thousand miles of high-speed, multi-lane, limited-access highways, which were seen as much less vulnerable to bombing than railroads. The final link in the original system—the largest government public works project ever undertaken—was completed in 1993. Construction continues on additional stretches of the interstate highway system, which has been called one of the Seven Wonders of the United States.

As in ancient Rome, the road networks built by the U.S. government for military purposes came to be used primarily for personal and commercial purposes. Both networks led not only to increased economic development but also to expanded cultural interactions among the different sections of vast territories. But there is one big difference between the two systems. Roman roads and bridges have stood the test of time. During World War II, for example, General George Patton's tanks used several Roman bridges in Italy. The spectacular Rome bridge at Alcantara, Spain, continues to be used today, as does the aqueduct at Nîmes in France. But U.S. interstate highways are in a constant state of disrepair, resulting not only in travel delays but also in a proliferation of unanticipated repair expenditures.

Suggested Readings

Boatwright, Mary T., Daniel J. Gargola, and Richard J. A. Talbert. *The Romans: From Village to Empire.* Oxford: Oxford University Press, 2004. The rise of Rome, with particular attention given to Rome's early history.

Bradley, Keith. *Slavery and Society at Rome.* Cambridge, England: Cambridge University Press, 1994. A thorough discussion of slavery in the Roman world, including the significance of the revolt of Spartacus.

Cary, Max, and Howard H. Scullard. *A History of Rome Down to the Reign of Constantine.* 3rd ed. New York: Bedford/St. Martin's Press, 1976. A massive and detailed standard survey of the full extent of Roman history.

Crawford, Michael H. *The Roman Republic.* 2nd ed. Cambridge, Mass.: Harvard University Press, 2006. A survey of Roman Republican history from an expert on Roman coinage.

Errington, Richard M. *The Dawn of Empire: Rome's Rise to World Power.* Ithaca, N.Y.: Cornell University Press, 1972. The story of how Rome's armies conquered a larger and larger part of the Mediterranean world.

Lintott, Andrew. *The Constitution of the Roman Republic.* New York: Oxford University Press, 2003. The legal basis for the functioning of the government of the Roman Republic.

Syme, Ronald. *The Roman Revolution.* Oxford: Oxford University Press, 1939. A classic account of the role played by ambitious senators in the fall of the Roman Republic.

Websites

Vast collection of images and primary and secondary sources related to Roman history, **LacusCurtius,** at http://penelope.uchicago.edu/Thayer/E/Roman/home.html

Participatory website with extensive information on Roman history, life, and geography, **The Roman World,** at http://vlib.iue.it/history/europe/ancient_rome/index.html

On the Etruscans, including their origins and their language, **Etruscology,** at http://etruskisch.de/pgs/pn.htm

The Roman Empire, 27 B.C.E.–284 C.E.

CHAPTER OUTLINE

1500 B.C.E.	1000 B.C.E.	500 B.C.E.	1 B.C.E./1 C.E.

		14 C.E. Death of Augustus Roman Peace begins	60 Revolt of Boudicca	79 Eruption of Mount Vesuvius destroys Pompeii
27 B.C.E. Roman Empire begins		ca. 33 Jesus is crucified	69 Flavian Dynasty begins	96 Antonine Dynasty begins

40	20	0	20	40	60	80	100	120

Note: C.E. means "common era."

The Roman Empire in 117 C.E.

At its maximum extent, the Roman Empire stretched from Scotland to the Persian Gulf. The empire surrounded the Mediterranean Sea, which the Romans referred to as "Our Sea." Do you think that the Roman Empire was land-oriented or sea-oriented?

Roman territory, 44 B.C.E.
Territory added to Roman Empire by death of Augustus, 14 C.E.
Territory added by death of Hadrian, 138 C.E.
Territory gained and lost, with dates held
Parthian Empire
Major battle

Map Labels

York
BRITAIN
St. Albans
Colchester
London
GERMANIA (4–9 C.E.)
LOWER GERMANY
Cologne
Teutoberg Forest 9 C.E.
BELGICA
Bonn
Mainz
Paris
Alesia 52 B.C.E.
LUGDUNENSIS
Strasbourg
UPPER GERMANY
GAUL
RAETIA
Vienna
AQUITANIA
Lyons
ALPS
NORICUM
Budapest
DACIA (107–272 C.E.)
Bordeaux
NARBONENSIS
Milan
CISALPINE GAUL
PANNONIA
Belgrade
MOESIA
Nimes
Narbonne
Marseilles
Arretium
ITALY
Rome
DALMATIA
THRACE
Byzantium
BITHYNIA AND PONTUS
ARMENIA (114–117 C.E.)
SPAIN
TARRACONENSIS
CORSICA
Ostia
MACEDONIA
Salonica
CAPPADOCIA
ASSYRIA (116–117 C.E.)
LUSITANIA
Tarragona
SARDINIA
Pompeii
Mt. Vesuvius
Brundisium
ANATOLIA
GALATIA
MESOPOTAMIA (115–117 C.E.)
PARTHIA
Mérida
EPIRUS
Actium 31 B.C.E.
ASIA
Pergamum
CILICIA
Tarsus
Antioch
Palmyra
Córdoba
BALEARIC IS.
SICILY
Corinth
Athens
Ephesus
PAMPHYLIA
Ctesiphon
Seleucia
BAETICA
Syracuse
ACHAEA
LYCIA
SYRIA
Carthage
Malta
RHODES
CYPRUS
Damascus
MAURETANIA
NUMIDIA
AFRICA PROCONSULARIS
CRETE
JUDAEA
Jerusalem
Petra
Leptis
Cyrene
Alexandria
ARABIA
NORTH AFRICA
CYRENAICA
EGYPT
BAHRIYA OASIS
SAHARA
ARABIAN DESERT

North Sea
Baltic Sea
ATLANTIC OCEAN
Elbe
Vistula
Dnieper
Don
Volga
Caspian Sea
BOSPORAN KINGDOM
CAUCASUS MTS.
Rhone
Rhine
Ebro
Po
Danube
Adriatic Sea
Black Sea
Mediterranean Sea
Red Sea
Nile
Euphrates
Tigris

0   200   400 Km.
0   200   400 Mi.

---

500 C.E.   1000 C.E.   1500 C.E.   2000 C.E.

193 Severan Dynasty begins
212 Caracalla's citizenship grant
235 Imperial crisis begins
284 Imperial crisis ends

140   160   180   200   220   240   260   280   300

Choice

Boudicca

Some of the strongest resistance to Roman expansion came from the Celts. In Britain, Celtic resistance was led by Boudicca, queen of the Iceni. In 1905, this bronze sculpture showing Boudicca and her two daughters was erected in London to symbolize all British resistance against invaders. (Courtesy, Gary Houston)

Boudicca Chooses to Revolt Against Rome

During the early years of the Roman conquest of Britain, Boudicca, the queen of the Celtic people known as the Iceni, decided to lead a revolt against the mighty Roman Empire. Boudicca's husband, Prasutagus, had been a client king whom the Romans had allowed to continue to rule as long as he acknowledged Roman authority. Prasutagus had hoped to leave his kingdom to his two daughters when he died, but he was afraid the Romans would simply annex it. In his will he therefore left half his kingdom to the emperor Nero, hoping that Nero would then allow his daughters to rule the rest. But Prasutagus's plan failed. According to the Roman historian Tacitus, after Prasutagus's death in 60 C.E., "the kingdom was ransacked by soldiers as if it was conquered territory. The king's wife Boudicca was beaten, and his daughters were raped. The leaders of the Iceni were stripped of their property, and those close to the king were enslaved." The Romans had decided to demoralize the Iceni in every way that they could, using rape to humiliate their leaders, and to occupy the entire kingdom.

Boudicca, whose name may be derived from Boudiga, the Celtic goddess of victory, took over the leadership of the Iceni. She faced a difficult dilemma: she could permit the Romans to loot and occupy the kingdom, or she could rebel. If she led a revolt, she knew the odds were against her, for almost all past resistance against Roman occupation had failed. But she also would have known of the victory of Arminius, who had successfully resisted the Romans in Germany forty years earlier. Unwilling to suffer further disgrace at the hands of the Romans, Boudicca chose to revolt. She convinced other Celtic peoples to do the same, and at first the rebels had great success. The Roman city of Colchester was captured and the inhabitants slaughtered. One Roman legion was ambushed and destroyed, and another was so terrified that it hid in camp and refused to march against the rebels. Paulinus, the Roman commander in Britain, evacuated London, which the Celts then sacked and burned in a fire so hot that a ten-inch layer of melted red clay still can be found fifteen feet below London's streets. The only other Roman city in Britain, St. Albans, also was destroyed. In the end, the Celts were said to have killed 70,000 Romans and Roman sympathizers, and it appeared that their uprising would succeed.

Paulinus then gathered what was left of the Roman army. In the decisive battle, 10,000 Romans faced nearly 100,000 Celtic warriors accompanied by family members and encumbered by wagons filled with loot. According to Tacitus, Boudicca, riding in her chariot with her daughters in front of her, addressed her army thus:

> Just as I have summoned each of the peoples, it also is customary for the Britons to be led by women in war. I come to avenge not my kingdom and riches but my lost liberty, my wounded body, and my ravished daughters.

The lusts of the Romans have grown to the point that they respect the bodies of no one; they leave untouched neither old age nor undefiled virginity. Now, the gods of avenging justice are at hand. One legion that dared to fight us already has been destroyed; the others have fled or are hiding in their camps. We must conquer in the line of battle or fall. That is the fate of this woman; let men live on as slaves if they wish.

The wild Celtic charge then was met by the disciplined Romans, who were drawn up on a hillside with forests protecting their flanks and rear. The Britons were thrown back, became entangled in their own wagons, and then were slaughtered. It was said that 80,000 Celts were killed, but only 400 Romans.

Boudicca, like Cleopatra before her, committed suicide to avoid the disgrace of being paraded in a triumph in Rome. After this last attempt at independence, the British Celts accommodated themselves to Roman rule. In modern times, Boudicca, also known as Boadicea, became the symbol of British resistance to any foreign invader.

Introduction

The empire Boudicca was attempting to resist began in 27 B.C.E., when Octavian, the winner of the civil wars of the Roman Republic, received the title of augustus, which he then used as his name. As the first Roman emperor, Augustus created the principate, the first phase of the Roman Empire. He ensured that he and his successors were able to maintain control of the army. He created a system of frontier defenses. He gained the support of the Senate by claiming that he had restored the Republic and was sharing power with the senators. He gained the support of the people in the provinces by allowing them the opportunity to become Roman citizens. The empire incorporated many diverse peoples. Some peoples willingly opted to come under Roman authority. Others, such as Boudicca and the Britons, momentarily resisted. But ultimately a multitude of peoples were gathered peacefully under Roman rule.

The Roman emperors created the most successful empire that the western world had yet known. What made it work was the belief of its inhabitants that the best interests of the empire were their own best interests. The first two centuries of the Roman Empire are known as the Roman Peace. The empire was well governed, well defended, and economically prosperous. People throughout the empire lived in peace and harmony and felt they shared in the benefits and opportunities the empire had to offer. It was possible for provincials to rise in society and even to become emperor. A common Mediterranean culture gave people a sense of shared identity, especially in cities.

The most important development during the Roman Empire was the rise of Christianity, a religion that grew out of Judaism and spread from Palestine throughout the Roman world. Ease of travel during the Roman Peace facilitated the spread of new religious ideas, and Christianity filled spiritual and social needs that other religions failed to address. It developed a large following, especially in urban areas and among underprivileged people. But some of its beliefs and practices brought it into conflict with the Roman government, leading to occasional persecutions.

By the third century, however, new problems, including economic decline and an unruly military, confronted the empire, problems that the methods introduced by Augustus could no longer effectively solve. The result was a period of imperial crisis that nearly destroyed the empire.

Augustus and the Creation of the Roman Empire, 27 B.C.E.–14 C.E.

↓ How did Augustus attempt to unify the Roman Empire?
↓ How did Roman government function during the principate?

The year 27 B.C.E. marks the beginning of the Roman Empire and the beginning of the reign of Augustus, the first Roman emperor. Augustus was a singularly talented administrator who was largely responsible for establishing the principate, as the first phase of

Chronology

31 B.C.E. Octavian defeats Antony and Cleopatra at Battle of Actium	**69–96** Flavian dynasty rules Roman Empire
30 B.C.E. Cleopatra and Antony commit suicide	**79** Eruption of Mount Vesuvius destroys Pompeii
27 B.C.E. Roman Empire begins when the Senate gives Octavian the title of Augustus	**96–192** Antonine dynasty rules Roman Empire
27 B.C.E.–68 C.E. Julio-Claudian dynasty rules Roman Empire	**193–235** Severan dynasty rules Roman Empire
9 C.E. Germans defeat Romans at Teutoberg Forest	**203** Perpetua is martyred for being a Christian
14 Death of Augustus	**212** Caracalla grants Roman citizenship to everyone but slaves
14–192 Peace and prosperity prevail during the Roman Peace	**227** New Persian Empire begins
ca. 33 Jesus of Nazareth is crucified	**235** Imperial crisis begins
60 Boudicca leads British revolt against Roman Empire	**250** Decius institutes loyalty oath
64 Great fire burns part of Rome	**270** Aurelian begins to restore the Roman Empire
	284 Imperial crisis ends
	Note: C.E. means "common era."

the Roman Empire is known. He shrewdly gained the support of both the army and the Senate. He created an image of the emperor as the embodiment of Roman virtue and of Rome itself. The measures he introduced not only gave him the powers that made him an emperor but also brought unity to the previously disorganized Roman world. It was largely as a result of his efforts that the Roman Empire became the most successful empire that the world has ever known.

Augustus the Emperor

In 30 B.C.E., after the suicides of Antony and Cleopatra, Octavian, the adopted son of Julius Caesar, was left in undisputed control of the Roman world. He commanded eighty legions, and all of his significant opponents were defeated or dead. He faced some difficult choices, such as whether he should retire or try to hold on to power. According to the Roman biographer **Suetonius,** Octavian "thought that he himself would not be safe if he retired and that it would be dangerous to trust the government to more than one person." He would have realized that to protect himself and to keep the peace, he would have to retain

control of the army, and to do that, he had to stay in power. Octavian was a shrewd politician, with a good sense of what would work and what would not. Sulla and Caesar had tried to stay in power by using the office of dictator, but their approach was considered by the other senators to be unconstitutional and autocratic and had created great opposition. Octavian could not repeat their example.

To remain in power peacefully, Octavian knew that he needed the support of the people and the Senate. After sixty years of civil war, the people wanted peace, and, therefore, being a better administrator than a general, Octavian committed himself to creating a peaceful world. Gaining the support of the Senate was even more crucial. The senators were the only experienced military and civil administrators; they controlled most of the economic resources of the Roman world; and as the most influential pa-

Suetonius (ca. 70–ca.135 C.E.) Secretary of the emperor Hadrian who wrote biographies called *The Twelve Caesars.*

trons, they also were able to mobilize the Roman people. The Senate also represented all the ancient traditions of Rome, including the power to oversee legislation and the election of officials. Octavian could not rule without them. So, to gain support from the Senate, Octavian portrayed himself as the representative of Roman tradition and virtue, as a supporter of the rights of the Senate, and as the restorer of the Roman Republic.

Octavian soon was confident that the Senate would support any legislation that he desired, thus ensuring that anything he did was legal. In 27 B.C.E., he offered to give up all his powers, but the Senate not only declined this proposal but also granted Octavian additional honors, including the title of **augustus** ("the revered one"), which was not a power or an office but a mark of great admiration and respect. Octavian was so proud of this new title that he used it as his name, and it later became a title used by subsequent Roman emperors. Augustus, however, claimed neither to have established the Roman Empire nor to have become Roman emperor, but to have restored the Republic. But in spite of this pretense, it is clear that the Roman Republic was dead and that one individual, the emperor, now controlled the army and was in charge of the government.

The Roman Empire thus is said to have begun in 27 B.C.E. In this form it is called the **principate,** from the emperor's title of *princeps,* the highest-ranking member of the Senate. There always had been a *princeps,* so the emperor could claim he was still just another senator. The principate was based on the understanding that the emperor and the Senate governed as partners. To hold on to the real power without upsetting the Senate, Augustus initially proposed to serve as one of the two consuls every year. Being consul allowed him to command the army, with the power of imperium, and to introduce laws. But by monopolizing the highest office, Augustus aroused the same kind of jealousy that Sulla and Caesar had experienced. Therefore, in 23 B.C.E., Augustus adopted a new solution. He stopped being consul and had the Senate grant him the power of a proconsul with a "greater" imperium that allowed him to outrank any other general. Augustus also received the power of a tribune, allowing him to introduce legislation and to veto the actions of other officials. The knowledge that he had veto power meant that he never had to use it, for any senator planning to introduce any legislation made sure to clear it with Augustus in advance. Augustus also took over the censor's right to appoint new senators, which allowed him to pack the Senate with his own supporters. He also became *pontifex maximus,* the head of the

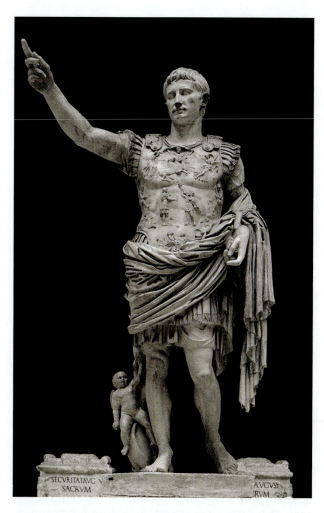

A statue from Prima Porta in Italy shows Augustus with Cupid, the son of Augustus' supposed distant ancestress Venus. By subtly showing that he was descended from gods, Augustus was able to lay claim to divine authority for his rule. *(Scala/Art Resource, NY)*

Roman state religion, the only actual office that he held. His general policy of holding powers rather than offices allowed him to keep a low profile and to avoid seeming arrogant or autocratic.

augustus   (Latin for "the revered one") Title given to Octavian in 27 B.C.E. that he used as his name; also used as the title of all subsequent Roman emperors.

principate   (based on Latin *princeps,* "first man") Roman Empire from 27 B.C.E. to 284 C.E., as established by Augustus.

Augustus created a model of empire that was used by his successors. The powers of a proconsul and a tribune became the two primary sources of the authority of the Roman emperors during the principate, permitting them to control the army and the laws while at the same time keeping a low profile. Everything the emperor did was done according to the Republic's constitution. The Senate still met; consuls still were appointed; and being a senator or consul continued to be a great honor. But the Senate, senators, and consuls no longer had any real power. Augustus's restoration of the Republic was a fiction, but a fiction that everyone was happy to go along with.

The Unification of the Roman World

Augustus used his authority to bring stability and unity to the Roman world and to create internal cohesiveness where none had existed before. He turned what in the past had been problems, such as the army and the provinces, into opportunities for unity. The most important institution in the Roman Empire was the army, for the empire could not succeed if the army was not fully integrated into the life of the empire. The army was responsible for defending the empire from foreign attacks and for maintaining internal order (there was no civil police force). It was by far the biggest drain on the imperial treasury. There also was a constant threat of its becoming involved in politics. The emperor's top priority always was to maintain the army's loyalty, and Augustus created a standing, professional army that was loyal directly to him. To minimize expenses, he reduced the army to twenty-eight legions—about 140,000 men—a number considered barely sufficient for defense plus a single offensive campaign. To keep the army out of politics, Augustus stationed it on the frontier, as far away from Rome as possible. The only troops in Italy were the **Praetorian Guard,** an elite 10,000-man unit camped on the outskirts of Rome.

The army was responsible for overseeing thousands of miles of frontier. During the Republic, there had been no coherent plan for expansion or defense. Augustus changed that. He terminated the practice of helter-skelter expansion that had characterized the Republic. He expanded the empire to fixed boundaries that were easy to defend and then stopped. In the south was the Sahara desert. To the east lay the Parthian Empire, which extended from the Euphrates River to India. Augustus realized there was nothing to be gained by attacking the Parthians, so he negotiated a favorable treaty and established peaceful relations. The most dangerous frontier was in the north,

where Celtic and Germanic peoples posed threats of raids, if not organized invasions. To safeguard the northern border, Augustus expanded the Roman frontier to the Danube River, but an attempt to expand to the Elbe River in Germany ended in 9 C.E., when the Germanic leader Arminius ambushed and destroyed three Roman legions in the Teutoberg Forest. The Romans withdrew to the Rhine River, and the Danube and the Rhine became the permanent northern frontier. Border areas not considered important enough to annex were left in the hands of client kings, such as Herod (r. 41 B.C.E.–4 E.C.) in Judaea, who were permitted to remain in office as long as they did not antagonize Rome. After this period of strategic expansion, Augustus focused on guarding the frontiers, regulating commerce and interaction with the outside world, and consolidating the territories that Rome controlled. This policy was followed by nearly all of his successors. The Roman army became a **garrison army,** spread out along the frontiers but doing little actual fighting. This single line of defense worked well as long as no enemy was able to break through and make its way into the undefended inner regions of the empire.

The army also held the empire together and unified it in other ways. Roman army camps brought **Romanization,** the extension of Roman culture, to the very edges of the empire. Augustus allowed provincials to serve in the army, and the first thing these soldiers had to learn was Latin. Romanization also was promoted by the elaborate Roman road system, which had been designed for military transport but was used primarily for personal and commercial traffic. In addition, during Augustus's reign, eighty colonies were established for hundreds of thousands of army veterans who received land in Spain, North Africa, and Greece, creating additional centers of Roman culture in the provinces. The army was a constant presence in the Roman world, but often a benign one. It was rarely used for internal peacekeeping; in fact, there were only two rebellions against the Romans after a province had been completely conquered—both by the Jews—a remarkable record for an empire supposedly based on military might. The army was

Praetorian Guard Ten thousand–man elite Roman army unit stationed at Rome.

garrison army Professional army stationed permanently in the same place that does little fighting.

Romanization Extension of Roman culture throughout the empire.

more likely to be engaged in constructing defenses or building roads than in fighting.

The empire now consisted of some twenty-five provinces and a population of between 40 and 60 million persons. Augustus tried to unify the many different peoples of the empire in several ways. He standardized the provincial administration. Governors and army generals were chosen from the members of the Senate on the basis of their ability. Augustus established a permanent civil service in both Rome and the provinces. Many officials were equestrians, including the **praetorian prefect,** the commander of the Praetorian Guard in Rome, and procurators who supervised tax collection. To remove tax inequities, Augustus replaced the tithe with fixed tribute in all the provinces. He also implemented a regular census that required all inhabitants of a province to register their property, thus providing a basis for fair tax assessment. City councils, whose members were known as **decurions,** continued to be in charge of local government in the provinces.

An effective integrating tool developed by Augustus and his successors was the Roman coinage system, which served both economic and propaganda purposes. A system of interchangeable copper, silver, and gold coins facilitated economic exchange inside the Roman Empire and well beyond the imperial frontiers. The coinage was based on the denarius, a silver coin that the emperors used primarily to pay the army. The salary of a soldier in the legions was 225 denarii per year. Copper denominations included the large sestertius (four per denarius) and the as (sixteen per denarius). A gold aureus, worth 25 denarii, was issued for special occasions, such as when a new emperor was named. Coins also conveyed a multitude of messages to a mass audience. Their words and images announced military victories and building projects, reminded people of the emperor's virtues, and reassured them of the army's loyalty. Table 6.1 summarizes the Roman coinage system.

Augustus also wanted to integrate the inhabitants of the provinces fully into the Roman world, to give them a sense of shared identity, and to allow them to feel that Rome's interests were their own. To provide provincials with a unified voice, he established provincial councils, where city representatives met annually to convey their concerns to the emperor. Augustus also established the **imperial cult,** the worship of the divine nature of living emperors and of deceased emperors who had been defied by the Senate. Even though Augustus and later emperors did not claim to be gods, the imperial cult implied that there was something godlike about the emperor's spirit. People participated in the imperial cult in temples

Table 6.1

The Roman Coinage System

Metal	Denomination	Value
Gold	aureus (aurei)	25 denarii = 100 sesterces = 400 asses
Silver	denarius (denarii)	4 sesterces = 16 asses
Copper	sestertius (sesterces)	4 asses
Copper	as (asses)	

honoring Rome and Augustus located in provincial capitals throughout the empire. Taking part in the imperial cult was more of a political than a religious act. By dropping a pinch of incense into a fire on the altar, people symbolically renewed their loyalty to Rome and to the emperor. Standard rituals like these gave the people of the empire a shared sense of belonging.

The benefit that gave the people of the provinces the greatest sense of identification with Rome was Roman citizenship, a privilege that few provincials had been able to obtain under the Republic. Augustus opened citizenship to two classes of people who served the empire: decurions and soldiers. Decurions could become citizens by requesting citizenship from the emperor, who granted it to encourage influential provincials to identify their interests with Rome. Once they became citizens, decurions could work their way up to being equestrians or even senators. Augustus also allowed provincials to become citizens by serving in the Roman army—not in the legions, which were open only to citizens, but in the auxiliary forces. The auxiliary forces were specialized troops (such as Numidian cavalry) and skirmishers (lightly armed troops sent into battle first). After twenty-five years of military service, provincials received citizenship. They and their descendants then likewise had opportunities to advance in Roman society.

praetorian prefect Commander of the Praetorian Guard.

decurions Members of the city councils in the provinces.

imperial cult Worship of the divinity of living and deified emperors in which provincials renewed their loyalty to Rome and the emperor; carried out in temples of Rome and Augustus.

After his death, Augustus, like Caesar before him, was deified. In the upper register of this carved cameo gemstone, known as the Gemma Augustea and now in Vienna, Augustus, seated next to the goddess Roma, is enrolled as one of the gods. In the lower register, the Roman soldiers raise a victory trophy over defeated barbarians, demonstrating where the real power of the emperors lay. *(Kunsthistorisches Museum, Vienna/Art Resource, NY)*

The Age of Augustus

Augustus was a master of public relations. In law, literature, art, and architecture, he created an image of himself as the restorer of peace, stability, virtue, and morality. He believed that conservative Roman virtues had gained the support of the gods and created the greatness of Rome. It was his responsibility, he felt, to provide a model for these virtues. In his memoirs, Augustus expressed his pride in a golden shield that the Senate had hung up in his honor, "testifying to his virtue, mercy, justice, and piety." Using his authority as censor, he encouraged other Romans to live up to his ideals of virtue and morality and promoted an ancient version of family values. He was particularly worried about sexual morality and passed legislation against adultery, fornication, and homosexuality. He tried to reduce prostitution by taxing it. He promoted marriage not only because it encouraged appropriate sexual behavior but also because it produced offspring who could join the Roman army. Widows and widowers were required to remarry within three years. Mothers and fathers of large families received tax exemptions. Augustus's implementation of his moral agenda was undercut, however, by the behavior of his own family, as he had to send his own daughter Julia into exile for adultery.

To promote his image of Rome further, Augustus became a patron of the arts. His sponsorship brought the height of the Golden Age of Latin literature. The works of writers whom he subsidized conveyed the glory of Rome, with Augustus as the divinely supported leader. In 17 B.C.E., Augustus celebrated the ancient secular games, which were held only every 110 years and marked the beginning of a new age each time they were held. In honor of the occasion, the poet Horace wrote a hymn that identified Augustus as the leader who had permitted "virtue, long dishonored, to return." Horace also wrote satires that described conventional morality and everyday life in Rome and showed that, with Augustus, everything had returned to normal. The poet Vergil composed an epic poem, the *Aeneid,* that recounted the story of the founding of Rome and was memorized by every

Aeneid   Epic poem, written in the late first century B.C.E. by the poet Vergil, describing the origins of Rome and Roman virtue.

The literature of the Golden Age of Roman literature provided a common cultural meeting ground for educated persons throughout the Roman world. A second-century North African mosaic shows the poet Vergil, the author of the Aeneid, the greatest of all Roman literary works, flanked by the muses Clio and Melpomene, writing the Aeneid on a papyrus scroll. *(Ancient Art & Architecture Collection)*

Roman schoolchild. Vergil stressed Aeneas's sense of duty, and readers recognized that their emperor had the same qualities. The historian Livy authored a massive history of Rome that commenced with the city's foundation and showed how the reign of Augustus was a continuation of the Roman Republic. There also was a flowering of poetry by poets such as Ovid, whose *Metamorphoses* provided a summary of Greek and Latin mythology that placed Rome in the context of the ancient Greek classical tradition.

Augustus also demonstrated his commitment to tradition by building and remodeling many Roman buildings, especially temples. In his memoirs, he stated, "I rebuilt in the city eighty-two temples of the gods, omitting none that needed to be repaired." One of these temples, honoring Mars, was located in the new Forum of Augustus, which adjoined a forum built by Julius Caesar. Augustus also built an Altar of Peace that showed Augustus, his family, and the Senate performing a religious sacrifice and portrayed

Augustus as the person who had brought peace to the Roman world. Augustus did additional remodeling work on the Senate house, the Capitoline temple of Jupiter, and Julius Caesar's basilica in the Forum. He also built a great circular mausoleum to hold his own remains and those of his family and successors. Augustus's efforts to adorn and beautify Rome were so extensive that he claimed he had changed Rome from a city of brick into a city of marble.

Finally, Augustus also showed his devotion to the Roman people by presenting many kinds of entertainments. He reported that he paid for eight shows of gladiators in which 10,000 men fought and twenty-six wild beast hunts in which 3,500 animals were killed. Later emperors followed his example by sponsoring building projects and extravagant entertainments in Rome.

Beginning with Augustus, therefore, the emperor became the patron of the Roman world, whose inhabitants became his clients. The emperor provided honors and offices for the senators and equestrians, salaries and employment for the soldiers, citizenship for the provincials, and public works and entertainment for the people of Rome.

The Roman Peace, 14–192 C.E.

↓ Describe how the Roman Empire functioned during the Roman Peace.

↓ Describe the life of an average citizen during the Roman Peace.

The first two centuries of the principate are known as the Roman Peace, the period when the Roman Empire was at its height. The Roman world was well administered by generally able emperors. With a few exceptions, the army was kept under control, and there was little threat of foreign invasion. Nearly all the empire's inhabitants had chances for social advancement. Urban life flourished, and economic opportunities abounded. A unified culture and society extended from Britain in the northwest to Arabia in the southeast.

The Successors of Augustus

The empire created by Augustus brought a long period of peace and prosperity known as the **Roman Peace.** The empire reached its absolute height during the Antonine dynasty (96–192 C.E.), named after the emperor Antoninus (138–161 C.E.), whose reign was so uneventful that it is curiously undocumented. Antoninus was so popular with the Senate that it granted him the title pius ("dutiful"), which, like the title augustus, was used by many subsequent emperors.

One of Augustus's most difficult tasks had been to find someone to succeed him. Because Augustus claimed that he had reestablished the Republic, there was no constitutional position of emperor and thus no constitutional process for **imperial succession,** the choosing of a new emperor. Augustus had to satisfy both the Senate and the army. To please the Senate, he had to do everything legally. Therefore, before he died, he had the Senate grant to his intended successor, his stepson Tiberius, the same powers that he had. To please the army, he had to designate a family member, preferably a son, for in Rome, loyalty, including military loyalty, was inherited. Augustus did not have any blood sons, so to show the army whom he wanted to succeed him, he adopted Tiberius. This method for choosing a successor by satisfying both the Senate and the army also worked for Augustus's

successors, but only when an emperor had the foresight to put his successor in place before he died. If he failed to do so, a crisis could arise if the Senate and different armies around the empire disagreed over who the next emperor should be.

Augustus died in 14 C.E. at the age of seventy-eight. He was immediately deified by the Senate, and Tiberius smoothly succeeded him as emperor. It now had been more than seventy years since the Republic had actually worked. Few remembered it as anything but ancient history, and everyone expected that Rome henceforth would be ruled by emperors. The succeeding Roman emperors are organized into families known as dynasties (shown in Table 6.2); Augustus was the first emperor of the Julio-Claudian dynasty (27 B.C.E.–68 C.E.).

Several important political developments occurred during the principate, including the increasing influence of the army, the declining importance of the Senate, and the growing power of the emperor. The emperors were well aware that their power was based on the army, and newly appointed emperors felt compelled to give the soldiers a gold offering known as a **donative** to ensure their loyalty. When an emperor died without naming a successor, the power of the army became even clearer. Even though the Senate had the legal authority to grant the powers that made an emperor, it rarely acted quickly. Thus, it was almost always the army that took the lead in finding a new emperor. In 37 C.E., Tiberius died without having named his successor. The Praetorian Guard in Rome immediately hailed Tiberius's nephew Caligula (r. 37–41 C.E.) as the next emperor, and the Senate had no choice but to agree. In 41 C.E., the army acted even more directly by assassinating Caligula and naming his uncle Claudius (r. 41–54 C.E.) as emperor. Once more, the Senate had to concur. A more serious crisis occurred in 68 C.E., when **Nero,** the last Julio-Claudian emperor, died without naming a successor. There were no family members left to succeed him, and when armies around the empire sponsored their own candidates, civil war broke out. The winner was Vespasian (r. 69–79 C.E.), a general who was in

Roman Peace   Period from 14 B.C.E. until 192 C.E., when the Roman Empire was at its height.

imperial succession   Means by which power was transferred from one emperor to the next.

donative   Gift of gold coins distributed to soldiers by new emperors.

Nero   (r. 54–68 C.E.) Roman emperor who blamed the Christians for a great fire in Rome in 64 C.E.

Table 6.2

Dynasties of Emperors

Julio-Claudian Dynasty (27 B.C.E.–68 C.E.)

Augustus (27 B.C.E.–14 C.E.)
Tiberius (14–37 C.E.)
Caligula (37–41 C.E.)
Claudius (41–54 C.E.)
Nero (54–68 C.E.)

Flavian Dynasty (69–96 C.E.)

Vespasian (69–79 C.E.)
Titus (79–81 C.E.)
Domitian (81–96 C.E.)

Antonine Dynasty (96–192 C.E.)

Nerva (96–98 C.E.)
Trajan (98–117 C.E.)
Hadrian (117–138 C.E.)
Antoninus (138–161 C.E.)
Marcus Aurelius (161–180 C.E.)
Commodus (180–192 C.E.)

Severan Dynasty (193–235 C.E.)

Septimius Severus (193–211 C.E.)
Caracalla (211–217 C.E.)
Elagabalus (218–222 C.E.)
Severus Alexander (222–235 C.E.)

for trading privileges. He kept Dacia, however, for its gold. Otherwise, the empire remained on a defensive footing, and the army was a garrison army. Hadrian, for example, strengthened the empire's defense with a program that included putting the army to work building a ninety-mile wall, known as Hadrian's Wall, across northern Britain to control traffic across the frontier. The emperors also used the army on public works projects such as building roads, bridges, and aqueducts. Many soldiers went their entire careers without fighting in a single war.

More and more authority fell into the hands of the emperor, for he was the person who had the power to get things done. The emperor assumed control of foreign affairs and took charge when emergencies arose, such as foreign attacks, food shortages, or natural disasters. The imperial bureaucracy expanded as emperors took on responsibility for dealing with additional administrative details. The Senate simply implemented the emperor's will; if the emperor requested a law, the Senate passed it. During the second century C.E., the emperors assumed the right to issue laws in their own name, bypassing the Senate altogether. Before making decisions, emperors consulted not with the Senate but with their *amici* ("friends") and with a private council made up of high officials and legal specialists. Thus, even more authority fell into the hands of the emperor. One of the few independent rights the Senate had came after an emperor's death. If the Senate liked an emperor, it would deify him, but if the Senate despised an emperor, it passed a decree of "damnation of memory," which permitted his name and images, on coins and statues, to be mutilated—an act that ordinarily was an act of treason.

Most emperors followed Augustus's lead by ruling responsibly according to law. Some, however, were less suited to rule. Emperors who had a suspicious nature listened to informers known as **delators,** who accused people of treason and received one-fourth of the property of any condemned person they had informed on. Some emperors acted irrationally or autocratically. Caligula, for example, reportedly made his horse consul and believed that he was the

the process of putting down a revolt by the Jews in Palestine when his soldiers declared him emperor. After he defeated his last rival, the Senate granted him the powers of an emperor and he founded the Flavian dynasty (69–96 C.E.). A series of effective emperors then successfully kept the army out of politics until 192 C.E.

Only two emperors violated Augustus's policy that the empire should cease expanding, and both were motivated by a desire to increase the empire's economic resources. Claudius undertook the conquest of Britain in the belief that it contained pearls and silver mines. After the revolt of Boudicca in 60 was suppressed (see Choice), southern Britain was successfully incorporated into the empire. But the Romans found little silver and few pearls. **Trajan** (r. 98–117) conquered Dacia, on the north side of the Danube River, for its gold mines and captured Mesopotamia from the Parthians. His successor, **Hadrian** (r.117–138), realized that Mesopotamia could not be defended and returned it to the Parthians in exchange

Trajan   (r. 98–117 C.E.) Roman emperor whose conquests of Dacia and Mesopotamia violated the policy of Augustus against foreign conquests.

Hadrian   (r.117–138 C.E.) Roman emperor who concentrated on defending the empire and built Hadrian's Wall.

delators   (from Latin for "betrayers") Informers who accused people of treason and received part of their property at their conviction.

god Jupiter. Domitian (r. 81–96 C.E.) liked being addressed as "lord and god." And Commodus (r. 180–192 C.E.) portrayed himself on coinage as the Greek hero Hercules and fought as a gladiator. Emperors who exhibited such extreme behavior ran the risk of being assassinated, as in fact happened to the three just mentioned.

Society and Culture

During the Roman Peace, a unified society and culture extended from Britain in the northwest to Arabia in the southeast. The extension of Roman culture to the provinces was balanced by continued Roman assimilation of provincial culture. The culture of the Roman Empire usually is called **Greco-Roman culture** but might be better called Mediterranean culture, for the culture of the Roman world was an amalgamation of the cultures of all the peoples incorporated under the Roman umbrella, including not only Romans and Greeks but also Egyptians, Syrians, Jews, Germans, and many others.

The two things that bound Roman society together were Roman citizenship and urban life. Those who enjoyed both were fully integrated into a homogeneous Roman system. But even noncitizen country dwellers and foreigners felt the impact of Roman culture. During the Roman Peace, legal and political privileges were extended to larger numbers of people, and many provincials attained Roman citizenship, intensifying the sense of collective identity. This process culminated in 212 C.E., when the emperor **Caracalla** (r. 211–217) granted citizenship to everyone (except slaves and certain ex-slaves) who did not yet have it. Foreigners who settled within the empire also became citizens. Everyone in the empire was under the same legal system—even slaves had legal rights.

Political power also filtered out from Rome into the provinces. By the beginning of the second century C.E., emperors such as the Spaniards Trajan and Hadrian were coming from the provinces. The Senate included North Africans, Greeks, and Syrians along with Italians and other western Europeans. People living outside Rome saw themselves as Romans first and Greeks, Gauls, or Egyptians second. In a speech entitled "To Rome," the Greek orator Aristides expressed to the emperor Hadrian the sense of satisfaction provincials felt: "No one fit for office or a position of trust is an alien. There exists a universal democracy under one man, the best prince and administrator. You have made the word Roman apply not to a city but to a universal people." Aristides was speaking, of course, primarily for the privileged male

population of the empire, which was able to enjoy the benefits of Roman citizenship to its fullest extent. Only males, for example, were able to hold office or be members of the Senate.

Other previously disadvantaged segments of the population gained new rights. It became easier for both sons and daughters to get out from under the authority of their fathers and establish their legal independence. Women gained greater authority to choose their own husbands. A **jurist** stated, "Engagements, like marriages, come about by the consent of the parties and, therefore, the consent of a daughter of a family is needed for an engagement just as it is for a marriage." Some women could even act in court without a guardian. The lot of many slaves had also improved. They were now much more valuable than they had been in the days of the Republic, for the wars of conquest and the cheap slaves they brought as spoils were long gone. Slaves' legal rights included the opportunity to accumulate money to buy their freedom. The regulations for slaves on one imperial estate stated that baths and hospitals were to be provided and that slave women were to be set free after bearing a specified number of slave children. But not all slaves were treated well. The enslaved gold miners of Dacia, for example, spent their lives chained underground and were left lying where they died.

The empire also offered career opportunities. The emperors sponsored an extensive education system, for the expanding imperial bureaucracy had an insatiable need for educated civil servants. There were municipal and imperial salaries for teachers of grammar and public speaking. The school curriculum was purely literary, based on studying texts such as Vergil's *Aeneid,* with little inclusion of mathematics and science. Law became the most popular field of advanced study; even if orators had fewer chances to rise in politics than in the Republic, they still could argue cases in court.

The period from 14 C.E. until about 200 C.E. is called the **Silver Age** of Latin literature. Around 100 C.E.,

---

Greco-Roman culture Composite culture shared by people living in the Roman Empire.

Caracalla (r. 211–217 C.E.) Roman emperor who raised the pay of the soldiers and gave Roman citizenship to almost everyone in the empire.

jurist Legal expert who commented on the law and advised emperors.

Silver Age Period of Latin literature lasting from the death of Augustus until the end of the second century C.E.

Tacitus, the greatest Roman historian, examined the times from Caesar through Domitian in the *Annals* and the *Histories.* Shortly thereafter Suetonius, secretary of the emperor Hadrian, wrote a collection of biographies of emperors called *The Twelve Caesars.* Much of the literature, moreover, was practical in nature. The rhetorician Quintilian's manual on oratorical training became a standard school text. Pliny the Elder, a Roman admiral who died while investigating the eruption of Mount Vesuvius in 79 C.E., authored a massive *Natural History* that dealt with geography, ethnography, zoology, botany, and geology. In the second century, the astronomer and geographer Ptolemy of Alexandria refined Hipparchus's concept of an earth-centered universe to create the complex Ptolemaic model, which was so convincing that it remained the standard model of the universe for the next seventeen hundred years. Ptolemy also created a world map and compiled a star catalogue containing 1,048 stars organized into 48 constellations whose names still are in use. And around 180 C.E. the physician Galen of Pergamum, who had gained extensive knowledge of human anatomy by serving as the imperial physician to gladiators, wrote the most important medical works of antiquity, including books called "On the Natural Faculties" and "On the Use of the Parts of the Human Body."

Urban Life

Urbanism provided another unifying factor, for life during the principate was centered on cities. The countryside, of course, remained important, for farming was the backbone of the Roman economy. But cities were the focus of cultural, social, religious, and economic development. Of all the cities in the empire, Rome was easily the most important and provided a model for urban life elsewhere. Rome now was home to 1 million inhabitants who had come from places both within and outside the empire. In the streets, one would encounter Greeks, Celts, Egyptians, and Syrians as well as red-haired and blue-eyed Germans, black Africans, and dark-skinned Arabs and Indians. Commercial goods flowed in from throughout the world, as did foreign languages, cultures, and religious practices. About the year 100 C.E., the Roman satirist Juvenal wrote, "The Syrian river Orontes now flows into the Tiber, bringing its language and customs." Rome had become a melting pot of peoples and cultures.

Rome was the showcase of the Roman world as emperors continued to adorn the city. Vespasian's Forum of Peace portrayed Vespasian, like Augustus, as one who had brought peace after a period of civil war. Vespasian and his sons sponsored the construction of the Flavian Amphitheater, commonly known as the Colosseum, one of the most enduring Roman monuments. Trajan built baths, a forum, and a market used for the distribution of subsidized food. Hadrian constructed the circular Pantheon, a temple of "all the gods," and a new mausoleum for himself and his successors. Caracalla built a huge public bath complex that is still used for opera performances. Many emperors contributed to the upkeep of roads, bridges, aqueducts that brought in fresh water from up to forty miles away, and a sewer system that flushed Rome's waste into the Tiber River. The most destitute residents of Rome could expect the emperor to provide basic foodstuffs, such as bread and olive oil, and perhaps even some occasional cheese and wine. On special occasions, such as an imperial birthday, the emperors even distributed money.

Outside Rome, city life also formed the basis for the enjoyment and extension of Roman culture. Many western European cities, such as Lyons in Gaul, had been created out of nothing to meet the needs of the Roman administration, and they now served as focal points for the dissemination of Roman civilization. So did colonies of Roman citizens that had been established early in the empire, such as Merida in Spain, and the restored cities of Carthage in North Africa and Corinth in Greece. Even on the frontiers, army garrison posts gave rise to cities such as Bonn, Mainz, Strasbourg, Vienna, Budapest, and Belgrade. By the second century, Alexandria in Egypt, Antioch in Syria, and Carthage in North Africa had populations of over a quarter of a million. Members of city councils, the decurions, patterned themselves on the Senate of Rome and manifested their civic pride by competing with one another to endow their cities with the same amenities as Rome, including theaters, amphitheaters, temples, town halls, and libraries. Aqueducts delivered fresh water, which was made available at streetcorner fountains. Public latrines were equipped with constantly flushing toilets. And elaborate public

Tacitus (ca. 56–117 C.E.) Roman historian who ca. 100 C.E. wrote histories from Julius Caesar through the emperor Domitian.

Ptolemy of Alexandria (ca. 90–168 C.E.) Astronomer and geographer who favored an earth-centered universe and created a star catalogue and world map.

Galen of Pergamum (ca.129–200 C.E.) The most influential medical writer of antiquity.

amphitheater Large circular structure with seats around a circular arena, used for entertainments.

baths provided enormous hot and cold pools along with exercise and massage rooms, libraries, and lecture halls. The emperors often aided cities with imperial assistance for public works projects, and army troops sometimes provided the labor.

The noise, smell, and dust in a Roman city were overpowering. In spite of sewer systems, the trash and filth that accumulated in the streets, much of it left behind by draft animals, bred insects, rodents, and disease. The rich did their best to shut the city out by building homes with blank external walls and elaborate central gardens. But the living quarters of an average laborer would have been a single room, without running water or indoor plumbing, on the fifth or sixth floor of a downtown apartment building. Such an individual would be fortunate to earn one denarius a day when working, an amount that provided little more than the most basic necessities— two sets of clothing, some pottery kitchen utensils, and a few pieces of furniture. The average person's diet consisted primarily of olive oil, wine diluted with water, and grain, which was made into bread or porridge. Bread was eaten with honey, cheese, or sausage. Vegetables included cabbage, asparagus, onions, and radishes. Fish and pork, if one could afford them, were the most common meats and had to be eaten immediately, before they spoiled. Honey was a common sweetener. The Romans particularly enjoyed strongly flavored sauces. The main meal was eaten at noon; morning and evening meals were often little more than snacks.

City governments in large cities also provided entertainments, including theatrical productions, mime performances, and athletic contests such as footraces. Violent forms of entertainment were very popular. Chariot races, which often featured disastrous wrecks, were held in circuses. Blood sports took place in an amphitheater on a sand-covered arena where wild beasts and gladiators (both male and female) fought against each other in different combinations. Public entertainment in arenas also was provided by the execution of condemned criminals who were not Roman citizens: they might be hunted down by starved wild animals, gored to death by bulls, or forced to fight each other. The provision of food and entertainment served a useful purpose: by keeping the urban population preoccupied and content, emperors and city governments ensured that there would be no bored and starving mobs rioting in the streets. In all of the cities in the empire, one encountered the same kinds of institutions and services, all of which gave people a sense of unity and shared identity.

Today's most extensive knowledge about life in Roman cities comes from **Pompeii.** At the beginning

In this view of the site of Pompeii, Mt. Vesuvius overlooks the ruins of the city. The theater lies in the foreground, and city streets stretch out beyond it. Archaeological excavations of Pompeii, which still continue, provide an intimate look into the everyday life of a typical Roman city. (*O. Louis Mazzatenta/National Geographic Image Collection*)

of the Roman Empire, Pompeii was a thriving city of about twenty thousand people, located on the Bay of Naples at the base of Mount Vesuvius, a volcano that had produced earthquakes but no recent eruptions. All this changed on August 24, 79 C.E., when the volcano erupted. A cloud of superheated gas, ash, mud, and rock known as pyroclastic flow surged down the mountainside, slamming into Pompeii at a temperature of about 650 degrees Fahrenheit. Ash filled the air and made it impossible to see. Some people fled to

Pompeii City on the Bay of Naples destroyed by an eruption of Mount Vesuvius in 79 C.E.

the seacoast and were rescued by Roman naval vessels. Others took refuge underground, where they were asphyxiated by the poisonous gases. Still others died in collapsing buildings or in the streets. The entire city was buried under thick layers of rock, mud, and ash. Over ten thousand inhabitants were killed. The city was not rediscovered until the eighteenth century, and excavations of the site are still going on.

The city preserves the tiniest details of everyday life. Like most Roman cities, Pompeii had a forum, a theater, an aqueduct, public baths, a senate house, a temple of the imperial cult, and even its own small amphitheater for putting on gladiatorial contests. The poor lived in large apartment buildings, the rich in villas built around a central garden. The streets were laid out on a grid plan, at right angles to each other. Steppingstones allowed inhabitants to avoid the animal droppings and other refuse that littered the streets; sewers under the streets carried away the waste when it rained. Streetcorner lunch counters served soup, vegetables, and beverages. Vendors sold round loaves of bread. Street musicians entertained passersby. A mosaic at the front entrance to one house depicts a dog and the warning, "Beware the Dog." Graffiti carved into the walls preserve the actual words of inhabitants, such as "Restitutus was here with his brother," "Marcus loves Spendusa," or "Money has no odor." Like no other Roman remains, Pompeii brings the Romans back to life.

Economic Activity

Even though cities have the greatest visibility in the literary and archaeological source material, they could not exist without the produce of the countryside. The Roman economy remained primarily rural, and most of the population lived in rural areas. Ninety percent of the government's tax income came from the tax on agricultural land. Some farmland was owned by small farmers, but most was consolidated into the large *latifundia* of senators. Initially, *latifundia* had been farmed primarily by a combination of slave and day labor, but by the second century C.E., there was an increasing use of tenant farmers known as *coloni,* who paid a portion of their crop to the landowner and kept the rest for themselves. Many senators were absentee landlords and left the administration of their estates to privileged slaves. The largest landowner of all was the emperor, whose estates grew ever larger as a result of purchases, bequests, and confiscations. These, too, often were overseen by high-ranking imperial slaves.

Manufacturing and trade expanded dramatically during the Roman Peace, as an empirewide free market was facilitated by two centuries of peace and lack of government restrictions. The second century C.E. was the great age of the Roman middle class. Ease of travel by water, by both sea and river, made it possible to ship bulk products great distances, and the Roman road system, which extended to the most distant frontiers, made land commerce much less costly than it had been. Road tolls and port dues were low, banditry had been suppressed, and piracy was virtually eliminated. A unified and trustworthy currency system facilitated monetary transactions. Long-distance commerce also was supported by imperial subsidies that kept frontier armies well supplied with foodstuffs and material goods. Much of the trade was in the hands of easterners, primarily Greeks, Syrians, and Jews, resulting in a gradual shift of the economic center of the empire from the western Mediterranean to the east.

The trade in luxury items such as gold, spices, and gems was complemented by large-scale commerce in smaller-value items ranging from agricultural products such as wine to manufactured items such as pottery, glassware, and clothing. Different regions were known for different kinds of products. Italy and Gaul were recognized for their ceramics; Sidon in Phoenicia and northern Gaul were famous for glass; Spain and Britain were centers of mining. Amber was imported from the Baltic Sea area and exotic animals from sub-Saharan Africa. The most important grain-growing areas were Egypt, North Africa (which was heavily irrigated), and Sicily. Every year, a huge grain fleet departed from Alexandria and struck out across the Mediterranean for Rome to help to meet Italy's voracious need for grain. In addition, olive oil was produced in North Africa, Italy, and Spain; wine in Italy and southern Gaul; and a popular fish sauce in Spain.

Rome's economic reach extended beyond the frontiers, to the peoples the Romans knew collectively as barbarians. For the Romans, as for the Greeks, barbarians were people whose culture was different from their own. None of the northern barbarian peoples had any written history prior to their contact with Rome. Greek and Roman accounts are full of stereotypes about them—they dressed in skins, liked to fight, and smelled—and offer little information on the actual details of their lives and customs independent

---

mosaic Work of art made from small colored pieces of stone or glass cemented together.

coloni (Latin for "tenants") Tenant farmers who worked sections of large estates in exchange for a percentage of their crops.

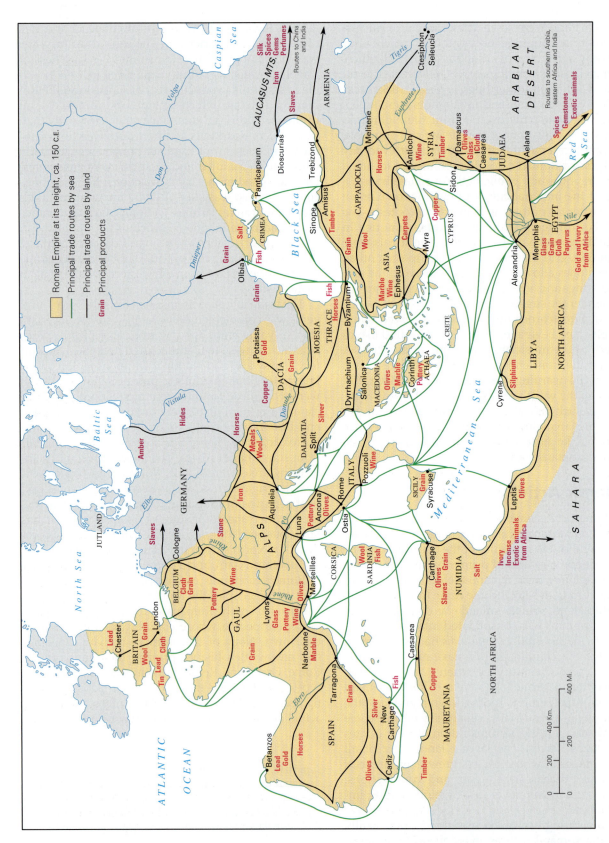

MAP 6.1 **Trade Routes of the Roman Empire** In exchange for trade goods such as textiles, glass, pottery, wine, and silver coinage, the Romans imported products from as far away as the Baltic, India, and Africa. Roman economic influence thus extended far beyond the frontiers of the empire and resulted in extensive cultural exchange with foreign peoples.

of Mediterranean influence. The most numerous barbarians were on the northern frontier, for in the south was the sparsely populated Sahara desert and to the east were the Parthians, who were just as civilized as the Romans. The northern barbarians, mostly Celtic and Germanic peoples, were settled farmers and had been living in contact with the Romans for centuries, so they were not uncivilized savages. Roman and barbarian traders and travelers exchanged not only trade goods but also elements of culture, and barbarians could not help picking up Roman culture, including the Latin language. A third-century historian remarked, "The barbarians were adapting themselves to the Roman world. They did not find it difficult to change their lives, and they were becoming different without realizing it." Rome's influence extended even to modern Poland, where an iron-working industry fluctuated according to economic and political conditions within the empire. Hoards of Roman coins found hundreds of miles beyond the frontiers also demonstrate Rome's economic reach.

Roman trade routes extended to the Far East, India, and even China. Roman gold, silver, fabrics, glassware, and wine were exchanged for eastern silks, spices, gems, and perfumes. The emperor Trajan dredged out a canal between the Nile River and the Red Sea, and every year a fleet of over a hundred trading ships set out from Egypt to the east. The journey from Italy to India took about sixteen weeks. An Indian poet of the second century wrote, "Drink the cool and fragrant wine brought by the Greeks in their vessels." In 166 C.E., traders claiming to be the representatives of the emperor Marcus Aurelius (r. 161–180) visited the Chinese court. One consequence of all this foreign commerce was a huge trade deficit of some 550 million sesterces per year—enough to pay the annual salaries of the entire Roman army three times over. So many silver denarii flowed out of the empire that the denarius became the standard coinage used in India.

Religion in the Roman Empire and the Rise of Christianity

↓ Describe the religious practices and beliefs of the early Roman Empire.
↓ How did early Christians relate to the Roman world?

The principate was a period of great religious development and change, caused, in part, by the expanded contact among peoples of different religious beliefs under a unified government. Eastern religious practices, including mystery cults, philosophical beliefs, and Judaism, spread throughout the Mediterranean

world. But the most important religious development of the principate was the appearance of Christianity, a religion that grew out of Judaism and would shape the development of western civilization.

State and Private Religion

Nearly all the people living in the Roman world were polytheists, worshiping many gods. Polytheistic religions included both state religion and private religion. State religion was exercised in public and revolved around the imperial cult. Emperors served as *pontifex maximus* and made regular sacrifices on behalf of the Roman people to Jupiter, Juno, and Minerva, the gods who looked after the welfare of Rome. For the general population, participation in the imperial cult was a political act, a way of declaring loyalty to Rome and the emperor, and did not entail a great deal of spiritual devotion.

In private religion, people sought personal religious satisfaction within a small circle of family and friends. Romans were exposed to many different kinds of private religious practices. Many participated in mystery cults, such as the cult of Isis, that promised an afterlife to their initiates. Magic, which allowed people to feel that they were empowered by the gods, was widely practiced. Astrology was used to cast horoscopes that predicted the future outcome of people's lives. It was illegal, however, to cast the horoscope of an emperor for fear that a bad forecast could lead to unrest or revolt. The study of philosophy continued to bring spiritual satisfaction. Stoicism, with its focus on duty and responsibility, had great attraction for the Roman ruling class. One stoic was the emperor Marcus Aurelius, whose *Meditations* preserve his personal thoughts on what it meant to be emperor. Some philosophers went to extremes to put their beliefs into practice. For example, a Cynic philosopher named Proteus burned himself alive to show that death was nothing to be feared.

People also believed in "divine men" who were able to use the power of the gods to perform miracles, including curing disease, raising the dead, and controlling the weather. The most famous miracle worker was Apollonius, a native of Anatolia who lived in the first century C.E. Apollonius attracted disciples and

hoard   Coins that were hidden, usually in the ground, either as a means of saving or in times of trouble.

Marcus Aurelius   (r. 161–180 C.E.) Roman emperor who fought German invasions and practiced Stoicism.

healed the sick. He was believed to have overpowered a vampire and to have expelled a demon that was bringing the plague. It even was said that he could be in two places at the same time. Some supposedly divine men, however, were opportunists who took advantage of people's gullibility. The satirist Lucian made fun of "swindlers who deal in magic; they will guide your love life, defeat your enemies, find you treasure, or get you an inheritance." Lucian also suggested, "These scoundrels are completely unprincipled. They understand that human life is ruled by fear and hope, and that anyone who can control these two things will become rich."

By the third century, as a result of religious syncretism, the many different polytheistic gods were seen as being part of a single universal deity. Many believed that the sun, worshiped as Jupiter, Apollo, or the Unconquered Sun, represented a single, primary god. The emperor Aurelian (r. 270–275 C.E.) even attempted to make the Unconquered Sun into the main god of the Roman Empire, and December 25, when the sun began to rise higher in the sky, was declared to be his birthday.

The Jews in the Roman World

Of all the peoples living in the Roman world, the Jews were the most resistant to assimilation and were, in fact, the only provincials to engage in organized resistance to Rome. They continued to await the arrival of a Messiah who would restore their political independence. In general, the Roman government was tolerant of the Jewish insistence on worshiping only a single god and exempted the Jews from making sacrifices to the imperial cult. But some emperors offended Jewish religious sensibilities. Caligula ordered a statue of himself to be set up in Jerusalem, and the Jews were at the point of revolt until a sensible Roman official refused to implement the order. In 66 C.E., Jewish dissatisfaction with Roman rule broke into open rebellion. Four years later, Titus, the son of the emperor Vespasian, captured and sacked Jerusalem, destroying the Jewish Temple. Many Jews fled Palestine and settled elsewhere in the empire, adding to the continuing Jewish Diaspora. Following Jewish uprisings in Egypt and Palestine in 117 C.E., the emperor Hadrian introduced anti-Jewish measures that included prohibitions on circumcision, reading of the the law, and observance of the Sabbath. In 132 C.E., Hadrian announced his intention to build a temple of Jupiter on the site of the Jewish Temple in Jerusalem. The Jews revolted again under Simon bar Kochba ("son of the star"), whom many Jews believed to be the Messiah, and it took the Romans three years to

suppress the rebellion. A Roman colony then was built on the site of Jerusalem, and thousands more Jews were expelled from Judaea, resulting in a further expansion of the Diaspora. By the second century C.E., there was scarcely a city in the empire that did not have a Jewish community.

In spite of Roman efforts to destroy Jewish unity, Jews living in the Roman Empire maintained their unique identity. After the Bar Kochba revolt, a new Sanhedrin assembled outside Jerusalem and continued to receive Jewish contributions that previously had gone to the temple. The Jewish leader, now called a patriarch, served as an intermediary between the Jewish people and the Roman government. With the Temple gone, synagogues became the centers of Jewish religious life in cities with a Jewish population. There Jews met under the guidance of a **rabbi** to pray, hear preaching based on scripture, and read and study scripture and commentaries on scripture. Learned Jewish rabbis met in Palestine to discuss and write down interpretations of God's will. About the year 200 C.E., oral interpretations of Jewish law were collected into a volume known as the **Mishnah,** which became part of a larger collection of Jewish teachings called the **Talmud,** a comprehensive guide to Jewish life that included oral tradition, interpretations of the Law of Moses, statements on faith and morality, biblical commentaries, and historical narratives. Jews preserved their way of life by living according to **Halakha,** a set of guidelines that determined how Jews related to God and to fellow human beings. Halakha established a common bond among all Jews everywhere.

The Talmud shows that Jews were ambivalent about Rome. According to one passage, "Rabbi Judah said, 'How excellent are the deeds of this nation. They have instituted market places, they have instituted bridges, they have instituted baths.' Rabbi Simeon ben Yohai answered, 'All that they have instituted they have instituted only for their own needs. They have instituted market places to place harlots in them, baths for their own pleasure, bridges to collect toll.'" Whether they admired the Romans or not, Jews were living in a Roman world. And some Jews

rabbi Respected Jewish teacher who decides questions of ritual and law.

Mishnah Written collection of interpretations of Jewish law, compiled ca. 200 C.E.

Talmud Collection of Jewish teachings that serve as the comprehensive guide to Jewish life.

Halakha Guidelines that specify how Jews relate to God and people.

Roman emperors often erected triumphal arches meant to commemorate their achievements. An arch built by the emperor Titus shows scenes of the Roman sack of the Jewish Temple in Jerusalem in 70 C.E. Here, Roman soldiers carry off Jewish sacred items including the seven-branched Menorah that was used at Hanukkah to celebrate the liberation from the Seleucids by the Maccabees. *(Scala/Art Resource, NY)*

did benefit, for the Jewish interest in commerce depicted in this passage reflects the unparalleled opportunities to pursue business activities that were open to Jews in cities throughout the Roman world and beyond that had Jewish communities.

The Teachings of Jesus of Nazareth

The most significant religious development of the early principate was the appearance of Christianity, a religion that grew out of Judaism and was based on the teachings of **Jesus of Nazareth.** Knowledge of the life of Jesus comes mainly from Matthew, Mark, Luke, and John, the first four books of the **New Testament** of the Bible, known collectively as the Gospels. The next book, the Acts of the **Apostles,** discusses the activities of Jesus's disciples after his **crucifixion.** The remainder of the New Testament consists of letters

(or epistles) written by followers of Jesus. From a historical perspective, the evidence of the New Testament is considered to be very reliable.

Jesus of Nazareth was born at the end of the reign of the Jewish king Herod, a time when many Jews were expecting the arrival of the Messiah, a word

Jesus of Nazareth (d. 33 C.E.) Founder of Christianity, whom Christians believe was the Son of God and the Jewish Messiah.

New Testament Books of scripture that the Christians added to the Hebrew Bible.

Apostles Original twelve disciples of Jesus Christ.

crucifixion Form of execution in which the victim is hung from a wooden crossbar and left to die a lingering death; Jesus was crucified.

A sixth-century manuscript from Rossano in Italy shows Jesus on trial before Pontius Pilate. On Pilate's left, Jews cry out for the condemnation of Jesus. Pilate disclaims responsibility for his order that Jesus be crucified by washing his hands. *(Scala/Art Resource, NY)*

translated into Greek as Christos, or **Christ.** According to Christian scripture, Jesus's mother, Mary, had been told by the angel Gabriel that even though she was a virgin, she would conceive by the Holy Spirit and give birth to the Son of God. Mary thus already was pregnant when she married Joseph, a distant descendant of King David and a carpenter in the town of Nazareth. Christian tradition placed the birth of Jesus on December 25 in a stable in the town of Bethlehem. Jesus's humble origins also were indicated by his early life as a carpenter.

When he was about thirty years old, Jesus was baptized in the Jordan River by his cousin John the Baptist, a Jewish holy man whom some Jews had already identified as the Messiah. The book of Luke said of Jesus, "The Holy Spirit descended on him as a dove, and a voice came from heaven, 'You are my beloved Son; with you I am well pleased.'" Jesus then began to take his message to the people. He gathered twelve disciples from varying backgrounds who accepted him as their rabbi. Several, such as Peter, were fishermen. Matthew was a tax collector and thus disliked by many people. Simon belonged to the Zealots, a group that advocated the violent overthrow of the Romans.

Christ   (from Greek "Christos," or "anointed") The Greek translation of the Hebrew word for the messiah, and the name given to Jesus of Nazareth.

For the following three years, Jesus traveled about Palestine, teaching in synagogues like any Jewish rabbi and also preaching in the streets. He carried his message not just to the rich and educated but also to the poor and oppressed. He taught that the kingdom of God was open to all equally, including people who were customarily looked down on, such as prostitutes and tax collectors. He also taught that the kingdom of God was coming quickly and that people needed to prepare themselves for it. People of high social status would not have any special privileges, as indicated by Jesus's lesson that it was easier for a camel to go through the eye of a needle than for a rich man to enter the kingdom of Heaven. Jesus recommended that the rich should give their wealth to the poor. He taught that the old Jewish covenants of Abraham and Moses with Yahweh now were replaced with a new covenant based on faith in the **grace** of God. As a demonstration of the power of God, he performed miracles such as changing water into wine, expelling demons, curing the sick, and raising the dead. Many of the most important points of Jesus's teachings appear in his Sermon on the Mount, delivered on a hillside to his disciples and a large crowd. Jesus made clear his message of peace and love, saying, "You have heard that it was said, 'You shall love your neighbor and hate your enemy.' But I say to you, love your enemies, bless those who curse you, do good to those who hate you, and pray for those who spitefully use you and persecute you." Unlike other Jewish popular leaders, however, and consistent with his message of peace, Jesus did not preach rebellion. When asked whether it was proper for Jews to pay taxes to the Romans, Jesus responded, "Give to Caesar the things that are Caesar's and to God the things that are God's," thus clearly expressing his teaching that the world of God was separate from the world of politics.

Those who believed Jesus's message saw him not only as the Messiah but also as the Son of God, but many Jews, especially Jewish leaders, saw him as a dangerous revolutionary. In the third year of his ministry, around the year 33 C.E., Jesus entered Jerusalem a few days before Passover, a Jewish spring holy day that commemorates the Exodus. Many Jews hailed him as the Messiah, causing the Sanhedrin, which oversaw Jewish religious and civil administration, to feel threatened by his increasing influence and to plot against him. Jesus foresaw his own death, and called his disciples together for a meal. He distributed to them bread and wine, which he told them to interpret as his body and blood, saying, "This is my blood of the new covenant, which is shed for many for the remission of sins." The Sanhedrin bribed one of Jesus's disciples, Judas, to identify him, and on that night Jesus was arrested and questioned by the Sanhedrin. Witnesses testified that Jesus had blasphemed against God, a capital crime under Jewish law. But only the Roman governor had the authority to impose the death penalty, so on Friday Jesus was brought before Pontius Pilate, the Roman **prefect,** or governor, of Judaea, who sentenced Jesus to death. Because Jesus was not a Roman citizen, he was subjected to the humiliating punishment of crucifixion. He died that evening and was buried in the tomb of one of his followers. Two days later, on Sunday, the Gospels report that Jesus rose from the dead. In the book of Matthew, Jesus appeared to his disciples and commanded them, "Go and make disciples of all nations," thus making it clear that his message was to be delivered not just to Jews but to all the people in the world. Forty days after his resurrection, his followers believed, Jesus rose to heaven.

Early Christian Communities

After Jesus's death, his followers, who were known as Christians, or the followers of Jesus the Christ, continued to **proselytize**—that is, to seek converts—for his teachings. The spread of Christianity was helped by three factors. First and foremost, Christianity met spiritual and social needs that other religions failed to address. Second, it attracted gifted adherents who were able to communicate its message and convince polytheists to convert. And third, it arose at a time when travel was easy and religious ideas could spread among multitudes of people. Initially, efforts at conversion were directed mainly at Jews, but this changed under the leadership of Paul of Tarsus, also known as Saul. A Jewish Pharisee and also a Roman citizen, Paul originally had persecuted the Christians and had stood by when Stephen, the first Christian **martyr,** was stoned to death by Jews in Jerusalem. While on his way to Damascus to arrest Christians, Paul had a vision in which Christ said to him, "Saul, Saul, why do you persecute me?", causing Paul to convert to Christianity and become one of its greatest

---

grace   The gift of God by which people receive salvation.

prefect   Equestrian military and tax collection official, or a governor of a small province.

proselytize   To recruit new members actively for an organization or belief.

martyr   (Greek for "witness") One who suffers for his or her faith.

promoters. Paul convinced the Christians of Jerusalem that Gentiles (non-Jews) who converted to Christianity should not be required to follow the Jewish laws, which would have required circumcision and adherence to a multitude of dietary and other restrictions. The primary requirement of converts was that they have faith in Christ, an emphasis that allowed Christians to deliver their message to all the peoples of the empire and beyond.

Paul tirelessly spread Christ's teachings throughout the Roman world, preaching that in the Christian world, there was "no Gentile and Jew, no circumcised and uncircumcised, no barbarian and Scythian, no slave and free freeman, but Christ in all things." During the 40s and 50s C.E., Paul visited Anatolia, Greece, and the Levant. He pursued his mission not just with visits, but also with letters—addressed to peoples such as the Galatians, the Hebrews, and even the Romans—in which he clarified the nature of Christian belief and the Christian life. Several of his letters later were incorporated into the New Testament. In the late 50s C.E., Paul was accused of plotting revolt and was arrested. He exercised his right as a Roman citizen to appeal his case to the emperor and was transported to Rome, where he continued to preach. According to Christian tradition, he eventually was tried, found guilty, and beheaded, an execution that befitted a Roman citizen.

Early Christians felt that Christianity offered them a much greater feeling of personal identity and spiritual fulfillment than the polytheistic religions. Like the mystery religions, Christianity promised an afterlife, but it also offered much more. Christians believed that Christ died to gain forgiveness for their sins. But they also believed it was their Christian duty to try not to sin, for Christianity offered a moral code according to which they were expected to live. The Christian message that all were equal in the sight of God regardless of wealth or social rank gave Christianity a degree of inclusivity that made it popular among less privileged people such as slaves, women, and the poor. Christianity also provided a sense of community, for along with offering the opportunity for private spirituality, Christianity also had a communal side. Christians met together to worship, very often in someone's house. Unlike Jewish synagogue meetings, which favored men, men and women participated together in early Christian worship services. Christian communities supported the poor, elderly, and sick. Early Christians also lived in the expectation that Christ soon would return. They believed that this Second Coming, also known as the **Apocalypse** and Judgment Day, would bring the kingdom of God and the destruction of the earthly world.

The early Christian church recognized two sacra-

ments, rituals that symbolized the bestowing of God's grace. One was baptism, which Christians believed washed away their past sins. Some Christians felt that people should wait to be baptized until they were old enough to profess their faith publicly; but others thought that infants should be immediately baptized because even they were tainted with the **original sin** of Adam and Eve, who had disobeyed God's command not to eat the fruit of the tree of knowledge in Eden. The other sacrament was the Eucharist, also known as Communion, a distribution of bread and wine based on Christ's Last Supper with his disciples. By taking Communion with each other, Christians shared their sense of community in God's grace. The worst punishment that could be inflicted on a Christian was **excommunication,** denial of the right to take Communion with other Christians. Christians who repented of sins committed after baptism were expected to confess them publicly before the other members of the Christian community. The penance that Christians performed to atone for their sins also was performed publicly. In this way, a sinner was reintegrated into the Christian community.

Christianity prospered earliest in urban environments for several reasons. The communal nature of early Christianity required a sufficiently large population, not found in the countryside. Cities also had diverse and often rootless populations looking for spiritual fulfillment. In cities, the Christian refusal to participate in traditional Roman religious practices did not attract as much attention as it would have in the countryside. In addition, the Jewish communities from which Christians often came were located in cities. The fact that early Christians often competed with Jews for converts may be one reason why the writers of the Gospels placed the blame for Christ's death not on the Romans but on the Jews, a consequence of which has been centuries of **antisemitism.**

Many Roman cities, especially in the east, gained Christian communities during the first few centuries of the principate. Christian congregations in each city

Apocalypse   The revealing of Jesus as the Messiah, a reference to the Second Coming of Christ, also known as Judgment Day.

original sin   Sin committed by Adam and Eve when they disobeyed God's command not to eat from the tree of knowledge.

excommunication   The denial of Communion to a Christian; later, the exclusion from other Christian sacraments as well.

antisemitism   Racial, religious, or ethnic hostility directed against Jews.

were under the overall authority of a male **bishop.** Christians believed that their bishops received their authority by **apostolic succession**—that is, by being the direct successors to the Apostles of Christ. Lower-ranking Christian clergy included priests, who oversaw spiritual matters, administered sacraments, and mediated between God and the congregation, and **deacons,** who initially could be either male or female and whose duties included managing church property, caring for the poor, and overseeing the instruction of new converts. The first Christian communities had little contact with each other. They often used different scriptures, had different rituals, and based their practices as much on oral tradition as on written texts.

The Christians in the Roman World

At first, the Romans took little notice of the Christians and had difficulty distinguishing Christians from Jews. But it soon became clear that there were differences. Christians, for example, met not on the Jewish Sabbath (Saturday) but on "the day of the Sun" (Sunday). Like the Jews, the Christians refused to worship other gods—a potential problem, for the imperial government saw participation in the cult of Rome and Augustus as the test for loyalty to the state. Jews were exempt from participation, but Christians were not. Normally, only high-ranking dignitaries were expected to sacrifice during cult rites, so Christians rarely had to worry about being tested. But if Christians were accused of atheism (not believing in the gods) or disloyalty, they could be ordered to sacrifice. If they refused, they could be found guilty of treason and executed. Because Christianity was different from other religions, misconceptions arose among the general public. Unlike polytheists, Christians worshiped in private, out of the public view, leading to suspicions that they were a secret society engaged in subversive activities. It also was thought that Christians were cannibals because they ate the flesh and drank the blood of their god (a misunderstanding of the sacrament of Communion) and that they practiced incest because they called each other "brother" and "sister."

When the Roman government noticed the Christians at all, it sometimes was tolerant. In 111 C.E., for example, Pliny the Younger, a Roman governor in Anatolia, consulted the emperor Trajan about how to deal with Christians. Trajan replied, "These people must not be hunted out; if they are brought before you and the charge against them is proved, they must be punished, but anyone who denies that he is a Christian, and makes this clear by offering prayers to our gods, is to be pardoned." Even in Trajan's lenient policy, Christians who refused to sacrifice to the state gods still were liable to execution. On other occasions, Christians were harshly treated. The historian Tacitus reports that in 64 C.E., a great fire incinerated a section of Rome where the emperor Nero had wanted to build a new palace. When suspicions arose that Nero himself had ordered the fire to be set, he blamed the Christians, and many were executed in what came to be known as their first **persecution.** Christians also were persecuted in other parts of the empire at other times. In 250 C.E., for example, the emperor **Decius** proposed to use religion to reunify the empire. He ordered all citizens to revalidate their loyalty by sacrificing at the altar of the imperial cult. Many Christians were martyred when they refused to sacrifice, although others did sacrifice and later were accused by other Christians of **apostasy,** or abandoning their faith.

Convicted Christians often were sentenced to die in the arena because they were noncitizens and therefore not entitled to a more honorable form of execution, such as decapitation. Those who were executed became martyrs and were revered for having died for their faith. Many martyrs also became **saints,** who lived model Christian lives and were believed to have the power to intercede with God. Two early martyrs and saints were the Apostles Peter and Paul, executed in Rome during the reign of Nero. Items associated with martyrs, such as their bones and clothing, were called **relics** and were thought to possess miraculous powers. The official court records of Christians' trials sometimes were preserved and later served as the basis for biographies known as "lives of the saints," which provided models for Christian behavior. One well-known such biography, that of Vibia Perpetua, included her own autobiographical account of the events leading up to her martyrdom at Carthage in 202 C.E.

bishop   Leader of the Christian community in a city.

apostolic succession   Belief that Christian bishops receive their authority by being direct successors to Jesus's Apostles.

deacons   Christian clerics responsible for overseeing church finances and carrying out good works of the church.

persecution   The seeking out and punishing of Christians by the imperial government.

Decius   (r. 249–251 C.E.) Roman emperor who sought to reunify the empire by ordering all citizens to sacrifice at the altar of the imperial cult.

apostasy   A Christian's denial of his or her faith.

saint   (from Latin, "holy") Christian martyr believed to be able to intercede with God.

relics   Pieces of the bodies or clothing of saints, thought to possess miraculous powers.

Voice

Vibia Perpetua Records the Events Leading to Her Martyrdom

Vibia Perpetua was a young Christian woman of Carthage in North Africa. In 202 C.E. she was arrested, convicted of being a Christian, and sentenced to fight wild animals in the arena. Her first-person account of the events leading up to her martyrdom on March 7, 203 C.E.—including her trial before the Roman procurator and several visions she had during the course of her imprisonment—is preserved in The Passion of Sts. Perpetua and Felicitas, from which the following selection is taken. The following day Perpetua was sent into the arena to die. When a mad cow failed to kill her, she guided the executioner's sword to her throat with her own hand. Her account then provided a model for later Christians for how to live their lives.

➡ *What kinds of pressures are put on Perpetua to sacrifice?*

➡ *What role did dreams play in the ancient world?*

➡ *Does Perpetua show any fear? Why or why not?*

➡ *Why does Perpetua see herself as a male gladiator?*

➡ *What does the "Gate of Life" signify?*

Another day we were suddenly snatched away to be tried; and we came to the forum and a very great multitude gathered together. We went up to the tribunal. The others being asked if they were Christians, confessed. So they came to me. And my father appeared there also, with my son, and tried to draw me from the step, saying, "Perform the sacrifice; have mercy on the child." ➡ And Hilarian the procurator said: "Spare your father's gray hairs; spare the infancy of the boy. Make sacrifice for the emperors' prosperity." And I answered, "I am a Christian." Then Hilarian passed sentence on us all and condemned us to the beasts; and cheerfully we went down to the dungeon. ➡ The day before we fought, I saw in a vision that Pomponius the deacon had come to the door of the prison and knocked hard on it. And I opened to him, and he said to me: "Perpetua, we await you; come." And he took my hand, and we went through rugged and winding places. At last he led me into the arena. And he said to me: "Be not afraid." And he went away. And I saw many people watching closely. ➡ And because I knew that I was condemned to the beasts I marveled that beasts were not sent out against me. And there came out against me a repulsive Egyptian, to fight with me. Also there came to me comely young men as my helpers. ➡ And I was stripped naked, and I became a man. And my helpers rubbed me with oil as their custom is for a contest. And there came forth a man of very great stature, wearing a purple robe and holding a green branch on which were golden apples. And he besought silence and said: "If this woman shall conquer the Egyptian, she shall receive this branch." And he went away. And we came close to each other. The Egyptian tried to trip up my feet, but with my heels I smote his face. And I rose up into the air and began so to smite him. And I caught his head, and he fell on his face; and I trod on his head. And I went up to the master of gladiators and received the branch. And he kissed me and said to me: "Daughter, peace be with you." ➡ And I began to go with glory to the gate called the Gate of Life. And I awoke; and I understood that I should fight, not with beasts but against the devil; but I knew that mine was the victory. Thus far I have written this, till the day before the games; but as for the deed of the games themselves let him write who will."

Source: Excerpt from "Vibia Perpetua Records the Events Leading to Her Martyrdom," W. H. Shewring, trans., *The Passion of Perpetua and Felicity* (London: Sheed & Ward, 1931). Reproduced by kind permission of Continuum International Publishing Group.

Christianity sometimes was thought to be a form of sun worship, as seen in this depiction of Christ as the sun god in a third-century mosaic from a Christian mausoleum beneath St. Peter's basilica in Rome. The head of Christ is surrounded with the halo of the sun god, which inspired the later Christian halo. *(Scala/Art Resource, NY)*

As of the late second century C.E., there were growing enclaves of Christians in cities throughout the Roman world. Christianity had shown remarkable staying power, not only enduring, but even being strengthened by periods of persecution. Christian intellectuals known as **apologists,** some of them converted polytheists, made an intellectual case for Christianity to the larger polytheist population. They argued that Christian teachings were compatible with the teachings of polytheistic philosophers such as Plato and that Christians were responsible subjects of the emperor. In addition, Christianity was gradually becoming part of the mainstream of Roman religion. For example, many people thought the Christians were sun worshipers because they met on the day of the Sun and their god had the same birthday as the sun. Even some Christians had a special reverence for the sun. But there still was no feeling among the general public that Christianity would ever be anything more than just one more eastern mystery religion.

The Roman Empire in Crisis, 193–284 C.E.

> ↓ In what ways did the principate no longer work in the third century C.E.?
> ↓ How did the army contribute to the empire's instability?

By the third century C.E., the principate was not functioning as well as it had in the past. New political and economic problems arose that the approach of Augustus could not solve. The supposed partnership of the emperors with the Senate fell apart as the emperors exercised more and more direct authority. At the same time, the army became more difficult to control, and the coinage lost much of its value. The inability of emperors to deal with these problems resulted in a period of civil wars and invasions that nearly destroyed the empire.

The Emperors and the Army

Beginning in the late second century C.E., the Roman Peace began to break down. During the reign of Marcus Aurelius, soldiers brought back a devastating plague from a Parthian war. And for the first time, there were serious problems on the northern frontier. Marcus spent most of his reign campaigning against Germanic peoples who were seeking to move south of the Danube, and by the time of his death, in 180 C.E., the Germans had been pushed back. But difficulties again surfaced after the assassination of Marcus's son Commodus in 192 C.E. Different armies named their commanders emperors. Civil war broke out, and the winner, **Septimius Severus** (193–211 C.E.), established the Severan dynasty (193–235 C.E.).

Severus was a native of Libya, and his wife, Julia, was a Syrian. They had little in common with the senators of Rome, who had supported one of his rivals and ridiculed his African accent. Realizing that he was completely dependent on the army, Severus began to abandon the pretense that he ruled in partnership with the Senate. The army had also changed. Few Italians enlisted anymore. Most soldiers came from the provinces, especially from the backwoods of the Rhine and Danube Rivers. To meet the need for troops, barbarian units from beyond the frontiers

apologists   Christian intellectuals who attempted to defend Christianity against attacks by polytheists.
Septimius Severus   (r. 193–211 C.E.) Roman emperor who looked to the army rather than the Senate for his support.

sometimes were hired. These soldiers had little in common with their cultured senatorial commanders and were much more difficult to control. They were less interested in defending the idea of Rome than in seeking personal gain.

The last emperor of the Severan dynasty was Severus Alexander (r. 222–235 C.E.), only thirteen years old at the time he came to power. He was much too young to rule on his own, and the government therefore was in the hands of his aunt and mother, both named Julia, who both received the title of **augusta.** This was the closest that Rome ever came to being ruled by women. Alexander's mother attended meetings of the Senate and attempted to restore its authority to counteract the growing influence of the army.

The Ruin of the Roman Economy

Septimius Severus was said to have advised his two sons, "Treat the soldiers well, and despise everybody else." He followed his own advice by granting the soldiers additional privileges. He allowed them to marry while still in service—making them happier but also less mobile, for they became reluctant to serve far from home. He also raised military salaries from 300 to 500 denarii a year. His son Caracalla (r. 211–217 C.E.) followed suit and increased military pay to 750 denarii per year. The treasury did not have nearly enough income to meet these increases.

To deal with the financial crisis, the emperors debased the money—that is, they mixed copper in with the silver. Soon the coins were only 50 percent silver, and their value fell accordingly. In addition, more than twice as many coins as usual were being poured into circulation every year. As the value of the coins decreased and the money supply increased, the cost of goods and services went up, resulting in runaway inflation. To make matters even worse, people hoarded the old all-silver coins and used the new debased ones to pay their taxes. Thus, every year when the incoming coins were melted down, there was less and less silver with which to mint new coins. In repeated cycles of debasement and inflation, the silver coinage lost almost all its value. By 260 C.E., the amount of silver in the coinage had fallen to 5 percent, and the salaries of the soldiers, rather than being increased, became virtually worthless.

Financial catastrophe also hit the cities, many of which had been misspending and overspending as a consequence of poor management. Some cities had begun massive building projects, such as new aqueducts and amphitheaters, that they could not pay for. The emperors often made up the difference, resulting

in another drain on the treasury. In some cases, emperors appointed caretakers to oversee a city's finances, thus increasing the size of the imperial bureaucracy. There also were problems with tax collection, which traditionally had been in the hands of the decurions. Shortfalls, which occurred more and more often, had to be made up by the decurions from their own resources. In addition, philanthropy by decurions that in the past had been optional, such as sponsoring entertainments, by the third century C.E. had become mandatory. As a consequence, being a decurion sometimes no longer was the great honor it once had been, and the emperors were in danger of losing local support.

The Imperial Crisis

In 235, the unruly army murdered Severus Alexander, marking the beginning of one of the most disastrous periods in Roman history, the **imperial crisis.** For several reasons, armies throughout the empire went out of control and began naming their commanders as emperors. First, the uncultured soldiers just could not be effectively commanded by cultured senators. In addition, because their salaries had become virtually worthless, their only meaningful pay became the gold donatives received when a new emperor was named, a situation that naturally encouraged them to make new emperors. Armies abandoned their frontier posts and marched on Rome to try to defeat the current emperor and force the Senate to recognize their candidate. No emperor was able to get the army back under control or to establish a new dynasty.

The borders could not have been left unguarded at a worse time, for several powerful enemies were menacing the frontiers. Germanic peoples north of the Rhine had coalesced into larger, more formidable coalitions, the **Franks** ("swordsmen") on the lower Rhine and the **Alamanni** ("all men") on the upper Rhine. The **Goths,** a Germanic people living north of the Black Sea, threatened Roman provinces on the Danube. And in the east, the Parthians were over-

---

augusta   (feminine form of "augustus") Title given to imperial women.

imperial crisis   Period of civil war and foreign invasions, between 235 and 284 C.E.

Franks, Alamanni, and **Goths**   Barbarian peoples who threatened Rome's northern frontier in the third century C.E.

New Persian kings advertised their achievements on a large scale. In this rock carving from Naqsh-e Rostam in Iran, the captured Roman emperor Valerian begs for mercy from King Shapur I, who had captured Valerian in 260 C.E. Valerian spent the rest of his life as a slave of the New Persians. *(Ancient Art and Architecture Collection)*

thrown in 227 C.E. by the Persians, who created the **New Persian Empire** and proposed to reestablish the Persian Empire of the fifth century B.C.E. The Persians laid claim to Egypt, Palestine, and Anatolia, resulting in an immediate state of war with the Roman Empire. All these foreign enemies were eager to take advantage of Roman weakness.

Disaster followed on disaster. The Franks, Alamanni, and Goths broke through the frontier defenses and ravaged the heart of the empire. In 251 C.E., the emperor Decius was killed by the Goths, an event that the Christians interpreted as the judgment of God against this persecuting emperor. The New Persians invaded the eastern provinces and captured and enslaved a Roman emperor. The provinces of Gaul, Spain, and Britain broke away and established their own empire. Then, just as it seemed that the empire was about to collapse, emperors known as the **soldier emperors,** who had risen through the ranks in the army and then been made emperor by their

troops, began to get the army back under control and put the empire back together. Aurelian (r. 270–275 C.E.), who gained the nickname "the Restorer of the World," drove the Goths and other invaders back across the Danube. In the east, he defeated Queen Zenobia of the desert city of Palmyra, who had declared her independence and seized several Roman provinces. Palmyra was destroyed, and the proud queen was taken captive. The Gallic empire capitulated without a fight. The empire now was on the road to recovery. In 284 another soldier emperor came to throne and definitively ended the imperial crisis.

New Persian Empire   Eastern empire extending from Mesopotamia to Iran that succeeded the Parthian Empire in 227 C.E.

soldier emperors   Emperors during the latter part imperial crisis who had risen through the ranks in the army and been made emperor by their troops.

Summary

Review Questions

↑ In what ways was the Roman Empire successful or unsuccessful during the principate?

↑ In what ways did the people living in the Roman Empire have a shared sense of identity?

↑ How did various religions meet the needs of people in the Roman world?

The Roman Empire, established by Augustus in 27 B.C.E., was the most successful empire the world had yet seen. Augustus established the empire in a form known as the principate, based on the concept that the emperor had restored the Republic and was sharing power with the Senate. Augustus and his successors were remarkably effective in being able to encourage people under Roman rule to feel that Rome's interests were their own interests. The empire brought peace and prosperity, and people throughout the provinces were able to share in the opportunities the empire offered. Even though the empire was based on the military might of the Roman army, the army was hardly ever visible, and instead of oppression it offered many Romans the opportunity for social advancement. The empire became more unified in several ways. Citizenship became available to all. Provincial men could become senators or even emperors. Previously disadvantaged groups, such as women, foreigners, and slaves, gained greater rights under the law than persons in any other ancient society. Trade and urban life flourished. A common culture extended to the most distant frontiers.

In this context of empirewide peace and security, a new religion arose, Christianity, based on the teachings of Jesus of Nazareth. Christianity began as a movement within Judaism but quickly developed as a separate religion. It met the spiritual needs of large numbers of people, and it attracted converts who were effectively able to spread its message. There soon were Christian communities in most of the large urban centers of the Roman world. But Christians also came into conflict with the Roman government when they refused to sacrifice to the imperial cult. Many were martyred, and it was not clear whether Christianity would be able to survive in the face of Roman persecution.

During the third century C.E., the empire established by Augustus began to fall apart. Emperors became more dependent on the army, and the Senate was shut out of power. The empire and its cities fell into financial difficulties. The government lost control of the armies, which revolted and made their own commanders emperors. Civil wars broke out, which gave foreign enemies the chance to raid and invade the empire. Parts of the empire were lost to invaders or to secession. By the middle of the third century C.E., it appeared that the empire might not survive. But then soldier emperors, who had spent their lives in the army, began to regain control of the armies and restore the empire.

← Thinking Back, Thinking Ahead →

Compare the effectiveness of the Roman Empire with the effectiveness of other empires of the ancient world.

ECHO ECHO ECHO ECHO ECHO

From Roman Gladiators to Boxing and Wrestlemania

The practice of ritual fighting to the death arose among the Etruscans as a means of appeasing underworld demons. The Romans copied it, and the first gladiators appeared in Rome in 264 B.C.E. at a senator's funeral. As a form of mock warfare, gladiatorial combats found a ready audience among the Romans, who were raised on stories of military bloodletting. During the empire, gladiators were the most popular entertainers in the Roman world, and many cities had their own gladiatorial teams. Some gladiatorial shows were truly spectacular: the emperor Trajan sponsored games with ten thousand combatants.

Gladiators were recruited from slaves, war captives, condemned criminals, and even freeborn persons—including senators, equestrians, and women—looking for fame and excitement. They swore an oath "to be burned, bound, beaten, and killed by the sword." Gladiators were classified according to their weapons. For example, some fought from chariots; some were armed like Gauls and wore large helmets decorated with a fish; and others were equipped with a net and trident. Female gladiators fought as Amazons, the female warriors of Greek legend.

If a gladiator was badly wounded, the crowd screamed "Hoc habet!" ("He's had it!"). If they turned their thumbs down, he was put to the sword, but if thumbs went up, he lived. Most combats did not end in death—after all, gladiators were expensive to train and maintain. An individual gladiator might fight only two or three times a year. Victorious gladiators were the sports heroes of their day. They enjoyed lengthy periods of leisure, receiving hero worship from the crowd, access to good food, and other forms of pleasure before training for their next combat. It was not uncommon for enslaved gladiators to be set free by popular demand after just a few victories.

The spirit of Roman gladiators lives on in many modern-day sports. Boxing matches often end with one or both contestants bloody and battered and the bloodthirsty crowd screaming for more. But for showmanship, the closest modern equivalent to gladiatorial contests would be professional wrestling spectaculars, where the crowd likewise screams for blood, but where—as must have been the case with many Roman gladiatorial matches—the fighting is well choreographed, with little real danger to the participants.

Suggested Readings

Balsdon, John P. V. D. *Romans and Aliens.* Chapel Hill: University of North Carolina Press, 1979. The role played by non-Romans in the evolution of Roman society.

Cary, Max, and Howard H. Scullard. *A History of Rome Down to the Reign of Constantine.* 3rd. ed. New York: Bedford/St. Martin's Press, 1976. A massive and detailed standard survey of the full extent of Roman history.

Dodds, Eric R. *Pagan and Christian in an Age of Anxiety: Some Aspects of Religious Experience from Marcus Aurelius to Constantine.* New York: Cambridge University Press, 1990. A discussion of the social, cultural, and emotional aspects of the period when Christianity and paganism had their greatest conflict.

Garnsey, Peter, and Richard Saller. *The Roman Empire: Economy, Society, and Culture.* Berkeley and Los Angeles: University of California Press, 1987. A study of the Roman Empire from the perspective of economic, social, and cultural development.

Millar, Fergus. *The Emperor in the Roman World (31 B.C.–A.D. 337).* Ithaca, N.Y.: Cornell University Press, 1992. The significance of the emperor for the evolution of the government of the Roman Empire.

Webster, Graham. *The Roman Imperial Army of the First and Second Centuries A.D.* 3rd ed. Norman: University of Oklahoma Press, 1998. The role played by the Roman army in the first two centuries of the empire.

Whittaker, C. R. *Frontiers of the Roman Empire: A Social and Economic Study.* Baltimore: Johns Hopkins University Press, 1994. An important study that emphasizes the role played by frontier peoples in the development of Roman politics and culture.

Websites

On the role played by Roman coinage, **Roman Numismatics, Art History, and Archaeology,** at www.romancoins.info

Detailed biographies of all the Roman emperors, including maps and battle summaries, *De Imperatoribus Romanis* **(On the Rulers of Rome),** at www.roman-emperors.org

More than one thousand photographs of artifacts related to the Roman Empire, **The Roman Empire,** at www3.flickr.com/photos/44124324682@N01/sets/31666

Late Antiquity, 284–527

CHAPTER OUTLINE

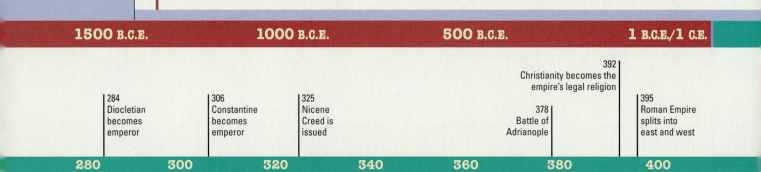

1500 B.C.E.	1000 B.C.E.	500 B.C.E.	1 B.C.E./1 C.E.

392
Christianity becomes the
empire's legal religion

284
Diocletian
becomes
emperor

306
Constantine
becomes
emperor

325
Nicene
Creed is
issued

378
Battle of
Adrianople

395
Roman Empire
splits into
east and west

280	300	320	340	360	380	400

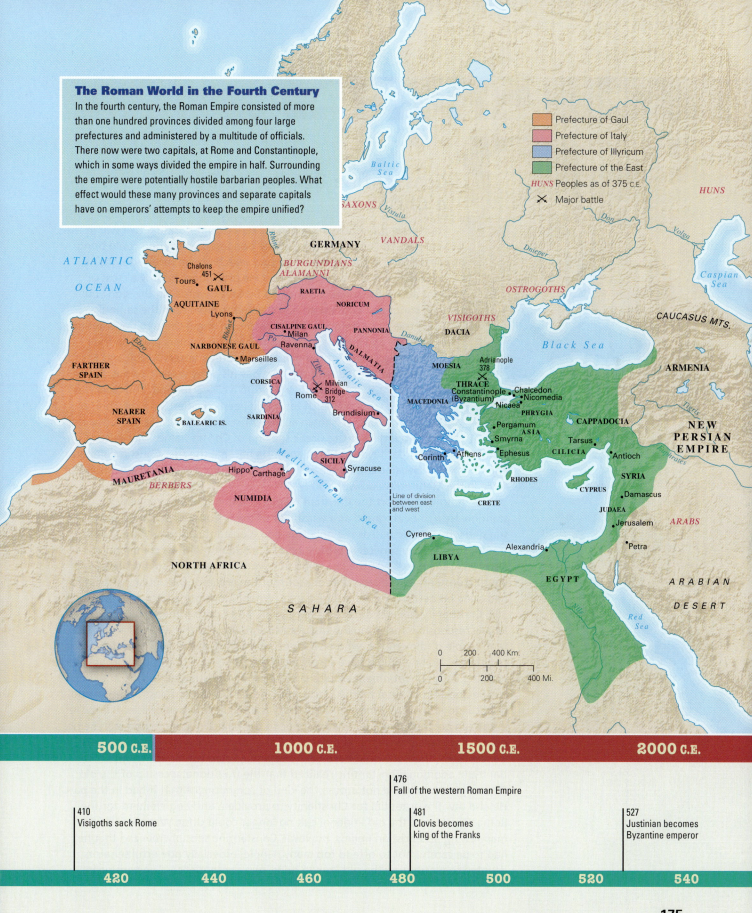

The Roman World in the Fourth Century

In the fourth century, the Roman Empire consisted of more than one hundred provinces divided among four large prefectures and administered by a multitude of officials. There now were two capitals, at Rome and Constantinople, which in some ways divided the empire in half. Surrounding the empire were potentially hostile barbarian peoples. What effect would these many provinces and separate capitals have on emperors' attempts to keep the empire unified?

Prefecture of Gaul
Prefecture of Italy
Prefecture of Illyricum
Prefecture of the East

HUNS Peoples as of 375 C.E.

✕ Major battle

ATLANTIC OCEAN

Baltic Sea

SAXONS

Vistula

GERMANY

VANDALS

BURGUNDIANS
ALAMANNI

Don

Volga

HUNS

Dnieper

OSTROGOTHS

Caspian Sea

Chalons 451 ✕
Tours • GAUL

RAETIA

NORICUM

Danube

DACIA

VISIGOTHS

Black Sea

CAUCASUS MTS.

AQUITAINE
Lyons •

CISALPINE GAUL
• Milan
Ravenna •

PANNONIA

MOESIA

Adrianople 378 ✕

ARMENIA

NARBONESE GAUL
• Marseilles

DALMATIA

Adriatic Sea

THRACE
Constantinople (Byzantium)
Nicaea

Chalcedon
• Nicomedia

NEW PERSIAN EMPIRE

FARTHER SPAIN

Ebro

CORSICA

Rome • Milvian Bridge 312 ✕

MACEDONIA

PHRYGIA

Tigris

Tarsus •

CAPPADOCIA

NEARER SPAIN

SARDINIA

Brundisium •

Pergamum •
ASIA
Smyrna •

CILICIA

• Antioch

Euphrates

SYRIA

BALEARIC IS.

Corinth •
• Athens

Ephesus •

CYPRUS

• Damascus

MAURETANIA
BERBERS

Hippo •
• Carthage

SICILY
Syracuse •

RHODES

Mediterranean Sea

CRETE

JUDAEA
• Jerusalem

ARABS

• Petra

NUMIDIA

Line of division between east and west

Cyrene •

Alexandria •

ARABIAN DESERT

NORTH AFRICA

LIBYA

EGYPT

Nile

Red Sea

SAHARA

0   200   400 Km.
0   200   400 Mi.

500 C.E.   1000 C.E.   1500 C.E.   2000 C.E.

476
Fall of the western Roman Empire

410
Visigoths sack Rome

481
Clovis becomes king of the Franks

527
Justinian becomes Byzantine emperor

420   440   460   480   500   520   540

Choice

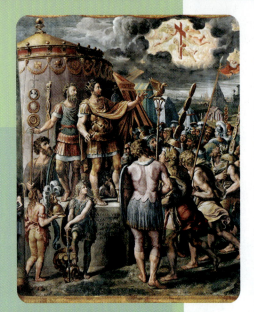

Constantine

Raised to worship the sun, Constantine became Roman emperor when Christianity was a persecuted religion. Soon afterward, he began to support Christianity. Several stories circulated about why Constantine had made this decision. Some believed he had received signs directly from God, as seen in this fresco of ca. 1500 in the papal palace in Rome by Raphael Sanzio showing Constantine seeing a vision of the Christian cross in the sky. (Scala/Art Resource, NY)

Constantine Decides to Become a Christian

Fourth-century Christian historians report that during a civil war in the year 312, the emperor Constantine pondered which god could bring him victory. In the course of his soul searching, he received signs he believed were divine revelations. One afternoon, he saw a cross of light above the sun, accompanied by Greek words "In this sign you shall conquer." Those with him claimed to have seen the same sign. Then, the night before a crucial battle, an angel came to Constantine in a dream and commanded him to have his soldiers place on their shields a sign made of the overlapping Greek letters X (chi) and P (rho). Constantine obeyed, and the next day his army was victorious. Everyone thought that the signs came from a powerful god. The cross was seen as the cross on which Jesus had been crucified, and the chi-rho sign, a symbol later known as the Christogram, was interpreted as the first two letters in the Greek spelling of Christ's name. Thereafter, Constantine showed great favor to Christianity. He became the first Christian emperor; and Christianity became the dominant religious, cultural, social, and even political force in the Mediterranean world.

The choice to support the Christian religion could not have been easy for Constantine. He had been raised as a worshiper of the unconquered sun, a militaristic sun god who was viewed as the only true god. Constantine's family had a long tradition of military service. A profession of Christianity, with its command to "love your enemies," was the last thing one would expect of a soldier. In his youth, Constantine had served at the court of the emperor Diocletian, who later had done his best to eradicate Christianity. When Constantine became emperor in 306, Christianity still was a persecuted religion, and Constantine would have been legally responsible for enforcing the persecution. Most of the wealthy and important people of the empire, whose support Constantine particularly needed, were polytheists. No one would have suspected that someone with this background and working in this environment would have turned to Christianity.

The question of what made Constantine suddenly abandon past tradition and political good sense to embrace Christianity is difficult to answer. His earlier belief in the sun god had made him sympathetic to the belief in a single god, and he no doubt was familiar with the popular belief that Christians were sun worshipers. Conceptually, then, it would have been but a small step for him to adopt Christianity. In addition, Constantine realized that the traditional worship of the old Roman gods simply did not arouse the kind of commitment that it had in the past. He also saw the potential for Christianity to provide a unifying element for the Roman world that the old imperial cult no longer could offer. When it came to manifesting his Christian beliefs, however, Constantine sensibly realized that he had to be careful not to offend too many people, especially powerful senators devoted to worshiping the old Roman gods. As a consequence, Constantine initially did not make his religions preferences obvious. For example, when he erected an arch of triumph in Rome, he attributed his victory to "the will of the divinity," without specifying which divinity. He also waited until he was on his deathbed to be baptized as a Christian, leading some to suggest he was not a committed Christian, although it was common at the time for Christians to delay baptism until the last moment in the belief that a person would then die without sin and go directly to heaven. If Constantine had not decided to become a Christian, and if the Roman government had continued to suppress Christianity, western civilization would have taken a different course. Later, because of his support for Christianity, he was called Constantine the Great.

Introduction

Constantine's decision to favor Christianity was the most striking of several significant changes that affected the Roman Empire just before and after the year 300. During fifty years of nearly constant civil war in the third century, the empire had seemed on the verge of extinction. Beginning in 284, it was largely the reforms of two able emperors, Diocletian and Constantine, that allowed the empire, which now can be called the Late Roman Empire, to survive. Yet some of these emperors' reforms had an unforeseen consequence: instead of unifying the empire, they led to greater fragmentation.

The middle of the third century marks the beginning of the period known as Late Antiquity, which lasted until the mid-seventh century and fills the gap between the Greek and Roman classical world and the Middle Ages. Whereas the principate was a time of social, political, and cultural stability and uniformity, Late Antiquity was marked by change and diversity. Political authority became decentralized, and the empire gradually split into eastern and western halves. Christianity became a favored religion with the full support of the imperial government. The emperor sometimes saw himself as the leader of the church, but powerful bishops contested this claim. Christian bishops took over many responsibilities that in the past had been held by civil officials. But the Christian church, which was intended to unify the empire, was itself racked by debates over authority and belief. The character of urban life changed as resources, that once had been expended on municipal public works, were reallocated to church building and as aristocrats reduced their support for the central government and withdrew to the countryside, where they were able to consolidate their influence.

During the fifth century, the western empire was infiltrated by non-Roman barbarian peoples from the north and east who sought security and a better life. Through a process of military conquest and largely peaceful settlement, the barbarians ultimately established independent kingdoms that later would develop into several modern-day European nations. The eastern part of the empire, however, continued as before and even prospered, in the form known today as the Byzantine Empire. In general, the Mediterranean world, once unified by Rome, now was breaking up.

The Restoration of the Roman Empire, 284–337

↓ What did Diocletian and Constantine do to try to restore order in the Roman Empire?
↓ How did the administration of the empire change during the late Roman period?

In 284, the Roman Empire still was in crisis. The army had spent fifty years in repeated revolts: there was no effective method for choosing emperors, the borders were under attack by barbarian peoples, and many people felt disadvantaged or alienated. In addition, the economy was in a shambles, imperial control over the army was shaky, the expanding bureaucracy was increasingly difficult to pay for, and the imperial cult no longer fulfilled its unifying purpose. Beginning in the 270s, a series of soldier emperors brought some stability. Order was fully restored under Diocletian and Constantine, who introduced many reforms. They brought the army back under control, devised ways to revive the failing economy, and assumed a much greater level of personal responsibility for the survival of the empire.

Chronology

284 Diocletian becomes emperor	**395** Roman Empire splits into eastern and western halves
303 Great Persecution begins	**406** Barbarians cross Rhine River
306 Constantine becomes emperor	**410** Alaric and the Visigoths sack Rome
312 Constantine defeats Maxentius at Battle of Milvian Bridge	**437** Theodosius II issues Theodosian Code
313 Edict of Milan grants religious freedom to Christians	**451** Romans defeat Huns at Battle of Chalons; Council of Chalcedon condemns the Monophysites
325 Nicene Creed states official Christian beliefs	**476** Western Roman Empire falls
337 Constantine is baptized a Christian	**481** Clovis becomes king of Franks
364 Valentinian I becomes emperor	**489** Ostrogoths invade Italy
378 Visigoths defeat Romans at Battle of Adrianople	**527** Justinian becomes Byzantine emperor
387 Augustine baptized as a Christian	
392 Theodosius I makes Christianity the legal religion of the empire	

Diocletian and the Return to Order

In 284, **Diocletian,** a tough Balkan soldier, was named emperor by the Roman army. Diocletian's origins were obscure: some said he was the son of a clerk, others that he was a freed slave. Like many Romans who wanted to improve their positions, he joined the army, where he rose through the ranks and did well. According to one Roman historian, "He was crafty, but also very wise and insightful. He was disposed to cruelty, but was nonetheless a very able ruler." Like the first Roman emperor, Augustus, Diocletian was a better administrator than general, but a competent administrator was just what the empire needed. Diocletian believed that it was the emperor's duty to oversee every aspect of life within the empire to ensure its future. First, he needed to end the military revolts, after which he could implement other long-term reforms. Diocletian's reign marks the beginning of the period known as the **Late Roman Empire.**

To reduce the threat of rebellion, Diocletian raised the status of the emperor from *princeps* ("first man") to *dominus* ("lord and master"), thus transforming the emperor from a high-ranking senator into a virtual living god. As emperor, Diocletian exchanged the general's cloak for a floor-length purple robe encrusted with gemstones and wore a pearl diadem as a crown. Everything associated with the emperor's person—the laws, the government, the coinage, his every word—became "sacred." Those who met with Diocletian were expected to fall facedown before him. These changes made it more difficult for potential rivals to pass themselves off as emperors.

As another means of reducing the possibility of a revolt, Diocletian limited the power of possible rivals and took away all remaining power from the Senate. Political authority now belonged to the emperor and army alone, and the Senate was reduced to the status of a city council for Rome. To lessen senators' influence even further, Diocletian also limited the oppor-

Diocletian (r. 284–305) Emperor who began the creation of the Late Roman Empire.

Late Roman Empire Second phase of the Roman Empire, from 284 to 480, and the first phase of Late Antiquity.

dominus (Latin for "lord and master") Title of Roman emperors during the Late Roman Empire.

tunities for senators to hold high-ranking government posts, especially military ones. He divided up possible sources of power. He split the army by pulling the most able troops back from the border and creating a mobile field army stationed in the interior, leaving the remaining troops as a border army guarding the frontier. He separated civil careers from military careers so provincial governors did not command troops and generals did not govern provinces. By subdividing the provinces, he increased their number from fifty to one hundred, thereby decreasing the power of each governor. These subdivisions of authority helped end the cycle of revolts but also greatly increased costs. Soon there were approximately 40,000 officials on the imperial payroll, and the army had a paper strength of about 450,000.

Once Diocletian had solidified his authority over the army and the government, he turned his attention to the economy. Tax income had been reduced because farms in border areas had been abandoned owing to the constant warfare. In addition, the debased silver coinage was virtually worthless; soldiers complained that their entire annual salary was used up on one small purchase. Taxes paid in these coins were hardly worth collecting. There was not enough gold and silver in the treasury to issue good gold and silver coins, so in an attempt to make the money worth something again, Diocletian issued a large copper coin coated with silver. No one, however, was fooled. He then tried to restore value to the money by issuing a law that set maximum prices for goods and services, but the law was blatantly disregarded.

Diocletian finally recognized that the value of the money could not be restored, so he required that the land tax be paid in produce rather than in the worthless coinage. A farmer, for example, paid roughly 20 percent of a harvest as taxes. Sheep owners paid in wool; the owners of iron mines paid in iron. Foodstuffs and other raw materials were gathered into imperial storehouses, processed in imperial factories, and used to pay soldiers with food rations, clothing, and weapons. A soldier's only significant monetary compensation was the donative, which now was issued in pure gold and silver at five-year intervals. This system was cumbersome, requiring an even larger bureaucracy, but it worked. In a further attempt to keep the empire going, Diocletian identified compulsory services that had to be performed. These who performed these occupations, such as soldiers, bakers, decurions, and tenant farmers, were prohibited from changing jobs, and their children were required to hold the same jobs. Enforcement of this requirement, however, proved virtually impossible.

Like earlier emperors, Diocletian believed that participation in the imperial cult could be used to unify the empire. But this belief brought him into conflict with Christianity, which rejected participation in the imperial cult and which Diocletian therefore saw as a direct threat to the well-being of the empire, all the more so because Christianity now attracted not just less privileged persons but also soldiers and even the occasional senator. As a result, Diocletian began in 303 what became known as the **Great Persecution.** Christians were ordered to sacrifice in the imperial cult or die. Some Christians actually were executed, especially in the east, and were added to the growing catalogue of Christian martyrs. But in most parts of the empire, the orders were ignored. Christianity by now had become too popular and widespread to be eliminated.

The Rise of Constantine

Believing that the empire was too large and complex to be governed by a single emperor, Diocletian divided it into four parts and appointed three of his army colleagues as co-emperors. Doing so created the **Tetrarchy,** shown in Table 7.1. Two emperors, Diocletian and Maximian, had the rank of augustus (senior emperor) in the eastern and western halves of the empire, respectively, whereas the other two, Galerius and Constantius, were their junior emperors and had the title of caesar. To create family ties among themselves and cement their alliance, the emperors married one another's daughters. Constantius, for example, was compelled to dismiss his concubine **Helena** to marry Maximian's daughter Fausta. Each emperor's court, consisting of his household, chief officials, and bodyguard, accompanied him wherever he went. The multiple emperors dealt effectively with matters of internal and external security. Maximian, for example, crushed rebellious peasants in the west, and Galerius defeated the New Persians and brought peace to the eastern frontier. But it always was clear that Diocletian was in control. His personal authority forced his three colleagues to rule peacefully together.

This system of multiple emperors also gave Diocletian a way to deal with the imperial succession,

Great Persecution   Last official persecution of Christians, begun by Diocletian in 303 and ended by Constantine's Edict of Milan in 313.

Tetrarchy   (in Greek, "rule by four") Four-emperor system established by Diocletian.

Helena   (ca. 250–330) Mother of the emperor Constantine who believed she had discovered the cross on which Christ was crucified.

A statue in porphyry (a purple stone), originally in Constantinople but now in Venice, shows the four emperors of the Tetrarchy demonstrating their solidarity with each other. The message is that even though there are four emperors, there is only one empire. Each emperor has one hand on his sword, demonstating the source of his authority. *(Alinari/Art Resource, NY)*

Table 7.1

The Tetrarchy

	Augustus	Caesar
East	Diocletian (r. 284–305) (Anatolia, Syria, Egypt) (retired in 305)	Galerius (r. 293–311) (the Balkans) (promoted to augustus in 305)
West	Maximian (r. 286–305) (Italy, Africa, Spain) (retired in 305) Son: Maxentius	Constantius (r. 293–306) (Gaul, Britain) (promoted to augustus in 305) Son: Constantine

Maxentius and **Constantine,** the sons of Maximian and Constantius. There was muttering in the army, which had always preferred emperors to be succeeded by their sons. A year later, while visiting York in Britain, Constantius became very ill. Before dying, he recommended his son to his soldiers, who then loyally proclaimed Constantine emperor.

The Tetrarchy then collapsed. Its fatal flaw was that it could not overcome the army's preference for sons to succeed their fathers. In Rome, Maxentius also was declared emperor, making a total of six emperors. Civil war again erupted as each emperor attempted to expand his authority. In 312, Constantine attacked Maxentius and, following his famous visions (see Choice), defeated and killed him at the battle of the **Milvian Bridge** just outside Rome. The next year, in early 313, Constantine demonstrated his support for Christianity by issuing the **Edict of Milan,** which decreed religious freedom for Christians and returned confiscated Christian property, thus bringing the persecutions to an end. By 324, Constantine's rivals were dead. Once again a single emperor controlled the empire.

Constantine the Great   (r. 306–337) Roman emperor who completed the restoration of the Roman Empire and made Christianity a favored religion.

Milvian Bridge   Battle in which Constantine attributed his victory over Maxentius, outside Rome in 312, to the support of the Christian God.

Edict of Milan   Law issued by Constantine in 313 making Christianity a legal religion.

which had been the greatest cause of instability during the principate. Diocletian decided that the successor of each senior emperor would be his junior emperor, who then would become the new senior emperor and name a new junior emperor. In 305, claiming that he had ruled long enough, Diocletian took an unprecedented step: he retired and made his co-augustus Maximian do the same, thus ensuring that his system for dealing with the imperial succession took effect. A second Tetrarchy was formed: Galerius and Constantius assumed the rank of augustus, and they appointed two new caesars. A potential difficulty with this arrangement, however, was that it ignored

URBS CONSTANTINOPOLITANA NOVA ROMA.

Constantinople is depicted in the *Notitia dignitatum*, a list of Roman offices compiled ca. 400 C.E., showing the city's protected location on a heavily fortified peninsula. A large round church dome emphasizes the Christian orientation of the city. The legend reads, "The City of Constantinople, New Rome" *(Bodleian Library, University of Oxford)*

Constantine and Late Roman Government

Constantine faced the same problems as Diocletian, but he tried some different solutions. For example, he reversed Diocletian's policy toward senators by welcoming them into imperial offices in the hope that they then would support the imperial government. Regarding the economy, Constantine decided that a trustworthy hard currency was needed to meet the expanding needs of the army and bureaucracy. Rather than trying to revive the discredited silver coinage, he put the empire on the gold standard by introducing a new gold coin, the **solidus.** Taxpayers who preferred the convenience of cash to payments in produce could pay in gold. Other taxes, such as the merchants' income tax, were assessed in gold. These policies resulted in a recycling of the gold coinage: it was constantly paid out in expenses and received back in taxes. The solidus was so successful that it was the standard means of exchange in the Mediterranean world for nearly seven hundred years.

Constantine recognized that the empire's greatest source of economic and population resources lay in the east. Therefore, in 330 he established a second imperial capital on the site of the old Greek city of Byzantium on the Bosporus, the strategic strait that linked the Mediterranean and Black Seas and controlled traffic between Asia and Europe. He named the new city **Constantinople,** after himself. In many ways, Constantinople (modern Istanbul) was a carbon copy of Rome. It soon had its own imperial administration and officials as well as its own chariot racecourse, the **Hippodrome.** New senators were created to populate a new Senate. Constantine also made Constantinople into a purely Christian city, in contrast to Rome, by building churches such as the Church of **Hagia Sophia** and a cross-shaped Church of the Holy Apostles, where he planned to be buried. But Constantine did not neglect Rome. Along with his triumphal arch, he also built churches, such as the Church of Saint John Lateran, which became the official church of the bishop of Rome. And he completed the construction of a large basilica that he used as an audience hall, the last monument to be built in the old Roman Forum.

solidus   (Latin for "solid") Gold coin introduced by Constantine, weighing 1/72 pound.

Constantinople   Second capital of the Roman Empire, established by Constantine in the east in 330.

Hippodrome   (from Greek for "running horse") Chariot racecourse in Constantinople and a site for gatherings of the people.

Hagia Sophia   (Greek for "holy wisdom") Church built in Constantinople by Constantine.

Constantine established a method for choosing emperors on the basis of dynastic succession that proved to be remarkably stable. Whenever possible, fathers were succeeded by sons. If an emperor had no sons and the position became vacant, the army had the authority to acclaim a new emperor. The reigning emperor or emperors also had the authority to create new emperors. The Senates of Rome and Constantinople had no role in choosing emperors except to deliver congratulations. Male emperors still bore the title augustus, and imperial women could be granted the title augusta. Women were not constitutionally excluded from ruling although for more than four hundred and fifty years no woman ruled in her own name.

Late Roman government was cumbersome, but it worked. The government had civil and military branches. The highest-ranking generals were the **masters of soldiers,** and the chief civil officials were the four praetorian prefects. Ranking below them were many layers of other officials. The Late Roman Empire, including the emperors themselves, continued to be ruled by law. Emperors preferred to deal with problems by issuing laws, many thousands of which survive. Every word that came from the emperor, even brief replies to questions, had the force of law. All of this legislation makes the Late Empire look like it regulated all aspects of Roman life, such as who could marry whom or who could pursue what kind of career. In reality, however, emperors were unable to enforce all these laws, and the laws often were disobeyed. They worked well enough to keep the empire going, but not so well that it became a complete dictatorship.

When Constantine died in 337, his new succession policy went into effect, and the empire was divided among his three sons. The empire appeared as sound and stable as it had been in the time of Augustus.

The Christian Empire, 312–415

↓ How did the Roman Empire change after Christianity was legalized?

↓ In what ways did people express their devotion to Christianity?

The most momentous change that occurred during Late Antiquity was the growing influence of the Christian church. Constantine himself is best known as the emperor who began the process of making Christianity into the predominant religion of the Mediterranean world. His example and initiatives had a profound effect on the life, culture, and religion of the Roman world. With startling rapidity, in only eighty years, Christianity went from a persecuted religion to the only legal religion (aside from Judaism) in the Roman Empire. Conversions to Christianity, that in the past would have occurred in an atmosphere of fearful secrecy, now were celebrated with joyous publicity. Christianity soon pervaded late Roman culture, society, and politics.

Constantine and the Church

Like his predecessors, Constantine believed that religion could be used to unify the empire, but he also felt that Christianity was a better choice than the imperial cult. If Christian support could be acquired, the organizational structure, standardized doctrine, and public services of the Christian church could be mobilized on behalf of the empire. Constantine, therefore, favored the Christians in various ways, such as exempting Christian priests from burdensome service on city councils; making Sunday, the Christian day of worship, an official day of rest; and forbidding Jews from keeping Christian slaves. At the same time, social services, such as the care of the sick and poor, something the emperors had never had the resources or resolve to undertake, were delegated to the church. In addition, Constantine's support for Christianity allowed him to confiscate polytheist temple treasures and use the gold to mint his new gold coins and also to finance the magnificent churches he constructed in Rome, Constantinople, and elsewhere.

But Constantine soon discovered that he had been mistaken in assuming the Christians were unified. The Christian community in each Roman city was in many ways an independent enclave under the authority of its bishop. Christians in different parts of the empire spoke different languages. There were no higher-ranking church authorities to enforce unity. Christians did not even agree on which books belonged in the Bible. The church was racked by disputes over **theology,** practices, and authority. To deal with these issues, Constantine assumed the responsibility for encouraging, or even compelling, churchmen to settle their disputes. Just as the emperor had appropriated authority from the Senate during the principate, Constantine now began to appropriate authority from the church, and as a result he accumulated even greater power.

masters of soldiers Highest-ranking generals in the late Roman army.

theology Study of religious teachings and beliefs.

The most troubling Christian conflict of this time involved questions about the nature of the Christian God. In the book of Matthew in the Bible, Jesus told his disciples to baptize "in the name of the Father, and of the Son, and of the Holy Spirit." This instruction gave rise to the understanding that God consisted of three persons, known as the Trinity. Conflict over how the three related to each other burst forth in the 320s when an Alexandrian priest named Arius taught that Christ the Son was subordinate to and of a different nature from God the Father. This teaching became known as Arianism. Many others, however, believed that the Father and Son were equal in status and of the same nature. Constantine, the only one with enough authority to settle the dispute, convened an ecumenical church council attended by bishops of cities from throughout the empire who were told to come up with a definition that everyone could agree with. Thus, in 325, 318 bishops assembled at the Council of Nicaea, a city in northwestern Anatolia, and condemned Arianism as a heresy, an illegal belief. The bishops issued the Nicene Creed, which stated what all Christians were expected to believe and became the official statement of faith of the Roman Empire. The council also adopted for the church an administrative hierarchy based on the Roman model. Each city in each province was placed under the spiritual authority of a bishop and each province under the oversight of a higher-ranking bishop called an archbishop. The bishops of three cities—Alexandria, Antioch, and Rome—were given the even higher rank of patriarch, as were the bishops of Jerusalem and Constantinople soon afterward. The bishop of Rome, the original capital city of the empire, claimed the greatest status of all based on apostolic succession from the apostle Peter, the first bishop of Rome. But many bishops, including those who had their own apostolic succession, refused to acknowledge this claim.

Constantine's last official act left a troublesome legacy, for his deathbed baptism in 337 was carried out by an Arian bishop who, in spite of his refusal to repudiate his belief, had risen in the emperor's favor. Shortly after Constantine's death, Arian bishops gained much influence, and it appeared that Arianism might yet triumph. The Goth Ulfilas learned the Arian form of Christianity while living in the empire and returned home to convert many of his people. They and other barbarian peoples then adopted Arianism.

The Impact of Christianity

The expansion of Christianity in the fourth century induced great personal and spiritual soul searching. Many people rethought their religious beliefs and the role that religion played in their lives. Christianity continued to offer the same attractions it had in the past: a moral code, communal worship services, a sense of community, economic support, an emphasis on personal spirituality, and hope of an afterlife. To this list now was added government preference, which resulted in increasing social and even official pressure for non-Christians to convert.

Christians also now had the opportunity to seek converts more openly than in the past. Conversion efforts were focused within the empire, where large numbers of people, especially in the countryside, clung to the religious practices of their ancestors. In addition, the senators of Rome, who believed that Rome's past successes were the result of faithfulness to the ancient Roman deities, continued to support traditional Roman religious practices. Convincing people such as these to change their religious identity was difficult work. There was little official interest, therefore, in converting foreigners. Conversions of foreign peoples, such as the work of Ulfilas the Goth, usually were carried out privately. Another private missionary was Patrick, a native of Britain who undertook to convert the Irish to Christianity around 430. Not until the sixth century, when most of the rural population of the empire finally had been brought into the Christian fold, was formal missionary activity initiated outside the Roman world.

There continued to be alternatives to Christianity. Paradoxically, the rise of Christianity led to a momentary revival of polytheism. When Constantine's nephew Julian succeeded to the throne in 361, it turned out that he had been a secret sympathizer with polytheism. He abandoned Christianity and openly worshiped the traditional gods, thus gaining the nickname "Julian the Apostate." Julian attempted to weaken Christian influence. For example, he prohibited Christian professors

---

Trinity   The three persons—Father, Son, and Holy Spirit—making up the Christian God.

Arianism   Form of Christian belief introduced by the priest Arius, who taught that Christ the Son was subordinate to God the Father; condemned at the Council of Nicaea in 325.

ecumenical   Relating to church councils made up of bishops from throughout the Christian world.

heresy   A prohibited form of Christian belief as defined by church councils and the imperial government.

Nicene Creed   Standard statement of Christian belief, issued at the Council of Nicaea in 325 and still recited in many Christian churches.

Patrick   (ca. 385–450) British missionary who brought Christianity to Ireland.

Christianity was not the only late Roman religion that offered believers salvation gained through baptism. In this scene, the Persian god Mithras slaughters the bull in whose blood initiates into the cult were baptized. The cult of Mithras, a sun god whose birthday was on December 25, was especially popular in the Roman army, but in the competition with Christianity it was doomed by its exclusion of women. *(Werner Forman/Corbis)*

from teaching classical literature, arguing that it was hypocritical to teach about gods in whom one did not believe. He also used the Christian church as a model for an organized polytheist church. But Julian's efforts failed, for Christianity had gained too strong a hold on the devotion of the people. In 363, during an invasion of the New Persian Empire, Julian was killed—some said by a Christian soldier in his own army. He was the last non-Christian ruler of the whole empire. All serious hope of imperial support for the old Roman religion died along with him.

Other non-Christian forms of belief and worship continued to attract followers. Neoplatonism, which had evolved from the teachings of Plato, was the most influential philosophical teaching of Late Antiquity. It viewed the universe as a hierarchy, with earthly matter at the lowest level of existence and a single, impersonal, divine principle called "The One" at the highest and most distant level. An adherent's duty was to try to leave earthly existence behind and attain a higher level of consciousness. Neoplatonism's stress on morality and self-discipline made it attractive to Christians. On the other hand, the cult of the Persian sun god Mithras was particularly popular with soldiers. The cult shared many aspects with Christianity, such as a moral code, group worship, communal meals, and baptism (in the blood of a slaughtered bull). Mithras's birthday, December 25, was even adopted by the Christians as the birthday of their own god, giving additional support to the idea that Christians were sun

worshipers. Mithraism's appeal was limited, however, by its exclusion of women. In the case of Neoplatonism and Mithraism, the attractiveness of a non-Christian belief was influenced by how much it resembled Christianity, indicating the degree to which Christianity had become the standard by which other religions were measured.

The only non-Christians who successfully retained their ancestral beliefs were the Jews. There still was a sizable Jewish population in Palestine, overseen by the Jewish patriarch. In addition, the Diaspora had placed Jewish communities in many cities in the empire and beyond, including over a million Jews living under New Persian rule in Babylon. Two versions of the Talmud were created by the Jews, who valued scholarship more than any other activity: a Palestinian one, which was completed in the late fourth century; and a Babylonian one, which was in circulation by around 500 and continues to be the authoritative basis for Jewish life. Even though the Christian population generally acknowledged the Jews' right to practice

Neoplatonism Late Roman philosophical belief descending from Plato that taught the existence of a single overall god and stressed morality and self-discipline.

Mithras Persian sun god popular with the Roman army.

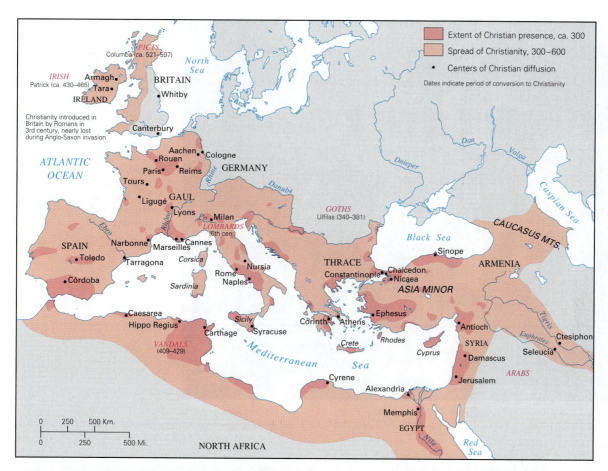

MAP 7.1 **The Spread of Christianity to 600 C.E.** During the first six centuries C.E., Christianity spread throughout the Roman world, with the greatest acceptance of Christianity coming after Constantine began making it into a favored religion after 312 C.E. Christians and Zoroastrians interacted in the New Persian Empire.

their religion, sporadic attempts were made to convert them to Christianity. Roman emperors attempted to pressure Jews to convert by issuing legislation that prohibited them from holding government posts, from making wills, from receiving inheritances, and from testifying in court. In 425, the Jewish patriarchate was abolished. Few Jews, however, abandoned their faith, and there continued to be a Jewish presence in virtually all the cities of the Roman world.

The Christian Life

The imperial acceptance of Christianity brought an end to the old distinction between personal and state religion. Regardless of whether one was worshiping privately at home or publicly in church, the same scriptures were used and the same God was being worshiped. Christian worship included personal, pri-

vate, communal, and ceremonial elements. Christians also rethought their role in the Roman world. Now that Christianity was becoming a favored religion, Christians began to treat non-Christians in a more disparaging manner. They described the believers in the traditional gods as **pagans,** a word meaning "country dwellers".

Eventually nearly everyone in the Roman world, except for the Jews, converted to Christianity. Certain kinds of behavior were expected of them. Attendance at Sunday church services was considered an outward demonstration of a Christian's internal devotion, and the presence of a church in a city, town, or

pagans (from Latin *paganus,* "country dweller") Term used by Christians to describe participants in traditional religious practices.

Beginning with Constantine, Roman emperors sponsored the construction of many Christian churches. Constantine himself built churches in both Rome and Constantinople. The round church of St. Costanza (Constantina) in Rome was built under Constantine as a tomb for his daughters Constantina and Helena but later was converted into a church. *(Scala/Art Resource, NY)*

village demonstrated the existence of an active Christian community. The simplest kind of church could be a converted house. Churches in cities, on the other hand, could be very large. Some were built in the shape of a cross, but most were constructed in the basilica style that in the past had been used for large public audience halls. **Chapels** often were attached to the sides of larger churches and dedicated to particular saints. Churches could be elaborately decorated, with fine mosaics or frescoes on the walls and marble columns. The holiest section, or **chancel,** was on the east end. The chancel housed the altar and was accessible only to the clergy and choir. A screen divided the chancel from the remainder of the church, or **nave,** where the congregation of men and women stood to worship. The main entrance was on the west end, where a baptismal font, or baptistery, for the performance of baptisms often was located. Many churches also had an underground crypt, usually below the chancel, for burials and the preservation of relics.

Christian church services in Late Antiquity included prayers; readings from scripture; the singing and chanting of hymns and biblical psalms by both choir and congregation; and sermons by bishops and priests, who often were trained speakers. The church calendar included saints' days that marked the date

of the death of Christian martyrs and other holy men and women. Social life increasingly revolved around the church, with people visiting with one another before and after the service. In these ways, Christianity differed greatly from paganism, which had no concept of regular attendance at religious services.

Christians also were expected to live a virtuous private life. In addition to the three Christian virtues of faith, hope, and charity (Christian love), Christians adopted the Greek and Roman cardinal virtues of temperance, prudence, courage, and justice. Private worship involved prayer and fasting, and Christians also were expected to perform good works. Christians were taught to distribute their wealth to the poor and to make offerings to the church. Christians also believed that the only acceptable sexual relations were those sanctified by the marriage bond and undertaken for the procreation of children. Senior Christian clerics,

chapel Small building or room used for Christian worship, often in association with a larger church.

chancel Part of a church containing the altar.

nave Main part of a church, especially the long, narrow central section.

such as bishops and priests, were expected to give up sexual relations even if they were married.

Christians continued to live in constant expectation of the Second Coming of Christ. Apocalyptic literature, such as the biblical book of Revelation, attempted to predict when the end would come. Some Christians combined the creation of the world in seven days with the scriptural passage that "every day is like a thousand years" to predict that the Apocalypse would occur around 400 or 500 C.E. Others thought that sinister signs would predict the approach of the Apocalypse. For example, Bishop Cyprian of Carthage wrote, "Wars continue to prevail, death and famine accumulate, the human race is wasted by the desolation of pestilence. The Day of Judgment is now drawing near, the censure of an indignant God."

To prepare themselves for the Last Judgment, many Christians experienced a second conversion, after which they devoted their lives completely to religion. One of these was **Augustine,** a North African who was raised as an unbaptized Christian and also received a classical education based on the traditional Greek and Latin authors. Augustine became a successful teacher and public speaker but felt there was something lacking in his life. In the midst of a spiritual crisis, he heard a child chanting "Tolle, lege" ("Take up and read"). He therefore picked a random spot in the Bible and read, in Paul's letter to the Romans, "Arm yourself with the lord Jesus Christ; spend no more thought on nature's appetites." Taking this passage as a sign, he committed himself to religion and was baptized on Easter Day, 387, by Bishop **Ambrose of Milan.** Augustine's later account of his conversion, known as the *Confessions,* is the most important autobiography to survive from antiquity. Augustine later was named bishop of Hippo in North Africa and wrote a great many letters, sermons, theological tracts, and interpretations of scripture. One of his most important teachings was that, because humanity was polluted by the original sin of Adam and Eve, people could not receive eternal life through their own efforts but only by receiving God's gift of grace. Many of Augustine's teachings on the church's authority, the Christian view of history, and Christian doctrine became the standard views of the Christian church and continue to influence Christian thought.

Christian Asceticism and Monasticism

Some Christians believed that to reach a higher level of spirituality and become closer to God, they had to separate themselves from the everyday world. These Christians practiced **ascetism,** or physical self-denial. Christian ascetics rejected earthly pleasures, such as comfortable living quarters, fine food and clothing, and sexual relations. The greater self-deprivation one suffered, the greater the degree of holiness and spiritual authority one was thought to have gained. As early as the third century, some Egyptian ascetics gave up all contact with the ordinary world and lived as hermits in isolated huts and desert caves, becoming the first **monks.** Other monks soon began living communally in monasteries. Male monasteries were directed by **abbots** and female monasteries by abbesses. Ascetic and monastic practices soon were adopted in the west by persons such as **Martin of Tours,** who in the fourth century abandoned a military career and became a hermit. Some monastic communities attempted to re-create the isolation of the desert, whereas others concentrated on performing charitable services. Monasticism created an alternate world, separated from urban life. Monks also attempted to distance themselves from the authority of bishops, who resided in cities, and in this way contributed to a decentralization of church authority.

Famous Christian ascetics, known as holy men and women, gained great moral and spiritual authority. Because they distanced themselves from earthly concerns and were thought to be in close touch with God, they were seen as impartial arbitrators, advisers, and judges. As a result, women, who were excluded from holding church offices, and unprivileged men could have great authority outside the normal channels of church or government jurisdiction. For example, the holy man Simeon, the son of a shepherd, sat exposed to the weather atop a column in northern Syria for thirty years and was consulted by rich and poor alike on account of his reputation for holiness. And Matrona of Constantinople, to escape her abusive

Augustine   Bishop of Hippo in North Africa from 396 to 430; one of the most important Christian writers and thinkers, author of the "City of God".

Ambrose of Milan   Bishop of Milan from 374 to 397; one of the leading teachers of the Christian church; established Christian authority over Theodosius the Great.

ascetism   A life of physical deprivation.

monks   (from Greek for "solitary") Christians who withdrew from society to live together in monasteries.

abbot   Head of a male monastery; abbesses were the heads of female monasteries.

Martin of Tours   (ca. 316–397) Soldier who converted to Christianity, became a monk, and later served as bishop of Tours.

husband, disguised herself as a man and entered a male monastery. She later became abbess of a female monastery and had such great spiritual power that she instructed the emperor on church teaching.

The Expansion of Christian Authority

The impact of Christian beliefs and practices was felt everywhere. Christians even asserted that the Roman Empire itself had arisen by the will of God. According to Augustine, "He who is the one true God gave a kingdom to the Romans when He wished. He who gave power to Augustus gave it also to Nero." As the Roman Empire became a Christian empire, Christian ideologies made their way into public life. The church used church councils assembled under imperial authority to establish official positions on matters of authority, belief, and proper behavior. The canons, or rulings, issued by church councils were collected into an increasing body of church law known as **canon law.** After much debate, an official list of books to be included in the Christian Bible was agreed on. Some books that were excluded, such as the Gospels of Peter and Thomas and the Revelation of Peter, continued to be used, however, by heretical Christian sects. Around 400, the Old and New Testaments were translated from the original Hebrew and Greek into Latin by the priest **Jerome** of Bethlehem in a definitive form known as the **Vulgate,** which gradually replaced earlier versions of the Latin Bible used by different churches.

What went on in the Roman world came to be viewed not from a Roman imperial perspective but from a Christian perspective. Powerful Christian clerics such as Ambrose of Milan exercised great influence even over Roman emperors. Ambrose represented a new kind of bishop. Rather than humbly rising through the ranks of the church, he was the son of a Praetorian prefect. Like his father, he embarked on a career of government service and was appointed as a governor in Italy. But his career took an about-face when the people of Milan, an imperial capital in northern Italy, elected him bishop even though he had no previous experience in the church. Like any good bishop, he adopted an ascetic lifestyle. But he also brought to the office his experience in the world of Roman politics.

Ambrose soon became engaged in a power struggle with the emperor **Theodosius I.** Theodosius was a strong supporter of Nicene Christianity and an open opponent of Arianism. In 381, the second ecumenical church council, which he convened at Constantinople, again condemned Arianism, which then faded among the Roman population even as it prospered among barbarians. But Theodosius angered Ambrose by ordering Christians who had destroyed a Jewish synagogue to restore it. Subsequently, Ambrose blamed Theodosius when Roman soldiers in Greece massacred seven thousand rioting citizens. Ambrose excommunicated the emperor, and Theodosius was not readmitted to Christian Communion until he had publicly and humbly begged forgiveness from God. The sight of this powerful and determined emperor's humiliation by an equally powerful and determined bishop demonstrated the high status of Christian clerics and the degree to which the church was able to act independently of imperial control.

Theodosius then issued pro-Christian legislation that culminated in 392 with a law definitively prohibiting all pagan practices. As a result, Theodosius was surnamed the Great by the Christian community, and Christianity became the only legal religion, except for Judaism, in the Roman Empire. Zealous Christians now persecuted non-Christians, and in 415, **Hypatia,** the first female head of the school of Neoplatonic philosophy at Alexandria, was assaulted and torn limb from limb by a band of fanatical Christians. Pagan statues were either smashed or "converted" by having crosses carved on their foreheads. Many pagan temples were demolished, sometimes against violent opposition. Others, such as the Parthenon in Athens and the Pantheon in Rome, were converted into Christian churches.

Late Romans and Their World

↓ How did late Romans find security and new opportunities?

↓ How did Christianity affect culture and society during the late Roman period?

Unlike the people of the principate, who thought of themselves as citizens of Rome, the people in Late

---

canon law   Law of the church, as issued by church councils or, later in history, by the bishop of Rome.

Jerome   (ca. 347–420) Priest of Bethlehem and translator of the Vulgate Bible; one of the leading teachers of the Christian church.

Vulgate   Standard Latin translation of the Bible, made by Jerome around 400.

Theodosius I the Great   (r. 379–395) Emperor who made Christianity the only legal religion of the empire.

Hypatia   Head of the Neoplatonic philosophy school of Alexandria who was murdered by fanatical Christians in 415.

Antiquity tended to identify themselves as Gauls, Italians, Egyptians, and so on. The empire no longer unified people as effectively as it once had. Nor did the empire protect people as well as before. The government issued laws attempting to strengthen the empire and to protect everyone's interests, but the laws were full of loopholes and exceptions and were regularly disregarded. Powerful persons often operated outside the law. The loss of imperial legal protection made it important for everyone, privileged or not, to look for a more powerful protector. Increasing numbers of the poor became dependents of the rich and powerful. But the changing times also brought new opportunities. Ambitious individuals from all segments of society could better themselves if they had enough initiative, good luck, and the right friends. The Christian church in particular provided new prospects for personal expression and social advancement to men and women, rich and poor alike.

The Pursuit of Personal Security

By the fourth century, everyone living in the Roman Empire was looking for physical, spiritual, and economic security that the Roman government was less able to provide. Powerful persons such as senators could be threatened by government demands or by rivals willing to take the law into their own hands. The less privileged were threatened by influential individuals who would take advantage of them in any number of ways. Declining trade reduced economic prosperity. Everyone was threatened by barbarian attacks.

The most influential people in the empire were still the senators, but there now were many more of them, both male and female, and many ways to become one. The easiest ways to become a senator were to be the child of a senator or for a woman to marry a senator. In addition, holding a high imperial office or being a Christian bishop automatically made a man a senator. Anyone with enough money could purchase senatorial rank from the emperor. Eventually an empirewide aristocracy of thousands of senators arose that stood in stark contrast to the elite six-hundred-member senate of the early principate. Senators still possessed great economic influence: the wealthiest had incomes of over two thousand pounds of gold a year. But because the Senates of Rome and Constantinople had no real power, senators were less committed to making the empire work. They continued to hold high government offices, which emperors granted to secure their support, but senators often saw these offices as a way to pursue their own self-interest rather than the good of the empire as a whole.

Instead of living in Rome or Constantinople, most senators now resided in the provinces, where they kept their distance from the emperor. Especially in the west, senators expanded their landholdings, consolidated their local authority, and pursued a life of leisure in the security of their self-sufficient country **villas.** They did their best to avoid paying taxes and often defied the law. Some recruited bands of armed retainers who were little better than hired thugs. Most senators preferred being big men at home to being under the thumb of the emperor. As a result, the central government had less authority in the provinces, and the empire became less unified.

Lower on the social scale were the decurions, whose primary responsibility continued to be tax collection. Because many senators refused to pay their taxes, decurions had to squeeze what they could out of the rest of the population, and for this they were hated. In addition, the imperial government forced more responsibilities for local administration onto them, such as carrying out expensive road repairs. Municipal offices, once an honor, now became a burden. Many decurions attempted to escape their duties. Some claimed to be senators or became Christian clerics, groups exempted from serving as decurions. Others simply ran away. As a result, city services suffered, and many cities fell into decline.

As more and more wealth, in particular landed property, was concentrated in the hands of the wealthy, the gap between the rich and poor became even greater. Less privileged people faced increasing economic hardship. The gold standard was convenient for the wealthy but did nothing to benefit the poor, for whom a single solidus represented four months' wages. The value of the copper coinage, the only form of small change, continued to decline. By the late fourth century, it took 450,000 tiny copper coins to purchase one solidus. People whose businesses used small change found it difficult to make a living. For merchants, opportunities shrank. The trend toward local self-sufficiency brought a decline in long-distance commerce. When troops were pulled back from the borders, government subsidies for trade to frontier areas were lost. And the construction of imperial factories for supplying the army meant an end to military contracts.

Small peasant farmers who owned their own land often fell into debt, transferred their property to land-hungry aristocrats, and became *coloni* (tenant farmers) on land they once had owned. *Coloni* were legally

---

villa   A largely self-sufficient country estate of a wealthy aristocrat.

During the Late Roman Empire, local life became centered on self-sufficient fortified villas such as this fifth-century villa in North Africa that belonged to a landowner named Julius. By withdrawing to their villas, senators could pursue local authority outside the direct oversight of the emperor and imperial officials. *(Gilles Mermet/akg-images)*

tied to the land unless they could repay what their patrons had invested in them, and in this regard they anticipated the serfs of the **Middle Ages.** But restraints on their freedom were usually outweighed by the security they gained from having a regular livelihood and being under the protection of a powerful aristocrat. They had few other options, except to become migrant laborers traveling from job to job.

Some slaves, on the other hand, experienced an improvement in their living conditions. Now that tenant farming was the preferred method for cultivating large estates, some landlords promoted slaves to *coloni* so they would not have to feed, clothe, and shelter them. Among the most valued and privileged slaves were castrated males known as eunuchs. Because castration was illegal in the empire, most eunuchs had to be imported, usually from Persia and the east. Eunuchs were used by the wealthy, mainly in the eastern empire, in positions of trust, and they could rise to have great authority. In the imperial palace the "Keeper of the Sacred Bedchamber" had to be a eunuch; he had the ear of the emperor and empress and often had great influence. In general, slave owners liked to believe that slaves were happy: in a fifth-century comedy, a slave stated, "For us, there are daily parties, and merrymaking with the maid-servants.

Because of this, not all slaves wish to be set free." In fact, however, it was quite common for slaves to be set free, especially on the death of their owners.

New Opportunities

The rise of the Christian church brought new social and economic opportunities for men and women. Less privileged persons could find work in churches as doorkeepers, readers, and gravediggers. Some even became deacons, who oversaw church finances, or priests, who provided spiritual guidance. But the greatest honor was the office of bishop. As the most important institution in the Roman world, the church became increasingly wealthy as a result of offerings and bequests made by emperors, aristocrats, and the general public. The person who controlled that wealth—the bishop—thus had great economic and political authority as well as spiritual authority. Bishops served for life, and **episcopal** office became increasingly at-

> **Middle Ages** The broad historical period between the ancient and modern periods.
>
> **episcopal** Relating to a bishop.

tractive to talented and ambitious individuals, such as Ambrose and Augustine, as an alternative to state office. Indeed, a prominent pagan senator reportedly said, "Elect me bishop of Rome and I'll become a Christian, too." Bishops were elected by the people, and intense, sometimes violent, politicking could go on before an election as the supporters of different candidates lobbied for support.

Episcopal office allowed bishops not only to display their Christian piety but also to demonstrate their public spirit and to enhance the local authority they cherished. Bishops supervised the care of the poor, elderly, and sick for which the church now was responsible. They intervened on behalf of those accused or even convicted of crimes. They ransomed captives. They were permitted to judge some kinds of civil and criminal cases. They also could influence public opinion by speaking out during church services, in contrast to the days of the principate, when public assemblies had been regulated carefully by the government. These activities gained bishops status and supporters.

Women, whose activities continued to center on the family, also found new opportunities in Christianity. It often was the women in the family, for example, who converted male pagan senators to Christianity. Moreover, women who devoted themselves to the Christian life were able to escape traditional subordination to males. Spending their money on charitable works gave single women and widows greater control over their property than they would have had if they were married. Imperial women provided role models for female piety. One was Helena, the mother of Constantine, who rose from humble beginnings as a stable girl to become the concubine of Constantine's father, Constantius. After Constantine adopted Christianity, Helena also took up the Christian life. She decorated churches, gained freedom for prisoners, and supported the poor. While on a **pilgrimage** to the **Holy Land,** she believed that she had discovered the True Cross on which Jesus had been crucified. The Cross then became one of the most sacred relics of the Christian church. Part of it was placed in the **Church of the Holy Sepulcher** in Jerusalem, which Helena had built on the site of Christ's tomb; the rest was taken to Constantinople.

Other rich and influential women also demonstrated Christian piety. Some built churches; others cared for the poor. For example, the Roman aristocrat **Melania** the Elder, daughter of a consul, made a pilgrimage to the Holy Land after the deaths of her husband and two of her three children. To minister more freely to the poor, she dressed in slave clothing. When she was arrested by a provincial governor who did not know who she was, she boldly addressed him: "I am the daughter of the consul Marcellus, but now I am the servant of Christ. I can dress any way I choose. You can't threaten me or take my money without getting into real trouble." The governor apologized and ordered that she be allowed to carry out her charitable works. Melania then established two monasteries, one for men and one for women. Around 400, she returned to Rome and converted her granddaughter, Melania the Younger, to the ascetic life. After the deaths of her two children, the younger Melania convinced her husband to live chastely with her. They sold most of their property and used their wealth for charitable works in Italy, Sicily, and North Africa, where they met Augustine and established men's and women's monasteries. Seven years later, they moved to the Holy Land, met with Jerome, and remained. Melania built a monastery for herself, virgins, and ex-prostitutes. In the 430s, she went to Constantinople, where she converted her uncle, a devoted pagan, to Christianity.

Literary Culture

Late antiquity was an age of great literary creativity. Some of it was due to the efforts of senators who took pride in participating in and supporting intellectual endeavors. The senators of Rome, for example, sponsored the work of the last great historian of antiquity, Ammianus Marcellinus, whose history went up to the year 378 and painted a glowing picture of the pagan emperor Julian. With their own hands, senators made **manuscript** copies of the literature of the past.

But the greatest expansion of literary creativity took place in the Christian church, to which many of the brightest minds were attracted. Christian writers such as Augustine, Ambrose, and Jerome wrote sermons, letters, theological treatises, commentaries on scripture, and even Christian versions of Roman history that had an immense effect on Christian belief and practice. Christian intellectuals debated the role pagan literature should have in the Christian world, some

pilgrimage   Journey made to a holy place for religious devotion.

Holy Land   Areas around Jerusalem and Bethlehem mentioned in the Bible.

Church of the Holy Sepulcher   Church built by Helena in Jerusalem on the site of Christ's tomb.

Melania   the Elder (d. 410) and the Younger (d. 439), grandmother and granddaughter; famous for leading lives of Christian asceticism and good works.

manuscript   (from Latin for "written by hand") Handwritten document or book.

One of the strengths of Christianity was that it, like Judaism, had teachings that were preserved in writing, meaning that different communities around the Roman world used the same scriptures. Christian scriptures originally circulated in Greek, as exemplified by this page from the Book of John from a parchment codex of the fourth century C.E. Latin translations of Greek scripture also circulated widely in the western part of the empire. *(British Library, Add. 43725 f. 247)*

arguing that the Greek and Latin classics should be abandoned. Jerome, who was afraid of being condemned for his classical education, reported a dream in which he saw himself standing before God at the Last Judgment and being told, "You are not a Christian. You are a Ciceronian." But the influence of classical tradition was irresistible. Augustine and Ambrose recognized that the Greek and Roman literary education, with its emphasis on grammar, public speaking, and argumentation, could be pressed into the service of the church. With suitable caution, the wisdom of pagan writers also could serve a useful purpose. For example, many Christian concepts, such as the idea of single transcendent god, were found embedded in the teachings of Neoplatonism. Of course, Christian thinkers sometimes disagreed with their pagan predecessors. For example, in his *City of God*, Augustine promoted a progressive, linear concept of history, which moved from a beginning (the Creation) to an end (the Second Coming of Christ), as opposed to the classical view that history was cyclical and constantly repeated itself.

Thanks to Augustine and other like-minded Chris-

tians, the church ultimately became the primary means by which Greek and Latin classical literature was preserved in the Middle Ages and transmitted to the modern day. Christian monks and clerics copied and recopied manuscripts that previously had been copied by and for Roman senators. In general, the preservation of both Christian and pagan writings was promoted by the use of the **codex,** the modern-day book format, as opposed to the scroll. For writing material, ccodices used virtually indestructible parchment, made from preserved sheep and calf skins, rather than from papyrus, which tended to become fragile and disintegrate.

The Changing Landscape

The changing social, political, and religious situation of Late Antiquity was reflected in the material culture. Roman senators and local elites concentrated more on expanding and embellishing their country estates than on maintaining cities. They decorated their estates with works of art, including sculptures, frescoes, and mosaics modeled on those of the Greek and Roman past. City populations shrank as rich and poor sought security in the countryside. At the same time, the withdrawal of much of the Roman army from frontier areas caused the cities that had arisen to support the army to decline. The result was a contraction of urban life. In Gaul, the areas of cities protected by defensive walls were as little as a tenth of what they had been in the second century.

But cities did not vanish. They still functioned as administrative centers and as the seats of bishops, who by the fifth century had assumed many responsibilities for local administration, including the upkeep of city services and the administration of justice. There also was a great deal of new building activity, but it had a different orientation. Resources that previously had been devoted to constructing public meeting halls, bath complexes, theaters, amphitheaters, and aqueducts now were used for building churches, which became a city's primary architectural monuments. Personal charitable contributions also were directed toward the church. Whereas in the past a rich benefactor might have funded a town hall, now he or she underwrote the construction of a basilica. In Gaul, for example, the wife of the bishop of Clermont built a church of Saint Stephen, choosing pictures from an illustrated copy of the Old Testament to be painted on

codex (pl. **codices**)   Modern book format, as opposed to the scroll.

the walls. Earlier public monuments that fell into disrepair were quarried for materials to be used in church building. Thus the old urban centers decayed at the same time that Christian centers, often located outside the old city limits, prospered. Some cities even reoriented around the churches, and the old city center was just abandoned.

The Fall of the Western Roman Empire, 364–476

↓ How did Romans and barbarians interact during Late Antiquity?
↓ What were some of the causes of the fall of the western Roman Empire?

In many ways, in 364 the empire looked as peaceful and prosperous as it had been in the first century C.E. But appearances were misleading. Forces were in motion that soon would produce the most significant political development of Late Antiquity: the fall of the western Roman Empire. By 395, the empire had effectively split into eastern and western halves. The eastern empire proved more durable than the western one. During the fifth century, bands of foreign barbarians carved the western empire into independent kingdoms, and by 476, it was no more.

Rome's Last Golden Age

In 364, soon after the death of the last member of Constantine's family, the army selected one of its officers as emperor. Valentinian I (364–375 C.E.) immediately made his younger brother, Valens (364–378 C.E.), co-emperor and gave him responsibility for the eastern provinces while he took the west. Valentinian's reign was looked on as the third Golden Age of the Roman Empire (the first two were the reigns of Augustus and Trajan). The borders were securely defended. The empire still extended from Scotland in the northwest to the Euphrates River in the east. Rural life flourished on large western villas and on smaller farms in the east. Now that Constantine's gold standard had been established, the imperial treasury had enough income to meet expenditures. Disputes among Christians were subdued, and debates between pagans and Christians were politely conducted. It looked like the empire would last forever.

But there were ominous signs of looming difficulties. Military recruitment continued to be a problem. Landowners, who were responsible for providing recruits as part of their tax assessment, either sent men unsuited for army life or chose to pay an exemption fee. Men eligible for military service sometimes cut off fingers or thumbs in an attempt to avoid it. In addition, in distributing resources, the government sometimes favored the eastern part of the empire at the expense of the west. This made sense, because the east was more defensible, more economically prosperous, more populous, and even more cultured, but the west suffered as a consequence. In addition, conflicts of interest could arise between the imperial administrations at Rome and Constantinople. Sometimes, one half of the empire adopted policies that were detrimental to the interests of the other half. There, thus, was an accelerating tendency for the two halves of the empire to go their own ways.

The Barbarians and Rome

The most worrisome problem faced by late Roman emperors was the barbarians. The Romans had dealt with barbarian peoples successfully for centuries, but barbarians now became a much greater threat, in part because it was no longer just barbarians on the frontier who impacted Rome but also those living farther away. (See Table 7.2.) The empire was surrounded by barbarians. In Ireland and Scotland, there were Celtic peoples who had never been incorporated into the Roman Empire. North and east of the Rhine River were west Germans such as the Franks, Angles, Saxons, and Alamanni. In eastern Europe lived east Germans such as the Visigoths, Ostrogoths, Vandals, and Burgundians. Farther east, on the Central Asian steppes, were nomads such as the Huns, a Mongolian

Valentinian I (r. 364–375) Emperor responsible for the last Golden Age of the Roman Empire.

Valens (r. 364–378) Co-emperor of the eastern empire during reign of Valentinian I; killed by the Visigoths at the Battle of Adrianople.

Franks West Germanic people living near the lower Rhine River who established the Merovingian dynasty in the fifth century.

Visigoths East Germanic people who crossed the Danube into Roman territory in 376 and in 418 established a kingdom in Aquitaine.

Ostrogoths East Germanic people from north of the Black Sea who invaded Italy in 489 and established their own kingdom.

Vandals East Germanic people who invaded the Roman Empire in 406; their destructiveness gave rise to the term vandalism.

Huns East Asian barbarian people originally from Mongolia who invaded the western Roman empire in 451.

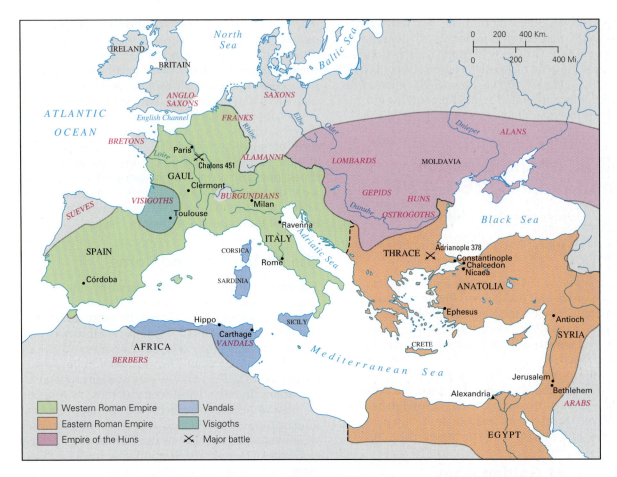

MAP 7.2 **The Barbarians and Rome** By the middle of the fifth century C.E., the occupation of the western Roman Empire by various barbarian peoples was well underway. The Anglo-Saxons, Franks, Visigoths, Burgundians, Sueves, and Vandals already had established independent kingdoms on Roman territory. At the same time, the entire Roman world was threatened by the Huns.

people who had been forced westward out of Mongolia centuries earlier. As the Huns continued to move west, they created a barbarian empire and came ever closer to Roman territory.

Table 7.2

Barbarian Peoples

West Germans	East Germans	Steppe Nomads
Alamanni	Visigoths (west Goths)	Huns
Franks	Ostrogoths (east Goths)	
Angles	Burgundians	
Saxons	Vandals	

Cultural interchange between barbarians and Romans continued. As already discussed, several Germanic peoples picked up the Arian form of Christianity from the Romans. And Romans adopted aspects of barbarian culture. Barbarian long hair and dress, such as trousers, fur coats, and boots, became all the rage in Rome. The Roman army even adopted the barbarian custom of raising a newly acclaimed ruler on a shield.

The primary point of contact between Rome and its barbarian neighbors was the Roman army. When barbarians were not fighting against the Roman army, they were serving in it. Faced with profound recruitment difficulties, late Roman emperors employed barbarian mercenaries. Bands of Franks and Alamanni, for example, would be hired for a campaign and then return home, bringing back Roman coinage, commodities, and culture, along with tales of the riches, prosperity, and opportunity that lay

This panel of a two-sided ivory plaque, known as a diptych, depicts Stilicho, a half-Vandal, in the uniform of a Roman general in the early fifth century, and illustrates how barbarians were becoming part of the Roman army. Stilicho married Serena, the daughter of the emperor Honorius, but his hope that his son Eucherius would become emperor did not come to pass. *(Alinari/Art Resource, NY)*

principate. By the middle of the fourth century, Roman and barbarian armies were using the same personnel and the same tactics.

In 375, a group of defeated Germans with whom Valentinian was meeting were so insolent that the emperor became enraged, suffered a stroke, and died. A year later, Valens was faced with a momentous decision. A large group of Visigoths fleeing from the Huns had appeared on the banks of the Danube River. The Visigoths offered military service in exchange for the right to settle on deserted lands located safely inside the Roman frontier. Valens agreed, believing that doing so would allow him to find more army recruits and also to get more land into cultivation and on the tax rolls. But, once inside the empire, the Visigoths began raiding and looting. Assembling the eastern Roman army, Valens attacked the Visigoths. In 378, at the Battle of **Adrianople,** northwest of Constantinople, his army was virtually annihilated and he was killed. His successor, Theodosius I, was unable to defeat, much less expel, the Visigoths. The best he could do was to recognize them as Roman allies. This face-saving measure left the Visigoths free to roam about under their own leaders, one of whom was the able general Alaric. The barbarian invasions of the Roman Empire had begun.

The Disintegration of the Western Empire

When Theodosius died in 395, he was succeeded by his two young sons. The empire was divided between them, and the split of the empire into eastern and western halves now became permanent. Constitutionally, there still was only one empire, and the emperors continued to issue laws and coins in each other's names. But in reality, the eastern and western empires had their own emperors and administrations and looked out for their own interests. During the fifth century, the eastern government watched as the west collapsed.

At the beginning of the fifth century, the barbarian invasions that initially had affected the east soon struck the west even more forcefully. Although the barbarian peoples had no unity and no common agenda, the attacks of several different peoples at the same time overwhelmed the west. First, a band of Visigoths led by Alaric invaded Italy. Then, on the last day of 406,

within the empire. Some barbarian chieftains even rose to the rank of master of soldiers in the regular Roman army. The large-scale recruitment of barbarians resulted in the loss of the Roman military superiority that had been taken for granted during the

Adrianople   Battle in 378 in which the Romans were disastrously defeated by the Visigoths.

after Roman troops had been withdrawn from the north to defend Italy, a horde of barbarians, including the Vandals and Burgundians, walked across the frozen Rhine River. They traveled south, looting and burning as they went. The Vandals made their way into the fertile, undefended provinces of Spain. In 410, Alaric and the Visigoths captured and sacked Rome. The pillaging lasted only three days, and the churches were left untouched, but the point had been made. "Unconquered Rome," as it had been called, was no longer unconquered. The psychological damage was even greater than the material destruction. The emperor Honorius, who had retreated to the safety of Ravenna in the swamps of northeastern Italy, eventually got the Visigoths out of Italy by allowing them to settle in Aquitaine in southwestern France. They soon established an independent kingdom on Roman soil, the first of several barbarian peoples to do so.

The disintegration of the western empire continued during the reign of the emperor Valentinian III (r. 425–455). The Vandals left Spain and occupied North Africa, depriving Italy of its best grain supply. The Huns continued to move west. In 451, they invaded Gaul, led by their ferocious king **Attila.** The Roman master of soldiers Aëtius, sometimes called "the last of the Romans," patched together a shaky alliance of Romans, Visigoths, and Franks. At the Battle of **Chalons,** the previously undefeated Huns were put to flight, but they returned the next year to invade Italy. An embassy led by **Leo the Great,** the powerful bishop of Rome, convinced the Huns to withdraw—Leo may have paid Attila off.

> **Attila** (r. 435–453) King of the Huns who terrorized the eastern Roman empire and was defeated at the Battle of Chalons.
>
> **Chalons** Battle in 451 in north-central France in which the Romans under the master of soldiers Aëtius defeated the Huns.
>
> **Leo the Great** Bishop of Rome from 441 to 460, who persuaded Attila the Hun to withdraw from Italy.

Voice

Ammianus Describes the Huns

The Romans' fear of the barbarians often led them to portray barbarians as uncouth savages who represented the opposite of everything a civilized Roman or Greek stood for. For Romans of the late fourth century, the Huns, who had only recently appeared on the Roman frontiers, were the most savage barbarians of all, hardly better than animals. In the following selection from his Histories, *the late Roman historian Ammianus Marcellinus, a former army officer who personally observed all kinds of barbarians, describes the Huns as they appeared to the Romans in the 390s. His account is full of stereotypes and would have made the Romans feel justified in the repugnance that they felt toward the Huns.*

The people of the Huns exceed every degree of savagery. Because the cheeks of the children are deeply furrowed with steel from their very birth, in order that the growth of hair may be checked by the wrinkled scars, they grow old without beards and without any beauty, like eunuchs. ➜ They all have compact, strong limbs and thick necks, and are so monstrously ugly and misshapen that one might take them for two-legged beasts. They are so hardy that they have no need of fire nor of savory food, but eat the roots of wild plants and the half-raw flesh of any kind of animal whatever, which they put between their thighs and the backs of their horses, and thus warm it a little.

They are never protected by any buildings, but they avoid these like tombs. Roaming at large amid the mountains and woods, they learn from the cradle to endure cold, hunger, and thirst. They dress in the skins of field mice sewn

➜ Why are the Huns compared to beasts?

➡️ What role did horses play in the life of the Huns?

➡️ How does Ammianus portray Hun government?

➡️ Does does Ammianus's description of Hun fighting tactics compare to Roman tacticsy?

➡️ How does Ammianus portray the life of the Huns as being different from Roman life? Why does he do so?

➡️ Why might you decide not to believe all of what Ammianus says about the Huns?

together. When they have once put on a faded tunic, it is not taken off until by long wear it has been taken from them bit by bit. ➡️ They are almost glued to their horses, and sometimes they sit on them woman-fashion and thus perform ordinary tasks. From their horses every one of that nation buys and sells, eats and drinks, and bowed over the narrow neck of the animal relaxes into sleep. ➡️ And when deliberation is called for, they all consult as a common body on horseback. They are subject to no royal restraint, but they are content with the disorderly government of their important men.

➡️ You would not hesitate to call them the most terrible of all warriors, because they fight from a distance with missiles having sharp bone, instead of the usual metal points. Then they gallop over the intervening spaces and fight hand-to-hand with swords, regardless of their own lives; and they throw nooses over their opponents and so entangle them that they fetter their limbs.

➡️ No one in their country ever plows a field or touches a plow-handle. They are all without fixed abode, without hearth, or law, or settled mode of life, and keep roaming from place to place, accompanied by the wagons in which their wives weave their hideous garments, cohabit with their husbands, bear children, and rear them to the age of puberty. None of their offspring, when asked, can tell you where he comes from, because he was conceived in one place, born far from there, and brought up still farther away.

➡️ In truces they are faithless and unreliable. Like unreasoning beasts, they are utterly ignorant of the difference between right and wrong; they are deceitful and ambiguous in speech, never bound by any reverence for religion or for superstition.

Source: Reprinted by permission of the publishers and the Trustees of the Loeb Classical Library from *Ammianus Marcelinus: Volume III*, Loeb Classical Library Volume 331, translated by J. C. Rolfe, pp. 380–381, Cambridge, Mass.: Harvard University Press, Copyright © 1939 by the President and Fellows of Harvard College. The Loeb Classical Library® is a registered trademark of the President and Fellows of Harvard College.

But avoiding conquest by the Huns was the west's last victory. After Valentinian III's death in 455, the western throne was occupied by nine emperors known as the **puppet emperors** because they often were manipulated by their barbarian masters of soldiers. What remained of the western empire was occupied by barbarians. In 476, the boy emperor **Romulus,** nicknamed "Augustulus" ("little Augustus"), was deposed by the barbarian general **Odovacar,** who called himself King of Italy and notified the eastern emperor Zeno that the west no longer needed its own emperor. Romulus was the last emperor to rule in Rome, and the year 476 generally is said to mark the fall of the western empire, even though some areas still resisted. Britain, for example, continued to fight the Angle and Saxon invaders. Led by warlords such as **Arthur,** the Britons held out until about the year 500, when they became the last of the western Romans to fall to the barbarians.

Interpretations of the Fall of the West

The question of why Rome fell has been debated ever since it happened. In antiquity, religious explanations were common. Pagans argued that Rome fell because the Romans had abandoned their old gods. Some Christians suggested that the fall of Rome was God's punishment of Christians for their immoral lives. Augustine proposed in his *City of God* that what happened on earth was God's will and had to be accepted by Christians; what was really important was what took place in God's "heavenly city."

In the late eighteenth century, the British historian Edward Gibbon wrote *The Decline and Fall of the Roman*

puppet emperors   Western Roman emperors between 455 and 476 who were manipulated by barbarian generals; a puppet ruler also is any ruler manipulated by another person.

Romulus   (r. 475–476) Last emperor of the western empire; deposed in 476; nicknamed "Augustulus" ("little Augustus").

Odovacar   (r. 476–493) Barbarian chieftain who deposed Romulus, the last western emperor, in 476 and became king of Italy.

Arthur   A sixth-century ruler in Britain; stories of his exploits and companions were popular in the Middle Ages and into modern times.

Empire, which described the fall of the western empire as the "triumph of Christianity and barbarians." He suggested that Christianity had weakened the will of the Romans to resist, opening the way for invasions by more warlike barbarians. This explanation now is seen as overly simplistic. After all, most barbarians were Christians themselves. And as for the invasions, the emperors had dealt effectively with barbarian threats for centuries. Aside from the Battle of Adrianople, the barbarians did not win many significant military victories. The west was occupied more by means of infiltration, peaceful settlement, and persistence than by military conquest. The real question, it seems, is what made it possible for barbarians to succeed in the fifth century when in the past they had been unable to occupy virtually any Roman territory.

More recently, historians have proposed many interrelated causes. Some suggestions, ranging from drastic climatic change to ethnic mixing to lead poisoning, can easily be dismissed. More plausible suggestions include the withdrawal of senatorial support for the emperors, increased administrative decentralization, too many barbarians in the army, economic collapse, excessive taxation, corruption, military recruitment shortages, excessive bureaucracy, poor leadership, lack of organized resistance, and just plain bad luck. In addition, any explanation for the political decline of the west also must explain why the east did not fall. In this regard, it is clear that the east had more secure geographical frontiers, a stronger economy, a larger population, and a more dependable Roman military recruitment base. In view of the east's advantages, it may be that the once the empire split in two, the downfall of the west was inevitable.

The Post-Roman World, 400–527

↓ How did Roman and barbarian populations and customs become integrated?
↓ How did eastern emperors survive the challenges of the fifth century?

By the beginning of the sixth century, the Mediterranean world was vastly different from what it had been in the time of Augustus. The unity so carefully constructed by the Romans had disappeared. The western part of the Roman Empire had been partitioned among several barbarian peoples. The most powerful were the Visigoths, who occupied Aquitaine and Spain, and the Vandals, who held the rich provinces of North Africa. Elsewhere, the Angles and Saxons settled in Britain, the Franks on the lower Rhine, the Alamanni on the upper Rhine, the Burgundians in central Gaul, and the Ostrogoths in Italy. During the sixth and seventh centuries, the western European world evolved into what we now call the Middle Ages. But the eastern half of the Roman Empire, the Byzantine Empire, continued and even flourished, adapting to changing times as it had in the past.

Romans and Barbarians in the Post-Roman West

By the end of the fifth century, the government of the western Roman Empire was gone, but the west remained populated by Romans who had to respond to the barbarian presence. Some fled, some were killed, and others faced captivity or enslavement. Most simply became free citizens of the kingdoms in which they resided and made whatever private peace they could with their new rulers. In most respects, life went on as before, but now with barbarians not only as rulers but also as neighbors, social acquaintances, and marriage partners. For many Romans, barbarian kings provided new sources of rewards, patronage, and career opportunities. Some powerful senators may even have preferred a local barbarian ruler who respected their property rights to a distant, yet intrusive, Roman emperor.

The barbarian peoples adopted Roman ways as they created their own nations on Roman soil. Barbarian kings realized the necessity of maintaining the goodwill of their Roman subjects, for there were many more Romans than barbarians. If they lost the support of the Roman population, in particular of the Roman senators, they risked provoking uprisings in which they might be overwhelmed. Thus, except in Britain, all the barbarian rulers used the Roman Empire as a model, adopting Roman administrative practices. Barbarian kings also accepted the Roman concept of the rule of law: they issued laws in their own names but also recognized the validity of Roman law. Romans continued to serve as city administrators, military governors, and royal advisers. None of the kingdoms, however, had a bureaucracy that was nearly as complex as that of the Roman Empire, especially at the local level. As a result, even more of the responsibility for local government fell into the hands of Christian bishops, who undertook most of the duties that in the past had been performed by government officials and city councils. Many European cities were transformed into centers of Christian administration and worship.

A potential incompatibility between Romans and

some barbarians involved religion. Barbarians such as the Visigoths, Burgundians, and Vandals were Arian Christians, whereas the Romans followed the Nicene Creed. In practice, however, Arian and Nicene Christians were generally tolerant of one another and even attended each other's services. Eventually all Arian barbarians eventually converted to Nicene Christianity. In addition, unlike Roman emperors, barbarian kings usually stayed out of theological disputes, leaving those to churchmen, although they sometimes interfered in the election of bishops.

Another possible source of conflict concerned property. Incoming barbarians were primarily seeking land on which to settle, and barbarian kings provided land for them in several ways. Sometimes, in a process called hospitality, barbarians received one-third of the land of a large Roman landowner. The Roman then was confirmed in the ownership of the rest. Barbarian kings also granted to their supporters property that had been abandoned by Romans who had fled or land that had fallen behind on its taxes. Barbarian governments also controlled the Roman tax collection structure and could use tax money collected from Romans to purchase land. Only rarely, as in North Africa or Britain, did barbarians forcibly evict Roman landowners. As a result, the barbarian settlement was much more peaceful than it might have been.

With the exception of Britain, Roman culture continued as before in the barbarian kingdoms. Latin remained the predominant language, eventually evolving into modern **Romance languages** such as Italian, French, Spanish, Portuguese, and Romanian. Classical literature was appreciated and preserved by the educated elite, both Roman and barbarian. It was once thought that the creation of the barbarian kingdoms resulted in a period of cultural barrenness known as the Dark Ages, but this attitude arose largely from a failure to appreciate the importance of the new Christian literature of the early Middle Ages. It is more accurate to speak of the transformation of the Roman world, not its decline and fall, terminology that refers only to politics. Western Europe undeniably went into a period of reorganization during the barbarian settlement. But in many ways it was the Roman Empire itself, not its aftermath, that was the anomaly. Rome had brought to western Europe an artificially high degree of administrative and economic complexity that was designed to suit the needs of the empire. When the western Roman Empire collapsed, it took its administrative and economic superstructure with it. Western Europe returned to a condition that was more suited to western European needs. European culture during the early Middle Ages was not necessarily worse than classical culture, but it was different. As time went on,

any sense of ethnic or cultural identity separating Romans and barbarians became meaningless. The peoples of western Europe created a hybrid culture that both preserved and reinterpreted classical culture.

The Barbarian Kingdoms

The kingdom of the Visigoths included Aquitaine and Spain. As the first barbarians to settle on Roman soil, the Visigoths readily adapted themselves to Roman practices. They issued a law code that contained selections from existing Roman law; thus Roman law became Visigothic law. Visigothic kings also issued new laws in their own names, which likewise applied to all of the people in their kingdom. Visigoths and Romans created a culture so integrated that it is virtually impossible to distinguish Visigoths from Romans in archaeological remains.

The Franks originated as several independent groups located on both sides of the lower Rhine. They were united by King **Clovis,** a member of the **Merovingian** family, which gave its name to the first dynasty of Frankish kings. Clovis lived in an age of strong men, and he was ruthless in his quest to unify the Franks, murdering several relatives who ruled their own Frankish subgroups. Clovis's reputation for brutality was enhanced when he split the skull of a Frankish warrior who objected to returning a stolen silver vase to a church. But Clovis also was politically savvy and knew how to use diplomacy when diplomacy suited his purpose. Advised by his wife, Clotilde, around 496 Clovis shrewdly adopted the Nicene Christian faith. According to the historian **Gregory of Tours,** "Clovis proceeded to the baptismal font like a new Constantine. Having confessed omnipotent God in the trinity, he was baptized in the name of the Father, the Son, and the Holy Spirit." As a consequence of becoming a Nicene Christian, Clovis gained support from the Roman population. In 507, he defeated the Visigoths at the Battle of Vouillé, and the Franks occupied most of Gaul. Like Germanic kings, Clovis

Romance languages   Modern European languages that derive from Latin.

Clovis   (r. 481–511) King of the Franks who converted to Christianity in 496 and defeated the Visigoths in 507.

Merovingian   Family name of the Frankish kings, named after a fifth-century king Merovech.

Gregory of Tours   (538–594) Bishop of Tours who wrote ten books of histories of his times and many accounts of saints.

The barbarians who settled in the Roman Empire in the fifth century initially were either pagans or Arians, creating problems of assimilation with the Roman population. Around 496 C.E., Clovis, the king of the Franks, chose to be baptized as a Christian, as shown in this re-creation by an unnamed French artist known as the Master of St. Gilles. By adopting the same religion as most of the Roman population, Clovis then was portrayed as a "new Constantine" and gained a political advantage over his barbarian rivals. *(Master of Saint Giles, The Baptism of Clovis. Samuel H. Kress Collection, Image © 2007 Board of Trustees, National Gallery of Art, Washington.)*

issued a law code, the **Salic law.** It incorporated a Germanic practice whereby the perpetrators of crimes like murder, theft, or vandalism made fixed payments to their victims. Not long afterward, Clovis's sons annexed the Burgundian kingdom, and the Franks thus became the most important power in Gaul, eventually giving their name to modern France.

In Italy, Odovacar was defeated and killed in 493 by **Theoderic the Great,** king of the Ostrogoths, who had invaded from the Balkans. The Ostrogoths then created a kingdom that looked much like the Roman Empire. Theoderic made the Roman imperial city of Ravenna his capital and worked closely with the wealthy and powerful Italian senators, issuing legislation virtually indistinguishable from that of the empire. Many of the highest-ranking officials in the kingdom were Romans, and the Senate of Rome even regained some of its old powers, such as the right to issue coins. The bishop of Rome, freed from imperial supervision, expanded his authority and began to monopolize the title of **pope,** which in the past had been applied to any distinguished bishop.

A few barbarian peoples, however, were less conciliatory. The Vandals of North Africa simply confiscated large tracts of Roman land and savagely persecuted Nicene Christians. And in Britain, the Roman population was forced to move out, to Wales or to Brittany in western France, by the Angles (whose name survives in modern England) and Saxons who, for the time being, retained their own Germanic culture.

The Byzantine Empire

During the fifth century, the eastern half of the Roman Empire, which can now be called the **Byzantine Empire** (after Byzantium, the original name of Constantinople), experienced many of the same problems as the west, but it was better equipped to deal with them. The emperor **Theodosius II** (402–450 C.E.), the grandson of Theodosius the Great, ruled for nearly half a century. Theodosius was more of a scholar than a soldier. He expanded the university at Constantinople to contain thirty-one professors teaching law and philosophy along with grammar and public speaking. Greek became the preferred language, with Latin

Salic law   Frankish law code introduced by Clovis in the early sixth century, named after the Salians, one of several Frankish peoples.

Theoderic the Great   (r. 493–526) Ruler of the Ostrogothic kingdom in Italy.

pope   (from Latin for "father") Title originally used for any distinguished bishop; by the sixth century, referred mainly to the bishop of Rome.

Byzantine Empire   The continuation of the Roman Empire in the east after 476.

Theodosius II   (r. 402–450) Byzantine emperor who issued the Theodosian Code in 437.

used mainly by administrators and lawyers. In 437, Theodosius issued the Theodosian Code, a comprehensive compilation of the legislation of Roman emperors going back to the time of Constantine. A treasure trove of information on administration, society, and the economy, it provides insights into what the emperors thought were the most important issues of their day.

The east, like the west, was threatened by barbarian attacks. In 400, the people of Constantinople responded to the barbarian menace by massacring several thousand Visigothic mercenaries. Theodosius then strengthened Constantinople's defenses by building massive walls on the city's landward side, doubling the size of the city. The greatest pressure came from the Huns, whose king, Attila, was kept from attacking with bribes of thousands of pounds of gold. After Theodosius's death in 450, the Byzantines stopped the tribute payments. The Huns then turned to the west, where, as already discussed, they were defeated in 451. In 453, Attila died, mysteriously, on his wedding night. The power of the Huns was broken forever when their subjects revolted and defeated them the next year. For the time being, the barbarian threat to the Byzantine Empire was reduced.

During the fifth century, Byzantine relations with the New Persian Empire improved. The New Persians also were menaced by the Huns, and therefore the two empires made peace so each could concentrate on the more serious threat. The New Persians, who were Zoroastrians, also ceased persecuting their Christians subjects. By the early fifth century, Christians had become a tolerated minority in the New Persian Empire. Some Jews and dissident Christians even fled Byzantine religious oppression and took refuge with the New Persians.

Economic prosperity returned to the Byzantine world at the end of the fifth century. The introduction of a copper coinage that was interchangeable with the gold coinage restored confidence in the small-change currency that facilitated exchange at the local level. Revitalized trade brought increased tax revenues. Political problems, however, surfaced in the early sixth century with the growth of mob politics. Chariot-racing fan clubs known as the Blues and the Greens (from the colors that the racing teams wore) became thinly veiled political activist groups. They met in the Hippodrome and often used violence to support their views on matters ranging from theology to imperial appointments. During one riot, an emperor presented himself bareheaded and offered to resign. The mob, impressed by his bravery, declined the offer.

In contrast to the west, where Christians were gen-

erally content with the Nicene faith, eastern Christians continued to dispute the nature of Christ, and the emperors often were compelled to intervene. The **Nestorians,** named after Nestorius, bishop of Constantinople, argued that while on earth Christ was just a man and was not divine until after the Crucifixion. This viewpoint angered Nicene Christians, who believed that the divine and human natures of Christ were mixed and who viewed Mary as the Theotokos, or "mother of God." In 431, at the third ecumenical council, summoned by Theodosius II at Ephesus on the Anatolian coast, Nestorianism was condemned. Many Nestorians then chose to go into exile in the New Persian Empire; some eventually even made their way to China, where eight hundred years later the Italian traveler Marco Polo claimed to have met their descendants.

Discussions about the nature of Christ were revived by the **Monophysites,** who denied that Christ had any human nature at all. In 451, a fourth ecumenical council, held at Chalcedon, just east of Constantinople, confirmed the belief that the divine and human natures of Christ were intermixed and declared Monophysite teachings to be heresy. But the Monophysites refused to surrender their beliefs and continued to have a wide following in Egypt (where they survive as the modern Copts), in Syria (where a few thousand survive as the Jacobites), and in the New Persian Empire. The Council of Chalcedon also granted the bishop of Constantinople a status equal to that of the bishop of Rome. Bishop Leo the Great of Rome and his successors refused to accept the bishop of Constantinople as an equal, creating dissension between the eastern and western Christian churches.

By 527, when the emperor Justinian came to the throne, the Byzantine Empire seemed secure. Economic prosperity had been restored, the barbarian threat had been contained, and religious dissent had been suppressed if not completely eliminated. It seemed that the empire in the east had avoided the misfortunes that caused the fall of the west, and its inhabitants could look to the future with optimism.

Nestorians Christians who believed that the divine and human natures of Christ were completely separate; the belief was condemned at the Council of Ephesus in 431; named after Nestorius, bishop of Constantinople.

Monophysites (from Greek for "single nature") Christians who believed that Christ had a single, divine nature; the belief was condemned at the Council of Chalcedon in 451.

Summary

Review Questions

↑ How did the official acceptance of Christianity change the Roman Empire?

↑ In what ways did living a Christian life change how people thought about themselves and their world?

↑ Why did the western part of the Roman Empire fall but the east survive?

During Late Antiquity, momentous changes occurred in the Mediterranean world. The political and cultural unity created by the Romans disappeared and was replaced by diversity and fragmentation. New governments and religious institutions were introduced that continue, in various forms, to the modern day. The empire recovered from the civil wars of the third century and was revived by able emperors such as Diocletian and Constantine. During the Late Roman Empire, emperors took personal responsibility for ensuring the continued survival of the empire by issuing thousands of laws intended to deal with problems they identified. But their efforts were hindered by difficulties in military recruitment, declining support from senators, and a growing split of the empire into eastern and western halves. At the same time, a growing inability of the imperial government to provide security led many people to look for it elsewhere, such as under the protection of a powerful person.

The most significant development of Late Antiquity was the expansion of Christianity beginning in 312, when the emperor Constantine began to favor the Christians openly. In a remarkably short period, Christianity evolved from a religion that was persecuted by the government to a universal state-sponsored religion that transformed the politics, society, and culture of the Roman world. Christianity also changed how individual people thought about themselves and their world. Many people lived Christian lives that emphasized self-denial, personal spirituality, and community service. For many, the church now provided a place to find forms of spiritual and economic security the empire no longer was able to provide.

In the middle of the fourth century, it looked like the Roman Empire was as sound as it had ever been, but this changed in 378, when the Roman army was defeated by the Visigoths at Adrianople, marking the beginning of the barbarian invasions. During the fifth century, barbarian peoples settled in the western half of the empire and established independent kingdoms, some of which eventually evolved into modern nations such as France and England. The synthesis of Roman and barbarian culture preserved classical culture, and western Europe evolved into an era known as the Middle Ages. In the eastern Mediterranean, what remained of the Roman Empire continued in the form now known as the Byzantine Empire. By the beginning of the sixth century, the unified political and cultural world created by the Romans had disappeared.

← Thinking Back, Thinking Ahead →

During the course of the ancient world, many empires rose and fell. From the examples presented here, do you think that all empires are doomed to fall? Have any modern empires followed a similar pattern?

ECHO

Sunday Blue Laws

Beginning with Constantine, Roman emperors issued laws intended to make Sunday a day of worship on which commercial activities, legal processes, and entertainments were prohibited. A law of 372 declared, "On the Lord's day, which is the first day of the week, the pleasures of the theaters and games are to be kept from the people in all cities, and all the thoughts of Christians and believers are to be occupied with the worship of God." Fourteen years later, another law decreed, "Let all law suits and all business cease on Sunday, and let no one try to collect either a public or a private debt, and let there be no hearing of disputes by any judges." But even Constantine made exceptions to his law—for example, he permitted legal business on Sunday for the purpose of freeing slaves.

The idea of Sunday as a day of worship persisted in the Middle Ages, when agricultural work was prohibited by church councils and kings. Subsequently, some Christian sects were more rigorous than others in their observance of Sunday. One of the strictest was the English Puritans, who brought their beliefs to North America in the seventeenth century. The Puritans issued so-called blue laws (perhaps named after the blue paper on which they were printed) that specified what could and could not be done on Sunday. The blue laws prohibited trade, commerce, public entertainment, travel (except to go to church services), hair cutting, and drunkenness on Sunday, and some of the laws were incorporated into state law codes in the early years of the United States.

Many blue laws remained on the books into the twentieth century. As recently as the 1920s, for example, sporting events and movies were forbidden on Sunday in some parts of the United States. Even more recently, most stores had to remain closed. Over the past fifty years, however, most blue laws have been repealed. All forms of entertainment are now regularly scheduled on Sunday, although complaints still arise, especially in regard to youth events. Stores now are permitted to open on Sunday nearly everywhere. One of the most deeply entrenched of the blue laws was the prohibition of sales of alcoholic beverages on Sunday, and even now many states prohibit Sunday liquor sales. The only remaining universal blue law, however, a direct descendant of Constantine's Sunday legislation, is the closing of nearly all government offices on Sunday.

Suggested Readings

Barnes, Timothy D. *The New Empire of Diocletian and Constantine.* Cambridge, Mass.: Harvard University Press, 1982. A detailed discussion of the ways in which Diocletian and Constantine created the Late Roman Empire.

Bowersock, Glen W., Peter Brown, and Oleg Grabar, eds. *Late Antiquity: A Guide to the PostClassical World.* Cambridge, Mass.: Harvard University Press / Belknap Press, 1999. A massive compilation of information about the late antique world, including both long essays and short dictionary-style discussions.

Brown, Peter R. L. *The World of Late Antiquity: A.D. 150–750.* New York: Harcourt Brace Jovanovich, 1974. The standard book on Late Antiquity, which established Late Antiquity as a major historical period.

Cameron, Averil. *The Later Roman Empir, A.D. 284–430.* Cambridge, Mass.: Harvard University Press, 1993. A balanced survey of the history of the later Roman Empire up to 430.

Clark, Gillian. *Women in Late Antiquity: Pagan and Christian Life-Styles.* New York: Oxford University Press, 1993. On the importance of women in late antique society.

MacMullen, Ramsay. *Corruption and the Decline of Rome.* New Haven, Conn.: Yale University Press, 1988. A comprehensive argument for the role played by official corruption in the decline of the western Roman Empire.

Wolfram, Herwig, *The Roman Empire and Its Germanic Peoples.* Berkeley and Los Angeles: University of California Press, 1997 A survey of barbarian peoples and their relations with the Roman world.

Websites

Artwork, architecture, and political significance of the Arch of Constantine, **The Arch of Constantine,** at http://sights.seindal.dk/sight/299_Arch_of_Constantine-2.html

Texts of the writings of many early Christian writers, including Augustine, Ambrose, Jerome, and Leo the Great, **The Early Church Fathers,** at www.ccel.org/fathers2

Detailed biographies of all the Roman emperors, including maps and battle summaries, *De Imperatoribus Romanis* (**On the Rulers of Rome**), at www.roman-emperors.org

CHAPTER

The Eastern Mediterranean, 500–1000

8

CHAPTER OUTLINE

1500 B.C.E.	1000 B.C.E.	500 B.C.E.	1 B.C.E./1 C.E.

| | | 622 Muhammad moves to Medina | | 732 Franks defeat Muslims at Tours | |
| | 527 Justinian becomes Byzantine emperor | Beginning of the Muslim calendar | 632 Death of Muhammad | 711 Muslims begin conquest of Spain | 754 Council of Constantinople forbids veneration of icons |

500	550	600	650	700	750

Three Civilizations, 800

Out of the old Roman world emerged three civilizations. In western Europe, the barbarian kingdoms adapted the Latin language. In Constantinople, the new center of the old empire, the people spoke Greek. To the south, the Muslims introduced Arabic to North Africa, Syria, and Palestine. Was peaceful coexistence henceforth possible?

Boundary of Roman Empire, 395
Byzantine Empire, ca. 500

Successors to the Western Roman Empire

Frankish Kingdom, 486
Areas conquered by Clovis, by 511
Visigothic Kingdom
Burgundian Kingdom
Ostrogothic Kingdom
Vandal Kingdom
IRISH Other peoples, ca. 500

Islam, 661

500 C.E. 1000 C.E. 1500 C.E. 2000 C.E.

787
Second Council of
Nicaea restores
veneration of icons

988
Kievan Rus
accept Christianity

1075
Seljuk Turks
defeat the
Byzantine army

800   850   900   950   1000   1050   1100

205

Choice

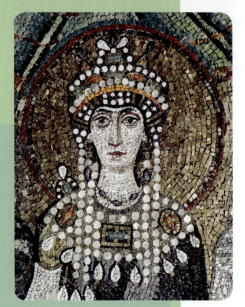

Theodora

Empress Theodora served as one of the closest advisers to her husband, Emperor Justinian. Though her enemies deplored her humble origins and her Monophysite beliefs, she won the loyalty of ordinary subjects, many of whom shared her religious tendencies and received her protection. In hindsight, Byzantine observers believed she had exerted a moderating influence over Justinian, who, after her death in 548, grew increasingly intolerant of religious doctrine deemed heretical. (Scala/Art Resource, NY)

Empress Theodora Changes Emperor Justinian's Mind

In January 532, rioting throughout the city of Constantinople shook the imperial court to the core. Crowds attacked and burnt down the great church of Hagia Sophia, rebuilt by Constantine II in the 350s. Emperor Justinian I and the empress Theodora had barricaded themselves, with their supporters, in the royal palace, fearful of what would happen next. In the preceding days, Justinian's soldiers had tried to stop the violence that had broken out between the Greens and the Blues—the rival fans of chariot-racing teams who also held competing political and religious views. The emperor and empress preferred the Blues, but no one really knows what this uprising, which came to be called the Nika Riot, was about. The only person to write about the riot was the historian Procopius, who simply condemned the passions of all who confused their enthusiasm for sports and entertainments with politics and religion.

Nevertheless, the crowd was now contemplating an overthrow of the political order. The rioters forced two nephews of a previous emperor to join in their plans, which were to attack the imperial palace and kill the imperial couple. The danger to Justinian and Theodora increased by the hour. When the emperor and his advisers were told that the army could not guarantee his safety, Justinian decided to evacuate the city and try to regroup on the opposite side of the Bosporus.

But at this moment, according to Procopius, the empress Theodora made a courageous decision that Justinian was unable to make on his own: she urged her husband and his advisers to remain and fight. With great dignity, the empress reasoned:

> If now it is your wish to save yourself, O Emperor, there is no difficulty. For we have much money, and there is the sea, here the boats. However, consider whether it will not come about after you have been saved that you would gladly exchange that safety for death. For as for myself, I approve a certain ancient saying that royal purple is fitting for a burial shroud.

With Theodora's support, Justinian resolved to stay in his palace. Summoning his general Belisarius, he ordered that the rioters be put down. Belisarius succeeded, but only by killing tens of thousands of the people of Constantinople. When the slaughter ended and peace returned to the capital, Justinian undertook the rebuilding of Hagia Sophia, this time on an unprecedented scale. The emperor and the empress entered the newly restored church five years after the Nika Riot. Thanks in part to Theodora's cool head and brave heart, the people of Constantinople once again accustomed themselves to the rule of this imperial couple.

It may seem surprising that Theodora should have been the one to give her husband courage, because nothing in her background suggested she would succeed in any endeavor other than the popular theater. Her father reputedly worked in a circus, an atmosphere associated with prostitution and rough customers. Be-

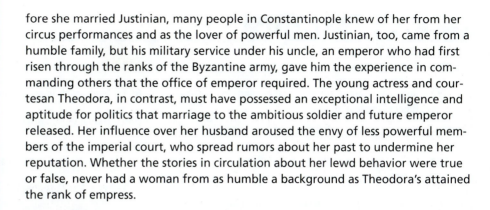

fore she married Justinian, many people in Constantinople knew of her from her circus performances and as the lover of powerful men. Justinian, too, came from a humble family, but his military service under his uncle, an emperor who had first risen through the ranks of the Byzantine army, gave him the experience in commanding others that the office of emperor required. The young actress and courtesan Theodora, in contrast, must have possessed an exceptional intelligence and aptitude for politics that marriage to the ambitious soldier and future emperor released. Her influence over her husband aroused the envy of less powerful members of the imperial court, who spread rumors about her past to undermine her reputation. Whether the stories in circulation about her lewd behavior were true or false, never had a woman from as humble a background as Theodora's attained the rank of empress.

Introduction

The violence of the Nika Riot lived in memory as an exception, for the residents of mid-sixth-century Constantinople felt safe within the city's stout walls. In contrast, the western provinces of the old Roman Empire no longer had an emperor. A barbarian king ruled most of Italy, and North Africa, too, was under barbarian rule. The attacks in the east by the New Persians must have seemed far away. Those who lived in Constantinople sensed they were living at the center of an ancient and thriving empire. The emperor Justinian, however, surely saw the situation differently. Despite the pride he took in his accomplishments—the construction of the greatest building the world had ever seen, the commissioning of a highly technical law code, the reconquest of territory that had slipped out of imperial control—he understood that he had stretched his empire's resources as far as they would go. An empty treasury and enemies on the borders indicated that the empire was not really secure.

And indeed it was not. Justinian's successors were victorious over the Persians, but, in the seventh century, they could not halt the advance of an army that surged northward from the Arabian Peninsula. The armies of Islam heralded the arrival of a new civilization that changed the balance of power in the Mediterranean from then on. The newcomers were quick learners. Unlike the Christians, they enthusiastically absorbed the philosophy and science of ancient thinkers. As their armies moved across the landscape of the old Roman Empire, the Muslims subdued the populations in their path through a combination of brute force and persuasion. First, they conquered them; then they hired them. Many people chose to adopt the religion of their new masters. Islam spread westward across Africa into Spain and northward up to the gates of Constantinople. The Christian world was challenged by a formidable adversary.

Even without the threat from the Muslims, the Byzantine emperors—as the rulers in the east are now called—faced problems that threatened to provoke political unrest and even civil war. Theological controversies were so serious that they destabilized the government. In the eighth century, an emperor's ban against the use of images, or icons, in Christian worship deeply divided the empire's subjects. The only Byzantine woman ever to rule in her own right, the empress Irene, received the credit for reintroducing icons into Christian worship, but the fact that she was a woman—and ruthless—was more than the more traditional members of the political and military elite could bear. The internal weaknesses of the Byzantine Empire made the Muslim conquest of Byzantium that much easier. The empire also fell prey to Seljuk Turks from the east. By the eleventh century, the old Roman Empire had irreversibly dissolved into political blocs, divided between Christian and Muslim. The political and religious unity that had been so important to Justinian and his predecessors was gone, as was the idea of the Mediterranean world as Roman.

Justinian and the Revival of Empire in the East, 500–650

↓ What were the causes and consequences of Justinian's attempt to reunify the old empire?

↓ What were the lasting achievements of Justinian's reign?

Of all the emperors to rule the Byzantine Empire, Justinian left the longest-lasting legacy. When he ascended the throne in 527 at age forty-five, he shared it with his uncle, Justin I, an old peasant from the

Chronology

527	Justinian becomes emperor
532	Justinian's forces kills tens of thousands in the Nika Riot in Constantinople
533–563	Body of Civil Law is issued
534	Vandal kingdom of North Africa falls to Byzantine forces
542	Bubonic plague devastates Constantinople.
552	Ostrogothic kingdom in Italy falls to Byzantine forces
ca. 570	Birth of Muhammad
610	Heraclius becomes emperor
613	Persians capture Jerusalem, destroy Church of the Holy Sepulcher
622	Muhammad flees to Medina in the Hejira; beginning of the Muslim calendar
628	Heraclius defeats Persians
630	Heraclius returns relic of the True Cross to Jerusalem; Muhammad returns to Mecca
632	Muhammad dies in Medina
656	Election of Ali as caliph
658	Defeat of Ali's army at Basra
661	Death of the caliph Ali and beginning of Umayyad dynasty, based in Damascus
711–714	Muslims conquer Spain
730	Leo III forbids use of icons in liturgical services
732	Franks halt Muslim advance at Tours
750	Umayyad dynasty is overthrown; Abbasid dynasty begins, based in Baghdad
787	Second Council of Nicaea reinstates veneration of icons
802	Removal of the empress Irene from power
803	Death of the empress Irene
988	Kievan Rus officially accept Christianity
1071	Turks defeat Byzantine army at Manzikert

Balkan region in the western provinces who had risen through the ranks of the army and been acclaimed emperor for lack of any legitimate heirs or stronger candidates. The co-emperors ruled together for only one year before Justin died. From then on, Justinian's most trusted adviser was his wife, Theodora, and together they set out to restore lost territory to imperial rule and to unify the people under their rule in one church. Recovered territory, glorious new monuments adorning the largest city in the empire, and the codification of ancient imperial law all represented a level of achievement not experienced within living memory. That Justinian managed to stay in power for nearly half a century and die of old age should by itself be considered an accomplishment, given the fate of many Roman emperors before him.

Justinian's Ambitions

From an imperial perspective, the old Roman Empire was gone. Barbarians had established kingdoms in Italy, Spain, Gaul, Britain, and the provinces of North Africa. The western provinces had not had an emperor for nearly half a century, while many eastern provinces had fallen into the control of the Persians. When **Justinian I,** a common soldier from the Balkans, succeeded to the imperial throne, he would have seen restoring the empire as his mission.

Reconquering territory was accomplished in arduous stages. After his first target, the Crimea, succumbed easily, Justinian turned his attention to the Vandal kingdom of North Africa, which fell to the forces of his brilliant general **Belisarius** in 534. The conquest of

Justinian I   (r. 527–565) Byzantine emperor noted for his reconquest of lost territory, building program, and comprehensive law code.

Belisarius   (505–565) Sixth-century general who led the Byzantine army to successes in Persia, North Africa, and the Italian peninsula.

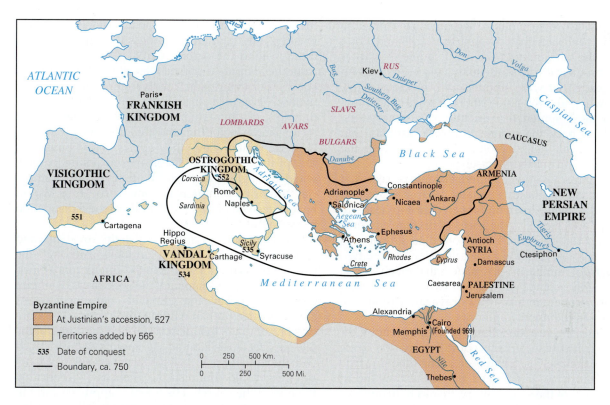

MAP 8.1   Justinian's Empire Out of the old Roman world emerged three civilizations. In western Europe, the barbarian kingdoms adapted the Latin language. In Constantinople, the new center of the old empire, the people spoke Greek. To the south, the Muslims introduced Arabic to North Africa, Syria and Palestine. Was peaceful coexistence henceforth possible?

Italy, now in the hands of the Ostrogoths, proved much more difficult. Belisarius arrived in 535; it took seventeen years to end Ostrogothic rule. Though Italy once again came under Byzantine rule in 552, the triumph was costly. Not only were Italy's cities and countryside devastated, but the Byzantine army and treasury were also much weakened.

Justinian's insistence on recapturing Italy put an enormous strain on the empire's resources. He sometimes had to cancel the salaries of his own troops for lack of funds—and then put down their rebellions. With his attention focused on the western provinces, he was compelled to pay off the Persians in the east to discourage them from invading. By building costly fortifications along the border, he managed to keep the **Slavs** on the far side of the northern frontier. But his treasury's resources were stretched to their limits. As the old Romans knew, maintaining an empire never came cheaply.

Maintaining the emperor's dignity was also difficult, especially since this emperor did not come from an aristocratic family. Unprecedented grandeur and increased rigidity in court ceremonies, designed to instill an unquestioning obedience to the emperor, may have been Justinian's way of asserting his legitimacy to rule. In every aspect of his person—from his appearance to his role in church policy—Justinian projected his belief that he ruled with God's sanction. Even his daily life was orchestrated to impress on those around him the measure of his authority. While visitors waited in the large rectangular audience hall in Constantinople to see him, he and the empress **Theodora,** dressed in sumptuous robes of royal purple bordered in gold, entered an area behind a curtain. On the other side of the curtain, the hushed, the

Slavs A loose confederation of peoples originating in eastern Europe who pressed into the empire at various times, becoming a serious threat in the seventh century.

Theodora (497–548) Emperor Justinian I's wife and empress, who had much influence on her husband's political and religious policies.

expectant crowd would have had time to examine the imposing mosaics that covered the walls and floor. Behind the curtain, after the royal couple took their places on their thrones, attendants placed crowns on their heads that were studded with precious gems. Then, when all was ready and the royal attendants sensed the heightened expectations of the visitors, they drew back the curtain to reveal Justinian and Theodora in all their awesome splendor. Instantly the supplicants prostrated themselves.

For all the majesty the imperial couple projected, it annoyed some visitors, especially the aristocrats, that they had to bend down and touch their foreheads to the floor and then kiss the knees of first the emperor and then the empress. Being forced to grovel was bad enough. Acting like a cowering slave before two people from humble origins made it that much worse. Never before, some believed, had two people of such base origins demanded such extravagant displays of submission to imperial authority.

Their insistence on excessive homage notwithstanding, Justinian and Theodora had reason to be proud of themselves. It had been a long time since the empire's fortunes had looked as good as they did in the first half of the sixth century, thanks to Justinian's energy and Theodora's mostly beneficial influence on her husband.

The Search for Christian Unity

Long before Justinian came to the throne, leaders of the church had taken notice of imperial court ceremony. Recognizing the power of presentation, they designed churches to resemble the emperor's audience hall, placing the altar at one end of a long rectangular room, screened from public view by a curtain. By staging most important elements of the Communion ceremony behind the curtain, out of sight of the congregants, they heightened the mystery of the **Mass.** Once the priest had consecrated the bread and wine and given Communion to the clergy around the altar, he passed through the curtain to dispense Communion to the **laity** waiting on the other side. Imperial pomp and ceremony had provided a model to the clergy seeking to enhance the central mystery of the Christian religion. And Justinian fully supported whatever strengthened the church.

The respect commanded by the emperor—no matter how low his social origins—bore a close resemblance to the authority owed a bishop or priest. Justinian, as a successor of Constantine the Great, claimed the right to convene and preside over church councils—something no barbarian king in the west had the right to do. Although he could not celebrate the Mass or administer the sacraments, the emperor was the only layman to witness the Eucharist ceremony behind the curtain that separated the people from the altar area, and he was allowed to preach in church. For this reason, the Byzantine emperors saw themselves as on a par with the patriarch of Constantinople and thus equal to all other patriarchs and archbishops, including (most controversially from a western point of view) the pope, who saw himself as the spiritual head of all Christendom. Justinian, then, wielded religious authority that enhanced his imperial authority, although no one at the time would have perceived or much less understood a distinction between the two.

Theology was one area in which this royal husband and wife diverged in their outlooks. Although the Council of Chalcedon in 451 had formally condemned the Monophysites, many people in the eastern empire continued to believe that Christ had only one nature—a divine, not a human nature. The empress Theodora was one of them. Justinian, a staunch supporter of the Nicene Creed, disliked all viewpoints that disagreed with the church, but he believed that persecuting Monophysites would diminish the chances of reconciling them with the church. His tolerant approach early in his reign was also influenced by his Monophysite-leaning wife. Theodora protected Monophysite monks, **nuns,** and clergy who faced persecution from local **ecclesiastical** authorities, harboring them in isolated monasteries and nunneries where there were sympathizers. It was the empress who made it possible for Monophysites to form churches in Armenia, Egypt, and Syria.

Nonetheless, Justinian had to enforce the church's condemnation of Monophysites. When his attempts to bring prominent Monophysites into line with church teachings failed, he sent them into exile. In regard to other religious and philosophical systems, he showed a strong inclination to stamp out those who did not adhere to church teachings or to the church itself. On his orders, Jews and followers of pre-Christian religions suffered persecution. Although earlier Christian thinkers had produced valuable theological works

Mass Christian liturgical ceremony in which the officiating priest symbolically reenacts Jesus's Last Supper with his disciples.

laity (adj. **lay**) Collective term used to refer to everyone except the clergy.

nun Woman who has entered a monastic order for women to lead a life of prayer and contemplation.

ecclesiastical Pertaining to a church.

that employed Platonic philosophy, Justinian forbade the study of any pre-Christian philosophy. He closed Plato's Academy in Athens at the same time that the clergy in the west were disparaging what little they knew about Plato. In an intellectual environment that discouraged critical examination of non-Christian texts, Christian thinkers placed those ancient works on their library shelves and forgot about them.

The Codification of Roman Law

Early in his reign, Justinian commissioned legal scholars to gather into one work the legislation of previous Roman emperors and the canon law of all the church councils as well as the legal opinions of Roman jurists. The project, which sought to extend the great Theodosian Code of the early fifth century, lasted decades, from the issuance of the first volume in 533 to the publication of the most recent laws in 565. This **Body of Civil Law** provided a systematic approach to law that had as its underlying principle: "Justice is the constant and perpetual wish to render to every one his due." The Civil Law remained the law of the Byzantine Empire until the fifteenth century and became the foundation of every modern-day legal system in continental Europe.

One basic distinction laid down by Justinian's law was that between a free person and a slave. A free person was someone endowed with the right to conduct affairs in civil society. A slave was the opposite: not quite a "thing," but not a person either, endowed with freedom by nature but deprived of civil rights by human society. Roman law proceeded on the convoluted logical grounds that a slave could not own property because he was property. A free man could not be property because he could own property. In this way, when Justinian's commissioners began to work out which ancient laws fit into their framework of legal principles, they provided the institution of slavery—already long in existence—with a rationale that governments would also rely on for more than a thousand years.

Family life also profoundly felt the impact of Roman law. At the heart of this legal system was the **patria potestas,** the legal head of household. In Justinian's day, the head of the household was the guardian of everyone in his household, all of whom were legally subordinated to his will, including not only his family but also his servants and slaves. A husband governed his wife, his children, his servants, and his slaves in the same way a ruler governed his people. In contrast to women in western Europe, however, Byzantine women enjoyed property rights and retained ownership over their dowries after mar-riage, although their husbands had the authority to manage their investments.

By regulating the relationship between people and property, Roman law also had a deep and lasting effect on commerce. By the sixth century, the head of a family who wanted to transfer property in a way that ensured that enforcement of the agreed-on terms (such as price or length of possession) would resort to a **contract.** Contracts, most of which were verbal but just as binding as written ones, invoked the power of the law in case one party did not abide by the terms. Traders made the greatest use of them, but contracts were also used in the transmission of property within and between families. In his lifetime, a father would hand over property to children by means of a contract but resort to the laws relating to succession and inheritance to direct the distribution of his property after death. Marriage amounted to little more than a contract to sanction the legal union of members of two families so that the couple's children would have a legal right to inherit both families' property. Because it provides instruments to manage relationships between people and between people and property, Roman law remains the foundation of legal systems throughout western Europe and the United States.

Constantinople: The New Rome

Standing under the immense dome of Hagia Sophia in Constantinople, a subject of Justinian might be forgiven for thinking that this was the center of the world. Under severe financial constraints when he rebuilt the basilica following its destruction in the Nika Riot of 532 (see Choice), Justinian hired two amateur builders whose daring must have horrified professional architects of the time. Indeed, that immense dome, 180 feet above the stone pavement, would collapse in 558, only to be rebuilt even more steeply within a few years.

To the ordinary person, the effect of standing under the dome in the immense central nave must have

Body of Civil Law   Justinian's three-volume codification issued between 533 and 563, containing the laws and jurist opinions of the Roman Empire and the canons issued by church councils.

patria potestas   (in Latin, "paternal authority") Legal authority of a head of household, usually a father, over the members of his household, including his family, servants, and slaves.

contract   Framework of rules and legal remedies for an agreement.

Hagia Sophia's immense dome was meant to instill in the visitor a sense of awe. When the Ottoman Turks converted the church into a mosque in the fifteenth century, they replaced many of the mosaics of Christian imagery with Quranic quotations. *(Erich Lessing/Art Resource, NY)*

Justinian's Hagia Sophia (Holy Wisdom) stands out in the skyline of modern Istanbul just as it did in the sixth century. *(Vanni/Art Resource, NY)*

been spectacular. The awed observer would have noticed subtle gradations of colors in the marble walls and, on the flat surfaces at the top of arches on either side of the nave, mosaic images depicting sacred figures against a shimmering background of gold leaf. Light entered through arched windows set around the base of the dome and the exterior walls. Hagia Sophia made worshipers feel God's majesty.

Crowds standing outside Hagia Sophia in the hot sun felt no less a sense of overwhelming majesty. The immense bulk of the building dominated the space around it, with the imperial palace complex on one side, near the Hippodrome, itself capable of seating thousands of spectators at the chariot races. To the east was the Sea of Marmora. A merchant sailing into port would have seen Hagia Sophia first, for it towered over the city. With its exceptional harbor, the Byzantine capital drew merchants not only from the Mediterranean but also from as far away as India and Scandinavia. Spices, glass, ceramics, silks, furs, and

timber—almost anything a person might want— were for sale in the city's **bazaars.** For the people of Constantinople, if Hagia Sophia was the center of the world, then their city was the epicenter of commerce.

The commercial world was a very masculine place. Men of all ages, origins, and social status crowded the narrow streets lined with low, flat-roofed buildings and bazaars. Respectable Byzantine women stayed out of sight in the women's quarters of their households and wore veils when they ventured into public. Servant men and women did the household shopping. Only disreputable women, such as actresses, prostitutes, slaves, and tavern keepers, circulated freely and unveiled in the streets of cities and towns.

Constantinople reflected the achievements of Justinian's reign in the jostle of the market crowds, the white marble of its monuments, and the throngs of

bazaar   Market in a Muslim city that can be either enclosed or in the open.

galleys moored in its harbor. But its very density made it vulnerable to natural disasters. In 542, the same year in which an earthquake flattened parts of the city, a horrifying epidemic of **bubonic plague** devastated the population. It killed indiscriminately, ceased, and then flared up again somewhere else. By some accounts, nearly half the population living around the Mediterranean died during the following thirty years. Once-bustling cities seemed empty of residents. In the Syrian city of Antioch, a man by the name of Evagrius left an account that reveals an elementary idea of contagion.

> Some perished by merely living with the infected, others by only touching them, others by having entered their chamber, others by frequenting public places. Some, having fled from the infected cities, escaped themselves, but imparted the disease to the healthy. . . . Some, too, who were desirous of death, on account of the utter loss of their children and friends, and with this view placed themselves as much as possible in contact with the diseased, were nevertheless not infected; as if the pestilence struggled against their purpose.

The high mortality rate led to hardship throughout the empire. Landowners took possession of lands left vacant by the epidemic and ruthlessly pushed peasants off their small plots of land and into poverty. Heavy taxation forced many others to give up farming. The landless peasants moved to urban centers in the hope of finding work or at least charity. Once there, they found soaring prices and rents, but also higher wages, because labor had become scarce. In 544, the emperor attempted to halt the rise in the cost of living by issuing an edict prohibiting wage and price increases: "In the future no businessman, workman, or artisan in any occupation, trade, or agricultural pursuit shall dare to charge a higher price or wage than that of the custom prevalent from antiquity." Such stern measures in hard times barely kept a bad economic situation from becoming much worse.

Justinian, who lived until his seventies, brought back into the empire territory it had lost; he constructed some of the most beautiful churches and public monuments his subjects had ever seen; and he and his wife had averted their overthrow by mobs. Plagues and earthquakes, however, disrupted his ability to lay down a solid basis for the empire's continued geographical expansion and military defense.

The Empire After Justinian

The pressures on the empire only increased after Justinian's death in 565. Even if his successors had been his equal in energy, administrative ability, and shrewdness, ruling the empire was not an enviable task. The **Lombards,** a people from northern Europe, began their gradual conquest of the Italian peninsula after Justinian's death. By the end of the eighth century, they had taken most of northern Italy. Large bands of people living beyond the borders of the empire pressed harder and harder on the frontiers. Epidemics of plague continued to weaken the empire's economy and reduce its population. Tensions among Christians with divergent views of Christ's nature increased and became entrenched along regional lines. The long decline of the Byzantine Empire had begun.

By the time of **Heraclius,** in the seventh century, the empire was in sore need of a strong military leader. What began as a migration of Slavs into the empire looked more and more like an invasion when they resisted efforts to hold back their advances. The **Avars,** a people related to the Huns, also tried to force their way over the frontier. They pushed into the Balkans and, by 617, had reached the outskirts of Constantinople. At the same time, the Persians on the eastern flank chipped off pieces of Mesopotamia, Syria, and Armenia. In 613, the capture of Jerusalem by the Persians stung the Christian empire, particularly when Persian soldiers looted and destroyed the Church of the Holy Sepulcher, founded by Helena, Constantine the Great's mother, in the fourth century. The Persians took away with them what the faithful believed to be a piece of the True Cross on which Jesus had been crucified. The problem for Heraclius, then, was to stop further erosion of the empire's territory and to reclaim land already lost, especially Jerusalem.

With an almost empty treasury, Heraclius devised ways to generate the revenue he needed to maintain an army in the field. These methods did not make him popular, but they helped him achieve his goals. He confiscated church furnishings made of precious metals to melt them into much-needed coinage. He reformed the tax system, making it harsher but more efficient. Extensive as these and other measures were,

bubonic plague   Disease caused by the bacillus *Yersina pestis* that attacks the lymph glands and is nearly always fatal if not treated with antibiotics.

Lombards   A northern German people who crossed the Alps and in 572 established a kingdom based in northern Italy.

Heraclius   (r. 610–641) Emperor who recovered the Byzantine Empire's eastern provinces and defeated the Persian Empire.

Avars   A people originally from western Asia who settled in eastern Europe in the sixth century.

they were barely enough. It took Heraclius more than fifteen years to recapture all the lands lost to the Persians. The situation looked grim when the Avars to the north allied with the Persians to the east and attacked Constantinople. After bribing the Avars to cease their attack, Heraclius turned his attention to the Persians. He pushed them so far back into their own territory that their utter defeat in 628 took place close to their own capital of Ctesiphon.

Humiliated, the Persians returned the relic of the True Cross, which Heraclius himself carried back to Jerusalem. In 630, the emperor entered the holy city, reportedly dressed as a humble pilgrim, walking barefoot into the old, ruined Church of the Holy Sepulcher. There he prostrated himself on the floor before placing the relic, now sealed in a protective container, back in its original place.

Neither the relic, nor the church, nor Jerusalem remained in Christian hands for long. No sooner had Heraclius achieved his goal of regaining the territory lost to the Persians than he had to face a surprising and even more formidable threat from the south: a new religion called Islam.

The Rise of Islam, 600–700

> ↓ What did Muhammad view as necessary to a worthy life?
> ↓ In which ways did Muslims view the world similarly to the way Christians and Jews viewed it, and in which ways did they view it differently?

In the late sixth century, few people in the Byzantine Empire remembered the ties they had once had with the people in the western half of the old Roman Empire. Not even a shared faith kept alive the bond that had once existed. The demise of the western empire reoriented the Byzantines toward Syria and Palestine, where Christianity began and where the empire's frontiers needed protection. In the markets of Jerusalem, merchants from Byzantium encountered traders from the Arabian Peninsula, Egypt, and even as far away as India. The mix of people of many faiths and from many cultures created an atmosphere of religious and cultural exchange whose influence could be felt across the entire region. In this spiritually fertile environment, a new religion took root and flourished.

The Arabian Peninsula

Located between Africa to the west and the Persian Empire to the east, the Arabian Peninsula had long been accustomed to seasonal **caravans** of traders and pilgrims. It was, and is, a harsh, forbidding desert land. The western coastline of the Red Sea contains the peninsula's only fertile soil, and in the seventh century even that land was sparsely cultivated. The area's chief value was that it lay on the route from the Syrian and Persian market centers in the north and east to the markets across the Red Sea in Egypt and Libya. Few cities enlivened the barren landscape.

Instead of relying on agriculture, the Arabian peoples were nomads who depended for their food largely on date palms and goats. Left pretty much to themselves, the people of the coastal plain, including communities of Jews, lived and worked in places where caravans stopped to sell their wares. Unlike the cities of Asia Minor, which were teeming with visitors, merchants, traders, and pilgrims, Arabian towns saw only traders on their way to the ferries that crossed the Red Sea or pilgrims coming to worship at local shrines dedicated to gods believed to reside in sacred rocks and trees. The region seemed so uninviting that even would-be conquerors, like the Romans, did not spend much time there. Indeed, Arabian towns benefited from the disruptive warfare to the north between the Byzantine and Persian armies, which compelled traders to find safer southern routes to the distant markets of Africa.

At the center of the town of **Mecca,** located about fifty miles inland from the Red Sea, stands a fifty-foot-high cube-shaped building called the **Kaaba.** It has only one door, seven feet above the ground on its northeastern side, which leads into a room containing only hanging lamps and inscriptions on the wall. Embedded in the outside wall of the building's eastern corner is a black rock—perhaps made of lava, or even meteoric—that today is held together by a band of silver. No building is holier to Muslims than this cube, surrounded by a broad plaza and a covered walkway. It stands at the heart of Islamic ritual and at the heart of Islam itself. Tradition has it that it was built by Abraham, whom Muslims call "the first submitter," the first human to submit to the will of God. Having long served as a shrine for the local gods, the Kaaba

caravan   Group of merchants traveling with their wares to distant markets.

Mecca   City of Muhammad's birth, located in the western part of the Arabian Peninsula, toward which Muslims pray.

Kaaba   Shrine in the form of a large cube—its name derived from the Arabic word for *cube*—located in Mecca (today, in Saudi Arabia).

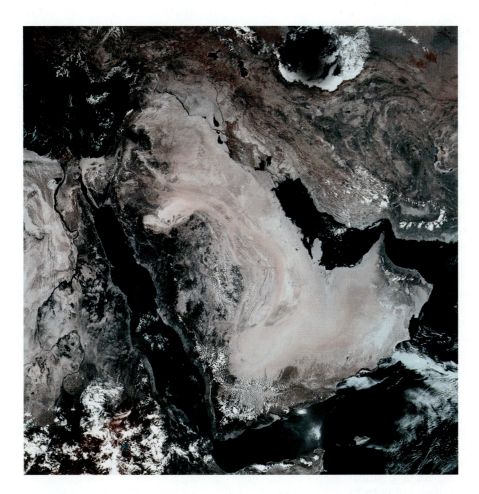

Nearly all of the fertile land in the Arabian peninsula lies on its western coast along the Red Sea. A trade route connected Jerusalem to Medina and Mecca. *(Getty Images)*

almost certainly predates the city of Mecca itself, which grew up around the shrine. By the end of the sixth century, one large tribe or clan, the Quraysh, dominated the town's economy. Among the wealthiest merchants in Mecca, the Quraysh also served as political leaders. Given their role as guardians of Mecca's pilgrimage and caravan trade, the Quraysh elders would not have approved of anyone who threatened to undermine their economic dominance, even if the threat came from one of their own.

The Life of Muhammad

About five years after the death of Justinian in Constantinople, the life of a man who would found one of the great monotheistic religions of the world began in this town of Mecca, far from the centers of cosmopolitan living in the Byzantine Empire. Around the year 570, **Muhammad,** whom Muslims call the Last Prophet, was born into a humble family belonging to

the Quraysh tribe. Orphaned early at an early age, Muhammad had the good fortune to marry a merchant's widow, Khadidja, for whom he was working. By taking over the management of Khadidja's trading business, he improved his social standing. Occasionally, he traveled to Palestine and Syria, where he encountered Christians and Jews, whose sacred writings impressed him greatly.

After he turned forty, Muhammad's conception of the world and of humanity's duties toward God began to take clearer shape. He often withdrew to a remote place on the outskirts of Mecca to meditate. One day, he believed he had a vision of the archangel Gabriel standing astride the horizon in the distance.

Muhammad   (570–632) Founder of Islam; Muslims believe he was the last prophet in a line of biblical prophets stretching back to Abraham.

The angel three times commanded, "Muhammad, recite!" When he opened his mouth, Muhammad began to utter the sayings Muslims believe to be the words of God. Eventually Muhammad's recitations, called **sura,** were written down by his followers and compiled to form the **Quran.** They expressed a belief in one God—Allah—and described the path to achieving salvation.

At first, the messages Muhammad received went no farther than his own household. His wife, Khadidja, became Islam's first convert. But others, too, began to find Muhammad's exhortations to live lives of prayer and charitable purpose appealing. Muhammad was offering the Meccans Allah as a substitute for the tribal gods and, ultimately, for tribal loyalty. As the number of converts grew and Muhammad began to speak out against the traditional gods of Mecca, the town's powerful families, who benefited financially from the pilgrimages to the Kaaba, viewed Muhammad with increasing hostility.

As tensions between Muslims and the authorities in Mecca grew, it seemed likely that Muhammad and his followers would be banished. Just then, the people of **Medina,** a smaller town a few hundred miles to the north, invited Muhammad and his followers to come and lead them. The prominent families of Medina, who frequently engaged in disputes that threatened the peace of the town, felt the need for an objective outsider to come among them as a mediator. The Medinans were looking for a political leader, not a religious one. Instead, they got both in one man. The year Muhammad left Mecca to go to Medina, 622, marks the beginning of the Muslim calendar, and his journey there is called the **Hejira.**

Muhammad brought political and religious unity to Medina, primarily by forcing out the Jews, most of whom would not convert to his new religion. Up to that point, the early Muslims had prayed facing the direction of Jerusalem, since they, like the Jews, revered the holy city. But not long after he and his followers moved to Medina, Muhammad substituted the town from which they had been exiled, Mecca, as the focal point of worship, thereby reducing Jerusalem to the rank of second most holy city of Islam. But Muhammad was determined to become a political and economic force whom the leaders of Mecca could not afford to ignore. To undermine the Meccan economy, he conducted raids on caravans heading there. Eventually, in 630, the leaders of Mecca had to negotiate with Muhammad. At the head of his community of followers, Muhammad returned to Mecca and took up the role as head of the Quraysh clan and the ruler of the city. Now the political leader of both

Built prior to Muhammad's lifetime, the Kaaba is constructed of bricks and mortar, draped with a cloth embroidered with Quranic quotations, and serves as the focus of pilgrims to Mecca. *(The Bridgeman Art Library/Getty Images)*

Medina and Mecca, Muhammad set out to convert the tribes of Arabia to his new way of life.

By the time he died in Medina in 632, Muhammad had very nearly realized his ambition. The peoples of Arabian Peninsula had accepted him as their spiritual and political leader, and in his last years, he had established the rituals and practices of Muslim life. Nine days before his death, Muhammad passed on his last recitation to the supporters whose responsibility was to write them down.

sura   Quranic verses representing the word of God.

Quran   Sacred book of Islam (formerly written in Roman letters as "Koran").

Medina   Town to which Muhammad and his followers emigrated from Mecca and where he served as a civic leader.

Hejira   Muhammad's flight, or "pilgrimage," to Medina in the year 622, the first year in the Muslim calendar.

The Religion of Islam

It is important to understand that Muhammad's role in Islam is not analogous to Jesus's role in Christianity. Instead, Jesus is to Christianity what the Quran is to Islam: both are believed to be physical manifestations of God's Word. Christians understand the New Testament Gospels as divinely inspired historical witnesses of sacred events, but Muslims view the Quran itself as a sacred event. In other words, it represents the very words of God, which came through the mouth of a mortal man, Muhammad, for whom Muslims claim no supernatural powers.

The words *Islam* and *Muslim* share a common linguistic root, which means "surrender" or "submission to God's will." In establishing his new religion, Muhammad envisioned a new way of life that would enact that obedience to God's will. A worthy life proceeds from the **Five Pillars of Islam,** actions that shape every individual Muslim's life and the life of the Muslim community as a whole. The first pillar is the admission that "there is no God but God and Muhammad was his prophet," the first line heard in the calls to prayer that ring out at set times during the day in **mosques** everywhere. This profession of faith is so important to Muslims that the only action necessary to convert to Islam is to repeat the admission three times in the presence of qualified witnesses.

Once God is acknowledged, every Muslim has a duty to pray five times throughout the day, the second pillar of Islam. Muslims pray for the same reasons that Christians and Jews pray: to express their devotion to God. Facing in the direction of Mecca (no matter where they are in the world), Muslims kneel and press their heads to the floor several times before sitting upright on the back of their heels with their outstretched palms opened on either side of the body. The third pillar of Muslim life is fasting. Muhammad intended fasting to be a reminder of how temporary life is and how inconsequential material possessions are. During **Ramadan,** the ninth and holiest month in the Islamic calendar, Muslims fast during the daytime, not eating until after sunset. Muhammad designated charity as the fourth pillar in the belief that Muslims were responsible for one another and for the Islamic community as a whole. More than a set of beliefs and a set of practices, Islam involved political allegiance from the very beginning. In this respect it is unlike Christianity, which did not become the exclusive religion of the Roman Empire until nearly three centuries after the death of its founder.

Finally, Muhammad expected every believer to make at least one pilgrimage to Mecca—the **Hajj.**

But, by not making the pilgrimage strictly mandatory, he took into account the limited means of the poor and sick to fulfill this obligation. Over the course of a set week in the Muslim calendar, pilgrims who do go to Mecca perform a series of rituals established by Muhammad in the last year of his life. Muhammad meant for the five pillars of Islam to give shape to the lives of all Muslims by uniting them in common purpose and action.

People of the Book

According to the Quran, Muslims, Jews, and Christians are all people of the book—namely, the Hebrew Bible. All three religions consider themselves descendants of the biblical patriarch Abraham, whose god became the God of Jews, Christians, and then Muslims. Muhammad acknowledged the figures in the Hebrew Bible and Jesus as prophets, but he did not believe, as Christians do, that through Jesus's death and resurrection God offered salvation to humanity. In Muhammad's view, humans still had not heeded God's injunctions to live righteous and moral lives. Since Muslims revere as prophets the same biblical figures that Jews and Christians do and believe in the same God, Muslims consider the Hebrew and Christian Bibles (the Old and New Testaments) to be sacred texts, but in their view, the compilation of God's messages in the Quran is the final and most authoritative divine statement.

From the start, religious authority and political authority in Islam were the same. When Muhammad became the political leader of Arabia, the religious and the political aspects of his authority, and that of his successors, blended into one. In contrast, in the western church, political authority over Christians came to be mediated through kings and emperors. Jesus never held political power, and his religious authority until his death was limited to a small group of followers. Because the church developed independently of the authority of kings in the west, it

Five Pillars of Islam   The basic duties of every Muslim: acknowledgment of one God, prayer five times a day, fasting at set times of the year, charity, and a pilgrimage to Mecca at least once in a lifetime.

mosque   Building where Muslims worship together.

Ramadan   Ninth and holiest month of the Muslim lunar calendar when Muslims fast during the day.

Hajj   Pilgrimage to Mecca expected of all Muslims at least once in a lifetime.

Muslims include Jerusalem among the holy cities of Islam. They believe that Muhammad ascended to heaven from the rock covered by the dome of this mosque. *(Scala /Art Resource, NY)*

remained distinct from political institutions even where it assumed political responsibility in cities with weak governments. Consequently, a Christian in living somewhere in western Europe looked to the king for protection and justice, while a Muslim in Damascus looked to religious leaders. Regardless of these differences, both Muslims and Christians thought of themselves in the first place as sons or daughters of the city or province in which they were born. Within the Muslim and Christian worlds, local culture and language distinguished people from one another more than religion united them. But when Muslims and Christians met, they would have regarded each other first in terms of their Muslim and Christian identities.

At first, Muslim relations with Jews and Christians were friendly. The Quran suggests that Muhammad tried to accommodate the beliefs and rituals of Judaism early in his residency in Medina. But the period of tolerance did not last, since the Jews refused to recognize Muhammad's religious leadership. Before the Muslims returned to Mecca, the Jews of Medina faced the choice of converting or emigrating, and most chose to emigrate. Although the first Muslims did not encounter many Christians before their conquests took them north to Palestine and Syria, they maintained a stance toward them similar to the one they held toward Jews.

This half-respectful, half-critical attitude toward Judaism and Christianity meant that Muslims much preferred Jews and Christians to adherents of polytheistic religions yet considered Judaism and Christianity to be inferior to Islam. In practice, although Jews and Christians living under Islamic rule paid more taxes than Muslims, they were allowed to worship as they pleased as long as they did not proselytize. Labeled **dhimmi,** they were thus able to survive,

dhimmi   Arabic word for people of the book—that is, Jews and Christians.

and at times prosper, within Muslim society. Some even became wealthy and politically influential. Quranic prohibitions against Muslims lending money at interest to fellow Muslims presented opportunities to Jewish and Christian moneylenders to offer credit to Muslim merchants. And members of both groups entered the employment of city governments as administrators and financial managers. On the whole, more Jews and Christians prospered under Muslim rule than Jews or Muslims did in Christian lands.

Muslim Families

Muslim families lived according to certain rules that placed them within the Judeo-Christian tradition. Like Jews, Muslims both prohibited the eating of pork and required their sons to be circumcised. Unlike Jews, however, they banned alcohol. Sharing a fear of idolatry with Christians and Jews, Muslims prohibited images of living creatures partly on the grounds that such depictions competed with God the Creator. And like the Byzantine Christian women, Muslim women wore veils in the presence of men who were not their kin and were confined to sections of their homes where male guests were not permitted.

But Muslims set themselves apart from the traditions of those older religions by allowing **polygamy,** the practice of multiple spouses. Muhammad set a limit of four wives for every Muslim man, but he himself did not take more than one wife until after the death of his first wife, Khadidja. Islam accords a place of honor to Khadidja, a capable woman who had been married to a prosperous merchant before marrying Muhammad. After her death, Muhammad took other wives in part as a way to cement alliances with the heads of other powerful families in areas of the Arabian Peninsula. To mark a tribe's acceptance of Muhammad's religious and political leadership, the tribal head would offer him a female relative in marriage. Muhammad's last wife, Aisha, played a significant role in the power struggles among Muhammad's successors, even leading an army into battle.

Before Muhammad revolutionized Arabian society with his new code of living, women occupied a low rung on the social ladder. They could not own property outright, and their legal rights amounted to little more than those of children. In this respect, they were not much worse off than women in Christian lands, who likewise had limited property rights and lived perpetually under the guardianship of a father, husband, or other male relative. As in Judaism, divorce was an option in Arabian society for both men and women, although men more easily initiated an end to their marriages than women did. The practice of hav-

ing multiple wives existed prior to Islam, but only wealthier men with the financial resources to support a large household could avail themselves of the right.

In Muhammad's lifetime and thereafter, the Muslim family became an even more private realm than before. The word **harem** has come to mean in the west a group of women, including wives, concubines, and slaves, segregated in quarters closed to the outside world. In Arabic, however, *harem* means "protected" or "forbidden" and refers to any space deemed a sanctuary or refuge and closed to certain groups thought to be potential threats or polluters of holy ground. Thus, the region around Mecca and Medina is "harem" to non-Muslims in the same way that women's quarters in private homes are "harem" to men who are not closely related to the women living there. What appears to non-Muslims as constraints on women's behavior and mobility Muslims themselves perceive as protection of women.

Undoubtedly, such protection felt like a burden to many women. After Muhammad's lifetime, Muslim laws pertaining to women grew increasingly harsh. Stoning became the punishment for a woman's adultery. Women now prayed in a segregated area of the mosque screened from the sight of men. Divorce became an option that only men could initiate. Women had to veil themselves whenever they moved outside the harem of their homes—in theory, to diminish the sexual temptation they posed to men. The seclusion and veiling of women had existed in certain circles prior to Muhammad's lifetime, and the Quran indicates that Muhammad's wives followed these practices. But sequestration and veiling became widespread in Islamic territory only in the period following Muhammad's death. In the view of many Muslims, men and women, the veil stood for a woman's sobriety, modesty, and virtue. It constituted her protection and her badge of honor.

Despite the restrictions placed on them, Muslim women played an active role in the management of their family's property. Occasionally, women even appeared in court to defend their own rights, although their testimony counted less than men's. Because men considered the proper place of women to be in the home, many women succeeded in wielding considerable moral authority within that sphere,

polygamy   Practice of taking multiple spouses.

harem   (in Arabic, "sacrosanct") A protected and inviolate area, often women's quarters in a Muslim home, but also the area around Mecca and Medina, forbidden to non-Muslims.

particularly if they had sons whose choices in life they could influence.

The Expansion of Islam, 700–800

↓ Identify some of the causes and consequences of Muslim expansion.

↓ What aspects of Islamic culture did Muslim conquests spread from Baghdad to Spain?

In the same year that Muhammad and his followers returned to Mecca, the Byzantine emperor Heraclius returned the relic of the True Cross to the ruined Church of the Holy Sepulcher in Jerusalem. With the Persians crushed and their empire extinguished, Heraclius may have believed Byzantine Christian rule secure. But when the city of Damascus, seat of a Christian bishop, fell to the armies of Muslim Arabs in 635, Byzantine imperial and religious unity was threatened anew. A century later, far to the west, even Frankish kings grew alarmed as adherents of this new religion pushed into their territory. Within just one hundred years, the religion of Islam and armies of Muslim Arabs had captured Egypt, raced across North Africa, and seized Spain. The Mediterranean had ceased to be Roman.

The Caliphate and Arab Invasions

Muhammad died in 632 before indicating clearly who would succeed him as leader of the Muslim community. From a field of four candidates, Muslim leaders chose Abu Bakr, one of Muhammad's fathers-in-law and a highly respected member of the Quraysh, to become the first **caliph,** or successor. The caliph, a position patterned after Muhammad's role among his followers, served as both the political and the spiritual leader of the community. For two years until he died in 634, Abu Bakr carried on the campaign to bring all Arabian peoples under Muslim authority. Another of Muhammad's fathers-in-law, Umar, next served as caliph for ten years. During this time Muslim forces conquered Byzantine Syria, Palestine, and Egypt. Old Persian lands, in disarray following defeat by Heraclius, fell to them, too.

After internal dissent led to the murder of the third caliph, Uthman, in 655, tensions among the Muslim leaders intensified. Some believed Ali, Muhammad's cousin and son-in-law, stood next in line to be elected Uthman's successor. Because only he among the Muslim leadership belonged to Muhammad's family, Ali claimed to be the rightful leader of the Muslim community. In his and his supporters' view, the first three caliphs had been illegitimately chosen. Others, however, wished to reserve the office for senior members of the Quraysh tribe. Ali's election as caliph in 656 did not end the disagreement. A civil war ensued between the supporters of Ali (the Shiites) and the Quraysh-led majority sect of Islam (the Sunni) that led to the defeat and murder of Ali and the beginning of the **Umayyad dynasty** of caliphs in 661.

The **schism** between the Shiites and the Sunnis came at a time when the leaders of Islam increasingly resorted to military conquest to extend their authority. Making no distinction between their political and religious authority, the religious leaders were also rulers of territory as well as people. Like most rulers, they sought to expand the territory they controlled. More territory meant more wealth for the leaders of Islam. The Umayyad caliphs' decision to relocate the capital of Islam from Mecca to Damascus in 661 after the death of Ali was as much a military decision as an economic one. Damascus, the capital city of Syria then and now, was situated on the path of a number of intersecting trade routes running east to west and north to south. Once the Muslim leaders conquered Syria, they benefited not only from improved lines of communication, as Muslim armies moved westward along the North African coast, but also from increased commercial revenue.

Within thirty years after Muhammad's death, Arab armies had conquered the lands stretching from Iran in the east to the Black Sea in the north as well as around the Mediterranean from Antioch to Alexandria. Not since the time of Alexander the Great had an army moved so far so fast. The dissatisfaction of populations subject to Byzantine rule made the Muslim conquest relatively easy and quick. High taxes and harsh treatment had undermined Byzantine authority in Syria, Palestine, and Egypt. Once those provinces were conquered, Muslim rule imposed taxes that were lighter than those the conquered people had paid to the emperor. Moreover, the Muslim authorities proved to be more tolerant of their subjects' religious diversity than the Byzantine emperor or patriarch of Constantinople had been. Although some Christians fled following Muslim conquests, many chose to remain.

---

caliph Spiritual and political leader of the Muslim community.

Umayyad dynasty First line of hereditary caliphs whose capital was in Damascus.

schism (in Greek, "split") Division in a religion or church on theological principles.

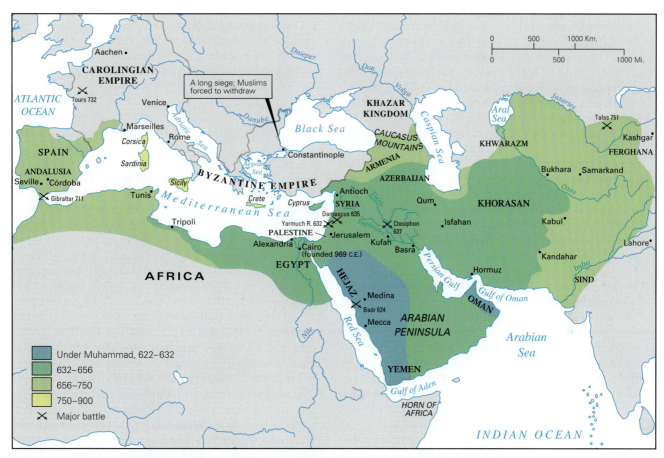

MAP 8.2 **The Spread of Islam** After the death of Muhammad in 632, Muslim forces brought the Arabian Peninsula, Syria, Palestine, all of northern Africa, and the Iberian peninsula under Muslim rule within one hundred years. How much of this vast territory had once formed part of the Roman Empire?

Under Muslim rule, Monophysite Christians no longer had to worry about persecution. The rebuilt Church of the Holy Sepulcher remained Christian.

When the Muslims brought new territory under their rule, they continued local political bodies but placed them under the supervision of a small number of Muslim military administrators. As a result, the newly created provinces of the Islamic empire enjoyed a degree of autonomy that lessened the humiliation of being conquered. At the height of its power, during the relatively short period of political and religious unity from the death of Muhammad to the early eighth century, the Muslim world embraced distinct cultural units whose people all turned in prayer toward Mecca.

Across Africa and into Spain

Having conquered the eastern provinces of the Byzantine Empire, the Muslims set out to capture Constantinople itself. Twice, from 674 to 678 and from 717 to 718, Muslim armies under Umayyad caliphs laid siege to the city. Both times they failed. The fall of Christian Constantinople to a Muslim army was still seven hundred years in the future. For now, Muslim leaders focused on extending Islam westward.

Quickly Muslim armies moved west across the North African coast, which had been under Byzantine rule since Justinian's army brought down the Vandal kingdom in the mid-sixth century. The Muslims' advance succeeded in part because of the leaders' ability to recruit new soldiers along the way, and the **Berber** people in North Africa were willing converts. In 711, Muslim forces under **Tariq ibn Ziyad,** a

Berbers An indigenous people of North Africa in modern Algeria and Tunis.

Tariq ibn Ziyad (d. 720) Muslim general who led the invasion and conquest of the Iberian Peninsula.

general of Berber origins, crossed the narrow straits from Africa to Spain, seizing the mountain that eventually bore his name, **Gibraltar** (Gibr al-Tariq, Arabic for "Mountain of Tariq"). Basing his army there, Tariq advanced to conquer Spain, under the rule of Visigothic kings since the beginning of the sixth century. His first conquest was Toledo, the capital of the Visigoths' kingdom. By 714, he had conquered all of Spain. To the Christians in neighboring Gaul, the Muslims appeared unstoppable, but in 732 the Franks stopped them at **Tours.**

When news of the conquest of Spain reached Damascus, the Umayyad caliph placed the territory under the command of the governor of North Africa and ordered that land be distributed to supporters. The first allotments went to Muslim military leaders, but Berbers from North Africa and Arabs from the Arabian Peninsula, including members of the Quraysh tribe, also migrated to Spain to claim land for themselves. A fifth of all revenue from Spain belonged to the caliph in Damascus, and his portion passed through the hands of the governor of North Africa, an arrangement that did much to increase the governor's wealth. In time, the provinces of Spain and North Africa became separate administrative districts, and governors of Spain were allowed to keep most of the revenue that once had gone to North Africa and Damascus.

Resistance to the Muslims in Spain was minimal in the first centuries of their rule. As long as Christians paid a poll tax and did not proselytize or in any other way undermine the Muslim faith, they could keep their property and practice their faith. Muslim authorities offered the same condition to the Jews, who had suffered from periodic persecutions under the Visigoths and may have aided the Muslims during their conquests.

From the mid-eighth century on, the empire created by the caliphs proved very difficult to rule from one center. The same techniques of conquest that allowed for a degree of local autonomy also weakened a centralized Islamic empire, with the caliph ruling from a capital. Problems in long-distance communications and regular tax collection plagued the caliphs just as they had the Roman emperors. When the Umayyads were overthrown in 750 and the new **Abbasid dynasty** moved its capital to Baghdad, Muslim leaders in Spain took advantage of the political chaos in Syria to establish a **caliphate** of their own in the **Iberian** city of Cordoba. For the first time since its inception, Islam had no political center or single caliph. The Abbasid caliphs in Baghdad looked to expand eastward. The caliphs of Spain aspired to crossing the **Pyrenees** into the Frankish kingdoms. These break-

away caliphates encouraged the development of local cultural traditions. Islamic religious unity had ended shortly after Muhammad's death. Now the political unity of Islam was at an end.

Islamic Civilization

From Persia in the east, through Mesopotamia and Arabia, north to Palestine and Syria, west through Egypt, arcing across North Africa and penetrating Spain to the Pyrenees, Muslims ruled a vast portion of the old Roman Empire—more, in fact, than Justinian had in his control when the Byzantine Empire was at its greatest extent. As the Muslims came into contact with older civilizations, they absorbed aspects of these cultures that enriched Islamic thought, art, and society. Muslim philosophers translated many philosophical and medical works of ancient Greek writers, which had survived in Syrian monasteries. Astronomers provided maritime traders with the elements of celestial navigation. Mathematicians studied Euclid's geometry and developed trigonometry and calculus. The Arabic origin of the word *algebra* demonstrates how much western mathematics owes to Muslim scientists. The very concept of zero, unknown in the Roman system of numerals, was developed by these thinkers. Later, in the fourteenth century, when Arabic numerals were adopted in the west, all kinds of new mathematical calculations became possible.

Through intellectual pursuits and law, Islamic society achieved a cultural unity that was visually apparent in its distinctive style. Rejecting representations of human figures, Islamic art favored a highly ornamental form of decoration that used brilliant colors, images of lush foliage, and elaborate curved lines to display calligraphic Quranic quotations on manuscript pages, ceramics, metalwork, and the walls of buildings. The architecture and decoration of mosques and public and private structures in Islamic Spain at

Gibraltar (from Jabal Tariq, "mountain of Tariq") Mountain at the southern tip of Spain.

Tours Battle in 732 in which the Franks defeated Muslims advancing north from Spain.

Abbasid dynasty Second line of hereditary caliphs, who came to power in 750 and moved the political center of Islam to Baghdad.

caliphate Muslim state ruled by a caliph.

Iberia Peninsula in southwest Europe today comprising Spain and Portugal.

Pyrenees Mountain chain separating France from the Iberian Peninsula.

Islamic architecture and art retained its distinctive features throughout the Muslim world. By the ninth century, the style and details of this mosque in Cordoba, Spain would have reminded a Muslim from Syria of the mosques he knew at home. *(Werner Forman /Art Resource, NY)*

one end of the Mediterranean displayed features similar to those found in Syria at the other end.

The greatest masterpieces of Muslim literature—lyrical and passionate love poems, biting political satire, and profound religious enquiry—were written during the Abbasid dynasty, after 750, when a high standard of composition in the Arabic language was attained. The poetry of **Abu Nuwas,** considered the best in that period, reflected the urban culture that flourished in Baghdad. The popularity of this poet's drinking songs makes it clear that, prohibitions against drinking alcohol notwithstanding, life in Muslim cities had much in common with cities in the west.

Following its start in the town of Mecca, Muslim civilization continued to be urban and commercial. In fact, commercial prosperity underlay much of the wealth and power of Muslim society. The Abbasid caliphs promoted trade and intellectual pursuits in all regions regardless of religion. Muslim prosperity drew merchants from western Europe, particularly from the Italian port cities, to the ports and markets of Egypt, Palestine, and Syria. The traders from far away brought ideas and skills as well as products. By 793, for instance,

Central Asian traders had brought from China to Baghdad the technique of papermaking, whose inexpensive manufacture made manuscripts and notebooks available more cheaply to literate people.

Though centralized control was lax, the one feature all Muslim provinces shared was a new language of religion, learning, and administration. When the peoples around the southern rim of the Mediterranean accepted the Muslim religion of their new rulers, they had to learn Arabic, the language of the Quran. Because Muslim leaders had decreed that the word of God as revealed in the Quran must remain untranslated, Arabic was the only language of worship and study. Those who did not convert had incentives to learn Arabic, too, since the Muslims used it in their political administration. Thus, the Muslim advances of the seventh and eighth centuries brought

Abu Nuwas (ca. 747–813) Poet of Persian descent who lived in Abbasid Baghdad, considered one of the greatest poets in the Arabic language.

about an Arabization of conquered lands that was linguistic as well as religious. Arabic, once spoken only in the Arabian Peninsula, became the dominant language wherever Islam made itself the law. In the eighth and ninth centuries, however, with political unity increasingly fragmented, the Arabic language took on local characteristics, each region developing a dialect of its own.

Middle Byzantine Period, 600–1071

↓ In what ways did the Byzantine Empire decline?
↓ How did debate at the highest levels of political and church authority over the use of icons in worship touch ordinary people?

The Muslim conquest of the southern and eastern regions of the Byzantine Empire brought far-reaching and permanent changes. With the loss of Syria, Palestine, and Egypt, three of the most important cities of Christianity—Jerusalem, Antioch, and Alexandria—no longer had Christian rulers. In losing them, the Byzantine Empire also lost important revenue. Despite territorial decline, the Byzantine Empire had energetic emperors in the seventh and eighth centuries. Sending missionaries north to convert the people living along the Volga River, they spread Byzantine culture. Some emperors attempted to shore up their defenses along the frontiers and to strengthen the imperial army. But societies need more than missionaries and military might to prosper. As Muslim raids from the south and Slavic harassment from the north continued, sheer survival became the emperors' most pressing priority. These external pressures, in addition to more outbreaks of plague, had economic, military, and cultural repercussions that made life precarious and strained the empire itself, in what is known as its middle period.

Losses and Reforms

A mere four years after the death of the founder of Islam, in 632, the caliph Umar led Muslim forces to confront the emperor Heraclius's army at the river of Yarmuck in Syria. Muslim chroniclers of the time estimated that tens of thousands of Arabian combatants faced hundreds of thousands Byzantine, Armenian, Mesopotamian, and Syrian soldiers in a showdown for possession of the Byzantine province. Despite the daunting odds against them, the Muslim forces smashed their opponents, and Heraclius had no choice but to retreat to the safety of Constantinople. Syria

became, and would remain, in religious, political, and cultural terms, a Muslim land.

The Byzantine emperors relied on three methods to hold off the threats to the empire's borders. First, to maintain the Byzantine army in the face of diminishing revenues, lost when Egypt, Syria, and eastern Anatolia fell to Muslim forces, Heraclius's grandson, **Constans II,** divided the empire into administrative units called **themes** and placed each *theme* under a military governor who commanded a battalion garrisoned there. As each battalion had to provision itself from the revenue of the *theme* in which it was stationed, the burden of maintaining an army of three hundred thousand was distributed across the empire. The system also partially relieved the imperial government in Constantinople from having to administer such far-flung provinces.

Second, Constans's successors extended his efforts to strengthen Byzantine defenses by building a navy and reorganizing the cavalry. Muslim Arabs were now raiding the Anatolian coast, coming uncomfortably close to Constantinople by way of the **Dardanelles Strait.** In response, the imperial navy made effective use of **Greek fire,** which had been invented by a Christian refugee from Syria. Believed to be made of petroleum-based substances that water could not extinguish, Greek fire launched from Byzantine ships forced the Muslim Arabs to withdraw. Though Greek fire was dangerous to launch and used sparingly, its lethal reputation constrained Byzantium's enemies for the time being. Beginning in the seventh century, heavy cavalry, known as **cataphracts** and recruited mainly from the more affluent levels of the peasantry, played an important part in the Byzantine land forces. Together, the Byzantine fleet and cavalry gained for

Constans II (630–668) Emperor responsible for extensive administrative and military reforms of the Byzantine Empire.

themes Administrative units of the Byzantine Empire corresponding to the dispersal of military battalions throughout the empire.

Dardanelles Strait The water passage connecting the northern Aegean Sea to the Sea of Marmora and Constantinople.

Greek fire Petroleum-based substance that ignited on contact with water; used by the Byzantine army in warfare.

cataphracts Units of heavy cavalry that dominated Byzantine military tactics on land by the seventh century.

Invented in the seventh century by Callimachus, a Syrian engineer, Greek fire was a mixture formed from petroleum, sulfur, saltpeter, and lime that ignited on contact with water. *(Institut Amatller d'Art Hispanic)*

the empire a reputation as a formidable military state. The Byzantine Empire also became known for its third method of protecting itself: military intelligence and subterfuge. Military leaders created dissension among Byzantium's enemies through spying and bribing one foe to attack another.

The administrative reforms and strengthening of the military in the empire gave the impression to Muslim and western Christian observers of a large superpower with unlimited resources. In reality, by the end of the eighth century, the Byzantine Empire had been reduced in size and population. If there was more religious unity, it was only because the loss of Syria, Palestine, and Egypt had removed the major dissenters from the orthodoxy of the eastern church. What remained of the old Roman Empire was scarcely recognizable to its inhabitants or to its enemies.

The Waning of Byzantine Society

Though its territory was shrinking, the Byzantine Empire from the seventh to the eleventh centuries had a stronger economy than did western Europe, and its subjects had a higher standard of living. The city of Constantinople, the center of urban life, retained its awe-inspiring powers. Long-distance trade in luxury goods and agricultural products between Christian

and Muslim lands continued in the eastern Mediterranean, while commercial traffic toward western Europe had begun to decline even before the advent of Muslim merchants. In contrast to the great number of cities in the Muslim world, however, the Byzantine Empire had very few urban centers apart from the capital city. Rarely did Byzantine traders venture with their merchandise very far from Constantinople. Instead, traders came to them.

But when the Middle Byzantine period is compared to the fifth and sixth centuries, a decline in almost all aspects of society can be seen. Most catastrophically, periodic outbreaks of the plague reduced population everywhere. By the ninth century, Constantinople's population had dropped from nearly 500,000 to around 100,000. Nearly every other city in the empire similarly shrank in size and population. Some disappeared altogether. Athens no longer resembled at all the classical city-state that had produced the philosophers Socrates and Plato and graceful temples like the Parthenon. Only the city of Thessalonica prospered a little in hard times. Most people resided in small villages out in the countryside, where livelihoods and diets were restricted. Villagers ate bread from local grain as well as beans, honey, and olives. For meat and dairy products, they relied on sheep and goats. Imported spices, dried fruits, and other products were rarely available outside of Constantinople, so the difference in the quality of life between Constantinopolitans and provincial peasants was stark.

The high level of cultural and intellectual expression attained during the Roman Peace was no longer possible. Higher education had mostly disappeared by the seventh century, after Justinian I closed Plato's Academy in Athens, but few people had access to education at any level. The primary and secondary schools that remained offered practical vocational training. But from then on, education, which had always been private, declined. By the seventh century, it would have been very unusual to meet a man of great learning anywhere outside of a small social circle in Constantinople. Even church intellectuals did not exhibit the mastery of texts and theological thinking that earlier Christian thinkers had.

As fewer people could read and write, the quality of literature declined. Byzantine writers produced no works of enduring fame or merit. Even the copying of ancient manuscripts to preserve classical works fell behind, and many writings of the ancient Athenians thus disappeared. Knowledge of Latin became scarce. Byzantine lawyers read Justinian I's great Body of Civil Law not in the language in which it was written—Latin—but in a simplified Greek version. The Christians of the east read the Bible in Greek, the language in which most of the books of the New Testament had been written. But very few could read at all, and those who could were most often clergy. To a merchant from Baghdad—a city famous for its writers, physicians, astronomers, and artists—Byzantine culture would have seemed unsophisticated and, if he was a snob, lacking in taste.

Increasingly over the sixth, seventh, and eighth centuries, the Mediterranean populations of the old Roman Empire made distinctions between themselves and others. How people defined themselves depended on whom they were defining themselves in relation to. A fisherman living in the eighth century in the port city of Antioch, situated on the coastline where Asia Minor meets Syria, might have thought of himself as a Christian when he was dealing with the tax collectors of his Muslim rulers. But as a Monophysite, he knew he would not be welcomed in lands ruled by Christians. He spoke to his Muslim and Jewish neighbors in Aramaic or Arabic, but he did not know Greek well enough to talk to visiting Christian and Jewish traders from the empire or farther west. All the new political and religious divisions apparent in the world made life very complicated and confusing. It was difficult to know where people's allegiances lay.

In either the Christian or Muslim worlds, the wonder was that any one facet of a person's identity, like religion, could count for so much, given that gender, birthplace, language, and social rank sometimes made more of a difference in daily life than did prayers and devotions. Nevertheless, religion became the standard that Christians and Muslims carried into battle against each other over the succeeding centuries.

The Controversy over Icons

The extraordinary variety of sights, colors, and sounds common today make it difficult to imagine the spectacular impact a church interior could have had on an ordinary person in the Byzantine Empire. A woman coming to pray for her sick child, for example, would have paused at the entrance to let her eyes adjust to the darkness. There were few windows, and the only light came from candles, whose smoke stains had made the interior even darker over time. But then, illuminated by candlelight, she might have stopped to study the stern faces of the early **church fathers,** depicted on the walls in frescoes. If the church had wealthy patrons, she could have gazed up at scenes from the life of Christ, portrayed in richly decorated mosaics against a background of gold. Above her, embedded into the surface of the central dome, there might be a huge mosaic of a forbidding rather than a compassionate Christ, in keeping with the Byzantine emphasis of Christ as ruler rather than as dispenser of mercy. At eye level, she would have seen **icons,** paintings made on panels of wood showing Christ; his mother, the Virgin Mary; or the saints—all close enough to touch or to kiss in the fervency of prayer. The flickering candlelight would animate the gold and multicolored pigments in these portraits. It is little wonder that, for many, these icons made visible the presence of the holy figures they represented. In her devotions, the mother of the sick child may have prayed to the Virgin in the icon, taking comfort in the Virgin's closeness even as the church interior evoked in her a deep sense of awe and humility.

By the middle of the eighth century, however, people's attachment to icons had made some high-ranking members of Byzantine society uneasy. Most prominently, Emperor **Leo III** was preoccupied with the biblical commandment against the worship of

church fathers Early Christian writers, such as Augustine, Ambrose, Jerome, and Leo the Great.

icon A representation of sacred figures on wood panels, mosaics, or wall paintings.

Leo III (r. 717–741) Byzantine emperor who took the first steps toward the prohibition of icons.

Few icons survived the period of Iconoclasm. Only icons in monasteries located far from the heart of the Byzantine Empire managed to escape destruction. This depiction of Jacob's ladder dates to the twelfth century. *(Erich Lessing/Art Resource, NY)*

"graven images": Were icons, as the focus of believers' prayers, almost the same as idols—objects embodying the "false gods" that the Hebrew prophets of old had warned against? Then, in the summer of 726, a volcano erupted in the middle of the Aegean Sea, spreading ash and smoke as far as northern Greece. God was evidently highly displeased with the people of the Christian empire, concluded Leo, and he removed an icon of Christ on the Chalke Gate, at the entrance to the imperial palace, that was greatly revered by the people of Constantinople. Riots ensued. The emperor had struck a nerve in the city populace, but he continued to urge the people to give up their icons and to pressure the clergy to remove icons from their churches.

Debate over the sinfulness—or righteousness—of religious images escalated into a full-scale church controversy. Those who persisted in their attachments to icons argued that the Old Testament prohibition of images had never been strictly observed, as angels were depicted in the Temple in Jerusalem. More positively, they argued that the birth of Christ, the God-Man, removed the old prohibitions. As the theologian John of Damascus explained, "In former times, God who is without body, could never be depicted. But now when God is seen in the flesh conversing with men, I make an image of the God whom I see." In other words, Christ's human nature deserved to be shown in the form God himself had chosen. Nevertheless, the church hierarchy fell into line with the emperor's wishes. In 730, Leo banned all icons depicting holy figures, except the Cross, reinforced by a subsequent ban in 754 by the Council of Constantinople. In reaction, the church in western Europe dissented, following Pope Gregory II's lead, and declared iconoclasts ("smashers of icons") and the doctrine of **iconoclasm** to be heretical. Thus, the division between the eastern and the Roman church deepened.

Leo III's son and grandson took the policy further and persecuted those who venerated icons. Monks and nuns, whose spiritual authority among the poor and the rural population rested in part on their association with revered icons, went into hiding. But when Leo's grandson, Emperor Leo IV, died in 775, and his widow, **Irene,** became **regent,** ruling until her nine-year-old son, Constantine VI, would be old enough to be named emperor, imperial policy toward icons changed. An ambitious woman, Empress Irene sought to consolidate her power by initiating the theological reform she knew would win her support from many clergymen and ordinary people. In 784, when the office of patriarch of Constantinople became vacant, Irene appointed a man who wished to end the policy of iconoclasm. Three years later, in 787, the Second Council of Nicaea debated the matter, and the leaders of the eastern church reversed themselves. At its concluding session, Irene and her son, Constantine VI—now twenty-one years old and ruling in his own right—signed a declaration officially restoring the use of icons in religious services and worship in the Byzantine Empire. The iconoclasm

iconoclasm   Policy initiated by Emperor Leo III in 731 forbidding the veneration of icons in religious worship.

Irene   (ca. 752–803) Widow of Emperor Leo IV, who usurped power from her son, Constantine VI, to rule in her own right.

regent   Person authorized to rule in the name of a monarch who has not yet come of age.

Voice

VoidVoiceVoiceVoice

Church Councils Condemn and Restore the Use of Icons

Although the iconoclastic movement lasted one hundred years, it had an impact that can be partially measured by how very few icons made prior to 730 survived past the ninth century. Thousands of icons cherished by men and women throughout the empire were destroyed when Leo III forbade the use of icons in liturgical services. Painters closed their workshops. Families risked hiding their beloved icons or surrendered them to authorities to be destroyed. Imperial troops cleared monasteries of the icons that people had traveled great distances on pilgrimage to visit. Few icons, mostly those housed in remote monasteries, such as St. Catherine's in the Sinai peninsula or in Russia, escaped destruction. The first selection here, from the Council of Constantinople's condemnation of icons in 754, sets out the rationale for the banning of icons. The second selection, from the Council of Nicaea in 787, explains the council's reasons for restoring the veneration of icons.

➡ Who are meant by "creature" and "Creator"?

➡ What is the basis of the argument against icons?

➡ If *demiurgos* means "maker," who does the term refer to in the document?

➡ Who are the "faithful Emperors"?

➡ What sinful gain does the painter derive from icons?

➡ What is the argument in favor of icons in religious worship?

From the Council of Constantinople in 754

➡ Satan misguided men, so that they worshipped the creature instead of the Creator. ➡ The Mosaic law and the prophets cooperated to undo this ruin; but in order to save mankind thoroughly, God sent his own Son, who turned us away from error and the worshipping of idols, and taught us the worshipping of God in spirit and in truth. As messengers of his saving doctrine, he left us his Apostles and disciples, and these adorned the church, his Bride, with his glorious doctrines. This ornament of the church the holy Fathers and the six Ecumenical Councils have preserved inviolate. ➡ But the before-mentioned demiurgos of wickedness could not endure the sight of this adornment, and gradually brought back idolatry under the appearance of Christianity. ➡ As then Christ armed his Apostles against the ancient idolatry with the power of the Holy Spirit, and sent them out into all the world, so has he awakened against the new idolatry his servants our faithful Emperors, and endowed them with the same wisdom of the Holy Spirit. . . .

➡ What avails, then, the folly of the painter, who from sinful love of gain depicts that which should not be depicted—that is, with his polluted hands he tries to fashion that which should only be believed in the heart and confessed with the mouth? He makes an image and calls it Christ. The name Christ signifies God and man. Consequently it is an image of God and man, and consequently he has in his foolish mind, in his representation of the created flesh, depicted the Godhead which cannot be represented, and thus mingled what should not be mingled. Thus he is guilty of a double blasphemy—the one in making an image of the Godhead, and the other by mingling the Godhead and manhood.

From the Second Council of Nicaea, 787

➡ We define with all accuracy and care that the venerable and holy icons be set up like the form of the venerable and life-giving Cross, inasmuch as matter consisting of colours and pebbles and other matter is appropriate in the holy

church of God. . . , as well as the image of our Lord and God and Saviour Jesus Christ, of our undefiled Lady the Holy Mother of God, of the angels worthy of honour, and of all the holy and pious men. For the more frequently they are seen by means of pictorial representation the more those who behold them are aroused to remember and desire the prototypes and to give them greeting and worship of honour—but not the true worship of our faith which befits only the divine nature—but to offer them both incense and candles, in the same way as to the form of the venerable and life-giving Cross and to the holy gospel books and to the other sacred objects, as was the custom even of the Ancients.

controversy was at an end. Symbolically, Irene replaced the Christ icon at the Chalke Gate, but very few other icons had survived. Irene's popularity rose, in large part because the people of the empire viewed her as responsible for restoring their beloved icons.

The Empress Irene

When, in 769, Emperor Constantine V had chosen Irene to marry his son Leo, designated heir to the imperial throne, the young woman from a provincial family in Athens must have been terrified. Life in the great palace complex in Constantinople, a labyrinth of reception rooms, galleries, gardens, churches, stables, and military barracks, would mean an unending series of exhausting ceremonies. From now on her days would be filled with prescribed movements and rituals, with coronations, judicial sessions, receptions for dignitaries, commemorative Masses, holy **feast days,** and other occasions that created a mystical aura around the emperor's person. So elaborate had the public and private court rituals become that specially trained courtiers oversaw their performance and instructed the imperial family in their proper roles.

The court specialists who trained Irene were likely tall, long-limbed, blond, and beardless eunuchs. Since they were unable to procreate, the eunuchs were trusted with access to the women's quarters, acting as servants and advisers to the female members of the imperial family. Irene would spend much of her life largely in the company of these court servants, many of whom she appointed to key positions in her government.

The empress Irene, once regent, enjoyed the power she wielded while her son was underage. Unlike previous imperial mothers who promoted their sons' interests, she had no intention of letting her son assume his role as senior emperor. Although of age to assume full control of the state, Constantine lived under a form of house arrest in Porphyra, the imperial palace

paneled with slabs of purple marble where he was born. In 788, his mother sent a commission of judges throughout the empire to find him a wife from among his subjects. With a list of ideal standards in hand, the judges measured the physical and moral qualities of young aristocratic women presented to them for inspection. These **bride shows** produced about thirteen possible candidates, from which Irene chose Maria, a young woman from the province of Armenia, to be her son's wife. The marriage turned out badly, in part because Constantine saw his wife as his mother's ally. After having two daughters but no son to succeed him, Constantine divorced Maria and married Theodote, his mistress, actions that church leaders strongly condemned but were unable to prevent.

In 790, with the support of military regiments unhappy with Irene's rule, Constantine took control of the government, alienating key sectors of Byzantine society. By 792, Irene had managed to rally enough support for her return to the position of empress mother. Constantine had no choice but to allow his mother a place in his court. Within a few years, support for Constantine had once again eroded. Relations between mother and son became so tense in 797 that Constantine fled, was captured, and, on the order of his mother, blinded, a common punishment for conspirators and political rivals. He did not die, but Irene ruled the empire alone for five more years. However, important segments of the army were still opposed to being ruled by a woman, and Irene's own connivances contributed to the growing instability of the throne and the empire. A group of military

feast day   Holiday marking a religious date, like the birth of Jesus or the birthday of a saint.

bride shows   Presentation of prospective brides to imperial representatives charged with finding a bride for an unmarried emperor or heir to the throne.

commanders deposed her and installed one of their own as emperor. Exiled to an island in the Aegean Sea, Irene died eight months after her deposition in 802. The son she had had blinded outlived her by a few years.

Irene's reign was an experiment that was not repeated. For the rest of the Middle Ages, no other woman in the Byzantine Empire or in western Europe came as close as she had to exercising the full power of a monarch.

A Reorientation to the North

Even as Byzantine authority and control were declining, Byzantine culture was expanding in response to continued threats on its northern border. Over the tenth century, the Kievan **Rus,** a Scandinavian-Slavic people, pushed deep into the Byzantine Empire to raid, trade, and settle. On trading expeditions, they brought timber, furs, and slaves from the north and took back with them silver in the form of coin and vessels. When raiding, they carried their terror farther and farther into Byzantium. They continued their ancestors' tradition of taking captives to sell in the ports where they found customers. Their attempts to settle in the interior caused the displacement of people and chaos in the empire.

Whether the Rus traded or raided, all observers, Muslims and Christians alike, reported the harsh conditions in which they lived. Groups of ten or twenty, crammed into small wooden structures along the Volga River, engaged in sexual behavior that greatly shocked Christian and Muslim visitors. Women wore pendants from their neck that indicated the social rank of the husbands. From childhood, their breasts were bound to discourage their growth. Equally shocking was the Rus custom of cremating their dead in boats. A wealthy man could count on sailing into the afterlife with his horse, dog, and one of his slave women, who would be slain and laid beside him. When all was ready, the boat with all its contents was set on fire and shoved into the sea. The advent of Christianity, with its emphasis on bodily resurrection, slowly changed these customs.

To confront the problem of the Rus pressing against their border, the Byzantine emperors devised a three-pronged strategy: diplomacy, military recruitment, and conversion. Diplomacy seemed the wisest course to all observers at the time and, in fact, did prevent the Rus from engulfing the empire. In the face of attacks and threats of siege, the emperors continued granting trading privileges, but these only stimulated the Rus to seek new advantages. Ultimately, the Rus extended their dominion over territory along the Volga and in Bulgaria. Military recruitment also failed.

Although the Rus supplied a relatively reliable source of troops and once, in 989, even rescued the emperor from a plot, they also (much like the barbarian contingents of the Roman army in earlier centuries) were increasingly attracted to Byzantine salaries and Byzantine culture—and were an increasing menace.

Conversion to Christianity seemed the best way to deal with the peoples north of the border. When the Byzantines sent missionaries, Christianity took root in Kiev. The brothers **Cyril** and **Methodius** are credited with introducing Christian worship in Slavonic, the language of the people they missionized, and providing the Slavs with an alphabet derived from the Greek, called **Cyrillic.** In 988, after missionaries brought Christianity to neighboring peoples, Kiev also became a Christian land when its rulers and people converted, and Byzantine culture now penetrated beyond the Volga River. Ancient customs were prohibited; like Christians elsewhere, the Rus buried their dead in the ground, in hopes of bodily resurrection. But as much as the Byzantine emperor and the patriarch of Constantinople would have liked to bring the Rus completely under the control of the eastern church, the new Kievan church instead developed its own liturgical customs and language, Old Church Slavonic.

Meanwhile, in the south, the Muslim threat strengthened. By the beginning of the ninth century, the Byzantine Empire encompassed little more than Anatolia and the mainland of what is today Greece. Then **Seljuk** Turks, newcomers from the steppes of Asia, threatened even Anatolia. When they soundly defeated the Byzantines at the Battle of **Manzikert** in 1071, the Byzantine Empire lost its core territory. With only the Greek peninsula south of the Danube River under its control, plus the islands of Crete and Cyprus, the emperor decided to seek assistance from the west.

Rus   Scandinavian-Slavic people who established themselves in Novgorod and Kiev by the late ninth century.

Cyril (ca. 827–869) and **Methodius** (ca. 825–885)   Missionaries and brothers sent to the Kievan Rus to oversee their conversion; they created the Cyrillic alphabet.

Cyrillic alphabet   System of letters, named for the ninth-century missionary Cyril, used to write Ukrainian, Russian, Bulgarian, and other Slavic languages.

Seljuk   Turkic people from the steppes of Central Asia who migrated westward into Byzantine territory and eventually converted to Islam.

Manzikert   Battle in 1071, in which Seljuk Turkic forces defeated the Byzantine army and extended their control into Anatolia.

Summary

Review Questions

⬆ How would a Christian traveler know he or she was in a Muslim city?

⬆ How did Byzantine and Muslim authorities each deal with religious diversity?

⬆ When the memory of the Roman past receded, what cultures emerged and spread beyond the old empire's borders?

The people of the eastern empire still thought of themselves as Roman in the ninth century, but so much had changed in the preceding three centuries that a Latin-speaking resident of the city of Rome would not have understood the Greek-speaking inhabitants of Constantinople, "the New Rome." Rumors of barbarian kingdoms to the west and the north circulated among the sophisticated members of Byzantine society, but no one knew much about them. They were too far away for anyone to care deeply. More important to them were local issues—taxes, trade goods, and the precious icons that they once again prayed before.

Disagreements over the nature of Christ had not diminished. The Christians of sixth-century Constantinople had very strong and conflicting opinions about Jesus's humanity and divinity, which Emperor Justinian and Empress Theodora at first tried to ignore. Eventually, after the Nika Riot disrupted the capital in 532, the emperor suppressed those who disagreed with church doctrine, as threatening to Christian unity. Ironically, the regions where the majority of Christians did not follow church teachings about Christ's nature gained freedom of belief only when they came under the rule of people of another faith altogether, the Muslims.

Founded by Muhammad, who recited what he believed to be God's word to humanity, Islam drew on Jewish and Christian traditions, but the new religion had from its start a firmer political and cultural foundation in the Arabian Peninsula than Christianity had enjoyed in the Roman Empire. After an initial period of conflict between believers and nonbelievers, the founder of Islam united the people of the Arabian Peninsula under his political and religious leadership. By the ninth century, Muslim territory encompassed more territory than had the Roman Empire. Muslims from one end of the Mediterranean to the other all turned toward Mecca when they knelt to pray. They also shared in the acquisition of a new language of worship, Arabic, that allowed them all, no matter where they lived, to read the same holy text. A religion that relied on one language stood in strong contrast to Christianity, whose sacred texts and commentaries existed in both Greek and Latin. Fewer and fewer Christians could read both. While Christians unsuccessfully sought unity of belief and practice, Muslims also fought unsuccessfully to maintain the unity they began with. The division between the Sunnis and Shiites and the breakaway caliphates in the eighth century signaled the end of religious and political unity in Islam.

By the eleventh century, only the most educated clergy members would have remembered that the empire had once been united under one Christian emperor. Nearly everyone had forgotten the imperial past. For a time, the eastern and western halves of the old empire could not agree on whether to allow icons in liturgical services. The empress Irene gained lasting praise for ending the official ban on their use, but she herself alienated the traditional military elements of Byzantine society, who forced her off the throne in 801. The Greek alphabet and the rites of the eastern church traveled with missionaries to the land of the Slavs and the Kievan Rus in the tenth century.

Increasingly, sacred languages, practices, and leaders divided the people of the old Roman Empire. Religion was now a matter of loyalty as much as it was of belief.

← Thinking Back, Thinking Ahead →

Given their political strengths and weaknesses, how do you think the three civilizations—western European, Byzantine, and Islamic—will negotiate access to Mediterranean trade and engage in cultural and religious exchange after the year 1000?

ECHO ECHO ECHO ECHO ECHO

Sunnis and Shiites

In the late twentieth and early twenty-first centuries, distinctions between the Sunni and the Shiite sects of Islam achieved a higher level of visibility in the west than ever before. Unfortunately, it has taken war and acts of terrorism in the United States and abroad to spark interest in the history of Islam, despite the millions of U.S. citizens who are Muslim. The revolution in Iran in 1979; the wars conducted by Iraq's leader, Saddam Hussein, on neighboring Iran and his own nation's Shiite population in the 1980s; and conflicts between Iraq's Sunni and Shiite populations in the aftermath of the U.S. invasion in 2003 have shown that what began as a dispute over the caliphate in the seventh century has evolved over the centuries into divergent traditions of spiritual authority.

The majority of the world's Muslims—900 million, by some estimates—belong to the Sunni sect, which traditionally favored choosing its leaders from among Mecca's Quraysh elite. Today, in contrast to Shiite Muslims, who believe their leaders (imams) must be direct descendants of Muhammad through Ali and his sons, Sunni Muslims in nations with secular rulers select their religious leaders through consensus. The prosperity of Sunni Muslim nations ranges widely, from oil-rich countries like Saudi Arabia, Dubai, and Qatar to countries with great disparities of wealth, such as Morocco, Algeria, and Malaysia. Shiites have faced discrimination in many Sunni countries where they are the minority, most notably in Saddam Hussein's Iraq, where they made up the majority of the population.

The 60 or 70 million Shiites around the world represent approximately 10 percent of the world's Muslims. They constitute a minority in most Islamic countries, where Sunnis form the majority. The first modern Shiite state, established in Iran in 1979 after the overthrow of the U.S.-supported shah (an ancient Persian word meaning "king"), is considered by most western observers to be governed by Shiite imams, who have the power to overrule the country's constitutionally elected president and parliament. Within Islam, the Shiites' reputation for protecting the poor and the weak contributed to the sect's growth among poor and oppressed populations, while the Sunni sect remained dominant among ruling elites.

Since the U.S. invasion of Iraq in 2003, Shiites have dominated the newly constituted government there. By 2007, tensions between the country's Shiite majority and Sunni minority had led many observers to consider Iraq to be in a state of civil war.

Suggested Readings

Ahmed, Leila. *Women and Gender in Islam: Historical Roots of a Modern Debate.* New Haven, Conn.: Yale University Press, 1993. An examination of the position of women in Muslim societies, past and present, by a prominent scholar of Islam.

Browning, Robert. *The Byzantine Empire.* Washington, D.C.: Catholic University of America Press, 1992. A combined political and cultural history of Byzantium by one of the finest scholars of the Byzantine Empire.

Evans, James A. S. *The Empress Theodora: Partner of Justinian.* Austin: University of Texas Press, 2002. A good overview of Theodora's life and political influence in the reign of Justinian I.

Herrin, Judith. *Women in Purple: Rulers of Medieval Byzantium.* Princeton, N.J.: Princeton University Press, 2004. An accessible introductory overview to the women rulers of the Middle Byzantine period by a scholar of great erudition.

Lings, Martin. *Muhammad: His Life Based on the Earliest Sources.* Rev. ed. Inner Traditions, 2006. An engrossing narrative of Muhammad's life that relies on the Quran and other ancient Muslim sources.

Moorehead, John. *Justinian.* New York: Longman, 1994. The best starting point for an introduction to the emperor and his reign.

Peters, Francis E. *The Hajj: The Muslim Pilgrimage to Mecca and the Holy Places.* Princeton, N.J.: Princeton University Press, 1996. Fascinating descriptions and photographs of the rituals enacted during the pilgrimage, past and present.

Websites

Primary documents for the Byzantine Empire, **Internet Medieval Sourcebook, Byzantium,** at: www.fordham.edu/halsall/sbook1c.html

Accessible and useful primary sources for the history and religion of Islam,

Internet Medieval Sourcebook, Islam, at www.fordham.edu/halsall/sbook1d.html

Links to art history sites that offer excellent illustrations of Byzantine and Muslim civilizations, **Art History Resources on the Web,** at http://witcombe.sbc.edu/ARTHLinks.html

The Kingdoms of Western Europe, 500–1000

1500 B.C.E.	1000 B.C.E.	500 B.C.E.	1 B.C.E./1 C.E.

511
Clovis's lands are divided among his sons

476
Fall of the western Roman Empire

525
Benedict founds monastery at Monte Cassino

ca. 563
Columba founds monasteries in Scotland and Britain

400	450	500	550	600	650	700

Europe and the Mediterranean, ca. 800

In the Treaty of Verdun, Charlemagne's grandsons, Louis the German, Lothar, and Charles the Bald, divided the Frankish kingdom among themselves. They continued the Frankish inheritance custom of dividing kingdoms equally among male heirs. Looking at the map, what do you think were the disadvantages of dividing Charlemagne's empire?

Legend:
- Frankish Kingdom, 768
- Areas conquered by Charlemagne, by 814
- Tributary peoples
- Byzantine Empire, 814
- Muslim territory, ca. 850
- Kievan Rus, ca. 888
- Norse, ca. 888

Map labels:

ATLANTIC OCEAN, SIBERIA, FINNS, Novgorod, Baltic Sea, BALTS, PRUS, KIEVAN RUS, VOLGA BULGARS, WALES, ENGLAND, London, DANISH MARCH, Canterbury, FLANDERS, SAXONY 804, POLES, Kiev, Dnieper, KHAZAR KHANATE, BRITTANY, Rouen, Aachen, AUSTRASIA, SLAVS, Paris, NEUSTRIA, Tours, ALEMANNIA, BAVARIA 788, AQUITAINE, Lyons, BURGUNDY, Milan, VENETIA, ISTRIA, Venice, DALMATIA, CROATIA, BULGAR KHANATE, MAGYARS, GASCONY, Roncesvalles, SPANISH MARCH 811, Marseilles, LOMBARDY, Ravenna, PAPAL STATES, Danube, SERBS, Aral Sea, Syrdarya, Samarkand, Amu Darya, UMAYYAD CALIPHATE, Toledo, Barcelona, Corsica, Rome, Naples, DUCHY OF BENEVENTO, Córdoba, Sardinia, Balearic Is., Tyrrhenian Sea, Mediterranean, Black Sea, Caspian Sea, PERSIA, Ceuta, Sea, Palermo, Ionian Sea, Aegean Sea, Constantinople, ARMENIA, Tahert, Tunis, Sicily, Crete, Cyprus, Antioch, Euphrates, Baghdad, Hormuz, Tripoli, Damascus, Basra, ABBASID CALIPHATE, Alexandria, Jerusalem, Persian Gulf, Muscat, SAHARA, EGYPT, HEJAZ, Medina, ARABIAN PENINSULA, OMAN, Arabian Sea, Red Sea, Mecca, YEMEN, Aden, INDIAN OCEAN

Scale: 0 400 800 Km. / 0 400 800 Mi.

Timeline:

500 C.E.   1000 C.E.   1500 C.E.   2000 C.E.

- 732 Franks defeat Muslims at Tours
- late 700s Viking raids begin
- 751 Pepin becomes king of the Franks
- 800 Charlemagne becomes emperor
- 843 Treaty of Verdun divides empire among Charlemagne's grandsons
- 962 Otto I becomes emperor

750   800   850   900   950   1000

Choice Choice Choice

Charlemagne and His Wife

Charlemagne, seen here in this manuscript page with his wife, was the first ruler in the West to bear the title of emperor in over three hundred years. (Erich Lessing/Art Resource, NY)

The Pope Crowns Charlemagne Emperor

Pope Leo III stood waiting, off to the side in front of the altar in the ancient Church of Saint Peter's in Rome. The priests assisting him at the Christmas Mass in the year 800 were helping Charles, king of the Franks and king of the Lombards, don once again the robes and symbols of his royal authority. Earlier in the Mass, the king had divested himself and prostrated himself before the altar as a humble gesture of an ordinary man—which he most definitely was not. The king was as proud a man as they come.

All his life, Charles exhausted everyone he came into contact with. Tall for his time (a little more than six feet) and burly, this new emperor in the west wore out officials, armies, horses, clergy, and family. From the time he became king in 768 until he died as emperor in January 814, Charles spent every year of his reign except the last four conducting war and conquering territory. His empire stretched from the Pyrenees Mountains in the southwest of Gaul to the river Elbe in eastern Europe. He conquered the Aquitainians, Lombards, Romans, Friulians, Saxons, Bretons, Beneventans, Bavarians, Slavs, Avars, Bohemians, Linonians, Abodrites, Alamannians, Gascons, Catalans, Pannonians, Dacians, Dalmatians, and others too many to name. Wherever he conquered, he forced his new subjects to convert to Christianity. The king seemed never to rest. The Byzantines, nervously pondering where lay the limits of Charles's ambitions, had a proverb: "Have a Frank as a friend, never as a neighbor."

Now, his prayers finished, the time had come for Charles to reassume his mantle and crown. Pope Leo took the crown from the altar and prepared to set it again on the king's head. He had done the same at Christmas Mass in years past, when Charles had come to Rome in the winter after safeguarding the pope's lands and position in central Italy. But this time, the pope deviated from past practice. Setting the crown on the king's head, Leo declared that Charles was now emperor of the Roman Empire, the first to bear that title in the west since the end of the fifth century.

When the news that the pope had crowned Charles emperor reached Constantinople, it made the Byzantines especially uneasy, for their ruler at the time was the empress Irene, and to some—in both the east and the west—rule by a woman meant that the throne in Constantinople might as well have been vacant. To call Charles emperor was at least presumptuous; at the worst, it could be threatening. There was little, however, the Byzantines could do about it, under pressure as they were from invaders on their southern borders.

The monk Einhard, Charles's biographer, claimed much later that Charles reluctantly accepted the title of emperor, "which at first he disliked so much that he stated that, if he had known in advance of the pope's plan, he would not have entered the church that day, even though it was a great feast day." As unlikely as it was that Charles did not know in advance what the pope intended to do,

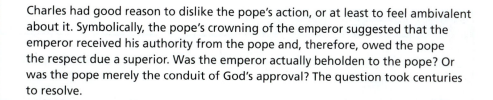

Charles had good reason to dislike the pope's action, or at least to feel ambivalent about it. Symbolically, the pope's crowning of the emperor suggested that the emperor received his authority from the pope and, therefore, owed the pope the respect due a superior. Was the emperor actually beholden to the pope? Or was the pope merely the conduit of God's approval? The question took centuries to resolve.

Introduction

The pope's conferral of such a grand title on a king on Christmas Day in 800 set a precedent that western emperors in the future resisted, though they liked to think of themselves as rulers with an aura of old Rome. But in the eighth century, in the territory that was once the Roman Empire, three very different civilizations dominated. Strong centralized authority persisted in the Byzantine Empire and also characterized the rule of the caliph over Muslim territory. But rule in the western part of the Roman Empire was decentralized. Almost no one had the power to defend public order beyond a city wall or a village boundary. By 750, constant warfare among rival Frankish kings and nobles had undermined what little prestige the title of King of the Franks held.

To the peasants who made a meager living off the land, the men who called themselves kings acted more like warlords with troops they could barely control. There was little anyone could do to prevent crops from being burned or trampled by armies. Increasingly, peasants belonged to plots of land that belonged to a lord, for whom they were compelled to work. Hardened by custom over time, relationships between people of different social status grew rigid. No matter how low or high their rank, every person had obligations to someone more powerful. When the pope asserted the right to legitimize kings, even kings came to feel they had obligations to a higher order, but they also resisted these obligations.

What little sanctuary existed from disaster and arbitrary violence was provided by the church. At its least effective, the church promised the distressed and poor a better world to come. At its most effective, it filled the gap left by the disappearance of public authority. Missionary monks fanned out across the northern lands to persuade the people living there, first, that they needed salvation and, second, that no salvation was possible without the church. Kings saw church teachings as a way to bolster their subjects' loyalty and obedience to public authority. In southern Europe, bishops stepped into the role of municipal leaders and ferociously defended the people under their care against kings and lords.

Charlemagne, king of the Franks and subsequently emperor, brought a greater security to the inhabitants of his lands by setting up a system of inspections to look after the lands and by taking war to his neighbors rather than by waging war in his empire's heartland. He brought the forces of church and government together to create a period of relative peace and stability for the people living in his empire.

But then order and security disappeared again, as Charlemagne's grandsons and great-grandsons fought among themselves over land and power. Only in the eastern portion of Charlemagne's old empire was one king, Otto I, able to restore some semblance of order. The system he devised to rule his empire, however, created problems of its own by coming to rely on the clergy for its personnel. In the newly revived empire, the clergy served one master, the emperor, a situation a subsequent generation of popes would find hard to accept. There and elsewhere in western Europe, rulers and popes began their long competition for the loyalty of their subjects.

Regional Rule, Local Views, 500–750

⬇ What caused the fragmentation of political power in the west?

⬇ How did the decline in long-distance trade affect the cities of western Europe?

Although no one realized it at the time, Romulus Augustulus, deposed in 476, would be the last Roman emperor in the west. When that office remained vacant in the late fifth century, rulers in the western provinces, once labeled "barbarian" by their Roman masters, stepped forward to lead their people off on their own. Partially as a result, the world became local. No longer did the peoples of the western interior look to the Mediterranean for direction or innovation, and no longer did the lands bordering the Mediterranean

Chronology

507	Franks defeat the Visigoths, who then migrate to Spain
525	Saint Benedict founds monastery
552	Byzantine forces conquer Ostrogothic Italy
ca. 563	Columba founds monasteries off Scotland and in northern Britain
572	Lombards establish their capital in Pavia, Italy
ca. 590s	Columbanus begins missions to Germanic tribes
597	Pope Gregory I sends Augustine to establish Christianity in British Isles
718	Muslim armies end Visigothic rule of Spain
732	Charles Martel defeats Muslim forces at Tours.
751	Pepin consecrates himself as king of the Franks
ca. 750s	Donation of Constantine supposedly puts pope in charge of western empire
768	Charlemagne becomes king of the Franks
774	Charlemagne proclaims himself king of the Lombards
late 700s	Viking raids begin
800	Pope Leo III crowns Charlemagne emperor
813	Charlemagne has son Louis crown himself co-emperor
816	Pope Stephen V recrowns Louis emperor
843	Treaty of Verdun divides Charlemagne's empire among his grandsons
878	King Alfred of Wessex defeats Danes in Britain
899	Magyars cross Alps and enter Italy
c. 924	The title of emperor falls into disuse in the West
936	Otto become king of eastern Franks
962	Pope John XII crowns Otto I emperor

give direction. Europe underwent a long, difficult transformation as Rome slipped further back into memory and new, smaller political units emerged. Western Europe was turning inward.

These new political units were often violent and unstable. In Gaul, the Merovingians managed to build the longest-lived kingdom in the political vacuum created by the collapse of the western empire. In contrast, the Visigoths in Spain and the Lombards in Italy lasted for little more than a century.

Kingship and Rule in Merovingian Gaul

Unlike the Ostrogoths, whose adoption of Roman methods of rule, nonetheless, did not protect them from conquest by the Byzantines in 552, the Frankish kings seemed unable to adopt a consistent Roman model of rule. The order maintained by the Roman frontier garrisons and the municipal services administered by provincial governors disappeared when the Romans withdrew from northern Europe. The Frankish kings and their warrior supporters were not interested in ruling or in overseeing the welfare of ordinary people. They sought only to increase their own land and wealth. The disorder that ensued actually suited them, because becoming a powerful warlord depended on the absence of order. Thus it took centuries for order and security to return to western Europe. From the sixth to the seventh centuries, the Franks repeatedly expanded into new regions and then withdrew, but out of the ensuing chaos the society and culture of the Middle Ages was born.

Today a kingdom calls to mind a tract of territory over which one king or queen rules the people who live in it, as the monarch of Great Britain (a territory) reigns over the people living in Great Britain today. Such was not the case in Merovingian Gaul. A king viewed the territory in which his subjects lived as his personal estate, which he would bequeath to his heirs. This Merovingian attitude came into clearest focus at the death of a king. When Clovis, king of the Franks, died in 511, each of his sons inherited—and

The sword hilts pictured here reveal the high quality of Frankish crafts during the Merovingian dynasty. The delicate gold leaf on the handle indicates that the king who wielded these weapons used them for display more than for battle. *(Erich Lessing/Art Resource, NY)*

and the people who lived on it. A king was only as powerful as he was wealthy and forceful, so he was always at war, always on the move in search of gain. Wherever he was, there was the government, but governance involved little more than rewarding supporters with land. This kind of kingship and rule encouraged instability and continual warfare. Only slowly, over the course of the sixth, seventh, and eighth centuries, did kings evolve from warrior chieftains to rulers of subjects. But when kings designated towns or castles as their seats of government, royal authority increased. These places, where they kept treasuries and records and from which they issued decrees, provided some stability. In the meantime, the overwhelming majority of the population working on the land hoped to escape the notice of passing armies and thereby survive.

The Iberian and Italian Peninsulas

Following their defeat by the Franks in 507, the Visigoths retreated over the Pyrenees to the Iberian Peninsula, where they found the population easier to subdue. As a province of the Roman Empire, Spain had had close cultural and religious ties to the imperial city. The upper levels of society were descendants of Roman military and civilian administrators and people indigenous to the region. These Christians looked to the bishop of Rome as their spiritual leader. The Visigoth kings, who were Arian Christians, came to understand that as long as they appeared to be heretics in the eyes of their subjects, their legitimacy would be in question. So, they converted to Roman Christianity. Thereafter, Visigoth kings cooperated closely with the bishops to bolster one another's authority. The arrival of the Muslims in 711 and the Muslim conquest of the peninsula in 718 brought Visigothic rule and society to an end.

In the same period the Lombards from the north of Germany crossed the Alps into northern Italy and drove the Byzantines out. The Italian cities that had survived the collapse of the western empire owed their existence largely to their bishops, who assumed many of the responsibilities as well as the grandeur of imperial power. Now the Lombards used the municipal buildings and organizations they found in these cities to good effect, trying to rule as they imagined the Romans would have done. Once they had established their capital at the inland town of Pavia in 572, they gave themselves the titles, offices, and authority of the old Christian Roman Empire. Not surprisingly, the bishops did not welcome these new competitors for civic authority, some of whom were Arian Christians and therefore, in their opinion, heretics. The ill

became king of an equal portion of the land their father had conquered. This division of a father's estate was custom, and custom had the force of law. In other words, the division of Clovis's kingdom was not so much a political division as a familial one.

Thinking of a kingdom as a family's estate makes it easier to understand why the temptation to restore the father's territory overcame brotherly affection in nearly every generation after Clovis. The Merovingian kings of the seventh century spent much of their time and wealth conducting wars against family members. Every time a king died, his sons fought each other, each seeking to acquire the power and wealth their father had possessed. The result was constant violence and murder. With alarming predictability, brothers slaughtered brothers, mothers attempted to kill daughters, and uncles massacred nephews.

Thus, Merovingian kings were not so much rulers of territories who sought to govern as they were warrior chieftains who sought to seize and subdue land

The Visigoths converted to Arian Christianity centuries before they settled in Spain. Their conversion to Roman Christianity made them more acceptable as rulers to the people of the Iberian Peninsula. *(Foto Marburg /Art Resource, NY)*

will between bishops and kings went both ways, as the Lombard kings rejected the church's claims to authority within the cities. Whereas the Visigoth kings saw cooperating with the bishops as a means for gaining power, the Lombard kings viewed bishops as impediments to their rule. The pope, in particular, became their target. As bishop of Rome, he ruled most of central Italy. Good relations between the Lombard kings and the church seemed impossible while the pope had the central portion of the peninsula in his control.

This threat to the pope, however, drew the attention of the Frankish kings in Gaul, who did not welcome the Lombards' attempts to take possession of the entire Italian peninsula. Just as it took Muslim invaders to bring down the Visigothic kingdom, it would take an invader from the north to put an end to the Lombard kingdom in Italy at the end of the eighth century.

The Decline of Trade

Merovingian warfare and political instability throughout the region contributed to a decline in trade between western Europe and the Mediterranean. What is more, as commercial contact between east and west dwindled, the Frankish kings had less cause to maintain cultural and political contacts with Greek Byzantium. The arrival of Muslim raiders in Mediterranean waters in the early eighth century further dampened enthusiasm for travel and trade around the Mediterranean. Up to that point, the axis of long-distance trade routes ran on sea and land from northwestern Europe in a southeasterly direction toward Constantinople. Now the dangers of long-distance trade caused a shift in the principal trade routes to an axis running north-south within western Europe, from the Baltic Sea to the shore of the Mediterranean.

These economic and political changes in the old Roman world had three effects on western Europe: a decrease in the quantity of luxury goods that reached the royal and aristocratic courts of eighth-century Gaul, a change from gold to silver coins, and a heightened self-sufficiency in the population of western Europe as a whole. Merchants still brought wares from the east to markets near the residences of nobles and bishops, but in smaller quantities and less often. Spices, gold, silk cloth, and ceramics became extremely difficult to find in the markets of the west. Trade became increasingly local and regional as western Europe increasingly came to rely on its own resources.

By the eighth century, people in Europe had little access to or use for gold coinage. What little there was entered Europe from Byzantine and Muslim lands, since Europe's only gold mines had been depleted by the eighth century. Moreover, because trading occurred most frequently on a local level, ordinary people found it more convenient to use a silver coin, the solidus, for their purchases. Gold coins were sim-

The Lombard kings' desire to rule the area of central Italy traditionally ruled by the bishops of Rome aggravated relations between the Lombards and the Frankish kings, who saw themselves as the pope's defenders. *(Vanni/Art Resource, NY)*

ply impractical for the small purchases people typically made. The switch to silver coins from gold reveals much about the kinds of commercial transactions taking place in early medieval Europe.

The use of silver coins does not mean that these transactions always involved coinage. Often coinage only supplemented exchanges of goods. For example, a peasant woman might want to purchase a pig from a neighbor. She had only three hens and some rough woolen cloth she wove herself to give for the pig, but those items did not come close to what a pig was worth. Pigs were valuable, and therefore expensive, not only for their meat but also for their low maintenance, since they wandered freely and could feed themselves off the growth in pastures and forests. The peasant woman did have some silver coins, which she could use to make up the difference between the value of her goods and the value of the pig. Barter, or exchange in kind, predominated in very isolated areas where coins were rarest and persisted throughout the early Middle Ages, particularly among people of humble status.

In general, people had less need of markets than they had had in the past. Markets had become places where peasants made purchases or bartered to supplement the foods they grew. There they encountered neighbors, and perhaps a few traders displaying locally or regionally produced goods. But there were no traders hawking wares from distant lands. And the peasants did not purchase much. Whether in times of plenty or of famine, people produced most of their own food and clothing.

The Decline of Cities

The decline in trade contributed to a decline in both the number and size of cities in western Europe. This decline began in the fifth century and lasted until the end of the tenth century. Under Roman rule, cities had been seats of provincial governments and military garrisons, with markets drawing merchants from far away. Residents of cities in the Roman world saw themselves as cosmopolitan and distinguished themselves from the humbler, less cultivated folk who toiled in the countryside. Living in a city meant, for those more sophisticated men and women, access to a wider range of goods in the market, better clothing, better housing, and the benefits of the services municipal governments provided, like courts of justice. Lyons, located in central Gaul where the Saône and Rhône Rivers converged, became an important market city connecting the Mediterranean with the north.

When warfare among the Merovingian kings made life insecure and trade with the eastern Mediterranean declined, city dwellers gradually dispersed to the relative safety of the countryside, where, even if their quality of life diminished, they at least could avoid marauding armies and grow their own food. In the countryside they would also be more likely to avoid epidemics like those that had devastated the Byzantine Empire in the sixth and seventh centuries. The cities of Britain started to shrink and then disappear as early as the late fifth century, once the Romans withdrew from the island. On the continent, the contraction of city size and population began in the sixth and continued into the seventh century. With no one needing services—few merchants and even fewer bureaucrats and royal officials—the service economy underlying the basis of most cities dried up. Public authority shifted away from cities to the countryside, where the lords resided. Bandits in the forest or simply a more powerful stranger encountered on a path could prey on the defenseless without much fear that any public authority would pursue them. Troops following ambitious leaders in search of loot and land posed as great a danger as did the bandits and ordinary thieves.

The cities that survived the economic shifts in western Europe shared certain features. In northern Italy, those cities whose bishops had assumed municipal authority and those that served as capitals of the Lombard kingdom made the transition to the medieval period. Roman buildings and monuments were put to new uses or were torn down for the stone, which was then used for new structures. Italian cities maintained portions of the gridlike street plans the Romans imposed on the cities they founded. Even some of the old city sewer systems built by the Romans lasted into the seventh century. North of the Alps, however, fewer Roman cities survived the end of the empire, for the Frankish rulers lacked the resources to maintain the city walls, streets, drainage systems, and roads provided by Roman imperial rule.

Even to call the places where a few hundred or thousands of people lived in this era cities seems an exaggeration. Certainly to a visitor from far to the east—rare enough in the Merovingian period—the muddy settlements would not have qualified as cities. Jewish merchants, practically the only traders who still occasionally came from the Byzantine world to the Frankish kingdoms, would have thought them primitive. To the people of Constantinople, the west had little appeal. Its rude living conditions, limited diet, and lack of personal hygiene were in strong contrast to the urban centers of Islam, with their learning and lively markets.

Urban life in the west ultimately began to revive, but at different times in different places. Britain, one of the first places where cities declined, experienced the earliest revival. In the seventh century, even as Frankish cities were beginning to contract, London and other urban settlements showed signs of increased activity, especially with an upsurge in trading

via the North Sea. The cities of Italy that managed to survive the decline in trade had to wait until the tenth century for better times, when the port cities took up trading with Muslim countries on distant shores of the Mediterranean. Not until the warfare among Frankish kings died down could rulers in the old Roman province of Gaul turn their attention to protecting and regulating trade in cities.

The Western Church, 500–800

↓ How did the church provide continuity between the old Roman world and the new Frankish one?
↓ What role did monasteries play in the preservation of learning?

At first, in the aftermath of the empire's collapse in the west, no one seemed to be in charge. Public authority had dwindled to nothing. The Germanic tribes hacked away at one another's territories in bids to increase their own holdings, thereby aggravating the violence and insecurity that marked the lives of all who lived in the western lands once ruled by Rome. Only in the northern Italian peninsula and southern Gaul could people feel a sense of continuity and a little security between the old world and the new. There, leaders of the church stepped into the breach created by the disappearance of municipal institutions and administrators. In northern Europe, the Roman past quickly receded and, along with it, the church, which had barely been established there. It would take an invasion of missionaries to resuscitate Christianity in the extreme reaches of the old Roman Empire.

The Christianization of Northern Europe

Across the channel from the Frankish kingdom, the newly arrived Angles and Saxons pushed the Celts and descendants of the Roman population to the margins of the island or off it altogether. Those who remained vied to dominate Britain. By the late sixth century, the region was divided among numerous kings whose fortunes rose and fell. A Saxon kingdom took shape in Wessex in the southwest and another in Northumbria in the north. In the southeast, King **Aethelbert** of Kent established his capital in the town

Aethelbert (r. ca. 593–ca. 617) King of Kent, a region in southeastern Britain bordering on the English Channel.

of **Canterbury,** and his kingdom lasted a century. Then the kingdoms of Wessex in the south and Mercia in the Midlands overtook the kingdom of Kent, and they in turn were overpowered in the mid-seventh century by the Northumbrian kings. Rivalry among Britain's kingdoms meant almost constant warfare in the island. In the midst of the fighting, groups of monks walked tirelessly across the land, seeking to speak of the Gospels.

These sixth-century monks had not yet withdrawn completely from the world. Though monasticism remained connected to the asceticism of the eastern Mediterranean, the monks of western Europe perceived a greater need for active proselytizing and seeking support for the establishment of new monastic communities. To them, there was still much to be done to extend and deepen the Christian religion among the rulers and the common people of the British Isles and the land of the Franks.

In 597, **Pope Gregory I** dispatched a small group of missionaries to the British Isles, headed by a monk who had adopted the name **Augustine** in honor of the early fifth-century Christian thinker from North Africa. Although Christianity had long before reached the Anglo-Saxon territory in Britain, Augustine and his companions worked to improve the people's understanding of the religion and extend its influence. Augustine converted King Aethelbert to Christianity and became the archbishop of Canterbury. From then on, even after the kingdom of Kent declined, the archbishop of Canterbury remained the spiritual and administrative leader of the church in all of Britain.

Augustine's mission has received most of the credit for initiating the spread of Christianity in Britain, but his missionaries received powerful support from royal women. When King Aethelbert married **Bertha,** daughter of a Frankish king, to reinforce an alliance with the Merovingians, he allowed her to practice her religion and to promote it through the churchmen who accompanied her as a bride to her new home. Similarly, Edwin, king of Northumbria, agreed to accept Christianity when he married Aethelbert's daughter. The missionaries who had accompanied Bertha north then began to convert the followers of Edwin. Thus, marital alliances between powerful families combined with missionary activity ensured the gradual spread of Christianity throughout England.

Missionaries in the British Isles encountered monks from Ireland, which Patrick had Christianized a century before. Since then, the church in Ireland had developed in relative isolation, depending on abbots more than on bishops for pastoral and administrative services. The Irish calculated the date of Easter differ-

Pope Gregory I not only sent missionaries to convert the peoples of northern Europe and the British Isles, he also wrote theological works and biographies of saints that led to his inclusion among the Church Fathers. *(SEF/Art Resource, NY)*

ently from the method followed in Rome, a distinction that caused considerable tension among Pope Gregory's missionaries and the Irish monks when they met in the courts of the British kings. In the end, representatives of the pope convinced Oswy, the king of Northumbria, to follow their calculation at the **Synod of Whitby** in 664, and Roman Christianity

Canterbury   Capital of the kingdom of Kent and seat of the archbishop and head of the English church.

Gregory I   (r. 590–604) Pope who dispatched missionaries to northern Europe and wrote theological works and saints' biographies.

Augustine   (d. 604) Augustine of Canterbury, a monk who converted King Aethelbert to Christianity and became the first archbishop of Canterbury.

Bertha   (539–ca. 612) Christian daughter of a Frankish king who married King Aethelbert and helped establish Christianity in Britain.

Synod of Whitby   Meeting in 664 at which Roman usages and the date for Easter were adopted, thus bringing English Christianity into the Roman tradition.

took the first step toward becoming the dominant form in England.

Columba, an Irish monk, crossed the Irish Sea around 563 to establish monastic communities, first on islands off the coast of Scotland and later in northern Britain, that became important centers of learning. In the 590s, another Irish monk, **Columbanus,** with a group of assistants from his homeland, traveled through the Frankish kingdom, founding monasteries wherever he went. One of them, **Luxeuil,** on the site of a Roman town in eastern France that had been destroyed by Attila in 451, became renowned as a center of learning. Columbanus's success depended in large part on the financial support and encouragement of the Merovingian rulers and aristocracy.

Another monk from the British Isles, **Boniface,** began the conversion of the northern Germanic peoples. Born with the name Winfrid, this missionary received in 719 the title of bishop from Pope Gregory II, who conferred on him the new name of Boniface to mark

his exalted status. Boniface set out to make converts out of the Frisians, Hessians, and Thuringians in what is today northern Germany. His efforts complemented the efforts of the Franks to submit the non-Christian German peoples to their rule. Christianizing the people of the north made it easier to integrate them into the Christian Frankish kingdom.

Columba (521–597) Irish monk who founded monasteries off the coast of Scotland and in northern England.

Columbanus (543–615) Irish monk who founded monasteries in the Frankish kingdoms.

Luxeuil Monastery founded by Columbanus in 590 in modern northeastern France that became a famous center of learning.

Boniface (ca. 672–754) Missionary appointed by Pope Gregory II to oversee the conversion of the northern Germanic peoples.

Voice

Pope Gregory Sends Instructions to a Missionary

In the 720s, Boniface, an English-born bishop appointed by Pope Gregory II to proselytize among the Germanic tribes, wrote to Rome to ask for advice. In spite of some years in the north, Boniface still did not have a solid knowledge of the practices of the church and its rituals. The pope's letter is important evidence of eighth-century religious practice. Gregory demonstrates, too, an understanding of how to win the trust and confidence of people.

➡️ Why does Gregory call the people of Germany uncivilized?

➡️ What does it mean to be in "a state of continence"?

You ask first within what degrees of relationship marriage may take place. We reply: strictly speaking, in so far as the parties know themselves to be related they ought not to be joined together. ➡️ But since moderation is better than strictness of discipline, especially toward so uncivilized a people, they may contract marriage after the fourth degree. ➡️ As to your question, what a man is to do if his wife is unable on account of disease, to fulfill her wifely duty: it would be well if he could remain in a state of continence. But, since this is a matter of great difficulty, it is better for him who cannot refrain to take a wife. He may not, however, withdraw his support from the one who was prevented by disease, provided she be not involved in any grievous fault. . . .

In the celebration of the Mass, the form is to be observed which our Lord Jesus Christ used with his disciples. He took the cup and gave it to them, saying: "This cup is the new testament in my blood; this do ye as oft as ye take it." Wherefore it is not fitting that two or three cups should be placed on the altar when the ceremony of the Mass is performed. . . .

You ask further, if a father or mother shall have placed a young son or daughter in a cloister under the discipline of a rule, whether it is lawful for the child after reaching the years of discretion to leave the cloister and enter into marriage. This we absolutely forbid, since it is an impious thing that the restraints of desire should be relaxed for children offered to God by their parents. . . . ➡

Lepers, if they are believing Christians, may receive the body and blood of the Lord, but they may not take food together with persons in health.

➡ You ask whether, in the case of a contagious disease or plague in a church or monastery, those who are not yet attacked may escape danger by flight. We declare this to be the height of folly; for no one can escape from the hand of God.

➡ Finally, your letter states that certain priests and bishops are so involved in vices of many sorts that their lives are a blot upon the priesthood and you ask whether it is lawful for you to eat with or to speak with them, supposing them not to be heretics. We answer, that you by apostolic authority are to admonish and persuade them and so bring them back to the purity of church discipline. If they obey, you will save their souls and win reward for yourself. ➡ You are not to avoid conversation or eating at the same table with them. It often happens that those who are slow in coming to a perception of the truth under strict discipline may be led into the paths of righteousness by the influence of their table companions and by gentle admonition. You ought also to follow this same rule in dealing with those chieftains who are helpful to you.

> ➡ What does this say about the degree of authority parents had over their children?

> ➡ How might Pope Gregory's understanding of contagious disease differ from our own?

> ➡ What can you infer from this letter about the standards of behavior imposed on the clergy?

> ➡ How would you describe the role of the priest and bishop in a community of people not yet well acquainted with the church and Christianity?

The Bishops

Boniface's elevation to the office of bishop of the German lands reflects the kind of work bishops undertook in northern Europe, where there were not yet many practicing Christians. In these regions, bishops resembled missionaries more than they did ecclesiastical administrators. In southern Gaul, Spain, and Italian cities, on the other hand, bishops became the caretakers not only of the early medieval church but also of early medieval society. In addition to overseeing the spiritual care of the Christians living under their jurisdiction, they became the effective rulers of many Italian and southern French cities. The bishops of Milan and Lyons acquired reputations for their courts of justice. In northern Europe, bishops acted more as advisers to kings in the absence of other officials. The bishops of a region met occasionally to discuss and address problems in their areas. But their primary role centered on their status as spiritual head of an administrative unit called the **bishopric** or **diocese,** which had authority over local churches, in smaller administrative units called **parishes,** within it. Parish priests assigned to local churches to perform religious services answered to the bishop in whose diocese their churches were located. The bishopric was centered on a city, and at the heart of the bishop's

city stood the **cathedral,** the principal church of a diocese, and at the heart of the cathedral were preserved the relics and tombs of local holy figures considered saints by ordinary people. The cathedral of Tours attracted pilgrims from all over Gaul who desired to pray to Saint Martin, a Roman soldier-turned-monk whose remains and relics lay under the altar. The proximity of sacred relics to the bishop's seat by the altar was meant to instill pious obedience in the hearts of the men and women living in the bishopric.

A bishop's authority nevertheless rested on more than an aura of holiness. His spiritual authority derived as well from worldly wealth and political power, in the form of revenue from land belonging to the bishopric. Throughout the Middle Ages, the church was the single largest landowner, if all the land belonging to bishoprics and monasteries is counted. Other sources of income also contributed to a bishop's authority. When bishops allied themselves to the

> **bishopric/diocese** Ecclesiastical administrative unit over which a bishop presides.
>
> **parish** Smaller ecclesiastical administrative unit, in which a parish priest serves a local church.
>
> **cathedral** Official church of the bishop's authority.

ruling and noble families of western Europe, they received gifts of land from wealthy men and women who wished to have **commemorative Masses** performed for the benefit of their souls or those of their relatives after they died. Bishops also relied on **tithes,** a tax placed on all Christians for the maintenance of the church. Bolstered by revenue from land and the tithes, and endowed with the gifts of the royal and noble patrons, bishops became very wealthy.

The bishops' wealth, combined with the authority delegated to them by kings, made these churchmen very powerful in both ecclesiastic and **secular** spheres. They exerted influence over ordinary Christians by virtue of their role as spiritual pastors. Bishops oversaw the instruction of the laity in Christian **dogma,** the administration of relief to the poor and and to the general populace in times of famine, and the supervision of the clergy in their duties. These ecclesiastical responsibilities alone afforded them considerable power. Everywhere in Europe bishops developed mutually beneficial relationships with rulers. Kings found in bishops capable advisers and administrators, and bishops looked to kings and their royal families for support in the extension and deepening of the Christian faith in western Europe. With the help of royal women, bishops organized missionary work and the establishment of new monastic communities. They served as judges in the kings' courts and oversaw the maintenance not only of churches but also occasionally of city walls and other municipal structures. To a modern eye, many Frankish bishops look very much like city mayors.

Because of the cooperation between rulers and bishops, Frankish kings felt they had the right to appoint churchmen to ecclesiastical positions within their kingdoms, although this notion went against long-established church law. In some respects, the kings' expectations were reasonable. After all, the duties of bishops extended far beyond the walls of their cathedrals, and, as practically the only literate people in society, the lower clergy such as priests and deacons performed critically important services in royal and municipal administration. Some bishops were inclined to agree with the king's view of appointments, but many bishops, and especially the pope, did not approve of secular appointments to church positions at any level, which they felt undermined the church's authority. Such appointments raised a question of loyalty: should a bishop owe his first loyalty to the church or to the layman who appointed him to his office? By the eleventh century, more and more people believed the health of the church depended on keeping the clergy out of the king's business and on keeping the king out of the church's affairs.

The Bishop of Rome

No one in the Christian world of the sixth through the eighth centuries denied the bishop of Rome his special place among the church's leaders. Bishops and archbishops in the east and west agreed that, through apostolic succession, he possessed the authority of Saint Peter, the Apostle to whom Christians believe Jesus conveyed his authority after his death. All Christians recognized the pope as an especially important bishop, but the Christians of the west viewed the authority of the pope directly descended from Saint Peter himself. To the Christians of the east, the pope did not rank quite as high. The pope, in their view, was no more than the first among equals and certainly not the supreme head of the church. The archbishops of Alexandria, Antioch, and Jerusalem each had a claim to apostolic authority by virtue of the Apostles who had worked and died in those cities. Constantinople's patriarch, in particular, claimed at least as much authority as the pope on the basis of his proximity to the emperor. Nevertheless, regardless of the details, all Christians everywhere turned to the pope as a figure of extraordinary spiritual and moral authority. Such was his prestige that clergy everywhere appealed to him to settle disputes over appointments and church property. The pope's court and staff, collectively known as the **papacy,** thus acquired a reputation in western Europe and in the east as a highly authoritative court of appeals.

The popes of the early Middle Ages and their officers saw their role in a different light. They came to believe that the office of pope was heir to the western half of the empire and viewed it as their right to take over many of the emperor's responsibilities and privileges. That sphere of jurisdiction included a sizable portion of the central Italy, the **Papal States,** over which they ruled as secular rulers. Sometime after the

commemorative Masses   Religious services during which the officiating priest prays for the souls of the dead.

tithe   Tax of one-tenth of property levied by the church on all Christians to help sustain its activities.

secular   Pertaining to the worldly as opposed to the spiritual or ecclesiastical realm; relating to the state as opposed to the church.

dogma   Official teachings of the church.

papacy   Institution that carries out the duties of the bishop of Rome, the pope.

Papal States   Large territory in central Italy ruled by the pope and from which the papacy derived a large proportion of its wealth.

year 750, a document came to light that gave the office of the pope the legitimacy it needed to rule territory. The **Donation of Constantine** purported to be a fourth-century agreement between the emperor Constantine the Great and the bishop of Rome, Silvester, in which Constantine, departing for his new capital in Constantinople, transferred to Silvester authority not only over the institution of the church but also directly over much of the territory of central Italy and indirectly over the secular rulers of the west. The document made it appear that Constantine was leaving Silvester in charge of the western half of the empire. In the fifteenth century, the Italian scholar Lorenzo Valla proved the document was a forgery, but even in the ninth century some doubted its authenticity.

The Donation of Constantine reveals, however, the high ambitions of the popes in contrast to the limits of their practical power. Frankish kings, in emulation of the eastern emperors, could still convene church councils, a prerogative that the pope claimed in principle exclusively for himself. Also, there was little the pope could do at this point to prevent kings from appointing bishops or prevent lords from appointing priests on their lands. Although they viewed the pope as the head of the church, western secular rulers and even bishops and archbishops outside of Rome felt no obligation to recognize, much less put into practice, the pope's laws. It would not be until the end of the twelfth century that the papacy would begin to realize its claim to hold supreme authority in spiritual and secular affairs. But the desire to do so had long been apparent.

Monasticism and Learning

In 525, in the vicinity of Monte Cassino, south of Rome, **Benedict of Nursia,** an educated man from a noble Roman family who had become a hermit, founded a small community of men who dedicated their lives to constant prayer. Benedict adapted and expanded on the **rules** of earlier monastic communities in Egypt and Syria to suit the conditions in which he and his fellow monks lived. The rules he put together—emphasizing poverty, chastity, and obedience and establishing a schedule of prayers, meals, and sleep—attracted others, who established further monasteries adhering to the Benedictine rule. Benedict made manual labor a daily obligation for the monks in his community. Each monastery had an abbot, whose authority was absolute.

The *Rule of Saint Benedict* gave structure to a monk's day. Benedict understood how the seemingly insignificant decisions in a spiritual life, such as what to eat, how to pray, and when to sleep, could undermine a community's peace if those decisions were left to individual choice. All monks took vows of poverty, chastity, and obedience. The fewer decisions the monks had to make about how to live together, so Benedict's thinking went, the fewer disagreements they would have. The Rule called for a regular rotation of religious services, called the **Divine Office,** that ensured the monks would recite the entire Bible at least once over the course of a year.

In the early Middle Ages, monks engaged in manual labor, such as farming, to support themselves. But as noble families donated more and more land to the monks in exchange for prayers, they did less and less manual labor. By the year 1000, monasteries had become self-sufficient, wealthy corporations engaged in a variety of revenue-producing activities, such as agriculture, milling, mining, and animal husbandry. In the two centuries following Benedict, a monastery's reputation depended on its strict adherence to his Rule; in the ninth and tenth centuries, monasteries became known instead for their wealth as well as their holiness. As monasteries grew wealthy and the violence and chaos of western Europe subsided, the monks secluded themselves in their **cloisters** to spend more time in prayer and study, leaving their duty to perform manual labor to their servants and the peasants living on their lands.

The monks' obligatory study of Holy Scripture had the effect of preserving some of Rome's literary heritage. With the decline of education in the post-Roman world, learning retreated with the monks behind monastery walls, where the only schools in the early Middle Ages persisted. The necessity of reading scripture in services prompted monasteries to maintain at least a minimal level of literacy among monks, who read and copied ancient works by Christian and non-Christian writers. In addition to the works of

Donation of Constantine   A forged mid-eighth-century document purporting to be a transfer of land and power in the western empire from Emperor Constantine to Pope Silvester.

Benedict of Nursia   (ca. 480–543) Founder of the Benedictine Order of monks who devised a mode of monastic living that proved successful and was widely adopted.

rule   Set of regulations followed by a religious community that established the schedule of worship and manual labor.

Divine Office   Daily cycle of prayers and services in a monastery.

cloister   Enclosed courtyard of a monastery; also the entire monastery itself.

Monks spent a portion of their day walking in silent contemplation around the cloister with their prayer-books. When the weather was inclement, they could walk under the portico. *(Scala /Art Resource, NY)*

Ambrose, Augustine, Jerome, and other early church fathers, monastic libraries contained the works of the great Roman authors, such as Cicero and Virgil. Some monastic **scribes** composed works of their own in addition to reading, copying, and commenting on works from the past. The pages of the manuscripts were made of either parchment or vellum—sheep and calf skins, respectively—that were treated to remove the hair and soften it. For a complete manuscript of the Bible, the skins of nearly two hundred sheep were required; only the very wealthy could afford such a luxury. In northern England, **Bede,** a monk in the isolated monastery of Wearmouth, relied on the ancient texts in his library to write a history of the English church. The monks of northern England and Ireland became known for their beautiful and intricate manuscript **illuminations,** decorations in gold leaf and brightly colored inks. Still, the monks' tendency to neglect the non-Christian works led to the permanent loss of many classical works.

Since women, too, had their own monastic communities, it was common prior to the tenth century for only a wall to separate women's monasteries from those of men, allowing the priest monks to celebrate the Mass in the women's section, as women were not allowed to do so. At the monastery of Luxeuil, a few women even served as abbesses of both the men's and the women's communities. But medieval society was always deeply suspicious of communities with both male and female members, even though sharing resources and providing mutual protection made sense in those violent and chaotic times. By the tenth century, conjoined religious establishments had been separated, and the religious women suffered materially. Unlike men's monasteries, women's communities could not attract lucrative donations to say commemorative Masses. With some notable exceptions, poverty burdened many women's monasteries throughout the Middle Ages.

Women's monasteries served a social function as well as a religious one. Royal and noble families unable to provide dowries commensurate with their status often compelled their daughters to become nuns.

scribe Someone who serves as a secretary or copies manuscripts in a formal script.

Bede (ca. 673–735) Monk known as the Venerable Bede for his great learning; author of *The Ecclesiastical History of the English People.*

illuminations Colorful decorations in gold leaf and brightly colored inks on medieval manuscripts.

The financial contribution required to place a woman in a monastery was more than most ordinary families could afford but less than the dowry expected of a noble bride. With no choice in the matter, noble daughters spent their lives in seclusion from the secular world. Widowed queens and noblewomen often chose to retreat from the world. The *History of the Franks*, by Gregory of Tours, indicated that entering a monastery meant the end of a Merovingian queen's political influence at court, but the start of a new life working for the poor and surrounded by kinswomen and attendants. One queen, Radegund, wife of King Chlotar I, left her husband to found a monastery in which she acquired a reputation for great sanctity and sacrifice.

Some women undoubtedly resented confinement in a secluded community. Others found that monastic life offered them opportunities for spiritual and intellectual growth not easily available in the lay world. Although women's monasteries did not possess libraries like those in men's monasteries, a nun nevertheless stood a better chance of learning to read and of having access to written texts than did a woman at the king's court. Since women's monasteries outnumbered men's in the early centuries of medieval Europe, the monastic life clearly had an appeal for women.

Charlemagne and the Revival of Empire in the West, 700–900

↓ How did the pope view his authority in relation to Charlemagne's?

↓ What factors helped revive the title of emperor in the west?

By the late eighth century, most people in western Europe associated the office of emperor with the Byzantine emperors. For the eastern emperors, there had been no break in continuity from the golden days of Rome to the less glorious present of a much-reduced eastern empire. But the Frankish king and nobility also remembered that there had once been a system of two emperors, one in the east and one in the west, and so the possibility of a revival of the western title existed. The time was especially favorable, because a woman occupied the imperial throne in Constantinople. For many in the west, that meant that the office of emperor was, in effect, vacant.

From Mayor to King

Over the seventh and early eighth centuries, the infighting among the Merovingians contributed to the decay of the office of king, as did pressure from powerful noble families. The nobles benefited from their position as the king's chief supporters, as the estates granted to them by the kings allowed them to create strongholds where they exercised authority equal to and eventually surpassing that of the kings. In fact, the kings became so insignificant politically that the most powerful nobles of the moment chose the king from the pool of Merovingian descendants.

As early as 600, the Frankish kingdom had consisted of three provinces—Neustria, Austrasia, and Burgundy. Each province had its own king, but a court official called the mayor of the palace, or **major domus,** effectively ruled in the place of the king. Instead of the kings fighting among themselves, the struggle for power shifted to the mayors, who fought for dominance over as much of one another's provinces as they could manage to acquire. The Merovingian kings had become little more than puppets for the ambitions of land-hungry mayors.

One family in particular rose to power from its base in Austrasia, the northeastern region of the Frankish kingdom. **Charles Martel,** the mayor of Austrasia, waged war against his fellow mayors in the adjacent regions and eventually brought the heartland of Europe under his rule. Once he had set up a puppet Merovingian king in Neustria, he turned his attention to east of the Rhine River. The populations there had had little previous contact with Frankish culture, nor had they yet converted to Christianity. When Charles incorporated them by force into his realm, he brought them into Christendom at the same time.

Charles Martel also battled for Christianity in the southwest, where he faced a Muslim foe. A little more than a century after conquering the Iberian Peninsula, Abd-ar-Rahman, the Muslim ruler based in the city of Cordoba, led an army over the Pyrenees and headed north, claiming the Frankish land he passed through by right of conquest. At Tours, in 732, Charles stopped the Muslim advance, and the invaders withdrew to the south. By the time he died in 741, Charles had more territory under his control than any Merovingian king had ever accumulated. Although he never

major domus (in Latin, "mayor of the palace") Merovingian kings' military commander and chief governor of a province.

Charles Martel (686–741) Known as "the Hammer," the mayor of the palace in Austrasia who established the Carolingian dynasty.

assumed the title of king, Charles lent his name to the **Carolingian** dynasty, founded by his son, **Pepin.**

Unlike his father, Pepin desired the title of king. The problem was how and under what pretext he could claim it, since the title of king had always belonged to the Merovingian family. It would have been unprecedented in Frankish history for it to pass to another family. Before he could resolve this problem, however, Pepin first had to reconsolidate his father's territory, as after Charles died, all the rulers of the conquered regions pulled away from his son's rule. Continual warfare marked the first eight years of Pepin's reign.

When he had achieved a relatively stable state of affairs in the kingdom, Pepin turned his attention to the title of king. Writing to Pope Zacharias in 750, he asked if it was right that a king should hold the title of king but not wield a king's power. The pope wrote back a convoluted answer that said, essentially, no, and he then ordered the Frankish bishops to consecrate Pepin as king. Pepin found the pope's validation useful, but he resisted the idea that the pope had the power to make (and, by implication, unmake) kings. Pepin locked away the last Merovingian king in a monastery and had himself consecrated king in a religious ceremony. The Carolingian dynasty had formally begun.

From King to Emperor

A change in dynasty did not lead to a change in inheritance customs. It would no more have occurred to the Carolingians than to the Merovingians to bequeath their kingdoms in one piece to one son, thereby disinheriting the other sons. When Pepin died, he left his territory to his two sons, Charles and Carloman, but before they began fighting each other for their father's territories they first had to subdue the rulers of these territories. Once accomplished, Carloman, very likely under pressure, turned his half of Pepin's kingdom over to his brother Charles. Charles's success at maintaining and even enlarging this kingdom would win for him immortality in history and legend as Charles the Great, otherwise known as **Charlemagne.**

Pepin's assumption of the title of king opened the door to a revival of the title of emperor in the west. In the old days, the Roman emperor could claim to be the ruler of nearly every people, or ethnic group, known to exist at that time. A conglomerate of different lands and different peoples under one rule indeed became the definition of an empire. Charlemagne had the title of emperor in mind when he took an innovative step and had himself crowned king of a people other than his own. In 773, he invaded the Lombard kingdom in northern Italy, partly as a favor to Pope

Charlemagne spent nearly his entire reign on military campaign. Only late in life did he give up life in camp and settle in his capital at Aachen in northern Germany. *(Giraudon/The Bridgeman Art library)*

Hadrian I, some of whose lands the Lombard king had taken. Instead of forcing regular payments of tribute or making the Lombard king swear allegiance to him—the usual choices for a conqueror after conquest—Charlemagne removed the Lombard ruler and proclaimed himself king of the Lombards in 774.

Carolingians   Dynasty (750–987) named for Charles (Carolus) Martel that replaced Merovingians as kings of the Franks.

Pepin   (c. 714–768) Son of Charles Martel, the first of his family to assume, in 750, the title of king of the Franks.

Charlemagne   (r. 768–814) Son of Pepin; king of the Franks who became emperor of the west in 800.

It made little sense to most people at the time, for Charlemagne was already king of the Franks. But it made sense to Charlemagne: as the king of a people other than his own, he was just a step away from calling himself an emperor of many.

Three factors were working together to create this possibility. First, Pepin's taking of the title of king from the Merovingian family, which had held it for two centuries, produced a different political understanding of kingship. After him, it was understood that the title of king could be transferred from one person or one family to another. Second, the diminished splendor and the much-reduced military might of the eastern empire opened Charlemagne's mind to the idea of restoring the old title of emperor in the west. So did the fact that ruler in Constantinople was a woman—Irene—and thus not regarded as legitimate by rulers in the west or by many in the east. Finally, an ongoing relationship of mutual support between the Carolingian kings and the pope created the possibility that the king of the Franks might claim to be the defender of the church, as Constantine the Great had done in the fourth century.

Toward the end of 800, Charlemagne and his army crossed the Alps to give aid to a pope, as he and his father had already done several times before. In this instance, the noble Roman families had physically attacked and expelled the unpopular Pope Leo III from the city of Rome. To restore order, Charlemagne first had to subdue the Romans. He then brought the unlamented Leo back to Rome, restored him to his position, and confirmed his possession of huge tracts of land stolen from him by the Lombards.

The situation in Rome now settled, the pope crowned the king as emperor at a Christmas Mass (see Choice). It was not only the first time the pope had formally conferred the title of emperor on a king but also the first time—in the west or the east—that a member of the clergy had placed a crown on the head of a king. In crowning Charlemagne, Pope Leo signaled that the authority of a pope, as God's representative, gave the king, or the emperor, his authority as a secular ruler. Thus, for Charlemagne, to be crowned emperor by the pope was something of a mixed blessing. He did not wish to be obligated to the pope for his imperial authority. On the contrary, Charlemagne felt the pope should be obliged to *him*. After all, the pope owed his position to Charlemagne's army. To make this point clear, thirteen years later, Charlemagne stage-managed a coronation ceremony of his own when he watched his son, Louis, crown himself co-emperor with no help from the pope.

To resist the idea that popes were the source of their authority, emperors thereafter came to view popes as mere messengers of God's will. They may have had the model of the Byzantine emperor's superior relationship to the patriarch of Constantinople in mind. But in neither the emperor's nor the pope's mind did government stand to one side and the church to the other. Today, church and state constitute two distinct entities. For most of the early Middle Ages, people made no such distinction.

Imperial Rule in the West

Charlemagne's reign represents a change in the expectations people in the Middle Ages had of their rulers. In contrast to the Merovingian kings, who felt little need to justify their possession of the title, Carolingian kings and emperors justified their rule by ministering to Christian society. Conceiving themselves as lay ministers, Charlemagne and his successors considered it their duty to defend and extend the church, bring justice to their subjects, punish their enemies, and make their own lives a moral example to others. **Ministerial kingship** became the standard by which medieval rulers measured themselves and were measured by others. Charlemagne viewed the church as well as his subjects to be under his care. Identifying himself as a Christian king and the source of social order, Charlemagne gained the loyalty of his subjects to a degree his Merovingian predecessors had been unable to achieve. Whether the emperor was always able to live up to his own expectations of his authority was different matter, but by overseeing government and church affairs, Charlemagne imposed a greater degree of order and peace in his kingdom than any of the earlier Frankish kings had done.

Still, government in Charlemagne's day amounted to little more than maintaining peace and granting justice. No bureaucracy yet existed to prepare reports, no courts to hear pleas, and no services offered to towns and villages. In practice, government accomplished little more than organizing the leading members of society for annual military campaigns, rewarding them for their work, settling disputes among them, and ensuring social order on a local level throughout the kingdom.

To these ends, Charlemagne delegated his authority to royal officials, or **counts,** whose wealth derived

---

ministerial kingship Concept of kingship introduced by Charlemagne in which the king assumes responsibility for government and church affairs.

counts Major landowners and supporters of Frankish kings; a count's territory corresponded to a county.

from the large tracts of land the king had granted to them as reward for their administrative and military services. To ensure that the counts were doing their job properly, he sent out royal emissaries, called **missi dominici,** to make inspections of his kingdom. The problem with this system of government, even with the help of the *missi,* is that it took a strong, energetic king to prevent the counts from viewing the authority they exercised locally as their own. While Charlemagne was alive, there was no question of who was in charge of the kingdom. After his death, power began to slip out of the hands of the kings and into the hands of the local counts.

Even before he was crowned emperor, Charlemagne wanted a cultural life around him that was reminiscent of the Roman Empire. Later in life, he no longer felt the need to be always leading his army to increase his conquests, and he spent more and more time in **Aachen,** a town in northern Europe once popular among the Romans for its hot springs. In his new capital, Charlemagne created a court life that became known for its learning and sophistication, and he encouraged intellectual and religious studies as they had once existed in earlier centuries. Viewing his office as a ministry, Charlemagne hoped to deepen understanding of Christianity within the ruling ecclesiastic and lay circles of his realm. To achieve these goals, he worked to improve the standard of literacy among the clergy and laypeople of high social status.

Even if government bureaucracy during Charlemagne's time was minimal, there was still a need for literate men who knew how to draw up documents. Although the number of **cartularies,** or records of royal law, did not significantly increase until the thirteenth century, people in the Carolingian period had a growing appreciation for writing down important information. The more often people turned to the king to settle their disputes, the greater the need for documents to preserve the outcome of those settlements. Charlemagne and his advisers recognized that his authority could not be imposed, or order in society brought about, without literate men. In an age when education had retreated to the monasteries, knowing how to read and, more rarely, to write became a skill scarcely found among the laypeople of the Charlemagne's empire. For this reason, Charlemagne relied heavily on clergymen to carry out the bureaucratic tasks of government. Yet the clergy in the service of the king found themselves in a potentially difficult position as the interests of the king increasingly diverged from the interests of the institutional church.

Charlemagne sponsored the establishment of schools throughout his kingdom, the most important of which was the one in his own court. To direct his palace school he chose the bishop **Alcuin of York,** reputed to be the greatest intellectual of the day. As head of the school, Alcuin promoted cultural reform that extended beyond the confines of Charlemagne's court. In addition to making the **liturgy** conform to the rites of the Roman Mass, he also revived the study of the **seven liberal arts** (grammar, logic, rhetoric, arithmetic, music, geometry, and astronomy), which had fallen out of use centuries before. Then he turned his attention to the Vulgate (the Latin Bible), eliminating the scribal errors and mistakes that had corrupted it over generations of copying and recopying since Saint Jerome completed his translation in the third century. Through this work and a program for copying manuscripts of religious and classical literature, Charlemagne and Alcuin helped ensure the transmission of late classical learning into medieval Europe's cultural heritage.

This program of preservation included a reform in script that increased legibility. Handwriting had deteriorated considerably in the last centuries of the Roman Empire and in Merovingian Gaul. At the height of the empire, Romans had used relatively clear capital letters with punctuation and breaks between words. By the beginning of the eighth century, not only had handwriting come to resemble today's cursive script, with each letter connected to the next, but word breaks and punctuation had disappeared. Some Merovingian handwriting was as difficult for monastic intellectuals of the early Carolingian empire to read as it is today. To improve handwriting, Carolingian scribes emphasized clarity in letter forms and divisions between words. They also modeled their letter forms on the inscriptions on the decayed Roman struc-

missi dominici   (in Latin, "emissaries of the lord") Inspectors appointed by Charlemagne to oversee how counts used his authority.

Aachen   Charlemagne's capital; today in northwest Germany and known to the French as Aix-la-Chapelle.

cartularies   A register of laws and varying kinds of documents used in monasteries and secular courts.

Alcuin of York   (ca.732–804) Important scholar and cleric appointed by Charlemagne to oversee the school established at his court in Aachen.

liturgy   Collection of Christian rites, like the Mass, performed in church services.

seven liberal arts   The classic course of study comprising the Trivium (grammar, rhetoric, and logic) and the Quadrivium (astronomy, geometry, music, and arithmetic).

tures and buildings. Their imitation of Roman capital letters was so successful that the fifteenth-century humanist intellectuals of Italy believed that the old and dusty manuscripts they were discovering in monastic libraries around Europe dated back to Roman times.

The Partition of Charlemagne's Empire

Like the Merovingian kings before him, Charlemagne submitted to custom regarding the inheritance of property and planned for an equal division of his empire among his three sons after his death. But two sons died before him, leaving only his third son, Louis, to inherit the empire. To ensure a smooth succession after his death, Charlemagne arranged in 813 for Louis, known to his contemporaries as **Louis the Pious,** to come to his capital at Aachen. There in the cathedral Charlemagne had Louis place a crown on his own head, making himself co-emperor with his father until his father's death would leave him sole emperor. This coronation without the pope would have set a lasting precedent had it not been for Louis' insecurity following his father's death in 814. Wishing to bolster his claim to the title, Louis reverted to his father's precedent. In 816, he had himself recrowned by Pope Stephen V in the cathedral at Rheims. From that point on, the central role of the pope in the coronation of all western emperors was established.

No doubt mindful of the premature deaths of his brothers, Louis began early in his reign to plan for the division of the empire after his own death. In 817, he allotted the bulk of the empire and the title of emperor to his oldest son, Lothar, who would hold a rank superior to that of his two younger brothers, Pepin and Louis. These last two were to receive smaller shares of their father's domain, a distinct innovation for its time. In 823, Louis had Lothar crowned co-emperor and king of Italy.

Thereafter, however, Lothar viewed his father and co-emperor as a rival, while the younger brothers resented both their emperor-brother and their emperor-father. When, after his first wife died, Louis had another son, **Charles the Bald,** by a second wife, the three older sons perceived this new brother as a threat to their inheritance. In 833, Louis' sons captured their father and placed him in a monastery. Louis gained his freedom and his authority in 835, but, in spite of the death of Pepin, the potential for warfare only increased. Louis' death in 840 signaled a new, violent phase in the civil wars of the Carolingian dynasty.

In the generations after Louis' death, the empire was divided up among succeeding Carolingian kings. The political divisions of modern Europe can be seen in the first important division among Louis' heirs. In the **Treaty of Verdun** in 843, his sons agreed to the partition of the Frankish kingdom into three segments. Charles claimed the western portion, corresponding roughly to modern France; Lothar, the central portion that covered the **Low Countries** (today Belgium and the Netherlands), the French provinces of Burgundy and Provence, and Italy. Louis' eastern portion became the basis of what would later be called the Holy Roman Empire and still later, Germany. The political divisions reflected linguistic ones as well. In the western kingdom, Latin mixed with local dialects gave rise to early dialects of French. German and Slavic languages emerged as the dominant languages in the eastern Frankish kingdom. The dialects in the northern Italian peninsula retained close relationships to Latin.

The treaty did not prevent further bloodshed. Each generation waged war against kinsmen to gain greater territory and wealth. The title of emperor was stolen from one branch of the family, passed from heir to heir for a couple of generations, and stolen once again by another branch of Charlemagne's descendants. In this maneuvering, the pope looked out for his own interests. The constant and debilitating warfare at the imperial level was made worse by the infighting among aristocratic families over their own acquisition of land and wealth. In the second half of the ninth century, the last vestige of the central authority once wielded by Charlemagne disappeared. Once again, kings were little more than military leaders constantly on campaign and minimally concerned with government. By 870, in another division of Charlemagne's empire that also soon collapsed, the old "Middle Kingdom" of Lothar was divided between Charles and Louis. By 924, even the title of emperor had fallen into disuse.

Louis the Pious   (r. 814–840) Charlemagne's only surviving son who had already assumed the title of emperor within his father's lifetime.

Charles the Bald   (r. 840–877) The king of the western Franks, a position inherited from his father, Emperor Louis the Pious.

Treaty of Verdun   Division of the Frankish empire in 843 among Emperor Louis' heirs into the three portions that laid the basis for the future political divisions of Europe.

Low Countries   Modern Belgium and the Netherlands, so described because they are on a low plain along the North Sea.

Order and Disorder in the Ninth and Tenth Centuries

↓ How did patterns of loyalty and obligation provide some sense of order and security in early medieval society?

↓ What were the forces for disorder?

Charlemagne had a notion of the orderly and highly cultured world of the Roman Empire in the west, but he could not restore it. Life on all levels of society had changed dramatically since the fifth century, when the last western emperor was deposed. In the face of almost perpetual warfare, relations between the powerful and the powerless had been fundamentally altered. Now, lords and kings—often no more than warlords—compelled peasants to supply them with goods and food in exchange for a small measure of security, and peasants had no choice but to agree. In addition, raiders from distant lands periodically brought death and destruction.

Lords and Vassals

In the early Middle Ages, kings devoted more time and energy to warfare than to governing. Only when Charlemagne set up his court at Aachen did the government find a permanent place in the kingdom—for a time. The highest lord in a realm, a king was only as powerful as he was wealthy, energetic, and ready to wage war. To wage war in a time when not much money was in circulation, kings developed ways to raise armies and ensure their loyalty through grants of land.

During the Carolingian period in the Frankish kingdoms north of the Alps, kings granted a portion of their land to their supporters, or **vassals.** This grant of property was called a **fief,** and in exchange, a vassal swore an **oath of fealty** that obligated him to provide military support to the king. At first, the concession of a fief to a vassal made it possible for kings to raise an army without having to pay for it out of their own pockets: the oath of fealty required vassals to bring their troops to the field of battle for their king for specified lengths of time, usually forty days a year, and to spend time at their own expense in the king's court, where they advised the king on matters pertaining to his kingdom. More than elsewhere in western Europe, the Frankish kings relied on this system of land grants in exchange for military service, otherwise known as **feudalism,** but, even among the Franks, there were many variations of this system. In general, however, vassals retained a large portion of the fief and disbursed the rest to their own supporters, who thus became vassals of the king's vassals. **Subinfeu-**

dation, as this secondary grant of fiefs is called, sometimes led to complications. Nobles who swore an oath of fealty to one lord in exchange for land could then swear an oath to another lord to acquire even more land. If a vassal's two lords went to war against each other, the vassal was at risk of forfeiting part of his lands. Only exceptionally did women become vassals, usually when they had no brother to inherit their fathers' commitments.

Feudal armies—made up of vassals performing their obligatory military service to their king—were notoriously unreliable. The strength of a sworn oath rarely overcame the reluctance of most lords to leave their lands to go fight their king's battles. Over time, the great nobles of the Frankish kingdoms greatly preferred to make cash payments instead of performing military service, and kings came to prefer cash payments, too, since they could then hire an army of professional soldiers, or mercenaries.

In the ninth century, when the power of the Carolingian kings dwindled as a consequence of the warfare among Charlemagne's descendants, the nobility exercised powers within their fiefdoms that kings had once sought to regulate. Nobles dispensed justice without concern that a king would step in to impose royal law on them. Nobles kept more of the taxes they collected from the peasants living on their lands. Their armies functioned like militias, policing the fiefdom, guarding the borders, and occasionally raiding their neighbors' lands. Just as in the Merovingian period, the world of those without land or power—in other words, the vast majority of the population—had once again become local, violent, and arbitrary.

---

vassal   Typically, a man of combat who swore an oath of fealty to bring both fiscal and military aid to a lord, usually in exchange for property with which to support himself.

fief   Unit of property, usually real estate, granted by a lord to a vassal.

oath of fealty   Formal pledge of fidelity made by a vassal to his lord to support him in his military efforts.

feudalism   System of landholding whereby a lord grants property, usually land, to a vassal, in exchange for which the vassal must perform military service for his lord for an agreed-on period of time each year.

subinfeudation   The dividing up of a fief by a vassal among his own vassals, who become vassals of the possessor of the fief and subvassals of the lord who originally granted the fief.

feudal armies   In theory , a force comprising all who owed military service to the king or a lord, but in practice vassals rarely met this obligation.

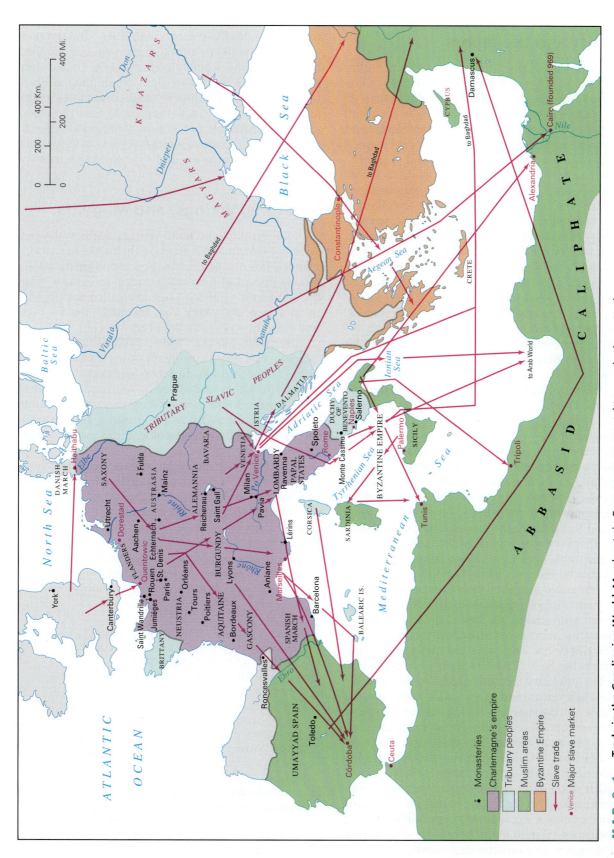

MAP 9.1 **Trade in the Carolingian World** Merchants in Europe never ceased to supply slaves to the Byzantines and Muslim. Captives were sold in the major slave markets of Constantinople, Cordoba, Rome, and Alexandria. Where did captives sold in the markets of the Mediterranean come from?

Peasants and the Manor

The king, his vassals, and all the nobles in the Carolingian kingdom depended for their material welfare entirely on the labor of the peasantry. More than 25 million people lived in western Europe in the ninth century, 98 or 99 percent of them peasants. Nobles and clergy made up the rest. To many, the world seemed naturally organized into lords, priests, and peasants.

And much of Europe's territory was divided into fiefdoms. A lord's fief might consist of various kinds of property typically found in a manor—a collection of peasant dwellings, a residence for the lord, and surrounding fields under cultivation. A manor resembled a village in that a community of agricultural workers tended fields belonging to the lord, but everything was designed to increase the wealth of the lord. The lord compelled peasants to work certain fields whose harvest he retained entirely, known as the **desmesne.** In addition, he required all peasants living on the manor to turn over a portion of what they grew for themselves to him and a portion to the church. Not only did he insist that the peasants take their grain to his mill to be ground and their food to his communal oven to be cooked, he charged them for it. Peasants had to put aside a portion of everything they tended, collected, or made—from hens' eggs to woven baskets—for the lord's rents. The manor was a revenue-generating machine that functioned for the benefit of the lord and solely through the work of the peasants.

Not all the people who lived on a manor had the same relationship to their lord. Some peasants were **serfs,** tied so tightly to the manor's agricultural obligations that they were not considered to be free and were said to belong to the manor rather than to the lord. The lord exacted more labor than rent from them. They could not leave the manor, and when the manor passed into the possession of another lord, the serfs went with it. Among their neighbors might be free peasants, who owed their lord goods or cash more than services. Both serfs and free peasants suffered from the heavy burdens their lords placed on them, but only free peasants had the right to bequeath whatever property they had to their heirs. At the bottom of the manor's society were slaves who had no rights at all and endured the grimmest existence. By the tenth century, however, slaves were extremely rare in the Carolingian kingdom. Overseeing the work of all free and unfree laborers on the manor, the **bailiff** stood at the top of peasant society. He represented the lord on the manor, making sure that the peasants' customary obligations were fulfilled.

Peasants spent their entire lives struggling to produce enough to live on after they turned over what they owed to their lord. Both men and women worked in the fields, although men usually handled the plowing and women the harvesting. In addition, peasants wove their own cloth, made their clothes, tended livestock, constructed tools, and built shelters and furniture—that is, if they could find the wood and other materials. No wonder children were set to work around the home almost as soon as they could walk. On the manor, the lord's requirements meant a lifetime of work.

Saracens, Vikings, and Magyars

As if life in ninth- and tenth-century northern Europe were not violent and hard enough, thanks to Carolingian warfare, the people also had to endure the harsh, bloody impact of three migratory populations: from the southwest came the Muslims (called Saracens by the people of the west); from the north, the **Vikings**; and from the southeast, the **Magyars.**

After their defeat at Tours, the Muslims returned to Spain, and they never again posed a serious threat to the Frankish rulers. But their raids continued. Just before Tours, they had seized Luxeuil and killed most of its monks. In the next century they sacked Monte Cassino and burned it to the ground. Their harassments around the Mediterranean discouraged maritime trade.

From the north came the Vikings of Scandinavia. Historians believe that overpopulation set the peoples of Scandinavia on the move in the late eighth century. At home, they were settled farmers. But after they planted their crops in the spring, they set off in their longboats, well designed for ruthless raiding and trading. These oar-propelled vessels, each with one main sail, were large enough to carry thirty warriors over rough seas but also shallow enough to carry

manor Collection of peasants dwellings and a lord's residence surrounded by agricultural land that the peasants cultivated for the lord.

desmesne Portion of an estate whose produce was reserved for the lord's use.

serfs Peasants whose residence on a plot of land that they cultivated for a lord was compulsory and hereditary.

bailiff Peasant who served as the lord's overseer and manager on a manor.

Vikings Scandinavian warriors who raided the coasts of Europe and the British Isles.

Magyars Nomadic people from Central Asia who invaded the Frankish kingdom and the Byzantine Empire; known eventually as Hungarians.

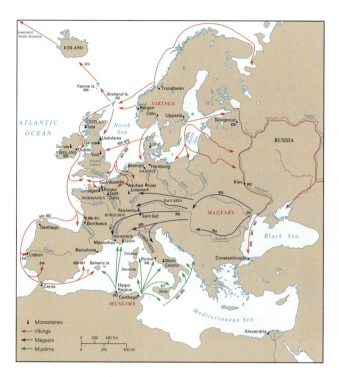

MAP 9.2 **The Migrations of the Vikings, Magyars, and Muslims.** In the ninth and tenth centuries, the Vikings, the Muslims, and the Magyars contributed to the disorder created by the wars between Carolingian heirs. Peasants received little protection from their lords. Monastic communities abandoned their cloisters and moved deeper into the Frankish kingdom. Which parts of the kingdom were most vulnerable to invasion?

them up rivers into Europe's interior. Wherever they went, they caused havoc, repeatedly sailing up the Seine River, for example, to attack, loot, and burn settlements all the way to Paris. When the season of raiding was over, the Vikings returned home to harvest their crops.

Viking pillaging was widespread along the coasts of northwestern Germany, the Low Countries, France, and Spain, and it occurred at a time when Carolingian warfare made organized defense impossible, though some local kings paid the raiders to leave them alone. Viking raiders from what is now Sweden headed for Russia, where they followed the Volga River south deep into the interior. There they settled and married into the local population to become the Kievan Rus, who harassed the Byzantines. The Danes headed west, raiding northern France and the eastern coast of England, while Northmen, as they were called by the people they attacked, raided the western coast of England and the eastern coast of Ireland. Some traveled as far as Iceland and Greenland; a few explored the

coastline of North America. At first, monasteries were their primary targets, and the Vikings seized their gold and silver liturgical objects, provisions, and even tools and implements. Many monasteries quickly moved deeper into the forested interior of Europe.

Well stocked with captured goods, Viking raiders became traders on their way home, selling their prizes when terrified Europeans were willing to deal with them. Some of the "prizes" were slaves, captured men and women who would be sold before their captors returned home. Most slaves were brought back to Scandinavia, however, where they were pressed into heavy labor during the summer growing and harvesting season, when the Viking men were on their raiding journeys.

Eventually, and only gradually, the various groups of northerners ceased returning to their homelands in the winter and instead settled near the areas where they regularly raided. For this reason, historians sometimes refer to the Viking experience as a migration instead of an invasion. Each time the Danes pushed their way into northeastern England, some managed to settle, in spite of the efforts of **Alfred,** king of Wessex, to prevent them. In 878, his army halted their advance into his southwestern region of the island. The Norwegians, or **Norsemen,** who settled on the northern coast of modern-day France, became so much associated with the region that it came to be called Normandy. As Normans, they would continue ventures of conquest—of England and Sicily—in the eleventh century.

By the time the Vikings began to settle down, both literally and figuratively, at the end of the tenth century, poet-singers had made them famous. The **sagas** of their adventures describe their violence and heavy drinking as well as their rough treatment of women. Yet Viking male society allowed women considerably more property rights and granted them more responsibilities outside the domestic sphere than other societies at that time. An accurate reflection of Viking life is found in the epic poem, *Beowulf,* written between 700 and 1000. It narrates the battles of a Germanic

Alfred (r. 871–899) King of Wessex in southwestern and south-central England who stopped the invasion of the Danes.

Norsemen Raiders and traders from the region now known as Norway who settled on the northern coast of modern France.

sagas Poems relating ancient stories.

Beowulf Epic poem written between 700 and 1000 in Anglo-Saxon that tells the story of a hero from Scandinavia who defeats the monster Grendel.

The isolated setting of the monastery at Conques in southwestern France near the Pyrenees Mountains is typical of monasteries seeking refuge from invaders and warlords. *(Erich Lessing/Art Resource, NY)*

hero from Scandinavia with the fearsome monster Grendel. Composed in the Anglo-Saxon language, the poem combines pre-Christian myths with Christian symbolism, reflecting the merging of pagan and Christian cultures that transformed Viking culture. Epics like *Beowulf* kept the Viking's reputation for brutality alive long after they had ceased raiding. As their thuggish behavior diminished, Vikings' customs and language blended into the regional cultures of the lands they had penetrated.

In southeastern Europe, another threat was emerging in the same period, this time from the Russian steppes. The Magyars, a nomadic people whose origins were much farther east in Asia, burst into the territory along the northern shore of the Danube River. Although the Bulgars, another steppe people on the move, had pushed them there, the Magyars aggressively preyed on the populations of the regions where they had been forced to migrate. Now known as Hungarians, the Magyars acquired a reputation for savagery similar to that of the Vikings. Some sold their services as mercenary soldiers to the Byzantine emperor and even to the Bulgar king who had forced them westward. The remainder crossed the eastern Alps and raided the towns of northern Italy in 899. Defeated by **Otto I,** king of the eastern Franks, at Lechfeld in 955, they withdrew to lands along the Danube and settled in the region that would one day be Hungary and Ukraine.

The Empire Under Otto

When Otto I, king of the eastern Franks, defeated the Magyars in 955, it had been some thirty years since a king had called himself emperor. But, following Roman practice, Otto's troops hoisted their king on their shoulders and proclaimed him Emperor Otto the Great. Seven years later, in 962, Pope John XII crowned Otto emperor in Rome in more dignified circumstances. As emperor, Otto grabbed firm hold of spiritual authority. Like his father and Frankish kings dating back to Pepin in the eighth century, he regularly marched an army over the Alps to come to the aid of a harassed pope in Rome. This practice had become a tradition, and it made the church reliant on kings, in particular on those ruling directly to the north of Italy, now heralded again as Roman emperors. Like the eastern emperor, Otto convened church councils and synods, something only an archbishop or the pope was supposed to be able to do. He, not the pope, appointed bishops, abbots, and archbishops in his lands. Wherever he conquered territory and compelled the people there to convert to Christianity, Otto established a diocese, whose bishop acted

Otto I (r. 936–973) King of the eastern Franks, crowned emperor in 962.

Seventy feet long and sixteen feet wide, a Viking long ship like this one shown here was capable of navigation over deep-sea water and up shallow river routes. *(University Museum of National Antiquities, Oslo)*

when the bishop was a member of Otto's family, as in the case of his brother Bruno, who was both the archbishop of Cologne and the duke of Lotharingia. The methods Otto developed to increase his authority in the empire disturbed the leaders of the church in Rome, but as yet they were unable to resist.

Kinship and spiritual authority did not always guarantee good relations, however. Otto frequently had to contend with his other brother, Henry, duke of Bavaria, and his sons, who seized what opportunities they could to undermine Otto's rule. In the early years of his reign, rebellions by the dukes, often stirred up by Henry, kept Otto from extending his realm eastward. After he had subdued his rebellious dukes or replaced them with churchmen, Otto could turn to other pressing matters, like the Magyar invaders. But rebellious dukes remained a problem for Otto I, his son Otto II, and his grandson Otto III, all of whom worked hard to integrate the church into imperial administration. They saw no contradiction in the emperor's acting as the head of the church in the west.

> **duke** (from Latin *dux*, "leader") A title similar to but superior in rank to that of count.

like a colonial governor. Bringing Christianity—as well as his dominion—to the peoples of eastern Europe preoccupied him, although the Magyar disturbances on his frontier distracted him from conquering and converting the Slavs and Danes.

Otto's empire in the heartland of the eastern Franks consisted of provinces ruled by **dukes,** all of whom made oaths of fealty to the emperor. To minimize dissension among them and to increase the number of obedient and compliant dukes, Otto installed bishops as dukes whenever a duke died. Thus he created a generation of dukes who owed their position to him and who, because as clergy they could not marry, would not produce successors, thus giving Otto even tighter control over the next generation of dukes. The benefits of using a bishop to administer territory increased

Summary

Review Questions

↑ What factors contributed to economic decline and social disorder in the west?

↑ How did a series of interlocking obligations, among kings, lords, vassals, bishops, priests, and peasants, define a person's place in the world?

↑ How did the emperor and the pope each view their authority with respect to the other?

The disappearance of imperial authority at the end of the fifth century ushered in an era of social disorder in the west. Kings—who were warlords more than rulers—and their supporters fought incessantly. In the north, the Franks fought among themselves and against the Visigoths for control of what had once been the Roman province of Gaul. The Lombards moved south over the Alps to establish a kingdom based in the northern Italian peninsula. It took more than three centuries for the barbarian armies to stabilize themselves in territory they constantly had to defend and fought so hard to extend. As a result of the chaos, interregional trade declined and cities contracted. Some cities in Italy survived, thanks to the energies of their bishops. For the peasants in the countryside, there was no protection from public authorities.

Even the church could provide little protection. Too often the pope himself called on the Frankish king and his army to save him from Lombard invaders. The communities of monks scattered throughout the kingdom fell prey to raiders, invaders, and warring nobles. By the tenth century, they had moved deep into the interior, as far as possible from the paths of armies. In spite of the danger, monasteries continued to grow rich, since they still received the bounty of royal favor. No longer poor, the monks spent more and more time studying sacred texts. As the texts of old manuscripts were transferred to new parchment, new life was given to old learning. For the most part, however, the learning stayed within the walls of monasteries.

Charlemagne was the first Frankish king to seek that long-hidden knowledge. He succeeded in instilling memories of the glorious past in the powerful families who supported his kingship. Once, they learned, an emperor had ruled in the west. The king's revival of the title of emperor led to the revival of—or at least the pretension to—imperial culture. Charlemagne had little to work with. There were no merchants to bring the gold and silver and expensive cloth from the markets of the eastern Mediterranean. But Charlemagne did ensure the survival of the memory of the Roman Empire, though following his reign his empire was divided and warfare returned.

To carry out their wars, kings devised a system of granting land to supporters in exchange for their military aid. In principle, the distribution of fiefs to vassals was meant to furnish an army at little expense to the king, but once in possession of their fiefs, vassals proved reluctant to leave their estates. Kings found it more convenient to accept cash payments from their vassals in lieu of military service. The western emperor, Otto I, turned to an even more convenient way depending on his vassals. He appointed bishops—many of whom also happened to be his relatives—to the position of duke, the rulers of the provinces into which his empire was divided. In this way Otto ensured that the bearer of the title would not produce an heir. Emperor Otto, the Carolingian kings of the Franks, and their vassals used their armies to fight among themselves and to confront incursions by Vikings, Magyars, and Muslims into their territories. In the ninth, tenth and eleventh centuries, the ordinary people of western Europe could expect little protection from the invaders. No one—not the powerful armies nor the clergy—seemed capable of securing the peace necessary for developing trade, reliable harvests, and the prosperity of families.

← Thinking Back, Thinking Ahead →

What potential conflicts of loyalty for the clergy developed when kings and emperors came to rely on them to carry out the tasks of government?

ECHO ECHO ECHO ECHO ECHO

The Beginning of Time

How do we measure time? When do we say it begins? Civilizations and cultures often look to their own founding to fix the beginning of time. The Romans set their calendar with the founding of Rome as year 1. But to the medieval world, Rome was said to have been founded in 753 B.C. ("before Christ"), because Christian Europe looked to a new event to mark the beginning of time—the birth of Jesus. Starting with this event, Christians designated time as A.D. (*anno domini,* "in the year of Our Lord"). But the year of Jesus's birth is based on a calculation that is in error.

This year was calculated by Dionysius Exiguus ("Dennis the Little"), an early sixth-century abbot of a monastery in Rome who was steeped in scripture and the Latin literature of old Rome. Dionysius received assignments from the pope that very few others had the literary skills to do. He compiled the canons of all the church councils prior to the sixth century, and he also calculated the date of Easter, the feast day commemorating Jesus's resurrection. Because the date is tied to the lunar calendar—the phases of the moon—

Dionysius devised a method for calculating when it would fall each year. Not all groups of Christians accepted his method, but it served as an important starting point. The Greek and Russian Orthodox Churches continued to follow the old method of calculating the date of Easter.

Dionysius replaced the Roman calendar with a calculation based on the year of Jesus's birth, basing his calculation on the year of King Herod's death—753 years after the founding of Rome—the year the New Testament indicates Jesus was born. Not since Julius Caesar sponsored the calendar reform that bore his name (the Julian calendar) in 46 B.C. had such a radical recalculation taken place. In the sixteenth century, however, Dionysius was shown to have miscalculated the year of King Herod's birth by four years. So, according to the Christian calendar, Jesus most likely was born about the year 4 B.C.

As an acknowledgment that not everyone in the world calculates time according to the Christian calendar, a new set of designations has recently been adopted and is used in this textbook: B.C.E. ("before the common era") to refer to dates prior to the traditional birthdate of Jesus Christ and C.E. ("common era") to refer to time thereafter.

Suggested Readings

Collins, Roger. *Early Medieval Europe, 300–1000.* New York: Palgrave, 1999.

A detailed narrative account of the transition from the Roman Empire to a Frankish-dominated Europe.

Dutton, Paul Edward, ed. *Charlemagne's Courtier: The Complete Einhard.* Peterborough, Ont.: Broadview Press, 1998. A collection of text and documents pertaining to Charlemagne's biographer, the monk Einhard, that contains the biography as well as letters illustrative of the ecclesiastical concerns of Charlemagne and his son, Louis.

Fichtenau, Heinrich. *Living in the Tenth Century: Mentalities and Social Orders.* Translated by Patrick J. Geary. Chicago: University of Chicago Press, 1993. An interesting exploration of daily life and the social customs of the late Carolingian period.

McKitterick, Rosamund. *The Frankish Church and the Carolingian Reforms, 789–895.* London: Longmans, Green, 1977. The standard work on the growth of the church during the Carolingian period.

McKitterick, Rosamund, ed. *The Early Middle Ages: Europe, 400–1000.* New York: Oxford University Press, 2001. In this collection of essays, each author addresses presents an overview of the most recent scholarship on particular themes in early medieval history.

Smith, Julia M. H. *Europe After Rome: A New Cultural History, 500–1000.* New York: Oxford University Press, 2005. An up-to-the-minute overview of the cultural and social changes in the wake of the Roman Empire's end in the west.

Wickham, Chris. *Framing the Early Middle Ages: Europe and the Mediterranean, 400–800.* New York: Oxford University Press, 2005. An authoritative and dense assessment of the evidence for the changes in long-distance trade and the economy of the Frankish kingdoms; an invaluable reference work.

Websites

For medieval documents (including Einhard's biography of Charlemagne), saints lives, law texts, and maps, **Internet Medieval Sourcebook,** at www.fordham.edu/halsall/sbook.html

Entertaining and educational site relating to the archaeology and history of Viking York, **Jorvik Viking Centre,** at www.jorvik-viking-centre.co.uk/

An informative site that provides information about the major Christian and Muslim pilgrimages today whose roots lie in the early medieval period, including the Hajj to Mecca, **Sacred Destinations,** at http://www.sacred-destinations.com/index.html

The High Middle Ages, 1000–1300

CHAPTER OUTLINE

1500 B.C.E.	1000 B.C.E.	500 B.C.E.	1 B.C.E./1 C.E.

1066
William, duke of Normany, conquers England

962
Otto I becomes emperor

1076
Pope Gregory VII excommunicates Emperor Henry IV

1095
Pope Urban II's sermon provokes the crusading movement

960	980	1000	1020	1040	1060	1080	1100	1120	1140

Merchants, Pilgrims, and Migrants on the Move, 1000–1300

By the end of the eleventh century, people at different ends of the Mediterranean came once more into contact with one another, mostly through trade, but sometimes through holy war. Which cities under Byzantine and Muslim rule drew traders and pilgrims from Europe to the east and why?

ICELAND

IRELAND

WALES

ENGLAND

London

North Sea

DENMARK

SWEDEN

Uppsala

Revel

Riga

FINNS

LIVONIANS

ESTONIANS

LITHUANIANS

Königsberg

PRUSSIANS

Baltic Sea

KIEVAN RUS

Kiev

GERMANY

HOLY

Cologne

Rouen

Paris

Metz

Mainz

Worms

Speyer

Ratisbon

Prague

BOHEMIA

Vienna

POLAND

Kraków

Buda

Pest

HUNGARY

ATLANTIC OCEAN

FRANCE

Cluny

Lyons

Basel

ROMAN

Milan

Genoa

BURGUNDY

CUMANS

Black Sea

Trebizond

LEÓN

NAVARRE

PORTUGAL

CASTILE

ARAGON

Toledo

Albi

Barcelona

Marseilles

EMPIRE

ITALY

Assisi

PAPAL STATES

Rome

Venice

Naples

Amalfi

KINGDOM OF THE TWO SICILIES

Palermo

Durazzo

BYZANTINE EMPIRE

Constantinople

Nicaea

SELJUK EMPIRE

LESSER ARMENIA

Edessa

COUNTY OF EDESSA

Antioch

SYRIA

PRINCIPALITY OF ANTIOCH

Lisbon

Córdoba

Granada

ALMOHAD CALIPHATE

Tunis

Mediterranean Sea

Candia

Limasol

Tripoli

COUNTY OF TRIPOLI

Tyre

Acre

KINGDOM OF JERUSALEM

Jerusalem

Alexandria

AYYUBID CALIPHATE

EGYPT

Red Sea

Roman church	→ First Crusade, 1096–1099
Eastern church	→ Second Crusade, 1147–1149
Crusader kingdoms, 1140	→ Third Crusade, 1189–1192
Islam	→ Fourth Crusade, 1202–1204
Pagan areas	→ Baltic Crusades, 12th–13th centuries

✶ Massacres of Jews, 1096
— Holy Roman Empire, 1175
— Other boundaries, 1175

500 C.E.   1000 C.E.   1500 C.E.   2000 C.E.

1163
Construction of Notre Dame Cathedral begins

1187
Saladin defeats the Crusaders

1204
Constantinople falls to Fourth Crusade

1215
Fourth Lateran Council sets new standards
King John signs the Magna Carta

1291
Acre, last Christian outpost in east, falls to Muslims

1160   1180   1200   1220   1240   1260   1280   1300   1320   1340

Choice Choice Choice Choice

The murder of Thomas Becket, archbishop of Canterbury, in 1170 by knights in the service of King Henry II outraged defenders of the liberties of the church. Three years later, he was declared a saint. Depictions of his murder appear in stained glass windows, in manuscript illuminations, and on objects like this casket pictured here. (HIP/Art Resource, NY)

Thomas Becket Defends the Liberties of the Church

On the evening of December 29, 1170, Thomas Becket, archbishop of Canterbury, had unexpected visitors. Four armed knights approached the archbishop in his cathedral—and murdered him. They believed that they were acting according to the wishes of their king, Henry II of England. With this murder, a long-standing quarrel between Thomas and his king over the church's freedom from secular interference came to an end. It did not, however, put an end to the problem.

Thomas and Henry had not always been enemies. As Henry's chancellor, Thomas had administered Henry's government, assisting him in a variety of judicial, fiscal, and military reforms. Thomas was one of the so-called new men—literate commoners elevated to positions of power by virtue of their skills in the exercise of government. Originally from London and of Norman descent, Thomas was a tall man and fond of lavish display. He aroused the resentment of the English barons, who felt that new men were unworthy of powerful and lucrative positions in the king's service. But Thomas was also in the service of the church. Prior to entering Henry's service, Thomas had served Theobald, the archbishop of Canterbury, and in 1154—the same year that Henry made Thomas his chancellor—Theobald made Thomas cathedral archdeacon. Yet, Thomas had served Henry faithfully, even supporting the king's attempts to curtail the authority of the church. Theobald, who was slowly dying, regretted his archdeacon's activities.

Upon the death of the old archbishop, Henry appointed Thomas archbishop of Canterbury, intending that Thomas would retain his position as chancellor as well. But as archbishop, Thomas experienced a political, personal, and ultimately spiritual transformation. As archbishop, he was head of the church in England, and in this position Thomas decided that his interests were no longer the same as the king's. The role of an archbishop, it was now clear to him, lay in the defense of the church's liberties against the attempts of the king to limit them. Thus, Thomas gave up being a king's man, resigned the position of chancellor, and took up the role of church defender.

A confrontation was soon in coming. In a departure from canon law and tradition, Henry claimed the right to try clergymen suspected of crimes in his royal court rather than in ecclesiastical courts, where they usually received lighter penalties. Thomas immediately objected and set himself against the will of the king. The hostility between the two men forced Thomas into exile in France and at the pope's court in Rome for six years. The geographic distance did not lessen their enmity. Henry confiscated the archbishop's property and forced his relatives into exile. Thomas excommunicated Henry and all those who supported him in his cause. The bishops of England were split on the matter, but most came down on the side of the king.

Eventually, Henry, fearing isolation from his fellow Christian rulers, met with Thomas and agreed that Thomas would return to Canterbury. When he did so, Thomas was greeted by cheering crowds. But he would not overturn the excommunications he had issued against Henry and those who supported him, and Henry took that as an insult. It was at that point that Henry's knights sped to Canterbury and murdered Thomas.

Almost immediately, Thomas Becket's grave in the cathedral became a focal point for pilgrims. So strong was Thomas's reputation for holiness and defense of the church that Pope Alexander III canonized him three years after his murder in 1173.

Introduction

By resisting the king's domination of the church, Thomas Becket became the most important martyr in a cause begun a century before his death by a succession of reform-minded popes. The church's dependence on secular rulers for protection and its inability to prevent lay interference in ecclesiastical appointments had undermined its role as supreme authority in Christian society. To become the spiritual leader of society, the church needed to live up to its own standards, set standards of behavior for everyone under its authority, and regulate the expressions of devotion among the common people that so easily got out of hand. It would take a reform movement that engaged everyone from the pope to the laity to bring these changes about.

Secular rulers, on the other hand, recognized that to extend their authority they had to impose much-needed order in society. The only way to restore social order was to dispense justice, prohibit private warfare, and collect taxes. To regularize the harvesting of crops and the collecting of revenue from the harvest, peasant families needed to live without fear of being plundered by land-hungry knights. How to contain the warlike impulse of the nobility was a problem that preoccupied kings and popes.

The pope saw a solution to the problem in holy war. Encouraging large numbers of nobles and knights to conquer Jerusalem discouraged them from fighting closer to home. But the establishment of Christian rule over the birthplace of Christianity came at a high cost. From the eleventh century on, even though merchants trading with Muslims in eastern Mediterranean ports brought to Europe a wider and more expensive range of goods to sell in markets, relations between Christians and Muslims were strained.

Those people who stayed close to home slowly began to feel the changes in the wider world. Peasant families had more to eat, found more in their local market to look at if not to buy, and had more obligations to the church than did people at the start of the twelfth century. As later generations of peasants saw more people on the road—merchants, wandering monastic scholars, royal messengers as well as troops—they heard about towns, which aroused their hopes for something better than what they could find on the land. Many laymen and -women chose a life of holiness as they understood it, not as the church had taught them. Others attacked Jews and Muslims out of a conviction that the world should be entirely Christian, no matter the cost. Still others sought new worlds through the life of the mind. Not in centuries had the people of western Europe had such a variety of opportunities to choose from.

Church Reform and Spiritual Renewal

↓ What goals did reform-minded popes set for reforming the Church?

↓ How did laypeople take a greater role in religious life?

By the year 1000, the standards the church had set for itself had sunk on all fronts. Rich monasteries, ecclesiastical offices for sale, married priests, and secular rulers appointing bishops all indicated that the church was losing sight of its mission. Some clergy were determined to turn the church around. Their campaign for reform inspired many laypeople to dedicate themselves to God's work among the poor and infirm. Yet church leaders also worried that religious enthusiasm would create an atmosphere in which the church's essential role in salvation would be ignored. The task was to find a way for the laity to participate more fully in the life of the church without challenging its authority.

Chronology

910	Monastery of Cluny is founded
987	Capetian dynasty replaces Carolingians in France
1049	Leo IX elected pope
1076	Pope Gregory VII excommunicates Emperor Henry IV
1095	Pope Urban II's sermon prompts crusading movement
1096	First wave of Crusaders sets off for Jerusalem
1098	Cistercian Order is formed
1099	Jerusalem falls to First Crusade
1120	Order of the Templars is founded in Jerusalem.
1163	Construction on Notre Dame begins
1182	Philip II expels Jews from France
1184	Church condemns Peter Waldo
1187	Saladin crushes crusading army at Hattin
1191	Richard I of England and Philip II Augustus of France capture Acre
1192	Richard I and Saladin conclude three-year truce
1204	Constantinople falls to Fourth Crusade
1208	Pope Innocent III calls for crusade against Albigensian sect
1209	Pope Innocent III approves Franciscan Order
1215	King John I signs Magna Carta; Fourth Lateran Council
1216	Dominican Order is founded
1291	Acre, last Christian outpost in east, falls to Muslims

Reform from Within

Since the Merovingian period, monasteries had grown wealthy. Many derived large incomes from land they had received from noble and royal patrons, and they acquired reputations more for opulence than for austerity. Gold and silver liturgical instruments adorned monastic altars. Servants tended to the needs of the monks. Abbots resembled noblemen more than leaders of contemplative communities.

The wealth of monasteries was bound to offend those still committed to the Benedictine ideal of poverty, charity, and obedience. In the tenth century, some church leaders had taken steps to restore discipline among the clergy living a monastic life and to advocate for similar reforms among the parish priests. They took their inspiration from **Cluny,** a monastery founded in 910 in central France that had set a standard for austerity. There monks adhered to a rigorous schedule of prayers that required them to rise several times during the night. So popular did this reform-minded monastery become that monks everywhere sought permission from Cluny's abbot to found monastic houses obedient to him. By the thirteenth century, the abbot of Cluny headed more than three hundred affiliated monasteries across Europe.

Cluny's renewal of the monastic ideal included instilling in its monks the necessity for church reform. In the eleventh century, highly educated monks helped direct church and papal policy. They prescribed a stricter adherence to celibacy, a minimal level of literacy, and a ban on the purchase of ecclesiastical office. Viewing human sexuality in mostly negative terms by associating all that is good with the spirit and all that is bad with the flesh, the church in western Europe reinforced its long-standing requirement that the clergy be chaste and unmarried. The requirement, dating back to 390, had been increasingly ignored, as priests and deacons had taken wives and concubines and had children by them. In the late eleventh and twelfth centuries, a series of church councils invalidated such marriages and reduced the wives and children of priests and deacons to servile status.

At the same time, the reformers instituted a rule that required clergymen to be literate enough to be able to read the Bible and the prayers involved in the liturgy. They also put on notice those clergymen who

Cluny   Influential reform-minded monastery founded in 910, known for its austerity.

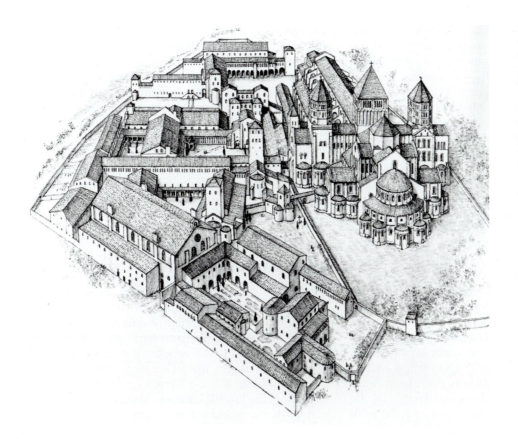

The largest structure in western Europe for most of the Middle Ages, the monastery attached to the church at Cluny provided the papacy with its most stalwart supporters of Church reform. *(Based on a drawing from* Cluny des Églises et la Maison du Chef d'Ordre, *by R. J. Conant. Courtesy, Medieval Academy of America)*

had purchased their positions, a practice known as **simony.** It had been customary for lords to accept fees from priests in exchange for the rights to officiate in the churches located on the lords' lands, despite the fact that bishops claimed to control these rights. Some bishops and archbishops even accepted payment for the lower-ranking offices in their jurisdiction. Now, all such payments were condemned.

Like most successful reform movements, over time the products of reform became themselves in need of reform. By the end of the eleventh century, the Cluniac Order, too, had become rich. The abbey church at Cluny was the largest structure in Europe, and the monastery resembled more a bustling city than a sanctuary for silent prayer. Cluny's influence can be measured by the great number of papal, royal, and noble delegations—similar to the elaborate ceremonial visits secular rulers paid each other—sent to pay respects to the order's abbot. Important visitors required accommodations and banquets befitting their exalted status. The order's own high standards had collapsed under the weight of its success.

A new set of reformers then sought to revive the standards the Cluniac Order had attempted to set. In 1098, monks from a monastery associated with Cluny established the Cistercian Order, which acquired a reputation for austerity it never lost. One of the most famous preachers of the Middle Ages, **Saint Bernard of Clairveaux,** belonged to this community in central France. He not only helped establish other Cistercian communities but also became an influential adviser to the French kings of the early twelfth century.

The Church and Secular Authority

The German emperor Henry III's selection of German-born **Leo IX** as pope in 1049 made few people happy. Supporters of reform within the Church viewed the emperor's role as interference. In Rome, the noble families had trouble accepting a non-Roman pope

simony   Purchase of ecclesiastical office from a layperson or church official.

Saint Bernard of Clairveaux   (1090–1153) Cistercian monk who was an influential preacher and adviser to French kings and the pope.

Leo IX   (r. 1049–1054) Pope who initiated the church reform movement.

over whom they exercised little influence. Bishops who had purchased their office were particularly nervous about the arrival of a man known to be intolerant of simony. Ordinary priests with wives feared that this new bishop of Rome might compel them to give up their families. They were right to be worried.

From the start, Leo set the tone for reform by dressing in the humble garb of a pilgrim. One of his first official acts was to depose the bishops and priests who had attained their positions through simony. He was equally aggressive in attacking clerical marriage. The response of the married clergy was clear and heartfelt: they accused the church hierarchy of driving them into poverty. Who, they cried, would tend to their material needs while they ministered to spiritual ones? Who would make and wash their clothing, clean their house, brew their ale, and in general maintain their household if not women? Affection undoubtedly entered into the clergy's concerns, but the ban's repercussions had a practical side as well.

Leo IX's successor, **Pope Gregory VII,** continued to raise standards for the clergy and also expanded papal authority, protecting the liberties of the church against interference from secular rulers. The greatest obstacle to the new pope's plans was Henry IV, the emperor who, like his father Henry III, considered it his right not only to appoint the pope but also to appoint clergy to church positions within his empire. Intending to end that custom, Gregory decreed in 1075 that only the pope had the authority to appoint clergy to offices. He also forbade secular rulers from conferring the symbols of a bishop's authority on newly appointed bishops, a ceremony known as investiture. Enraged, Henry responded by removing Gregory from office and calling for the election of a new pope. To punish the emperor, Gregory excommunicated him in 1076. "I release all Christian men from the allegiance which they have sworn or may swear to him, and I forbid anyone to serve him as king," the pope declared. Relations between the emperor and the pope could hardly have been more tense.

In the winter of 1077, wearing the garb of a penitent pilgrim, Henry went to meet the pope at Canossa, a village in the mountains of central Italy where the pope was visiting the castle of a powerful family. For three days, it was said, Henry stood barefoot in the snow waiting for the pope to receive him. In the face of such a public act of contrition, the pope was compelled to forgive the seemingly penitent emperor. The **Investiture Controversy,** as the confrontation between Gregory VII and Henry IV is known, appeared to be over.

In fact, the battle for an end to lay interference in Church affairs was just beginning. A compromise between Gregory's and Henry's successors was reached in the **Concordat of Worms** in 1122, which distinguished between the earthly and spiritual powers of a bishop. From then on, the emperor would confer the symbols of a bishop's temporal authority over lands and property, and church authorities would invest bishops with the symbols of their spiritual jurisdiction. Despite the clarity of the compromise, the liberties of the church remained an important issue as popes continued to challenge the right of not only the emperor but also kings, dukes, counts, and barons to interfere in church affairs.

Innocent III and the Fourth Lateran Council

The Gregorian reform lived much longer than its namesake. In the early thirteenth century, another pope, this one a young, highly skilled lawyer, turned reform into law. The reform legislation of **Innocent III** was intended to define what it meant to be Christian and to distinguish Christians from the non-Christians living among them. In 1215, with Innocent presiding, the **Fourth Lateran Council** issued seventy canons that set standards for clergy behavior, declared the pope to be the preeminent bishop in Christendom, condemned heresy, and required all Christians to confess their sins to a priest once a year. But it was the council's pronouncements on marriage and the presence of Jews in Christian society that had the greatest impact on ordinary Christians.

Since Carolingian times, the church had had an unofficial role in the formal arrangements of marriage,

Gregory VII   (r. 1073–1085) Pope who expanded papal authority, raised clerical standards, and protected the church from interference by secular rulers.

Investiture Controversy   Conflict between Pope Gregory VII and Emperor Henry IV over the secular role in the investiture, or appointment, of bishops.

Concordat of Worms   Agreement between the papacy and the emperor in 1122 that allowed the emperor to confer secular, but not spiritual, authority on bishops.

Innocent III   (r. 1198–1216) One of the most influential popes of the Middle Ages, responsible for the Fourth Lateran Council and the crusade against heretics within Europe.

Fourth Lateran Council   Church council of 1215, presided over by Pope Innocent III, whose decrees set standards for the clergy, declared the pope to hold supreme authority in the church, and required all Christians to take confession once a year.

usually no more than a priest's blessing of a couple wed by contract. As in the Roman world, marriage signaled an alliance between families and the passage of property between them. By the eighth century, the church had made the consent of the couple, not of their families, the defining feature of a legal marriage. Starting in the twelfth century, to prevent marriages between close kin, priests required the publishing of banns, a public announcement of a couple's intention to marry that invited anyone with information that would hinder the marriage to come forward. Clandestine marriages—unions contracted between a man and a woman in secret—were strongly condemned by the church. After the Fourth Lateran Council, marriages had to be announced publicly in advance, contracted openly, and publicly acknowledged; they were also forbidden between closely related kin.

In seeking to reinforce Christian identity, the council decreed that Jews and Muslims must wear distinguishing clothing in public. In addition, on the grounds that only Christians should exercise authority over Christians, Jews were barred from holding public office. Finally, Jews who had converted to Christianity were forbidden to return to their former religion. At this time Jews in the Diaspora lived mainly in the German territories, southern France, and Sicily, working as merchants, moneylenders, cobblers, and tanners. The constraints placed on them only increased from this point forward.

Innocent died in 1216, less than a year after the council adjourned. The church had benefited from having such an able canon lawyer as pope for eighteen years. The reforms that Leo IX and Gregory VII had fought for took on substance in the legislation Innocent III shepherded through the council sessions. Not all of his measures would succeed in the long run, but he provided the papacy with the legal and theological instruments to impose order on the church and Christian society and to delineate the boundaries of Christian identity.

Lay Leaders and Friars

Starting in the late tenth century and throughout the eleventh, wandering monks carried the spirit of reform through the towns and villages of western Europe, preaching and engaging laypeople in the movement to define what it meant to be Christian and live accordingly. Inspired by the biblical text "If you wish to be perfect, then go and sell everything you have, and give to the poor" (Matthew 9:21), many lay people formed communities dedicated to prayer and helping the sick and poor. Unlike monasteries, the new lay communities did not withdraw from but worked in the world and lived according to rules they devised for themselves.

The church welcomed these initiatives but worried that untrained preachers might misrepresent the teachings of the church. So laypeople had to receive permission to preach. Permission became an issue in the French city of Lyons, when, in the late twelfth century, the public preaching of a merchant, Peter Waldo, attracted attention. Waldo sought permission to preach from the archbishop of Lyons and from the pope but was denied. This refusal led him to question the church's authority and, later, the necessity of the sacraments for salvation. When he continued to preach, the church formally condemned him in 1184. This condemnation caused the Waldensians to question the value of some of the sacraments, at which point the church undertook their suppression with vigor. Members of the sect were declared heretics, imprisoned periodically, excommunicated, and, finally, in the early thirteenth century, expelled from the region.

In the mid-twelfth century, another heretical sect, the Cathars, adopted a dualist conception of the world, seeing everything of the spirit as good and the material world as evil. Also known as Albigensians (for the southern French town, Albi, where many lived), Cathars rejected the special role of the priesthood in salvation. By the early 1200s, Catharism had spread over much of southern France and into Spain. In many towns, under the protection of noblemen who had joined the sect, Cathars set up their own churches, which attracted more people than did the Roman churches.

Although missionary efforts aimed to bring the Cathars back into obedience failed, the church did not always discourage new religious orders, provided they respected church authority and adhered to church teaching. In the early thirteenth century, the spirit of reform combined with a new religious enthusiasm among the laity to produce a new kind of religious order, the mendicants, who repudiated property ownership and embraced poverty. Unlike monks in

banns   Declaration by a priest of a couple's intention to marry.

Peter Waldo   (ca. 1170s–1218) Devout merchant in Lyons, France, who defied church authorities and exhorted Christians to live more piously.

Cathars   Heretical religious sect, also known as Albigensians, who rejected the role of the priesthood in salvation.

mendicants   (from Latin, "beggars") Members of religious orders that repudiated the ownership of personal and communal property.

Innocent III, seen here, was the first to turn the weapon of crusade against inhabitants of western Europe when he called for a crusade against the Cathar sect. *(HIP/Art Resource, NY)*

isolated monasteries, **friars** lived according to a monastic rule in the world and carried out the church's mission, working or begging to provide for their very simple needs.

The Order of the Minor Brothers, commonly known as the Franciscan Order, vowed obedience to the pope, renunciation of property, and chastity. Relief of the poor and preaching stood at the center of their mission. Their founder, **Francis,** was born in 1182 in Assisi, a hill town in central Italy, to a family of prosperous cloth merchants. After serving in a war, he renounced his claim on his father's goods in 1207, gave away all his clothing and goods, and dedicated his life to the poor and infirm. The powerful example of his conversion convinced many of his friends to join him. Within two years, in 1209, Pope Innocent III approved the rule Francis wrote. The Franciscan friars wandered over Italy, preaching repentance and aiding the sick; within ten years, they numbered in the thousands. Their wanderings took them not only across Europe but also to Muslim territories, where they sought converts. Women followed a more traditional path in the order. With support from Francis, a young woman from Assisi, **Clare,** founded an order of nuns in 1212 that became known later as the Order of the Poor Clares. Unlike the friars, however, they lived in strict seclusion.

Although Francis resisted pressure from members of his order to modify his principle that Franciscans could own no property, either individually and collectively, he reluctantly lessened the physical hardship the brothers were expected to endure in their life of poverty. After his death in 1226 from years of physical self-deprivation, the Franciscans became divided between those who wanted to follow Francis's original rule to the letter and those who believed the order needed to own some property to be able to function. The majority of the members and the papacy favored a modified rule that permitted the order to acquire missions and schools to teach their members how to preach and convert. By the start of the fourteenth century, the Franciscans had brothers working in missions as far away as Africa.

friars (from Latin, "brothers") Members of mendicant orders.
Francis of Assisi (1182–1226) Founder of the Franciscan friars, the first mendicant order.
Clare of Assisi (1194–1253) Follower of Francis of Assisi who established an affiliated order of nuns, the Poor Clares, in 1212.

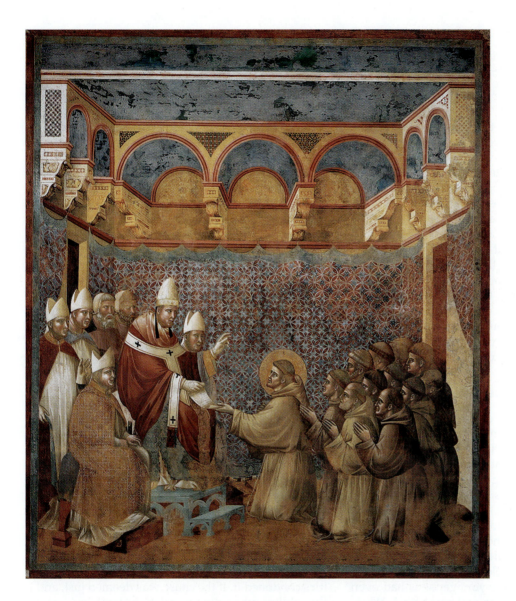

Francis of Assisi received the blessing of Pope Innocent III and launched his Order of the Lesser Brothers, as the Franciscans are officially called. *(Erich Lessing/Art Resource, NY)*

A Spanish contemporary of Francis, **Dominic Guzman,** founded another order of mendicant friars, the Order of Preachers, or the Dominicans. In contrast to the Franciscans, few of whom were priests, the Dominicans were an order of priests who specialized in preaching with the special aim of combating heresy, in particular the Cathars. Founded in 1216, the Dominican Order proved so effective against heretical groups that bishops relied on theologically trained Dominican friars to interrogate possible heretics and apostate Jews—Jews who had converted and later renounced Christianity. Dominicans placed great value on education in theology as a way to combat religious beliefs at odds with church doctrine.

The friars' work made a deep impression on religious life in Europe. By setting an example of apostolic poverty, they made people question their attachment to material things and made them more sympathetic to the poverty surrounding them. They placed a greater emphasis on learning. They also participated in the papacy's campaign to impose uniformity of belief on Christian society.

Dominic Guzman   (ca. 1170–1221) Founder of the Order of Preachers, or Dominican Order.

The Crusades

- ↓ What were the causes and outcomes of the Crusades?
- ↓ How did the Crusades change relations between Christians and Muslims?

The belief that Jerusalem—the holiest spot in Christendom—needed rescue gave a focus to an enthusiasm few people suspected lay behind the spirit of reform. Beginning in the late eleventh century the church—until then an advocate of peace—sent armies across the continent for the purposes of war and conquest. Thousands left homes and families to travel great distances and fight non-Christians for possession of land they thought of as theirs but that, in fact, had not been under Christian rule since the seventh century. Crusading armies attacked not only Muslims but also Jews, other non-Christians, Christians believed to be heretics, and the Christians of the Byzantine Empire. The march of Christian armies changed the nature of the Christian religion and created deep and lasting enmities that persist to this day.

A War to Renew the Church

Beginning in the eleventh century, the papacy had campaigned for reform on many fronts. In addition to raising the standards of clerical behavior and defending the liberties of the church, reformers also felt compelled to do something about the near-constant warfare among the nobles of western Europe that they perceived as harmful to the well-being of the church and its members. Noble families had long engaged in combat to seize land and build wealth. Now, as the custom of **primogeniture** began to take root in northern Europe, with the eldest son inheriting his father's entire estate, landless younger sons had even more incentive to make war and seize land. While some served as **knights**—in this period, little more than soldiers in the households of other nobles—others fought almost constantly. Few people felt secure.

Secular rulers did not have the means to control this violence, since their armies were made up of the same men they sought to rein in. But the pope, who saw himself as the shepherd of an enormous flock, nobles and commoners alike, looked for ways to redirect the violence elsewhere. At local councils, bishops declared Truces of God, outlawing violence on certain days, and the Peace of God, prohibiting attacks on clergy, women, and the poor. These measures proved only partially effective, however,

In 1095, **Pope Urban II** received a letter that allowed him to give the nobility a new focus for their

hostilities. The Byzantine emperor, **Alexius I Comnenus,** asked for aid against the Seljuk Turks, who had seized land in Asia Minor, Syria, and Palestine from both Byzantine and Muslim rulers. Instead of appealing to the German emperor or the king of the French, Alexius applied to the pope, whose status in western Europe he understood to resemble his own in his empire. Even before receiving Alexius's request, the pope had heard that the Church of the Holy Sepulcher had been destroyed in 1010 by a Muslim ruler of Jerusalem. Rumors about the mistreatment of Christians there were widespread in the west. In reality, the Muslims, who by then had ruled Jerusalem for centuries, and Seljuks, who replaced them, benefited economically from the great number of pilgrims who came to worship at Christian shrines and so were inclined to leave the Christians in peace. The pope was in possession of mistaken and outdated news.

Yet, on November 25, 1095, Pope Urban II preached a sermon to a large crowd in Clermont, in central France, where he had been presiding over a local council. Enemies of the faith, he reportedly declared, were intent on conquering the Holy Land. He urged "men of all ranks whatsoever, knights as well as footsoldiers, rich and poor, to hasten to exterminate this vile race from our lands and to aid the Christian inhabitants in time." He promised a remission of sins for any of those who went to fight non-Christians, making war an act of penance. Christians fighting Muslims for control of the Iberian Peninsula would also have their sins remitted. This war, said the pope, unlike the noblemen's violence, was a **just war.**

The church taught that war in itself was not sinful, especially when it was defensive. Since Saint Augustine in the fourth century, Christians had considered violence, when necessary, lawful if the proper authorities condoned it, if the cause was deemed just, and if the soldiers themselves meant good by it. In Alexius's letter, Urban saw an occasion for a just war that met all those criteria.

primogeniture   System of inheritance that directs the majority of or the entire estate from a father to his eldest son.

knights   Armed supporters of nobles who lived and served in the households of their lords.

Urban II   (r. 1088–1099) Pope who in 1095 inspired the crusading movement.

Alexius I Comnenus   (r. 1081–1118) Byzantine emperor whose request for aid from the west served as the pretext for the Crusades.

just war   The idea and theological explanation of when it is legitimate to wage war.

In this fourteenth-century manuscript illumination, Pope Urban II arrives at the council and gives the sermon that galvanized thousands to march to Jerusalem. *(Bridgeman-Giraudon/Art Resource, NY)*

Crusading Armies and Crusader States

When monks spread word of Urban's sermon throughout Europe, the response was dramatic. Within a year, two armies—one hardly more than a mob of knights and peasants, the other contingents of knights led by noblemen—planned to depart. In the first wave, tens, possibly hundreds, of thousands of people incited by the sermons they had heard set out for Jerusalem, the city they believed to be in need of rescue. Jerusalem had for centuries been a city that Christians in western Europe dreamed of seeing but which only pilgrims willing to endure the dangers of a ruinously expensive journey ever reached. Now pious determination mixed with the allure of plunder and the thirst for adventure in the crowds that set out to rid Jerusalem of people who were not Christian. "Deus le volt!" ("God wills it!") became the rallying cry of the masses marching east.

Some saw enemies closer to home. In numerous cities, mobs massacred the only non-Christians in their midst, the Jews. One witness described how pilgrims in the northern French city of Rouen "armed themselves, rounded up some Jews in a church—whether by force or by ruse I don't know—and led them out to put them to the sword regardless of age or sex. Those who agreed to submit to the Christian way of life could, however, escape the impending slaughter." The massacres were the first widespread violence against Jews in western Europe. Having accomplished what they believed God desired, many crusading Christians returned home, but thousands pushed on. When they reached Constantinople in 1097, Emperor Alexius did not recognize in these ragged, mostly unarmed, and mostly poor men and women a response to his request. His army quickly escorted them out of his territory. On a road in Asia Minor, the Seljuk Turks put a bloody end to what became known as the Poor People's Crusade.

Meanwhile, more seasoned soldiers prepared for a military undertaking endorsed by the pope. The First Crusade, led by nobles from France, Germany, and southern Italy, lasted over two years, during which the Crusaders besieged walled towns, fought Muslim powers that stood in their way, and slaughtered indiscriminately—even Christians, whose faith they either ignored or were unaware of. Enduring hardship and starvation, more Crusaders died of disease than in combat. After capturing the port of Antioch from a Muslim ruler, they reached the walls of Jerusalem in June 1099. Since their journey began, however, not only had rival Muslim powers in Egypt expelled the Seljuks from Jerusalem but now Muslims, Jews, and Christians once again coexisted under Muslim rule in the city they all considered sacred. Nevertheless, on July 15, 1099, after a month-long siege, the Crusaders captured the city and massacred nearly the entire population.

Voice Voice Voice Voice

Anna Comnena Describes the Crusaders

Around 1120, Anna, the daughter of the Byzantine emperor Alexius I Comnenus, wrote The Alexiad, *an admiring history of her beloved father and the events of his reign. The last five of the fifteen chapters describe the First Crusade (1099–1102), and Anna's account of the crusading warriors who showed up unannounced at the gate of Constantinople provides insight into the way western Europeans were perceived in the old, highly ceremonial culture of the Byzantine court. In addition to calling them Franks, as most Byzantines did, Anna also calls them Kelts (Celts). In her world, northern Europe was populated by primitive "barbarian" peoples whom Roman geographers had labeled long ago.* ➡ ➡

➡ *What does Anna appreciate about the Crusaders and what does she dislike?*

➡ *How would you describe the Byzantine court based on what Anna says?*

➡ *What is it about the language Anna uses that tells you her impressions of the Crusaders are mostly negative?*

➡ *Why does Anna object to the way the Crusaders speak to her father?*

➡ *Does Emperor Alexius show diplomacy or a lack of sensitivity in dealing with the Crusaders?*

➡ The Keltic counts are brazen-faced, violent men, moneygrubbers and where their personal desires are concerned quite immoderate. These are natural characteristics of the race. They also surpass all other nations in loquacity. So when they came to the palace they did so in an undisciplined fashion, every count bringing with him as many comrades as he wished; after him, without interruption, came another and then a third—an endless queue. Once there they did not limit the conversation by the water-clock, like the orators of ancient times, but each, whoever he was, enjoyed as much time as he wanted for the interview with the emperor. ➡ Men of such character, talkers so exuberant, had neither respect for his feelings nor thought for the passing of time nor any idea of the by-standers' wrath; instead of giving way to those coming behind them, they talked on and on with an incessant stream of petitions. Every student of human customs will be acquainted with Frankish verbosity and their pettifogging love of detail; but the audience on these occasions learnt the lesson more thoroughly—from actual experience. When evening came, after remaining without food all through the day, the emperor would rise from his throne and retire to his private apartments, but even then he was not free from the importunities of the Kelts. They came one after another, not only those who had failed to obtain a hearing during the day, but those who had already been heard returned as well, putting forward this or that excuse for more talk. ➡ In the midst of them, calmly enduring their endless chatter stood the emperor. One could see them there, all asking questions, and him, alone and unchanging, giving them prompt replies. But there was no limit to their foolish babbling, and if a court official did try to cut them short, he was himself interrupted by Alexius. He knew the traditional pugnacity of the Franks and feared that from some trivial pretext might a blaze of trouble might spring up, resulting in serious harm to the prestige of Rome. It was really a most extraordinary sight. Like a statue wrought by hammer, made perhaps of bronze or cold-forged iron, the emperor would sit through the night, often from evening till midnight, often till third cock-crow, sometimes almost until the sun was shining clearly. The attendants were all worn out, but by frequently retiring had a rest and then came back again—in bad humour.

The new kingdom of Jerusalem established by the Crusaders could not depend on western kings for consistent, timely support, so early in the twelfth century professional soldiers came to be garrisoned in immense stone fortifications, like the imposing Krak des Chevaliers in Syria. These soldiers were not ordinary knights. They belonged to religious orders of laymen who had taken vows similar to those taken by monks. Their original purpose had been the care of sick pilgrims, but now, in addition to their vows of poverty, chastity, and obedience, these monk-knights considered the defense of the Crusader kingdom to be their primary responsibility.

One such order was the **Knights Hospitaller** of Jerusalem, which acquired a reputation as a superior military unit. Another, which took its name from the location of its headquarters near the ruins of what was reputedly Solomon's Temple, was the **Knights Templar.** Bernard of Clairveaux praised "the new knighthood" for its services to Christendom, but the Templars engaged in far more than relief of the poor and military defense. Their military skill made them the ideal guards of money moving between western Europe and Palestine, and they gained immense wealth from moneylending.

As creditors of kings, the Knights Templars had not only wealth but also political influence. In 1305, one of the Templars' debtors, King Philip IV of France, charged them with heresy and homosexual activity, confiscated their vast properties, imprisoned all the Knights Templar in his kingdom, and burned many of them as heretics at the stake. Their destruction produced a windfall of cash for the nearly empty royal treasury.

For nearly a century, the Franks maintained Crusader states in the cities they conquered in Syria and Palestine. These were multicultural societies with legal and political institutions that blended western European and local traditions. But the Crusaders' presence, brutality, and ignorance of the religion and customs of the people in the land they had conquered galvanized opposition to them.

Crusades in the East and in Europe

Meanwhile, a Second Crusade had organized to support the gains of the First. The German emperor Conrad III gathered his troops and pressed the kings of Poland and Bohemia to join him. With **Louis VII** of France, accompanied by a host of other nobles, the Crusaders arrived in Syria in the spring of 1148, where they chose to attack Damascus, the one city in the region whose Muslim ruler was most inclined to join forces with the Christians. The resulting siege was a disaster. The arrival of a massive Muslim army from the south forced the Christian kings to retreat and find their way home. The failure of the Second Crusade had a devastating impact on the morale of Christians in western Europe. Bernard of Clairveaux attributed the failure to the sins of Christians, many of whom were willing to accept the blame.

It took a while for the Muslims of the region to unify behind a leader, but when they did, the **jihad,** as holy war is called in Islam, brought an end to Christian rule in the Near East. The Muslim leader was **Saladin,** a legend in both the Muslim and Christian worlds. Saladin drew the crusading armies into a trap. On July 3, 1187, his army crushed the Frankish army, weakened by internal rivalries, on ground between two hills, the Horns of Hattin, near the Sea of Galilee. Only one Crusade leader survived the battle. Saladin then took possession of the cities under Frankish rule one by one until he finally entered Jerusalem in October, a loss that deeply shocked the Christian west. Barely alive, Frankish refugees retreated to the ports of Tyre, Tripoli, and Antioch.

To recapture Jerusalem, **Richard I,** king of England, and **Philip II Augustus** of France led the Third Crusade, but they succeeded in seizing only the port of **Acre** on the coast of Palestine in 1191. King Philip shortly returned to France. For nearly a year, Richard and Saladin fought indecisive skirmishes. But when reports of problems at home reached Richard and reports of disagreements among his allies reached

Knights Hospitaller   (from the Hospital of St. John in Jerusalem) Monastic order of knights formed to defend Christian possessions in Syria and Palestine.

Knights Templar   Military order founded in the 1120s in Jerusalem to defend the land the Crusader forces had captured.

Louis VII   (r. 1137–1180) King of France, first husband of Eleanor of Aquitaine and leader of the failed Second Crusade.

jihad   Religious duty imposed on Muslims to defend and extend Islam.

Saladin   (r. 1169–1193) Muslim leader, of Kurdish ancestry, who defeated the Crusaders at Hattin and captured Jerusalem.

Richard I   (r. 1189–1199) Son of Henry II of England and Eleanor of Aquitaine; king of England and leader of the Third Crusade; known as Richard the Lion-Hearted.

Philip II Augustus   (r. 1179–1223) King of France and co-leader of the Third Crusade.

Acre   Mediterranean port, today in Israel; last Christian territory in the Holy Land to fall to Muslims, in 1291.

Saladin, the two warriors looked for a way out of the war. They agreed to a three-year truce in September of 1192 that ended shortly before Saladin died in 1193, but Jerusalem remained out of reach for the crusading armies. Meanwhile, a hospital set up by a group of German merchants to assist Richard and his forces in the siege of Acre was transformed, within a decade, into the **Teutonic Knights,** an order whose military mission was identical to that of the Hospitallers and the Templars but whose members came from German lands.

In Rome, Pope Innocent III called for a Fourth Crusade to the Holy Land. But in 1204, instead of fulfilling the mission defined by the pope, the crusading army seized Constantinople, the capital of the Byzantine Empire. It was the first time in a thousand years that the mighty walls had been breached by invaders. Once inside, the army burned and pillaged the city. Churches, palaces, libraries, and public buildings were ransacked and stripped of their treasures. The crusading leaders then divided the old empire among themselves. The principal funder of the crusade, Venice, received the island of Crete and two ports on the southern coast of the Peloponnesus. There eastern clergy were compelled to recognize the pope as their spiritual leader and the Christian population was made to feel like conquered people. The crusading movement had now become an open hunt for plunder and territory.

Closer to home, the crusade to seize Spain from the Muslims continued. Known as the **Reconquista,** the effort to bring all of the Iberian Peninsula under Christian rule succeeded in limiting Muslim rule to the province of Granada in the south by 1236. In 1208, Pope Innocent III also called for war against the Cathar heretics, thus using crusading as a tool to impose religious uniformity in western Europe. Responding to his call, knights from England and nobles from northern France undertook the **Albigensian Crusade,** attacking Cathar cities and massacring thousands. It took several armies and nearly twenty years to suppress the Cathars.

The Teutonic Knights now applied their crusading zeal to the conquest and conversion of the peoples of eastern Europe. In 1211, they arrived in Hungary to serve the king, Andrew II, whose kingdom suffered from incursions from a non-Christian people, the Cumans. The knights next subdued and converted the Prussians and in 1226 received permission to settle. Within fifty years they were masters of the region, controlling the lucrative grain trade to the Baltic Sea. In eastern Europe, the land-rich, commercially active Teutonic Knights remained a military, political, and economic force.

Meanwhile, all attempts to reestablish a Christian presence in the Holy Land stalled. In 1215 King Louis IX of France, later Saint Louis, led a crusade to Egypt as its target, but, like his great-grandfather, Louis VII, he went home in defeat. The few remaining Christian outposts in Syria and Palestine survived until 1291, when Acre, the last city in the region under Christian rule, fell to Muslim forces.

The Impact of the Crusades

Two centuries of fighting had resulted in a tremendous loss of life, on all sides. By openly endorsing the idea of slaughter as penance, the papacy created the conditions for legitimating violence toward Jews, Muslims, other non-Christians, and Christians who did not recognize the pope as the head of the universal church. The massacre of Jews at the start of the Poor People's Crusade was only the first episode in centuries of violence against them. Although Christians and Muslims had fought against each other in centuries past, now their confrontations were cast in starkly sectarian terms. For each side, it was a matter of "we the believers" against "the **infidels**"—the nonbelievers—despite the fact that for centuries Muslim and Christian merchants had done business on largely peaceful terms in eastern markets. In the northern reaches of Europe, whole peoples joined the church when faced with the choice of conversion or death. In southwestern France, the Cathars were destroyed. Christians living in the conquered Byzantine Empire thought of the Crusades as the last of the barbarian invasions. Following the Crusader conquest, eastern clergy were no longer allowed to be ordained according to the Greek rite. With the Crusades, reform of the church had come to mean uniformity of belief and practice, and western Christianity became a militant religion.

Many profited from the Crusades. The merchants of western Europe, especially in Italian cities, bene-

---

Teutonic Knights   Order of German knights founded in Jerusalem who shifted their area of operation in 1211 to eastern Europe to convert non-Christians.

Reconquista   (from Spanish, "reconquest") War to bring all Muslim territory in Spain under Christian rule.

Albigensian Crusade   War waged in the first half of the thirteenth century against the Cathar sect in southwestern France.

infidel   (from Latin, "unbeliever") From a Christian or Muslim perspective, anyone who is not a member of their religion.

fited from contact with the markets of Palestine and Syria. Following close behind the crusading conquerors in the First Crusade were Italian merchants, who immediately established trading outposts in the Crusader states. Venetian traders predominated in the port of Tyre, while merchants from Amalfi, Pisa, and Genoa traded in Jerusalem, Acre, and other Christian strongholds. Having access to local markets where traders from as far away as India and even China brought their goods meant that the Italian merchants could now create a demand in European markets for luxury goods: spices, silk and linen fabrics, carpets, and brassware. In the twelfth century northern Italian cities began to produce their own silk instead of importing it from the east, setting the conditions for the rise of the silk industry in the next century. The great distances between Italy and the Levant gave rise to banking techniques for the long-distance transfer of credit instead of coin, always vulnerable to theft and piracy. Thus, the Crusades accelerated the pace of economic changes that had already begun prior to the fall of Jerusalem in 1099.

The Growth of Royal Authority

> ↓ By what means did kings manage to centralize and increase their authority?
>
> ↓ Describe the different government structures in France, England, and the Holy Roman Empire.

In the eleventh century, kings had limited power over their kingdoms. The disorder created by the warring nobility made it difficult for any authority, except that of the church, to extend beyond a local level. Even the authority of the emperors had eroded since Otto I in the tenth century. But in the next two centuries, kings imposed their authority. They brought additional land into direct royal possession, replaced customary law with royal law, claimed the exclusive right to declare and wage war, and asserted their right to tax subjects. By the end of the thirteenth century, the imposition of royal authority had brought stability to the lives of ordinary people, and secular rulers had created within their kingdoms the mechanisms of strong and lasting monarchies.

From Weak Kings to Strong Monarchs

In France, royal authority rose in direct proportion to the increase in the royal domain. When France's

longest-lasting line of kings, the Capetians, replaced the Carolingians in 987, kings were poorer and weaker than their nobles. Although in theory the kingdom of the Capetian kings consisted of most of the land of modern-day France, their income derived principally from the region around Paris, which formed the royal domain. The rest of their kingdom was parceled out to the great lords who were their vassals. Over the twelfth and thirteenth centuries, the French kings added much territory to the royal domain—mainly by confiscating their chief vassals' lands—and made significant progress in turning royal law into the law of the kingdom. In the thirteenth century, the French kings convened their judicial court, called **Parlement,** where they and their judges took the counsel of vassals, tried cases reserved for royal justice, and heard appeals from the towns and provinces.

In England, the consolidation of royal authority occurred more swiftly than in France. Following invasions by Angles and Danes in the ninth and tenth centuries, at **Hastings** in 1066, **William,** the duke of Normandy, defeated the Danish king of England. After this **Norman Conquest,** William and his successors ruled England from Normandy until the early thirteenth century by delegating the tasks of government in England to royal representatives. Their main concern was to raise money. After a long contest among William's heirs, **Henry II** restored order in part by adapting pre-Norman administrative structures to his needs. He instituted a system whereby royal representatives in the counties, known by their Anglo-Saxon name as **shires,** collected taxes and delivered them to the royal treasury, called the **Exchequer.**

Parlement   In the fourteenth century, the French king's court of appeals located in Paris.

Hastings   Battle in 1066 in which William, duke of Normandy, defeated the Danish king of England.

William I   (r. 1066–1087) King of England, who, as duke of Normandy, invaded England, defeated the Danish king, and assumed the crown; known as William the Conqueror.

Norman Conquest   Invasion and conquest of England in 1066 by William, duke of Normandy, and his army of Norman nobles.

Henry II   (r. 1154–1189) King of England who, through his marriage to Eleanor of Aquitaine, held in vassalage a large portion of the French kingdom.

shire   Administrative unit in England equivalent to a county, represented to the king by the sheriff.

Exchequer   English royal treasury, so-called for the checked cloth covering a table on which accounts are calculated.

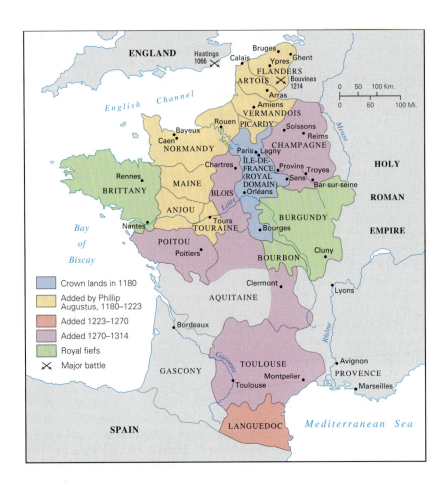

MAP 10.1   The Growth of the Kingdom of France The French king's revenue derived from the royal domain. At the start of the twelfth century, the royal domain consisted of mainly the region surrounding Paris. Over the succeeding two centuries, the royal domain grew larger as the king took land away from his vassals. Which regions did the French kings first set out to confiscate?

Henry and his sons, Richard I and **John I,** all tried to curtail the ability of their nobles to wage war against them by prohibiting the construction of castles without royal license. Henry's relations with the church were marred by his fight with Thomas Becket, archbishop of Canterbury. Though Henry hoped Becket's loyalty to him would survive his appointment to the highest church office in his kingdom, the archbishop defended the liberties of the church, and lost his life (see Choice).

In France and England, kings launched military campaigns more easily than they managed to raise regular funds from their subjects. Throughout the Middle Ages, direct taxation—that is, the levying of taxes on individuals rather than on goods and services—was associated with low social status and local authority. Kings expected financial support from their vassals, but the amounts set by long-standing custom were tiny in comparison to royal fiscal needs. Beyond the customary financial aid, nobles viewed the royal treasury as the personal concern of the king. The church was exempt from all taxation. Not sur-

prisingly, then, royal pressure on the nobility and the church to contribute more often led to rebellion.

When the demands of England's King John I exceeded the limits of what he was owed by custom, a group of nobles compelled him to sign the **Magna Carta** in 1215. Although this document restored the traditional rights of the barons and the clergy, especially protection from the king's excessive fiscal demands, its defense of "free men" created a powerful precedent for the rights of all subjects of the king, not just the nobility. Later generations used it to protect themselves from unlawful seizures and oppressive government. The king's need for financial aid from his free, property-owning subjects played a role in the

John I   (r. 1199–1216) King of England who lost most of his territory in France and was forced by nobles to sign the Magna Carta in 1215; known as John Lackland.

Magna Carta   A document confining the English king to his traditional rights and obligations, signed by King John in 1215.

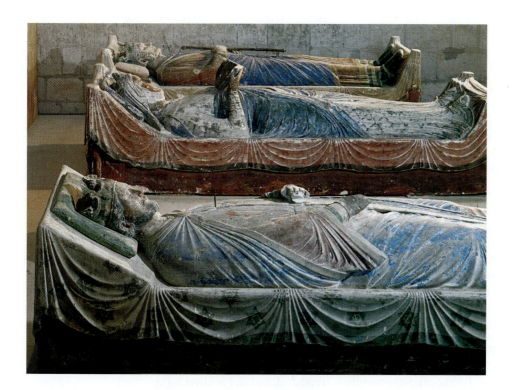

Whether Richard I, king of England, would have preferred being entombed so near his father is doubtful, but he would probably have appreciated laying next to his mother, Eleanor, his main support and ally in his wars against his father. *(Erich Lessing/ Art Resource, NY)*

emergence of a representative assembly, the English **Parliament.** When the king needed money, he met with representatives from the nobility, clergy, and merchants to request the amount. When these representatives used the meetings to raise issues of concern to them with the king, the interaction became a negotiation, though the king usually maintained the upper hand. In France, by contrast, the king never instilled in the nobility the expectation of financial support.

The Politics of Dynastic Families

Because the dowries of royal and noble daughters consisted of large amounts of money and even land, marriages at that social level often had important political consequences. Deprived of a direct role in political life, royal and aristocratic women served as the vehicles that transferred property from one family to another. The custom of not allowing women in possession of large amounts of territory to inherit noble and royal titles led to some of the period's most disruptive conflicts within and between families.

When **Eleanor,** the heiress of the duke of Aquitaine, married the heir to the French throne in 1137, the land she brought to the marriage more than doubled the size of the kingdom. Over fifteen years of marriage, Eleanor and Louis VII produced several daughters, but no sons. She acquired a reputation for bold, even

scandalous behavior at her husband's court, which was only heightened when she accompanied him to Syria on the Second Crusade and stayed close to the fighting. Well-educated, Eleanor gathered around her poets and intellectuals. For reasons having mostly to do with the lack of a male heir to the throne, Louis and Eleanor's marriage was **annulled** by the pope in 1152. She took all her lands with her out of the marriage. Louis married twice more before he had a son, Philip II Augustus. Two months after the annulment, Eleanor married Henry Plantagenet, duke of Normandy, count of Anjou, soon to become Henry II, king of England, in 1154. The new king and queen of England now held more land in the French kingdom than did Eleanor's former husband, Louis VII, king of the French.

Politics shaped King Henry's relations with his wife and children. He saw four of his five sons and three daughters all married to wealthy, titled men

Parliament   The representative assembly of England.

Eleanor of Aquitaine   (1122–1204) Queen of France and later queen of England, who inherited the province of Aquitaine in southwestern France.

annulment   Invalidation of a marriage as if it had never existed.

and women. The daughters married a German duke, a Spanish king, and a Neapolitan king. After his eldest son died, Henry had the next son, his namesake, crowned king in 1170. Eleanor made her third son, Richard, the duke of Aquitaine. Another son, Geoffrey, became the duke of Brittany through his marriage to the heiress of the province. Only John, the youngest, had to be content with nothing for the time being, thereby earning the nickname John Lackland. Henry's refusal to allow his sons a role in ruling the territories attached to their titles alienated both his sons and his queen. Henry the Young King led one unsuccessful revolt against his father and died during another. The surviving brothers continued to plot against their father. As punishment for her support of her rebellious sons, Henry had Eleanor imprisoned, where she remained for sixteen years until Henry died, in 1189. While her son Richard I was on crusade in the east, Eleanor ably administered the government of England. Richard's brother and successor, John I, could not prevent Philip, the French king, who was looking to increase the French royal domain, from capturing most of his land in France and thereby reducing his income by a third. By the mid-thirteenth century, the English kings held little more than Gascony in southwest France.

Over the thirteenth century, dynastic marriages between the French and English royal families punctuated an almost continuous state of hostility between the two kingdoms. In 1299, King John's grandson, Edward I, took as his second wife Margaret, the sister of France's King Philip IV, and married his son, the future Edward II, to Isabelle, the French king's daughter. The two marriages represented attempts at peace in recurring wars over Gascony. Tensions between the two kingdoms intensified in 1328, when the last of Philip IV's sons died. A long struggle for the French crown between descendants of the French royal family was about to begin.

The Holy Roman Empire and Frederick II

In the western empire, the successors to Otto III reinforced imperial control over church appointments. Not only had bishops become provincial governors, but the emperor had acquired a free hand in choosing the pope. With Emperor Henry III's selection of Leo IX, the first pope to make church reform a priority, the empire became the first battleground in the church's struggle to gain independence from secular interference. Despite seeming resolutions in the Investiture Controversy and the Concordat of Worms, the pope

and the emperor continued to contest each other's authority over clergy in the empire.

In the early twelfth century, a new dynasty, the Hohenstaufen, restored prestige and authority to the office of emperor. The ongoing rivalry between the papacy and the emperor over whose authority was superior made the new emperors highly conscious of their title's symbolic power, and so the empire now acquired a new name, the **Holy Roman Empire,** a political entity that would last until 1806. In the twelfth century, the designation *holy* signaled the emperor's claim to defend the church and to involve himself in its affairs. The first to designate the empire as "holy," **Frederick I** reinforced imperial power by claiming the same rights and laws wielded by the ancient Roman emperors, which became known collectively as **regalia.** Frederick's revival of Roman imperial authority was as short-lived as it was ambitious. He died, apparently of a heart attack, on his way to join the Third Crusade in 1190. His son who succeeded him, Henry VI, married Constance, heiress to the Norman kingdom of Sicily, who, because she was a woman, could wear the crown only as consort of her husband, not in her own right.

In 1198, Henry VI died. When his son, **Frederick II,** an infant, became the ward of Innocent III, the pope hoped to raise an obedient son of the church, but he was disappointed. Frederick's kingdom consisted not only of the Holy Roman Empire in the north but also, in the south, Sicily and southern Italy. In between lay the Papal States. In 1215, the year before he died, Innocent gave his approval to Frederick's being crowned emperor in Aachen—Charlemagne's old capital. Soon Frederick attempted to join the two portions of his empire by depriving Innocent's successors of their lands. He marched his armies through the Italian peninsula, causing the cities of Italy much suffering from urban warfare between factions loyal to him and to the pope. He also forced the Muslims from Sicily to leave the island and settle in a village in southern Italy, where he allowed them to practice their religion without hindrance but required them to pay heavy taxes and serve in his armies.

Holy Roman Empire   Name first used for the old eastern Frankish empire from the twelfth century on.

Frederick I   (r. 1155–1190) Emperor of the Holy Roman Empire known as Barbarossa ("Red Beard").

regalia   Instruments and symbols of either ecclesiastical or secular authority.

Frederick II   (r. 1197–1250) Emperor of the Holy Roman Empire and ruler of Sicily and southern Italy who engaged in a long war against the papacy.

Because he began his reign at such a young age, by the time Frederick II died in 1250 at least two generations of people living in the empire and in Italy could not remember a time when he had not been emperor. His great learning, military exploits, and reputation for both good and bad government led the people of his time to call him Stupor Mundi ("Wonder of the World")—an epithet he had no reason to reject.

The Instruments of Rule

As kings in France, England, and the Holy Roman Empire sought to centralize their authority, and popes sought to maintain theirs, written records became increasingly useful and in the thirteenth century proliferated. By 1300, many people in western Europe had reasons to consult a written document at least once in their lives. Managers of estates kept account books of inventories and sales of estate produce. Knights preserved charters to show they had rights to the land granted to them by their lords. Noblemen sent instructions to their vassals in letters. Merchants relied heavily on written documents to communicate with their partners and employees traveling on business and to keep accounts of the business they conducted.

By far, the record offices of secular rulers and popes produced the most documents. The chief secretary of a king's or pope's records acquired the title of **chancellor.** His responsibility was to draft letters in response to requests for the king's advice. At the start of the thirteenth century, the records of the French king traveled with him. By the end of the same century, the king's business had become so complex that it was necessary to store his correspondence and account books in a fixed, permanent place.

The commercial culture of Italian cities gave rise to needs that brought about changes in record keeping and legal documents for which customary law had few answers. Merchants looked to the law of the Roman Empire, specifically the Body of Civil Law, to supply legal formulas that would protect the interests of both parties to contracts. Two merchants forming a company or a short-term business venture called on a **notary**—a public official charged with drawing up legal documents—to write a contract with the proper legal formula. The revival of Roman business law and practice in the thirteenth century made merchants adept at the intricacies of loans, bills of sale, receipts, wills, and other documents involving the management of property.

Universities began to specialize in teaching law. At the University of Bologna, the most famous and prestigious of law faculties in the Middle Ages, law students absorbed principles of law and legal remedies through the study of Justinian's Body of Civil Law. Once graduated, as jurists, they applied their learning by writing opinions in court cases that judges referred to when making their decisions. Similarly, jurists reconciled Roman law with canon law. The law of the church governed the clergy, ecclesiastical property, and procedures against heretics, but it also covered matters of intimate concern to laypeople, such as penance, marriage, and wills. In many places in western Europe, inheritance and marital disputes were decided in ecclesiastical courts.

The influence of Roman law did not reach far north of the Alps. In southern France, Provence adapted Roman law to the needs of its merchants. Feudal law combined with royal law and statutory law prevailed in northern Europe. England developed a judicial system that had no comprehensive code book like the Body of Civil Law but relied instead on the accumulation of decisions rendered in past cases. England's **common law** was made applicable everywhere in the kingdom as the law common to all. Itinerant justices made regular circuits of the shires to hear the civil and criminal cases under the king's jurisdiction. Out of this system of law evolved the English legal system and, much later, that of the United States.

The Growth of Towns and Trade

> ↓ How and why did economies begin to grow in the eleventh century?
> ↓ How did trade encourage the growth of towns?

The expansion of church and royal authority from the eleventh through the thirteenth centuries owed much of its success to generally improved conditions in the countryside and to the growing concentrations of population at key points along expanding trade routes. More surplus on the land meant more food, but also more rents to pay to landowners. Merchants brought merchandise from the eastern end of the Mediterranean to sell to kings, nobles, and church officials. Negotiating one's way through the world was becoming increasingly complex—new technology, new courts,

chancellor Office of chief secretary in a king's household.

notary Public official who draws up private legal documents, like deeds and wills.

common law Body of English law and case precedents applicable to all free persons.

documents, taxes, and financial obligations. New opportunities for trade led some to traffic in human beings.

Expansion in Agriculture

Throughout the Middle Ages, land was the measure of most aspects of life. A person's wealth was measured by the amount of land in his or her possession. The amount of land under cultivation determined how much food was available. Toward the end of the tenth century, an increase in the amount of crop-producing land was accompanied by an increase in population, with the potential for that number to rise even higher. The increase in agricultural production came about as a result of a combination of factors, the most prominent of which were changing methods of field management and improvements in agricultural technology.

For much of the early Middle Ages, peasants, like the Romans before them, had divided their fields in two, left one half fallow, or uncultivated, for a year, and planted their crops in the other half. Fallow land replenished its nutrients, but the practice meant that half the land produced nothing every year. In southern Europe—with its drier climate—this system of two-field crop rotation continued, but in northern Europe, peasants improved on this system by dividing their land into three parts. One they left fallow, another they planted in the spring, and the third they planted with winter crops. This three-field crop rotation, dependent on more rainfall than southern Europe received, meant that two-thirds instead of half of a peasant's land was under production in one year.

Related to the changes in crop rotation were improvements in plows and animal harnessing. More land under cultivation spurred experimentation in the construction of plows. Peasants attached wheels to their plows, which made it easier for oxen to pull them through the heavier, wetter soil of northern Europe. A vertical blade, or coulter, made a narrow slice through the soil, followed by the plowshare, an iron-covered blade that cut horizontally. The moldboard tipped the cut soil over, creating the ridge of a row. Wheels made it possible for a plow to move more quickly down a row—provided it had a speedy animal pulling it.

Oxen are slow and unintelligent compared to horses. But because the strap that circles an ox's neck under a yoke would strangle a horse, peasants could not use horses to pull plows until they devised a different kind of harnessing. With a harness resting on its shoulders rather than its neck, a horse could be used to plow, and horses could walk more quickly and work longer hours than oxen. They also required

less guidance, since they understood verbal signals from the plower to turn or to stop.

Heavier, wheeled plows pulled by suitably harnessed horses meant that peasants could work more land in a day than ever before. Whether an increase in population across western Europe, but particularly in the north, stimulated innovations or whether such innovations contributed to a rise in the population, the cumulative effect of these changes in agriculture made itself apparent in the tenth century. Conditions in Europe were ripe for an economic and cultural upsurge.

Revival of Trade and Town

Even before the Crusades brought western Europe into increased contact with the people and markets of the eastern Mediterranean, trade and towns were on the rise. Travel was still dangerous, but merchants were willing to risk transporting goods long distances. By the late thirteenth century, a few merchants from Italy, like the Venetian Marco Polo, had even reached China. Greater surpluses in crops meant people had more to sell at market. More people and goods led to regularly held markets in the most populated location in a region. It would be impossible to say whether trade gave rise to towns or vice versa. What is clear is that each fostered the other in conditions of greater social stability.

Travel on trade routes increased, and some towns sprang up to provide rest and refreshment to traders. The distance between towns often corresponded to the distance that traders could cover in a day. Merchants kept their eyes open for customers with money to spend. Kings, lords, bishops, and their household dependents were good customers, eager to buy the luxury items merchants had for sale. Thus, royal, noble, and ecclesiastical residences became sites of markets for local and long-distance traders. In Champagne, in northeastern France, six large annual markets attracted merchants from all over Europe during the twelfth century. Their different currencies prompted the first development of banking techniques. With the use of coins now the norm, money-changers daily posted changing exchange rates so that merchants would know the worth of their coins in relation to the worth of other merchants' coins. The fairs of Champagne declined in the 1200s, when merchant galleys reached northern Europe through the Strait of Gibraltar. By 1300, trade had transformed life for the better throughout western Europe.

Italian seaports benefited from their proximity to the markets of the eastern Mediterranean. They became urban far faster than most towns north of the Alps. Because of their location, merchants from Genoa,

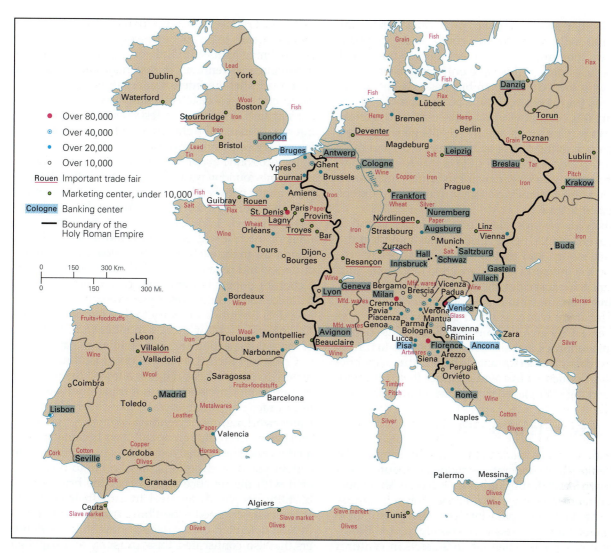

MAP 10.2 **Population and Economic Centers** Improved agricultural techniques contributed to the rise in population across most of Europe. Cities grew in size and population between the tenth and twelfth centuries, but few had more than a few thousand inhabitants. Which cities were the largest cities?

Venice, Pisa, and Amalfi functioned as middlemen carrying goods from the eastern Mediterranean to north of the Alps. In northern Europe, urbanization occurred at a slower pace. Towns grew fastest in the cities of **Flanders,** a region in modern-day Belgium, whose merchants took an active part in trade with the British Isles, the Baltic region, and, eventually, Italy. Starting in the thirteenth century, Flemish textiles, made with imported wool from England, were sold in markets all over Europe and the Mediterranean. By the beginning of the fourteenth century, commerce and manufacturing industries experienced explosive growth throughout western Europe.

Merchants and craftworkers organized themselves into **guilds** according to the goods they specialized in. Guilds for goldsmiths, masons, leatherworkers, furriers, carpenters, glassworkers, drapers, and many other skilled workers as well as merchants wrote

> **Flanders** Most urban region of northern Europe in the Middle Ages, today a province of Belgium.
>
> **guilds** Associations of merchants or craftworkers for mutual protection and regulation of their field of business.

statutes that governed their professional behavior and built halls in which they could meet. Members relied on their guilds to represent them to municipal authorities. Some guilds were only for master craftsmen, who owned their own businesses. Others also admitted **journeymen,** those who had completed apprenticeships and now worked in a master's business for a wage. Craftsmen and merchants generally had shops open to the public on the street level and their private residence above. In spite of the expertise they could acquire working in their husbands' businesses, women were generally excluded from guilds, except in the textile trade.

Urban life required new forms of government. A city government's highest priority was to protect the city's economy, and that almost always meant protecting the interests of its wealthy merchants and craftsmen. In most cities, the craft and merchant guilds effectively became municipal governments: what was good for trade was considered good for the city, and vice versa. City governments assigned guilds such as large warehouses that also served as hostels to traveling merchants; others granted them entire neighborhoods in which to live and conduct their business. The working poor played no political role in their cities.

The Interests of Business

For long-distance trade and manufacturing to be profitable, some cooperation among competitors was necessary for all the businesses to be secure. Merchants and craftworkers in western Europe formed companies that directed capital into potentially profitable ventures. Often business was a family matter. Brothers and sons pooled their family's assets in ventures designed to turn a profit. The younger male members of a family spent years working in the family's branch offices throughout Europe and the Mediterranean. Galleys bearing cargo and business correspondence voyaged several times a year in convoy for mutual protection against pirates.

To protect themselves from the hazards of sea travel and piracy—in addition to the risky nature of business ventures—merchants developed various kinds of contracts that allowed investors different degrees of involvement and profit. One kind of contract between two merchants promised greater profit to the partner who supplied most of the funds but stayed home than to the one who contributed fewer funds but traveled to purchase goods elsewhere. Early forms of insurance also offered merchants protection. Traders who understood how profitable long-distance trade could be also came to recognize how intricate the methods of turning a profit had become.

Not everyone who wished to conduct business had the means to do so. Borrowing money at interest enabled merchants with little or no capital to embark on commercial ventures. If they made back what they borrowed plus the interest and still had profit, their venture was a success. The church's view was different. On the basis of the Old Testament ban on charging interest, or **usury,** the church forbade interest-bearing loans between Christians. Since credit was essential to the economic expansion of the thirteenth century, merchants found ways around the prohibition. Written agreements between lenders and borrowers recorded only the amount to be repaid, thereby hiding the interest charged. Long-distance-trade merchants hid rates of interest—12 percent on ordinary loans was standard—in the exchange rates of loans made in one currency and repaid in another. What began as protection of poorer traders from richer ones inhibited bold economic initiatives. Over time, the church adjusted its definition of usury to the charging of *excessive* interest, to allow money to move into the hands of those who needed and were willing to pay for it.

Christians turned over the job of lending money mostly to Jews, whose religion allowed them to take interest from Christians but not from other Jews. For Jews practicing humble crafts like shoemaking and leatherworking, moneylending offered a chance for prosperity. Even though not all Jews became moneylenders and Christians, too, lent money at interest in certain places and periods, Jews came to be associated with the practice and to bear the brunt of the hostility people always feel toward their creditors. When cash-strapped King Philip Augustus of France in 1182 defaulted on his debts to Jewish moneylenders, he also confiscated their property and expelled them from his kingdom. He was not the only Christian king to deal with debt in this way.

The Trade in Slaves

Throughout the Middle Ages, goods from the Muslim world were in greater demand in western Europe than goods from the Christian world were in Muslim countries. Christian merchants supplied Muslim traders with three basic commodities: furs, timber, and slaves. Since the Carolingian period, Christians

journeymen (from French, "day") Skilled, salaried workers who labored for master craftsmen.

usury Originally, the charging of interest on a loan, revised in the later Middle Ages to mean the charging of excessive interest.

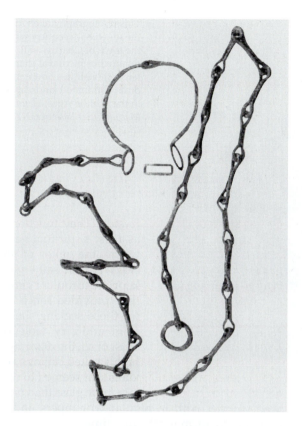

A slave trader restrained his captive by slipping the chain through the loops in the neck collar (top), fastening it securely, and then attaching the chain to the captive's limbs. Similar devices for controlling slaves while allowing them to walk were later used in other parts of the world. *(Courtesy of the National Museum of History, Sofia)*

from western Europe had sold slaves to Muslims on the southern shore of the Mediterranean. As long as western merchants had minimal contacts with their Muslim counterparts, the trade persisted on a small scale. When long-distance trade intensified over the eleventh and twelfth centuries, Christian merchants once again found the sale of slaves to Muslims a good way to make a profit—only, this time, they now found a growing market for slaves at home as well.

The word *slave* is derived from the word *Slav*, a general term for someone from eastern Europe or Russia. At certain times, Slavs constituted the majority of captives sold into slavery, but never for long. Yet the association between slavery and Slavs stuck. Traders native to the forested regions around the Black Sea captured men and women in the same places they logged for timber and hunted for animal fur. They made the slaves haul the timber and furs to Black Sea ports, where they sold them. Raiders stripped the is-

lands and coastlines of the Aegean Sea of its occupants and carried their captives to markets in Constantinople, Thebes, and Crete. Genoese and Venetian traders dominated the slave trade in the eastern Mediterranean, while the Catalans from Barcelona controlled the trade from North Africa at the western end.

In the twelfth century, most of the slaves Christian merchants sold came from North Africa, Sardinia, and Corsica. After the Fourth Crusade in 1204, Greeks, Turks, Tatars, Bulgars, Abkhazians, Georgians, Russians, Circassians, and many others fell victim to slavery. The old Viking trade in slaves along the Volga River continued well into the tenth century. Christian merchants met Muslim merchants in the slave markets of the old Byzantine ports around the Aegean Sea and in North African ports. Both were willing to pay high prices for slave women from north of the Black Sea, but Muslim merchants also bought large numbers of men to use as rowers on galleys and soldiers in their armies. The young women who constituted the majority of slaves sold to Christians in Italian and Spanish markets worked as domestic servants, unskilled laborers in crafts and trades, and sexual servants of their masters.

Muslims were forbidden to enslave other Muslims, and Christians of the Roman rite could not enslave other Christians of the Roman rite or, later, someone of western European descent. Nor were Christians allowed to sell Christians to Muslims. But Christian merchants defined *Christian* narrowly. For example, until the early fifteenth century, they considered Greek Christians to be heretics and so beyond the protection of the church. After the fall of the Byzantine Empire, the growing power of Turkish states in Asia Minor inspired Italian cities to bring Greeks within the circle of those protected by law from enslavement.

During the economic expansion of the thirteenth century, the number of slaves increased and the demand for them rose, especially in Italy and Spain. In 1300, the French conquerors of Italy sold the Muslims whom Frederick II had transported to southern Italy. Those cities with the most slaves were the same ones whose merchants dominated the trade: Barcelona, Genoa, Venice, and Palermo. The high cost of slaves made them luxury items, symbols of status. Great distances and the destitute origins of most slaves made redemption by relatives highly unlikely. At the close of the thirteenth century, the Mediterranean trade in slaves had not yet reached its peak. Before the focus of the slave trade shifted to Africa, both Christian and Muslim slave traders had swept up whole populations of the eastern Mediterranean into servitude. It was just getting started.

This photograph, taken in the nineteenth century when the town of Chartres still retained its medieval character, demonstrates how cathedrals dominated landscapes in the Middle Ages. *(Foto Marburg /Art Resource, NY)*

The Building of Cathedrals and the Spread of Learning

⬇ What did cathedrals do and symbolize?

⬇ How did knowledge and learning change and grow?

In the twelfth century, signs of increased prosperity were apparent not only in the marketplaces and the wealth of royal courts but also in the towns of western Europe, where enormous cathedrals were begun and new universities attracted communities of scholars and students. As townsfolk watched enormous churches rise up to the sky, they were aware of the benefits wrought by increased trade, better diets, social stability, and increased money in circulation. Teachers and scholars took learning to new levels and changed the nature of intellectual debate.

The Great Cathedrals

A trader with goods to sell approaching a large town in western Europe would have seen its cathedral first. These enormous churches, the seat of the bishop, were always taller than any other structure, though in the twelfth century many were still under construction. Cathedrals were an integral part of the revival of cities. Their magnificence reflected the growing wealth of the church. Their construction gave work to hundreds of people and drew workers in from the coun-

tryside. They functioned as a city's spiritual heart, where the relics of the city's patron saint were kept. In turbulent times, they provided sanctuary for those seeking shelter from arbitrary violence. Most of all, the dizzyingly high vaulted ceilings and walls that seemed to contain more glass than brick evoked wonder both in regular worshipers and in those who saw them for the first time.

In the early Christian period, churches tended to be built first and decorated later. Flat walls went up before mosaics and paintings were applied to them. In the tenth century, decorative stone sculpture on entries and columns required planning from the outset of construction. Two styles of cathedral architecture emerged. Incorporating elements taken from ancient Roman arches, the **Romanesque** style, popular in the eleventh century, had rounded arches over doors and window tops. The small windows and broad, unbroken wall space of cathedrals built in the Romanesque style made them resemble fortresses. Emerging in the mid-twelfth century, the **Gothic** style's central features were pointed arches on doorways and windows and ceilings pushed up to unprecedented heights. Because walls consisting more of brilliantly colored stained glass windows than of brick could not sup-

Romanesque   Style of architecture beginning in the eleventh century that evoked features of ancient Roman structures.

Gothic   Style of architecture that emerged in the mid-twelfth century and diverged from the slightly earlier Romanesque style in its pointed arches and the use of much more stained glass made possible by flying buttresses.

Notre Dame became one of the most recognizable buildings in the world. Even in the Middle Ages, when people associated the cathedral closely with the city of Paris. *(David R. Frazier/Photo Researchers)*

port heavy timber roofs, braces called flying buttresses propped up the exterior walls.

Such large buildings required innovative feats of engineering, and their costs put severe strains on episcopal and municipal treasuries. The long stretches of time when construction ceased for lack of funds help explain why cathedrals took a century or more to complete. In 1163, construction began on **Notre Dame de Paris,** one of the most impressive Gothic cathedrals in western Europe. Twenty years later, the area around the altar, the apse, was completed, followed nearly fifteen years later by the central aisle, or nave, which was covered by a timber roof 115 feet above the floor. It took another half century to complete the enormous round stained-glass window on the western wall and the decorations on the cathedral's façade. Generations of Parisians passed their lives in the shadow of a never-ending construction site. Only someone born after 1250 would have seen the cathedral that we still see today. Finished or not,

once the great towers went up, their visibility from a great distance gave a focus to travelers approaching Paris. In later years Notre Dame would be the site of coronations, royal weddings, and the most important public ceremonies in France.

From Cathedral Schools to Universities

In the late eleventh century, as part of the movement for church reform, cathedrals established schools where young men could prepare to become clergy. Aspiring scholars, too, found teachers in cities like Paris, Bologna, Pavia, and Salerno, whose bishops

Notre Dame de Paris   Cathedral of Paris, begun in 1163 and completed in the late thirteenth century.

licensed men who had demonstrated their expertise in a subject such as logic or theology to give lectures and organize students' readings. These masters acquired reputations for their deep knowledge of a subject or ancient author. When cathedral schools first started, students worked with one master until they were ready to move on to a master of another subject, who might live in another, distant town. By the mid-twelfth century, it became common for masters and students to converge on cities, like Paris or Bologna, where the one group would always be sure of finding the other.

The career of John of Salisbury, a secretary of Thomas Becket and a famous intellect in his own right, offers a good example of the education of a wandering scholar of the twelfth century. Born in England, in the 1130s John arrived in Paris as a young man to study under the most illustrious minds teaching in Europe at that time. There he studied with a succession of eight different masters of theology for more than ten years before, in 1150, he took the position of secretary to the archbishop of Canterbury in England. His education under those eight masters consisted of the seven liberal arts. When he had completed all seven courses, John achieved the level of master of arts, the ancestor of the modern postgraduate degree today.

By 1200, the large number of students seeking higher education forced the replacement of the loosely related cathedral schools with the more organized structure of a university. Universities acquired specialties. The University of Paris, founded in the late twelfth century, became the preeminent place to study theology. Bologna's university attracted students from all over Europe who wished to study law. Following study at one of these universities, young men entered not only church positions but also government service, as expanding royal bureaucracies needed men trained in letters and law.

But before they finished school, students worked and enjoyed themselves as much as their modern-day counterparts do. Twelfth- and thirteenth-century students stayed up too late, caroused, neglected their studies, and caused havoc in the cities. A group of cleric scholars, the Goliards, wandered from city to city, singing songs that celebrated gambling, drinking, and revelry.

When we are in the tavern,
do not think how we will go to dust,
but we hurry to gamble,
which always makes us sweat.
What happens in the tavern,
where money is host,

you may well ask,
and hear what I say.

Some gamble, some drink,
some behave loosely.
But of those who gamble,
some are stripped bare,
some win their clothes here,
some are dressed in sacks.
Here no-one fears death,
but they throw the dice in the name of Bacchus.

New Learning, New Thinking

Meanwhile ancient texts, both classical and Christian, continued to be preserved and copied in monastery libraries. The epics of the Roman poets fascinated the monks, who sought in such works as Virgil's *Aeneid* foreshadowings of the birth of Christ. They had copies of a few of Plato's works, which the fourth-century writings of Saint Augustine helped them to understand, but they struggled to understand Aristotle. Only a few of his texts were preserved in the west, and the isolation of monasteries made it difficult for monastic scholars to communicate with one another about their studies. Moreover, the monastic scholar's goal was to know a text and its author thoroughly, not to question them. The reasoning underpinning the text tended to be accepted at face value.

Beginning in the tenth century, however, a new generation of clerical scholars began to pay greater attention to how philosophy worked—in other words, to reasoning. Instead of relying on scriptural authority, scholars now aimed to support arguments with logic, the systematic principles of reasoning. Their aim to uncover the mysteries of the universe through applied logic came to be called Scholasticism. Scholastics like Anselm of Bec and Berengar of Tours believed the mind possessed the tools needed to understand God, while other intellectuals believed that God's essence could not be contained within human understanding. Anselm devised a famous proof of God's existence in the formula that God is "that than which no greater can be conceived." It was a brave attempt to apply logic to faith but easily refuted, as other scholars pointed out that the ability to imagine something, however great, did not mean that it necessarily existed. Other thinkers came up

logic   Systematic study of philosophical and theological propositions.

Scholasticism   School of theology that applied logic to matters of faith.

with logical proofs of God, but none withstood close analysis. Fierce debates galvanized students and scholars on one side or the other.

The career of one of the most brilliant scholars of the Middle Ages exemplifies the intensity of debate. **Peter Abelard,** who first described his field of study as theology, believed in the power of logic to answer all questions, and he put logic to use to debate and defeat his teachers with an arrogance that gained him enemies. While previous scholars had followed the prayer of St. Augustine—"I believe in order to understand"— Abelard reversed the sequence, asserting he wanted to understand in order to believe. His approach put him at odds with many church leaders, who insisted that faith had to remain a mystery. In their view, having proof of God's existence deprives humanity of the free choice to believe in a supreme being. Abelard, however, had his mind set as much on the means of his intellectual reasoning as he did on the ends. Higher learning's purpose was no longer exclusively spiritual. Abelard loved learning for learning's sake.

Abelard also loved a young woman named Heloise, whose reputation for great learning was widespread among the intellectuals of Paris. In addition to an excellent command of Latin and a knowledge of Greek, she could even read a little Hebrew, a language that practically no Christian in western Europe knew. Her uncle, a clergyman attached to the Cathedral of Notre Dame, hired Abelard to tutor her, and as Abelard admits in his autobiography, their tutoring sessions became love-making sessions. Their marriage, after she gave birth to a son they named Astrolabe, put an end to Abelard's career in the church. When Heloise's uncle learned of their marriage, he sent his niece to a convent and a band of men to Abelard's rooms, where they castrated him. Abelard retreated to a monastery, where he tried to revive his school, but church leaders vehemently opposed him. Called to an inquiry, he supplied an intellectual basis for faith and church doctrine. But his works were condemned and burned.

Debates over the utility of logic to answer questions of faith continued, however, especially after new translations into Latin, from Arabic, made Aristotle's *Metaphysics* and other previously unknown works available. These addressed the relationship of the natural world to the soul, and they forced monastic scholars to reconsider all they thought they had understood about Aristotelian logic. To help them understand these works, they also had commentaries written by Muslim scholars, translations of which reached them around the turn of the thirteenth century. The earliest commentator was **Avicenna,** a physician and philosopher in early eleventh-century Persia. His writings on Aristotle's medical and scientific works reached the scholars of Spain and then France in translations around the time Aristotle's new works arrived. Another Muslim philosopher, **Averroës,** wrote his influential interpretation of Aristotle's philosophy in Cordoba, Spain, where he was a judge and a jurist in the late twelfth century. In the same period in the same city, a Jewish philosopher and physician, **Moses Maimonides,** wrote interpretations of Aristotle's work in both Hebrew and Arabic. In his *Guide for the Perplexed,* he reconciled Aristotle's thinking with Judaism so clearly that Jewish communities across Europe and around the Mediterranean requested copies of the work. When the works of these three thinkers had been translated into Latin by Christian scholars working in Spain, they gave the scholars in northern Europe and in Italy much to ponder about the natural world and the role of God in it.

In the thirteenth century, a Dominican friar, **Thomas Aquinas,** became well known for his effort to reconcile Christian doctrine with Aristotelian philosophy. Thomas excelled at composing **summae,** treatises containing the "highest," or most complete, summary of a given topic. The most important of these was his *Summa Theologiae,* which he meant to be a complete statement of Christian philosophy. Although Thomas's brilliance gave him enormous influence over theological debates of this time, some church leaders objected to his attempts to render God and human existence perfectly intelligible. In 1270, a few years before he died, Thomas stood accused of trying to do the impossible: reconcile reason with faith. The bishop of Paris condemned as heretical portions of his *Summa* but accepted Thomas's essential position that logic prepares the mind for faith rather than determines it.

Peter Abelard (1079–1142) Brilliant theologian and charismatic lecturer in Paris, notable for his attempts to reconcile faith and reason.

Avicenna (ca. 980–1037) Persian physician and philosopher who specialized inAristotle's work relating to medicine.

Averroës (1126–1198) Important Muslim philosopher, born in Muslim Spain, whose interpretation of Aristotle's work were influential in Christian Europe.

Moses Maimonides (1135–1204) Jewish philosopher and physician from Muslim Spain whose *Guide for the Perplexed* and other works influenced Christian scholars interested in Aristotelian philosophy.

Thomas Aquinas (1225–1274) Dominican theologian whose works are a synthesis of Aristotelian philosophy and Scholasticism.

summae Works that seek to be the most complete statements about a subject.

Summary

Review Questions

↑ Describe the contest for authority between the papacy and secular rulers.

↑ How did Christian identity develop and change during the High Middle Ages?

↑ What new opportunities were available to the people of western Europe in this era? What new restrictions constrained them?

From the eleventh through the thirteenth centuries, church leaders carried out reforms aiming to set higher standards of behavior and belief for the clergy and the laity and to end lay interference in church affairs. Most notably, in the late eleventh century, Pope Gregory VII challenged Emperor Henry IV's right to invest the bishops in his empire with the symbols of their authority. Although Henry yielded to the pope's demand that he cease from interfering, secular control of church appointments continued to plague relations between the papacy and secular rulers. In 1215, the energetic Pope Innocent III oversaw the Fourth Lateran Council, whose decrees turned reform measures into law. At the same time, the laity, too, embraced the ideals of reform, taking vows of poverty and chastity to display the spirit of reform in their own lives. The papacy welcomed these efforts as long as the faithful acknowledged the church's spiritual authority.

At the end of the eleventh century, enthusiasm for an expedition to rid Jerusalem of nonbelievers surged beyond the power of the church to control it. Crowds headed east; some were armed, some were not, and some chose to attack perceived enemies of the faith closer to home, such as Jews, Muslims in Spain, and heretics in southern France. To the Byzantines and Muslims in the east, the Crusaders seemed like invaders. Shedding the blood of infidels and heretics in the name of God—holy war—became a growing obsession among many Christians and one more way in which the church extended its authority over Christian society in Europe.

Kings also sought to expand their authority, but their power did not increase at the same pace or in a uniform fashion. The new Norman kings of England benefited from institutions already in place when they conquered the island in 1066. In France, the kings applied brute force to increase their authority, capturing as much land as possible from the vassal who held more land within the kingdom than did the king himself. This vassal was the king of England, however, and thus was set in motion a contest that would continue into the following centuries. Meanwhile, successors of Otto started calling their empire the Holy Roman Empire to reinforce a claim to defend the church and to be actively involved in church affairs.

Kings of western Europe could extend their authority in large part because more of their subjects had property worth taxing. Improved agricultural technology increased food supplies. Long-distance trade revived, and towns grew. Merchants, craftsmen, and those who supplied services to them had more money than previous generations to spend on goods from near and far, to invest in business ventures, and to educate themselves. The church and inhabitants of the young cities devoted some of this wealth to building cathedrals, monuments to the glory of God. At new universities, scholars debated new approaches to learning and faith. In the High Middle Ages, everyone from peasants and townsfolk to kings experienced an improvement in the conditions of their lives. The question was: how long would it last?

← Thinking Back, Thinking Ahead →

What are some of the long-lasting consequences of the Crusades?

ECHO

Crusade

On September 16, 2001, in the wake of attacks by terrorists, President George W. Bush announced that the United States was going to war against terrorism. He cautioned the American people, "This crusade, this war on terrorism, is going to take a while." His use of the word *crusade* provoked a strong reaction from people in Arab nations, while it evoked barely a comment from people in the United States.

Osama bin Laden, leader of al-Qaeda, an alliance of the terrorist organizations, did not hesitate to turn the phrase back on the American president in issuing a call for jihad: "Bush left no room for doubts or the opinions of journalists, but he openly and clearly said that this war is a crusader war. He said this before the whole world to emphasize this fact." Bin Laden's perception of history and international policy rests on the enduring image of crusading in Muslim countries of the Middle East. The word *crusade* recalls the time when their lands were invaded by Christian armies, but Bin Laden also connected it to the early twentieth century. "Following World War I," he stated in his call, "which ended more than eighty-three years ago, the whole Islamic world fell under the crusader banner—under the British, French, and Italian governments." The reference is to European intervention in lands with majority Muslim populations, including Syria, Iraq, Saudi Arabia, and Lebanon. While the extreme views of Bin Laden do not reflect those held by the overwhelming majority of the world's Muslims, his reference to the Crusades of the twelfth century and the colonies of the twentieth century was comprehensible to Muslims in the Middle East in a way that it was not to Christians and Jews in the United States.

The power of words and history to incite people continues to complicate relations among Christians, Jews, and Muslims. When, in a university lecture in 2006, Pope Benedict XVI quoted a Byzantine theologian's negative assessment of Islam, Muslim leaders took it as an insult to their religion. Some Muslims saw the pope's words as further proof of the long-standing enmity the Christian west has displayed toward Islam. Why the series of armed migrations of western Europeans toward the east nearly a millennium ago still resonates in relations between Christians and Muslims is a question that the study of history can help answer.

Suggested Readings

Blumenthal, Uta-Renate. *The Investiture Controversy: Church and Monarchy from the Ninth to the Twelfth Century.* Philadelphia: University of Pennsylvania Press, 1988. A succinct introduction to the broad scope of the movement to reform the church.

Clanchy, Michael T. *Abelard: A Medieval Life.* Cambridge, Mass.: Blackwell, 1999. An insightful biography of one of the most brilliant minds of the Middle Ages.

Duby, Georges. *The Early Growth of the European Economy: Warriors and Peasants from the Seventh to the Twelfth Century.* Translated by H. B. Clarke. Ithaca, N.Y.: Cornell University Press, 1974. A classic of medieval economic history.

Radding, Charles, and William W. Clark. *Medieval Architecture, Medieval Learning: Builders and Masters in the Age of Romanesque and Gothic.* New Haven, Conn.: Yale University Press, 1992. A case for a change in the way intellectuals and architects of the Middle Ages reasoned based on the design of and space within cathedrals; filled with illustrations.

Richard, Jean. *The Crusades, c. 1071–c. 1291.* Translated by Jean Birrell. New York: Cambridge University Press, 1999. A comprehensive survey of the crusading movement from its origins to the fall of Acre.

Warren, Wilfred L. *Henry II.* New Haven, Conn.: Yale University Press, 2000. The standard history of the reign of one of England's most important kings.

Websites

Examples of medieval art from the best medieval museum in the United States, **The Cloisters, the Metropolitan Museum,** at www.metmuseum.org/events/ev_cloisters.asp?HomePage Link=collections_cloisters_l.

The British monarchy's webpage with an interesting overview of its own history, **History of the Monarchs of the United Kingdom,** at www.royal.gov.uk/output/Page5.asp.

Website and search engine with links to bibliography, sources, and other information relating to the crusading movement, **Crusades Encyclopedia,** at www.crusades-encyclopedia.com/index.html

CHAPTER 11

Reversals and Disasters, 1300–1450

CHAPTER OUTLINE

1500 B.C.E.	1000 B.C.E.	500 B.C.E.	1 B.C.E./1 C.E.

	1215 King John signs the Magna Carta				1305 Avignon papacy begins	1337 Hundred Years' War begins

1200	1220	1240	1260	1280	1300	1320	1340

Course of the Black Death

- ● City or area partially or totally spared
- Summer 1347
- June 1348
- December 1348
- June 1349
- December 1349
- June 1350
- December 1350

Fourteenth Century Peasant Revolts

- ✳ Main centers of popular revolt
- Main areas of rural uprisings
- Main area of the Peasants' Revolt in England, 1381
- Maximum area of Mongol control, 1259

Europe Ravaged from Within

Along the trade routes and sea lanes that linked Europe to the Middle East and Asia traveled merchants, pilgrims, and armies. These travelers also brought deadly diseases that killed a third to half the population of Europe. How long did it take the plague to travel from Italy to northern Europe?

500 C.E.   1000 C.E.   1500 C.E.   2000 C.E.

1347
Black Death first appears in Italy

1356
French defeated at Battle of Poitiers

1378
Great Schism begins

1417
Great Schism ends

1453
Fall of Constantinople
Hundred Years' War ends

1360   1380   1400   1420   1440   1460   1480

Choice Choice Choice

Joan of Arc

Key to the story of Joan of Arc are the men's clothing she wore. It was considered improper for women to dress like men, because it implied their ability to act like men. Though trial records indicate Joan wore male attire to her death, the illuminator depicts her at her execution in women's clothing. (Bridgeman-Giraudon/Art Resource, NY)

Joan of Arc Recants, Then Retracts Her Recanting

In 1428, Joan of Arc, a peasant girl around sixteen years of age from the French province of Lorraine, claimed to hear the voices of Saints Michael, Catherine, and Margaret. They told her she must convince the leaders of the French forces fighting the English to put her at the head of the army. Joan sought out the captain of the French army garrisoned near her village to ask him to send her to the dauphin, the late French king's uncrowned son and commander of the army. When the captain refused, Joan returned home. A year later, she tried again and this time received permission to make the eleven-day journey to the castle where dauphin was lodged. Dressed in men's clothing, Joan, accompanied by six armed escorts, reached the dauphin's court.

Perhaps the most extraordinary aspect of her story is that Joan, who had never before traveled far from her village, much less fought in a battle, succeeded in convincing the dauphin to let her lead the troops in an attack on the walls of Orléans in 1429. Against tremendous odds, the troops she led raised the siege. Still dressed in men's clothing and armor, Joan led French troops into other battles and opened the way into captured territory so that the dauphin could be crowned King Charles VII at the Cathedral of Rheims, the traditional site of royal coronations in France.

A year later, Joan was captured and kept prisoner by England's Burgundian allies. A court of English and Burgundian judges condemned her as a witch— someone who, they claimed, had dealings with the Devil—and a heretic. The judges sought to end the inspiration she could provide to the French, for the English were slowly losing ground to France in a war that would eventually last more than one hundred years. Just nineteen years old, Joan stood her ground before the judges. She refused to exchange her men's clothes for women's and to deny that the voices she heard came from Heaven. She refused to tell the judges what she had said to the dauphin to convince him to let her lead the French armies. She refused to acknowledge that the church's authority took precedence over the instructions she received from the voices. The judges threatened her with torture and made it clear that if she did not cooperate, she would be burned at the stake.

But after Joan was found guilty of witchcraft and heresy, and turned over to the secular authorities for execution, her courage faltered. Terrified of being burned at the stake, she signed a document in which she recanted, renouncing her voices and admitting that her claim to having heard them was heretical. The judges condemned her to life imprisonment and required her to give up the men's clothing she had worn since she first led the French army. Dressed once again in women's clothing, Joan entered her prison cell.

A few days later, her jailers found her in men's clothing once more. She put on the clothes she wore in battle to symbolize her decision to retract her recanting and once more to obey the voices of the saints that she believed she had heard. The possession of courage, it must be remembered, does not mean the absence of fear. Joan bravely went to her death at the stake in terror of the agony she was about to endure. After the war against the English ended, the people of France cherished the memory of Joan's short life and career as a soldier for her king. She became a symbol of France and in 1920 was canonized.

Introduction

Joan of Arc's appearance at the siege of Orléans at the head of the French army in 1429 coincided with a period in western European history when patriotic sentiments more than ever before bound people to their rulers. In previous centuries, that bond was often strained and weak, as the people of western Europe felt unprotected, even abandoned, by their rulers and also by the church. The change, however, had less to do with the order reestablished by rulers in their realms during the fifteenth century than it did with the government's and the church's manipulation of people's attachment to their town, region, country, and now their ruler.

The fourteenth century was a time of reversals and disasters. The growth of towns and trade slowed as colder, wetter weather in the north had a catastrophic effect on agriculture. Famine was ever-present, and then a terrifying illness, first seen in the port cities of the Mediterranean, spread across Europe. Men, women, and children, high and low, died in days, overnight, within hours. Meanwhile France and England were engaged in a long war, and in the east, Turks and Mongols made advances against the surviving portions of the Byzantine Empire. Three kings of England waged war on the Welsh, Scots, and the Irish when they were not fighting their own rebellious barons. To finance the fighting that was taking place all over the continent, rulers stretched their sources of revenue to their limits. Heavy taxes burdened people already oppressed by the climate changes and failed crops.

New, extended wars and new threats from the east made life seem much more precarious than it had been in the thirteenth century. The common people bore the brunt of the consequences of their rulers' territorial ambitions. From far away, reports of infidels marching right up to the frontiers of Christendom alarmed both governments and their subjects. The ancient Byzantine Empire was dwindling away under the pressure of first the Mongol and then the Turkish advances. A new empire ruled by the descendants of the warrior chieftain Osman took its place. The reality of the expanding Ottoman Empire pushing right up against Europe's borders put secular rulers and the pope on alert. After the process of steady economic expansion slowed and as the borders of Europe seemed threatened, few looked into the future with optimism. Survival was all.

Famine and Plague

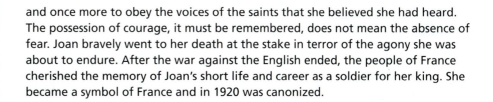

↓ What factors caused widespread death throughout Europe?
↓ What were the economic consequences of the plague?

By 1300, the benefits of more land in cultivation, increased long-distance trade, and strengthened royal authority were felt by many throughout western Europe. Population expanded: some 4 million people lived in the British Isles and 10 million or so in the Italian peninsula. More towns and villages dotted the landscape. People had a little more to eat, better clothes to wear, and a wider range of goods to buy. As long as the harvests were plentiful and families well nourished, the peasantry and townsfolk could look forward to living longer than previous generations.

The Spread of Hunger

Then, around the start of the fourteenth century, the weather and even the climate changed noticeably. Winters were colder and longer. Heavy rains poured down summer after summer on France, Germany, the Low Countries, and England, depriving crops of warmth and sunlight. The seasonal changes peasant farmers relied on to determine when to sow their crops grew undependable. Cities on the coastlines of northern Europe experienced severe flooding. In the North Atlantic, sheets of ice permanently covered Greenland, so named when its land had been green, not white. The inhabitants of England and the Low Countries turned to brewing beer instead of making wine once the colder weather put an end to grape

Chronology

1261	Michael VIII Palaeologus recaptures Constantinople
1301	Pope Boniface VIII issues *Unam sanctam*
1305	Clement V becomes pope; Avignon papacy begins
1323	Flanders revolt begins
1346	English defeat French at Battle of Crécy
1347	Black Death first appears in western Europe
1356	English defeat French at Battle of Poitiers
1358	Jacquerie revolt takes place in France
1360	Truce ends first phase of Hundred Years' War
1361	Ottomans conquer Adrianople
1378	Gregory XI returns papacy to Rome
1378	Great Schism begins
1378	Ciompi Revolt takes place in Florence
1381	Peasants' Revolt takes place in England
1402	Timur (Tamerlane) invades Anatolia
1409	Council of Pisa attempts to solve problem of multiple popes
1415	Henry V defeats French at Battle of Agincourt
1415	Revolt in Bohemia following the execution of the religious reformer John Hus
1417	Council of Constance resolves Great Schism; Martin V becomes pope
1429	Joan of Arc defeats English at Orléans
1453	Constantinople falls to Ottomans; Hundred Years' War ends

cultivation there. The **Little Ice Age** had descended on northern Europe.

To make matters worse, much of the previous century's increase in agricultural production had occurred in regions with rocky, unsuitable soil. Signs of soil exhaustion appeared early in the fourteenth century. Because it now took more seed to yield the same amount of crops as before, peasants had to put aside a larger share of their grain for the next year's sowing. Meager harvests in the years when rains did not wash away the entire crop meant less food for the peasant family and less to sell at market. A ten-acre plot of land would have fed a peasant family a generation earlier, but no longer. The land was overworked.

By 1315, rain, colder weather, and soil exhaustion had created the conditions for a severe famine across much of northern Europe. Failed crops and the difficulties of transporting food from where it could be found to where it was needed meant that most people experienced the pain of hunger, and thousands starved to death. Those who lived were weak and malnourished. The famine lasted three years, faded, and then recurred intermittently in succeeding decades whenever harvests were poor. Livestock, too, declined, and peasants resorted to eating whatever they could

find: cats, dogs, rodents, and horses. By the middle of the fourteenth century, northern Europe's population increases had been reversed.

Fear of starvation set people in motion. From the northern English city of York to the trading posts of Poland, rain, flooding, and perpetual winter turned thousands of people into refugees. Villages became ghost towns, while cities became temporarily overcrowded, until their populations, too, succumbed to starvation. Entirely dependent on grain imports to feed its inhabitants, the population of the manufacturing city of Ypres in the Low Countries fell drastically in 1317. Bands of beggars roamed the countryside, while in cities most crimes involved theft of food. Municipal authorities ordered the town gates locked at night. Like the Frankish kings of the early Middle Ages, secular rulers could offer little protection to their subjects. Disorder prevailed, and for most people, the situation could not have gotten much worse.

Little Ice Age   Period of cooler weather in Europe beginning around the start of the fourteenth century.

The Specter of Death

And then it did. In the summer of 1347, a deadly plague, later called the **Black Death,** swept across western Europe. The symptoms were unlike any seen before. Swollen, bruised lumps on the lower abdomen, in the armpits, or on the throat were the first indicators. Lymph glands swelled to the size of an egg or larger in the groin and armpits. If the glands burst, causing internal hemorrhaging, the suffering was unbearable and death was inevitable. If they did not, then the victim might survive, but most often they burst. Someone retiring to bed in the evening with a slight fever might never wake up. An airborne form of the bubonic and pneumonic plague affecting the lungs could bring death within hours. Other symptoms— bruises and spots appearing all over the body—led some physicians (and a few modern historians) to wonder if more than one disease was at work.

Most historians agree that the disease that made death a daily, if not hourly, possibility was the bacillus *Yersinia pestis*, or bubonic plague, so called for the inflamed swellings, or buboes, of the lymph glands. Beginning in Central Asia, spreading westward into the Byzantine and Turkish territories, the plague was carried—though its victims did not know it at the time—by fleas on rats. Rats hidden on vessels heading west carried the disease to the Aegean Islands and then to Sicily, where it was first seen in September 1347. Six months later, the disease had spread north to Florence, where it killed half the population between March and September 1348. Over the course of 1349, the plague spread across Spain and northern Europe, reaching eastern Europe in 1350. Between a third and a half of the people of Europe died.

The cities and towns of Italy were hardest hit, for they had the greatest concentrations of population. In Florence, the devastation was reported in *The Decameron* by the poet and storyteller **Giovanni Boccaccio:** "Many dropped dead in the open streets, both by day and by night, whilst a great many others, though dying in their own homes, drew their neighbours' attention to the fact more by the smell of their rotting corpses than by any other means. And what with these, and the others who were dying all over the city, bodies were here, there and everywhere." After the first wave, the plague repeatedly flared up and then died down again. It recurred every ten years or so until the early fifteenth century, when the number of outbreaks increased even more.

Physicians had few remedies for the suffering taking place around them. Weakened immune systems made people vulnerable to other diseases, such as smallpox and influenza, the symptoms of which com-

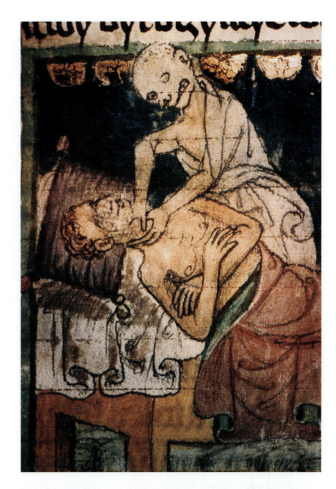

This fourteenth-century illumination from a collection of sermons by Thomas of Stitny, a Czech cleric, depicts strikes at people's fear about the bubonic plague. The disease could take hold so quickly that people died in their sleep hours after contracting it. *(Werner Forman/Art Resource, NY)*

plicated physicians' understandings of what they observed in their patients. Because the number of deaths in heavily populated areas was so high, physicians believed the disease spread by contact between persons. Because everyone, not just physicians, lacked an understanding of germs, poor hygiene and filth contributed to the spread of disease. The only option open to medical men and the women who worked more informally as healers was to fall back

Black Death Epidemic of bubonic plague that killed one-third to one-half of the people of Europe between 1347 and 1351.

Giovanni Boccaccio (1313–1375) Influential Florentine author of *The Decameron* and other literary works.

The "Dance of Death" became a common scene in manuscript illuminations, frescoes, and statuary. Even though the poor died in greatest numbers, the figure of Death is depicted here leading off to the afterlife people of all social ranks, including, as seen here, a pope, an emperor, and a noble woman. *("The Dance of Death"[detail], 1463, attributed to Bernt Notke. St. Nicolai's Church, Tallinn, now the Niguliste Museum)*

on methods familiar to them: astrology, bloodletting, and herbal medicine. Inadvertently, some of these methods may have helped in certain situations, but in general, physicians proved to be as helpless as the rest of the population in the face of the plague's virulence. Mostly, they simply urged people to flee the congested areas where the plague was rampant. But the working poor and the destitute had nowhere to go, and so the plague claimed more victims among the humble than among the rich, who fled to their country estates. Parents abandoned their children, children abandoned their parents, and priests deserted their flocks.

Endurance and Adaptation

In the face of so much suffering and death, the people of Europe searched for spiritual comfort and some means of understanding the disasters. Rulers could do little for their people; nor could the church offer much in the way of physical relief. Locally, the comfort church services and rituals could provide depended largely on the survival and courage of local priests. Many laypeople sought a deeper involvement in religious life. Others, believing that God had abandoned humanity because of its sins, assumed a despairing, cynical attitude toward life. In the face of so much inexplicable death, it took fortitude to survive.

Death preoccupied everyone everywhere. Poets personified death in their poems, and writers such as Boccaccio described the devastation. In *The Canterbury Tales,* the English poet **Geoffrey Chaucer** created characters who were hardened by the deaths of so many around them.

Some felt the need to take responsibility for the catastrophe by joining penitential groups. Believing that the plague represented God's punishment for their sins, people living mainly in cities flocked to join **confraternities,** associations dedicated to the performance of acts of charity and whose processions through city streets were now meant as public penance. A few groups went to extremes by ritually whipping themselves in public. When the **flagellants,** as they were called, drew blood with their scourges, they drew the admiration of some and aroused the revulsion of

Geoffrey Chaucer (1343–1400) English poet most famous for *The Canterbury Tales,* a collection of stories in verse.

confraternities Associations dedicated to the public performance of acts of charity and penance during the plague.

flagellants Groups who ritually whipped themselves in public to atone for the sins of humanity during the plague.

others. Groups of flagellants had existed in the thirteenth century, but their popularity waned after the church condemned their activity in 1261. After the plague hit, flagellants went from town to town in processions, scourging themselves as they walked, until, in 1349, Pope Clement VI again condemned the activity.

Others felt the need to blame someone else, and Jews proved to be convenient scapegoats. Across Europe, whole communities of Jews died at the hands of rioting Christians who believed that the Jews had poisoned the water supply or in some other mysterious way introduced the disease. Such persecutions caused some Jews to leave western Europe, migrating east toward Poland and Russia, where they remained in large numbers until the twentieth century, or southeast toward Muslim lands, where they received a slightly warmer welcome.

Economies Under Stress

At first the commercial boom of the thirteenth century continued into the fourteenth century. The economic outlook in long-distance trade looked much brighter than did the outlook in local agricultural production. Refinements in merchants' arrangements, improvements in navigation, and the development of new commercial techniques in the decades prior to the arrival of the plague helped keep economies going during difficult times. Long-distance trade had become so complex that merchants reorganized the ways in which their companies operated. Each company delegated its business among the merchants who remained at the company's base to manage the business, the operators of the ships that conveyed the company's goods from market to market, and the agent-representatives residing in foreign cities who oversaw the buying and selling of those goods. Regular convoys of galleys bearing goods and mail between merchants and their home offices made the networks of trade run more smoothly and profitably.

The same commercial networks benefited from improvements in navigation. Not only were oar-driven galleys redesigned to hold more cargo, but a new type of vessel was introduced to the Mediterranean trade. Round-hulled sailing vessels called cogs, which, with their small crews and great storage capacity, had been developed for the rough waters of the Atlantic Ocean and the Baltic Sea were adapted for use in the smoother waters of the Mediterranean. Still, galleys, whose oars offset the disadvantages of low wind, remained the principal means of Mediterranean naval transport until the eighteenth century. In the fourteenth and fifteenth centuries, the governments of Venice, Genoa, and Florence annually sponsored enormous convoys of merchant galleys to Flanders, England, Crete, the Black Sea, and the ports of the Levant.

The two major trading regions continued to be the Mediterranean and the Baltic Sea. In the Mediterranean, the merchants of Venice, Genoa, and Barcelona dominated maritime trade. Nobles, kings, manufacturers, and even popes took advantage of the credit services offered by Florentine merchants, whose interest rates for loans were far below those of merchants elsewhere. In Florence, too, the government promoted schools where aspiring merchants learned basic arithmetic, bookkeeping, and business practices, a policy that Genoa and Venice emulated. On the Baltic Sea, the city of Lübeck (in present-day northern Germany) was unrivaled in the import-export traffic that passed through its port. In 1358, it became the official headquarters of the Hanseatic League, an association of German merchants with branches throughout the Holy Roman Empire.

Yet even before the plague hit western Europe, trade with the eastern end of the Mediterranean had begun to decline, and economies were weakening. Migrations and disturbances far to the east in Central Asia and China made the long treks to the markets there increasingly difficult. Muslim conquest of the Black Sea region also hampered Christian trading in the east. Venetians, Genoese, and Catalans still traveled to the Black Sea to do business, but Muslim merchants offered them stiff competition. Then, with famine and plague, population decreases and the disruptions of warfare, the demand for luxury goods decreased. Many trading companies went bankrupt.

Overall, the economic consequences of the plague were mixed. Death emptied rural areas of workers, causing rents to fall. At the same time, although some cities experienced an increase in population—mostly refugees from the countryside—the scarcity of labor drove up wages. Skilled and unskilled workers earned more than ever before, but had less to buy than they would have had at the start of the century. By the middle of the fifteenth century, population levels had still not recovered, trade with the east was still difficult, and the people of Europe had learned to endure the new realities of a frightening world.

---

scapegoats   Any group that innocently bears the blame of others.

cog   Sailing cargo ship with a rounded hull.

Hanseatic League   (from German *hansa*, "trading association") Association of north German merchants formed to protect their trading interests.

One Hundred Years of Warfare

> ↓ What caused the Hundred Years' War, and why did it last so long?
>
> ↓ How did the war create national sentiment in the English and the French?

Famine and plague arrived in the midst of a war between France and England that continued, intermittently, for more than one hundred years. The war began for dynastic reasons, created at the time of the Norman Conquest, when William, the duke of Normandy, added king of England to his titles and lands across the English Channel to his realm. Henry II inherited his great-grandfather's lands in northern France and, through his marriage to Eleanor, assumed control of the Aquitaine, making him a greater landowner in France than the French king. By the end of the thirteenth century, the French king had deprived the English king of most of his lands in France and was intent on taking them all.

Buildup to War

Frustrated by their loss of land and revenue in France, the English kings of the thirteenth century looked northward to Scotland to compensate for their losses. Scottish barons resisted English sovereignty over Scotland in a series of rebellions between 1295 and 1304. Prominent among the rebel lords was **Robert Bruce,** who exploited the dissension among the barons to claim the throne of Scotland. He was crowned in 1306, an event that did not stop Edward I—and afterward his son, Edward II—from pressuring the Scottish king to become a vassal of the English king. With France's support, King Robert's army inflicted a decisive defeat on the English army at Bannockburn in 1314. Another fourteen years passed before, in the Treaty of Northampton, the English crown formally—but, in practice, only temporarily—recognized Robert as king and renounced all claims to overlordship in 1328.

By then, a new king sat on the throne of England. Only sixteen years old in 1328, **Edward III** was too young to reign on his own, but not too young to marry. The regents—his widowed mother, Queen Isabella, sister of the French king, and her lover, Roger Mortimer—arranged Edward's marriage to Philippa of Hainault to cement an alliance with William, count of Hainault and Holland. The marriage sent a signal to the French king, Charles IV, not to make further incursions into **Guyenne,** the English territory in southwestern France that included Gascony and the

Aquitaine, and to cease undermining English authority there. But then Charles's death, with no male heir to succeed him, caused a dilemma. The French nobles could choose the late king's cousin or his nephew, son of his sister. In addition to a prejudice against the female line of succession, crowning the nephew posed a special problem because the nephew was Edward III, already king of England. Thus the majority of French noblemen instead supported his cousin, who was crowned king of France in 1328 as Philip VI, the first of the Valois dynasty.

To most observers of these dynastic disputes, war between the English and French kings, with Scotland in alliance with France and the Low Countries sympathetic to England, seemed increasingly likely from this point on.

An Occasional War

Within a decade, the conflict had begun. The nobles of Guyenne were divided between those who supported King Edward's overlordship and those who preferred the direct lordship of the king of France. Each side repeatedly tested the limits of authority, leading to occasional outbreaks of violence. By the late 1330s, Edward III believed the only way to compel the French king to accept England's sovereignty over Guyenne was to defeat him in war. In 1337, what would eventually be known as the **Hundred Years' War** began.

In 1338, Edward arrived in Flanders with an army, hoping that his presence on France's northeastern frontier and his army in Guyenne in the southwest would squeeze the French king into compliance. But the first six years of war produced little result. Short of money and soldiers and now calling himself king of France, Edward avoided the French king's larger army until August 1346, when, at **Crécy,** he arranged

Robert Bruce   (r. 1306–1329) King Robert I of Scotland, who successfully resisted English attempts to impose lordship over his kingdom.

Edward III   (r. 1327–1377) King of England whose claim to the throne of France was largely responsible for the Hundred Years' War.

Guyenne   Region in southwest France, originally a part of Aquitaine, under English rule from the twelfth to the mid-fifteenth century.

Hundred Years' War   (1337–1453) The long conflict between the kings of England and France.

Crécy   Battle in 1346 between English and French armies in which the English gained advantage with the longbow and France lost much of its nobility.

At the battle of Crécy in 1346 in northeastern France, the six-foot tall long bow, carried by the archers in the right-hand foreground of this fifteenth-century manuscript illumination, played in instrumental role in the English army's devastating victory over French forces. *(Bibliothèque Nationale de France/The Art Archive)*

his troops across a low rise and faced oncoming French forces. He had only 4,000 men-at-arms and 10,000 archers, but the archers had **longbows** that shot arrows faster and farther than the crossbows of the French archers. A shower of English arrows destroyed the first contingent of French crossbowmen and then the cavalry of French nobles. Their superior position and the success of the longbows allowed the English army to wipe the much larger French army from the field, where France's greatest nobles lay dead. Ten years later, Edward III's son, Edward—called the Black Prince for the color of his armor—repeated his father's victory at **Poitiers** in 1356: the longbowmen again overwhelmed an attack of mounted French nobles, with the same lethal results. This time, the king of France, John II, was captured, taken to England, and held for ransom. The humiliation of the French aristocracy and monarchy seemed complete.

After the catastrophic French defeat at Poitiers, diplomacy produced a truce in 1360. Despite provocation, neither side was prepared to continue the fight. Edward III's death in 1377, one year after the death of his son, the Black Prince, meant that Edward III's grandson, Richard II, a boy too young to lead a war, ascended the English throne. The war seemed to be over.

But it was not yet half over. In its first phase the war was not so much between the countries of England and France as it was between the kings of England and France. To persuade his subjects to finance his war through taxation, Edward III fostered a connection between the crown and the people by holding a series of public pageants to celebrate his army's victories. As long as the English army was winning, he succeeded. Since the French were unable to mount an invasion of England, the English people did not suffer from warfare as did the people of France. In France, on the other hand, support for the war had never been strong. From the start, the people of northern France, where most of the fighting occurred, viewed

longbow Bow six feet high that had been used by the Welsh to resist the English and then adopted by the English army, where it proved decisive in Edward III's battles in France.

Poitiers Battle in 1356 that marked the second defeat of the French army by the English, during which the French king was captured and held in England for ransom.

In a fifteenth-century chronicle of the Hundred Years' War, an illumination shows soldiers opening barrels of wine, drinking from them, and carrying off the furnishing of a house in Paris. Soldiers' violence against civilians caused nearly as much harm as their warfare. *(Erich Lessing/Art Resource, NY)*

were captured by noblemen of the opposing army, they could also expect financial ruin from the enormous ransoms their families would have to pay to liberate them from captivity. Common soldiers taken captive by nobles could expect death. Evading capture at all cost—even if that meant leaving the field prematurely—led to chaos on the battlefield.

King Edward of England, in contrast, led a different type of army. He hired commanders through contracts binding their service. The commanders promised to recruit a certain number of troops, equipped with agreed-on types of weaponry, for predetermined lengths of military service. Long experience had taught the kings of England that relying on the feudal army meant going to war with an insufficient number of troops and that recruiting commoners led to an armed population capable of rebellion. A system of paid contingents was expensive, but more reliable.

During the Hundred Years' War, deliberately inflicted violence became military policy. The Black Prince instituted a strategy of terror to undermine the morale and economic resources of the French. Companies of mounted fighters and foot soldiers stormed throughout northern France, burning crops and houses they came across and randomly killing anyone they encountered. These campaigns of terror, known as *chevauchées,* were a brutal way to wage

the dispute as their ruler's problem. Sieges of ports and cities focused the hardship of warfare on civilians as much as on soldiers. When the French king was captured, the government of his eldest son, known as the **dauphin,** exacted heavy taxes from the population to raise the huge ransom. By 1360, the people of France had had enough of the war—but the periods of peace were beginning to take their toll as well.

Violence Against Civilians

Military commanders in the fourteenth century faced considerable difficulties in controlling their armies on and off the field of battle. The source of their difficulties lay chiefly in methods of recruitment and in the periods of demobilization. Feudal service, mass **conscription,** mercenary forces, or a combination of all three each had advantages that were often outweighed by the disadvantages of poor accountability, the political consequences of an armed peasantry, and the chaos created by out-of-work professional fighters.

The French army was made up largely of noblemen and their troops who fought out of loyalty to their king, to whom they owed feudal service. Military discipline did not emerge easily from the feudal army, bound together as it was by a loose sense of common purpose among quasi-autonomous troops under the French king. Although an informal code of **chivalry** meant noble combatants could expect mercy if they

dauphin   Title of the eldest son of the king of France, usually the heir to the throne.

conscription   Military draft; involuntary recruitment of soldiers from among the people.

chivalry   Code of military and courtly conduct among the nobility that valued mercy in battle, Christian duty, and defense of women.

chevauchées   (in French, "horse charges") Mounted warriors whose purpose was to destroy crops and terrorize the people of the countryside.

1337
(before the Battle of Crécy)

English holdings
French holdings
Extent of English holdings after Treaty of Paris, 1259

1360
(after the Battle of Poitiers)

English holdings
French holdings
✕ Major battles

ca. 1429
(after the siege of Orléans)

English holdings
French holdings
Burgundian lands allied with England to 1435
✕ Major battle

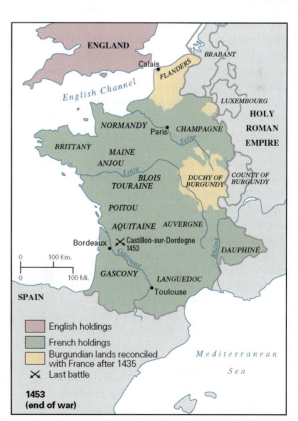

1453
(end of war)

English holdings
French holdings
Burgundian lands reconciled with France after 1435
✕ Last battle

MAP 11.1 **Hundred Years' War** As the sequence of four maps showing the stages of the Hundred Years' War indicates, a large proportion of the kingdom of France came under the rule of the English king after 1360. By the 1430s, France stood in danger of becoming entirely a possession of the English king.

war that stood in contrast to the often gallant consideration knights and nobles showed to enemy combatants of their own social rank. This form of warfare extended far beyond the boundaries of battlefields.

Many parts of France had no peace, for people had as much to fear from the cessation of fighting as they had from pitched battles and long sieges. If the soldiers were not fighting, they were not paid. So between military campaigns, companies of unemployed soldiers moved from place to place, looting as they went or demanding to be paid off instead. It was abundantly clear that neither the king nor the nobility could provide protection for their subjects or for the kingdom as a whole.

The Final Stage

In 1399, Edward III's grandson, the former boy-king Richard II, had alienated his nobles so severely that they forced him to abdicate at the age of thirty-two. In his stead, his cousin, Henry of Bolingbroke, leader of the rebel nobles, became King Henry IV. Viewed as a usurper of the English throne by many, Henry successfully put down Scottish raids on the border, Welsh assertions of independence, and powerful English nobles who made their own attempt to capture the throne. In 1413, Henry IV died with his claim to the English throne and his son's succession secured.

This son, **Henry V,** revived the claim to the French throne. Since Henry needed money and moral support to carry out his military ambitions, he organized a campaign to win the hearts of all his subjects, noble and commoner alike. Priests delivered sermons espousing justifications for war. The bishop of Rochester even insisted to his congregation that since God was an Englishman, they had a duty to fight for England. Triumphal processions filled with colorful floats carried religious and royal symbols whenever the king left for war or returned from France. The crowds lining the streets to see the processions were moved to feel pride and loyalty. The people of England came to think of themselves as united in being English.

After forming a secret alliance with the duke of Burgundy, for a while the regent ruling in place of the intermittently mad French king Charles VI, Henry V took his army across the English Channel. In September 1415 at **Agincourt,** the French army went down to defeat for the third time. Henry quickly annexed Normandy while the dauphin organized an army in the south of France. When the English army laid siege to Orléans, southwest of Paris, the town's stiff resistance slowed their advance. That was when **Joan of Arc** (see Choice) convinced the dauphin that the voices she heard told her she could raise the siege. Inspired by her courageous leadership, the French army gained decisive victories that undermined the alliance between the English and the Burgundians. After the duke of Burgundy made his peace with Charles VII in 1435, the French army slowly recaptured nearly all the territory that the English had taken. When the French army captured Guyenne in 1453, all the English king had left in France was the port of Calais. The conflict that had lasted more than one hundred years was over.

The peoples of England and of France paid a heavy price for their kings' century-long war. Overtaxed, the English grew tired of King Henry's military adventure. Overburdened and underfed, the French endured sustained and serious losses in crops, income, and lives. Yet, despite the suffering, the peoples of England and of France now each regarded their kings as symbols of their country. The kings' needs to rally support and raise funds for the war forged a new bond between rulers and their subjects, the strength of which was tested repeatedly. For France, the ultimate victor despite losing so many battles, the war also united French territory, at least theoretically.

Resistance and Revolt

↓ What elements did the revolts of the fourteenth century have in common?
↓ From which ranks of society did the rebels emerge?

Famine, plague, and war brought the people of Europe much to endure. When bonds between kings and their subjects strengthened, many were emboldened to ask their rulers for greater freedom and political participation, especially since they had to pay heavy taxes. But when their hopes for protection, relief, and political rights were disappointed, many vented their frustrations on those they held responsible for their problems. Across Europe, and throughout the fourteenth century, revolts broke out and were ultimately put down.

Henry V (r. 1413–1422) King of England who revived the Hundred Years' War.

Agincourt Battle in 1415 in northern France in which the army of Henry V defeated the army of Charles VI of France.

Joan of Arc (1412–1431) Peasant girl who led French troops to victory over the English at Orléans in 1429; later captured by the English and burned at the stake as a witch.

Flanders

The cities of Flanders, just beyond France's northeastern border, were among Europe's largest by the end of the thirteenth century. Bruges was a commercial hub. Ghent, with more than sixty thousand inhabitants, ranked second only to Paris in population. These cities owed their size and economic vitality to the textile industry. From England came vessels carrying bales of raw wool, which would be washed, carded, spun, woven, fulled, dyed, and finished as cloth before being sent out from Flemish cities along trade routes heading south toward the Mediterranean and north toward the Baltic ports. The process of turning wool into cloth involved both rural and city workers. Although textiles made many Flemish cloth producers wealthy, the economy nevertheless depended largely on agricultural production, mainly grain, and on livestock on rural estates belonging to the merchant families in the cities. Whoever ruled Flanders stood to benefit richly from custom duties and taxes.

By 1320, the Flemish found themselves caught between the French king, on the one hand, and the English king, on the other. Their own ruler, Louis, count of Flanders and a vassal of the French king, favored the French, though it was clear that the French king was interested primarily in revenue from taxation and customs duties. Louis' subjects felt differently. Dependent heavily on the wool trade with England, Flemish peasants and merchants resented the heavy tax burdens the count imposed on them as well as the pressure the French king put on their economy. They had already pushed the French out of their territory when a Flemish army defeated the French king's army at Courtrai in 1302. Just when their economy was improving, not only were the count's taxes crushing them, but his corrupt government was making him wealthy at their expense.

In 1323, peasant farmers in the countryside rioted against the count's oppressive taxation. Well-to-do textile merchants and less well-off workers in the city allied with them and forced the governors of their cities to flee. Ghent, Bruges, Ypres, and other cities of Flanders formed a federation of rebel governments, with city councils and an administration made up of rebels from the upper levels of Flemish peasant and urban society. The first action the new rulers took was to cancel tax collection. They organized themselves into an army that met and defeated the count's forces on more than one occasion.

The Flanders revolt that began in 1323 changed character over the five years it lasted. What began as a tax revolt of prosperous merchants and peasants against the count of Flanders eventually gained the support of poorer peasants and workers in the cities. Ordinary people spoke out against the privileges of the nobility. Popular preachers delivered sermons that advocated social equality. Once the revolt took on characteristics of a social revolution, the count and the Flemish nobles appealed to the French king for help.

In the summer of that 1328, the French king sent an army through the cities and countryside of Flanders, slaughtering tens of thousands of people as they went. The rebellion was brutally suppressed, but it had already gone on far longer than any other subsequent rebellion in the fourteenth century. One change initiated by the rebels was lasting. When they first assumed control of a city at the start of the revolt, the merchants experienced political power for the first time. Although the end of the revolt ended their dominance of Flemish politics, merchants continued to hold seats on the governing councils of their cities. By the mid-fifteenth century Bruges was losing its preeminence in the Mediterranean and Baltic trades, as its river silted up. Its place was taken by Antwerp, to the north.

France

In contrast to Flanders, whose merchants and peasants fought for a greater say in the management of their economy and government, the dire conditions in France made peasants desperate and angry. Following the French defeat at Poitiers, when the English massacred or captured almost all of the nobles, including the king himself, the peasants were forced to raise the king's ransom. The situation was worse in the areas where the English armies conducted their *chevauchées*, as the land was ravaged. More than any other rebellion of the fourteenth century, the rebellion of the **Jacquerie**—so called for the name the nobles called peasants, "Jacques"—arose from the ranks of the much-oppressed peasants.

The violence began in May 1358 as resistance to plundering soldiers near the town of Compiègne. It very quickly turned into an expression of rage toward the nobility. Soon peasants from all over northeastern France attacked and destroyed castles and slaughtered nobles and their families. Word of the rebels' violence spread far beyond the region affected. As rebels traveled along the Loire and the Seine Rivers, moving in the direction of Paris, noble families fled.

In the same period, the city of Paris was experiencing political turmoil of its own. There the need to

Jacquerie Peasant revolt of 1358 in northern France directed mainly at the nobility.

raise the king's ransom had forced the government to make political concessions to the merchants of Paris, who sought reforms in the way they were governed. Very reluctant to cede any authority to the Parisians but much in need of their money, the captive king's government, led by the dauphin, granted some of the merchants' demands in February 1358, but the concessions were not enough. The leader of the Paris merchants, Etienne Marcel, quickly found himself heading a rebellion against the king's government. Within days, tensions turned to violence; two of the dauphin's closest advisers were murdered by a mob that invaded the royal palace. Paris remained poised on the brink of revolt for three months. Then news of the Jacquerie reached Paris. Marcel hoped to ally the rebels of Paris with the rebels moving quickly toward the capital. Instead, in June 1358, a combined force of peasants and Parisians occupying the city of Meaux was defeated. A month later, Marcel was assassinated.

The Jacquerie rebellion was suppressed within weeks of its start. The suppression was brutal, inflicting new suffering on an already much-burdened population. But chroniclers who wrote about the war for their noble patrons, such as Jean Froissart, attributed the brutality to the rebels, and that is what the French people remembered.

Florence

As in Flanders, the workers and well-to-do inhabitants of Italian cities grew increasingly dissatisfied with the way they were being governed, taxed, and excluded from political decisions. More and more people questioned—in private, for the most part—the privileges that aristocratic families demanded as their due. Periodic riots against city governments contributed to a growing sense of disorder, most notably in Florence.

Florence was governed by a system of councils, chief of which was the Signoria. Made up of representatives from the city's twenty-one major and minor guilds, it acted like an executive council overseeing all the other councils charged with governing the large mercantile city. The rotation every two months of the guild members on councils looked from a distance like a republican government, as so many of Florence's guild members proudly insisted that it was. In reality, a small group of wealthy merchants and their male relatives and clients were repeatedly elected to the city's public offices, and guilds representing the most prestigious occupations—lawyers, merchants from the textile trade, bankers, shopkeepers, and furriers—dominated Florentine political life. Middling businessmen, artisans, and poor skilled workers belonging to smaller and less prestigious guilds were not represented on the city council. Entirely excluded from power, workers and peasants sought power in republican Florence in the only way available to them—through force.

The **Ciompi Revolt** of 1378 began as a revolt of the wool carders, the *ciompi,* who combed out the wool into manageable strands prior to its being woven. The production and sale of woolen cloth made the city wealthy, but not all of those who worked in the industry benefited equally. The *ciompi* ranked lower in Florentine society than weavers and wholesale woolen merchants. Their radical inclinations had up until then caused the Signoria to forbid them to form a guild. Shut out of political life, they grew increasingly frustrated.

When their anger finally exploded into riots in the summer of 1378, other workers, who felt shut out of Florence's political life, joined them. In the same period, the divisive competition among the major guilds for dominance on the councils made it easier for people in the lower social levels to push forward their demands. For a few weeks that summer, Florentines flooded the streets with riotous demonstrations or they hid in their houses. Crowds milling around in the **piazza** of the Palace of the Signoria called for the government to lower taxes, abolish the public debt, and allow the *ciompi* to form their own guild. The city council refused to compromise. Finally, on July 22, 1378, a crowd pushed into the large, fortresslike palace and took the council room and its occupants by force. The minor guilds gained the political power they had long desired, and the *ciompi* at last announced the formation of their own guild.

The minor guilds dominating the new government despised lower-class *ciompi* just as the major guilds had when they were in power. Moreover, they proved inefficient and unresponsive to changes in the economy. The wool carders soon felt themselves again pushed to the margins of political power. Within a month, conflict once more threatened to engulf the city. To avert another civil war, the lesser guilds on the city councils suppressed the wool carders' guild and thus ended their participation in Florence's government. But the minor guilds themselves, despised by the more prestigious guilds, did not last long in power.

Four years later, in 1382, the major guilds regained control of the city council, expelled the lesser guilds,

Ciompi Revolt (in Italian, "wool carders") Revolt in Florence in 1378 instigated by wool carders.

piazza Public square in an Italian city.

On the right of this illumination, King Richard II persuades the army of the Peasants' Revolt of 1381 to follow him outside London's walls. To the left of the illumination, once outside the city wall's, the king watches his guards murder Wat Tyler, the leader of the rebels. *(HIP/Art Resource, NY)*

and pushed the middling and lower ranks of Florentine society out of political power. An oligarchy of wealthy guild members monopolized civic authority in Florence once more.

England

In 1381, contingents of horsemen and men on foot, armed with bows and pikes, marched along the roads of Essex and Kent toward London, recruiting artisans and farmers as they went. They were men of property intent on seeing that someone would suffer for the heavy taxes imposed on them by the king's ministers. Earlier that year, the government had imposed the third **head tax** in four years on all property owners. Finally, they had had enough. Wars, famine, inflation, and disease placed the heaviest burden on the poor, but the social standing of the people on their way to London reflected the profound changes taking place in English society.

Well-to-do peasants, merchants, artisans, and craft-workers profited from the low cost of real estate, abandoned property, and the shortage of food. By buying land cheaply or simply taking possession of abandoned farmland and by selling the food produce they grew at inflated prices where food was scarce, they earned more than they ever had before. Some of the marchers were technically still serfs, even if they were quite well off. Reeves, or managers of noble estates, came from the countryside north of London to

join in with the rebels. In their towns and villages, they were respectable men of modest property but they had no political representation at the king's court and wanted some say about taxes. The **Peasants' Revolt** of 1381 represented the first large-scale rebellion of commoners demanding greater participation in the political life of the kingdom in which they were tax-paying subjects.

To the dismay of the government, the rebels behaved like a trained army, as indeed, in some ways, they were. Although the war with France had entered a period of relative inactivity, the government of England still feared an invasion from across the English Channel. **Militias** organized in the towns and villages of Essex and Kent had gathered in local pastures to practice archery; some men actually served as archers in the king's army. These trained men now became a rebel army, marching to London in an orderly manner to rid their young king of ministers they viewed as corrupt.

Along the way, the rebels stopped to burn down the homes of particularly unpopular noblemen and to interfere with the work of the king's tax collectors. In London, they decapitated the archbishop of Canterbury and murdered the king's chancellor. Rushing to London's Newgate Prison, notorious for its barbaric conditions, the rebels forced open the gates to release all those imprisoned in it. By the time King Richard II, fourteen years old at the time, and a company of his

head tax Fixed tax all residents of a locality are expected to pay.

Peasants' Revolt An uprising in the summer of 1381 of commoners from mainly southeast England seeking greater political liberty that was quickly suppressed by King Richard II's forces.

militia An armed group of people from one town or region whose self-appointed or assigned purpose was to protect their locality.

nobles had organized to put down the revolt, the rebels had gone on to murder London merchants and set fire to portions of the city. With a small troop for protection, the young king on horseback confronted the leaders of the revolt, **Wat Tyler** and the renegade priest John Ball, inside the city walls. To show their loyalty to their king, the leaders and their rebel army followed Richard through the city gates and into a field. He knew they would follow him, because they had made it clear their complaints were directed at the king's officials, not him. But Richard led them into a trap. His army was waiting for them. The rebels who were not slaughtered that day were later executed.

Like the revolts in Flanders, France, and Florence, the English uprising ended without having significantly altered the society that the rebels sought to change. The hopes and radical ideas of the rebels did not disappear entirely, but the conditions for their fulfillment still lay far in the future.

A Worldly Church

↓ What factors contributed to the papacy's loss of prestige?
↓ How did the mystics reflect the religious sentiment of ordinary people?

To many in western Europe in the fourteenth century, it seemed that raising funds, not saving souls, had become the papacy's first priority. The popes saw things much differently. The papacy still claimed authority over ecclesiastic and secular rulers, but, lacking the resources to make its political claims effective, it turned to adornments—to gold, silver, marble, and silk vestments—that would give the impression of authority. Secular rulers of western Europe were either indifferent to, or irritated by, the papacy's claim that its power was superior to theirs. Ordinary people, alienated by the papacy's opulent appearance and apparent corruption, sought ways to privately and publicly express their own spirituality.

Papal Ambitions

Like most political or administrative capitals, Rome's population consisted of wealthy, modest, and poor families, all of whom depended on the city's biggest employer—the church—for jobs, patronage, and business. It now took a manager as much as a spiritual leader to oversee the bureaucracy of the papacy. The pope had the authority to appoint clergy to lucrative positions within the church, and the competition among clergy for positions with good incomes, called **benefices,** was not only fierce but corrupt. Bribes paid

to papal officials opened doors for those who had the money. The noble families of Rome pressured the pope to favor their kinsmen. The pope had his own kinsmen to give positions to, as did the cardinals.

When Pope Nicholas IV died in 1292, the cardinals of the church withdrew into a **conclave** to elect a new **pontiff.** A process that usually consumed a few days or occasionally a few weeks at most, the conclave this time lasted until 1294. One faction prevented the election of an opposing faction's candidate, with the result that the cardinals could not agree on anyone. After two years of stalemate, they settled on an elderly monk with no talent for administration. Six months later, Celestine V became the only pope in history to **abdicate,** an action that did not prevent his canonization in 1313. Fearful of another deadlock, the cardinals quickly elected **Boniface VIII,** an elderly canon lawyer and diplomat who was also a good administrator. In spite of these qualities, Boniface's sharp temper alienated the cardinals. His popularity sank even lower when he had the former pope, Celestine, put in prison, where the old monk soon died.

Despite his lack of support, Boniface energetically tackled the major problems facing the church. Of them, the fact that the papacy's income did not meet its expenses was the most serious. Though head of the extensive lands in the Papal States, the pope had difficulty exacting taxes from the nobles who ruled in his name but preferred to keep the revenue for themselves. Papal troops—always a major expense—had to be maintained there to keep order. Tithes, gifts, a tax to pay for a new crusade, and fees for appointments earned the papacy much revenue, but its expenses continued to outstrip what the church took in.

When, in 1296, Philip IV of France and Edward I of England taxed the clergy in their kingdoms despite the canon law exempting the church from taxation by secular rulers, the centuries-old dispute over the liberties of the church flared up again. Boniface threatened to excommunicate any clergy who paid the

Wat Tyler (d. 1381) Leader of the English Peasants' Revolt.

benefice Right to the income from a church office.

conclave Meeting of church leaders to elect a new pope.

pontiff One of the pope's titles, derived from *pontifex maximus,* the title of the chief priest of the state religion in pre-Christian Rome.

abdicate To resign from an office, usually one with a life term.

Boniface VIII (r. 1294–1303) Pope who reasserted the papacy's supreme authority over secular rulers.

idate the pope, who was residing at his summer home at Anagni, south of Rome. The eighty-six-year-old man died a few weeks later, after the French nobles reportedly physically mistreated him. His successor, Benedict XI, lived barely a year after his election, and discord among the cardinals in Rome left the papal throne once again empty for nearly two years.

The Avignon Papacy

When, in 1305, after two years of stalemate, the French king pressured the cardinals to chose the bishop of the French city of Bordeaux, the new pope—Clement V—was in no hurry to reach the papal palace in Rome. The city of Rome had become a contentious place, torn apart by the rivalries among the cardinals' families and now especially unhappy to have a pope who was not Roman. Resigned to waiting until the political climate in Rome improved, Clement settled in Avignon, a town on the Rhone River outside the borders of the French kingdom. But as a Frenchman and now within easy reach of Philip's letters and ambassadors, Clement gave the impression of being the French king's puppet. He made so many Frenchmen cardinals that they soon constituted the majority, thus ensuring that the succeeding seven popes all came from France.

What was intended to be a short stay at Avignon lasted more than seventy years. During the **Avignon papacy,** Clement V and his successors established a court that resembled the courts of the wealthiest secular rulers. Merchants from all over came to sell their luxury goods to the pope, the cardinals, and the bureaucrats. The Avignon popes bought sumptuous fabrics, spices, and foods for their banquets as well as gold and silver objects to adorn their rooms and chapels. A new palace that looked like an imposing fortress became their residence and workplace. Emissaries of secular rulers from all of Europe found in Avignon a papal court with all the attributes of a major center of diplomatic power.

Residence in Avignon made it difficult, however, for the pope to collect income from the Papal States, so they looked for new sources of revenue. Because the pope continued to receive appeals in ecclesiastical disputes, the papacy became an international court of

Arnulfio di Cambio made this bust of Pope Boniface VIII, which can be found today in the Vatican. The key Boniface holds in his left hand represents the one Christ gave to St. Peter and symbolizes the power of the pope to grant entry into the kingdom of heaven. *(Scala/Art Resource, NY)*

taxes. In turn, Philip and Edward promised to banish them if they did not. Philip also stopped all shipments of gold and silver coin to the papacy from leaving his kingdom. Starved of his revenue, Boniface backed down.

Five years later, in 1301, Philip tried a bishop in the royal court, also against canon law, which exempted clergy from trial in secular courts. Boniface condemned this act and, a year later, issued a bold statement of how he viewed his authority. In his statement, *Unam sanctam,* he claimed ultimate temporal and spiritual authority over all humanity. Boniface declared that "it is absolutely necessary for salvation that every human creature be subject to the Roman Pontiff." Since no one could attain salvation except through obedience to the pope, this meant that secular rulers were subordinate to him. The claim, in fact, had no force behind it. In 1303, determined to end Boniface's opposition to Philip's right to try a member of the clergy, the king sent a troop of noblemen to intim-

> *Unam sanctam* ("One Holy Church") Declaration issued by Pope Boniface VIII in 1302 that defined the supreme authority of the pope.
>
> **Avignon papacy** From 1309 to 1377, the period of the papacy's residence in the city of Avignon in what is today southern France.

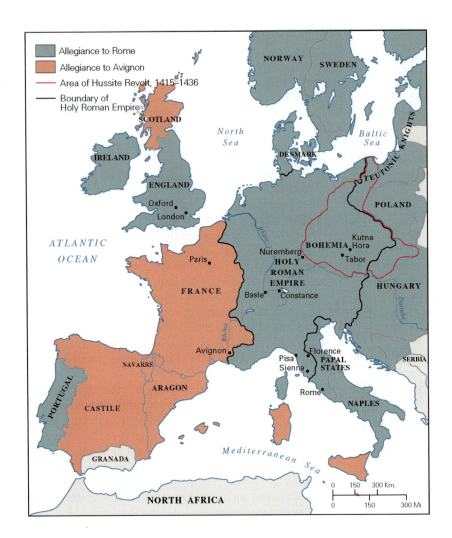

MAP 11.2   **The Great Schism**
The Great Schism, when the church was split between popes in Avignon and Rome, played into the political antagonisms of the late fourteenth century. The king of England and his allies supported the pope in Rome, while the French king and his allies backed the Avignon pope.

had to contend with the widespread conviction that the papacy had become a worldly institution more interested in its own financial health than in the spiritual health of ordinary Christians. Moreover, it remained mildly scandalous for the papacy to continue to remain in Avignon, far from its spiritual base in Rome. The longer the pope resided away from Rome, the greater the papacy was believed to have drifted from its mission to offer salvation to the faithful. The honorable return of the papacy to Rome became a problem to which church leaders gave increasing attention.

The Great Schism

When Clement V settled in Avignon in 1305, the departure of the papal bureaucracy sapped the life out of Rome. Bureaucrats and their families moved to Avignon or to other towns in search of employment. With so many of the church's higher clergy too far away to look after them, Rome's buildings and churches fell into decay. Ancient monuments, such as the Pantheon, were stripped of their marble for use in other buildings. An earthquake caused portions of the Coliseum to collapse, giving it the appearance it retains to this day. Marshland that had been filled in during the thirteenth century returned to its previous unhealthy condition. Without the papacy, Rome reverted to a small, run-down town of crumbling walls and malarial marshes.

> **indulgence**   Cancellation of any punishment still due to sin after the sacrament of penance.
>
> **Purgatory**   Place in which the souls of the dead spend time to atone for sins still remaining at the time of their death.

appeal to which both the clergy and laypeople could apply—for a fee. Aristocratic couples, for instance, who sought annulment of their marriages, or bishops who felt their privileges infringed in some way, sought the pope's authoritative ruling on their problems. In replies to written questions, the papal secretaries produced thousands of letters offering the pope's judgment. The Avignon popes found additional income by issuing **indulgences** to sinners seeking forgiveness. An indulgence was the wiping away of any punishment still owing in this life or in **Purgatory** for sins confessed and repented. The church's original acceptance of a contribution to facilitate the granting of an indulgence had grown into the their outright sale. As the papacy was much in need of money, the temptation to sell indulgences was too great to resist, although many laypeople and even church leaders deplored the crass exchange of money for salvation.

No matter how hard the Avignon popes tried to reassert the moral authority of their office, they always

Maintaining the papacy in Avignon had become so unpopular that Pope Gregory XI, another Frenchman, moved back to Rome in 1377. When he died soon after, the corruption and luxury of his successor, Urban VI, provoked the cardinals into invalidating their election of him and electing another Frenchman, Clement VII, who returned the papacy to Avignon. But in Rome, Urban VI refused to recognize his removal, and he excommunicated the newly elected pope, who, in turn, excommunicated Urban. Two men, each claiming to be pope, appointed their own cardinals and established rival bureaucracies. The enemies in the Hundred Years' War took sides, even though there had been little fighting in over two decades: the French king supported the pope at Avignon, and the English king supported the pope at Rome. By 1378, the split in the church and in Christian society in the west, known as the Great Schism, threatened to divide the Roman Church in two.

The Great Schism brought shame on the church, but the two popes and secular rulers found it to their advantage to let the situation continue. Theologians and cardinals tried to solve the problem. Even though only the pope had the authority to convene councils, the cardinals of both popes at last jointly convened the Council of Pisa in 1409 to settle the matter. They deposed both popes and elected a new pope, Alexander V. When the two popes refused to recognize that they had been removed from office, the cardinals faced the challenge of three men claiming to be pope. Another five years passed before the church was prepared to end the confusion. At the Council of Constance in 1414, the Roman pope was forced to resign, the Avignon pope continued to resist, and church officials imprisoned the third pope elected at Pisa. With two of three popes disposed of, removing the third depended on political maneuvering and timing. In 1417, when the last Avignon pope gave in, the council elected Martin V as pope. The church was at last reunited.

During the Great Schism, when the prestige of the papacy had sunk very low, some church theologians and lawyers argued for limits on the pope's authority. They studied the history of the church and concluded that ultimate church authority derived from councils, consisting of high church officials, including the pope. This position, known as conciliarism, surfaced in a period when the weakened papacy could do little to counter it. The conciliar movement had initiated the Councils of Pisa and Constance, and at the Council of Basel (1431–1439), new canons set limits on the pope's finances and his courts and reserved the right to hear appeals against his decisions. Although debate continues, official church doctrine holds that the pope is neither superior nor subordinate to councils, but instead stands in relation to them as the intellect relates to the soul. The council also officially endorsed seven sacraments.

The new pope and his cardinals tried to restore the papal authority that the schism had damaged. In 1420, Pope Martin moved the papacy back to Rome after instigating a program of urban improvement to make the city habitable. He also rejected the very process that had brought about his election. Thenceforth, he proclaimed, the pope would not answer to the authority of church councils.

The Laity and the Church

Laypeople, too, had their opinions about the state of the church. For many, religion was their only comfort in the face of starvation, disease, and random violence, but church leaders seemed too embroiled in the schism to minister to the people. Left to themselves, some men and women joined chaste communities dedicated to prayer. Like the mendicant orders of the thirteenth century, these laypeople chose to remain active in the world while carrying out acts of pious charity. In contrast to the cloistered Poor Clares, however, some women stepped into the public sphere to make an example of their spirituality.

The spiritual life of one such woman, Catherine of Siena, made many church leaders uneasy. Born to artisan parents, Catherine discovered a vocation for religious life at young age. She renounced marriage and, when she was eighteen, joined a Dominican order that allowed her to live in her parents' home while wearing the special tunic worn by members of the order. She became known for long fasts that over the years wore down her body's reserves. So famous for holiness did Catherine become that she felt free to express her opinions about the political events of her day. Although she never received an education, Catherine dictated hundreds of letters to a secretary. Her letters reached church leaders, rulers, and the pope. She gave

Great Schism (1378–1417) Split within the western church at the end of the Avignon papacy over the three rivals to the office of the pope.

conciliarism Theory that councils are the highest authoritative body in the church.

sacraments Religious practices or ceremonies that symbolize a deeper religious reality; the seven sacraments are baptism, communion (Eucharist), confirmation, confession (penance), ordination, marriage, and unction in sickness.

Catherine of Siena (1347–1380) Holy woman known for her long fasts and mystic religious experiences; canonized in 1461.

counsel to the mighty and comfort to the weak through her works and the prayers she composed.

Catherine's reputation for speaking out in public about the need for the Avignon papacy to return to Rome and her service as the pope's ambassador to Florence went against all notions of how a proper, devout woman should act. Religious women were not supposed to be heard, much less seen. They belonged, most people felt, in a nunnery or in their homes. Yet Catherine captured the affections of pious men and women throughout Italy and southern Europe, who tolerated her untraditional behavior because they believed her when she said that, in a vision, she had become a spouse of Christ. In 1378, when the papacy returned from Avignon to Rome, Catherine moved there and spent the last two years of her life helping the church reestablish itself. Only thirty-three years old but suffering from extreme physical self-deprivation, she died in Rome in 1380.

In contrast to the Scholastic theologians, whose intellectual efforts involved philosophical tools like logic, mystics such as Catherine spoke and wrote about the experience of religious passion and rapture. Her **mysticism** inspired a movement of clergy and laypeople who sought a direct experience of God that appealed to people's spiritual sensibilities instead of to their reason. In the Low Countries, laywomen, known as **Beguines,** took vows of chastity and lived in communities, although they could leave to marry if they chose. In 1415, a church council arranged for the Beguines' incorporation into the Franciscan lay order. Many mystics were highly educated men and women, one of whom, Meister Eckhart, a German Dominican, preached to laypeople about the mystery of God. Because he advocated that everyone, not just the clergy, should embark on his or her own spiritual searches, Eckhart came under suspicion for heresy.

When religious belief combined with anger toward the leaders of the church, the church's response was harsh. **John Wycliffe,** a theologian at Oxford University in England, wrote works that questioned clerical authority, excommunication, and monasticism. After his death, his followers, known as **Lollards,** endured persecution or went into hiding. A more serious challenge to church authority occurred in the Czech region of Bohemia, under the rule of the Holy Roman Emperor. **Jan Hus,** a theologian, expressed many of the same opinions as Wycliffe, but unlike the Lollards, the **Hussites,** as they were called, enjoyed the protection of the Bohemian nobility. After Hus was captured and burned at the stake in 1415, his followers led a revolt that drew support from all levels of the population. The Hussites developed a radical program of reform that dispensed with the distinction between clergy and laity. The popularity of the revolt among the Czechs and the strength of the rebels' army forced the emperor, as the church's defender, to negotiate a settlement in 1436. The success of the Hussite Revolt represents a turning point in the church's monopoly over lay religious expression.

The Contraction of Europe's Borders

↓ How did the old Roman Empire finally come to an end?
↓ Compare the multiethnic society of the Ottoman Empire to western Europe.

All too aware that Muslim states remained in Spain and on the southern shore of the Mediterranean, the people of the later Middle Ages learned of a new threat to their eastern borders. Turkish tribes were slowly destroying the Byzantine Empire. One tribe in particular, the Ottomans, came uncomfortably close to the frontier between the old empire and western Europe. Farther east and northward in Russia lay the lands of people whom the Roman Church scarcely considered Christian. Although some in the west, especially merchants, felt that distant markets represented opportunities, others felt that Christendom was contracting, and with it the boundaries of what was safe and familiar.

Old Empires and Newcomers

In 1261, thirty-six-year-old Michael VIII Paleologus, the emperor of the much-reduced Byzantine Empire, centered on the city of Nicaea, recaptured Constan-

mysticism Belief that God can be experienced directly through contemplation and prayer.

Beguines Laywomen, mainly in the Low Countries of northern Europe, who lived communally to devote themselves to a spiritual life.

John Wycliffe (ca. 1330–1384) Theologian from Oxford who questioned the fundamental teachings of the church.

Lollards Followers of John Wycliffe, whose beliefs and social agenda drew the condemnation of the church.

Jan Hus (ca. 1369–1415) Czech theologian and reformer condemned as a heretic and burned at the stake.

Hussites Followers of Hus, whose execution in 1415 sparked a revolt and led to the establishment of a Hussite government in Czech Bohemia and the Hussite church.

tinople from the Frankish rulers who had held it since 1204. From there, he fought to retake all the territory lost earlier in the century. His first priority was northern Greece. Unable to expel the Frankish rulers of the Peloponnesus, he forced them to recognize him as their overlord. Yet, expecting invasion from Turkish powers to the east, Slavs from the north, and armies from southern Italy to the west, the Byzantine emperor was surrounded by hostile forces.

With such pressure on his borders, Michael sent delegates to the Council of Lyons in 1274 to gain the support of the pope with a promise to reunite the Latin and Greek churches, which had formally ended relations with each other in 1054 mostly over the Greek church's refusal to recognize the pope as the supreme head of both churches. When the council and the pope agreed that the eastern church could continue some of its rituals, Michael authorized the union. The idea of union between the churches had long been unpopular among ordinary Byzantines and especially among the Byzantine clergy. But Michael had succeeded in depriving his enemies in southern Italy of a pretext to invade his empire. After his death in 1282, his son, Andronicus II, could afford to repudiate the union, because the southern Italians were forced to ally with him anyway against a new threat emerging from the east that menaced his empire and the Muslims in Syria and Palestine.

In the thirteenth century, with the arrival of **Mongols** from the east, the Muslims were placed on the defensive for the first time. The great Mongol leader **Genghis Khan** led his armies from their base in the heart of Asia all the way to Russia in the west and Beijing in the east. His successors drove their forces even farther. In 1240, they sacked Kiev. In the 1260s they ended Seljuk rule, already in decline, in Anatolia. The Abbasid dynasty in Baghdad fell in 1258, thus bringing to an end the centuries-old caliphate. Wherever the Mongols went, news of their terrifying mounted archers and savagery preceded them. Now, when merchants from Christian and Muslim territories reopened land routes to Asian markets, they had to pass through a new and unfamiliar empire whose borders seemed endless.

From eastern Siberia to western Russia, from Siberia in the north to Iran, modern-day Iraq, and Syria in the south and southwest, the Mongol Empire was so extensive that it could not be governed by a central power. So the Mongols established **khanates** that relied on local populations to do much of their ruling for them. Each of the khans reported to the great khan (the equivalent of the western title of emperor) based no longer in Mongolia but in China after the 1220s. The huge distances gave the khans a good

deal of autonomy. Political, cultural, or social cohesion was nearly impossible, given the size of the empire and the innumerable peoples, each with its own language, living within its borders. An empire like the Mongols' could be held together only by force and the cooperation of local elites. As with previous empires, however, the strains of ruling such far-flung provinces, together with the impact of the bubonic plague that devastated Asia before reaching western Europe in 1347, contributed to their decline in the mid-fourteenth century.

The fall of the Abbasid caliphate in Baghdad allowed for the emergence of other, independent caliphates in Egypt and India. In thirteenth-century Egypt, the position of caliph became the prerogative of the descendants of **Mamluks,** or slave soldiers, many of them Turkish in origin, who had gained control over the caliphs. Under the Abbasids, Muslim armies relied on slave soldiers who over time acquired influence over their masters to such a degree that they became, in effect, the rulers. Eventually in Egypt and in India, they replaced the caliphs altogether and established dynasties that lasted until the sixteenth century.

The Rise of the Ottoman Turks

When the Mongols put an end to Seljuk dominance of Anatolia, the Turkish warrior leader **Osman,** whose ancestors had probably arrived in Anatolia early in the thirteenth century, emerged as the strongest power in the region. By the time Osman died in 1324, he had conquered most of northwestern Anatolia. His successors, the Ottomans—whose name derives from Osman—steadily added new territory. They conquered Thrace in northern Greece after 1357 and Adrianople in 1361. Bulgaria came under their rule in 1389. They continued to whittle down the Byzantine Empire until it consisted of little more than its capital,

Mongols An Asiatic people whose empire at its height in the thirteenth century stretched from the Pacific to the Mediterranean.

Genghis Khan (c. 1204–1227) Mongol ruler who conquered northern China and established the Mongol Empire.

khanate Geographical unit ruled by a Mongol ruler, or khan.

Mamluks Slave soldiers in Muslim Egypt who first served the sultan ruler but later assumed power themselves.

Osman (1258–1324) Turkish founder of the Ottoman dynasty.

MAP 11.3   **The Spread of the Ottoman Empire and the Contraction of the Byzantines** The Ottoman Turks first ruled the region around Nicaea before expanding across Asia Minor, north into the Balkans and eastern Europe, and south into Muslim territories. Their expansion occurred mainly at the expense of Byzantine power, but the older Muslim dynasties ruling Egypt also succumbed to their might.

Constantinople, and the surrounding region. Even before the capture of the capital in 1453, the Ottoman **sultans** ruled an empire that stretched from Anatolia to the Balkans and would last more than six centuries, until the end of the First World War in 1918.

In the early fifteenth century, only the Tartar ruler **Timur** (Tamerlane, as he is known in the west), who conquered Persia and most of Central Asia, halted, temporarily, the Ottoman advance. In 1402, he invaded Anatolia with the intention of destroying the Ottoman state. Forced to turn his attention away from his conquests in eastern Europe, the Ottoman sultan Bayazid brought his army to meet Timur's at Ankara, today Turkey's capital, where he was soundly defeated. For the next decade the Ottoman state ceased to exist, as conquered lands reasserted their independence when they learned of Bayazid's defeat. But Timur's presence in Anatolia did not last long. When he died in 1405, the sons of Bayazid fought among themselves for the sultanate. Ten years

passed before one of them, Mehmed I (r. 1413–1421), united all the warring factions under his rule as sultan of the newly restored **Ottoman Empire.**

Before he could begin to reconquer the land that was lost, Mehmed reestablished the mechanisms of state that had existed in the first empire. He restored the bureaucracy and Islamic judicial system. He reinstated a system whereby he allotted a unit of land called a **timar** to a mounted soldier who was ex-

> **sultan**   Ruler of a Muslim country or empire called a sultanate.
>
> **Timur**   (ca. 1370–1405) Tartar conqueror, also known as Tamerlane.
>
> **Ottoman Empire**   Empire ruled by the sultan descendants of the house of Osman.
>
> **timar**   In the Ottoman Empire, a unit of property in exchange for which military service was required, similar to the western European fief.

Although the Venetian painter Giacomo Palma the Younger painted this scene a century after the fall of Constantinople in 1453, it captures the monumental undertaking that the conquest required of the Ottoman Turks. The painting shows on the left Ottoman forces breaching the city walls built by Theodosius II in fifth century. *(Scala/Art Resource, NY)*

In 1478, the Senate of Venice sent Gentile Bellini, a member of the talented family of painters, to visit the Ottoman court in Constantinople, where the Venetian painted the aged Sultan Mehmed the Conqueror's portrait. Here, Mehmed wears the large turban typical of Ottoman rulers. Men of lower rank wore smaller turbans. *(Erich Lessing/Art Resource, NY)*

pected to equip himself with its revenue. The sultan returned to the practice of seizing Christian boys from conquered territories, compelling them to convert to Islam, and raising them to serve in an elite unit of warriors known as the **janissaries.** Once the basic elements of state were in place, Mehmed set out to reconquer all the Balkan territory his predecessors had once ruled.

By 1450, the Balkan lands were once again under Ottoman rule. **Mehmed II** was determined to breach the thick walls of Constantinople and take the city. Help from the west was unlikely and unwelcome, as the Fourth Crusade's conquest of Constantinople and the Byzantine emperor's favor shown to Venetian and Genoese merchants to the disadvantage of Byzantine merchants had instilled a deep hostility toward the west in the subjects of the Byzantine emperor. The pope's insistence that the clergy of the eastern church recognize his supreme authority intensified the hostility.

Though representatives of the western and eastern churches had tried to achieve reunion at the Council of Florence in 1439, so many Byzantine Christians resented the agreement that the reunion had to be abandoned. But without friends in the west, the people of the Byzantine Empire had nowhere to turn.

Mehmed set about bringing down the capital of the Byzantine Empire and all the vestiges of the old Roman Empire. In addition to nearly 100,000 troops, he deployed a relatively new technology to achieve his goal: cannon. Mehmed's huge cannons, forged by Christian Hungarians in his employ, battered the city walls that had only twice before been breached. On May 29, 1453, Mehmed's janissary troops entered Constantinople through a hole the cannons had created in the walls. Its capital city conquered, the Byzantine Empire vanished.

janissaries Ottoman infantry composed mainly of Christian boys either captured or given in tribute to the sultan to be raised as Muslim soldiers.

Mehmed II (r. 1451–1481) Sultan who conquered Constantinople and established the city as the capital of the Ottoman Empire.

A Multiethnic World

While the people of western Europe often cast their world in terms of religion—Muslim or Jew versus Christian—the people of the Ottoman Empire experienced their world differently. Men and women of Turkish descent held a privileged position in Ottoman society, but not one that was exclusively theirs. The new empire encompassed lands occupied by many different ethnic groups that followed the Christian, Jewish, or Muslim religion. No matter their ancestry, converts to Islam entered fully into the rights and privileges of Muslim life. Even some who remained Christians and Jews achieved positions of wealth and power. But most of the non-Turkish population entered Ottoman society involuntarily and on an inferior social footing.

Slaves were central to the households of early Ottoman sultans and the ruling elite. Although most slaves performed menial labor, slaves also formed the backbone of the army, served as advisers and ministers in the bureaucracy, and bore the sultan's children. Slaves in the army and government had usually been brought as children from Christian and other non-Muslim lands to Ottoman territory. They were raised as Muslims and expected to display unswerving loyalty to the sultan. Endowed by Islamic law with limited power to act on their master's behalf, slaves could exercise some authority. At the level of the sultan, eunuch slaves served as officials in various departments of government.

Because of the prevalence of compulsory labor in Ottoman households and in the sultan's government, slaves factored heavily into sexual relations and reproduction in Ottoman society. It was common for slave concubines to bear their master's children, who inherited their free father's status. Once she gave birth to a boy, her position in her master's household was protected. The head of the household, whether the sultan or an Ottoman official, was not allowed to sell her once she had borne him a son, and at his death she would be freed. By the middle of the fifteenth century, the sultans had given up marrying and had children exclusively with slaves, whose offspring provided the sultan with a pool of potential heirs—and had also created conditions for their rivalry. Men of lower social rank continued to take legal wives.

After the fifteenth century, all Ottoman sultans had mothers who had been slaves in their father's household, which also means that sultans had mothers of different ethnic origins from their fathers, since Muslims are forbidden to enslave other Muslims. The mother of a ruling sultan often wielded great political power through her influence over her son. Mothers raised their sons in their harem quarters until they reached the age of twelve, when the sons were appointed provincial governors. When the father died, his sons, by tradition, fought one another for the succession to the sultanate, and the slave mothers conspired with their sons for the office of sultan. Through their sons and through the networks of informants and clients that they established in the sultan's household, the concubines could achieve a significant level of political power and influence.

Jews Under Christian and Ottoman Rule

The condition of Jews under Ottoman rule contrasts markedly to their life in the Christian west. Ottoman Turks regarded all non-Muslims as second-class subjects of the empire, but, like most Muslim societies, appreciated that, as People of the Book, Muslims, Jews, and Christians all venerated the ancient Hebrew prophets. Jews fared at times as well and as poorly as Christians under the sultan's rule.

But in the west, Christian antipathy toward Jews had been increasing ever since the massacres preceding the First Crusade at the end of the eleventh century. The Lateran Council of 1215 accentuated the isolation of Jews in Christian society by compelling them to wear badges that identified them in public. Beginning in the twelfth century, accusations of **blood libel**—false charges that Jews sacrificed Christian children at Passover to obtain their blood—incited attacks on Jews. Occasionally all the men of a community were arrested and executed, as happened in Trent in 1475. The hostility many Christians directed toward Jews made them easy scapegoats when explanations for the devastation caused by the plague were sought. Jews throughout the Diaspora in Europe endured the hardship of expulsion from the lands where they had lived and worked for generations. Edward I expelled them from England in 1290. They were expelled from France several times during the fourteenth century. In 1492, the rulers of the newly united Spanish kingdom expelled Jews and Muslims from their lands, initiating a migration of tens of thousands of **Sephardim,** or Spanish Jews, to the Low Countries; Italian cities; the northwestern frontiers in Poland, Lithuania, and Russia; and the Ottoman Empire.

> **blood libel**   Accusation that Jews sacrificed Christian children to use their blood in rituals for Passover, the commemoration of the ancient Hebrews' deliverance from slavery in Egypt.
> **Sephardim**   Jews expelled from Spain in 1492.

In between periods of violence and open hostility, the Jews of Europe, especially the communities in the German cities of the Holy Roman Empire, Italy, and southern France, lived productive and even prosperous lives in the narrow range of occupations they were permitted to enter, such as moneylending and shoemaking. German and Polish Jews, the **Ashkenazim,** spoke and wrote in **Yiddish,** a language derived from German and Semitic languages and written in Hebrew characters. A rich literary culture began to flourish in the twelfth century in the cities along the Rhine River and eastern Europe. Unwelcome and often persecuted, Jewish communities responded by emphasizing among themselves their bonds of kinship, common faith, and vibrant culture.

Ashkenazim   Jews of Europe who settled mainly in the Holy Roman Empire, Poland, Lithuania, and other eastern regions.

Yiddish   Language spoken by the Ashkenazim, derived from German and Semitic and written in Hebrew characters.

Voice

Eleazar of Mainz Writes His Last Testament

Mainz, Germany, was one of the cities whose Jewish population was massacred by crusading zealots in 1096. More than 250 years later, around 1357, a member of the small, barely revived Jewish community, Eleazar ben Samuel HaLevi, wrote a kind of last testament for his children known as an ethical will. Unlike most wills, which dispose of the testator's worldly goods among his or her heirs, ethical wills bequeath to the heirs the testator's moral and spiritual legacy. Eleazar's will is the last lesson in life that he passed on to his children.

➡ Who does Eleazar mean by "Gentile"?

These are the things which my sons and daughters shall do at my request. . . . ➡ Their business must be conducted honestly, in their dealings both with Jew and Gentile. They must be gentle in their manners and prompt to accede to every honorable request. They must not talk more than is necessary; by this will they be saved from slander, falsehood, and frivolity. They shall give an exact tithe of all their possessions: they shall never turn away a poor man empty-handed, but must give him what they can, be it much or little. If he beg a lodging over night, and they know him not, let them provide him with the wherewithal to pay an innkeeper. Thus shall they satisfy the needs of the poor in every possible way. . . .

➡ What does Eleazar consider to be the marks of membership among Jews?

➡ If they can by any means contrive it, my sons and daughters should live in communities, and not isolated from other Jews, so that their sons and daughters may learn the ways of Judaism. Even if compelled to solicit from others the money to pay a teacher, they must not let the young of both sexes go without instruction in the Torah. Marry your children, O my sons and daughters, as soon as their age is ripe, to members of respectable families. Let no child of mine hunt after money by making a low match for that object; but if the family is undistinguished only on the mother's side, it does not matter, for all Israel counts descent from the father's side. . . .

On holidays and festivals and Sabbaths seek to make happy the poor, the unfortunate, widows and orphans, who should always be guests at your tables; their joyous entertainment is a religious duty. Let me repeat my warning against gossip and scandal. And as you Speak no scandal, so listen to none; for if there were no receivers there would be no bearers of slanderous tales; therefore the reception and credit of slander is as serious an offense as the originating of it. The less you

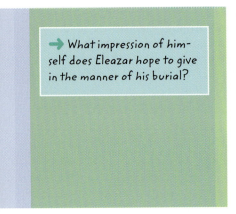

> ➡️ *What impression of himself does Eleazar hope to give in the manner of his burial?*

say, the less cause you give for animosity, while "in the multitude of words there wants transgression" [Proverbs 10:19].

➡️ I beg of you, my sons and daughters, my wife, and all the congregation, that no funeral oration be spoken in my honor. Do not carry my body on a bier, but in a coach. Wash me clean, comb my hair, trim my nails, as I was wont to do in my lifetime, so that I may go clean to my eternal rest, as I went clean to synagogue every Sabbathday. If the ordinary officials dislike the duty, let adequate payment be made to some poor man who shall render this service carefully and not perfunctorily. . . .

Put me in the ground at the right hand of my father, and if the space be a little narrow I am sure that he loves me well enough to make room for me by his side. If this be altogether impossible put me on his left, or near my grandmother, Yura. Should this also be impractical, let me be buried by the side of my daughter.

Source: Reprinted from Jacob R. Marcus, *The Jew in the Medieval World,* with permission of the Hebrew Union College Press, Cincinnati.

At the same time that the religious and political climate in Christian Europe worsened for Jews, it improved in the newly established Ottoman territories. While Christendom was unable to incorporate Jews as Jews, the Ottomans were willing to let Jews prosper in relative security. Ottoman cities such as Constantinople (now called Istanbul) and Edirne had Jewish residents. Thessalonica had had prosperous Jewish communities well before 1453.

The inclusion of Jews in Ottoman society was not entirely voluntary. Soon after the conquest of Constantinople, which had been depopulated and in decline in the years leading up to its capture, Mehmed II forcibly relocated Jews from the Balkans and Anatolia to his new capital to help revive the economy. Thereafter, he encouraged Jewish immigrants from the west. Jewish physicians, merchants, and bankers became much sought after in the new empire. Opportunities to live in peace, make a living, and even join the ranks of the wealthy (despite a tax rate higher than Muslims paid) were available to Jews under the Ottomans as they were not in the west.

Russia After 1000

Medieval Russia had been divided into principalities, each ruled by a prince. The descendants of Vikings and Slavs, Christianized in the tenth century, ruled the region surrounding the city of Kiev along the Dnieper River. With the city's commercial power and military strength, Kiev's princes dominated the other Russian princes until the arrival of the Mongols around 1237 drastically changed the political and economic landscape.

When Genghis Khan died in 1227, he was on the verge of entering the steppes north of the Black Sea and south of the land of the Russians. His sons and grandsons received a portion of his empire, the western portion falling to his grandson Batu, who ruled the population of Mongols, Turks, and Russians known to the west as the Empire of the **Golden Horde.** In 1240 Batu's army laid waste to the city of Kiev, the populous capital of trade and government. Only the death of his uncle, the great khan, stopped Batu from pushing farther westward.

Once Batu had conquered all the Russian principalities, he and his people settled in the steppes and south of the Volga River. As the overlord of the Russian princes, he organized the collection of tribute and the conscription of soldiers for the army of the Golden Horde. Important caravan routes—known as the **Great Silk Road**—connecting China with the Byzantine Empire passed through their land. Silk, spices, precious jewels, and ceramics came west to be exchanged for Scandinavian slaves, fur, hides, salt, and Caspian caviar in demand in the east. The khans granted Genoese merchants the use of Caffa, a port on the Crimean peninsula in the Black Sea, as a base for their trade in slaves and other commodities. The Venetians had the use of Tana, another port on the Black Sea, where they engaged in similar commerce.

To the north, in the lands of the Russian princes, the fur and timber of Russia forests attracted merchants from everywhere. The Baltic Sea served as a highway for the cogs sailing from Scandinavian and German ports, while rivers gave access to merchants

Golden Horde Collection of Tartar-Mongol tribes who conquered and ruled the land of the Rus from the mid-thirteenth to the late fifteenth century.

Great Silk Road Long trade route from China to the Mediterranean coast; so-called because it was the route by which silk goods arrived in the west.

from Christian Europe and Muslim lands. Whoever ruled this land—spectacularly rich in resources, with few towns and a relatively small and entirely rural population—had the potential of possessing great economic and political power.

The fall of Kiev and the princes who ruled it opened the way for other Russian leaders to emerge. Although Novgorod in the north survived the Mongol invasion, Moscow, once an isolated military post, began to emerge as a center of power in the late thirteenth century. **Alexander Nevsky,** prince of Novgorod and grand price of Vladimir, made sure not to alienate the khan of the Golden Horde but fought back Swedish, Lithuanian, and German troops from the west. His son, Daniel, was the first prince of a dynasty centered on Moscow in the principality of Muscovy, which would benefit from the political vacuum created by the fall of Kiev.

Alexander Nevsky (r. 1236–1263) Russian ruler who stopped the advance of German, Swedish, and Lithuanian troops from the west.

Summary

Review Questions

↑ Describe life, and death, in fourteenth-century Europe.

↑ How did the papacy and secular rulers contest each other for authority?

↑ Where did the loyalties of various ranks of people lie? How did they assert their rights and dignity and spirituality?

Plague, war, and social upheavals exist in every age, but at certain times in history, they can occur in such intensity and with such frequency that they leave a deep impression in memory and in culture. The fourteenth century in western Europe was such a period. Men and women of all ranks, but especially the poor, faced extraordinary challenges.

Prior to the beginning of the plague in 1347, most people of western Europe experienced hunger at some point in their lives. Weather changes in northern Europe brought wet summers, even colder winters, and extensive flooding. Bad weather destroyed crops. Poor harvests led to severe shortages of food in many regions. The price of grain soared, putting food out of reach of all but the wealthy. Weakened by malnourishment, the population fell prey to disease. An epidemic of the bubonic plague claimed the lives of a third to half of the population of Europe in the middle of the century.

Warfare conferred even greater hardship on peasants in the countryside and city dwellers alike. In the Hundred Years' War between the kings of England and France, the English armies trampled planted fields, set fire to villages, and besieged walled towns as a way to undermine support for the French king. Across the English Channel, the people of England were made to pay more and more through taxes for the war. After a long lull in the hostilities, when the English and the French resumed the fighting in 1415, the hold that kings had on their subjects' loyalty had strengthened. The path leading to a stronger sense of patriotism, though, was not a straight one. In the 1350s, discontented men and women began the Jacquerie, a bloody rampage in the countryside of France. In 1381, an army from the counties surrounding London tried to impose social change on the English king, Richard II, but was quickly defeated.

Beset by so many challenges, ordinary people turned to religion and spirituality to find comfort and fulfillment. The church, governed for most of the fourteenth century in Avignon, had become a huge bureaucracy concerned primarily with its own unhealthy finances. The reputation of the church while the papacy resided at Avignon sank low, but not as low as it would sink during the Great Schism. Some church leaders, however, saw in the scandal an opportunity to make the pope share some of his authority with the leaders of the church embodied in councils. For the papacy, this was taking reform too far.

On Europe's frontiers, the conquest of the last remnants of the old Roman Empire alarmed people in the West. The Ottomans had emerged from Anatolia by 1300 and slowly chipped away at the Byzantine Empire over the fourteenth century. When in 1453 the great city of Constantinople fell for the second time in its long history, it was to its new Muslim master, the Ottoman sultan Mehmed II. To the people of Europe, the Christian world now seemed a much smaller place.

← **Thinking Back, Thinking Ahead** →

How did the disappearance of the Byzantine Empire in the mid-fifteenth century change the possibilities for trade between Europe and Asia?

ECHO ECHO ECHO ECHO ECHO ECHO

The Black Death and AIDS

Until the influenza pandemic between 1918 and 1920, when nearly 100 million people around the world died within two years, the epidemic of diseases that swept across western Europe beginning in 1347 was the deadliest. The Black Death held a position in popular opinion in the west as the most physically and psychologically devastating catastrophe ever to strike a large population. That an estimated one-third to one-half of Europe's population died within a few years overwhelmed the imagination of people living in the twentieth century. What it must have been like to live in societies where people could die unexpectedly within hours of contracting a disease defies imagination today.

Acquired immune deficiency syndrome (AIDS) and the human immunodeficiency virus (HIV) first entered the consciousness of Americans during the early 1980s, when large numbers of homosexual men in the United States and a smaller number of people around the world began to die. Then the disease and the virus spread through sexual contact and blood transfusions to all sectors of the population and throughout the world. More than 25 million people worldwide have died from AIDS since 1981. As of 2006, more than 38 million people—over 21 million of them in sub-Saharan Africa alone—are living with AIDS or are HIV-positive. Unlike victims of the bubonic plague, those who are HIV-positive can live for years. Once they contract the full-blown disease of AIDS, they can last another few years. Although drugs can now prolong the lives of those infected by decades, the high cost of medication means that millions cannot afford treatment.

The long-term economic and psychological impact of AIDS has yet to be fully felt. Since the majority of those infected are between the ages of fifteen and sixty, a significant percentage of the workforce and student population of Africa have been incapacitated. Twelve million children have lost their parents. Households of children raised by grandparents are common. Just as the Black Death created ghost villages and set back the gains of the European economy in the twelfth and thirteenth centuries, so, too, is AIDS undoing many of the economic advances made in recent decades by countries such as South Africa, Zambia, Botswana, and Zimbabwe.

Suggested Readings

Boccaccio, Giovanni. *The Decameron.* London and New York: Penguin Classics, 2003. A collection of one hundred delightful tales filled with insights into daily life, the Black Death in Florence, and relations between men and women.

Cohen, Mark R. *Under Cross and Crescent: The Jews in the Middle Ages.* Princeton, N.J.: Princeton University Press, 1995 A comparison between the condition and status of Jews in Christian territory and those in Muslim countries.

Froissart, Jean. *Chronicles.* London and New York: Penguin Classics, 1978. A lively account of the first phase of the Hundred Years' War written in the late fourteenth century.

Herlihy, David. *The Black Death and the Transformation of the West.* Edited by Samuel K. Cohn Jr. Cambridge, Mass.: Harvard University Press, 1997. Still a reliable overview of the devastating plague that swept Europe.

Hilton, R. H. *Bond Men Made Free: Medieval Peasant Movements and the English Rising of 1381.* London: Routledge, 2003. A classic study of the Peasants' Revolt of 1381 and its origins.

Imber, Colin. *The Ottoman State, 1300–1650: The Structure of Power.* New York: Palgrave Macmillan, 2004. An excellent overview of the forming of the Ottoman government in its early centuries.

Muldoon, James. *Popes, Lawyers, and Infidels: The Church and the Non-Christian World, 1250–1550.* Philadelphia: University of Pennsylvania Press, 1979. A study of papal policy toward non-Christians.

Websites

Links to a wide variety of sites of interests to students of medieval warfare, **De Re Militari: The Society for Medieval Military History,** at deremilitari.org

Text of Giovanni Boccaccio's collection of tales and many interesting articles on aspects of life in fourteenth-century Italy,

Decameron Web, at www.brown.edu/Departments/Italian_Studies/dweb/dweb.shtml

On many aspect of Ottoman life and society, **The Ottomans,** at www.theottomans.org/english/index.asp

CHAPTER 12

The Renaissance in Italy and Northern Europe, 1350–1550

1500 B.C.E.	1000 B.C.E.	500 B.C.E.	1 B.C.E./1 C.E.

	1347 Black Death first appears in Italy				1417 Great Schism ends	1440s Gutenberg invents printing process
1340	1360	1380	1400	1420		1440

The Spread of New Cultural Expression, 1300–1500

In the fifteenth century, artists and thinkers across northern Italy produced extraordinary artistic and intellectual work that attracted attention throughout Europe. Byzantine refugee scholars brought previously unknown classical works with them to Italy. Which Italian cities played important roles in the promotion of the new forms of cultural expression?

Largest cities, ca. 1500

- ■ Over 125,000
- ◆ 100,000 to 125,000
- ● 50,000 to 100,000
- ○ 25,000 to 50,000
- • Other cities
- — Boundary of Holy Roman Empire

ATLANTIC OCEAN

IRELAND
Dublin
ENGLAND
London
Edinburgh
NORWAY
Oslo
SWEDEN
Stockholm
North Sea
Baltic Sea
DENMARK
Riga
TEUTONIC KNIGHTS
Danzig
Lübeck
MUSCOVY
Warsaw
POLAND-LITHUANIA
Kiev
KHANATE OF THE GOLDEN HORDE
Rotterdam
Antwerp
Ghent
FLANDERS
Rouen
Paris
Fontainebleau
FRANCE
Mainz
HOLY ROMAN EMPIRE
BOHEMIA
Prague
Cracow
Vienna
AUSTRIA
Buda Pest
HUNGARY
MOLDAVIA
SWISS CONF.
Lyons
SAVOY
Milan
Cremona
Genoa
Brescia
Verona
Venice
VENICE
Bologna
Florence
Urbino
Pisa
Siena
GENOA
Marseilles
Ragusa
OTTOMAN EMPIRE
Black Sea
NAVARRE
PORTUGAL
KINGDOM OF CASTILE AND ARAGON
Valencia
Córdoba
Seville
Granada
Cádiz
Ceuta
Corsica (Genoa)
Sardinia
PAPAL STATES
Rome
Naples
Salonica
Constantinople
Smyrna
MOORISH EMIRATES
Algiers
Tunis
Palermo
Sicily
Crete (Venice)
Cyprus (Venice)
Mediterranean Sea

0   200   400 Km.
0   200   400 Mi.

| 500 C.E. | 1000 C.E. | 1500 C.E. | 2000 C.E. |

1492
Columbus sets sail

1508
Michelangelo begins painting ceiling of the Sistine Chapel

1485
Henry Tudor defeats Richard III of England

1494
Savonarola institutes reforms in Florence

1516
Erasmus translates the Greek New Testament

1517
Luther condemns indulgences

1532
Machiavelli publishes *The Prince*

| 1460 | 1480 | 1500 | 1520 | 1540 | 1560 |

Choice Choice Choice

Although a few Renaissance painters matched his skill and talent, Leonardo da Vinci surpassed them all in vision, curiosity, learning, and expertise in an impressive range of subjects. In 1513, when he was sixty-one years old and living in Rome, Leonardo drew this self-portrait that shows the flowing hair and beard of an old man. (Alinari/Art Resource, NY)

Leonardo da Vinci Seeks Employment

In the spring of 1519, at the great age of sixty-seven, Leonardo da Vinci made his will. He died several days later, leaving his long-time trusted assistant, Francesco Melzi, a treasure trove of paintings and drawings. Their power to move and evoke awe has not diminished with the passing of centuries. Today, they are among the most valuable works of art in the world.

It may have been that this master draftsman and painter would have preferred to be remembered for his engineering feats, especially those applicable to the so-called art of waging war. Leonardo had long applied his talents to the service of the state, and since 1516 he had been living in a house granted him by the French king in Fontainebleau, France. He was far from Milan, where he had spent nearly two decades in the service first of Duke Ludovico Sforza and then of the military governor after the French invaded that city in 1499 and forced Sforza out. His deathbed was equally far from Tuscany, where he had been born in 1452 and spent his childhood and youth. After spending his teenage years and his twenties working as an apprentice to the master painter Andrea del Verrochio, the thirty-year-old Leonardo composed a letter to Ludovico Sforza, in which he detailed the skills he hoped to put to use in the duke's service. He offered to design bridges that could bear the weight of cannon and weaponry; to instruct Milanese captains in the techniques of siege warfare; to make a transportable cannon that fired rocks; and to build ships more suitable to naval warfare, as well as siege engines, catapults, and even an armored vehicle to transport troops. In the end, none of these plans were ever executed, but they demonstrate Leonardo's extraordinary imagination. Only in an incidental way did he mention the very talents for which he was already acquiring a reputation, painting and sculpture.

By portraying himself in this fashion, Leonardo ensured that he would not have to choose among his many and varied interests. Noble men and women all over Italy wanted him to paint their portraits. Monasteries commissioned him to paint altarpieces and frescoes. The city of Florence hired him to paint a large and complicated fresco painting of a battle for the city's freedom. The pope ordered paintings from him. But Leonardo simultaneously pursued his military interests. He drew topographical maps of contested territory for his employers. The government of Genoa paid him to survey the landscape in the city's hinterland and make recommendations on its defenses. In 1500, he inspected and suggested improvements to the eastern defenses of the Republic of Venice. Two years later, he prepared military maps and charts of the Papal States for the pope.

Leonardo's decision to emphasize his talent for military engineering in his letter to the duke of Milan was in his mind not much different from his decision to put his talent for painting in the service of the French king. Both rulers were willing to give him employment to create what the world

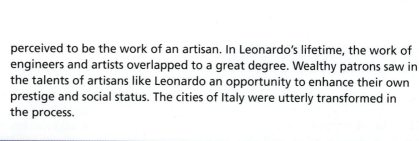

perceived to be the work of an artisan. In Leonardo's lifetime, the work of engineers and artists overlapped to a great degree. Wealthy patrons saw in the talents of artisans like Leonardo an opportunity to enhance their own prestige and social status. The cities of Italy were utterly transformed in the process.

Introduction

Even before Leonardo died, his fame was secured for his work as an artist, and it would soon be seen as part of the cultural flowering of art and literature that began in Italy and is known as the Renaissance. By the early sixteenth century, the new forms of expression affirming faith in God and the worth of human creativity had been developing for more than a century. Even before famine and plague afflicted Italy in the fourteenth century, its intellectuals and artisans had begun to explore new techniques, new ideas, and new ways to analyze old texts, and the hardships ahead did not hinder them. Over time, commerce and industry revitalize the Italian urban economies hurt by crop failures and population loss. A mutually beneficial relationship developed between wealthy families looking to display their high social status and talented scholars and artisans. The products of those relationships—extraordinary, lifelike paintings and bronze statuary, philosophical treatises displaying great learning, and breathtaking monuments to God or man—caught the attention of the rest of the continent.

No longer confined to the world of the clergy, scholars rejected the old methods of analysis in favor of a rigorous, questioning approach to the study of classical and Christian texts. In Italy, intellectuals discovered new joy in reading ancient Latin texts, taking pleasure foremost in the literary qualities of Cicero and Virgil instead of testing their compatibility with Christian doctrine. When Greek texts that no one in the west had previously read arrived in the baggage of refugees from the east, the scholars dedicated themselves with enthusiasm to the study of Greek. In northern Europe, the same love of inquiry drove scholars to reexamine with newly critical eyes authoritative Christian texts. The invention of the printing press made all these texts widely available to a far greater number of readers than ever before, prompting new levels of scholarly debate.

Both in Italy and in the north, painters, sculptors, and architects approached their work with the same open mind with which scholars viewed their texts. An enhanced appreciation of human potential and a desire to highlight in the human form the image of God inspired them to represent in their work men and women with a realism not seen in paintings and sculpture since ancient Rome. Italian painters relied on the precision of perspective, while the Flemish painters achieved similar effect with the warmth of color. The results stunned the whole of western Europe. Guided by scholarly insight into God's relationship to humanity and inspired by the astonishing creativity of the artisans now become artists, the rulers of Europe might now act like the wise princes so many of their subjects hoped they would become. They hoped in vain.

A New Climate of Cultural Expression

⬇ How did the humanists differ from monks and scholastic thinkers?
⬇ What factors caused artisans to emerge as artists?

Even before the Black Death completely subsided, an entirely new spirit began to be felt in Italy. Between the middle of the fourteenth and the middle of the fifteenth centuries, an explosion of cultural expression of astonishing and extravagant proportions permeated every aspect of life. No one, no matter how poor, could fail to notice. Whether passing the construction site of an enormous cathedral dome rising to an awe-inspiring height, praying before an altar painting of an unusually lifelike and colorful scene, or watching a bejeweled husband and wife clothed in rich fabric trimmed with gold embroidery, surrounded by a large entourage, pass by on a city street, even the most ordinary person was aware of living in an extraordinary time. People believed they, or at least their societies, had reached unprecedented wealth and ease. This impression was only partly an illusion.

The Spirit of Humanism

The new spirit began with a broadening of learning. Universities no longer held a monopoly on intellectual pursuits. Now laymen studied texts with private

Chronology

1356	Emperor Charles IV issues Golden Bull	**1485**	William Caxton publishes Malory's *Le Morte D'Arthur*; Henry Tudor defeats Richard III of England
1362	Lithuanians capture Kiev	**1494**	Ludovico Sforza becomes duke of Milan; The Medici of Florence enter exile
1380	Venice and Genoa fight War of Chioggia	**1496**	Savonarola assumes power in Florence
1417	Great Schism ends	**1498**	Savonarola is burned at the stake
1436	Brunelleschi's dome atop the cathedral of Florence is consecrated	**1508**	Pope Julius II reconquers Papal States
1440	Lorenzo Valla refutes authenticity of Donation of Constantine	**1508–1512**	Michelangelo paints ceiling of Sistine Chapel
1440s	Gutenberg invents printing press	**1512**	Medici return to power
1450	Francesco Sforza becomes duke of Milan	**1516**	Erasmus translates Greek New Testament into Latin; Leonardo settles in France
1455–1485	House of Lancaster and House of York fight Wars of the Roses	**1520**	Francis I becomes king of France
ca. 1455	Gutenberg Bible is published	**1532**	Publication of Machiavelli's *The Prince*
1470	Thomas Malory writes *Le Morte d'Arthur (The Death of Arthur)*		
1478	Lorenzo de' Medici survives assassination attempt		

tutors in the hopes of employment in the governments of Italian cities. Women from well-to-do families, too, studied philosophy and theology, but solely out of a love of learning, since careers outside of home and marriage were closed to them. Lay scholars became interested in exploring the question of what it meant to be human. They were called humanists because their intellectual interests centered on the study of humanity (*studium humanitatis*), or **humanism.** They esteemed the works of ancient Romans for their literary qualities rather than their usefulness for Christian theology. Their interest in language and the technical aspects of literature led them to criticize Scholastic thinkers for not paying closer attention to grammar and vocabulary in their interpretation of biblical texts. In general, however, they celebrated human potential and downplayed the theological emphasis on the sinful nature of humanity.

One of the earliest humanists, Francesco Petrarca, born in 1304 in Tuscany and known as **Petrarch,** belonged to the generation of scholars that joined the clergy to acquire a higher education. His father wanted him to study canon law, but a love of literature directed the young scholar toward poetry both in Latin and in the everyday **vernacular** language. Petrarch's poems made him famous throughout Italy, southern France, and eventually all of Europe, but his love of manuscripts made a greater impact on literature. As ambassador to the Avignon popes, Petrarch traveled all over Europe, stopping in monasteries along his way. A **bibliophile** of the first order, Petrarch searched

humanism   Philosophical and literary study of what it means to be human.

Petrarch   (1304–1374) Francesco Petrarca, one of the first humanist scholars, who was responsible for the recovery of numerous works of classical Latin Roman writers.

vernacular   In medieval and Renaissance Europe, the dialects spoken in everyday life, in contrast to the literary language of Latin.

bibliophile   Lover and collector of books.

through their libraries for old manuscripts and discovered lost works by Cicero. Writing to the ancient Roman as if he were alive, Petrarch chastised Cicero for contributing to the downfall of the Roman Republic. He emulated the style and content of the ancients with such success that readers took a new interest in the language and texts associated with Rome.

Ancient Greek texts benefited from the arrival of refugees from the Byzantine Empire in the 1390s. Fleeing the Ottomans, they emigrated to Italy and stimulated a great interest in the literature of the past. After a tour of Europe in 1394, the great Greek scholar **Emmanuel Chrysoloras** made Florence a new center of Greek learning, thanks to his skills as a teacher and to the manuscripts he brought with him. Other Byzantine scholars found employment elsewhere in Italy, where they not only taught Greek but also introduced intellectuals to the previously unknown body of scientific works by Plato, Aristotle, and others.

Not all intellectuals worked as papal secretaries or scribes in city government. Some worked directly for **autocratic** rulers and wealthy merchants who enjoyed the prestige that came with being **patrons** of humanists. These men employed scholars in their households, to instruct their children or to converse when visitors came to call. Humanist **clients** encouraged their patrons to collect manuscripts and, later, books that would form the basis of some of Europe's most important libraries. **Lorenzo de' Medici,** the ruler of Florence in the late fifteenth century, amassed an important collection of manuscripts and books under the guidance of the humanist scholars whose patron he was. Although humanists tended to embrace the values of the patrons for whom they worked, they admired Cicero's involvement in Roman public affairs and valued political engagement in city life. The Florentine humanists took from Cicero an appreciation for republicanism, which rejected autocractic rule in favor of government by the people. **Civic humanism,** the study of ancient texts to develop ideological support for Florence's republican government, gave the humanists an opportunity to express their patriotism. Through the study of these texts, the humanists sought to bring what they perceived to be the best of the ancient world to life again in their own time—hence their conviction that they lived in a period of rebirth, or **renaissance.**

From Artisan to Artist

By the end of the fifteenth century, when the Renaissance in Italy was at its height, patrons like Lorenzo de' Medici would have viewed the painter, sculptor, and architect **Michelangelo** much as we do today, as

an artist of outstanding genius. Two centuries earlier, the early-fourteenth-century Italian painter **Giotto** would have been viewed as an **artisan** of exceptional talent. The emergence of artists from the world of artisans had everything to do with the same cultural climate in which humanist scholars worked.

Giotto painted in a time when the function of a painting mattered as much as the beauty or creativity it displayed. The male and female patrons who hired Giotto would have specified what they wanted to see in the painting. Giotto's role in the process was simply to execute the patron's desire. Although Giotto received much praise for the beauty and spiritual qualities of his painting, he was only a craftsman in the eyes of the people who employed him. Religious and secular patrons hired artisan painters, sculptors, and architects to create devotional objects whose beauty was meant to enhance, reinforce, and remind viewers of what they should believe or do. Painted frescoes like the ones Giotto painted celebrating the life of Saint Francis in the basilica at Assisi (see image on page 271) depicted stories that taught the laity the elements of Christian belief. Sculptors created statues out of stone or bronze that portrayed holy or historical figures, celebrated warriors, or secular rulers. Craftsmen builders designed churches, government buildings, and private residences whose size or grandeur suggested the glory of God or its occupants. Even the finely crafted gold and silver objects on display in churches had practical uses in the Mass. All artistic creations had a purpose and a function.

Emmanuel Chrysoloras (1355–1415) Important Greek scholar who introduced the scientific works of ancient Greek philosophers to the west.

autocrat Ruler who possesses absolute power.

patron Person, usually wealthy or powerful, who financially supports the intellectual or artistic work of a client.

client Artist or intellectual supported by a wealthy patron.

Lorenzo de' Medici (r. 1469–1492, "the Magnificent") Ruler of Florence and patron of artists, poets, and humanist scholars during the Italian Renaissance.

civic humanism Study and appreciation of classical republican forms of government.

renaissance Literally, "rebirth," signifying a revival.

Michelangelo Buonarotti (1475–1564) Painter, sculptor, poet, and architect, considered in his time to be the greatest artist Italy had ever produced.

Giotto di Bondone (1267–1334) Best-known and most influential painter of the Middle Ages.

artisan Skilled craftsmen, such as a cabinetmaker, painter, or shoemaker.

For these reasons, those who painted portraits or religious works, made statues, and designed buildings would have described themselves as artisans, not as painters, sculptors, or architects. They were also businessmen. If a painter was successful, he very likely owned and operated his own workshop and employed other painters who assisted him, even to the extent of painting the background of a scene that would eventually be associated with his name alone. Gentile Bellini, a renowned Venetian painter and the son and brother of two other famous painters, was the master of his own workshop, where he and his assistants together painted scenes of Venice's ceremonial life. The contract he signed with his patrons specified precisely what images the painting would contain, the pigment colors that would be used, and the date when the project would be completed. Once all the conditions had been agreed upon, Bellini's assistants worked on drafting and painting the buildings in the background while the master focused his creative attention on the figures that required technical precision and artistic vision. Sculptors and architects made similar contractual arrangements with their patrons, who tended to view themselves as the real creative force behind artistic productions.

The workmanlike relationship between a painter and his patron changed slowly over the fifteenth century as the creative expression of the artisan became more highly valued. By the end of the century, not only did people think of painters, sculptors, and architects as artists, as we understand the term, but the artisans also began to regard their skills and talent more highly than previously. Michelangelo, a devoutly religious man, who painted the ceiling of the Sistine Chapel and designed Saint Peter's Church, both at the Vatican, evoked the highest praise of any artist in his time from his contemporaries, yet he revealed his ambivalence about the life of an artist in a poem:

My cherished art, my season in the sun,
name, fame, acclaim—that cant I made a run for,
left me in servitude, poor, old, alone.
O death, relieve me soon. Or soon I'm done for.

By the sixteenth century, the artisan had become an artist, and his work was now art. This change is reflected clearly in a collection of biographical sketches by a painter whose reputation rests more firmly on his writings than on his paintings. Giorgio Vasari's *The Lives of the Most Eminent Painters, Sculptors, and Architects*, published in 1550, preserves details about the life, work, and character of Renaissance Italy's most famous artists, from Giotto in the thirteenth century to Michelangelo in the sixteenth. In this work,

the stereotype of artist as temperamental genius emerges clearly for the first time.

Perspectives and Techniques

One man's career best personifies the changes in cultural expression and production during the Italian Renaissance. Filippo Brunelleschi, like most of his colleagues, did not confine himself exclusively to one creative medium. He was an exceptionally talented painter, metalworker, engineer, and architect, all in one. Born and raised in Florence, Brunelleschi became even in his own day one of the most famous artists Italy ever produced. His two most significant contributions to the cultural movements of his time related to his experiments with linear perspective in painting and to his engineering innovations in architecture.

Like the humanists, Brunelleschi believed the ancient Romans had much to teach him. His studies in the art and architecture of Rome led him to develop the mathematical principles of linear perspective that the Romans had used in their wall paintings to convey a sense of depth. Linear perspective creates the illusion of three dimensions on a two-dimensional surface. To convey a sense of depth or distance, the painter drew lines on the flat surface of his canvas or wall that all converged on one point, called the vanishing point. Brunelleschi's own paintings in which he demonstrated this technique have not survived, but his peers credit him with bringing the principles of linear perspective to the attention of working painters and sculptors. Among the very first to make use of perspective were Masaccio in Florence and Ja-

---

Gentile Bellini (ca. 1429–1507) Important Venetian painter whose subject matter mainly concerned Venetian political and religious history.

Vatican Area on the north side of the Tiber in Rome where the pope was living by the end of the fifteenth century.

Giorgio Vasari (1511–1574) Italian architect and artist who wrote biographies of Renaissance artists.

Filippo Brunelleschi (1377–1446) Outstanding architect, painter, and engineer who introduced linear perspective in painting and designed the dome of Florence's cathedral.

linear perspective Illusion of depth and three-dimensional space in an image achieved by drawing the lines of the composition toward a vanishing point.

vanishing point In a painting, the point at which all the lines converge to give the illusion of depth and three dimensions.

Masaccio (1401–1428) Italian artist notable for his early experimentation with linear perspective.

Brunelleschi's reputation rests on his engineering of the dome of Florence's cathedral, finished in 1436 and pictured here. Italians refer to cathedrals by their word for "dome," *duomo.* The Duomo stands out so clearly in Florence's skyline that it epitomizes the city today as much as it did in the fifteenth century. *(Scala/Art Resource, NY)*

copo Bellini, the father of Gentile Bellini, the prominent Venetian painter.

Brunelleschi's fame, in his own time and today, however, stems mainly from his architectural and engineering accomplishments. Although the foundation of Florence's cathedral was laid at the very end of the thirteenth century, it still lacked a roof and a dome in the first decades of the fifteenth century. In 1420, Brunelleschi, chief architect of the ongoing construction, implemented his plan to build an enormous and immensely heavy octagonal dome on top of the completed cathedral walls. It was a daring project, involving updated Roman engineering equipment and ancient brick and stone methods of construction. In the end, Brunelleschi's plan worked, and the dome was consecrated in 1436. A friend of all the great artists at the time, Brunelleschi represents the extraordinary combination of talent, skill, and great learning found in many of the artists who emerged in the fifteenth century.

Leonardo da Vinci rivaled Brunelleschi and Michelangelo in breadth of knowledge, skill, and talent. He worked as a painter of portraits and of the large frescoes in monasteries and civic buildings that only ecclesiastical institutions and governments could afford to commission. His skills as a military engineer made him just as well known (see Choice). He was a scholar, too, who read widely in many fields. The humanist quest to celebrate all that was human inspired Leonardo to investigate the inner workings of the human body through dissections of cadavers, an illegal practice condemned by the church. Understanding how tendons connected muscle to bone enabled him to depict human forms with detailed accuracy. Everything that was human fascinated Leonardo. His wide range of expertise and his genius made him the prototype of the Renaissance man.

The Pleasure of Things

The explosion of cultural creativity in Renaissance Italy was not confined to the works of art in churches and government buildings. All wanted to adorn themselves and their surroundings with more possessions than had ever been available before, but, as always, only a minority could afford to. When the economy began to revive after the reversals and disasters of the fourteenth century, a new acquisitive spirit took hold in Italian cities as trade, manufacturing, and a rise in imported goods provided people with opportunities to spend money on objects that pleased them, enhanced their status, or both.

Leonardo da Vinci (1452–1519) One of the world's greatest artists and engineers, most famous for his painting the *Mona Lisa.*

Before beginning his painting in 1482, the Adoration of the Magi, Leonardo sketched on paper its composition, using linear perspective in the architectural elements. The painting was never finished, but Leonardo's sketches have taught art historians much about how painters in the fifteenth century worked. *(Scala/Art Resource, NY)*

Domestic interiors in the late fourteenth century would have seemed as uncomfortable to someone at the start of the sixteenth century as they would to someone today. Medieval homes lacked good seating. Most families of modest means in the fourteenth century owned very few pieces of furniture. One or two beds sufficed for all members of the family; the servants slept on rushes piled on the floor. One table provided a surface to eat on, socialize around, or write on. Perhaps there was a stool or a wooden bench to sit on. Against a wall might be a rough-hewn wooden chest for storage. With so little furniture, families spent most of their days outside in the courtyard of a house, working in the fields, or sitting under a tree with their neighbors, whether they lived in the countryside or in a city. When they had to come indoors, family members piled on the bed for seating.

The home of a well-to-do family would not have contained a greater variety of furniture, although there were likely to be a few more seats, wooden chests, and tables. Nor was there much in the way of decoration. Only wealthy families could afford to have their walls hung with tapestries, whose main function was, in any case, to retain heat. Everyday utensils, like serving dishes and cookware, tended to be uniform and utilitarian in shape, color, and material.

As the fifteenth century progressed, people bought more and more things, because, in large part, there were now more things to buy. Italian cities were becoming societies of consumers, intent on spending money in ways that would show off their status and taste. The wealthiest families directed their money toward building palaces that would reflect their social status. Domestic architecture emerged as a style distinct from ecclesiastic and governmental architecture. Builders designed palaces for their patrons that looked magnificent and imposing from the outside and luxurious and ceremonial on the inside. Spacious reception rooms, where the members of the family met with visitors, now contained more kinds of furniture than before. Larger and more ornately decorated wooden storage chests lined the wall. More chairs were available. A sideboard held the family's silverplate in a room now specifically designated for eating. Framed devotional paintings or frescoes depicting all the members of the family and their patron saints filled in the spots on the wall not covered by tapestries. People spent their money on luxury goods that would impress a visitor with the family's wealth, prestige, and cultivated taste.

In addition to decorating their homes, consumers also spent a good deal of money on what they wore. Until the fifteenth century, people's social status could be judged by the quality of their clothes. Renaissance Italians now had a greater variety of apparel to choose from, and the clothes themselves became more ornate, more complex in design, and made of expensive material. This greater availability of luxurious clothing, however, caused social tension. When a greater variety of fabrics came on the market at prices humble people could afford, even the wife of a shoemaker could look like a member of the upper classes. People could no longer be sure of a stranger's social rank from his or her clothing. Many city governments in Italy passed **sumptuary laws** that prohibited people of middle and low social status from wearing the kinds of fabrics and accessories associated with the rich. Ordinary women, for instance, could not use mink to trim the necklines of their dresses. In Venice, only patrician men could wear a red *giubba,* the gown worn by men of the city's highest rank. Of course, these laws proved very difficult to enforce. The consumer societies coming into being in the fifteenth century had the unintended effect of blurring some social distinctions that the ruling elites depended on to maintain order in society and themselves in power.

In this study in Anderlecht, in modern-day Belgium, the humanist theologian, Desiderius Erasmus wrote his best-known works at this desk. The shelves above his desk hold books of a size typical in his time. On the writing stand, an inkwell holds a feather quill, like Erasmus would have used to write. *(Erich Lessing/Art Resource, NY)*

The Northern European Renaissance

↓ What distinguished Flemish from Italian painters?
↓ How did the invention of movable type and the printing press bring about a revolution?

The Renaissance in northern Europe contrasted sharply with the busy, chaotic workshops of Italian artists and the offices in government palaces occupied by busy scribes. In Flanders, France, and England, quiet chambers in universities and libraries lined with tall bookcases—with the soft light of northern Europe streaming through glass windows—characterized the more tranquil environment of intellectuals and artists at work. What was produced in the northern Renaissance struck contemporary observers as no less stunning, however, for its less dramatic and less noisy emergence onto the cultural scene. If northern Europe benefited much from exposure to Italian scholars and artists, then the people of the north more than balanced the exchange of innovation by providing everyone with the printing press.

Northern European Art

The other center of artistic innovation in the fifteenth century lay in northern Europe, particularly in the cities of Flanders, where a style of painting and decoration very much different from Italian painting evolved. Although Flemish and Italian painters were interested in one another's work, they took from the other basic ideas and molded them to fit their own cultural environment. So subtle was the cultural exchange that it has been a matter of considerable debate as to whether the fifteenth-century fashion for portrait painting began in Italy or in Flanders. By the end of that century, however, two distinct styles of painting and sculpture had emerged.

sumptuary laws Municipal legislation restricting modes and expense of attire according to social status, profession, and, in the case of Jews, religion.

Manuscripts from the late fourteenth century reveal the earliest signs of northern European artists' unique approach to representing the world around them. Wealthy women and men paid copyists to compile prayer books for use in daily worship and artists to illuminate the pages with designs and figures in brilliant colors and gold leaf. A so-called **Book of Hours** contained a calendar with feast days and saints' days marked, the Psalms, and readings from the Gospels. Typically, illuminating the calendar offered the artist an opportunity to use bright and costly blue, red, and gold pigments to illustrate a month. In the manuscript collections of the Psalms (**Psalters**) and the schedule of church services throughout the year, which were small enough to fit conveniently in the hand, artists rendered painstakingly detailed scenes of the banquets, hunts, and other recreations of the nobility and urban elites. *The Very Rich Hours of the Duke of Berry,* executed around 1416, offers an exquisite example of the artistry to be seen in northern Europe.

From the detailed miniature manuscript illuminations to oil paintings was a short step. Unlike Italian artists, who used paints made of pigments mixed with egg yolks—known as **tempera**—either on fresh wall plaster or on wooden boards joined to form a smooth surface, Flemish painters set their scenes in pigments mixed with linseed oil and on linen canvas. The practice of painting in oil migrated from Flanders to Italy by the start of the sixteenth century, once Italian artists saw the superb work of **Jan van Eyck,** court painter to Philip, duke of Burgundy, and other Flemish artists. Apart from this difference in painting medium, two other differences in technique between the Italians and the Flemish are immediately noticeable. Whereas Italian painters relied on linear perspective to convey depth and dimension, the Flemish used gradations in color and the optical effect of painted light to achieve the same effect. And Italian painters presented their paintings in an architectural frame within the painting that separated the viewers from the painting's subject, while Flemish painters placed their subjects in a setting that seemed to include the viewer of the painting in the same space.

In contrast to the monumental, spare quality of Italian painting, the oil painting of Flanders looked cluttered and busy, with too many objects claiming the viewer's attention. Nothing in the world around them—from sacred figures to the buttons on the jacket worn by a portrait's subject—seemed insignificant to van Eyck and his fellow painters. They sought to realistically depict things and people as they looked to the human eye. It was the ordinariness of life that interested them. Not everyone appreciated the effort.

Above, in his 1434 portrait of a newly-married couple, the Flemish painter Jan Van Eyck used light and color to achieve depth of field. In contrast, the Italian Fra Angelico, a painter and Dominican friar, employed linear perspective—the use of lines converging on a vanishing point—for a similar effect in his fresco of the Annunciation from the 1440s on the right (page 333). *(Above: Reproduced by courtesy of the Trustees, the National Gallery, London; Right: Erich Lessing/Art Resource, NY)*

Michelangelo, for one, thought Flemish painters were far too obsessed with the minutiae of life and not attentive enough to its spiritual essence. Yet the things that cluttered Flemish paintings possessed meanings not

Book of Hours   Book or manuscript containing a calendar, prayers, and biblical passages for private devotion.
Psalter   Book or manuscript containing the Psalms.
tempera   Egg-based medium that binds paint pigments, used in Renaissance Italy.
Jan van Eyck   (ca. 1390–1441) Influential Flemish painter whose pioneering use of rich colors and light conveyed unprecedented depth of field.

easily apparent. In his portrait commemorating the marriage of an Italian merchant residing in Bruges, the objects van Eyck placed around the wedding couple standing beside a bed include a little dog and one lighted candle in the chandelier, both objects seemingly irrelevant to the event the painting honored. To the people of the time, it has long been believed, the bed was a familiar symbol of the sexual union in marriage, the little dog recalled fidelity, and the candle signaled the presence of Christ at the marriage. Thus, the painting works on both literal and symbolic levels at the same time. Flemish artists invited viewers to look not just at the objects in their paintings but through the objects to find their symbolic meaning.

Northern Humanists

Scholars from all over Europe undertook the arduous journey through the mountain passes into Italy to learn from the humanist scholars, especially those in Florence, whose works displayed a refreshing approach to classical literature. Frenchmen, Englishmen, and scholars from the Low Countries, in particular, came to Florence, Pisa, Venice, and other cities, where they found tutors in Greek and specialists in Latin literature to study with. When they returned home, they took with them new methods for the analysis of texts, a deeper appreciation for Greek and Roman literature, and plans to apply their newly acquired learning in the service of the church. In contrast to the Italian humanists, who believed public

service was as important as private study, the scholars from the north mostly came from and returned to either the cloister or the university. Because they were not in the public eye, the impact they had on their societies was less obvious and provoked less fanfare, but it was equally profound.

Like many of the Italian humanists, the humanists of northern Europe focused on the languages and literature of the past, but their interests reflected their close ties to the church and universities. By examining the language and history of texts written by early Christian writers more closely than had been done before, these fifteenth-century Christian humanists placed Christianity in history. They traced the evolution of doctrine from the church's earliest days to their present. In France, Italian-trained humanists such as Jacques Lefèvre d'Étaples produced new editions of texts written by the early church fathers. Others, like John Colet at Oxford University in England, studied early Christian texts written in Greek and Latin. They were the first generation of scholars to question the accuracy of the translations from Greek into Latin of scripture and the writings of early church thinkers. These editing projects and textual analyses formed the basis of a new field, **patristics.** Likewise, German scholars studied early Hebrew texts to gauge their influence on the development of early Christian thought.

The new fields and methods of study were controversial. From the perspective of the Christian humanists, the texts they studied and edited suggested that the church had wandered far from its original mission. More controversially, a few questioned the translation of certain words and verses in the New Testament, a text whose accuracy the church prohibited anyone from questioning. **Desiderius Erasmus,** a theologian born in Rotterdam in the Low Countries,

patristics Study of the writings of the early church fathers, such as Jerome, Ambrose, Augustine, and Pope Gregory I.

Desiderius Erasmus (1469–1536) Dutch humanist, theologian, and textual scholar whose writings influenced the movement for church reform.

In 1523, Hans Holbein the Younger, one of the best known painters in northern Europe, painted this portrait of Erasmus. Even though he is shown indoors, he wears heavy robes and a hat. The interiors of houses in northern Europe were so difficult to heat that people dressed very warmly while indoors. *(Erich Lessing/Art Resource, NY)*

believed not only that literate lay Christians ought to read scripture in the languages they spoke, but also, that scholars ought to reexamine the Vulgate Bible, which he found to contain errors in translation from the Greek New Testament. After a number of years of comparing manuscripts of the Greek New Testament he found in western Europe, Erasmus produced in 1516 a corrected Greek version with an updated Latin translation and extensive notes. Even this corrected version did not satisfy the standards set by humanist scholars, including Erasmus himself, and in 1522 he issued an improved edition of his Greek Testament that corrected his own errors. Erasmus faced stiff criticism from church leaders, most of whom objected to his undertaking the translation without the authorization of the church. They also felt ambivalent about making scripture available in vernacular languages to people liable to read whatever they wished into the translations. Even many of Erasmus's friends warned him that allowing laypeople to read and interpret the Bible for themselves would lead to disorder and rebellion. Although he and his fellow humanists believed that reading scripture for themselves in their own language would strengthen laypeople's faith, Erasmus came to see that it would not necessarily lead to continued obedience to church authority.

Jewish scholars, too, participated in the humanist study of texts. Their works incorporating humanist principles into the study of Judaism and the Hebrew Bible drew the interest of some Christian scholars. The study of Hebrew texts posed a challenge to those who objected in principle to the idea that Judaism had any influence on Christianity. Anti-Jewish senti-

VoicVoiceVoiceVoiceVoice

Erasmus Defends His Translation of the Greek New Testament

Erasmus, a theologian and editor and translator of the Greek New Testament, faced strong criticism for undertaking his translation from church leaders and other theologians, who feared what would happen if laypeople studied the text on their own. Erasmus had an enormous circle of friends throughout Europe. All his life, he wrote letters to them in which he discussed whichever work he was composing at the time, debated with them about political trends, and defended his belief in church reform. In the following letter, written in 1515, he responds to Martin Dorp, a Dutch theologian who in a previous letter had questioned the need for and legitimacy of the New Testament translation that Erasmus was about to begin. In his reply, Erasmus aggressively defends his translation at the same time as he insinuates that someone like Dorp, who could not read scripture in its original language of Greek, was in no position to lecture a theologian who could.

➡️ **What does Erasmus seem to have learned from his reading of the church fathers?**

What you write about the New Testament really makes me wonder what's happened to you. . . . You don't want me to change a single thing unless an idea is expressed more significantly in the Greek, and you deny that in the edition we know as the Vulgate there is any error at all. You think it would be sacrilege to alter in any way a text authenticated by agreement over so many centuries and endorsed by so many councils. ➡️ But if what you say is true, let me ask you, most learned Dorp, why Jerome often cites scripture in a form that varies from ours, and Augustine in another form, and Ambrose in still another? Why does Jerome censure and correct many specific passages which still remain uncorrected in the Vulgate?. . . . Are you going to dismiss all these authorities to follow a manuscript that may be full of scribal errors? Nobody says that the scriptures contain lies, though you seem to assume this is my attitude; nor does the matter relate in any way to the various controversies between Jerome and Augustine. ➡️ But the situation cries aloud; it would be plain, as they say, to a blind man: often, because of the ignorance or carelessness of a translator, the Greek has been imperfectly rendered, and often the original true reading has been corrupted by an ignorant copyist. We see this happen every day: texts are changed by thoughtless or sleepy scribes. Who does more to promote a lie, the man who corrects and removes a mistake, or the man who, out of reluctance to make a change, lets it stand? Besides, it's the nature of corrupt texts that one error leads to another. For a fact, more of these changes that I've made relate to the emphasis than to the basic sense, though frequently the emphasis is itself part of the sense, and not infrequently the whole passage has been drawn out of shape. When such a thing happens, I ask you, where does Augustine turn, where do Ambrose, Hilary, and Jerome look, if not to the Greek original? . . .

➡️ **How did printing change the problems inherent in the process of manuscript copying?**

. . . I have translated the entire New Testament afresh from the Greek originals with a Greek text across the page for easy comparison. My annotations are separate; they show, partly on the evidence and partly on the authority of ancient theologians, that my emendations were not rashly undertaken, that they can be accepted with confidence, and that they cannot be lightly dismissed. I only hope I have succeeded in a venture which has cost me so much labor. . . . ➡️ Finally, I don't doubt that you too will congratulate me on the book you now deplore, provided only that you acquire a little taste of that language without which you can't possibly form a reasonable judgment of the matter.

➡️ **Why does Erasmus stress the need for Dorp to learn Greek before he can offer informed criticism?**

Source: From *The Praise of Folly and Other Writings* by Desiderius Erasmus, translated by Robert M. Adams. Copyright © 1989 by W. W. Norton & Company, Inc. Used by permission of W. W. Norton & Company, Inc.

ment within the church and among traditional scholars made ecclesiastical authorities look with suspicion on scholars like Johannes Reuchlin, a German theologian at the university in Württemberg, who studied the **kabbala,** a Jewish mystical text.

Neither northern humanists nor their Italian counterparts sought to challenge the authority of the church and the papacy. But to varying degrees, the humanist project in northern Europe and in Italy helped to create the conditions out of which powerful critiques of the church emerged in the sixteenth century.

Printing, a New Medium

Scholarship in both northern Europe and in Italy underwent a profound change when a new invention, the printing press, made it possible to reproduce

kabbalah   (From Hebrew, "tradition") Field of Jewish mysticism dating to the twelfth century but of greater interest in the sixteenth.

Printer's shops, like this recreation of Johannes Gutenberg's in Mainz, Germany, pictured here, were crowded places. The printing press took up most of the room. Printers hung freshly-printed pages on lines across the shop so that the ink would dry. In the background appear frames with many compartments in which letter types were stored *(Erich Lessing/Art Resource, NY)*

many identical copies of a work quickly for distribution. A goldsmith from the German city of Mainz, **Johannes Gutenberg,** is believed to have invented in the 1440s the process in which a printer pressed ink-coated movable type onto paper. Although the Chinese had centuries before devised a printing process by carving the characters that made up their written language onto blocks of wood, Gutenberg's innovation was, first, to cast small pieces of metal type, each with a raised face in the shape of a letter. A typesetter arranged the metal type, letter by letter, in horizontal rows to spell out the text to be published. Setting the type was the most time-consuming part of the printing process. After the rows were locked within a frame, the printer brushed the set type with ink, laid paper on it, and then slid it under a heavy press. When all the pages of the text had been printed, the metal type was disassembled so that it could be set again for another text.

The development of the printing process depended on the availability and low cost of paper in western Europe. Originally a product from China that Muslim merchants brought back along the caravan routes to the Mediterranean, paper attracted the attention of Christian merchants—and possibly the crusaders—who had dealings in the Muslim world. They recognized that paper, made from pulverized cotton cloth,

cost far less to produce than parchment and vellum, the treated sheep or calf skins that served as writing surfaces in western Europe. Depending on its size, a complete Bible consisting entirely of parchment or vellum pages could require the skins of nearly two hundred sheep or calves, which explains why manuscripts were so expensive to produce. By the late thirteenth century, paper production in Italy had begun. Scribes continued to use parchment and vellum for their luxury manuscripts, but in everyday life people increasingly used paper for their account books, records, and private documents.

The affordability of paper and the speed of printing on it brought about a revolution in ideas and beliefs in the sixteenth century, as unprecedented amounts of information were put into circulation. The first products of the printing press certainly included books, but short and inexpensive political pamphlets, religious tracts, and bureaucratic forms appeared for sale in Mainz's first printshops right away. The artistry and craftsmanship that went into large luxury books, like the beautiful three-volume Bibles Gutenberg printed around 1455, kept their price prohibitively high.

Johannes Gutenberg   (d. 1468) Inventor of the printing press, and printing from movable type, in the west.

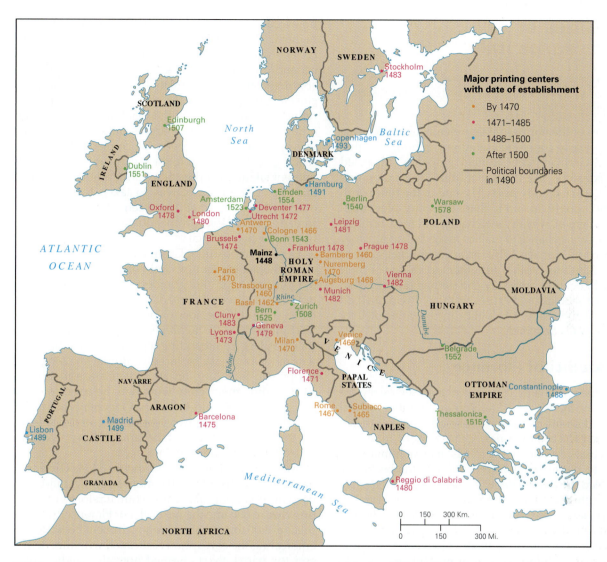

MAP 12.1 **The Growth of Printing** Bills of sale, sermons, bibles, and scholarly works were among the first printed texts that printers produced. The new invention quickly spread across western Europe. Within fifty years, Venice had more printing presses than any other city in Europe.

Printing shops spread quickly, first across Germany and then throughout Europe. Within a few years of Gutenberg's Bibles, the printing press reached other German cities—Strasbourg in 1460, Cologne in 1464. Sixty towns in Germany had printing shops by 1500. But in that same year Venice could boast of 150 printing presses. One Venetian printer, **Aldus Manutius,** joined with humanist scholars to print texts in the Greek alphabet that refugee scholars from the Byzantine Empire had brought to Italy.

Less than a century following the invention of movable type and the printing press, an estimated 9 million books were in circulation. Moreover, a great many more people knew how to read, especially in Italy, where literacy had accompanied the expansion of commerce and lay education. As the print culture expanded, reliance on memory and recitation diminished. The very way people thought and learned and remembered was changing.

Aldus Manutius (1449–1515) Important Venetian printer noted for publishing Byzantine texts in the Greek alphabet.

The Cities of Renaissance Italy

⬇ How were the cities of Italy governed?
⬇ What was the relation of the Papal States to the politics of Renaissance Italy?

The cities of the northern Italian peninsula took pride in their nearly complete autonomy, although in theory the German Holy Roman emperor still ruled them. For some, like the city of Milan, that autonomy had come at a bloody price. The end of the fourteenth century brought an end to that autonomy. Now military strongmen, wealthy merchants, and royal foreigners each saw a chance to grab as much Italian territory as they could manage. While an army brought some to power, fabulous wealth put others in charge of their cities. The republican liberty and human potential that humanist scholars and artists celebrated remained an ideal that the reality of politics in the cities of Italy nearly always defeated.

The Medici of Florence

Florentine merchants considered themselves the inheritors of the ideals of the Roman Republic, which they read about in history books now being written for their pleasure by a new generation of humanist intellectuals espousing the ideals of civic humanism. In reality, these city governments only inadvertently resembled the Roman Republic, because, like the small elite that had ruled Rome more than fifteen hundred years before, they, too, constituted a small minority of wealthy men who monopolized the political life of their cities. Within those small groups of mercantile families, competition to exert the most influence on the government was fierce. Wealthy patrons granted business and political favors to less wealthy clients, who then were expected to vote according to the interests of their patrons. A family's political power stemmed from such supporters, friends, and relatives who felt beholden to their benefactors and their families.

In Florence, the Medici family came to power through the steady and generous distribution of fiscal, political, and commercial favors to those less fortunate than they. Those favors bought the political loyalty of those who accepted the Medici's help. The first member to achieve nearly complete but unofficial dominance of the Florentine government was **Cosimo de' Medici,** who inherited his father's lucrative role as banker to the pope in addition to the responsibility of representing the family in Florence's public life. Cosimo was elected to the Signoria and other city councils, like many of his peers, but his real power far exceeded the authority of any public office he held. Through his network of clients, Cosimo directed—out of sight from public view—Florentine fiscal and diplomatic affairs. He dressed modestly, ate sparingly, and often retreated to Florence's most exclusive monastery, San Marco, spending days in quiet reflection and prayer. Behind that humble exterior lay a hunger for power as sharp as his splendid palace was opulent. The city governing councils did nothing relating to taxation, foreign policy, or the economy without taking their direction from Cosimo de' Medici. His supreme authority was so taken for granted—even if an open secret and resented by many—that foreign powers knew to negotiate directly with him, not the elected councils.

Despite opposition, Cosimo's grandson, Lorenzo, strengthened his family's hold on power. Called "the Magnificent" for the grandeur of his palaces and building projects, Lorenzo shared with his grandfather a similar passion for power. Displaying a subtle diplomatic skill, he prevented the pope and other Italian rulers from banding together against him, but within his own city he faced continual challenges to his power, including an attempted assassination in 1478. Although severely wounded, he lived to exact revenge on his would-be killers. Opponents of Medici rule had to wait until two years after Lorenzo's death in 1492 before they ousted the family from power and exiled them from the city.

After the ouster of the Medici in 1494, **Girolamo Savonarola,** a friar from the monastery of San Marco, used his great popularity as a church reform–minded preacher to become the next ruler of Florence. Savonarola's establishment of a new government dedicated to eradicating the corruption associated with the Medici and the papal court alarmed both the Medici allies and the pope. He ruled Florence with the support of the majority of Florentines, while a small faction of families conspired with the papacy to bring about his downfall. On the grounds that his calls for church reform constituted heresy, Savonarola was tried and burned at the stake in 1498. After four more years of turmoil in the city, the Medici returned to power in 1512.

Cosimo de' Medici (1389–1464) First important member of this wealthy family to make himself ruler of the city of Florence.

Girolamo Savonarola (1452–1498) Italian Dominican friar who tried to carry out church reform in Florence.

This map from 1480 shows that many of the landmarks that Florence is known for today were already in place. The Duomo and the public buildings appear in the center of the map. The expansion of the city across the river Arno, to the right, required extending the city walls. *(Erich Lessing/Art Resource, NY)*

Maritime Republics

The Florentines were not the only people of Italy who claimed their city embodied the classical virtues of civic humanism. Similar to the elites of Florence, small, hereditary groups of merchant families ruled the republics of Venice and Genoa by the end of the fourteenth century. The governments of both city-states consisted of councils, over each of which a **doge** presided as the official head of state. In Venice, the members of the ruling councils considered themselves to be nobles, but the term they used to describe themselves was reminiscent of ancient Rome—patricians. They represented only about 1 percent of the population of Venice, which fluctuated just above and below 100,000. A similarly tiny percentage of Genoa's population exercised complete political authority there. The families that rose to the top of Venetian and Genoese societies became wealthy through long-distance trade. Trading companies had extensive networks of branch offices around the Mediterranean and in the ports of northern Europe.

Economic competition between Genoa and Venice at times led to open hostilities and even warfare between the two republics. Four times—in 1258, 1298, 1350, and 1380—the fleets of the two cities met in sea battles in the vicinity of their trading operations in the east and in the Venetian lagoon. They fought over access to and commercial dominance of the Aegean Islands and the Black Sea. During the last and decisive conflict known as the **War of Chioggia** in 1380, the Venetians relied on cutting-edge military technology by mounting cannon on their war galleys, which they aimed both at attacking ships and at on-shore military defenses. Venice's victory over Genoa had as much to do with its advanced weaponry as it did with Genoa's internal weaknesses. Factional fighting among Genoa's ruling elite led to frequent changes in Genoa's government and the shifting of the responsibility for the city's overseas trade to the **Maona,** a private mercantile company in Genoa that assumed the role of the state in the Aegean Islands under Genoese rule. Genoa's instability gave the edge to Venetian merchants, who benefited from the stable and mature institutions of their government, which maintained a war fleet in the region that protected them. By the turn of the fifteenth century, Venice had emerged as the stronger power.

Of the two cities, Venice had the more illustrious—certainly the more notorious—reputation. By the fifteenth century, Venetians lived as much by means of the sea as literally in the sea. A city made up of more than a hundred tiny islands connected by bridges, Venice had thoroughfares that were either footpaths or navigable canals, punctuated now and then by a campo, or field, with a public well in its center. In the seventeenth century, when the campi were paved, the Venetian government banned horses and compelled Venetians to move around the city either on foot or by gondola, a long, black vessel propelled by an upright oarsman. Even in the fifteenth century, Venice exerted a fascination on people from elsewhere. Its jewel-like appearance, lying off the mainland and surrounded by a shimmering sea, impressed visitors. So did its growing reputation for vice. Contemporaries expressed astonishment as the number of prostitutes and **courtesans** in public view in certain quarters of the city.

Beginning with Petrarch in the 1360s, humanists received a warm welcome in Venice, provided they did nothing to disturb the oligarchic serenity of Venice's patricians. In the city itself, the lack of visible social unrest among the humble sections of its population and its ruling elite impressed visitors and Venetians themselves to such an extent that its government proudly called itself The Most Serene Republic in its official documents. The Aegean islands occupied by Venetian troops in the fourteenth century and the mainland Italian cities subordinated to Venetian authority in the fifteenth had a different experience of Venice's serenity. By the middle of the fifteenth century, as Ottoman Turks undermined Venetian authority in the eastern Mediterranean and Venice attempted to extend its territory on the mainland, the other Italian powers felt increasingly threatened.

Autocrats and Humanists

In the late fourteenth century, northern Italian city dwellers lived in fear of rioting workers, bloody **vendettas** between warring families, and the violent overthrow of civic institutions by ambitious men. Personal and collective liberty required from the city residents constant vigilance and active defense. Urban violence reached such alarming levels that city

doge   (from Latin *dux*, "leader") Head of state in Venice and Genoa.

War of Chioggia   Conflict between Venice and Genoa in 1380, in which Venice won a decisive victory.

Maona   Private mercantile company in Genoa that assumed the role of the state in the Aegean Islands under Genoese rule.

courtesan   A woman, very often highly educated and refined, who served as a mistress to wealthy men in exchange for support.

vendetta   Campaign of revenge fought between two factions or families.

authorities resorted to the services of professional military men—**condottieri**—to keep the peace. These captains and their salaried armies acted at first like a police force and a militia, but they soon made themselves lords of the cities whose safety they had been hired to defend.

These military rulers of Italian cities owed their power to brute force, but disguised it behind the elegant and refined behavior typical of a Renaissance court. Among humanists, two types of the ideal ruler took shape. *The Courtier,* a widely-read work published in 1528 by **Baldassare Castiglione,** a diplomat and intellectual from Milan, described the ideal ruler as a battle-tested as well as a highly educated commander with elegant manners. Castiglione's "Renaissance man" combined a chivalrous knight with a humanist scholar.

A Florentine presented another type of ideal ruler that reflected a grittier understanding of how the world worked. The son of a poor Florentine lawyer who belonged to a distinguished family, **Niccolò Machiavelli** gained considerable experience as a diplomat in Florence's government between the death of Savonarola in 1498 and the Medici's return to power in 1512. On the grounds that employment in Florence's government prior to their return made Machiavelli their enemy, the Medici family had him arrested and tortured. After a brief, painful period in prison, he went into exile. To win his way back to Florence, Machiavelli dedicated to the new Medici ruler his work *The Prince.* Published in 1532 only after Machiavelli died, *The Prince* offers political advice on how heads of states, particularly those who seize power, should govern. Machiavelli advanced a strategy for domination requiring rulers to show no mercy to their enemies, to act decisively and ruthlessly, and to rule by expediency rather than morality. The ends, Machiavelli famously argued, justified the means. Like the humanists, he looked to ancient Roman writers for solutions to the problems he saw plaguing the cities of Italy. But he studied those texts with the autocratic behavior he had witnessed when on diplomatic business for Florence in Milan and the Papal States in mind and came to conclusions that sat uneasily with humanist ideals.

Milan in the province of Lombardy enjoyed the rights and privileges of an autonomous city. A council made up of the leading Milanese families governed the city until 1311, when the **Visconti** family imposed its rule on the population. Under their rule, Milan grew into a powerful state founded on its rulers' military requirements. Its armaments and textile industries made the city wealthy. Milanese armor was in demand throughout Europe, and its silk cloth rivaled what Florentine weavers produced.

The Visconti family's ambition to govern did not stop, however, at the city walls. Throughout the 1380s and 1390s, Visconti forces conquered Siena and Pisa (both near Florence) as well as Verona and Vicenza (close to Venice), subdued the city of Bologna (a papal possession), and took control of the commercially important passes over the Alps. The alliance formed by Florence, Venice, and the pope to stop the Visconti was only partly successful. In 1447, when Filippo Maria Visconti died without a legitimate male heir, the people of Milan saw an opportunity to form a republic. Filippo Maria's son-in-law, **Francesco Sforza,** the condottiere hired to keep public order, had other plans. By 1450, attempts to form a republic had failed and Sforza had declared himself duke of Milan.

The new autocratic rulers of Milan enjoyed the prestige that came from patronizing the humanists and artists inspired by Renaissance ideals of republican liberty. In return, the republican-minded humanists, painters, and architects did not object to working in the military state that Milan had become. They easily found employment in the city's monasteries and ducal government. The most prominent artist of all, Leonardo da Vinci, spent nearly two decades in Milan in the employ of Ludovico Sforza, duke of Milan, who asked him to cast a bronze equestrian statue commemorating his father, Francesco, the first Sforza duke of Milan. His fresco of the Last Supper in the Convent of Santa Maria delle Grazie in Milan remains to this day one of the most recognizable paintings in the world.

The Papal States and the Church

Unlike Florence and Milan, where many people clung to republican ideals even when ruled by autocrats, the Papal States made no accommodation to those who would have preferred to live in a republic. In all of western Europe, only the pope could claim

---

condottieri   Mercenary captains employed by Italian city-states to maintain internal order.

Baldassare Castiglione   (1478–1529) Diplomat and humanist who wrote The Courtier (1528), in which he describes the "Renaissance man."

Niccolò Machiavelli   (1469–1527) Diplomat and political writer most famous for *The Prince,* a work instructing rulers on how to govern.

Visconti   The family of ruling Milanese dukes from 1395 until 1447, when replaced by the Sforza family.

Francesco Sforza   (r. 1447–1466) Mercenary captain hired to protect Milan; the first of a dynasty to rule Milan.

legitimacy dating back to Emperor Constantine in the third century, even if that claim had been discredited in certain circles. Over half a century before, in 1440, the humanist **Lorenzo Valla** performed a feat of scholarship that drew the admiration of scholars all across Europe, including Erasmus. Using humanist methods of textual analysis, he convincingly proved that the Donation of Constantine, on the basis of which the papacy laid claim to central Italy, was forged. Valla's work had little practical impact, as the papacy's power had been reinforced simply by the passage of centuries and the weight of tradition. The Papal States remained a theocratic and autocratic dominion until the nineteenth century.

When the papacy left Rome and settled in Avignon, the nobles who governed the Papal States on behalf of the papacy took the opportunity to extricate themselves from its lordship. During the fourteenth century, several of the cities and towns under papal rule, such as Bologna, refused to recognize the lordship of the Avignon popes. The Visconti family of Milan, whose territory abutted the northwestern borders of the pope's lands, also saw an opportunity to add to their territory. Resistance to papal overlordship grew so strong that the papacy's income dropped significantly. Hiring an army in the 1350s to reimpose papal rule over the rebel lands sapped the pope's treasury even more.

Initially, restoring order in the Papal States was the first order of business when the popes returned to Rome permanently at the end of the Great Schism in 1417. The popes of the fifteenth century appointed their own family members to secular and ecclesiastic offices in the cities of central Italy as a way of securing the loyalty of public authorities there. At the end of the century, Pope **Alexander VI** of the Borgia family put family loyalty ahead of the papacy's interests by creating a new, independent state carved out of the Papal States for his illegitimate son, Cesare Borgia, whom he had made a cardinal in 1493 when Cesare was not yet twenty. Five years later, Cesare exchanged his position as cardinal for that of military commander. The army he led conquered the three principal regions in the Papal States: Emilia, Romagna, and Umbria. When his father died in 1503, Cesare lost access to the funding he needed to pay his army. Without an army, and with a new pope intent on restoring dignity to the papacy and its lands, Cesare fell from power.

The death of Alexander VI's successor within a year of his election put Pope **Julius II** in charge of imposing papal rule over central Italy. Not content with hiring a mercenary army to enter battle for him, Julius led his own troops in 1508 to restore papal authority in the cities of Bologna and Perugia, contrary to church law, which forbade clergy to fight in wars.

Alexander VI's death and Cesare Borgia's inability to defend his possession of the Papal States had given Venice an opportunity to expand its mainland holdings. Now, in an alliance with other powers in Italy, Julius forced the Venetians out of his lands in 1509. Julius, the patron of the arts responsible for Michelangelo's ceiling in the Sistine Chapel, conquered the land that had been lost to the papacy since the Avignon popes of the fourteenth century.

Renaissance Ideals in Transition, 1400–1550

> ⬇ How did many of the cultural benefits of the Italian Renaissance reach France?
> ⬇ What factors contributed to their slow passage to England?

Pope Julius, the Sforza dukes, and the Medici demonstrated that the appreciation of humanist ideals could coexist with autocratic domination over their subjects. Similarly, the people of other countries and their rulers absorbed the cultural and intellectual innovations of Italy and Flanders at different rates and in their own ways. The French king admired the Italian Renaissance so much that, when he invaded the peninsula to conquer it, he made sure to acquire as many works of art—and artists—as he could along the way. For most of the fifteenth century, civil war distracted the nobility of England from the pleasures of patronage. In Germany, painters took some notice of the Italian and Flemish artists, but farther east, the Russians clung to the stylized forms icon painters had absorbed from the Byzantines long ago.

The Court of Francis I

Chivalry—the medieval code of heroism, piety, and the idealization of noblewomen—was the consuming passion of one man, whose interests and predilections shaped the character of the Renaissance in France:

Lorenzo Valla (1407–1457) Humanist scholar whose influential treatise, written in 1440, showed the Donation of Constantine to be a forgery.

Alexander VI (r. 1492–1503) Pope who was a member of the Spanish Borgia family and notorious for the promotion of his illegitimate children and the corruption of his papal court.

Julius II (r. 1503–1513) Pope who was a great patron of artists, especially Michelangelo, and who restored the Papal States to papal control.

King **Francis I.** As a fatherless teenager, heir to his cousin Louis XII, Francis took no interest in academic learning. Warfare and the ceremony associated with aristocratic knighthood absorbed all of the spoiled boy's attention. With no one able to guide him or restrain him apart from his mother, Francis trained himself to wage war rather than to rule.

When he succeeded to the throne in 1520, Francis I made his mother, Louise, regent so that she could rule in his absence and then left to conquer Italy. His first target was the duchy of Milan, under the rule of the Sforza family, whose forces he defeated. The French king was outmaneuvered by the adroit Pope Leo X, who took back possession of his territories in central Italy while recognizing Francis's overlordship. The Sforza duke of Milan achieved the same arrangement.

Francis failed to conquer Italy, but Italy, in a sense, conquered him. During his time at the papal court, the French king was deeply impressed with the culture of the Italian Renaissance and, over time, patronized some of its leading artists. He drew to his court in France the finest painters, poets, musicians, and scholars, who, perceiving their patron's chivalric passions, produced paintings, poetry, and songs that glorified the arts of war. Leonardo da Vinci and the sculptor Benvenuto Cellini were his guests. The royal place at **Fontainebleau** melded traditional French architecture with the new Italian style, and the king's lavish court life there was modeled on the magnificence of the great Italian courts in Florence and Milan. Moreover, Francis took an interest in the Christian humanists and their reform-minded critiques of the church. As an adult, he acquired the intellectual interests that his martial training in youth had precluded. The combination of chivalric ceremonial displays and his promotion of the arts and learning created a lasting legacy for Francis as his kingdom's Renaissance king.

England Before Its Renaissance

After the last battles of the Hundred Years' War in the mid-fifteenth century, English men and women associated king with country more than they had ever done, partly as a result of patriotic pageants, popular **ballads,** and other propaganda meant to rally financial and moral support for the war against France. Throughout the war, the **Arthurian legends** idealized knighthood and offered a powerful model of chivalric kingship in the character of King Arthur. After the war, in the 1470s, **Thomas Malory** reworked many of the old tales about the legendary king and his knights for the first time in English in an epic account of the Knights of the Round Table, *Le Morte d'Arthur* (*The Death of Arthur*). The printer **William Caxton** pub-

lished it in 1485, making it one of the earliest printed works of English literature. The stories about the adventures of King Arthur, Lancelot, Guinevere, and the knights offered a model of heroic kingship that the English looked for in their own king.

Henry V's son and heir, Henry VI (r. 1421–1461, 1470–1471), did not, however, inspire much confidence. Mentally unstable and unfit to rule for periods of time, he survived repeated attempts to remove him from power until kinsmen and rival claimants to the throne deposed him in 1461. The leader of his opponents and his cousin from the House of York ascended the throne as Edward IV (r. 1461–1470, 1471–1483). Henry fled to allies in Scotland but was captured and confined in the **Tower of London** in 1465. The new king Edward spent his entire reign fighting off supporters of the deposed Henry in the ongoing series of civil wars known collectively as the **Wars of the Roses** (1455–1485), after the red and white roses symbolizing Edward IV's York and Henry VI's Lancaster families. After his coronation, Edward ruled for ten years before his early death put his young son, Edward V (r. 1483), on the throne.

The young king's reign, too, soon ended. His uncle, Richard of York, imprisoned the young king and his younger brother in the Tower of London, where they both died under mysterious circumstances. Rumors that their uncle, now **Richard III,** had had his

Francis I (r. 1515–1547) King of France who centralized royal rule, created at his court a vibrant Renaissance culture, and unsuccessfully fought Charles V for control of Italy.

Fontainebleau Castle, or château, and chief residence of Francis I, king of France.

ballad Popular song that usually told a story.

Arthurian legends Stories associated with the deeds and lives of the mythical King Arthur and the Knights of the Round Table.

Thomas Malory (d. 1471) Author of *Le Morte d'Arthur,* an English-language collection of the Arthurian legends, published in 1485.

William Caxton (ca.1415–1492) England's first printer, who published Malory's *Le Morte d'Arthur.*

Tower of London Norman fortification situated on the banks of the Thames River where political prisoners were confined.

Wars of the Roses Civil wars between the descendants of Edward III for the throne of England, 1455–1485.

Richard III (r. 1483–1485) King of England after his young nephew, Edward V, died in captivity; defeated and killed by Henry Tudor at the Battle of Bosworth Field.

nephews murdered turned the nobles and the population against the king, thus presenting an opportunity for the supporters of Henry VI's House of Lancaster to reassert their claim to the throne. In 1485, Richard's chief Lancastrian opponent, Henry Tudor of Wales, defeated Richard at **Bosworth Field.** When Henry married Elizabeth of York in 1486, he united the Lancastrian and Yorkist factions. Crowned **Henry VII,** the founder of the **Tudor** dynasty set out to restore stability to England and replenish the nearly empty royal treasury. Only under later Tudors would England achieve its Renaissance.

The Holy Roman Empire and Eastern Europe

In the lands to the east of the French kingdom in the late fourteenth and fifteenth centuries, the flourishing trade among the Baltic Sea countries inspired the rulers in the region to consolidate their authority and claim their share of the profits. The Holy Roman emperors concentrated their efforts on their German lands. The princes of Moscow wrested control over their lands from their Mongol conquerors. The kings of Bohemia and Hungary insinuated themselves into the center of the Holy Roman Empire's political life, while new states were emerging along the northern shorelines of the Baltic Sea.

Unlike his predecessors, the Holy Roman emperor Charles IV (r. 1347–1378) faced the difficult truth that he could not sustain an empire that stretched from Germany in the north to Italy in the south. In a proclamation issued in 1356 and known as the **Golden Bull,** he laid out a system by which his successors would be chosen by seven permanent electors: the archbishops of three German cities and the rulers of four principalities. Three of the **prince electors** were German; the fourth was the king of Bohemia. Although Charles's plan provided political stability to the civil war–prone empire, the permanent exclusion of certain princely families deepened resentments and competition among the German nobles that had already led to sporadic warfare. Charles's choice of electors, however, had an unforeseen but timely impact on the empire's security. After deposing Charles' son and successor, the electors chose as emperor his grandson, Sigimund, king of Bohemia and Hungary in 1410 largely because his kingdom was viewed as the front line in the effort to hold back the Ottoman Turks, whose armies pushed the empire's eastern borders in the first half of the fifteenth century.

While the system of prince electors offered some stability to the empire, merchants in German and Slavic territories competed fiercely over trade in Scandinavian and Baltic lands. In the final decades of the thirteenth century, guilds of German merchants with branch offices in England and Flanders joined with German merchants based in the Baltic and Scandinavian regions to form the Hanseatic League, a commercial association whose purpose was to provide its members with protection against piracy at sea and to regulate trade in German cities and in the Baltic states farther north. They specialized in the major commodities of the Baltic region, especially in fish, timber, and furs. Because public order was conducive to trade, league members served as city managers and police forces in the hundred-odd cities in which they were based during the fourteenth century. But the lack of centralization among the branches of the Hanseatic League led to their decline in the face of the growing power of the states around them, particularly to the east.

On the eastern borders of the empire and the Hanseatic cities of Prussia lay Poland and, beyond it, Lithuania, whose duke, Jagiello, became king of Poland in 1386 when he married Poland's heiress to the throne, Jadwiga. Jagiello's conversion to the Roman church at his marriage ensured that the majority of Lithuanians adhered to the Roman Catholic Church rather than the Eastern Orthodox tradition. Although the two countries were ruled by the same man, they did not merge into one kingdom. Within a generation, Poland had one grandson of Jagiello's as king and Lithuania had another as grand prince. The power of conjoined Poland-Lithuania succeeded in defeating the military order of Teutonic Knights, the major competitor for conquering and ruling the unchristianized Baltic territory to the north. Based in Prussia, to the west of Poland and Lithuania, the order protected the Hanseatic cities and made incursions into Polish territory in

Bosworth Field   Battle in 1485 in which the Yorkist forces, led by the English king Richard III, was defeated by the Lancastrian faction commanded by Henry Tudor.

Henry VII   (r. 1485–1509) First Tudor king of England, who ended the Wars of the Roses and consolidated royal power.

Tudor   Dynastic family ruling England from 1485 to 1603.

Golden Bull   Decree issued by Emperor Charles IV in 1356 that established the method for electing the Holy Roman emperor.

prince electors   Noblemen and bishops with the hereditary right to elect the Holy Roman emperor.

an effort to claim land there. In 1410, Jagiello defeated the order in a battle that set back its efforts to occupy the northern parts of Lithuania. But it was only at the conclusion of a thirteen-year war in 1466 that the Teutonic Knights were finally and decisively defeated.

Even farther to the east, the grand prince of Moscow, **Basil I,** brought together Russian principalities under his rule by conquering his neighbors between 1392 and 1398. To discourage an invasion of his lands by the Mongol Empire of the Golden Horde—to whom he paid tribute to prevent just that possibility—he made an alliance with Lithuania in 1392. Within three years, a larger threat appeared on his eastern borders: Timur, the Tartar ruler, who attacked Basil's lands and inflicted even more damage on the Mongols. Basil's death in 1425 left his ten-year-old son, Basil II

(r. 1425–1462), to defend his inheritance of his father's lands from his uncles. Political stability came to Basil's Russian lands only after decades of warfare against his uncles and cousins, the slow collapse of the Golden Horde, and, once Basil had died in 1462, the coming to power of his capable son, Ivan III. By the end of the fifteenth century, Basil's heirs had transformed Moscow into the strongest power in the east, beholden to no other.

> **Basil I** (r. 1389–1425) Grand prince of Moscow who expelled the Mongols from Russia and maintained his independence from Lithuania.

Summary

Review Questions

↑ How did Renaissance ideals affect the expectations of the people and behavior of rulers?

↑ How did ideas about painters, sculptors, and architects change over the course of the Renaissance?

↑ What was the impact of printing?

Out of the long, bleak period of high mortality rates emerged a cultural movement that emphasized humanity's essential worth. Individually and collectively, the human species found its champions in the humanists, painters, sculptors, and architects who celebrated mind and body in their work. In the birthplace of the long-gone Roman Republic, scholars found a new inspiration that to many felt like a rebirth, a renaissance. The rediscovery of classical texts refreshed knowledge of a past world and stimulated a new type of critical textual analysis. Greek refugees from the east brought the opportunity to incorporate new knowledge from the even older Greek civilization.

Artisans, too, underwent an evolution in how they approached their work. As humanists, painters strove to depict the human form in lifelike dimensions, which included situating figures realistically within a painted scene. The human image was no longer an ideal type with indistinguishable, anonymous features but was now, in the hands of a master

painter, a recognizable figure with a name. The skills required were more than those of a technician. It took an artist to render the soul in human form.

In northern Europe scholars also found a new appreciation of ancient Roman authors, but their intellectual audacity led them to focus on the Bible and the writings of the church fathers. Humanists such as Erasmus came to believe that it was time to review the translations from Greek of the New Testament. They also believed that the main consequence of more people reading the Bible in the vernacular would be the strengthening of Christian faith. The spread of printing presses across western Europe assisted the humanists in their goals. Communities of scholars now had identical texts to study. The scientific works of ancient Greek philosophers reached a far wider audience of scholars than they would have in manuscript form. The greater availability of inexpensive printed texts created an incentive to learn how to read.

The work of humanists and artists appealed to the autocratic rulers of western Europe in spite of its ideals rather than because of them. The Medici family of Florence had no intention of sharing power with any others in a state that was republican in the Roman sense of the word. The republics of Venice and Genoa also discouraged dissent within their populations and conducted campaigns of conquest. When military strongmen assumed control of Milan, they ruthlessly squashed republican sentiment. Pope Julius II crushed all resistance to papal rule in the

Papal States. In ruling circles, the appeal of civic humanism was limited.

Elsewhere in Europe, the news of these cultural movements led slowly to similar changes. Francis I of France could not conquer Italy, but he returned with a great appreciation of the Renaissance and lured many of its artisans, like Leonardo, to follow him. The absorption of Renaissance ideals by the peoples of England, the Holy Roman Empire, and Russia occurred at a slower pace. Political stability and peace had to return to those war-torn regions before the influence of the Renaissance could be felt.

← **Thinking Back, Thinking Ahead** →

What were the possible consequences of the greater availability of printed Bibles in vernacular languages?

ECHO ECHO ECHO ECHO ECHO ECHO

Renaissance Art, Modern Art

What is art? If you walk into a museum today, you might find one gallery filled with huge canvases covered with stripes of color or splattered paint. In the next room might be portraits and religious scenes painted centuries ago. One kind of art seems like child's play, while the other seems to have required much skill in its creation. Can they both really be art? Must art involve craftsmanship and fine technique as well as beauty, as in a Renaissance painting? Or does anything that an artist does or makes that stimulates a response in a viewer qualify as art?

Such questions have long preoccupied artists, art critics, and the public. Renaissance artists meant to glorify God, in the first place, and humanity, in the second. Their aim was to faithfully represent the world they saw around them, and by "faithfully" they would have intended faithfulness to God and nature. In later centuries, artists abandoned the goal of accurately depicting the human form and expression and sought instead to depict an interior reality—what an emotion felt like, for example, or the fragmentation of modern life, or the chilling efficiency of machines and technology.

Since the Renaissance, the purpose or role of art in society has never ceased to change. Pablo Picasso, one of the most influential artists of the twentieth century, insisted that when he incorporated African and Asian-Pacific elements into his paintings and sculptures, he was seeking only to broaden the range of what was considered beautiful. His goal was to render new models of beauty accessible to people in the west. Still other modern artists renounced the ideal of beauty in art altogether. Barnett Newman, a twentieth-century artist, wrote in 1948, "The impulse of modern art is the desire to destroy beauty," a sentiment that stands in strong contrast to the objectives of Renaissance artists, whose aim was to exalt the human form.

Today the desire to create—even if to do so is to suggest destruction—continues to motivate artists to put their works before the public. The concept of art has become so broad that it can encompass the altarpiece painting that appeals to religious and nonreligious people alike and an abstract painting that consists of a solid block of color.

Suggested Readings

Abulafia, David. *The Western Mediterranean Kingdoms, 1200–1500.* London and New York: Longman, 1997. A useful study of mainly Italy and Spain.

Baxandall, Michael. *Painting and Experience in Fifteenth-Century Italy.* 2nd ed. Oxford: Oxford University Press, 1988. A work that helped establish the social history of Renaissance art.

Brucker, Gene. *Florence, the Golden Age, 1138–1737.* Berkeley and Los Angeles: University of California Press, 1998. A classic overview of Florentine history.

Epstein, Steven. *Genoa and the Genoese, 958–1528.* Chapel Hill, N.C.: University of North Carolina Press, 2001. A good introduction to the history of this merchant republic.

Goldthwaite, Richard A. *Wealth and the Demand for Art in Italy, 1300–1600.* Baltimore: Johns Hopkins University Press, 1995. An account of the rise of consumer culture that emphasizes Florence.

Lane, Frederic C. *Venice, a Maritime Republic.* Baltimore: Johns Hopkins University Press, 1973. Still the place to begin, despite having been written more than thirty years ago.

Nuttall, Paula. *From Flanders to Florence: The Impact of Netherlandish Painting, 1400–1500.* New Haven, Conn.: Yale University Press, 2004. A good introduction to northern influence on Italian art.

Websites

On Leonardo, a museum in his birthplace, **The Leonardo Museum,** at www.leonet.it/comuni/vinci

An excellent site to look at images of artwork, organized by the artist's name, **Web Gallery of Art,** at www.wga.hu/frames-e.html?/html

A group seeking to vindicate Richard III of the charge of murder offers many interesting features relating to the Wars of the Roses, **The Richard III Society, American Branch,** at www.r3.org/intro.html

CHAPTER 13

Europe's Age of Expansion, 1450–1550

1500 B.C.E.	1000 B.C.E.	500 B.C.E.	1 B.C.E./1 C.E.

1440s Gutenberg invents printing process		1462 Ivan III becomes tsar	1469 Marriage of Ferdinand of Aragon and Isabella of Castile	1485 Henry VII becomes king of England	1492 Columbus sets sail Jews expelled from Spain

1440	1450	1460	1470	1480	1490

The political boundaries of Europe in the year of Emperor Charles V's abdication indicate the power of the Habsburgs. In what ways do the size and location of his lands suggest potential threats to the independence and stability of other European states?

Lands of Charles V, by 1556
France
England
Ottoman Empire
Boundary of Holy Roman Empire

NORWAY

SWEDEN

ESTONIA

TEUTONIC
KNIGHTS

RUSSIA

SCOTLAND

DENMARK

Baltic
Sea

PRUSSIA

POLAND-LITHUANIA

IRELAND

North
Sea

Hamburg

BRANDENBURG

Elbe

Vistula

Dnieper

WALES   ENGLAND
Cambridge
Oxford
London

Amsterdam

NETHERLANDS
Antwerp

ANHALT
HESSE-
KASSEL

LUSATIA
SAXONY

SILESIA

Rhine

ATLANTIC

OCEAN

Paris

FRANCE

LUXEMBOURG
RHINE
PALATINATE
LORRAINE

UPPER
PALATINATE
WÜRTTEMBERG

BOHEMIA

MORAVIA

HUNGARY

BURGUNDY

FRANCHE-
COMTÉ

BAVARIA

Vienna
AUSTRIA

CHAROLAIS

SWISS
CONFED.

TYROL
SALZBURG

SAVOY

MILAN

REP. OF
VENICE

Po

GENOA

MODENA

REP. OF
VENICE

OTTOMAN

Danube

Black Sea

PORTUGAL

ANDORRA

Madrid

Corsica
(Genoa)

TUSCANY

PAPAL
STATES

MONTENEGRO

EMPIRE

Ebro

Tagus

SPAIN

Rome

Constantinople

Lisbon

Palos
Seville

BALEARIC IS.

SARDINIA

Naples

NAPLES

Otranto

Tangiers

Melilla
Oran

Algiers
Bougie

Bona
Tunis

SICILY

Crete
(Rep. of Venice)

0   200   400 Km.
0   200   400 Mi.

NORTH AFRICA

OTTOMAN
EMPIRE

Mediterranean   Sea

1515
Francis I crowned king of France

1552
Las Casas
publishes Brief
Account of the
Destruction
of the Indies

1510
Albuquerque
conquers Goa

1517
Charles V begins to rule in Spain

Luther condemns indulgences

Choice Choice Choice

Isabella of Castile

In this painting by an unknown artist, Queen Isabella is presented in modest dress, head covered. There is no hint of royal splendor in her appearance or expression. She appears, rather, as the woman head of household, a role she emphasized for her subjects. (Institut Amatller d'Art Hispanic)

Isabella of Castile Finances Columbus's Voyage Across the Atlantic

In January 1492, a forty-year-old Genoese sailor, Cristoforo Colombo, known in the English-speaking world as Christopher Columbus, appeared before Queen Isabella of Castile and her husband, King Ferdinand of Aragon. Columbus was seeking Spanish support for an ocean voyage to the eastern shores of Asia, which he believed were on the far side of the Atlantic Ocean. Twice before, Isabella had turned the Italian down. His third audience with the queen in 1492 was a desperate last attempt. Once again he presented his plans and described the benefits of the voyage. Once again, the queen refused. In despair, Columbus fled the court and galloped north, intending to ask the French king for help. But six miles out of town, royal guards stopped him and brought him back to the city. Isabella had changed her mind.

Later, Ferdinand would claim that he had convinced his wife to finance the voyage. Perhaps. As the only woman in the fifteenth century who ruled as a monarch, Isabella had to assert her royal will while not breaking the conventions of womanliness, which required submission to her husband. Throughout her reign, she acted as a dutiful wife involved in the traditional tasks of running a household, weaving cloth for the family's clothing, and repairing worn garments. Isabella also emphasized her faithfulness to Ferdinand despite his frequent infidelities. Ferdinand's claim that he had the final say in authorizing Columbus's voyage would fit with Isabella's role as the subordinate partner in their marriage.

But Ferdinand's account was challenged by one of Isabella's earliest biographers, the Dominican friar and bishop Bartolomé de Las Casas. Las Casas was an influential person at the court of Isabella's grandson, King Charles I, and had access to official documents and family papers. After Isabella's death, he wrote that the queen took the advice of her financial advisers when she recalled Columbus to court. This, too, is possible. Although Isabella embraced the gender expectations of her age, she was also highly effective in charting her own course of action. She herself had chosen Ferdinand as her husband, defying the wishes of her half brother, the king. The bride and groom were technically ineligible for marriage because, as cousins, they were too closely related in the eyes of the church. But Isabella went ahead with the union after documents were forged in the pope's name permitting an exception to Catholic marriage laws. Although independent when she needed to be, she preferred to work as a partner with Ferdinand, adopting as her motto, "The worth of one is the worth of the other—Isabella as Ferdinand." Isabella's motto cleverly proclaimed both her independence and her wifely relation to Ferdinand. It also emphasized the union of the two Spanish kingdoms that her marriage had achieved.

However she made her decision, Isabella announced that she would pawn her jewels to finance the voyage. (Pawning valuables was one way fifteenth-century monarchs could raise quick cash.) Finances settled, the queen could relish the gains from Columbus's voyage. Spain, like the rest of Europe, was hungry for the gold and spices of the east. But the country was cut off from a land route across Asia by the Venetians and their Muslim trading partners, and from a sea route around Africa by treaties with the Portuguese. A direct westward route was therefore the only one available to the Spanish. Moreover, both the Spanish and Portuguese had discovered and colonized islands in the Atlantic during the past seventy years. Perhaps Columbus would find more on the way to Asia, increasing the likelihood of riches.

Columbus's proposal also appealed to Isabella's fervent Catholic faith; a Spanish presence in eastern Asia would open the way for a Christian encirclement of the Muslim world and even the recapture of the holy city of Jerusalem. This vision exerted a powerful influence on a Spanish queen whose ancestors had extended their rule over a Muslim-dominated Iberian Peninsula. In fact, at the very moment Columbus appeared at court in 1492, Isabella and Ferdinand were celebrating their conquest of Granada, the last independent Muslim state on the peninsula. The Muslim defeat also provoked an attack on the other non-Christian people of the peninsula, the Jews. Shortly after Isabella offered Columbus the money he needed, she ordered the forced conversion or expulsion of all Jews in her lands. In the spring of 1492, just as the unconverted Jews were being shipped out of Spain, Columbus began preparing for his westward voyage.

Introduction

The Europe Columbus left in 1492 was bustling with renewed energy. The economic stagnation and population decline that had followed the trauma of the Black Death, the turmoil of the Hundred Years' War in France, and the Wars of the Roses in England was easing. By 1450, Europe's population was once again growing, and commerce revived. Both rural and urban dwellers profited from these upswings as increased demand for labor resulted in good wages, laying the foundation for an economically prosperous and expanding Europe.

The years after 1450 also saw a vigorous new generation of rulers in Spain, France, and England who consolidated state power and increased their control over their subjects, often with the help of new, professionally trained legal and financial experts. At the same time, these rulers continued to fight wars that drained their treasuries and forced them to tax and borrow at unprecedented levels. These European states were stronger and more centralized in 1550 than they had been in 1450 and exercised increasingly effective control over their inhabitants. In other parts of Europe, however, especially in Germany and Italy, the trend was toward smaller regional states instead of large, centralized ones. In the east, the rulers of

Moscow broke free from their Mongol overlords, conquered vast territories, and established a Russian empire that stretched from Poland to Siberia.

Europeans also extended their political and economic power over Africa, Asia, and the Americas. When the decline of the Mongol Empire disrupted Europe's land routes to Asia, the Portuguese sought new sea routes to the east and created a trading empire that stretched down the west coast of Africa, where they purchased gold and slaves. They also crossed the Indian Ocean to India and China, where they traded for spices, silks, and porcelain to sell in Europe, and ventured to the Western Hemisphere, where they established a colonial empire in Brazil based on African slave labor. The Spanish established an empire in the Caribbean, Mexico, and Peru that exploited the labor of Indians and then African slaves. Europe's territorial and economic expansion created the first global economy and turned many European states into colonial powers. It also raised the troubling issue of the relation of Europeans to the non-European peoples encountered in imperial expansion. While the peoples of Africa and the Americas experienced cataclysmic changes, the century between 1450 and 1550 was, for Europeans, marked by economic, political and territorial expansion. It was Europe's first modern age.

Chronology

1420	Portuguese begin the colonization of Atlantic islands
1462	Ivan III becomes tsar
1469	Ferdinand of Aragon and Isabella of Castile marry
1480	Ivan III declares Moscow's independence from Mongol rule
1485	Henry VII (Tudor) becomes King of England
1488	Bartholomew Diaz rounds southern tip of Africa and enters Indian Ocean
1492	Jews are expelled from Spain; Columbus sets sail
1500–1502	Muslims are expelled from Spain
1509	Henry VIII becomes king of England
1510	Alfonso de Albuquerque conquers Goa
1515	Francis I becomes king of France
1517	Charles V (Habsburg) begins rule in Spain
1519	Cortés lands in Mexico
1531	Pizarro invades Inca Empire
1533	Ivan IV becomes tsar
1542	Charles V issues New Laws for the Indies
1552	Las Casas publishes *Brief Account of the Destruction of the Indies*
1556	Charles V abdicates
1557	Portuguese establish trading colony at Macau
1559	French and Spanish sign Peace of Cateau-Cambrésis
1565–1572	Ivan the Terrible purges enemies in *oprichnina*

Economic and Social Change

> ↓ What effects did the rise in population after 1450 have on rural and urban communities?
> ↓ How did the revival of the European economy affect the lives of men and women?

From 1347 to 1351, between a third and a half of Europe's people died from the Black Death. For the next hundred years, population declined; outbreaks of plague, devastation caused by war, and failures of the grain harvest raised death rates to crisis levels and prevented a recovery. Then, about 1450, as plague, war, and famine subsided, the population once again started to grow. Population growth was also accompanied by an economic revival in both the countryside and towns.

Population Increase

Historians using the techniques of modern **demography** have determined that even in the good times after 1450, European death rates were shockingly high. Half the children born died before they reached their twenties. If a person made it to adulthood, however, the chances were good that he or she would live on for another thirty-five years. People over sixty, however, were rare, and the older they were, the stranger they were thought to be. Old people aroused fears: Why had they lived so long? Were they especially blessed by God, or (more likely!) had they made deals with the Devil? No social or economic group escaped these high **mortality rates.** Death cut down the families of kings and queens along with those of their humblest subjects, with no consideration of social distinctions or levels of wealth.

Once the crisis conditions in the century following the Black Death eased, the low population level created favorable economic conditions for those who had survived. Fewer people meant more available agricultural land, greater food supplies, and a higher demand for labor, which in turn produced higher wages. These favorable economic conditions affected marriage rates. In the lands of the Roman Catholic Church, a distinctive marriage pattern had emerged by the mid-fifteenth century. Women married in their

> **demography**   Statistical study of populations.
> **mortality rate**   The number of deaths per thousand in a given population.

Peter Bruegel the Elder's *The Harvesters* (1556) captures the beauty of a good harvest. Grain stalks shimmer in the sun as men scythe them, while men and women bind them. Other workers take a meal under a tree. This painting presents a powerful image of agricultural abundance and human wellbeing. *(Copyright © The Metropolitan Museum of Art/Art Resource, NY, The Metropolitan Museum of Art, New York, NY, USA)*

mid-twenties and men somewhat later, and about 10 percent of both men and women never married. This pattern contrasted with that of European Jews and Eastern Orthodox Christians, for whom marriage for women coincided with the onset of sexual maturity in the teenage years and was nearly universal. The reason for late marriage and significant rates of celibacy among the Christians of western Europe lay in the expectation that people should marry only when they could afford to set up their own household; it took time to establish economic independence, and some people never achieved it. After 1450, when land, food, and wages were abundant, more young people married and established their own households. When these better-fed, healthier people started their families, the **birthrate** rose in much of western Europe. The rise in

marriage and birth rates caused the increase in Europe's population. In 1450, Europe's population was about 60 million. In 1550, it was nearly 69 million.

Recovery in the Countryside

In 1450, Europe was still an overwhelmingly agricultural society. Ninety percent of Europeans lived in rural areas, where they engaged in some kind of farming. As in the past, agriculture depended on unpredictable weather conditions that could lead to

> **birthrate** The number of live births per thousand in a given population.

either abundant harvests or devastating crop failures. Yet despite the precarious nature of agricultural activity, times were good for rural people between 1450 and 1550.

After the Black Death, when population fell and labor was scarce, landlords' power over their peasants often decreased. Serfdom virtually disappeared in western Europe, where it was replaced with communities of free peasants who either owned their land, rented it from their lords, or worked as wage laborers. Below the lord was the peasants' **commune,** which set dates for planting crops and managed the meadows and woodlands belonging to the community as a whole. If the local lord tried to seize these common lands for his own use, the commune would organize villagers' resistance and even encourage riots in defense of them. In eastern Europe, however, landlords successfully reimposed serfdom on their peasants, seizing peasant lands, setting heavy work requirements, and forbidding peasants to leave their estates. Landlords were able to do this because the kings and other rulers in the region supported their actions.

In western Europe, the village of Langlade in southeast France shows how rural people responded to improved economic conditions. Like most communities, Langlade increased agricultural production to provide for a rising population. In addition to cultivating their grain fields, the villagers grew grapes for wine and moved into nearby hills, where they chopped down scrubby oaks and uprooted wild rosemary bushes. After pack animals had carried off the wood to nearby towns to meet a growing demand for fuel, the community planted the new land with wheat and olive trees.

In 1450, many rural communities were largely self-sufficient economically, since they produced most of the food, clothing, and other basic necessities they needed. Over the next hundred years, however, many rural people sold their agricultural surplus and bought many goods they had previously produced for themselves. Thus, they became integrated into regional or international markets. When the villagers of Langlade, for example, sold the wood they had cleared from their new fields to townspeople, they were losing their economic independence and becoming integrated in a market economy.

The growth of a market economy affected the value of people's economic activity. Previously, everything men and women did to maintain the material well-being of their families was considered work. With the growth of markets, however, the definition of work began to change. It was now defined simply as activity that produced goods for the market. This narrower definition of work affected men and women differently. Because women's economic activity focused primarily on their households, they no longer "worked." They simply did "housekeeping." Men were the "workers" because they raised crops for the market.

The devaluation of women's traditional household work was accompanied by the belief that women were incapable of skilled work. They were thought to be too awkward or ignorant to do complicated jobs. Therefore, anything they did was, by definition, unskilled. In fact, however, much of their activity involved considerable skill. For example, many rural women made butter or cheese. But the skill involved was not recognized. The same attitudes shaped men's and women's wages. At harvest time, when there was a high demand for labor in the fields, men were regularly paid twice what women were although they performed similar tasks.

Growth in the Cities

The developing market economy was also closely linked to the growth of cities. Beginning in 1450, Europe's cities grew until by 1550 about 10 percent of the total population lived in them. Since most cities were surrounded by their old walls, the rise in population made them ever more crowded. Houses were crammed next to each other, and streets were full of garbage. Sometimes garbage was dumped into wells, canals, or the local river, polluting the city's water supply, while at others it was piled just outside the city walls. These garbage piles could become so high that they threatened the city's defenses, since they could be used for scaling the walls. Human excrement also presented problems. Feces were placed next to front doors for sale to manure peddlers, who used them to fertilize nearby fields. Urine was sometimes collected in barrels outside leather shops, where it was used in the tanning process. All this waste created a huge stench; often travelers could smell a city long before they could see it. Overcrowding and filth also led to high urban disease and death rates. Throughout the sixteenth century, cities could never sustain their population levels but relied on a continuous stream of migrants from the countryside. Because of Europe's expanding population, the stream never dried up. Although cities were crowded and dirty, their inhabitants thought of them as organic wholes

commune An association of peasants supervising and coordinating the collective life of their village.

whose well-being depended on the harmonious interaction of all the people living in them. It was therefore the responsibility of the well-off to care for the needy by founding hospitals, orphanages, and homes for the elderly.

Men's work in sixteenth-century cities can be classified into four categories. Some men turned agricultural products like grain into food such as bread, the basic element in the urban diet. Bread was such a basic necessity that urban governments strictly regulated its price and tried to assure its availability in times of grain shortages, since they feared riots if the supply gave out. Others manufactured cloth and leather goods for clothing. Still others were engaged in construction; with urban populations growing and more buildings under construction, these men were in constant demand. Finally, some men made household furnishings or fashioned the tools that builders used. The most prestigious workers in a city, such as weavers of fine woolen or silk cloth or workers in gold, were organized into guilds. Guilds had originated in the Middle Ages but were in their heyday from 1450 to 1550. Like society at large, the guilds were organized on hierarchical lines; the men admitted to them were divided into masters, journeymen, and apprentices. Journeymen hoped someday to be admitted to the ranks of the masters, but often they were not, since masters worked to keep their membership limited. Guilds had originated as social clubs for artisans, providing opportunities for drinking and offering protection from a saint adopted as the guild's patron. In the sixteenth century, these older functions were still important, but the guild's main purpose was to regulate the manufacture of specific goods for the marketplace.

Membership in a guild was a prized source of male identity, and members proclaimed their skills and the perfection of their products. They thought of themselves as the backbone of the urban world and were concerned with maintaining an honorable position in society. To this end they carefully policed themselves, punishing the wayward for indecent or immoral behavior. Also, in line with the idea that the community should function as a harmonious whole, the guilds were required by law to maintain the quality of their products in the interests of consumer protection.

Guild work was considered skilled and, therefore, usually open only to men. In the Middle Ages, a few women had participated in guilds, but after 1500, most lost their place in them. As in the countryside, most women were confined to housekeeping or low-paid work. Women did, however, have a significant role in retail trade, operating stalls in marketplaces and

serving as city-appointed officers to certify weights, measures, and grain quality. They also worked as seamstresses and lace makers, skilled activities that, like butter and cheese making, were usually undervalued and poorly paid. Many women spun thread for weaving. Spinning was the slowest process in cloth production, and the need for spinners rose dramatically as weavers tried to meet the growing demand for cloth from a rising population. In the countryside, both men and women worked as spinners. In cities, however, men avoided this occupation as too low paying.

One group did break through the restrictions on women's economic activity—widows. A widowed woman could step in as the head of her dead husband's business and run it on her own. But if she remarried, or had male children who wanted to take it over, she usually returned to a subordinate economic position. Finally, prostitution was the one occupation always open to women. Because it dishonored her, a woman usually chose it only when nothing else was available.

The Port of Antwerp

Although cities all over Europe were growing, none could rival **Antwerp** in wealth and importance. Located at the western end of the North Sea, Antwerp was an ideal transfer point for the east-west trade that moved through the English Channel and the North Sea to the Baltic Sea. It was also a transfer point between northern Europe, the Iberian Peninsula, and the Mediterranean. By 1500, it was the most important commercial center in Europe. With its rise, European trade networks shifted northward, from the Mediterranean. Although Italian cities and merchants continued to play a central role in European trade, Mediterranean cities would never again dominate it.

The wharves of Antwerp were piled high with goods from Europe and Asia. One hundred thousand pieces of English woolen cloth were imported each year, and the city was ringed with huge bleaching vats preparing the cloth for finishing in the city's cloth guilds. Spain also sent its prized wool north for spinning and weaving. Next to the bales of cloth and wool were sacks of wheat, along with wood for

Antwerp City in the Netherlands that functioned in the first half of the sixteenth century as Europe's main trading center.

This painting by an unknown artist from the Netherlands shows the bustling commercial activity of Antwerp. The crowds examining goods for sale, the groups of men talking, and the carts carrying barrels of beer or wine give a lively sense of the city as Europe's leading commercial center in the sixteenth century. *(Musées Royaux des Beaux-Arts de Belgique)*

urban construction and shipyards, all from eastern Germany and Poland. The sixteenth-century population surge turned eastern Europe into a major supplier of grain and timber for the west. Bars of copper and silver from mines in south Germany were securely locked away in Antwerp's warehouses, waiting the arrival of Portuguese ships laden with spices brought around the southern tip of Africa from India and Southeast Asia. The metals would be exchanged for cinnamon, nutmeg, and pepper, and then exported to the Far East, where they would pay for another cargo of spices. Vaults also held chests of diamonds waiting to be cut and sold. Over a thousand representatives of foreign trading companies jostled each other on the city's streets as they inspected cargoes and bargained over prices.

In 1500, Antwerp boasted a population of over 100,000, making it one of Europe's largest cities. The city center was dominated by the Cathedral of Our Lady, the largest in the Netherlands, which covered more than two acres. Begun in the mid-fourteenth century, it was finished in the sixteenth and stood as a symbol of the city's wealth and pride. Nearby was the great square with its monumental city hall and imposing guild offices. On the city's outskirts were breweries supplying beer for thousands of thirsty workers.

The complex trade networks converging on Antwerp, involving thousands of merchant businesses spread over long distances, stimulated the development of the banking and credit networks, developed in the twelfth century, through which traders avoided the inconvenience of hauling about large sums of coins to cover their transactions. Instead, they signed notes promising payment from money kept at home. If a merchant's reputation was good, the notes would be accepted as a kind of paper money. The use of these notes laid the foundations for modern banking practices. Because Antwerp was the center for both inter-European and Far Eastern trade, it functioned as a center of exchange for an emerging world economy.

Resurgent Monarchies

↓ What steps did rulers take to strengthen their realms?
↓ What role did religion play in the advancement of royal authority?

While Europe's population and economy were expanding after 1450, new, energetic rulers extended their control over their subjects and centralized their governments. Civil wars were brought to an end, state control of justice increased, new officials enforced government decrees, and new sources of revenue were created. Above all, a period of warfare erupted in Italy, where the rulers of Spain and the Holy Roman Empire fought the kings of France for control of the peninsula.

Ferdinand and Isabella and the Rise of Spain

In 1469, **Isabella of Castile,** aged eighteen, married the seventeen-year-old **Ferdinand of Aragon.** Their kingdoms shared the Iberian Peninsula with Muslim **Granada** and Christian Portugal and Navarre, and neither was a first-rate state. Moreover, on Ferdinand and Isabella's wedding day, their kingdoms were torn apart by civil war as great nobles challenged the young monarchs' rule. Yet the marriage of these two teenagers laid the foundations for a spectacular rise in the power of Spain.

Within ten years, Ferdinand and Isabella had secured their rule, embarking on a tireless campaign of travel and direct appearances and relying on the persuasive power of face-to-face meetings with their unruly subjects. In early modern Europe, kings and queens, God's appointed rulers, were bathed in a sacred aura. As a result, even the most rebellious subjects could be coaxed into obedience when brought personally before the monarch. As a boy, the future historian of Isabella's reign, **Bartolomé de Las Casas,** was part of the crowd cheering the royal couple as they passed through his hometown of Seville on one of these journeys. In addition, the two rulers shrewdly calculated that their success depended as much on negotiation with their people and respect for each kingdom's traditional political institutions as it did on a show of royal grandeur. Thus they did not try to fuse Aragon and Castile into a single monarchy but respected the political independence of each kingdom.

In Aragon, Ferdinand accepted traditions that made him a limited, constitutional monarch. In Castile, the larger and more populous kingdom, he and Isabella took specific measures to strengthen royal power. The nobility was confirmed in its privileges and landed estates, and new titles of nobility were awarded to men who cooperated with the monarchs. At the same time, powerful but rebellious nobles were excluded from a direct role in government and were replaced by lesser nobles or commoners. These men were more dependent on royal favor for their success than the great nobles. Many had been trained as lawyers. Their legal training gave them orderly habits of mind and a commitment to carefully defined routines for state administration that made the monarchy more efficient. One of the first benefits of this rule of orderly lawyers was a more effective collection of royal taxes. Isabella and Ferdinand also worked out a policy of cooperation with the towns of Castile. They knew that they were tightly knit communities, jealous of their traditions and suspicious of outsiders who might upset them. Painstaking negotiation in the interests of peace after civil war was the way to bring them into working relations with the royal government. The monarchs also revived urban police forces to clear the country of bandits and established a workable local judicial system.

In 1482, Ferdinand and Isabella went to war with Granada, the last Muslim kingdom on the Iberian Peninsula, using the revitalized urban police forces as their army. The pope declared the war a crusade and sent a huge silver cross for troops to carry in battle. In 1492, the Spanish monarchs stood with their glittering court before the gates of the city of Granada to receive the defeated Muslim king, who came forward, kissed the hands of the monarchs, and surrendered the keys to the city. By the end of the day, Christian flags flew from the highest tower of Alhambra, the royal palace. With Granada's fall, the centuries-long Christian Reconquista of the Iberian Peninsula was complete.

The fall of Granada coincided with a new Spanish policy of religious intolerance. In the spring of 1492, Isabella and Ferdinand decreed that Jews were to convert to Christianity or leave their kingdoms. A century earlier, anti-Jewish riots had provoked mass

---

Isabella of Castile (r. 1474–1504) and **Ferdinand of Aragon** (r. 1479–1516) Rulers who launched Spain's rise as a major European power in control of a vast overseas empire.

Granada Last Muslim state on the Iberian Peninsula, conquered by Ferdinand and Isabella in 1492.

Bartolomé de Las Casas (1474–1566) Soldier turned priest and bishop who criticized the brutality of the Spanish conquest of America.

conversions to Christianity. But these **New Christians,** or **Conversos,** were often accused of secretly holding to their old Jewish ways. In response, the monarchs created the **Spanish Inquisition,** a church court authorized to examine Conversos about the genuineness of their Christian faith. Over the next dozen years, hundreds of them failed to prove their sincerity and were burned alive as heretics. Then, in 1491, news of a supposed atrocity swept across Castile. Some New Christians and unconverted Jews in the town of La Guardia were accused of murdering a Christian boy and ripping out his heart for use in magic. A story like this was a standard element in late medieval Christian attacks on Jews, and in 1491 it led to the execution of the accused men, despite the fact that no one in La Guardia reported a missing child. Faced with rising anti-Jewish passions, some Jews responded in kind, repeating old arguments that Christians' souls were created by the Devil. It was against this background that Ferdinand and Isabella ordered the forced conversion or expulsion of all remaining Jews. About fifty thousand converted, while some forty thousand fled to Portugal, Italy, and North Africa. Many of these refugees eventually returned and submitted to baptism. Thus the edict eliminated Jewish communities but greatly increased the number of New Christians, who continued to be accused of half-hearted conversion. The Jews who had fled to Portugal were expelled from that kingdom in 1497. Some then moved to Antwerp, where they established a thriving merchant community that prospered from the revival of European commerce. In 1494, Pope Alexander VI proclaimed Ferdinand and Isabella "Catholic Rulers" in recognition of their efforts to suppress non-Christian religions.

Finally, between 1500 and 1502, all remaining Muslims in Granada and Castile were also ordered to convert to Christianity or leave. Some, like the Jews, became Christians. But these **Moriscos** were no more well received than the Conversos, since the sincerity of their conversions was also questioned. Most who left went to North Africa. The forced conversion or expulsion of Jews and Muslims ended the religious pluralism and cultural diversity of Castile and Aragon. The war against Granada had united Castilians and Aragonese in a common Spanish crusade. The expulsion of the Jews and Muslims created a new, exclusively Christian Spanish identity.

As they consolidated their power and promoted a new identity among their subjects, Ferdinand and Isabella searched for a husband for their eldest surviving child, Joan. They themselves had made a good political marriage, and they wanted one for their daughter. Fortunately, they found an ideal match in the son of the Holy Roman emperor, Philip the Handsome. Joan brought Castile, Aragon, Granada, Naples, Sicily, and Sardinia to the marriage, while Philip brought the **Habsburg** family's land of Austria, inherited from his father, along with the Netherlands, inherited from his mother. Theirs was the royal wedding of the century. All that was needed was a child who would inherit this vast collection of territories.

Charles I of Spain, Charles V of the Holy Roman Empire

That child was born in 1500 and named Charles. Charles spent his early years in the Netherlands, where Joan moved after her wedding. A sickly boy, he inherited from his father a large lower jaw that stuck out beyond the upper one and made it difficult to chew food. This "Habsburg jaw" continued to be passed on in the family and can be seen in many paintings of Habsburg rulers, despite artists' attempt to downplay it. In 1517, after the death of his father, Philip, and grandfather, Ferdinand, Charles journeyed for the first time to Spain, where he was to rule as Charles I in place of Joan, who had developed mental problems that prevented her from governing. Charles quickly made Spain his primary place of residence, spending more time there than in his other lands. When not in Spain, he was usually back in the Netherlands, the country he loved the most.

The lands Charles inherited rivaled Charlemagne's empire in size, but they were never a united state. Like Ferdinand and Isabella, Charles recognized the political independence of each, respecting its local laws and traditions. Also, like his grandparents, he realized the importance of appearing personally before his subjects. Unlike them, however, he ruled over so many lands that he could never be in one of them long enough to satisfy people's desire to see him. This was a constant source of friction. "My life," he complained, "has been one long journey."

New Christians/Conversos Jews whom the state forced to convert to Christianity or face persecution and expulsion from Spanish territory.

Spanish Inquisition Church court originally established to try New Christians suspected of observing their old Jewish practices in secret.

Moriscos Muslims in Spain who were forced to convert to Christianity or leave.

Habsburgs Dynastic family originating in Austria that provided many rulers there, and also in the Netherlands, Spain, and the Holy Roman Empire.

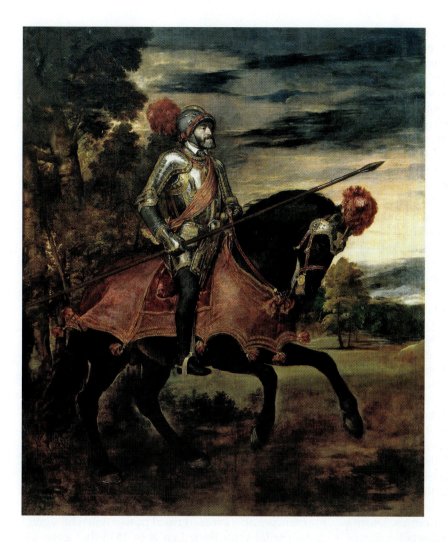

This portrait of Emperor Charles V by the Venetian painter Titian (1548) presents him as a warrior, a convention for depicting rulers that stretches back to the pharaohs of ancient Egypt. Charles' forceful gaze, the horse's prancing and fine plumes, and the thrusting lance all point to the Emperor's might. (*Museo del Prado*)

feudal armies no longer worked in the face of highly trained soldiers who made warfare their permanent profession. Moreover, weapons technology had changed with the introduction of gunpowder from China, brought west by Arab traders, which made bows and arrows obsolete. But mercenaries and firearms were expensive, and state budgets strained to finance them. For his Italian wars, Charles managed to field an army of 150,000 men, the largest Europe had ever seen, but he had to scramble to find ways to pay for it. One way was to push heavily on traditional sources of income like sales taxes and grants from representative assemblies of subjects like the Castilian **Cortes.** Gold also started to pour in from the Caribbean after Spanish conquests there. But taxes and **New World** wealth never provided enough, so Charles sold **Crown lands.** This was still not enough. He then turned to borrowing and contracted ever-larger debts

The journeys became even more frequent in 1519, when he was elected Holy Roman emperor on the death of his paternal grandfather, the emperor Maximilian. In the empire he was called **Charles V.**

Although Charles never united his territories into a single state, he did develop a common policy for them by consolidating his rule in each and making sure that none worked at cross-purposes with the others. Coordinating a common policy became particularly important during the long wars with France over Italy, where his role as Holy Roman emperor, along with his inherited lands in southern Italy, made him a central player. For sixty-five years, France and Spain fought for control of the Italian peninsula.

These wars were costly, and they were only one series of Charles's wars. By 1500, Europe's rulers faced a new military world. To win a war, it was necessary to fight with the best military forces, and that meant hiring **mercenary armies,** since the medieval

Charles V (r. 1516–1556) Heir of Ferdinand and Isabella in Spain and of the emperor Maximilian in the Holy Roman Empire; the most powerful European ruler during the first half of the sixteenth century.

mercenary armies Skilled professional armies under the command of generals who sold their services to European rulers.

Cortes In Castile, a representative assembly of Isabella's subjects that advised the queen and negotiated over taxes.

New World Term that Europeans used to refer to the Americas.

Crown lands Lands owned by a ruler as his or her family estate.

in the forms of **annuities**—long-term loans that guaranteed an annual payment to the lender.

Annuities turned out to be the way that cash-hungry sixteenth-century states managed to meet their financial obligations. The success of annuities depended on two things: the availability of lenders and the recruitment of managers to supervise states' growing indebtedness. The demographic and economic expansion of Europe from 1450 to 1550 ensured the former; prosperous times put money in the pockets of many people who then looked for relatively safe ways to invest it. Lending to a state seemed one way. Charles borrowed from bankers in Germany and the Netherlands who were financing the growing trade networks centered on Antwerp, the prize jewel in his inheritance. He also turned to individual subjects who had money to invest.

The rise of a professionally trained class of bureaucrats began with Ferdinand and Isabella's lawyers. Under Charles, men with expert skills were recruited to collect taxes more efficiently. Increasingly, trained managers supervised governments' growing debts and oversaw the new complexity of state borrowing in a time of escalating military costs. Borrowing from banks and subjects turned Charles, and other rulers who did the same, into royal credit risks whose credit ratings were closely watched by would-be lenders.

By 1550, Charles V was growing weary of rule. He had been personally involved in the Italian and French wars for thirty years. Moreover, the political and religious situation in the Holy Roman Empire was becoming destabilized with the rise of **Protestantism.** He suffered from gout and insomnia. During the sleepless nights, he tinkered with his collection of clocks, taking them apart and reassembling them over and over again. He sank into depression and wept like a child. Finally, in 1556, he decided to abdicate. He granted the position of emperor and his Austrian lands to his younger brother, Ferdinand. His son Philip received the Netherlands, the Italian possessions, the Spanish states, and Spain's vast new American empire. Charles then retired to a monastery in southwestern Spain, where he died in 1558.

Francis I and the Kingdom of France

In 1500, the French state, like Spain, was undergoing profound transformations. The Hundred Years' War had strengthened the French monarchy, which now possessed a regular source of revenue from the *taille* tax, a permanent royal army, and the beginnings of a state bureaucracy staffed by experts. But France was fragmented. Although the English had been driven out, except for a toehold around Calais, large swaths of territory, each ruled by a branch of the extended royal family, functioned as virtually independent units within the theoretically unified kingdom. Over the second half of the fifteenth century, however, these branches died out, their lands reverted to the Crown, and the amount of territory directly ruled over by the king almost doubled between 1450 and 1500. Habsburg lands had grown as a result of spectacularly successful marriages; the French state grew as a result of lucky deaths.

Francis I, who ruled from 1515 to 1547, was the most vigorous of the newly powerful French kings. His court was famous for its Renaissance culture. Like Charles V, he traveled throughout his realm, showing himself to his subjects and thereby cementing his rule. Unlike Charles, however, he ruled over a more unified state, since political centralization had increased when each previously independent territory reverted to direct royal rule. To further this new centralization, Francis ordered all courts, except church ones, to use the French dialect of Paris in their proceedings. Since this French was only one of several dialects spoken at the time, the edict promoted a single common language for use in public affairs throughout the kingdom. At the same time, French nobles stopped using their local dialects and started to speak the refined French of Francis's royal court. The growing use of standardized French, along with political centralization, created a new national identity for the people of the kingdom that slowly replaced older identities rooted in local customs and dialects.

Francis also increased royal power when he signed a **concordat** with Pope Leo X in 1516 that gave the king the right to nominate candidates for hundreds of high offices in the French church, thereby increasing the Crown's control of church personnel. In return, Francis repudiated the earlier French position that

---

annuities Long-term loans to European states guaranteeing an annual interest payment to the lender.

Protestantism Beliefs and practices of Christians who broke with the Roman Church in the sixteenth century.

taille French royal tax first levied during the Hundred Years' War.

Francis I (r. 1515–1547) King of France who centralized royal rule, created at his court a vibrant Renaissance culture, and unsuccessfully fought Charles V for control of Italy.

concordat Formal agreement between a pope and a ruler of a Catholic state.

the pope was subject to the authority of general church councils and recognized him as the supreme head of the Roman Church. Having reestablished good relations with the papacy, the king was now free to pursue his military ambitions in Italy.

By 1519, when Charles V had inherited the lands ruled over by his two grandfathers, Francis had one great fear: the Habsburgs. From the northeast to the southwest, wherever he looked beyond French borders, he saw Habsburg lands. Francis had tried to break Habsburg power by bribing the imperial electors in the Holy Roman Empire to choose him as emperor, but Charles was the grandson of the emperor Maximilian, and he had bribed the electors as well. Francis then turned to Italy and tried to make good the French claims to Milan and Naples. But he fared poorly, being captured on a battlefield and taken as a prisoner to Madrid. As the price for his freedom, he was forced to sign a humiliating peace in which he repudiated all his Italian claims and promised Charles the duchy of Burgundy, one of the territories that had reverted to the French Crown.

Back in Paris, Francis repudiated the peace and laid plans to continue the fight. Charles's victories in Italy had created a backlash that allowed Francis to form an anti-Spanish alliance with a number of Italian rulers, including the pope. Then in 1527, Charles won another victory when Spanish and German mercenary armies descended on Rome and sacked the city. Charles's reputation suffered badly from his troops' brutality, and he took his anger out on Francis, proposing, unrealistically, that the two should meet in a duel to settle their dispute.

After 1527, Francis continued the fight against the Habsburgs, but his strategy changed. Now Charles faced the threat of an expanding Protestant movement in the empire and the Netherlands. Although he was no friend of the Protestants in France, Francis allied with the German Protestants and then with the Ottoman Turks in his attempts to weaken Habsburg power. Francis's foreign policy undermined the medieval notion that Europe was held together by a common Catholic Christian faith. Now, it seemed, it was composed of a number of independent states, each of which advanced its own interests without regard to religious allegiance.

In 1547, Francis died, aged fifty-three and wracked by syphilis, a new disease from America. He was succeeded by his son, **Henry II,** who ruled until 1559. Although the king was new, French policy remained the same, since Henry continued the war against the Habsburgs. Finally, in 1559, the French and the Spanish signed the **Peace of Cateau-Cambrésis,** which brought

the long conflict to an end. The French renounced claims in Italy and ceded some territory to Spain. This settlement caused a good deal of grumbling among powerful French nobles who had shed their blood over three generations on behalf of the "king's just cause" in Italy. Henry, however, ordered festivities to celebrate the peace and participated in one of them, a joust in which men on horseback holding lances charged each other in hopes of dismounting their opponent. As the king's opponent made contact with him, his lance shot into a slit in the king's helmet and pierced his eye. Ten days later Henry was dead.

Consolidation in England Under the First Tudors

Defeat in the Hundred Years' War forced England's kings, for the first time in four hundred years, to confine their rule to their island possessions, except for the French port city of Calais. In 1485, when the Wars of the Roses ended with the death in battle of Richard III, **Henry VII** ascended the throne as the first king of a new royal dynasty, the Tudors. Like his counterparts in Spain and France, Henry embarked on a policy of consolidating royal power. Henry, a Lancastrian, also united Lancastrian and Yorkist factions by marrying Elizabeth of York in 1486.

The Tudors' roots lay in Wales, a semi-independent territory under English rule. Henry emphasized his Welsh heritage and presented himself as a truly home-grown ruler, the first since the Norman Conquest in 1066. In the year he became king, Sir Thomas Malory's *Le Morte d'Arthur* was published, recounting the legends about the Welsh king Arthur and his Knights of the Round Table. Drawing on them, Henry named his first son Arthur to emphasize his ancient British background. When Arthur was of age, Henry arranged his marriage to Catherine of Aragon, the younger daughter of Ferdinand and Isabella, to forge a Spanish alliance against England's old enemy, France. Henry ruled in conjunction with the Parliament, which

Henry II (r. 1547–1559) French king who pursued Francis I's wars in Italy.

Peace of Cateau-Cambrésis (1559) Treaty that ended the Spanish and French war for the control of Italy and established Spanish dominance there.

Henry VII (r. 1485–1509) First Tudor king of England, who ended the Wars of the Roses and consolidated royal power.

had gained power during the Hundred Years' War by granting the king taxes to pay for his military expenses. Like Ferdinand and Isabella with the towns of Castile, Henry coaxed the Parliament to cooperate in consolidating the new dynasty.

Henry became king at a particularly favorable time. England, like the rest of Europe, was experiencing demographic expansion and economic growth. Its heartland, the southeast, centered on London, was bustling with agricultural and commercial activity as population rose and ships loaded with wool crossed the North Sea to Antwerp. Henry took advantage of prosperous times to increase his royal income. He confiscated the property of his opponents in the Wars of the Roses and then made sure his new estates produced maximum revenue. Yet more money came from import and export fees, which rose with expanding overseas trade. The administration of justice also produced revenue, since courts charged fees and levied fines. Henry established a series of judicial councils that operated with streamlined rules and speedy efficiency. Understandably, they were popular with his subjects since they offered justice more quickly than older courts bogged down in top-heavy procedures.

Perhaps Henry VII's most important achievement was his imposition of English power on the other parts of the British Isles—Scotland and Ireland. Although Scotland was an independent kingdom, English kings had tried for centuries to bind it closely to their realm. Henry continued this policy by arranging for the marriage of his daughter, Margaret, to the Scots king, a marriage that laid the foundation for a union of the two kingdoms under a single ruler. Ireland had been under English rule since the twelfth century, when the pope had confirmed Henry II as its lord. In fact, effective English control was confined only to the area around Dublin. But even this area had slipped from the English during the Hundred Years' War and the Wars of the Roses. During his reign, Henry reestablished royal control there.

In 1509, Henry VII died and was succeeded by his younger son, **Henry VIII,** since Arthur had also died. Henry VIII had married Arthur's widow, Catherine of Aragon, to keep his father's Spanish alliance intact. He had to obtain a special papal dispensation to do so, since the church forbade marriage between a widow and her brother-in-law. Henry VIII wanted the marriage with Catherine for dynastic reasons: Catherine's chief job was to produce a male heir to the throne. At this she failed, since she gave birth to only one child who survived infancy, and it was a daughter, Mary. By the late 1520s, Henry was convinced that Catherine could no longer conceive and sought an annulment of his marriage. Eventually, in the 1530s, Henry

broke with the pope over the issue. He forbade papal control of the church in England, got Parliament to approve his divorce from Catherine of Aragon, and married a new wife, Anne Boleyn, the second of six, as it turned out. Like his father, Henry VIII expanded English control over the rest of the British Isles. He abolished Wales's semi-independent status and gave it seats in the English Parliament and got the Irish parliament in Dublin to decree that Ireland was an independent kingdom ruled by the king of England.

England's political control of ever-larger parts of the British Isles was accompanied by a growing cultural dominance as the English dialect of the court and the southeast spread throughout the Tudor realm. The rise of English was partly the result of a new literature, like Malory's Arthurian legends, which was printed in London and distributed throughout the kingdom. English was also spread by men graduating from the country's two universities, Cambridge and Oxford, which started to use it instead of Latin. The introduction of an English prayer book in churches after Henry VIII's break with Rome spread the use of the language even more. Political centralization and cultural unification laid the foundations for a new English identity that would develop fully during the long reign of Henry VIII's daughter Elizabeth I.

From 1450 to 1550, the monarchs of Spain, France, and England embarked on a policy of consolidating their political power at home by ending civil wars and strengthening royal government. If they fought foreign wars, they faced financial strains that forced them to search for new sources of revenue. The most important source came from borrowing. As a result, a new group of state creditors emerged in Europe. The management of strengthened royal governments and complex state finances fell increasingly on a new class of legally trained experts, often of non-noble birth. Finally, these states created new forms of collective identity for their subjects based on a common religion or a common language. As these developments took place, the older ideal of Europe united into one community, Christendom, gave way to a new reality, a Europe made up of independent states whose ambitions often brought them into armed conflict with one another.

Henry VIII   (r. 1509–1547) King who consolidated Tudor rule over the British Isles and, breaking with the pope over his divorce, launched the English Reformation.

MAP 13.1 **The Expansion of Russia, to 1725** From its beginnings as the small Principality of Moscow, Russia expanded to become one of the world's largest states. Ivan III's and Ivan the Terrible's acquisitions made Russia both a European and a central Asian power.

Map legend:
- Principality of Moscow, ca. 1300
- Acquisitions by Ivan III's accession (1462)
- Acquisitions under Ivan III (1462–1505)
- Acquisitions by death of Ivan the Terrible (1584)
- Acquisitions by Peter the Great's accession (1689)
- Acquisitions under Peter the Great (1689–1725)
- ✕ Major battle

characterized the political life of the peninsula for the next three hundred years.

Germany was even more politically fragmented. In theory, the Holy Roman Empire bound all of north-central Europe into a single state. But Emperor Charles IV's Golden Bull of 1356 had given the imperial electors a good deal of political independence, which was gradually claimed by the other rulers of the empire's more than three thousand separate territories, some large and powerful like Saxony or Bavaria, others comprising only a few acres. The Protestant Reformation of the sixteenth century added religious fragmentation to the previously existing political decentralization as the empire's states split into hostile Protestant and Catholic camps. As in Italy, regionalism was to characterize German political life until the nineteenth century.

In far eastern Europe, the decline of the Mongol Empire allowed peoples under Mongol rule to assert their independence. In 1462, the grand prince of Moscow, **Ivan III the Great,** began to consolidate power in a centralized Russian state. Ivan, who married the niece of the last Byzantine emperor, took the title of **tsar,** the Russian form of caesar, to proclaim that he

Italy, Germany, and Russia

By 1550, large centralized states covered parts of Europe, but other parts continued to be characterized by political fragmentation. Chief among them were Italy and Germany. In 1450, the Italian peninsula was dominated by five states: Milan, Venice, Tuscany, the Papal States, and the kingdom of Naples. In 1559, when the French and Spanish wars in Italy ended, Spain controlled Milan in the north and the kingdom of Naples in the south and thereby exercised the greatest influence over the peninsula as a whole, but the other states maintained their political independence. Thus regionalism, rather than centralization,

Ivan III the Great (r. 1462–1505) Grand prince of Moscow who conquered lands, took the title of tsar, and established a centralized state.

tsar (in Russian, "Caesar") Title taken by the early consolidators of a unified Russian state.

was the successor of the Byzantine emperors, whose court ceremonial he adopted. Moscow was to be the "Third Rome," succeeding Old Rome and Constantinople, now in Muslim hands. In 1478, Ivan conquered the city of Novgorod and more than doubled his territory, since Novgorod ruled lands that stretched east to the **Ural Mountains.** In 1480, he refused to pay tribute to the khanate of the Golden Horde and thereby formally declared Moscow's independence from Mongol rule.

Ivan III's conquests required a large army to defend his territories. He therefore expanded the army by awarding new soldiers grants of land in return for military service. He also resettled large numbers of landlords: men from Novgorod were moved into older Russian lands, while men from those lands were awarded land in Novgorod. This shift in elite populations lowered the chance of resistance to Ivan's rule by cutting landlords' ties with their old regional power bases while creating clusters of landlord elites in new territories, where they administered justice and collected taxes.

Throughout his reign, Ivan increased the tax burden of his subjects, starting a trend that continued into the sixteenth century. In fact, the government was so aggressive in raising taxes that it exhausted the ability of its subjects to pay. By the late sixteenth century, landlords and their peasants had started to flee east and south into frontier lands in hopes of a better life. The state responded by ordering peasants to remain where they were to guarantee landlords a workforce for their estates. The result was to turn more and more Russian peasants into serfs bound to the land. Raising armies, administering justice, and collecting taxes were tasks like those of the centralized monarchies of western Europe. But Ivan's wholesale resettlement of landlords involved a governmental interference in the lives of elite subjects that was unlike anything done in the west.

In 1533, Ivan III's grandson, **Ivan IV the Terrible,** became tsar. He continued his grandfather's policy of territorial conquest when he marched southeast to the Volga River to seize Mongol **Kazan** and **Astrakhan.** During his reign, Russians also started crossing the Urals to establish settlements in western Siberia.

In theory, Ivan IV's state was organized like a great family with the tsar as its stern but just patriarch. Thus the whole family suffered when the tsar went mad. In the 1560s, Ivan was engaged in the **Livonian War** against Livonia and Lithuania to gain access to the Baltic Sea. When the war went badly, Ivan blamed his nobles, some of whom he accused of treason. He then started to terrorize his subjects in a bloody episode

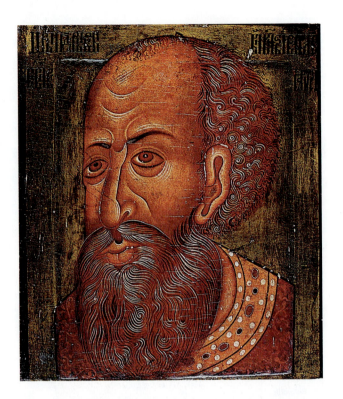

This anonymous portrait of Ivan the Terrible employs traditions of Russian religious art to depict the tsar. The text around his head and the stylized hair and beard echo the icons found in Russian churches. The artist's use of icon techniques is a way of depicting Ivan's majesty and divinely sanctioned rule. (*National Museum, Copenhagen, Denmark*)

known as the *oprichnina,* an ever-widening purge of the tsar's supposed enemies, carried out by some six thousand state agents. As the purge expanded, thousands were tortured and killed. Ivan exhibited violent mood swings, doing public penance for his sins by beating his head on church floors until the blood ran

Ural Mountains   Mountain range marking the border between the European and Asian parts of Eurasia.

Ivan IV the Terrible   (r. 1533–1584) Ruler of Russia and conqueror of Mongol Kazan and Astrakhan along the Volga River, southeast of Moscow.

Kazan and **Astrakhan**   Mongol khanates along the Volga River conquered by Ivan the Terrible.

Livonian War   (1558–1583) Russian war against Livonia and Lithuania, two states blocking Russia's access to the Baltic Sea.

oprichnina   (in Russian, "domain") (1565–1572) A period of mass terror and executions perpetrated by Ivan the Terrible that resulted in the deaths of thousands.

and then rushing to his palace, where he would preside over bands of executioners engaging in drunken, blasphemous orgies. The *oprichnina* convulsed Russia for seven years and then subsided. Ivan continued to suffer from fits of violent rage, during one of which he brutally killed his son and heir. He died in 1584, a year after his defeat in the Livonian War.

Despite its violence, the *oprichnina*'s lasting effects on Russia were minimal. Many old noble and landlord families survived the purge, while some of Ivan's agents, temporarily raised to power during this terrible episode, sank back into the class of modest provincial landowners. Ivan's attempt to rule despotically had failed. Like their counterparts in the west, Russia's rulers were most successful when they cooperated with their social and economic elites instead of trying to crush them.

When Ivan IV died, the tsar ruled over vast, culturally diverse lands. The northern peoples and those in western Siberia were non-Russians who spoke their own distinct languages and worshiped local, non-Christian gods. The people of the center were Slavs who had converted to Orthodox Christianity, while the peoples of the south, in the former Mongol lands, were either Muslims or pagans. The tsars' policy was to respect these religious differences. Although they were Orthodox Christian in religion, and claimed descent from the Christian rulers of Kiev and Constantinople, Ivan III and his successors officially forbade the Orthodox Church from systematic missionary activity among the non-Christian peoples of the emerging Russian Empire. This policy contrasted sharply with that adopted farther west by Ferdinand and Isabella of Spain.

Europe's Global Expansion

↓ What were the motivations of Europeans who sought long-distance trade and far-off territories?

↓ What were the unexpected outcomes of expansion?

Population and economic growth in Europe, along with the rise of strong states headed by energetic rulers, contributed to Europe's global expansion in the sixteenth century. Rising population and a strong economy led to increased demand for the products of Asia and Africa, while vigorous governments helped to organize and finance new commercial ventures. When technological developments turned the wish for new long-distance trade routes on the open seas into a practical possibility, a global economy based on trade began to emerge. At the same time, Portugal

and Spain created Europe's first overseas empires in Asia and the Western Hemisphere.

The Motives and the Means

Economic, political, and religious factors, along with technological developments, combined to bring about Europe's overseas expansion. After 1450, when population rose and the economy strengthened, Europeans once again demanded goods from Asia and Africa. By 1450, however, the realities of trade with those places had changed. Gone were the days when Marco Polo and other Europeans could travel under Mongol protection across Eurasia to trade directly with the Chinese. Now the Ottoman Turks barred the way, while Muslims in Africa kept Europeans out of trade there. Some Europeans benefited from the new realities; the Venetians established profitable trading posts in Syria and Egypt, where they worked with local Arabs to bring Asian goods to Europe. Others, jealous of the Venetians' success, sought new routes to the east. The Genoese, especially, looked for ways to recover the trade they had lost to the Ottomans on the Black Sea.

The rise of strong governments after 1450 also prepared the way for expansion. State sponsorship and financing were crucial in the search for new trade routes. The first states to offer this support were Portugal and Castile. Their location on the Iberian Peninsula positioned them for explorations down the coast of Africa and across the Atlantic. Moreover, Portuguese and Spanish sailors, who had fished in Atlantic waters for centuries and carried cargoes to and from northern trading centers like Antwerp, were accustomed to sailing ocean waters outside the protected Mediterranean. Often, it was the Genoese who organized this rising seaborne commerce. Columbus himself was Genoese.

Economic considerations drove states to support the ventures of their merchants, but religious motives were equally important. As Christians, most Europeans believed they were required to spread their faith to all parts of the world, following Jesus's command in the Gospel of Matthew: "Go therefore and make disciples of all nations, baptizing them in the name of the Father and of the Son and of the Holy Spirit." Kings, queens, merchants, and priests all wished to promote Christianity along with trade. Many believed that worldwide conversion to Christianity would prepare for the Second Coming—Jesus's return to earth, when he would judge the world and reign with his saints. Hopes for profits, the spread of Christianity, and Jesus's return, however,

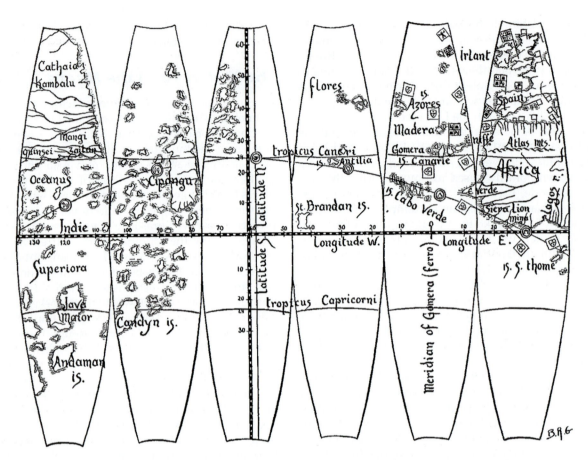

MAP 13.2 **Map of Martin Beheim, 1492** Martin Beheim, a fifteenth-century German map maker, showed the world as round in 1492. Africa and part of Europe are on the far right. The Madeira and Cape Verde Islands are identified, and then Cipongu (Japan). This is the information Columbus had when he set sail. *(From Admiral of the Ocean Sea by Samuel Eliot Morison. Copyright © 1942 by Samuel Eliot Morison; Copyright © renewed 1970 by Samuel Eliot Morison. By permission of Little, Brown and Company, Inc.)*

would have gotten nowhere had it not been for technological developments that made long-distance sailing on the open seas a practical possibility.

In the Middle Ages, Europe's ships were ill suited to long voyages on rough Atlantic waters. Propelled by oars or a simple sail, they were small, with only crude steering devices. By the end of the fifteenth century, however, ships had improved. They were larger, better constructed, fitted with improved rudders for steering, and supplied with a triangular **lateen sail,** popularized by Arab sailors, that allowed them to pick up the wind regardless of the direction from which it was blowing. They could also carry cannons and thus take advantage of the new gunpowder technology.

Navigational aids had also improved. Mapmaking became more accurate with the spread of navigational manuals and the development of **cartography,** which allowed mapmakers to accurately draw large portions of the known world. Sailors were also able to determine their north/south position (latitude) with greater accuracy, using **astrolabes** or **quadrants** for measuring the distance of heavenly bodies (the sun or known stars) from the horizon. Finding one's east/west position (longitude) was more difficult, but a skilled sailor could calculate it using a magnetic com-

lateen sail Triangular sail, first used by Arab sailors, that could swing to pick up wind coming from different directions.

cartography Science of mapmaking.

astrolabes and **quadrants** Devices allowing sailors to use the stars to find their north/south position (latitude) on the ocean.

pass, first developed by both Chinese and Arab sailors, along with an hourglass to mark off time and observations about the speed of the ship through the waters.

With improved ships, navigational manuals, maps, quadrants, compasses, and hourglasses, sailors ventured farther into the Atlantic and gained knowledge of ocean sailing. By the time of Columbus, they had a good sense of the wind patterns on the Atlantic and were learning how to use them to travel north and south as well as east and west. They had also discarded some earlier theories about global climate. In the Middle Ages, geographers knew that when one traveled south from Europe, it got hotter and hotter. They therefore reasoned that continuing south would eventually lead to parts of the earth so hot that no human being could survive there. Voyages down the coast of Africa gradually proved this theory wrong.

The Portuguese Empire

Sailors from the kingdom of Portugal, the westernmost state on the Iberian Peninsula, were the first Europeans to systematically explore Africa's west coast. For years, the Portuguese had resented Muslim control of the overland trade routes that carried gold from Africa to the Mediterranean. They were also eager to participate in the spice trade from Asia. In 1415, they captured the Muslim port of Ceuta in Morocco. Portuguese seamen then began inching down the African coast, looking for trading partners who would supply them directly with gold. At the same time, they bought black African slaves from local merchants. Both gold and slaves brought high prices back home, spurring other adventurers to join in the voyages. By the 1480s, the Portuguese had set up trading posts in **Guinea,** the center of the gold and slave trade. From the start, the kings of Portugal took an active part in the explorations, working closely with merchants and finally declaring a royal monopoly over the African trade. A member of the royal family, **Prince Henry the Navigator,** promoted the new technologies that made Atlantic sailing possible.

Portuguese traders did not seize large territories in Africa. Instead, they established fortified trading posts along the coast where they could exchange wine, guns, and wheat for gold and slaves. Life in these posts was difficult; the climate was harsh, and many traders died of tropical diseases, against which they had no immunity. Nevertheless, the trade prospered, and by 1500 Portugal was the chief supplier of gold and slaves to Europeans. In 1488, **Bartholomew Diaz** made it to the southern tip of Africa, rounding the Cape of Good Hope, as he called it, and sailing into the Indian Ocean. Faced with a mutiny by his crew,

he turned back to Portugal before reaching India itself. Then in1497, **Vasco da Gama** landed on the west coast of India, returning to Portugal in 1499 with a shipload of spices and cotton cloth. Da Gama's success launched the Portuguese drive into the Indian Ocean. Sailors soon discovered that the best winds for getting around southern Africa were picked up far out in the Atlantic. They therefore sailed due west of the Cape Verde Islands, found these winds, and then turned around and sailed to the southeast past the Cape of Good Hope. In 1500, on one of these trips, the ships sailed farther west than usual and sighted the coast of South America. Soon the Portuguese settled there, calling it Brazil after a local wood used for dying cloth.

The founder of the Portuguese Empire in Asia was **Alfonso de Albuquerque.** Appointed governor-general of Portuguese possessions along the Indian Ocean, Albuquerque sought to take over the spice trade with Europe. He attacked local Muslim merchants' ships at sea, pounding them with his superior shipboard cannons, and led armed expeditions on land against key trading posts. In 1510, he captured **Goa** on India's west coast, killing the Muslim men there and forcing their widows to marry his sailors to establish a Portuguese community. With Goa secured, he attacked the spice-trading center of **Malacca** on the Malay Peninsula. In 1557, the Portuguese established the first European settlement in China at **Macau.** Albuquerque mixed a passion for trade with hatred of Muslims. To him, they were liars and cheats; force, not friendship, was the only thing they understood.

Guinea   Area near the western bulge of Africa; in the sixteenth century, the center of gold and slave trade.

Prince Henry the Navigator   (1394–1460) Member of the Portuguese royal family who encouraged explorations along the coast of Africa.

Bartholomew Diaz   (ca.1450–1500) Portuguese sailor who in 1488 rounded the southern tip of Africa and sailed into the Indian Ocean.

Vasco da Gama   (1460–1524) First Portuguese trader to land in India and establish direct European trade.

Alfonso de Albuquerque   (1453–1515) Governor-general of Portuguese possessions along the Indian Ocean; founder of Portuguese Empire in Asia.

Goa   Portuguese colony on the west coast of India.

Malacca   Muslim port on the Malay Peninsula where goods from spice-growing islands farther east were collected and shipped westward.

Macau   Trading post on the south coast of China near Hong Kong.

His dispatches to Portugal reveal the kind of stereotyping that would feed western imaginations for centuries to come. For Albuquerque, smashing infidel control of Far Eastern commerce would allow for the triumphant planting of the cross of Christ in heathen lands. He was the perfect crusader trader.

The Spanish Empire

In the spring of 1492, **Christopher Columbus** began preparations for his westward voyage across the Atlantic. Columbus was no stranger to Atlantic waters. He had lived in Portugal for many years, marrying a Portuguese woman and sailing to the **Canary Islands,** the African coast, and the Madeira Islands, where his wife's family had estates. After failing to get Portuguese backing for a voyage across the Atlantic, he turned to Spain for help (see Choice). When that finally came, he began collecting crews and supplies for the three small ships Queen Isabella had given him. Local sailors were reluctant to sign on, not because they thought the world was flat and they would soon fall off its western edge (most Europeans knew the world was round) but because they were local tuna fishermen already making a good living in waters close to home. So Columbus had a hard time recruiting the ninety men he needed, some of which, in the end, were convicts. His task was made especially difficult because he had to work out of the small Spanish port of Palos; the larger ports were clogged with ships carrying away the recently expelled Spanish Jews. Finally, on August 3, 1492, just as a ship carrying the last of the Jews sailed from Palos, Columbus headed out of the port.

After reprovisioning his ships in the Canary Islands, in early September Columbus sailed west for thirty-three days, landing in the Bahamas on October 12. Since the Spaniards believed they had found islands in the East Indies, they called the local people Indians. Columbus then explored the islands of Hispaniola and Cuba, hoping to set up Portuguese-style trading posts. Finding no cities, he returned to Spain in January 1493, leaving some men behind on Hispaniola. Following a triumphant procession across Spain, witnessed by Bartolomé de Las Casas and his family, Columbus presented Isabella and Ferdinand with gold, parrots, spices, and captives, along with a pineapple, which Ferdinand happily ate. This was modest booty, but Columbus played up the potential for future profits and managed to get royal backing for three more voyages between 1493 and 1504. Las Casas's father, excited by the sight of Columbus's captives and booty, embarked on the first of them. In 1494, Spain and Portugal, with the blessing of the pope, signed the **Treaty of Tordesillas,** granting Spain control of Central and South America except for Brazil, which went to Portugal, along with Africa and Asia. Thus the entire world was divided into two zones for these first European empires.

Christopher Columbus   (1451–1506) Genoese sailor and explorer who captained the first European voyages to the Caribbean and South America and claimed lands there for Spain.

Canary Islands   Islands in the Atlantic Ocean colonized by Spain.

Treaty of Tordesillas   Arrangement in 1494 between Spain and Portugal drawing a north-south line west of the Azores; lands west of it went to Spain and lands east (plus Brazil) to Portugal.

Voice

Isabella of Castile Writes Her Last Will and Testament

On October 12, 1504, twelve years to the day after Columbus landed in the Bahamas, the dying Isabella began to dictate her last will and testament. In it she made arrangements for her burial and the disposition of her worldly goods. She also summed up the major achievements of her reign and asked her successors to honor them.

➡ I ask and order that my body be buried in the monastery of Saint Francis which is in the Alhambra in the city of Granada . . . dressed in the habit of the very blessed poor man of Jesus Christ, Saint Francis, in a lowly grave without any bust and only a plain slab on the ground containing an inscription.

➡ Why would Isabella ask to be buried in a plain grave in Granada?

➡ In addition, because I have wanted to order a simplification of the laws . . . , identifying the doubtful ones and eliminating the superfluous ones, in order to avoid doubts and any contradictions that have arisen concerning them and the expenses that they might impose on my kingdoms . . . I beg the king my lord, and I order and enjoin the said princess, my daughter, and the said prince, her husband, to bring together a learned and conscientious prelate with persons who are educated, wise, and expert in law, to examine the said laws and to reduce them into a briefer and less cumbersome code.

➡ Why does Isabella "beg" her husband and "lord" to carry out her wishes while "ordering" her daughter and son-in-law to do so?

➡ I command that the jewels which the said princess and prince, my children, have given me be returned to them. And that the relic I have of Our Lord's loincloth be given to the monastery of Saint Anthony in the city of Segovia. And that all my other relics be given to the Cathedral in the city of Granada.

➡ How does Isabella's gift of relics to Granada relate to her instructions for her burial?

And I entreat and command the said princess, my daughter, and the said prince, her husband, as Catholic princes, to take great care concerning the things that honor God and His holy faith, watching over and securing the faith's safety, defense, and glorification, since for it we are obliged to pledge our persons, lives, and possessions as is necessary. And that they be very obedient to the commandments of holy mother church, as they are obliged to be its protectors and defenders. And that they will not cease the conquest of Africa to fight for the faith against the infidels. And that they will always favor the work of the Holy Inquisition against heretical depravity.

➡ From the time when the Holy Apostolic See granted us the Islands and Mainland of the Ocean Sea . . . our first intention was, from the time we entreated pope Alexander VI, of blessed memory, who gave us the said grant, to attempt to persuade and cause the inhabitants there to convert to our holy Catholic faith, and to send to the said islands and mainland prelates and members of religious orders and clergy, and other learned and God-fearing persons, to instruct the inhabitants and residents there in the Catholic faith, and to teach and instruct them in good behavior, and to put in them the necessary diligence, taking the care stated more fully in the letters of the grant. To this end, I most affectionately beseech the king my lord and I charge and command the said princess, my daughter, and the said prince, her husband, to carry this out as their principal goal with much diligence. ➡ They must not in any way allow the Indians, the inhabitants, and the residents in the said islands and mainland to suffer any injury to their persons or property, but must be well and justly treated. And if they have received any injury, they must set it right.

➡ Notice Isabella's description of her motive for conquering new territories. To what degree was it shared by the Spaniards who went to these new territories?

➡ Why would Isabella express her concerns for the Indians in her will?

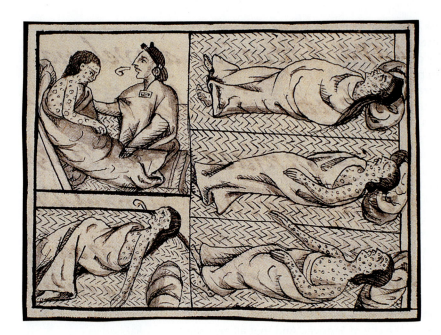

This drawing from about 1550 by an unknown Aztec artist shows the devastation that smallpox brought to the indigenous populations of the Western Hemisphere. At the upper left a local healer speaks to a sick person while others lie dying on mats. *(Biblioteca Medicea Laurenziana; Photo: MicroFoto, Florence)*

The **Taíno** people Columbus encountered on the islands of the Caribbean were friendly and provided him with food and information, but relations deteriorated when the Spaniards started to claim their land for Spain and rape women. Over the next twenty-five years, as more land was seized for farms, the Taíno, now virtually enslaved, were forced to work it. Even worse were the diseases, such as smallpox and influenza, that swept through the local population. Since the Western Hemisphere was isolated from Europe, local peoples had no immunity from the diseases the Spaniards brought, and millions died as epidemics swept through Central and South America, often in advance of any European's arrival. The Taíno, who may have numbered 300,000 in 1492, were virtually extinct by 1550, and, overall, the native population of the Americas fell by 90 percent in the century after Columbus's voyages—the greatest demographic catastrophe in recorded history.

For a quarter century after 1492, few Spaniards migrated to the Caribbean. Although some gold was found, it was difficult to grow sufficient food, and Spanish mortality rates were high as men succumbed to local diseases. Columbus himself died in Spain in 1506, disappointed by the meager results of his discoveries. Everything changed, however, in 1519, when a Spanish nobleman, **Hernán Cortés,** landed on the east coast of Mexico with six hundred men, sixteen horses, and six cannons.

Like those before him, Cortés was looking for gold. Unlike them, he embarked on territorial conquest; in

two and a half years his small force conquered the **Aztec Empire** of central Mexico. The Aztecs ruled over many states, which had to supply men and tribute to the emperor in the capital of Tenochtitlán. Cortés formed alliances with the most discontented states and augmented his own force with their soldiers. If local states refused to join the anti-Aztec coalition, they were intimidated by the invaders, who were mounted on horses, which the local people had never seen before, wore strange body armor, and wielded steel swords. In addition, the noise, smoke, and fire of Cortés's artillery, which was also unknown to the Aztecs, panicked the enemy, as did the attack dogs used in battle. (The Aztecs' only dogs were tiny, resembling modern-day chihuahuas.)

In November 1519, Cortés and his allies entered Tenochtitlán at the invitation of the emperor, Moctezuma II, who may have been influenced by Aztec traditions that prophesied the arrival by sea of a pale-

Taíno   Native people inhabiting the Caribbean islands visited by the Spaniards in the first period of encounter between Europeans and American Indians.

Hernán Cortés   (1485–1547) Spanish nobleman and conquistador (conqueror) who in 1519 conquered the Aztec Empire.

Aztec Empire   Federation of states in central Mexico ruled by an emperor from his capital, Tenochtitlán, the present-day Mexico City.

In this engraving, the Inca prince Atahualpa rises from his throne on his litter just before his capture by the Spanish at Cajamarca. He attempts to fend off a soldier while a Spanish friar raises a cross either in blessing or as protection against a pagan. The cannon in the foreground reminds the viewer of the withering Spanish fire power. *(Biblioteca Nazionale Marciana Venice/Dagli Orti/The Art Archive)*

skinned god, Quetzalcoatl. In June 1520, Moctezuma died under mysterious circumstances. Although probably murdered by his own people, the Aztecs blamed the Spaniards for his death and attacked Cortés. Withdrawing from the city, the Spaniards regrouped and made a successful assault in August 1521. Cortés now controlled the Aztec Empire, and one of his first acts was to demolish the sacred pyramid in the center of Tenochtitlán and replace it with a cathedral.

Cortés's conquest of the Aztecs launched the first New World gold rush. When news of Tenochtitlán's capture reached Europe, along with gold from Moctezuma's treasury, thousands of Spaniards flocked to Mexico in search of bounty. Among them was **Francisco Pizarro,** an illiterate laborer who had migrated to Hispaniola in 1502 and served in expeditions to Central America, including **Vaso Núñez de Balboa**'s trek across Panama to the Pacific Ocean. In

1531, Pizarro launched an expedition of 280 men and 55 horses against the **Inca Empire,** taking advantage of a political crisis among the Inca to conquer them.

In the late 1520s, the Inca emperor died, a victim of the European-induced epidemics that were raging though Central and South America. Two of his sons, Atahualpa and Huáscar, then fought each other for

Francisco Pizarro (ca. 1475–1541) Soldier who in 1531 conquered the Inca Empire with a small Spanish force.

Vaso Núñez de Balboa (1475–1519) Spanish explorer who crossed the isthmus of Panama in 1513 and sighted the Pacific Ocean.

Inca Empire Empire stretching from Ecuador to northern Chile and from the Pacific Ocean to the upper Amazon River.

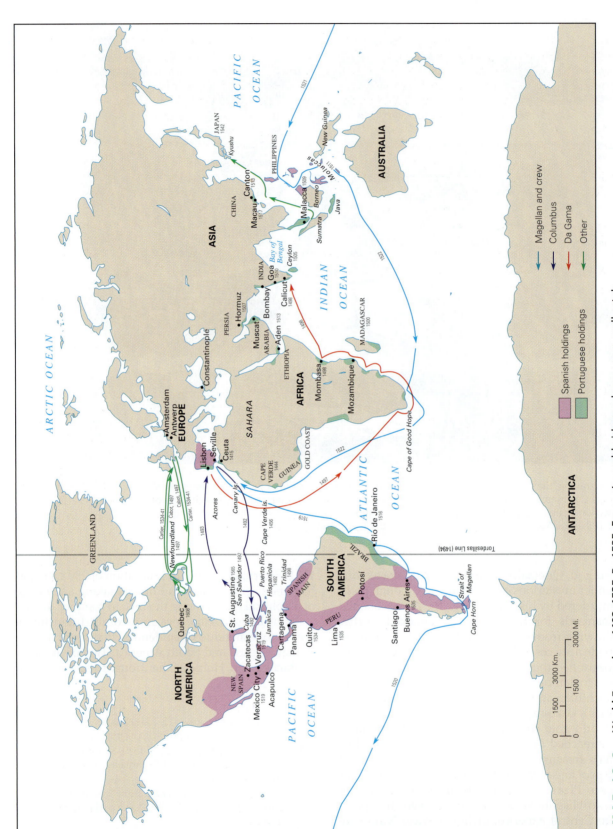

MAP 13.3 **World Expansion, 1492–1535** By 1535, Europe's worldwide sea-lanes were well established, following the voyages of Vasco da Gama, Christopher Columbus, and Ferdinand Magellan. Compare the size of Spain and Portugal with the size of their overseas empires.

control of the empire. Arriving during the civil war sparked by the sons' rivalry, Pizarro played the brothers against each other. He used his horses, cannon, and steel swords to slaughter over three thousand Inca soldiers at Cajamarca in present-day Peru after Atahualpa had unwittingly led them into an ambush. Atahualpa was taken prisoner. Huáscar was murdered in 1532, and a year later Atahualpa was also. Pizarro then set up a third brother as a puppet emperor.

Cortés's conquest of the Aztecs and Pizarro's of the Incas finally produced the precious metals that had driven the search for direct trade routes to Asia. It was silver, however, rather than gold, that flowed in ever-increasing quantities toward Spain from mines at Zacatecas in Mexico and Potosí in present-day Bolivia, both started in the 1540s. Following **Ferdinand Magellan**'s circumnavigation of the globe in 1519–1521, the magnitude of Columbus's voyages and subsequent Spanish conquests began to sink into the European consciousness.

Exploration, Expansion, and European Identity

↓ How did Europeans come to terms with the peoples of Africa and the Americas, whom they perceived as not like them?

↓ How did African slavery develop, and how was it justified?

Once it became clear that the peoples of the Western Hemisphere were not Asians but previously unknown inhabitants of a "New World," travelers' and missionaries' accounts appeared offering conflicting descriptions of these "Indians." In addition, the creation of Portuguese and Spanish Empires in the New World led to the importation of millions of black African slaves to replace the declining native populations as a labor force. Confronted with strange New World people and the emergence of African slavery in overseas empires, people in Europe were forced to rethink who they were in relation to others and outsiders.

Native Americans in the European Imagination

European attempts to understand Native Americans started with the assumption that there were universal standards for proper human behavior. Early travelers' and missionaries' accounts of New World people based on this assumption were positive. Native Americans were pictured as simple people who lived virtu-

ous lives. They had no private property and no money, and hence no reason to be greedy. They lived in harmony with nature and each other, solving disputes without need of laws and courts. They waged war, but only for just cause. In a word, the Indians were what Europeans ought to be. And so, in the end, these accounts were really about Europe, with the Indians providing a way for moralists to condemn abuses in their own society.

Alongside the picture of the "good Indian," an image of the "bad Indian" soon emerged. Indians were accused of eating disgusting things like spiders and worms. Because they wore no European clothes, they were accused of engaging in what Europeans thought were the vilest kinds of sexual behavior, including homosexuality and intercourse with animals. They had no true religion but worshiped satanically inspired idols. Worst of all, they practiced human sacrifice and cannibalism. Both the good and bad pictures of the Indians wove together bits of accurate information with misinformation and a host of European fantasies and fears, and both were believed. Gradually, however, the negative picture gained ground, and by the mid-sixteenth century, arguments were made that the Indians were not really human beings but **"natural slaves."**

The theory of the natural slave went back to the Greek philosopher Aristotle, who stated that there were creatures resembling human beings who nevertheless lacked fully rational minds. Although they could understand and communicate with real humans, they needed human masters to control them. If Indian behavior was as bad as some people said, then it was clear that the Indians were natural slaves, since fully rational human beings would reject the things the Indians supposedly did. Moreover, when the theory of natural slavery was applied to the Indians, the Spanish conquest and exploitation of them was fully justified.

The attack on the Indians reached a climax in the late 1540s, when Charles V's chaplain, **Juan Ginés de Sepúlveda,** defended the theory that they were natural slaves. Sepúlveda's endorsement of the "bad In-

Ferdinand Magellan (1480–1521) Portuguese commander of a Spanish fleet who circumnavigated the globe in 1519–1521.

"natural slaves" As theorized by the Greek philosopher Aristotle, semirational creatures resembling human beings who needed human masters to control them.

Juan Ginés de Sepúlveda (1494–1573) Charles V's chaplain, who denounced the American Indians as less than human.

This idealized portrait of Bartolomé de Las Casas is shows Las Casas as a Dominican friar. The artist gives him a noble but kindly face. He sits quietly writing in defense of the Indian populations he encountered first as a conquistador and then as a priest and bishop. *(Archivo de Indias, Seville/Mithra-Index/The Bridgeman Art Library)*

dian" theory provoked a response from Bartolomé de Las Casas. Las Casas was also an influential member of Charles V's court who had known both Ferdinand and Isabella. After 1492, he followed his father to the Caribbean, where he became a landowner, with many Indians working for him. But his true calling was to the church, and he became the first man to be ordained a priest in the Americas. Las Casas's experiences as a landowner had shown him just how brutally the Indians were exploited, and as a priest he campaigned for their better treatment. In 1542, he persuaded Charles V to stop the worst abuses by issuing the **New Laws for the Indies.** In 1545, Las Casas was consecrated a bishop and sent to Guatemala to introduce the New Laws, but local landlords' opposition to the reforms forced him to return to Spain. When Las Casas read Sepúlveda's attack, he demanded to face him in a debate.

Las Casas argued that men like himself, who had observed Indian culture directly, were the only persons qualified to determine whether Indians were fully human. And he argued eloquently that they were. Las Casas admitted that the Indians often behaved "badly," but he explained that this did not prove a lack of humanity. Their behavior resulted from evil customs that had taken root in their societies. In the past, Christianity had corrected Greek and Roman errors, and it would also correct Indian ones. In 1552, following his debate with Sepúlveda, Las Casas published his *Brief Account of the Destruction of the Indies*, a fiery description of Spanish brutality in the New World that was widely read and influenced many Europeans.

New Laws for the Indies   (1542) Laws issued by Charles V that attempted to stop Spanish exploitation of New World populations.

Las Casas's arguments were thoroughly **Eurocentric.** He believed in the superiority of European civilization and thought that the Indians' conversion to Christianity was the only way to save them from eternal damnation. His recognition of their full humanity and his demands for a just treatment of them, along with his sense of the superiority of European culture and religion, gave voice to many of the principles that guided European colonial expansion in subsequent centuries. Finally, Las Casas, aware of the labor shortage in the Americas created by the decline in local populations, urged his fellow Europeans to import African slaves to fill the gap, a position he later regretted.

The Labor of Africans

New World slavery had its origins in Portuguese exploration of Africa. Beginning in 1420, the Portuguese settled on **Atlantic islands** off Africa's west coast, while the Spanish occupied the Canary Islands. The islands' volcanic soil was ideal for growing sugar cane, and large **plantations** were established to produce it. During the Middle Ages, honey was Europe's chief sweetener. Medieval Europeans had known of sugar, which was imported in small quantities from Muslim lands and used as medicine or a sexual stimulant. With the colonization of the Atlantic islands, sugar became a European-controlled commodity and the demand for it rose rapidly. At first, the plantations' workforce consisted of Portuguese settlers as well as **indentured servants** fulfilling the terms of their contracts and slaves from the eastern Mediterranean and sub-Saharan Africa. By 1500, however, black African slaves predominated. For years, tribal warfare in West Africa had involved the capture and enslavement of enemies. Portuguese traders bought these slaves from Africans because they were relatively cheap and could be forced to do the harsh work on the island plantations that free Europeans eventually rejected.

Some African rulers opposed the Portuguese slave trade, but coastal merchants found it economically profitable and even invested in the sugar plantations. Over the sixteenth century, tens of thousands of slaves were brought to the Atlantic islands. Because they came from parts of Africa where agriculture was widespread, they were familiar with field work and could be trained to handle sugar cane. Soon the islands were the main sugar producers for Europe, sending sugar to Antwerp and other markets.

The Portuguese and Spanish not only pioneered the use of African slaves in a plantation system, they also adopted stereotypes about Africans developed first in the Muslim world, where a trade in sub-Saharan African slaves had persisted throughout the Middle Ages. These stereotypes condemned Africans as ugly, lazy, sexually promiscuous, stupid, and evil smelling. Christians had also long identified the color black with sin and the Devil and the color white with purity. The combination of these Muslim and Christian stereotypes laid the foundations for arguments about the racial inferiority of blacks to whites that were to have a long and vicious history.

Columbus, who had lived on the Madeira Islands before coming to Spain, took sugar-cane plants with him on his return to the Western Hemisphere in 1493. When settlers realized that cane grew well in Brazil and the Caribbean islands, plantations were established there, and the transatlantic importation of African slaves began. For the next three hundred years, more than 11 million Africans were carried across the Atlantic in one of the largest forced migrations in history.

Europeans justified African slavery in various ways. Some appealed to Aristotle's theory of natural slaves, while others cited Christian scripture, which showed that both the Israelites and the first Christians owned slaves. Others turned to Genesis and argued that Africans were the descendants of Noah's son Ham, cursed as a slave because he had seen his father drunk and naked. In a world that believed all human beings were slaves to sin, the idea that some were slaves to other men was easily accepted. In addition, Europe's hierarchical and patriarchal social order, in which wives, children, and servants were subject to the male head of household, made slavery seem like an extension of the general structure of society. As a result, few Europeans questioned it.

Slavery in the Western Hemisphere differed in important respects from the kind practiced in European and Muslim lands. First, slaves were increasingly thought of as black and African. Earlier forms of slavery had been colorblind, since people of many different racial and ethnic communities had been enslaved.

Eurocentric   Idea that Europe and European culture are either superior to or more important than the lands and cultures of other peoples.

Atlantic islands   The Azores, the Cape Verde Islands, the Madeira Islands, and São Tomé, where the Portuguese used African slaves to cultivate sugar for the European market.

plantation   A large-scale agricultural enterprise producing goods for the European market, often using slave labor.

indentured servants   Servants who agreed to compulsory service for a fixed period of time, often in exchange for passage to a colony.

In the Americas, most slaves worked on plantations or, after silver was discovered in the Spanish Empire, in mines. This work was in contrast to European and Muslim slavery, in which many different types of work were performed by slaves. Most important, slavery was increasingly considered a lifelong status and one that children inherited from their parents, thus creating a perpetually enslaved class of persons. The idea that one was "born" a slave, not "made" one by capture or some other force, fitted in with European ideas of Africans' racial inferiority.

The Problem of "the Other"

At the end of the sixteenth century, the new peoples Europeans had encountered in their expeditions for trade and wealth were so broadly recognized that the great playwright of the English Renaissance, **William Shakespeare,** put them on stage in his dramas. In Shylock the Jew, Caliban the slave, and Othello the African, Shakespeare provides insights into Europeans' thoughts about **"the other."** These unforgettable stage characters reveal traditional stereotypes but also portray the playwright's sense of their humanity and the injustices done to them.

In *The Merchant of Venice,* Shakespeare used traditional Christian stereotypes of the Jew to create Shylock, a miserly moneylender who proclaimed his hatred of Christians and wanted to destroy the Christian merchant Antonio. When Antonio's finances falter, Shylock agrees to loan him money, but at a price—a pound of his flesh if he fails to repay. This gruesome demand echoed traditional Christian fantasies and fears, like those that had surfaced at La Guardia in Spain, where Jews were accused of killing a child for magical purposes. The Christians of Venice repay Shylock's hatred in kind, spitting on him and calling him "dog" and "the devil in the likeness of a Jew."

When Antonio goes broke, Shylock demands his pound of flesh—to use as fish bait. But just at this point, Shakespeare gives Shylock one of the most famous speeches in the play:

> *Hath not a Jew eyes? hath not a Jew affections, passions? if you tickle us, do we not laugh? if you poison us, do we not die?*

Here, Shakespeare shows Shylock not as a monster but as a man crushed by Christian slander and contempt, and his words cut through the mutual hatred like a cry. Nevertheless, Shylock continues to demand his payment. In the end, he loses in court; Antonio keeps his flesh, and Shylock must surrender half his fortune to his daughter, who has run away with a Christian. Then he is forced to convert to Christianity.

Shakespeare used common anti-Jewish stereotypes to construct Shylock. But two details were his own: Shylock's plea to be treated as a human being and the renunciation of his religion by force. These both complicate the stereotype of the wicked and hated Jew.

Like Shylock, Caliban in *The Tempest* is a complex character. He was "king" of the island where he lived alone until Prospero, the deposed duke of Milan, was exiled there with his daughter. At first, Prospero befriended Caliban, teaching him to speak like a human. But when Caliban attempted to rape his daughter, he turned against him, enslaving him and calling him "a born devil, on whose nature nurture can never stick." Prospero also calls himself "lord" of Caliban's island.

Shakespeare had read European accounts of Native Americans. References in *The Tempest* show that he drew on them when he created Caliban, who has all the qualities of a natural slave—he is physically deformed, without speech until taught by a European, and a would-be rapist who must be ruled by force. Throughout the play Caliban uses his newfound speech to curse Prospero while plotting to murder him. He is dangerous and despicable. And yet, when Caliban describes the beauties of his island, which Prospero has seized from him, Shakespeare gave him some of the most beautiful lines in the play, and they are in poetry. Shakespeare normally reserved poetic lines for high-born or noble characters, while the low and bad ones speak prose. Caliban, like Shylock, embodied stereotypes of the hated "other." But, like *The Merchant of Venice,* there are occasions in *The Tempest* when Shakespeare cast the stereotypes aside to show the humanity of the injured character, if only for a moment.

In *Othello,* Shakespeare returned to Venice for the setting of his play. The title character is an African ex-slave serving as the mercenary commander of Venetian forces on Cyprus to defend the island against the "malignant and turbaned Turk." Shakespeare again used current stereotypes to create Othello, who is described by other characters in the play as having thick lips and being "sooty," "lascivious," "an old black ram," and "ignorant as dirt." He also drew on a contemporary account of Africans in English that called them savage, jealous, and easily deceived. The play

William Shakespeare (1564–1616) England's greatest playwright, author of *The Merchant of Venice, The Tempest, Othello,* and many other plays and poems.

"the other" Religious, ethnic, racial, or other outsiders who are feared and hated because they are said to embody all that a community rejects as bad or inhuman.

revolves around Othello's growing belief that his beloved Venetian wife, Desdemona, who is white, has been unfaithful to him. Once convinced of Desdemona's infidelity, Othello flies into a wild, jealous rage. In the end he strangles his wife. When he learns that she was, in fact, innocent, he kills himself. Othello is a great sinner, guilty of rage, murder, and suicide. But he is not the villain of the play. That label goes to Iago, who is white, Christian, and Venetian. Out of jealousy and hatred for Othello, Iago seduces the "Moor" into believing that Desdemona is an adulteress. He is one of Shakespeare's greatest villains—intelligent, crafty, and supremely evil. In the end, Othello the black outsider is a tragic hero, while Iago, the white insider, is led offstage in chains.

In Shakespeare's plays, debates about "others," carried on in learned circles by Las Casas and Sepúlveda, were presented to a wider audience in vividly dramatic form. Like Las Casas, Shakespeare wrestled with the problem by starting with assumptions of his own culture's superiority. But also like him, Shakespeare could argue that the hated and savage "other" was part of humanity. Medieval people had identified themselves as Christians and thought of the "other"—that is, Jews and Muslims—mainly in religious terms as people who had heard of but rejected the Christian gospel. Now "others" came to include Indians and African slaves, who had no prior knowledge of Christianity, and the problem of understanding who they were became acute.

Summary

Review Questions

↑ How did Europe's economic expansion create a global economy?

↑ What strategies did European rulers use to increase control over their territories?

↑ What factors shaped the formation of Europeans' individual and collective identities and those of the peoples they encountered in global expansion?

The growth of Europe's population, which began after 1450, stimulated an economic expansion based on increasing agricultural activity and the growth of new trading networks. From 1450 to 1550, most urban and rural workers benefited from a rise in wages, although rates of pay were sharply different for men and women because of prevailing notions about the relative value of men's and women's work. The gendered distribution of wages echoed the general patriarchal organization of society. Both urban and rural communities were headed by men. In addition, these communities were arranged hierarchically from the better sort to the lesser sort.

Although many communities became less economically self-sufficient as they were linked to large-scale trading networks, a strong sense of community identity and mutual responsibility characterized Europe's villages, towns, and cities. The community was conceived of as an organic whole in which anyone's fate was everyone's business. This view explains Europeans' commitment to public hospitals and welfare institutions. Communities also carefully guarded their local ways of life against outside intrusions.

Rulers in this early modern world benefited from Europe's rising economy, which allowed them to tax and borrow to meet their needs, but they also had to be careful to respect their subjects' rights and traditions, even as they sought to increase their control over them. Successful government involved cooperating and negotiating with local elites, whether nobles, landowners, or town fathers, in order to develop working relations with them. Rulers like Ivan IV, who tried to govern despotically, could throw their societies into turmoil, but their extreme policies usually met with failure.

One trend in government was the attempt to forge more centralized states. The means to this end varied. In Spain, a policy to respect the political independence of Castile and Aragon was balanced against the creation of a new, more homogeneous national identity. In France and England, it involved the introduction of standardized languages. In many states, it involved tying rulers as borrowers to subjects as lenders. It also involved administrative centralization in the hands of experts.

The creation of empires after 1450 was the most dramatic example of Europe's age of expansion. For Portugal and Spain, empire building was directly linked to trade. The creation of empires had enormous consequences for both Europeans and non-Europeans. For Africans, it had the disastrous effect of expanding and extending the trade in slaves from the small Atlantic islands to the huge plantation economies of the New World. In the New World, it involved not only conquest but also the destruction of whole societies, through the unforeseen and largely uncontrollable spread of new diseases. For Europeans like Cortés and Pizarro, empire brought new riches. For those like Las Casas and Shakespeare, it brought a new urgency to think through the problems of colonial domination and Europeans' relations with other peoples.

← Thinking Back, Thinking Ahead →

What were the long-term consequences of European overseas expansion during the sixteenth century?

ECHO

Christopher Columbus

Cristoforo Colombo, a Genoese sailor, died before the full impact of his voyages was understood in Europe. He certainly could not have known how famous he would become—or that he would be a symbol for all that later generations admired or condemned in the complex encounter between the "New World" and Europe that his voyages set in motion.

Curiously, this Italian who sailed for a Spanish Catholic monarch became a hero for nineteenth-century Americans, most of whom were staunchly Protestant. In their eyes, Columbus embodied all the virtues they most admired in themselves. He seemed to represent the rugged individualist whose contempt for hidebound traditionalists arguing that the world was flat led him on a heroic adventure across the unknown frontier of the Atlantic. This way of thinking reached a climax in 1892, when President Benjamin Harrison issued a proclamation for a national observance of the four-hundredth anniversary of Columbus's "discovery" of America.

In the first half of the twentieth century, Columbus was returned to his ethnic roots and became the darling of Americans of Italian descent, who campaigned for an annual national holiday in his honor. In 1937, President Franklin D. Roosevelt, who had recently won a landslide reelection victory with many Italian American votes, created the present holiday. (In 1971, the observance was changed to the second Monday in October to give workers the chance for a three-day weekend.)

In the second half of the twentieth century, Columbus became a contested symbol. Italian Americans continued to venerate him, but so did Hispanics, claiming that his voyages were "a thoroughly Spanish event." In 1996, both groups organized rival Columbus Day parades in New York City. On the other hand, Scandinavians complained that Columbus was a latecomer and called for a holiday honoring the first Norse "discoverers," who landed in North America around the year 1000. All three groups have also had to compete with Native Americans' counterimage of Columbus as the man who brought devastating disease, followed by slavery, to the peoples of the Western Hemisphere. In 1992, on the five-hundredth anniversary of his voyages, a protest holiday, Indigenous Peoples Day, was observed in some places by Native Americans and their supporters. Although seventy towns or districts in the United States are today named in honor of Columbus, the Genoese sailor continues to be a contested figure for people with different ethnic loyalties and conflicting historical memories.

Suggested Readings

Cameron, Euan, ed. *Early Modern Europe: An Oxford History.* Oxford: Oxford University Press, 2000. A recent general account.

Kamen, Henry. *Empire: How Spain Became a World Power, 1492–1763.* New York: HarperCollins Publishers, 2003. Detailed account of Spanish empire building in the Western Hemisphere.

Musgrave, Peter. *The Early Modern European Economy.* New York: St. Martin's Press, 1999. A recent survey.

Phillips, William D., Jr., and Carla Rahn Phillips. *The Worlds of Christopher Columbus.* New York: Cambridge University Press, 1992. Excellent on Columbus's life and times.

Postma, Johannes. *The Atlantic Slave Trade.* Westport, Conn.: Greenwood Press, 2003. An excellent introduction.

Riasanovsky, Nicholas V. *A History of Russia.* 6th ed. New York: Oxford University Press, 2000. The standard account in English.

Zinsser, Judith P., and Bonnie S. Anderson. *Women in Early Modern and Modern Europe.* Washington, D.C.: American Historical Association, 2001. A brief introduction.

Websites

For sections and links to readings on many of the topics discussed in this chapter, **Internet Modern History Sourcebook,** at www.fordham.edu/halsall/mod/modsbook03.html

A detailed listing of products traded in the emerging world economy, **Trade Products in Early Modern History,** at www.bell.lib.umn.edu/Products.html

More than a thousand images relating to the slave trade and slave life, **The Atlantic Slave Trade and Slave Life in the Americas: A Visual Record,** at www.hitchcock.itc.virginia.edu/Slavery/index.php

Reform in the Western Church, 1490–1570

CHAPTER OUTLINE

1500 B.C.E.	1000 B.C.E.	500 B.C.E.	1 B.C.E./1 C.E.

	1516 Erasmus translates the Greek New Testament	

1494 Savonarola institutes reforms in Florence	1517 Luther condemns indulgences	1527 Henry VIII breaks with the pope

1490	1495	1500	1505	1510	1515	1520	1525	1530

Catholics, Protestants, and the Eastern Orthodox in 1555

The Religious Peace of Augsburg in 1555 confirmed the division of western Christendom. Which religious community or communities were able to win over the majority of the population in the most parts of Europe, north and south, east and west?

Predominant religion in 1555

- Lutheran
- Calvinist (Reformed)
- Church of England
- Roman Catholic
- Orthodox
- Muslim
- ← Spread of Calvinism
- ▲ Huguenot centers
- Boundary of Ottoman Empire, 1566
- Boundary of Holy Roman Empire

Bergen

NORWAY

SWEDEN

Helsinki

Stockholm

ESTONIA

LIVONIA

Riga

RUSSIA

Baltic Sea

SCOTLAND

Edinburgh
John Knox

Penetration of Calvinism to England after 1558

DENMARK
Copenhagen

North Sea

IRELAND

Dublin

WALES ENGLAND

Oxford

London
Thomas More

Plymouth

Amsterdam

NETHERLANDS
Menno Simons

Antwerp

Brussels

Hamburg

Münster
Slaughter of Anabaptists, 1535

BRANDENBURG

Wittenberg
Martin Luther

PRUSSIA

POLAND-LITHUANIA

Warsaw

Leipzig

Marburg

Erfurt

SAXONY

SILESIA

ATLANTIC OCEAN

Rennes

Paris

Orléans

Worms
Edict of Worms, 1521

Speyer

Strasbourg

HOLY ROMAN
EMPIRE

Nuremberg

Stuttgart

BOHEMIA

Prague

MORAVIA
Jacob Hutter

Nantes
Edict of Nantes, 1598

La Rochelle

FRANCE

Basel

Zurich
Ulrich Zwingli

Augsburg

Munich

Vienna

AUSTRIA

HUNGARY

Buda   Pest

TRANSYLVANIA

Bordeaux

Geneva
John Calvin

Council of Trent, 1545–1563

Milan

Trent

Pavia

Genoa

Belgrade

Black Sea

Loyola
Ignatius Loyola

Toulouse

Avignon

Marseilles

Pisa
Florence
Girolama Savanarola

Venice
Jewish Ghetto, 1516

PORTUGAL

Ávila
Teresa of Avila

Madrid

ANDORRA

Corsica

PAPAL
STATES

OTTOMAN

Lisbon

Toledo

SPAIN

Barcelona

Valencia

Sardinia

Rome
Roman Inquisition established, 1542

Naples

NAPLES

Constantinople

EMPIRE

Seville

Granada

Balearic Is.

Sicily

ALGIERS

TUNIS

OTTOMAN
EMPIRE

Mediterranean Sea

0   200   400 Km.

0   200   400 Mi.

| 500 C.E. | 1000 C.E. | 1500 C.E. | 2000 C.E. |

1535
Anabaptists slaughtered at Münster

1536
Calvin's *Institutes* published

1540
Pope approves Jesuits

1545
Council of Trent opens

1555
Peace of Augsburg accepts split in western Christianity

1563
Council of Trent ends

| 1535 | 1540 | 1545 | 1550 | 1555 | 1560 | 1565 | 1570 | 1575 |

Choice

Teresa of Ávila

Teresa of Ávila, one of the Catholic Church's great reformers, reinvigorated her religious order, the Carmelites, and wrote spiritual works that were quickly recognized as masterpieces of devotion. As a woman, she faced huge obstacles because women were thought to be unsuited for such serious work. But she won over even her fiercest opponents and at her death was recognized as one of the pillars of the Roman Catholic Church. (Institut Amatller d'Art Hispanic)

Teresa of Ávila Chooses to Reform the Carmelites

In 1535, a twenty-year-old woman, defying her father, secretly left her family's house and entered a convent of the Carmelites, a religious order founded in the Middle Ages. There, as "Teresa of Jesus," she did not cease to follow her heart—challenging the male church authorities who oversaw orders of nuns, urging the Carmelites to adhere to poverty, and inaugurating a renewal of church life based in prayer and a personal union with God. Her accomplishments are testimony to the power of one woman's persistence and the strength of personal conviction even in an era dominated by an authoritarian church hierarchy.

Teresa de Cepeda y Ahumada was an unlikely candidate for a nunnery. She was born in 1515 to a wealthy Spanish family, aristocratic in status but also suspect for its recent conversion to Catholicism from Judaism. Many Spaniards thought that Jewish ancestry was a blot that not even Christian baptism could wash away. But Teresa's commitment to Christianity was genuine; even as a child she showed signs of the choice she would make later in life. She liked to "play church" with her brothers and sisters, pretending to be a holy hermit living in a cave. She even dreamed of a trip to North Africa, where she hoped Muslims would chop off her head and make her a Christian martyr.

As a nun, Teresa contended not only with her Jewish background but also with stereotypes that cast women as weak, the playthings of the Devil, and therefore especially prone to error and sin. Clerical enemies dismissed her as a "silly little woman" who had no business writing about monastic reform and the life of prayer. In a clever response, Teresa accepted these charges but turned them upside down, arguing that her ideas and plans must have come directly from God, since she herself was so weak, ignorant, and sinful.

At the same time, Teresa undertook a drastic reform of the Carmelite Order, which had not strictly obeyed its own rules concerning separation from the world. With support from the bishop of Ávila, her hometown, Teresa saw that it did. The nuns were to become the Discalced, or "Barefoot," Carmelites, giving up shoes for sandals and living a life of poverty. These reforms also provoked strong opposition, but she pursued them with firmness and common sense. Although she suffered from ill health, she traveled all over Spain seeking support from the rich and powerful. She regularly rose at five in the morning but often stayed up past midnight to write letters to those who could help or harm her cause. The turning point came when she won the support of the Spanish king, Philip II. Fourteen Carmelite convents accepted her reform program.

Like Catherine of Siena, Teresa was a mystic. Beginning in 1554, she started to experience visions of Christ during her prayers. "His Majesty," as she called Jesus, appeared to her frequently and spoke to her in her heart, as one friend to another. When Teresa told her father confessor and other male clergymen of these visions, they were alarmed and ordered her to write them down in detail so they could examine them for errors. She obeyed. These writings, which described her visions and offered advice on how to pray, soon brought her to the attention of the Spanish Inquisition. But she was able to convince the inquisitors and others that there was nothing heretical or devilish in her experiences or writings.

Soon after Teresa died in 1582, her friends collected her writings and published them. The recently invented printing press, which could rapidly spread an author's works throughout Europe, made Teresa famous. She was immediately recognized as a masterful guide for Catholics who sought a more perfect life of prayer and a closer union with God. In 1612, she was declared a saint of the Catholic Church. But the gender expectations of her age, which classified women lower than men, even shaped the decrees proclaiming her sainthood. She was labeled a "virile woman" with a "manly soul," as male clerics believed that, before Teresa could become an object of public devotion, she had to be made manlike. But her life and writings carried a different message. Here was an intelligent, capable woman who counteracted deep prejudices to renew the life of her religious order, write treatises on prayer that became instant classics of Christian spirituality, and lead church reform. In 1969, Teresa was the first woman to be proclaimed a doctor, or authoritative teacher, of the Roman Catholic Church.

Introduction

Teresa of Ávila's reform of the Carmelite religious order was part of a larger church renewal movement sweeping over Europe in the sixteenth century. Church reform had been a feature of Christian life throughout the Middle Ages, but the movement that gained strength around the year 1500 was unparalleled in intensity and scope. It also split the Catholic Church apart. One branch of reform, known as Protestantism, rejected the authority of the pope, who until then had been the head of western Christianity. The other branch remained loyal to the pope while insisting, like Teresa, on the need for basic change within the Catholic Church. Only the Orthodox churches of eastern Europe and the Middle East were largely untouched by these reforms.

In Germany, Martin Luther launched Protestant reform. He was followed by other Protestants who began reforms of their own that sometimes disagreed with Luther's. Thus Protestants had to choose which reformer to follow. The leaders in Catholic reform were the religious orders of the church and the Roman popes. Together they refashioned Catholicism in ways that lasted until the mid-twentieth century. Because Catholics could rally around the person of the pope, they remained more united than the Protestants, although they, too, experienced division and controversy, as Teresa of Ávila's struggles show.

As reform touched more and more people's lives, both Protestants and Catholics had to rethink what it meant to be a Christian. Both forged new identities while imposing undesirable stereotypes on their opponents. Catholics also launched the first worldwide Christian missionary movement, as priests followed conquerors and merchants into the Americas and East Asia. Both Protestants and Catholics expected Jews to be swept up into church renewal and looked for their conversion to Christianity. When this did not happen, a backlash developed that worsened the living conditions of Jews in western Europe.

In both Protestant and Catholic Europe, reformers expected the mass of Christians to accept the changes they proposed. Often Christians did, since there was wide popular support for many of the reforms. Sometimes, however, ordinary people had expectations of their own. When these clashed with those of the reformers, a period of unofficial negotiation took place in which reforms were modified or rejected by the community as a whole.

Chronology

1494	Savonarola institutes moral reforms in Florence	**1536**	Calvin publishes *Institutes of the Christian Religion*
1516	Jewish Ghetto is established in Venice	**1540**	Pope approves Jesuits
1517	Luther condemns church indulgences	**1541**	Calvin initiates reform in Geneva
1521	Luther is excommunicated and declared an outlaw in the empire	**1545**	Council of Trent opens
1522	Ignatius of Loyola becomes a church reformer	**1549**	Francis Xavier introduces Christianity into Japan
1524	Peasants' War breaks out in Germany	**1555**	Peace of Augsburg allows Lutheranism
1525	Luther marries Katherine von Bora	**1558**	John Knox introduces Calvinism into Scotland; Elizabeth I becomes queen of England
1527	Henry VIII breaks with pope		
1535	Catholic and Lutheran rulers slaughter Anabaptists at Münster Teresa of Ávila becomes a nun	**1563**	Council of Trent ends

The Context of Church Reform, 1490–1517

⬇ What developments prepared the way for the church reform of the sixteenth century?

⬇ What were the similarities and differences between Savonarola's and Erasmus's church reform programs?

The famine and plague that beset Europe in the fourteenth century intensified religious concerns and raised anxieties about God's wrath and judgment. Above all, people looked to the traditional head of the western church, the pope, for spiritual leadership, but when he did not provide it, they turned elsewhere for religious guidance. Some found it in the sermons of fiery preachers predicting God's punishment on sinful humankind, while others turned to new forms of piety and to the humanist movement for inspiration. By 1500, spiritual hunger and a growing sense that the western church was ineffective and worldly had set the stage for the waves of religious reform that swept over Europe in the sixteenth century.

Growing Discontent in the Western Church

Around 1500, a number of developments converged to provide the context for the reforming movements that spread throughout the western church during the sixteenth century. After 1450, the Roman papacy, the focal point of the church, tried to recover from the decline in prestige it had suffered during papal residence in Avignon and the Great Schism. Although the papacy successfully countered conciliarism's challenge that church councils held more authority than the pope, the popes of the late fifteenth century did not inspire confidence. People were looking for a pastor, but none of the men elected to the papacy lived up to their expectations. Some, like Alexander VI, shocked contemporaries with their sexual immorality by keeping mistresses who gave birth to their children. Others, like Leo X, behaved more like Renaissance princes than devout bishops. On hearing of his election to the papacy, Leo reportedly said, "God has given us the papacy and we intend to enjoy it!" Lack of spiritual leadership convinced many that the papacy had become corrupt and worldly.

Hope for a spiritual leader in Rome was fueled by the spread of **Christian humanism,** which emphasized the need to recover pure Christianity by turning to the Bible and the ancient church fathers. At the same

Christian humanism Humanist movement in northern Europe emphasizing study of the Bible and the early church fathers.

These two prints attack Pope Alexander VI. The left image, the first a viewer would see, shows the "official" Alexander in his papal robes, carrying a ceremonial cross and wearing the papal triple tiara. The caption reads "Alexander VI Supreme Pontiff." After lifting up the first image the viewer would see the right image of the "real" Alexander, a hideous, hellish monster. The caption reads "I am the pope." *(University Library Bern, Switzerland. Biblia. (lat.) Interprete Sebastiano Castalione, Basel; Johannes Oprinus, 1550, sign. Hosp. 44)*

time, laymen and -women in the Netherlands joined clergy to form the **Brothers and Sisters of the Common Life.** The brothers and sisters tried to live the life of Jesus's first disciples—a life of poverty while caring for the sick and feeding the hungry. Their activities and their intense personal devotion to Jesus offered religious comfort to a generation hungry for spiritual renewal. Their devotion also prompted a growing popular interest in the life of Jesus and in the Bible and a greater demand for preachers who could talk about scripture and describe Jesus's life and death.

Although the popes did not respond vigorously to rising demands for spiritual leadership, the lower clergy did. By 1500, many clergymen were better educated and more effective in performing their duties than they had been in the Middle Ages. Some installed **pulpits** in their churches to respond to the de-

mand for preaching. Traditionally, preaching had been the task of religious orders like the Franciscans and Dominicans. When **parish priests** began to preach, these orders resented their intrusion, and tensions led to charges of incompetence and immorality from both sides. Friars complained that parish priests were badly educated, while parish priests accused the friars of preaching to lure women into confession and then

Brothers and Sisters of the Common Life   Religious community founded in the Netherlands that cared for the needy, following the example of Jesus.

pulpit   Raised and enclosed platform for preaching.

parish priests   Clergymen in charge of church life in the basic local unit of the church, the parish.

use them sexually. Although many of these accusations were exaggerated, they fed a growing belief that the clergy as a whole, not just the pope, was corrupt.

In the absence of strong papal leadership, rulers in many parts of Europe tried to meet their subjects' religious expectations while strengthening their own control over the church in their lands. Ferdinand and Isabella in Spain, along with Francis I of France, showed what determined rulers could do in reforming perceived abuses and regulating relations with the pope. Their efforts inspired others to look to the state as an agent of religious reform.

Finally, the printing revolution that swept over Europe during the fifteenth century allowed for fast reproduction of inexpensive texts and illustrations in large numbers. It was in the Rhineland and the Netherlands that printing first became widespread. In the fifty years between 1450 and 1500, more books were produced using the new technology than during the previous thousand years. After 1500, church reformers quickly exploited the possibilities of rapid, widespread dissemination of their views that the printing press made possible.

God's Wrath and Church Reform

Fear of God's wrath, which lay behind movements like the medieval flagellants, continued to inspire movements of reform. In the 1490s, a Dominican friar in Florence, **Girolamo Savonarola,** denounced corruption in the city and church. He proclaimed that a divine day of reckoning was just around the corner on which the church would be judged and then renewed. Condemning the Florentines' worldliness, he organized "burnings of vanities." In a frenzy of communal purification, people tossed their fancy clothes and jewels onto public bonfires along with playing cards, gambling tables, and pornographic pictures. For Savonarola, this was the first act in a divinely scripted drama in which Florence would become a truly holy Christian city. He proclaimed that reform would increase Florence's wealth and prestige and would inaugurate a purification of the church throughout the world. Savonarola also prophesied that a French army would invade Italy and win an easy victory over the Italians. When, in fact, the French king Charles VIII invaded in 1494, many Florentines believed that Savonarola's prophesy had come true, and his prestige in the city soared. For the next four years he was Florence's spiritual dictator.

Savonarola denounced not only the "vanities" of the Florentines but also Pope Alexander VI's sexual immorality. Angered by the attack, Alexander looked for ways to silence him. Faced with mounting papal hostility, Savonarola called for a general council of the church to judge Alexander, thus resurrecting the theology of the conciliar movement that Rome had tried to quash. This was too much for the pope; in 1498, at Alexander's instigation, a church court condemned Savonarola. He was then tortured and burned at the stake.

Savonarola's dictatorship, which had widespread popular support, mixed Christian reform with a strong dose of local patriotism and a belief that a truly Christian Florence could prosper in this world. It expressed a yearning for Christ's return to earth as judge of the living and the dead that was as old as Christianity itself. It also reflected the traditional Christian view that earthly and heavenly things were inseparable; right relations with God led to an orderly, prosperous community life. Savonarola's commitment to a purified Christian community, his belief in a coming day of reckoning with God, and his sense that religion and all other aspects of life were tied together reappeared regularly in the later church reform movements of the sixteenth century.

Humanism and Church Reform

Humanism also contributed to the movement for church reform, thanks to **Desiderius Erasmus** of Rotterdam, the greatest Christian humanist of his generation. The illegitimate son of a priest, Erasmus lost both his parents to the plague when he was a child. His new guardians sent him to various schools, including one run by the Brothers of the Common Life. Later, he complained about the brothers' harsh routine, but their piety deeply influenced him. When his guardians insisted that Erasmus become a monk, he joined a religious order and was ordained a priest. The monastic life, however, was not to his taste, and in 1516 he obtained papal permission to live outside his monastery. Although he attended the University of Paris and lectured at Cambridge University in England, he was never drawn to the academic life. Rejecting both the monastery and the university, he set himself up as an independent scholar and traveled widely throughout western Europe. Erasmus shared the humanists' interest in studying the pagan and Christian literature of antiquity. His writings com-

Girolamo Savonarola (1452–1498) Italian Dominican friar who tried to carry out church reform in Florence.

Desiderius Erasmus (1469–1536) Dutch humanist, theologian, and textual scholar whose writings influenced the movement for church reform.

bined an elegant Latin style with biting humor. Like Savonarola, he was fiercely opposed to immorality, but unlike him, he expressed his opposition in wit and satire instead of fiery preaching. Also, like Savonarola, he wanted a reform but not a rejection of the Catholic Church, since he accepted the basic teachings of Catholicism, including the pope's preeminence.

Erasmus's version of reformed Christianity centered on what he called the philosophy of Christ, which was found in the ancient sources of Christianity—the scriptures and the commentaries of the early church fathers. Erasmus believed that the fathers, who were closer in time to Christ than his own generation, were also closer to the original meaning of scripture. Therefore, people should follow the example of Christ in the Gospels as the fathers presented it. Erasmus argued that if certain practices were not found in these early sources, like confession to a priest or clerical celibacy, they were not essential to Christianity.

Erasmus believed that education was the way to get people to accept the philosophy of Christ. He had huge faith in the power of education to change people's lives; study did not simply make people informed or skilled—it made them good. He therefore told teachers that they should teach the young by persuasion, not fear, and should avoid whipping bad students unless absolutely necessary. Since education was to teach the philosophy of Christ based on the scriptures, Erasmus prepared an accurate printed edition of the New Testament in its original Greek and made a correct translation into the more familiar Latin.

During his visit to England, Erasmus met the English lawyer and humanist **Sir Thomas More.** More was famous for his *Utopia*, a witty account of a fictional country where there was no private property, men and women saw each other naked before marriage to show that they were physically sound, and the incurably ill were encouraged to take their own lives. More, a devout Catholic, was not advocating these practices (*utopia* in Greek means "no place"). His intentions were to amuse his readers and to unmask the stupidity and greed of his own society. More also served in the English king's government as chancellor, the highest judicial official in the realm. His service appealed to Erasmus, who believed that Europe's rulers should be agents for church reform.

By the time Erasmus died in 1536, the Protestant Reformation was well under way. Although he remained a Catholic, his emphasis on scripture as the foundation of Christianity, his call for Christians to return to their ancient roots for standards of belief and action, and his faith in the power of education to make a better world were all embraced by reformers after him.

Martin Luther and the Protestant Reformation, 1517–1550

↓ How was Martin Luther's reform agenda similar to and different from that of his predecessors?
↓ What was the impact of Luther's reforms?

By the time Erasmus was a well-established critic of the church, another reformer, Martin Luther, had emerged and was carrying the reforming agenda in new directions. Eventually, Luther argued that reform of the church required a complete rejection of the Roman pope, and rupture with Rome, therefore, became the central feature of his movement. Historians call reformers who broke with the pope Protestants. With the establishment of Lutheran Protestant churches in north Germany and Scandinavia, the religious unity of western Europe was shattered.

Luther's Challenge to the Church

Martin Luther was a broad-faced German monk from peasant stock with a sharp tongue and a brilliant mind whose father had wanted him to become a lawyer. Like Savonarola, Luther was troubled by fears of sin, God's wrath, and judgment. In the summer of 1505, the fears came to a head when he was caught in a violent thunderstorm, during which a bolt of lightning threw him to the ground. He cried out in terror, "Help me Saint Anne! I shall become a monk!" After Luther gave up the law and took monastic vows, the head of his monastery ordered him to study theology, and in 1508 he was appointed professor of New Testament studies at the new University of Wittenberg.

For the next seven years, Luther studied the Bible. He had become a monk to lessen his fears about his sinfulness before God, but the old doubts continued to haunt him. He carefully observed the monastic life and regularly confessed his sins, but the promise of God's forgiveness, which came with the priest's **absolution,** seemed hollow, since he continued to feel

Thomas More (1477–1535) English lawyer and humanist, author of *Utopia* and friend of Erasmus.

Martin Luther (1483–1546) German monk who led a church reform movement in Germany that became the Lutheran form of Protestantism.

absolution At the end of confession, words spoken by a Catholic priest, acting as God's agent, that grant forgiveness of a person's sins.

Luther was fifty when Lucas Cranach the Elder painted this portrait in 1533. By then Lutheranism was spreading through much of Germany and Scandinavia. Luther gazes out of the picture toward something that would be on the viewer's right. His sturdy face and serene expression convey confidence and calm. *(Scala/Art Resource, NY)*

that they had performed a superabundance of good works, which overflowed into a treasury that Christians could draw on to supplement their own less abundant righteousness. An indulgence, issued by the pope, allowed the person obtaining it to use the righteousness of Christ and the saints to cancel out his or her own sins. At its best, the system of indulgences was something like a mutual-aid society based on compassion for sinners, but it often degenerated into an accountant's game of credit (works) and debit (sins) in which specific sums were shifted from the treasury to the sinful man or woman. Moreover, indulgences could be obtained for someone else, like a spouse or parent, who had died. These dead people were thought to be in **Purgatory,** where they were being punished for their earthly sins. An indulgence for them would cancel some of that punishment and thus hasten their passage into Heaven.

Luther's study of the Bible led him to reject the premises on which the practice of indulgences was based. For him, righteousness before God, called **justification,** did not begin when humans chose to do good works, which then earned God's grace. In fact, Luther believed that

unrighteous before God. In 1517, these private doubts burst into public protest when a Dominican friar, **Johannes Tetzel,** began to sell **indulgences** in the territories of the empire.

Indulgences were at the heart of late medieval Catholic religion, and they raised a particularly troubling question for Luther: "How can I become righteous in God's eyes?" The Catholic Church taught that righteousness resulted from two things: human effort and God's help, called **grace.** People could become righteous before God by choosing to do good deeds, called **works**—giving to the poor, going on a religious pilgrimage, and fasting. Above all, righteousness began when one received the **sacraments** of the church, like baptism, Communion, and confession, most of which had to be administered by a priest. When God saw this human effort, he rewarded it with grace, thus helping one to do even better.

In addition to one's own good works, one could become righteous by drawing on the good works of Christ and the saints. They had been so righteous

Johannes Tetzel (ca. 1465–1519) Dominican friar whose sale of indulgences angered Martin Luther.

indulgences Documents applying the good works of Christ and his saints to cancel the divine punishment of one's own sins or those of a dead friend or relative.

grace God's help in making a person righteous.

works Good deeds performed to become righteous in the sight of God.

sacrament Religious practice or ceremony that symbolizes a deeper religious reality; the seven sacraments are baptism, Communion (Eucharist), confirmation, confession (penance), ordination, marriage, and unction in sickness.

Purgatory The place where the souls of the departed were punished for their earthly sins before entering heaven.

justification Luther's teaching that righteousness before God comes from God alone, not from a combination of God's grace and human works.

while humans had **free will** in the sense that they could choose what they ate for breakfast, when it came to doing things that were good in God's eyes, they had no free will—their sinfulness always made them choose unrighteousness and made them incapable of doing good works. Justification therefore had no connection to good works. It was simply God's gift to human beings that made them righteous even though they were still sinners. Christians were simply to trust in this gift and the additional gift of faith that God alone made them righteous. Luther based his position on the apostle Paul, who had written, "He who through faith is righteous shall live" (Romans 1:17).

Tetzel came to the vicinity of Wittenberg selling indulgences to fund the building of the new Saint Peter's Church in Rome. He even had a slogan to motivate potential buyers: "When the coin in the change box rings, the soul from Purgatory springs!" When Luther heard of this, he was outraged. Tetzel stirred up the issues of works, grace, faith, and righteousness before God that had preoccupied Luther for years. Luther's response was to pen the **Ninety-five Theses,** propositions attacking indulgences, which were quickly printed up and distributed throughout Germany. They caused a sensation. At first the pope dismissed Luther as just another "drunken monk," but, as the seriousness of his challenge to indulgences sank in, a gulf opened up between Luther and the papacy.

The Impact of Luther's Challenge

The implications of Luther's teaching were profound: if works were irrelevant, and people were justified by faith alone, the whole structure of medieval Catholic piety—based on pilgrimages, fasting, alms to the poor, and indulgences—came tumbling down. Moreover, the sacraments administered by priests were no longer so central. Over the next five years, the rift between Luther and the Catholic Church deepened. In 1518, the pope condemned him as a heretic. In 1519, during the **Imperial Diet,** the Holy Roman Empire's legislative body, which elected **Charles V** emperor, Luther debated publicly with a papal representative, John Eck, and declared that neither the pope nor church councils had final authority to settle theological disputes. The pope then excommunicated Luther, who in turn publicly appealed to the princes of the empire to initiate reforms against indulgences. He argued that all believers, not just the clergy, were priests who were responsible for the well-being of the church. This doctrine of the **priesthood of all believers** posed another threat to Catholic Christianity, which made a sharp distinction between the ordained priesthood

and ordinary Christians. To gain support, Luther printed four thousand copies of his appeal. They sold out in a few days.

In 1521, Charles V, who had remained in Spain during these confrontations, made his first trip to Germany as emperor and summoned Luther to another Imperial Diet in the city of Worms. Asked directly to renounce his teachings, Luther refused, arguing that **scripture alone** was the only authority he would obey. He concluded dramatically, "Here I stand. May God help me! Amen." The emperor then declared him an outlaw, and Luther went into hiding.

The local ruler of Wittenberg, who had embraced Luther's theology, shielded him from the imperial authorities. Luther continued to develop his theology, arguing that in the Gospels, Christ had instituted only two sacraments, baptism and Communion, not the other rites that Catholics considered sacraments. Soon afterward, Luther began to translate the Bible into German, using Erasmus's edition of the Greek New Testament to make the ancient scriptural sources of Christianity available to ordinary men and women. He also composed hymns like "A Mighty Fortress Is Our God" for people to sing, thus bringing them directly into community worship and strengthening their sense of God's presence among them. And he continued to publish his protests; some three hundred thousand copies of his works were printed and distributed throughout the empire.

The Spread of Reform

Luther's ideas, spread by the printing press, inspired local reformers in both town and countryside. Like Savonarola, they believed that religion was linked to all other aspects of life, and their reform programs had political and social dimensions along with religious

---

free will   Teaching that people can freely will to do good works and thereby merit God's grace.

Ninety-five Theses   Luther's public attack on indulgences.

Imperial Diet   Holy Roman Empire's legislative body.

Charles V   (r. 1516–1556) Heir of Ferdinand and Isabella in Spain and of the emperor Maximilian in the Holy Roman Empire; the most powerful European ruler during the first half of the sixteenth century.

priesthood of all believers   Luther's teaching that all Christians exercised priestly functions in the Christian church.

scripture alone   Luther's teaching that the Bible was the only authoritative guide for Christian belief and conduct.

MAP 14.1 **Cities and Towns of the Reformation in Germany** This map shows the early spread of Protestantism in the cities and towns of the Holy Roman Empire. It also shows where the supporters of Roman Catholicism stopped the spread. At first, Protestantism was concentrated mainly in the center and southwest of the Empire. Eventually, it spread to the north and east, where it set down its most lasting roots.

ones. In the cities of southern Germany and Switzerland, local religious or political leaders encouraged men and women from the middle ranks of urban society to support reform. These were hardworking people who resented their exclusion from the ruling elite and thought of themselves as the backbone of the town on whom its collective well-being depended. After 1520, they produced a flood of printed pamphlets that, like Luther's, were circulated throughout Germany and constitute a kind of sixteenth-century public opinion poll. It shows that Luther's criticism of the pope and his priests was widely accepted. In the decentralized political world of Germany, papal taxes and clerical exemptions from them were often easily imposed and deeply resented. As a result, urban reformers attacked the privileges of the Catholic clergy, demanding that they be taxed like all other citizens.

The urban reformers also believed that community

life should be regulated by what they called the **pure gospel,** which stressed the equality of all Christians and rejected the idea that clergy or members of religious orders were somehow more genuinely Christian than laypeople. A number of specific reforms flowed from the idea of the pure gospel. The community, not the local bishop, would appoint clergy. Preachers were to preach on the Bible and nothing else. If disputes arose about the correct interpretation of scripture, the community would decide who was right. Acceptance of the pure gospel, which called for love of neighbor and commitment to the common

pure gospel Reform program of German Protestant reformers in the cities of the empire endorsing some of Luther's reforms but rejecting others.

good, would reinvigorate the collective identity and social solidarity of city dwellers. The reformers were, therefore, particularly receptive to Luther's theology of the authority of scripture alone and the priesthood of all believers. Faced with the demands of these urban reformers, which were often introduced with a wave of rioting, local municipal authorities had to decide what to do. Since they were concerned with maintaining public order, they more or less willingly went along with the reforms.

Events in the Swiss city of Zurich show how urban reform progressed. There, a local priest, **Huldrych Zwingli,** after reading Erasmus's attacks on corrupt clergy, urged the town council to inaugurate reform. Zwingli was supported by many townsfolk who believed that both the material and spiritual welfare of the city depended on a purifying reform of the church. Luther's actions influenced Zwingli, but he went beyond Luther when he banished images of Christ and the saints from the churches and argued that the bread and wine of Communion were not the body and blood of Christ but simple memorials of Jesus's Last Supper with his disciples. Protestant reform thus started to take different and sometimes conflicting paths.

By 1523, there were signs that urban reform was attracting rural followers. Calls for religious renewal to create a more just Christian community also appealed to German peasants, many of whom were experiencing economic hard times following crop failures and landlords' demands for more rent. Invoking the pure gospel, peasants demanded that their payments to landlords be lowered, that serfdom be abolished, and that they have greater access to common lands. During the summer of 1524, violence broke out in the **Peasants' War,** which engulfed much of southern Germany. In May 1525, an imperial army defeated a peasant force and massacred five to six thousand rebels. After that, the uprising collapsed.

The war shocked Luther, who had a firm respect for social order and obedience to civil authorities. In a pamphlet, *Against the Robbing and Murdering Hordes of Peasants,* he urged the troops to "smite, slay, and stab" the rebels. Because of the radical nature of its demands, historians have often regarded the Peasants' War as a revolution, though a failed one. It testified to a widespread hunger for fundamental religious and social reform that touched hundreds of thousands of ordinary men and women by the mid-1520s.

The years after 1525 saw the continuing spread of Luther's reforms, but the dynamic behind them had changed. No longer were church-based reformers the leaders in the movement, and no longer were German cities in its vanguard. Now the princes of the empire, like the dukes of Saxony and Bavaria, deter-

mined whether Protestantism would be adopted in their territories. Rulers also introduced Lutheran reforms in Denmark and Sweden. The state's increasing leadership in reform was partly a backlash following the Peasants' War, as princes and city councils decided that a popular reformation by peasants or the urban middle classes was too dangerous to tolerate. But Luther, under Erasmus's influence, had also prepared the way by calling on rulers to carry out reform.

As the empire split into hostile Catholic and Lutheran states, the emperor Charles V looked on in dismay. Although he wanted to stamp out the Lutheran movement, he was only one of many imperial princes, and he was never able to implement his policy, largely because of distractions from warfare with the Turks in the east and the French in the west. Between 1531 and his abdication in 1556, Charles tried many solutions to the problem of growing religious disunity in the empire: gaining time with a truce between the competing factions; calling for a general church council to resolve the matter; trying to establish a dialogue with the Lutherans; and, finally, in 1546, going to war against the Lutheran princes. None of these strategies worked, and in 1555 he turned the problem over to his younger brother, the archduke Ferdinand, who accepted the **Peace of Augsburg** in that year. It acknowledged Lutheranism as a religious option in the empire and allowed the rulers of each imperial state to determine whether the state would be Lutheran or Catholic. If the ruler chose Lutheranism, Catholics were free to emigrate to a Catholic state, and vice versa. In fact, emigration was often impossible because of family or economic reasons, and secret Catholic or Lutheran communities developed in a number of states. Thus, dissenting German Christians were forced into a situation rather like that of the Jews and Moors after their expulsions from Spain and Portugal—convert, leave, or practice one's religion in secret. State rulers now took the lead in reorganizing the church, policing the behavior of clergy, and maintaining Christian morality in the general population. In Catholic states, they still had to share

Huldrych Zwingli (1484–1531) Swiss reformer who accepted some of Luther's theological points but rejected others.

Peasants' War Uprising, 1524–1525, in southern Germany inspired by Protestant calls for a reform of church and society.

Peace of Augsburg First major treaty, 1555, to accept the split in western Christianity between Protestants and Catholics.

government of the church with the pope. In Lutheran ones, they ruled largely unchecked. Thus, the Peace of Augsburg permanently shattered the religious unity of Germany and established a pattern of Christian religious pluralism that would be one of the hallmarks of European life in subsequent centuries.

The Protestant Reformation Across Europe, 1520–1570

> ↓ What were the similarities and differences among the reform programs of Luther, the Anabaptists, and Calvin?
>
> ↓ What were the distinctive features of Protestant reform in England?

Along with Lutheranism, other forms of Protestantism developed. One movement, led by radicals, went even further than Luther and Zwingli in rejecting traditional Catholicism. Another, founded by the Frenchman John Calvin, proved to be the most rapidly expanding form of Protestantism. In England, an ambiguous type of reform was eventually introduced from above by the state.

The Anabaptists and Radical Reform

In the early 1520s, when Luther was condemned by the church for pushing church reform too far, he was also attacked by people who thought he had not gone far enough. These were the Protestant radicals. Though never a unified movement, the radicals shared a deep dislike of the ordained clergy and a strong sense that the church should exist for the benefit of ordinary men and women. They were at odds with Luther—a clergyman and university scholar—in rejecting scriptural interpretation by trained professionals. While Luther proclaimed the priesthood of all believers and wanted the Bible in people's hands, he believed the people needed expert guidance in understanding scripture. The radicals replied that every Christian man and woman was capable of correctly interpreting it under the direct guidance of the Holy Spirit.

The radicals were also deeply suspicious of Luther's policy of turning to city or state rulers to help introduce Protestantism. Arguing for a sharp separation of church and state, some also believed that true Christians should be completely separated from the sinful world surrounding them. Only adults who had received a divine call should become church members; consequently, the ancient practice of infant baptism should be abolished because babies were incapable of

receiving or responding to such a call. Soon these radicals were being denounced as **Anabaptists,** since they insisted on being rebaptized as adults in a true, voluntary baptism.

Anabaptism first emerged among the craftsmen of the Swiss city of Zurich. They preached adult baptism, called for a separated church, and refused to honor customary civic obligations like paying church taxes, holding public office, or serving in the militia. They even began to hold all their material goods in common, inspired by the first-century church in Jerusalem, which had implemented this form of Christian communalism, as described in the New Testament book of Acts. Anabaptist separatism was thus deeply subversive because it rejected the generally accepted idea that everyone in a given place should be a church member and that society would fall apart without the unifying force of a common religion. To suppress Anabaptism, Charles V issued an imperial edict in 1529 decreeing the death penalty for anyone who held a separatist view of church-state relations. In some states, executions were carried out by drowning, a punishment thought to fit the crime.

In the northwestern German city of **Münster,** the Anabaptists would not be suppressed. Elected to the city government in 1534, they declared all real estate common property, banned money, and decreed that house doors were to be unlocked and open day and night. Then polygamy was introduced. The reformers justified the practice of men's taking multiple spouses by citing the Old Testament, but the practice may have had more to do with remedying a gender imbalance in the Anabaptist community and the need to put women under male rule in individual households. When Münster's expelled bishop tried to retake the city by force but was defeated, the Anabaptists proclaimed the impending end of the world, with Münster designated as the New Jerusalem. As executions of the wayward began, Catholic and Lutheran rulers were so alarmed that they set aside their differences and joined forces to recapture Münster. Following their victory in 1535, they slaughtered almost all Münster's inhabitants in one of the greatest bloodbaths of the century.

The catastrophe in Münster permanently discredited all forms of violent Anabaptism. Following it, the

Anabaptists   (from Greek, "repeated dippers") Radical Protestants who practiced a second, adult baptism.

Münster   City in northwestern Germany where a violent Anabaptist movement was defeated by a combined Protestant and Catholic army.

radical remnant turned to leaders who denounced violence and embraced **pacifism. Jacob Hutter** provided the inspiration for those who fled to Moravia, where they continued to practice Christian communalism and prospered economically in the later years of the sixteenth century. By 1600, about 20,000 Hutterites lived in peaceful coexistence with their Catholic and Protestant neighbors.

In the northern Netherlands, **Menno Simons,** a Dutch ex-priest, organized churches as a refuge for those Anabaptists who had survived the slaughter of 1535. Simons's churches were based on voluntary membership and adult baptism, but he gave up the New Testament ideal of Christian communalism and called simply for mutual aid among church members. These Mennonites numbered about one hundred thousand at the end of the century. Like the Hutterites, they gained a degree of respectability in the eyes of their non-Anabaptist neighbors. Beginning in the eighteenth century, many began to emigrate to North America, where their descendants today make up the Amish and Mennonite communities of Pennsylvania and parts of the Midwest. They still live a life separated from the larger world.

John Calvin and Calvinism

John Calvin founded the third major Protestant community of the sixteenth century, **Calvinism.** Luther was already thirty-six when Calvin was born in northeastern France; Calvinism was thus a second-generation Protestant movement. Calvin was sent to the University of Paris to study theology, since his father wanted him to become a priest. Then, his father changed his mind and sent him to law school. During his school years, Calvin met men who had embraced Protestant reform. His father's death in 1531 freed him to make his own future plans, and he became a reformer. Calvin was more reserved and private than Luther, who talked openly about his spiritual trials. But he, too, believed that he had undergone a "sudden conversion" in which God subdued his "stubborn heart" and called him to Protestantism. In 1535, the pro-Catholic French government attacked Protestants in Paris, and Calvin was forced to flee under a false name.

In 1536, Calvin was in Switzerland, beyond the reach of French authorities. There he published the first edition of the *Institutes of the Christian Religion,* a work he revised and expanded for the next twenty-three years. It gained him an immediate European reputation. The *Institutes,* which presented Calvin's version of theology, came to serve as the blueprint for Calvinist reform. Calvin followed Luther on a number of points, condemning the pope and ar-

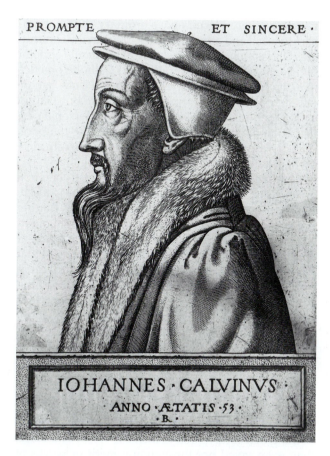

René Boivin's engraving (1562) shows Calvin at age fifty-three, as the Latin inscription at the bottom of the portrait indicates. The caption at the top, in French, asserts that Calvin is "active and honest," affirming his success as a religious leader. (*Genève, Département Iconographique, Bibliothèque de Genève*)

guing that scripture was the only source of authority for Christians. He did not, however, accept Luther's teaching on the priesthood of all believers. For Calvin,

pacifism   Opposition to armed force and warfare.

Jacob Hutter   (1500–1536) Anabaptist leader in Moravia who embraced pacifism and the practice of Christian communalism.

Menno Simons   (1495–1561) Leader of the Mennonite Anabaptist communities in the Netherlands who embraced pacifism but rejected Christian communalism.

John Calvin   (1509–1564) Frenchman who founded the Protestant movement known as Calvinism.

Calvinism   Teachings and church organization of Protestant churches that considered John Calvin their founder.

Institutes of the Christian Religion   Calvin's systematic presentation of his Protestant teachings, which served as a blueprint for Calvinist reform.

the clergy were placed above ordinary church members to teach and administer discipline in the community. His insistence that the church alone should appoint the clergy was closer to traditional Catholic practice than the procedures adopted in Lutheran lands, where the state controlled clergy recruitment. But Calvin joined Luther in increasing worshipers' personal participation in church services by translating the book of Psalms into French and setting the Psalms to simple tunes that the congregation could sing.

Calvin also agreed with Luther that everyone in a given territory should belong to the same church. But, because of his belief in the doctrine of **double predestination,** he did not think that all church members were necessarily saved. Predestination taught that before the world was created, God foresaw that human beings would sin and thereby merit damnation as the just punishment for their sin. God then decreed that some of these sinners were predestined for Hell while others were predestined for Heaven. Those predestined for Hell suffered just punishment for their sins, testifying to God's justice. Those predestined for Heaven were forgiven their sins and would be reunited with God, testifying to God's mercy. Calvin often argued that probably only one in a hundred would be saved. Like Luther, he believed that sin had corrupted people's wills so that they could do nothing that contributed to their salvation. Therefore, they were saved not through any merit or works of their own but solely as a result of God's loving kindness. Although a person's good works did not earn salvation, Calvin taught that they were a sign that God had chosen the person as one of **the elect** destined for salvation. Since impulses to act as good Christians were an assurance of salvation, Calvinists were quick to nurture their desire for church and state reform. Calvin also argued that hard work and thrift were signs of election. He believed that the doctrine of double predestination explained why some people refused to join the reformed churches. It also

assured believers that, in the end, God would triumph over sinners' opposition to him.

Calvin's opportunity to put his theology into practice came in 1541, when the town council of the little city-state of Geneva called him to reform the local church. For the next fourteen years, he argued, threatened, and maneuvered to get a reform to his liking. Calvin's cause was helped by an influx of religious refugees from his native country who fled to Geneva to avoid persecution by the French government. These Frenchmen, solidly behind their fellow countryman's agenda, were able to take over Geneva's government in 1555. It was then that Calvin finally gained full control over the church.

Because Calvin thought of the church in territorial terms, everyone in Geneva had to conform to church standards. To enforce reform, he created the **Consistory,** a body made up of Calvinist ministers and members of the city government. The Consistory scrutinized every aspect of Genevans' behavior, imposing fines or imprisonment for infractions. Everything people said or did was to be supervised and controlled. Like the advocates of the pure gospel, Calvinists in Geneva were trying to forge a new Christian identity based strictly on Protestant religious principles.

Throughout the period of Calvin's rule in Geneva, religious refugees from all over Europe continued to stream into the city. It is estimated that between 1550 and 1562 about seven thousand of the city's ten thousand inhabitants were foreigners. These refugees,

double predestination   Belief that God has predestined some human beings for damnation and others for salvation.

the elect   Those whom God has chosen (elected) for salvation.

Consistory   Assembly made up of Calvinist ministers and members of city government that enforced Calvinist standards of behavior in Geneva.

Voice

The Pastors of Geneva Establish Rules for Proper Christian Conduct

Beginning in 1541, the reformed clergy of Geneva, under the guidance of John Calvin, published rules governing the behavior of clergy and laity in Geneva. Calvinism's great strength lay in its ability to forge strong bonds and loyalties between members of a Calvinist community. This could be done by rewarding behav-

ior that conformed to Calvinist community norms while punishing behavior that did not. It could also be done by trying to reconcile quarreling members of the community. The rules of 1541 provided guidelines for carrying out all aspects of Calvinism's community building agenda.

➔ Vices which are intolerable in a pastor:
Heresy . . . Rebellion against ecclesiastical order . . .
Drunkenness . . . Dancing and similar dissoluteness.
Vices which can be endured provided they are rebuked:
Strange methods of treating Scripture which result in
scandal . . . Buffoonery, Deceitfulness . . . Rashness, Evil
scheming . . . Uncontrolled anger, Brawling and quarreling.

➔ *What picture of the pastor emerges from the prohibition of these vices?*

➔ FAULTS WHICH CONTRAVENE THE REFORMATION . . .
Those who are found in possession of . . . images for the purpose of worshipping them shall be sent before the Consistory, and besides the discipline which shall be imposed on them, they shall be sent to [the government].
Those who have been on pilgrimages or similar journeys.

➔ *Against whom are these prohibitions directed?*

➔ Any person who curses or denies God or his baptism shall on the first occasion be placed on bread and water for nine days; and for the second or third occasions he shall be punished with a more rigorous physical punishment, . . .

If anyone is found drunk he shall pay three sous on the first occasion and shall be summoned before the Consistory; on the second occasion he shall pay the sum of five sous; and on the third he shall be fined ten sous and be put in prison.

Anyone who sings indecent, dissolute, or outrageous songs or dances the fling or some similar dance shall be imprisoned for three days and shall be sent before the Consistory.

➔ *What is the picture of the model Calvinist that emerges from these rules?*

No one shall stir up rowdy scenes or altercations, under penalty of being punished according to the seriousness of the case.

If there is ill-will or altercation between any, the minister shall call the guards and shall endeavor, as is his duty, to bring the parties concerned to agreement, and if he is unable to achieve this, the matter shall be brought before the Consistory.

No one shall play dissolute games or any game for gold or silver or excessive stakes, under penalty of five sous and the forfeiture of the money staked.

Any who are found practicing fornication, if they are an unmarried man or an unmarried woman, shall be imprisoned for six days on bread and water and shall pay sixty sous into the public funds.

Although in ancient times the right of the wife was not equal with that of the husband where divorce was concerned, yet since, as the Apostle says, the obligation is mutual and reciprocal regarding the intercourse of the bed, and since in this the wife is no more subject to the husband than the husband to the wife, if a man is convicted of adultery and his wife demands to be separated from him, this shall be granted to her also, provided it proves impossible by good counsel to reconcile them to each other.

➔ On Sunday July 28 [1549] an ordinance . . . was announced in St. Pierre ordering that girls who had not kept their honor should not henceforward present themselves in church for marriage with the hat which virgins are accustomed to wear, but that they should have their heads veiled; otherwise they could be sent away.

➔ *Why would this shaming technique be necessary?*

Source: The Register of the Company of Pastors of Geneva in the Time of Calvin,
ed. and trans. Philip Edgcumbe Hughes (Grand Rapids, Mich.: William B. Eerdmans
Publishing Company, 1966), pp. 38–39, 56–59.

many of whom were nobility, wanted to introduce Calvin's reforms into their homelands, and their status was particularly important for Calvinism's future success. To meet the refugees' needs, Calvin founded a training institute for future Calvinist pastors, the Genevan Academy, where men were taught the theology of the *Institutes* and the best ways to form church communities, especially under persecution.

The Spread of Calvinism

Calvinism was the most dynamic form of Protestantism after 1550, becoming an international movement with headquarters in Geneva as missionaries left the city to establish Calvinist communities in their native lands. The first to return home were the French. In France, most Calvinists were recruited from the urban middle class, but members of powerful noble families also converted. It was often the women in these families who convinced their relations to embrace Calvinism. For example, **Jeanne d'Albret** introduced Calvinism into the tiny kingdom of Navarre, on the border between France and Spain. By 1560, about 10 percent of the overall French population was **Huguenot,** as the French Calvinists were called, while about 50 percent of the nobility had embraced the new faith. As the Huguenots' numbers grew, confrontations with Catholics also increased, and soon France was on the verge of civil war.

In the Netherlands, Protestantism was fiercely resisted by Charles V. Unlike in Germany, where he was often checked by other powerful imperial princes, Charles governed the Netherlands directly as the local prince, and no powerful noble factions emerged to promote the Protestant cause. When the Lutherans and Anabaptists tried to establish communities in the Netherlands, Charles's government effectively repressed them. By the time he abdicated in 1556, some five hundred dissidents had been executed for heresy. Nevertheless, Calvinist missionaries began to infiltrate the region, establishing secret communities, and, like France, the Netherlands was moving toward armed clashes between Protestants and Catholics.

In 1558, **John Knox,** returning from Geneva, successfully introduced Calvinist theology into his native Scotland and created a **Presbyterian** form of church administration that eliminated bishops. Knox had the help of powerful nobles who opposed the rule of Mary, Queen of Scots, widow of the French king Francis II and a committed Catholic. In 1559, Knox published *The First Blast Against the Monstrous Regiment of Women*, in which he attacked Mary and argued that female rule was unnatural. Knox's attack appealed to Scottish Calvinists, whose leaders, hard-

ened by organized persecution from Catholic authorities, were prepared to resist rulers if they opposed Calvinist reform. This position directly conflicted with Luther's views about obedience to rulers.

Reform in England

Calvinists in Scotland introduced religious reform from the bottom up. To the south, in England, it was introduced from the top down. In 1521, King **Henry VIII** published a treatise condemning Lutheranism. Shortly thereafter, the pope granted him the title Defender of the Faith in recognition of his service to Catholicism. Twelve years later, however, Rome excommunicated Henry, a surprising turn of events that occurred because succession problems were plaguing the king.

When the pope refused to grant Henry an annulment from Catherine of Aragon, the daughter of Ferdinand and Isabella, the king turned to the English clergy. With their support, he divorced Catherine and married her lady-in-waiting, Anne Boleyn, who was already pregnant with his child. Anne gave birth to Henry's second daughter, Elizabeth. When the pope learned of Henry's action, he excommunicated him. In retaliation, Henry, in the **Act of Supremacy,** proclaimed himself "the only supreme head on earth of the church of England," a title still held today by British monarchs. In 1536, Henry, still in search of a male heir, had Anne convicted of adultery and beheaded. Following her execution, Henry married four more times, finally having a son, Edward, by his fourth wife. All three of Henry's children were to rule England, as Edward VI, Mary, and Elizabeth I.

Although Henry VIII broke with Rome, he had no intention of breaking with traditional Catholicism.

Jeanne d'Albret   (1528–1572) French noblewoman who introduced Calvinism into the kingdom of Navarre.

Huguenots   (from German, "confederation") French Calvinists, so called because they formed a network of Protestant churches.

John Knox   (1505–1572) Leader of Calvinist reform of the church in Scotland.

Presbyterian   Form of church organization used in the Calvinist Church of Scotland in which ministers known as presbyters or elders were church leaders, eliminating bishops.

Henry VIII   (r. 1509–1547) King who broke with the pope over his divorce from Catherine of Aragon and marriage to Anne Boleyn, launching the English Reformation.

Act of Supremacy   Henry VIII's declaration that the king of England was the earthly head of the English church.

Throughout his reign, he resisted any attempt to turn the English church into a Protestant one. Nevertheless, the rift with the pope opened the door to more radical reform, which actually began under Henry. The greatest change came when the king ordered the abolition of English monasteries and the confiscation of their lands on the grounds that the monks and nuns in them were too closely tied to the pope. Most of these lands were then sold to aristocrats to pay for England's foreign wars, and these new owners—who constituted the kingdom's political, social, and economic elite—thus had a vested interest in keeping Roman Catholicism out of England. So Henry's divorce had huge consequences he had not intended.

When Henry died in 1547, he was succeeded by his son, Edward VI. Because the boy was a minor, a Regency Council, controlled by Protestant noblemen, was created to govern in his name. In 1552, the council instituted a compromise form of Protestantism in the English church when it imposed the **Book of Common Prayer,** a blend of Lutheran and Calvinist theology. Now congregations could participate directly in worship, using their own language instead of Latin. Had Edward VI lived, the reforms might have succeeded, but in 1553 he died, at the age of sixteen, and was succeeded by his older half sister, Mary, Catherine's daughter.

Mary had never accepted Henry's divorce of her mother and his break with the pope, and as queen she promptly restored the Catholic Church. To seal the restoration, she married Philip II of Spain, the Catholic Church's most energetic defender. Mary then proceeded to execute some three hundred Protestants, many of them Anabaptists, earning her the nickname "Bloody Mary," which has stuck to this day. In the end, England's return to Catholicism was short lived. In 1558, Mary died childless and was succeeded by the last of Henry VIII's children, **Elizabeth I,** the daughter of Anne Boleyn.

When she became queen, Elizabeth endorsed Protestantism and ended the decade-long alternations between the two forms of Christianity, depending on the ruler. Elizabeth's forty-three-year reign proved decisive in establishing an ambiguous form of Protestantism in England. In 1571, an official theology for the **Church of England** was proclaimed in the **Thirty-nine Articles,** which were silent on a number of hotly contested theological issues, such as Calvin's doctrine of predestination.

Elizabeth and her religious advisers were trying to find a middle ground between Catholicism, Lutheranism, and Calvinism. Political calculations played a central role in this policy. The queen feared a powerful Catholic faction in the English Parliament. She also feared popular agitation if reform went too far. It was Elizabeth's accomplishment to make England Protestant while keeping Catholic opposition fairly well contained. As her reign progressed, more and more Anglicans identified with the queen's theological middle way, seeing it as a distinctively English solution to the huge rift between Protestantism and Catholicism that had engulfed the western church.

By 1570, religious warfare between Catholics and Protestants had broken out in France and the Netherlands. These developments ruled out the possibility of any reconciliation between the rival forms of Christianity on the continent, where, for the next eighty years, there would be armed conflict between Protestants and Catholics.

Catholic Reform, 1500–1570

↓ What did Catholic reformers want to change in the church?

↓ What were the most important outcomes of Catholic Church reform?

As Protestantism spread in Europe, the Catholic Church underwent its own reform. In addition to the reform programs of Savonarola and Erasmus, an early sign of Catholic reform was the founding of new religious orders and the reform of old ones. By the 1530s, the papacy had also become involved in reform. Its most important act was to convene a church council in the northern Italian city of Trent. The Council of Trent defined traditional Catholic theology and condemned the Protestants. It also laid down guidelines for the internal reform of the church. Finally, the Catholics inaugurated Christianity's first major missionary campaigns overseas in the Spanish and Portuguese Empires.

Reform by Religious Orders

The reform of old religious orders and the foundation of new ones signaled renewal within the Catholic

Book of Common Prayer   Official service book of the reformed English church.

Elizabeth I   (r. 1558–1603) Daughter of Henry VIII and Anne Bolyn who ruled after the deaths of her half brother Edward VI and half sister Mary.

Church of England   Name given to the reformed church in England; also called the Anglican Church.

Thirty-nine Articles   Statement of the official theology of the Church of England during Elizabeth I's reign.

Church. Although their specific goals were often different, all the reforms aimed to increase Catholics' commitment to the moral and spiritual teachings of the church. Most began in Italy or Spain, where Protestantism was less widespread than in northern Europe. None was founded to counteract Protestantism, although some later took up the fight against it.

Teresa of Ávila's reformed **Carmelites** set the tone for women's orders (see Choice). Her convents were strictly separated from the larger world because of traditional disapproval of women working actively as teachers or preachers. These nuns maintained their dwellings and prepared their community's food, depending on donations to help with their upkeep. Social distinctions between rich and poor nuns, or noble and common ones, observed in many convents, were abolished. Although not all reformed women's orders adopted the strict poverty of Teresa's Carmelites, most followed separation from the world and a rigorous life of prayer, which, they believed, would strengthen the church as a whole. Recruitment to women's orders rose during the sixteenth century. For example, in 1427 two out of a hundred people living in Florence were nuns; in 1622, six out of a hundred were.

The largest reformed male order was the **Capuchins**, a branch of the Franciscans. The Capuchins took strict vows of poverty. They lived in mud huts, went barefoot, and begged in public for their food to show their detachment from worldly possessions and pleasures. They also preached lively sermons on street corners and in churches, urging Catholics to live more in accordance with Jesus's teachings and setting an example by caring for plague victims. In 1542, scandal rocked the order when its head moved to Geneva and became a Calvinist. Nevertheless, the Capuchins continued to attract new members. By 1600, there were almost nine thousand; by 1700, twenty-seven thousand.

The most dynamic new religious order was the **Society of Jesus,** or the **Jesuits.** Its founder was **Ignatius of Loyola,** a nobleman from northern Spain. As a young man he embarked on the classic noble career, service in the army. In 1521, aged thirty, he was badly wounded and forced into a long convalescence. During this period, Ignatius had a profound religious conversion and decided to become a spiritual soldier instead of a military one. In 1522, he offered his old sword to the Virgin Mary and symbolized his new life of dedication to God by exchanging his fine clothes for those of a beggar.

Ignatius wanted to convert Muslims to Christianity in the Holy Land, but an outbreak of plague delayed his departure. As he waited for better travel conditions, he formulated his *Spiritual Exercises,* a training program designed to strengthen one's will to

Jacopino del Conte painted this portrait of Ignatius of Loyola shortly after Ignatius' death in 1556. The artist bathes Ignatius's face in light to convey his holiness. Like the artists who depicted Luther and Calvin, Conte wished to show Ignatius's gentleness as well as his authority. *(Courtesy, Archivio A.R.S.I., Rome)*

fight for Christ. For thirty days, persons taking the *Exercises* examined their conscience to see where their will to obey God was weak and then concentrated on a word or deed of Christ to strengthen their resolve to

Teresa of Ávila   (1515–1582) Spanish monastic reformer and spiritual teacher.

Carmelites   Order of nuns reformed by Teresa of Ávila to be strictly separated from the larger world.

Capuchins   (from Italian, *cappuccio,* "hood") Largest reformed male religious order, named after the hood the friars wore as part of their religious garb.

Society of Jesus/Jesuits   Most important reforming religious order in the sixteenth-century Catholic Church.

Ignatius of Loyola   (1491–1556) Spanish nobleman and ex-soldier, founder of the Society of Jesus.

Spiritual Exercises   Ignatius of Loyola's training program, designed to strengthen one's resolve to serve Christ and his church.

follow him. Ignatius's emphasis on training the will to follow Christ was based on the traditional Catholic view that both human effort and God's grace brought about a person's salvation. This view contrasted with Luther's and Calvin's belief in the deep sinfulness of human wills.

For Ignatius, strengthening the will involved a form of prayer called **meditation,** in which one concentrated on a scene from Jesus's life as recounted in the Gospels, breathing the air, feeling the heat, and becoming part of the crowd in order mentally to meet Jesus face to face. Thus Ignatius, like Luther and Calvin, turned to the Bible for inspiration. But he never embraced their doctrine of scripture alone. In fact, part of the *Exercises* laid down "rules for thinking with the church." As a Catholic, Ignatius looked to church tradition and papal authority, as well as scripture, for religious guidance.

As Ignatius formulated the *Exercises,* he also modified his future plans, deciding that more education was necessary to be a successful missionary in the Holy Land. He, therefore, enrolled in a Spanish elementary school (as a nobleman, he had learned how to fight, but not how to read and write). Later he transferred to the University of Paris, where he began his studies in 1528, the year John Calvin entered law school. In Paris, he joined seven fellow students to found the Society of Jesus. In 1537, they were ordained priests and set off for Venice, intending to sail for the Holy Land. Once again, the trip was canceled, this time because of a war between Venice and the Turks. In 1540, the pope officially recognized the Jesuits, and Ignatius moved to Rome. From there he ran the order in a highly centralized way, rather like a general running his army. He also placed the order at the pope's disposal. From then on, it expanded rapidly and became the single most important reforming order in the church. Like the Capuchins, it concentrated on active service in the world.

The Jesuits' most successful service was in education. They founded secondary schools throughout the Catholic world, for boys from the middle and upper classes. They believed that, by instilling a deep sense of Catholic identity in these future social and political leaders, they could reinvigorate Catholicism and push back Protestantism. The Jesuits did not charge students tuition; instead, they expected local authorities to finance their schools and thereby build community involvement in their educational program. They also gave Ignatius's *Exercises* to students and their families, as well as to interested local clergy. The Jesuit schools were spectacularly successful. The quality of instruction was so good that even some Protestants went to them. The Jesuits attacked Protestants in print and from the pulpit, but they welcomed them into their schools in hopes of converting them.

Like the Protestants, the Jesuits and other Catholic reformers also promoted new forms of devotion for the laity. One of the most popular was the recitation of the rosary. Combining traditional veneration for Mary with meditation on Christ's life, death, and Resurrection, the rosary was a widely used means for instructing ordinary Catholics in the church's teachings, heightening their sense of spiritual union with God and forging a strong sense of Catholic identity. In 1556, when Ignatius of Loyola died, the Jesuits had almost a thousand members. Seventy years later, they had fifteen thousand members across the globe and ran 450 schools.

Reform in the Papacy

The pope who recognized the Jesuits was **Paul III.** Paul cautiously embraced church reform, and his reign proved a turning point for the Catholic Church. One of his first reforms was to appoint a special commission to evaluate papal administration. The commission's secret report, issued in 1537, argued that corruption in the church was caused mainly by abuses of papal power. Paul tried to ignore the report, but it was smuggled out to a local printer who made it public, once again demonstrating the power of the printing press. Shortly thereafter, Luther published it with his own scathing comments. Publicly, Paul appeared unruffled by the uproar, but privately he began appointing reformers to the **College of Cardinals,** the body charged with the election of future popes.

In 1542, Paul established the Roman Inquisition. Modeled on Ferdinand and Isabella's Spanish Inquisition, it investigated and punished heretics in Catholic lands. In 1549, another instrument of repression was set up, **The Index of Prohibited Books,** which listed works Catholics were forbidden to read. Eventually, many of Erasmus's works appeared on it. The creation of the Roman Inquisition and the *Index* signaled a change in outlook for the Catholic Church. Faced

meditation   Form of mental prayer developed by Ignatius that concentrated on a scene from the life of Jesus as recounted in the Gospels.

Paul III   (r. 1534–1549) Most important reforming pope of the Catholic Church.

College of Cardinals   Body charged with the election of new popes.

The Index of Prohibited Books   A list of books that Catholics were forbidden to read.

Titian painted *Pope Paul III and His Grandsons* (1546). The old pope, with an arresting face and piercing eyes, looks toward one grandson, an elegant courtier who bows to him, while the other grandson, a cleric, raises his hand in blessing while looking out at the viewer. Paul made both grandsons cardinals. *(Erich Lessing/Art Resource, NY)*

justification by faith alone, the council decreed that while God's grace saved people, Christians could choose whether they would cooperate with grace or resist it. This position was based on a verse in the Old Testament: "Thus says the Lord of hosts, 'Return to me . . . and I will return to you'" (Zechariah 1:3). The council, therefore, quoted scripture against Protestants to justify Catholic teaching about the roles of free will, works, and grace in determining a person's salvation and to counteract Protestant teaching about corrupted human wills and double predestination. The council's defense of traditional Catholic belief and practice dismayed Charles V, who saw his hope of reconciliation with the Protestants slipping away.

When the council next met, in 1561–1563, it reaffirmed the practice of indulgences while discouraging their sale, and it endorsed the traditional organization of the church with the pope as its head. Under him were the clergy and then—standing sharply apart—the laity. This last point was reinforced symbolically when the council decreed that at the Mass, the clergy alone would receive the cup of wine, the laity only the bread—a rejection of Luther's priesthood of all believers. The council also reaffirmed the church's seven traditional sacraments. In addition to restating doctrine, the council's last session also established guidelines for a thoroughgoing reform of the church. Trent ordered the establishment of **seminaries** in all

with Protestantism, it developed a fortresslike mentality, identifying itself as a militant church guarding against heresy. This new emphasis had a chilling effect on what many Catholics did or said in public.

Paul III's most significant act was to convene a church council in the city of Trent to address Protestantism and Catholic Church reform. He was not eager to convene the council, fearing it would get out of control or be ineffective, but he conceded to pressure from Charles V, who still hoped to restore religious unity in the empire. The **Council of Trent** met in three separate sessions from 1545 to 1563. The first two sessions (1545–1547 and 1551–1552) reaffirmed traditional Catholic theology. To counter Luther's doctrine of scripture alone, the council declared that *both* scripture *and* the traditions of the church were authoritative for Catholics. Moreover, it decreed that only the Roman Catholic Church, headed by the pope, had the right to interpret scripture. To counter the doctrine of

Council of Trent   Catholic Church council, meeting 1545–1563, that reasserted traditional Catholic teaching and created guidelines for Catholic Church reform.

In this engraving of the Council of Trent, cardinals, bishops, and papal representatives are shown on either side of the Council's Chancellor, who sits at a desk while the king of Spain's representative speaks. Representatives of other Catholic rulers are seated in the center. Behind them is a crowd of observers. *(Courtesy of the Trustees of the British Museum)*

Catholic **dioceses** for the training of new clergy. It also ordered bishops to visit every church in their diocese to make sure that the buildings were in good repair, that services were properly conducted, and that the clergy were living moral lives. Another decree reaffirmed the traditional position that all women in religious orders were to stay within their convents, separated from society. In 1564, the pope accepted all Trent's decrees while announcing that he alone had the authority to interpret them.

The reforms of Trent were implemented, slowly and unevenly, throughout the Catholic world. The greatest gains were made in dioceses where the bishop was a committed reformer. One of the first successes came in the northern Italian city of Milan, where the archbishop, **Carlo Borromeo,** founded a diocesan seminary, set up Sunday schools to teach the young the basics of Christian belief and practice, and established religious associations for laymen and -women. He also gained control over local religious orders, conducted thorough visitations throughout the diocese, and cared personally for the sick and needy. Despite strong opposition from people who profited

from the old system, including an assassination attempt, Borromeo was remarkably successful in making Milan a showcase of reform. He died in 1584, at age forty-six. In 1610, the pope proclaimed him a Catholic saint.

Borromeo showed the way for reforming bishops elsewhere in the Catholic world. A hundred years after the Council of Trent, that world had been largely transformed. The Catholic Church was more centralized than ever before. Vigorous leadership after 1534 strengthened the position of the Roman popes, while centralized and dynamic orders like the Capuchins and Jesuits spread new ideals and practices to Catholic communities all over the globe. Religious devotion

seminaries Schools for the training of the Christian clergy.

diocese Territory presided over by a bishop of the church.

Carlo Borromeo (1538–1584) Catholic archbishop of Milan who implemented the reforms of the Council of Trent in his diocese.

intensified as Teresa of Ávila's treatises on prayer were more and more widely read. Finally, a reformed Catholic identity was further advanced when the church issued new books for worship services that put Catholics literally on the same page throughout the year; all over the Catholic world, on any given day, people in church read and heard the same words during worship. Like the Muslims, whose worship was always in Arabic, the Catholics also shared a common religious language, Latin.

Catholic Missions Overseas

The Catholics were the first Europeans to embark on overseas missionary activity in the Americas and East Asia, believing that converts there could make up for the souls lost in Europe to the Protestant "heresy." Some also thought that spreading Christianity overseas meant the end of the world was near, since Christ's command "to make disciples of all nations" (Matthew 28:19) would finally be realized.

In the Americas, Spanish missionaries debated the best strategy for Christianizing the local people. Some followed Bartholomé de Las Casas in trying to protect them from harsh treatment by fellow Europeans and to preserve those features of their pre-Christian cultures that were compatible with Christianity. Others believed that local peoples were so lacking in human reason that they should be viewed as stubborn unbelievers, like Jews and Muslims. They should be forced to learn Spanish and live in settlements that reproduced European life, thereby replacing their old values and customs with European ones.

If missionaries in the Americas disagreed over strategies for converting local peoples, they all agreed that the process of conversion should be in European hands. Only in the eighteenth century did the church start to train large numbers of Indian men for the clergy. Before then, even the most well-disposed priests doubted that the Indians were ready to lead the church on their own. This attitude resulted from three factors: bewilderment at the complexity and strangeness of the Indians' cultures, a paternalistic sense of the church's obligation to protect or correct local peoples, and a racist sense of the innate superiority of Europeans.

Local peoples reacted to the missionaries' activities in various ways. Some tried to resist any changes in traditional culture. Others, particularly those who came from the old Indian elite, converted fairly easily to both Christianity and European customs. Many, however, found a middle way. They adopted those aspects of Catholicism and European culture that seemed useful and melded them with their older beliefs and practices, creating a new religious identity.

Thus, in Peru, local people went to church—after protecting the building by smearing animal blood on its foundations, an old Inca ritual. This modified Latin American Catholicism still exists, illustrating the complexity of the encounter that took place as the Catholic Church established itself in the Americas.

In Asia, Portuguese missionaries led in spreading Catholicism. One of the first was **Francis Xavier,** who with Ignatius of Loyola had founded the Jesuits. Xavier was active in India and Japan, using as his base the Portuguese trading post at Goa. In 1549, he also traveled to Japan and stayed two years, leaving behind a small Christian community made up of Jesuits and Japanese converts. This mission's success depended on the Japanese political elite. Some local rulers supported the missionaries in hopes of strengthening their commercial ties with the Portuguese. For their part, the Jesuits were careful to respect Japanese customs by dressing appropriately, bathing frequently, and eating only locally acceptable foods. The result was the establishment of a Christian community that numbered some 250,000 by 1600, or about 0.5 percent of the total population. But after 1593, when Spanish missionaries arrived from the Philippines, quarrels with the Portuguese caused the missionary effort to collapse in the face of imperial rivalries. In 1616, the Japanese government began suppressing Christianity and ultimately executed almost forty thousand men, women, and children, some by crucifixion. Japan then closed its doors to the west. Christianity was driven underground, where it survived for centuries as a secret religion passed on in families and local communities from generation to generation.

The Jesuits also initiated missionary activity in China. In 1552, Francis Xavier arrived there but died shortly after landing on an island near Hong Kong. The real founder of the Chinese mission was an Italian Jesuit, **Matteo Ricci,** who was born in the year Xavier died. Ricci learned Mandarin, dressed in Chinese clothes, and emphasized the similarities between Catholicism and the traditional Chinese philosophy of Confucianism. Like the Jesuits in Europe, Ricci concentrated on Chinese political and social elites, hoping for conversions in powerful places. He eventually resided at the imperial court in Beijing, where he gained a few converts, though most refused baptism. Thus, Ricci's influence in China was small, but his influence in Eu-

Francis Xavier (1506–1552) Jesuit who led Catholic missions in India and Japan.

Matteo Ricci (1552–1610) Italian Jesuit missionary in China who sent new information on Chinese civilization back to Europe.

Adam Schall, a German Jesuit dressed as a mandarin, was court astronomer for the Chinese emperor in Beijing. Schall calculated the astrologically best dates for the performance of Confucian rites at court. In assimilating aspects of Chinese culture, Schall represents the style of missionary activity in China that his fellow Jesuit, Matteo Ricci, established. *(Bettmann/Corbis)*

rope was considerable. The reports he and other Jesuits sent to Rome were soon published, providing a flood of new information about Chinese culture, philosophy, and history. Here was a people who were unquestionably "civilized" like the Europeans but who had developed without the benefit of Christianity. Debates over the meaning of this puzzle were to swirl about in European intellectual circles for decades to come.

After Ricci's death, the Catholic community in China continued to expand. By the early eighteenth century, Christians numbered somewhere between two hundred thousand and five hundred thousand, or about 0.2 percent of the total population. Chinese Christians never faced government repression like Japanese Christians, but they achieved only a marginal place in the larger Chinese world.

Reformation and Society 1517–1570

↓ How was religious reform put into practice?
↓ How did the actions of ordinary men and women shape the outcomes of reform?

From Savonarola on, both Catholic and Protestant reformers hoped that church renewal would bring about a renewal of society as a whole. Reformers, therefore, tried to impose new codes of conduct on their communities, and people had to decide whether to accept or reject them. The result was a negotiation between reformers and the population at large, during which some changes were accepted and others were modified or rejected. This process was at work in three areas: children's education, poor relief, and family life. Finally, both Protestants and Catholics reassessed their relations with the largest religious and social minority in Europe, the Jews.

Educating the Young

In the Middle Ages, primary schooling was mainly reserved for boys destined for careers in the church, the state, law, and medicine. As a result, many men, like Ignatius of Loyola before he decided to become a missionary, saw no reason why they should study or learn to read and write. Protestant reformers, however, began to question these traditional ways and to argue for popular educational reform. Luther's belief in the priesthood of all believers led him to promote elementary education for both boys and girls, along with the establishment of public libraries. His goal was to turn children into good Christians by teaching them how to read the Bible. In 1529, he also published a *Small Catechism* for them, which contained the **Lord's Prayer** along with simple statements of Lutheran theology. Calvin adopted a similar program in his *Geneva Catechism* of 1545.

Leaders in a number of communities adopted Luther's and Calvin's educational agendas, but only after modifying them. While primary schools for boys were established, those for girls lagged behind, reflecting current social values. Few people, including many girls, thought that women's social or work roles were the same as men's; their education could be limited to training as wives and mothers, since these were the only respectable roles left for them after the Protestants abolished religious orders.

Lord's Prayer The prayer Jesus taught his followers to use, found in the Gospel of Luke and the Gospel of Matthew.

Catholic reformers sometimes endorsed education for both boys and girls, often for the same reasons as Protestants. A new *Roman Catechism,* published in 1566, taught young people throughout the Catholic world how to recite the Lord's Prayer, the creeds, and the **Hail Mary.** Nevertheless, Catholics established even fewer schools for girls than the Protestants; a late-sixteenth-century educational survey in Venice listed 4,600 boy students but only 30 girls. Catholics, too, thought that cooking, sewing, and other household activities, all requiring little formal education, were women's usual work, although they continued to see life in a religious order as another option.

Catholic boys fared better than girls, since efforts were sometimes made to educate more of them than before. For example, the **Piarists,** a religious order founded in 1597 by a blacksmith's son, established primary schools for poor boys so they could meet the entry qualifications for the more advanced Jesuit schools. Since Piarist schools were free, the poor would be given an equal chance with the rich for a quality education. The Piarists met with opposition from people who thought that the lowborn should stay where they were. Overall, both Catholic and Protestant reforms of elementary education, along with the availability of printed reading material, hastened the spread of **literacy** throughout Europe.

Poor Relief

In Europe, the number of poor people grew during the sixteenth century, rising to nearly half the population in the hardest-hit urban and rural areas. It is, therefore, not surprising that Protestant and Catholic reformers called for a rethinking of the problem of poverty. The outcome was a change in attitudes about the poor and the ways communities should deal with them.

In the Middle Ages, the poor were given sacred significance. In the Gospel of Matthew, Jesus identified the hungry, the naked, and the sick with himself. Anyone, therefore, who cared for them was also caring for him. As a result, charity toward the needy made up a major portion of the good works medieval people performed; they looked after the sick and dying and provided food and shelter for the destitute. Above all, they gave to beggars. These practices came under attack from both Protestants and Catholics during the sixteenth century.

As early as 1522, Martin Luther issued an ordinance governing poor relief in Wittenberg. It outlawed all public begging and mandated that care of the poor was to be transferred from private individuals or groups to the city. Funds for poor relief were to be collected in all the city's churches and then distrib-

uted by the municipal government. Only those identified by the authorities as "deserving" would receive help, thus restricting aid to those who were truly unable to work because of age, disability, or sickness. People who simply chose not to work would be left to fend for themselves.

The guiding principle behind Luther's ordinance was his rejection of good works as a means toward salvation. No longer were people to think that giving to the poor helped to save them. Charity was simply a free act of love performed by Christian people for the benefit of other Christians. Luther's reform was rooted in his theology, but his decision to turn poor relief over to the city government had profound consequences: from then on, the state, not the church, was responsible for care of the destitute.

Catholic reformers also argued that the state should assume the task of poor relief. In 1526, **Juan Luis Vives,** a Spanish humanist living in the Netherlands, argued that municipal governments should administer all funds for the poor. Vives's work won the support of other Catholics, but his proposals were never fully implemented in Catholic lands. The old practice of individual giving to the poor was too strong to be swept away completely, as the success of the begging Capuchins shows. Moreover, the idea that charity was a praiseworthy good work was reinforced by the Council of Trent. As a result, Catholics tended to create a variety of different systems for poor relief. State authorities administered some funds, religious confraternities collected and distributed others, and private individuals continued to give. Like the Lutherans, Catholics usually tried to distinguish between the deserving and undeserving poor.

Calvin's program for the poor resembled both Luther's and Vives's, since the government of Geneva took responsibility for the needy. Calvin believed that all wealth came from God and was to be used for the benefit of the community as a whole. Thus the state should tax the rich for the benefit of the poor. He also thought that poverty was a sign of God's anger over sin, but he did not place the sin simply on the shoulders of the poor themselves. If there was poverty, it

Hail Mary   Roman Catholic prayer praising Mary and asking her to pray to Jesus on behalf of the one reciting it.

Piarists   Catholic religious order dedicated to the education of poor boys.

literacy   Ability to read and write.

Juan Luis Vives   (1492–1540) Spanish Catholic humanist living in the Netherlands who supported a state takeover of relief for the poor.

was because the community as a whole had sinned. Like Luther and Vives, Calvin was shifting poor relief from the church to the state. In the long run, state administration of poverty programs was to be a central feature of the modern European world.

Family Life

A third area in which Protestant and Catholic reformers tried to introduce new social attitudes and practices was family life. As with primary education and poor relief, communities accepted some reforms while modifying or rejecting others. The result was a melding of old and new that resulted from a prolonged contest between reforming elites and ordinary people.

In the western Catholic Church during the Middle Ages, family life was based on the institution of marriage. The church taught that the purpose of marriage was twofold: to provide an outlet for sexual impulses and to bring children into the world. Both purposes were considered acceptable but not ideal. The highest state for Christians was that of permanent sexual abstinence expressed in a life of celibacy, following the example of Jesus and the apostle Paul. Thus clergymen, monks, and nuns were thought to live a better kind of Christian life than married people. For the married, sexual intercourse was permissible only between husband and wife, only on certain days, and only in certain positions. Of course, there were many who failed to live up to these ideals, and some clergymen even expected that people would find it impossible to observe them. Thus many city governments established brothels, arguing that men, especially, were incapable of controlling their sexual passions and that use of brothels was better than rape and adultery.

Marriage itself was considered a sacrament that the bride and groom administered to each other through the exchange of vows. The free consent of the partners to marriage was thus required. The Council of Trent also required that the marriage take place in public before witnesses, including the priest in the parish where the agreement to marry had taken place. Marriages contracted secretly were not recognized as binding on the couple. Once a proper marriage had taken place, it would last until the death of one of the spouses, since divorce was prohibited. It was also widely agreed that after marriage, the husband was head of the family, with his wife and all others subject to him.

As in other areas of life, Martin Luther swept away many of these traditional attitudes and practices. He declared that marriage was not a sacrament but simply a God-given social institution. He saw it as the foundation of all social order, since it created the basic social unit, the family. All men and women, including the clergy, were now to be married, and religious orders, which promoted celibacy, were to be abolished. In 1525, he set the example by marrying an ex-nun, Katherine von Bora. Marriages were to be public events, and they had to be sanctioned by the couple's parents, not just the future spouses themselves. In these ways Luther narrowed the freedom of choice for couples. In another way, however, he expanded it by allowing for divorce under special circumstances. Although divorces were frowned on and expensive to obtain, they could be granted for such reasons as adultery, male impotence, a spouse's refusal of sexual relations, desertion, and conviction of a capital crime. Finally, Luther ordered the closure of brothels, arguing that men could control their sexual impulses and confine their sexual activities to marriage. Luther's reform of marriage served as a model for most other Protestant churches, although some modified various points. For example, the Church of England forbade divorce, while the Anabaptists often insisted on community, not just parental, approval of marriages.

Protestant reform brought changes to the lives of husbands and wives. On the one hand, those Protestants who married were no longer viewed as second-class Christians, since the old ideal of a celibate life was no longer accepted. In addition, marriage was viewed more positively than before. Its purpose was to increase affection and cooperation between spouses, not just to provide an outlet for sexual impulses or to bring babies into the world. Women were viewed as real partners with their husbands in running a household, increasing their honor in society. On the other hand, women lost some of their older religious options, since they could no longer enter a women's religious order. From then on, their adult roles were limited to those of spouse or spinster. Even legal prostitution as a choice was taken away when brothels closed.

Catholics also reformed marriage practices, although they kept more of the old ways than Protestants. Marriage was still viewed as a sacrament. In addition, the free consent of bride and groom remained the only essential act leading to marriage; parental consent was encouraged but not required. Marriages could not be secret; they had to take place in public before a priest. Divorce was still not allowed. The best one could hope for in a failed marriage was either a permanent separation or an annulment declaring that the marriage had never really existed. While Catholics differed from Protestants on the matter of divorce, they both agreed that marriage existed for something more than the release of sexual passion and the production of offspring. It was also the place where individuals could find companionship and

The woman in this sixteenth-century engraving represents, according to the caption, "A Virtuous Woman of Geneva." Her dress is sober and her head is covered. Her bowed head and clasped hands convey a prayerful attitude and the submissiveness that embodied Calvinist gender norms. *(Genève, Departement Iconographique, Bibliothèque de Genève)*

mutual support. Moreover, women's religious options were greater for Catholics than for Protestants. Special female saints could be invoked during conception, pregnancy, and childbirth, and women could still enter their own religious orders, where they largely governed themselves. In contrast, Protestant authorities had abolished religious orders and prohibited asking saints for their prayers.

Faced with the reforming agendas of both Catholic and Protestant clergy, the mass of people had to decide how to react. Many reforms were well received. There was popular support among Catholics and Protestants for closing brothels and for punishment of sexually promiscuous people. Public anger was highest against sexual acts that threatened to disrupt the family or bring dishonor on it, like adultery. Others, like same-sex acts, while technically capital offenses that were deeply offensive to most people, were less of a challenge to social order since they did not result in the birth of children and usually did not tear families apart.

Other reforms were less well received, especially if they seemed too novel or threatening. For example, Luther wanted early marriages as a safeguard against lust. In Germany, where marriages were usually late and took place only when the couple had saved enough money to establish their own households, this reform was rejected. Popular opinion also often won out over the issue of premarital sex. Reformers wanted sexual relations to begin only after marriage, but many couples began them right after their engagement to prevent ill-wishers from using magic that would prevent desired pregnancies, since most people believed that their enemies could draw on the Devil's power to inflict harm.

Jews in the Age of the Reformation

The late-fifteenth-century expulsions from Spain and Portugal left western Europe almost empty of Jews, since the Iberian Jewish communities were the largest in the Christian world. As Protestant and Catholic reform developed, anti-Jewish sentiment increased and led to further expulsions. In some states, however, authorities permitted Jews to live under severe restrictions.

Like Savonarola, Martin Luther believed that church reform would usher in Christ's return to earth. This belief led to attacks on the Jews. With the end of the world at hand, why did they still refuse to convert to Christianity and acknowledge Jesus as their Messiah? In 1543, Luther gave his answer in a pamphlet, *Concerning the Jews and Their Lies*, where he repeated all the anti-Jewish arguments Christians had made in the Middle Ages. As a result, the Lutheran reformation turned sharply against the Jews; rulers of Lutheran states in the empire ordered their expulsion along with Catholics. Calvin also endorsed the medieval view of Jews as Christ killers and therefore enemies of God. Protestant Europe, therefore, became increasingly hostile toward Jews. It was only in Catholic Italy that Jews found new places to resettle in the west.

In 1516, the government of the Republic of Venice allowed a permanent Jewish community on its territory. Jews were confined to one area of Venice, the **Ghetto.** As a result, some Spanish and Portuguese Jews migrated there from the Muslim lands where they had gone after the expulsions. Those who had been forced to convert to Christianity now returned to Judaism. "Ghettos," modeled on the one in Venice, were also established in Rome and other Italian cities.

Like Luther, reform-minded popes believed that the Jews' refusal to convert to Christianity made them God's enemies. The low point came in 1593, when the pope placed severe restrictions on Jews living in his territories. They were forbidden to sell meat or unleavened bread to Christians. They could not bathe or shave with Christians and could not employ them as servants. Cases they had previously settled in Jewish law courts were now transferred to the state's law courts, run by Christians. Jews could no longer serve as physicians to non-Jews, a role traditionally played by Jewish men in the Middle Ages. Now, their economic activity was confined to the secondhand clothes trade. Finally, they continued to be publicly identified and shamed by the yellow badges they were forced to wear on their clothing. The pope intended to humiliate the Jews, isolate them socially, and attack them economically. But Jews were not expelled from the Papal States. They were also allowed to live in other states in Italy, often on terms more favorable than those offered by the popes. While Rome shaped its policy for religious reasons, the other states took economic considerations into account. They wanted Jewish settlements for commercial reasons, since Jews had good business connections in the Muslim world.

Ghetto Originally, a district in Venice where Jews were allowed to settle in the sixteenth century.

Summary

Review Questions

↑ What motivated the leaders of church reform, whether Protestant or Catholic?

↑ How did Protestant and Catholic reform reshape the religious identities of both Christians and non-Christians in western Europe and overseas?

↑ How did religious reformers, rulers, and ordinary people interact in the business of reform?

Savonarola's and Erasmus's hopes for church reform were symptomatic of a growing demand for religious renewal in the western church, brought about by the spread of humanism, a decline in the prestige of the papacy and the clergy, a rise in lay-inspired devotion to Christ, and the ability of reformers to use the new technology of the printing press. Savonarola and Erasmus raised issues and proposed changes that shaped the programs of many later reformers. One of the first was Martin Luther, the founder of Protestant reform. Although other Protestants, like the radicals and Calvinists, disagreed with Luther on some points, their programs were similar enough to create a general Protestant movement. Lutheranism was the dominant form of Protestantism in northern Germany and Scandinavia. But in the second half of the sixteenth century, Calvinism became the most dynamic Protestant movement, spreading throughout Europe. After the fall of Münster, the radicals renounced violence and followed leaders who embraced pacifism. The outcome of Protestant reform was a permanent split in the western church, characterized by deep hostility on both sides.

Initially, Catholics who shared the general expectation of church reform did not shape their programs with an eye to the Protestant challenge. In the end, however, orders such as the Capuchins and the Jesuits combated Protestantism while reforming the Catholic Church from within. Along with the religious orders, the papacy led Catholic Church reform when Paul III convened the Council of Trent. The council reaffirmed Catholic teaching, thereby cementing the division between Catholics and Protestants, and created a blueprint for reform that was implemented over the next hundred years throughout the Catholic world. Finally, Catholics inaugurated the first overseas missions by western Christians. Missionaries often tried to impose European values on converts as they sought to make up for the souls lost in Europe to Protestantism. Some local people accepted Christian teachings wholeheartedly, while others rejected them or blended them into their old religions.

In Europe, the decisive factors determining the success of reform, whether Protestant or Catholic, were the choices made by rulers, nobles, and ordinary people. The choices of the elite were the most important in determining whether communities would become Protestant or remain Catholic, but the long-term success of reform within a community depended on popular reception. Many reformers thought their programs would restore a united church to a state of purity they believed had existed formerly. In this sense, they were looking backward. Some reformers thought that church reform and overseas missions would usher in Christ's Second Coming and thus the end of the world. One outcome of reform was the introduction into European life of some basic features of the emerging modern world—the spread of literacy, new state administration of poverty programs, and changing standards for family life.

← **Thinking Back, Thinking Ahead** →

What were the consequences of religious reform in Catholic and Protestant Europe for future generations of Europeans?

ECHO ECHO ECHO ECHO ECHO

Media Revolutions

The first modern media revolution took place in the second half of the fifteenth century with the invention of printing using movable type. Studies of printed material in the sixteenth century show that most publications dealt with religious matters. Catechisms, prayer books, Bibles, and saints' lives were turned out in ever-increasing numbers. Not only were more religious texts produced in shorter time, *mistakes* in texts were produced in a different way. When a scribe made one copy of a manuscript, his mistakes were in that copy alone. When the printing press churned out many identical copies of a single work, mistakes were repeated over and over again. In England, for example, a printer was summoned before a church court on the charge of blasphemy because of a mistake in his edition of the Bible. His text read, "Thou shalt commit adultery."

The use of print media to promote Catholic or Protestant reform meant that, for the first time, reading skills were necessary for the mass of Europeans. The ability to read and write therefore became a central aspect of European identity. Historians measure the growth of literacy by noting the percentage of personally signed documents in the surviving sources. By this indicator, literacy spread gradually throughout Europe in the seventeenth and eighteenth centuries, first in the northwest and then in the south and east.

Beginning in the late nineteenth century, when literacy was widespread in all parts of Europe, media revolutions followed each other in rapid succession. The silent motion picture and the phonograph, which were invented at about the same time, emphasized different channels of communication—sight and sound. In the early twentieth century, radio expanded sound communication even further. Then the two were united in the talking motion pictures. After World War II, the development of television brought sight and sound into the home. Now it was possible to get the daily news or enjoy a story without having to use reading skills, and some critics complained that people's reading ability would decline.

Today, communication via e-mail, online newspapers, and audiovisual streaming in real time links millions of people around the globe in radically new ways. But the Internet revolution is only the latest in a series of media revolutions that have changed people's lives. Compared to the Internet revolution, the printing revolution looks pretty primitive. But, in its time, its impact was equally profound.

Suggested Readings

Donnelly, John Patrick. *Ignatius of Loyola: Founder of the Jesuits.* New York: Pearson/Longman, 2004. A good biography.

Hsia, Ronnie Po-chia. *The World of Catholic Renewal, 1540–1770.* 2nd ed. New York: Cambridge University Press, 1998. A comprehensive guide to Catholic reform in Europe and overseas.

Kittelson, James M. *Luther the Reformer.* Minneapolis: Augsburg Publishing House, 1986. A readable biography.

McGrath, Alister E. *A Life of John Calvin.* Malden, Mass.: Blackwell Publishers, 1990. A biography that places Calvin's life and thought within the larger context of church reform.

Tracy, James D. *Europe's Reformations, 1450–1650.* 2nd ed. New York: Rowman & Littlefield, 2006. Good general coverage.

Wiesner-Hanks, Merry. *Christianity and Sexuality in the Early Modern World.* New York: Routledge, 2000. A wide-ranging study that examines the impact of church reform on ordinary people.

Williams, Rowan. *Teresa of Avila.* New York: Continuum, 1991. A brief account of Teresa's life and thought.

Websites

Basic information and many links to more specialized topics, **Internet Modern History Sourcebook / Reformation Europe,** at www.fordham.edu/halsall/mod/modsbook02.html#Protestant

More basic information and links, **The Reformation Guide,** at www.educ.msu.edu/homepages/laurence/reformation/index.htm

Illustrations of important Reformation people, **Reformation Picture Gallery—People,** at www.mun.ca/rels/reform/pics/people/people.html

CHAPTER 15

A Century of War and Wonder, 1550–1650

CHAPTER OUTLINE

1500 B.C.E.	1000 B.C.E.	500 B.C.E.	1 B.C.E./1 C.E.

1555
Peace of Augsburg accepts split in western Christianity

1562
French Wars of Religion begin

1566
Calvinist revolt in the Netherlands

1598
Edict of Nantes grants tolerance for French Protestants

1550	1560	1570	1580	1590	1600	1610

Europe in the Age of the Religious Wars

From 1550 to 1650, Europe was engulfed in a series of religious wars. One of the last was the Thirty Years' War, fought from 1618 to 1648 in the Holy Roman Empire. It pitted the Catholic Habsburgs and their German allies against the Protestants of the Empire. During the war Sweden, Denmark, the Dutch Republic, Spain and France were drawn into the fighting. Does the position of the Empire in relation to the other states of Europe suggest why this happened?

Legend

- Austrian Hapsburg lands
- Spanish Hapsburg lands
- Other German states
- Swedish lands by 1648
- Ottoman and Tributary States
- Boundary of Holy Roman Empire
- ✕ Major battle
- Siege

NORWAY
SWEDEN
FINLAND
RUSSIA
ESTONIA
LIVONIA

North Sea
DENMARK
JUTLAND
SCHLESWIG
Copenhagen
Baltic Sea
Vilna

IRELAND
Edinburgh
Dublin
ENGLAND
London
Hamburg
Lübeck
POMERANIA
Danzig
PRUSSIA
BRANDENBURG
Berlin
Warsaw

UNITED PROVINCES
Amsterdam
Essen
Magdeburg
Breitenfeld 1631
SAXONY
SILESIA
POLAND-LITHUANIA

ATLANTIC OCEAN
Antwerp
SPANISH NETHERLANDS
Cologne
Lützen 1632
White Mountain 1620
Prague
Rocroi 1643
UPPER PALATINATE
LOWER PALATINATE
BOHEMIA
MORAVIA
Paris
Nantes
Nördlingen 1634
BAVARIA
Vienna 1529
AUSTRIA
Buda
Pest

Dnieper
Dniester
CRIMEA

FRANCE
FRANCHE-COMTÉ
Augsburg
Salzburg
HUNGARY
TRANSYLVANIA
Zurich
Geneva
SWITZERLAND
Trent
SLAVONIA
Black Sea
SAVOY
Venice
REPUBLIC OF VENICE
Belgrade
PIEDMONT
MILAN
GENOA

PORTUGAL
SPAIN
Madrid
Lisbon
Tagus
TUSCANY
PAPAL STATES
Corsica (Genoa)
Rome
NAPLES
Naples
Adriatic Sea
MONTENEGRO
Constantinople
OTTOMAN EMPIRE

SARDINIA
Balearic Is.
Palermo
SICILY
Athens
Lepanto 1571
Mediterranean Sea
Crete (Rep. of Venice)

MOROCCO
ALGIERS
TUNIS
TRIPOLI
CYRENICA
EGYPT

0 200 400 Km.
0 200 400 Mi.

Timeline

500 C.E. 1000 C.E. 1500 C.E. 2000 C.E.

1618 Thirty Years' War begins

1629 French Wars of Religion end

1648 Thirty Years' War ends

1649 Charles I is executed, England becomes a republic

1660 Monarchy is restored in the British Isles

1665 Sabbatai Sevi is proclaimed the Messiah

1620 1630 1640 1650 1660 1670

Choice Choice Choice

IACOBVS CALLOT
CALCOGRAPHVS AQVA FORTI NANCEII IN LOTHARINGIA,
NOBILIS.

Jacques Callot

Jacques Callot was one of the greatest artists and printmakers of his generation. Born into a noble family, he spent his early years documenting the pageants and festivities of European rulers in works that pioneered remarkable new techniques of fine line etching and were printed on the new printing press. In his last years, Callot produced scenes portraying the horrors of war that have inspired generations of antiwar protesters. (Lucas Vorsterman, Flemish, 1595–1675, *Portrait of a Man* [Jacob Callot]. Princeton University Art Museum. Gift of Junius S. Morgan. x1934-367a. © 2007 Trustees of Princeton University)

Jacques Callot Publishes "The Miseries and Misfortunes of War"

In 1633, Jacques Callot, nearing the end of his life and suffering from a painful stomach disorder, published eighteen large etchings depicting "The Miseries and Misfortunes of War." Military scenes had always been part of his artistic repertory, but the "Miseries" were something different. With them, the respected portrayer of elite life in early-seventeenth-century Europe revealed himself as one of the most powerful protesters against the dark side of war.

Callot was born in 1592 into a noble and devout Roman Catholic family in the duchy of Lorraine. His artistic talent was apparent at an early age, and in his teens he joined a band of gypsies heading south to Rome, where he worked as an assistant in a printshop specializing in religious images at a time when the campaign against Protestantism gripped the city. The papacy urged the Catholic faithful to come to Rome to reinforce their faith through visits to the tombs of saints and the city's magnificent churches. When they left, these pilgrims were eager to take home souvenirs, and prints like Callot's of the famous paintings they had seen in churches were especially prized.

In 1611, Callot moved to Florence to serve the grand duke Cosimo II and his mother, the grand duchess Christine, who, like Callot, was from Lorraine. Cosimo's court was one of the most brilliant and intellectually distinguished in Europe, and Florence was filled with artists and scientists in the grand duke's employ. Here Callot perfected his etching technique using the extra-hard varnish Italian violin makers put on their instruments. This varnish allowed Callot to prepare his copper printing plates by cutting fine, clear lines with his etching needle. The result was a remarkably detailed and precise etching ready to pick up ink for printing. In Florence, Callot continued to produce religious prints, but he also documented the lives of the grand dukes and their lavish court—scenes of operas, precision marching, and tournaments. Soldiers also figured prominently in these works because the rulers of the time were expected to project an image of warrior power. Callot's soldiers were dashing and heroic, mounted on prancing horses and glittering with finely polished armor.

In 1621, Cosimo II died, and the grand duchess Christine, reducing state expenditures, dismissed Callot and other court artists. Callot returned to his father's house in Lorraine, which, in 1630, the French invaded. They invaded again in 1632 and in 1633, when they finally annexed the duchy to France and demanded an oath of loyalty from all locally prominent people, including Callot.

The invasion of Lorraine brought the harsh facts of warfare directly into Callot's family. Plague swept through the duchy, brought in by French soldiers, and Callot's father fell victim to it. It was in this context that Callot decided to create his "Miseries and Misfortunes of War." The series of prints were published in 1633. The first shows an army recruiter luring men to sign up with promises of good pay. A fierce battle scene follows, and then come five prints showing the cruelty of soldiers against civilians as troops pillage a farm, attack a monastery, burn a village, and seize a stagecoach. In these scenes people are stabbed, shot, and burned alive. The next prints show the tables turned on the soldiers, who are tortured and killed by their commanders for military crimes such as desertion. Here men are tied to a rope and hurled earthward from a great height, shot by a firing squad, torn apart on a rack, or burned at the stake, while others hang by their necks like human fruit on the branches of a great tree. We then see wounded and mangled soldiers crowding a hospital, people dying by a roadside, and peasants attacking soldiers in revenge for their atrocities. The series ends with a conqueror rewarding his troops, implying that the horrors, now celebrated as a "victory," will start all over again. Callot presented his prints without any commentary, intending that his artistic skill alone should carry his bitter message; the moralizing lines now seen on many of them were added later.

In 1635, at the age of forty-three, Jacques Callot died in a Lorraine that was ravaged by wartime disease and famine. But his prints endured. They struck home to many of his generation who, like him, were deeply committed Christians, whether Catholic or Protestant, and who were also appalled by the horror and futility of the warfare that had torn Europe apart for nearly a century.

Introduction

Callot's Europe was indeed troubled and turbulent. Rulers fought increasingly expensive and destructive wars and, not content with battling their enemies at home, carried the struggles overseas. The Spanish and Portuguese fought to maintain their empires, while the French, English, and Dutch attempted to seize their rivals' wealth or establish competing empires of their own in the Western Hemisphere and Asia.

After 1550, the prosperity Europeans had experienced since the mid-fourteenth century ended. In both town and country, the numbers of the poor grew, while a small, well-to-do elite struggled to maintain control over the increasingly restless and riot-prone masses. Hard times produced widespread anxiety. People became obsessed with witches, who were feared as agents of the Devil bent on ruining society. Many believed that the troubles they were experiencing were a prelude to Christ's Second Coming to judge the world.

The church reforms of the sixteenth century had created two mutually hostile religious communities in western Europe. Neither the Protestants nor the Catholics accepted that religious unity had been shattered, and both fought ferociously to impose their own ways on their opponents. Capitalizing on his New World wealth and extensive European territories, Philip II of Spain, the son of Charles V, took the lead in the fight for Catholicism. The Netherlands, France, Germany, and the British Isles all saw religious warfare. In some wars, all Protestants joined to fight Catholics; in others, different types of Protestants fought each other. Both Protestants and Catholics committed terrible atrocities. The fierceness of the fighting shows how central the principle of religious unity was for the culture of early modern Europe.

Warfare accelerated economic decline, producing widespread famine and disease. In parts of Europe, population dropped by 50 percent. In the end, neither Protestants nor Catholics succeeded in eliminating their opponents, and religious disunity prevailed. By 1650, most Europeans had accepted it, often unwillingly, as a fact of life. Also by 1650, Spain, having exhausted its resources in the fight against Protestantism, had lost its preeminent position in Europe. France, weathering the crisis of its religious wars, now emerged as the dominant European power.

Although the Jews were not directly involved in disputes between Christians, they, too, experienced hard times when wars broke out in the lands where they lived. Nevertheless, the Jews' condition improved in western Europe, where they settled once again and often prospered. Yet, as a despised minority, Jews were sometimes subjected to terrible attacks. Some Jews saw the troubled times after 1550 as a sign that the long-awaited Jewish Messiah was about to appear and lead them to victory.

Chronology

1540s	Spain's silver mines in the Americas open
1555	Peace of Augsburg allows Lutheranism
1556	Philip II becomes king of Spain; Ferdinand I becomes Holy Roman emperor
1558	Elizabeth I becomes queen of England
1559	Francis II becomes king of France
1562	French Wars of Religion begin
1564	Maximilian II becomes Holy Roman emperor
1566	Calvinists rebel in the Netherlands
1571	Spain defeats Turkish navy at Battle of Lepanto
1572	French Catholics attack Protestants in Saint Bartholomew's Day Massacre
1588	Spanish Armada attacks England
1589	Henry IV becomes king of France
1598	Edict of Nantes grants religious toleration to Huguenots

1603	James VI of Scotland becomes James I of England and Ireland
1610	Louis XIII becomes king of France
1618	Thirty Years' War begins
1625	Charles I becomes king of Scotland, England, and Ireland
1629	Peace of Alès ends French Wars of Religion
1642	English civil war begins
1643	Louis XIV becomes king of France
1648	Peace of Westphalia ends Thirty Years' War
1649	England becomes a republic
1659	France and Spain sign Treaty of the Pyrenees
1660	Monarchy is restored in the British Isles
1665	Sabbatai Sevi proclaimed the Jewish Messiah
1667	War ends in Poland

Europe's Economy and Society

↓ What were the effects of overseas empire building and global trading on Europe's economy?

↓ What caused the decline in the standard of living for most Europeans, and what effect did this decline have on society?

Between 1550 and 1650, Europe's economy, which had boomed in the previous hundred years, began to stagnate. Silver from Spanish mines in the Americas caused inflation, which, combined with overpopulation, reduced the standard of living for most Europeans. Hardship was widespread, evident in protests and riots. As communities' traditional sense of solidarity crumbled, the well-to-do became obsessed with maintaining social order. Panic over witches was another symptom of the hard times that struck after 1550.

Europe's Continuing Overseas Expansion

During the sixteenth century, Portuguese and Spanish success in creating empires stirred similar ambitions in France and England. At first, the French and English were content to conduct raids against Spanish shipping. In 1523, a French ship sized three ships loaded with Moctezuma's personal treasure and the booty collected by Hernán Cortés's army. Since France and Spain were at war for most of the sixteenth century, this attack was considered part of the larger struggle. In the late sixteenth century, when relations between England and Spain deteriorated, Queen Elizabeth I commissioned the **privateer** Sir Francis Drake to seize Spanish treasure. These raids constituted the first phase of France's and England's entry into empire building in the New World, and by the early seventeenth century, permanent English and French colonies were being established.

In 1607, businessmen financed the first permanent English settlement in North America at Jamestown in

privateer Private vessel commissioned by a state to attack the commercial and naval ships of another country.

present-day Virginia. In 1625, the English colonized the Caribbean island of Barbados and imported African slaves to work sugar plantations there. The French state also sponsored colonial ventures in America. In 1608, Samuel de Champlain founded the city of Quebec on the Saint Lawrence River as the center of the new colony of Canada. In 1683, a French nobleman, Robert Cavalier, Sieur de La Salle, led an expedition from the Great Lakes down the Mississippi River to the Gulf of Mexico and claimed the lands along the river for France, naming them **Louisiana** in honor of the French king, Louis XIV. At the very end of the century, France claimed the western half of the island of Hispaniola and established sugar plantations there. The Dutch also established sugar plantations in the Caribbean as, like the English and French, they seized islands originally claimed by Spain. In Asia, the Dutch attacked the Portuguese and gradually replaced them as the major power in the spice trade.

Establishing colonies and attacking empires were costly adventures involving large investments and high risks. To raise the necessary money, Europeans developed a new form of business organization, the **joint-stock company,** in which individuals pooled their capital and received stock shares in proportion to the size of their investment. The joint-stock technique raised huge sums of money but limited the risk factor for each investor. Jamestown was founded by a joint-stock venture, the Virginia Company. The English **East India Company,** founded in 1600, established trading posts on the subcontinent of India, while the Dutch United East India Company, founded in 1602, was profitable for more than a century.

Nowhere were the effects of trade and colonization more far reaching than in the exchange between Europe and the Western Hemisphere. In the century after Columbus's voyages, many new food items were introduced into Europe: chili peppers, beans, pumpkins, squashes, tomatoes, peanuts, chocolate, maize, and potatoes. Maize and potatoes were to become staples in the diets of southern and northern Europeans, respectively. These strange foods provoked doubt and debate. Some argued that people should eat only foods mentioned in the Bible. Others wondered if potatoes and peanuts, which grew underground, should be fed to animals but not to humans, who were higher up in the ladder of creation. Tobacco, cultivated early in Virginia, provided a satisfying New World smoke, sniff, or chew after a New World turkey dinner, washed down with rum, an alcoholic drink made from American-grown sugar.

The exchange brought even more dramatic changes to the Americas. On his second voyage, Columbus brought wheat, melons, onions, radishes, grapevines,

sugar cane, cauliflower, cabbages, lemons (originally from Asia), and figs to the Western Hemisphere, along with the European rat. Horses, cattle, pigs, goats, dogs, sheep, and chickens came as well, changing forever the animal population of the Americas. Later European arrivals unknowingly brought weed seed with them in the form of Kentucky bluegrass, daisies, and dandelions, as well as the European honeybee. The European ox pulled plows through soils that had been too heavy to turn over with the Indians' hand-held tools.

Trade with Asia also brought more new products to Europe. The first shipment of tea from China arrived at the beginning of the seventeenth century, and rice, a staple in some Asian diets, was soon widely grown in Italy. By the end of the century, coffee, native to the Arabian Peninsula, was grown in the East Indies and then shipped to Europe. Soon it would also be grown in the Americas. The rich prized Asian ebony wood for furniture and delicate Chinese porcelains for their collections of rare items. At a less exotic level, Chinese zinc and Indian tin were imported in ever-increasing quantities. Thus, the entry of new states and private companies into Europe's overseas trade expanded the global trading networks linking America, Europe, and Asia that had begun in the sixteenth century. The result was the beginning of a new era in Europe's economic life based on commerce.

A River of Silver

Spain's silver mines in the Americas, opened in the 1540s, produced huge quantities of precious metal that flowed to Europe and Asia. Contemporary official estimates of silver exports from the Spanish Empire place the figure at some 17,800 tons, but smuggling and unofficial exports may have pushed it as high as 29,000 tons. This amount would have tripled silver supplies in Europe, where the metal was used mainly as money; when news of silver's discovery reached Europe, Charles V's credit rating soared. The most productive mine was in present-day Bolivia at San Luis de Potosí. The other main source was at Zacatecas in northern Mexico. Gold and emeralds were also mined.

The silver of Potosí was either minted into coins or

Louisiana   French colony in the Mississippi valley named after King Louis XIV.

joint-stock company   Company in which individuals pool their capital and receive stock shares in proportion to the size of their investment.

East India Company   English joint-stock company founded in 1600 to establish trading posts on the Indian subcontinent.

melted into bars and then transported to the Peruvian port of Lima. From there it went by ship to Panama, where it was hauled overland to the Caribbean for transfer to Spain. Some silver from northern Mexico was also carried to the Caribbean while the rest went to Acapulco on the Pacific, where it was loaded onto the **Manila galleon,** a large, square-rigged sailing ship sent to the Philippine Islands to purchase Chinese silks and porcelains. The galleon's annual round trip was the single most profitable voyage in the Spanish Empire, and the millions of silver coins used to pay for trade goods flooded Southeast Asia, where they became the standard international currency.

The silver for Europe, along with goods from China, was collected once a year by armed Spanish ships that arrived in the Caribbean in late summer. After wintering there, they joined up in Havana for the voyage home. This was the most perilous part of the trip, since the fleet's valuable cargo made it subject to seizure by independently operating pirates or privateers commissioned by the governments of Spain's enemies.

If the Spanish fleet managed to dodge attacks and survive storms at sea, it headed for **Seville,** Spain's largest and richest city. In theory, all precious metals from the Americas had to be registered with the port authorities and then taxed, but smuggling, bribery, false declarations of value, and other techniques were routinely used to evade this requirement. Nevertheless, the government *quinto,* or fifth tax on gold and silver, made up a quarter of the royal income. Other goods were stored on the wharves, but few merchants gathered there to buy them. Instead, goods were shipped north to the trading centers of Antwerp and Amsterdam. Thus, Seville never became a major hub in the global commercial network but served simply as a transit point for Spanish overseas riches.

Despite the sizable sum provided by the royal *quinto,* Charles V and then his son, **Philip II,** found that the ruling of their lands created costs even the river of silver from the New World could not completely pay. So Philip, like his father, borrowed. During his reign he overextended himself, borrowing more than he could repay and declaring bankruptcy four times. Each bankruptcy created a financial crisis throughout Europe. Lenders disappeared, and expenses piled up until a renegotiation of Spain's debt was worked out. The crisis solved, lenders returned—until the next bankruptcy.

A Revolution in Prices

Around the middle of the sixteenth century, Europe experienced **inflation,** a sharp rise in prices for land, food, and other basic necessities that had major effects on Europeans' day-to-day lives. Several factors explain this **price revolution.** The New World silver flowing into Spain soon spread through Europe, since the Spanish government sent it out of the country in the form of coins to pay for the costs of warfare in Italy, the Netherlands, and elsewhere, which never seemed to stop. As silver coins became more and more common, the value of the metal in them declined, and their purchasing power diminished. To counteract the declining value of silver, people with things to sell raised their prices.

The continuing rise in Europe's population after 1450 also caused the price revolution. At first, population growth stimulated the economy and led to increased agricultural and commercial activity, which benefited many urban and rural workers. By the mid-sixteenth century, however, as population continued to grow, Europe was experiencing a crisis of overpopulation that put pressure on the ability of people to sustain themselves. For example, in agriculture, the growing population required that more and more land had to be cultivated. By about 1550, good land was running out, and cultivation moved to marginal, less productive land. This process is evident in the little French village of Langlade. Vineyards were converted into wheatfields, and hilly land, once thought too poor for cultivation, was cleared and planted with wheat. But these efforts were still not enough to meet the surge in population. The result was an inadequate food supply and a rise in food prices.

The rise in the price of food led, in turn, to two other developments: first, fierce competition for food-producing acreage caused land prices to rise sharply, and second, a glut of workers in need of jobs caused wages to decline. The impact of declining wages might have been offset if rural workers could have raised enough food for themselves on their own plots, but most could not because their landholdings were too

Manila galleon   Spanish sailing ship that carried Spanish silver from Mexico to exchange for Chinese silks and porcelains in the Philippine Islands.

Seville   Spain's largest city and government-mandated port for all goods going to or coming from the Spanish Empire.

Philip II   (r. 1556–1598) King of Spain, the most powerful ruler in late sixteenth-century Europe and leader of the Catholic crusade against Protestantism.

inflation   Process by which the cost of goods and services increases and the value of money declines.

price revolution   Rise in prices for land, food, and other basic necessities in mid-sixteenth-century Europe.

In this etching by Jacques Callot, a blind beggar stands with his begging cup and canine companion. His attitude is humble; with head bowed, he quietly waits for help from passersby. The man's blindness would qualify him as one of the "deserving poor." *(Callot, Jacques,* Beggar with Dog. *Rosenwald Collection, Image © 2007 Board of Trustees, National Gallery of Art, Washington, D.C., 1949.5.302)*

small. To make ends meet, peasants borrowed from local moneylenders. As collateral, they would put up their land or anything else they owned. If they defaulted on the loan, the lender would seize the collateral. So another problem was rising peasant debt. Over the hundred years from 1550 to 1650, rural communities were gradually polarized between a few rich peasants who managed to keep or increase their landholdings and a mass of poor small-scale landowners, landless wage laborers, and sharecroppers who paid rent for the land they farmed by sharing its produce with their landlord.

Urban workers also suffered from rising prices and declining wages brought on by overpopulation. Guild members in the textile industry, which employed thousands in cities across Europe, were particularly hard hit because they faced fierce competition from merchants who hired needy peasants to weave in their homes for low wages and to produce cloth that was not subject to guild regulations. The result was a growing gap between the urban rich and poor that strained relief agencies.

To make matters worse, Europe was experiencing a period of climate change known as the **Little Ice Age.** Winters were colder and longer than previously; glaciers in the Alps advanced to cover inhabited land; in England, the Thames froze over. Colder, wetter years damaged crops, causing food shortages. Epidemics increased. Declining standards of living, vulnerability to disease, and the growing polarization between rich and poor weakened both rural and urban communities' sense of solidarity and mutual responsibility. The needy protested and rioted more frequently, while the well-off became obsessed with maintaining order among the masses.

The Hunt for Witches

Local political leaders shared the concern for maintaining popular order. In addition to economic hard times and social unrest, they also faced religious turmoil and spiritual anxiety as Europe split permanently into hostile Protestant and Catholic camps. Religious uncertainty lay behind rising beliefs that the world was coming to an end and that the Devil's attempt to destroy good Christians was intensifying. These fears led in turn to a search for **scapegoats** who could be blamed for the troubled times.

For centuries, Europeans thought that some people possessed magical skills that allowed them to cast harmful or helpful spells. These so-called cunning men and women were consulted by people at all levels of society. Both Catholic and Protestant reformers considered them nuisances and tried to draw their followers away from their "superstitious" practices, usually with little effect. By the sixteenth century, however, a belief spread that these cunning folk were not just magicians, but Devil worshippers. As it did, authorities in many parts of Europe inaugurated a crusade against **witches.**

Little Ice Age Period of cooler weather in Europe beginning around the start of the fourteenth century.

scapegoats People blamed for other people's bad behavior or embodying their fears.

witches People, usually women, who were believed to have made a pact with the Devil, whom they worshiped.

Belief in witches was long standing, but it was only in this period that a sustained campaign against them was launched. After 1550, a stereotype of the witch emerged. Witches were said to be cunning folk who sold their souls to the Devil. In their obscene night rituals, called witches' Sabbaths, they sacrificed infants to Satan, engaged in cannibalism, and performed disgusting sexual acts. In a world where most people's lives were increasingly insecure, fear of bad magic skyrocketed, encouraging people to accuse their neighbors of satanic witchcraft. As many as 200,000 witchcraft trials were held all over Europe, most leading to convictions. The number of trials varied from place to place. Where lawyers and church officials had strict standards for accepting accusations or were skeptical of them, there were fewer trials. In England, for example, legal procedures prohibiting torture to procure confessions lowered the rates of self-incrimination. Rates were also low in Spain, where the Inquisition held that the Devil had no power to seduce people into witchcraft. The greatest number of trials—three-quarters of all known cases—occurred in the Holy Roman Empire, in areas where local officials, rather than state or church authorities, were in charge of the process. There, community leaders, clergymen, and other members of the local social elite, fearing social disorder and panicked by their belief in Satan's subversion of society, carried out wholesale prosecutions of people accused of witchcraft.

The vast majority of those accused were older women, most of whom were widowed or single and therefore lacked male protection. Some had served as midwives. Most were poor, but some controlled their own property. Those who were quarrelsome or sexually independent were seen as transgressors against prevailing patriarchal values. Women accused of witchcraft were, therefore, associated with dangerous activities, or seen as an economic burden to their communities, or envied for their material wealth, or despised as violators of the community's norms of behavior. Their trials often involved torture to get them to confess their activity and then more torture to force them to name accomplices. In cities, torture often produced a chain reaction of accusations. As the numbers of accused grew, the victims bore less and less resemblance to the stereotypical poor-woman witch: men, the rich, and children were named. On average, half of those convicted were executed, while the rest were imprisoned or subject to other forms of punishment.

Beginning in 1650, witch trials declined dramatically, as more and more centralized states took jurisdiction away from local authorities. Lawyers also worked to end persecutions. Although most lawyers still believed in witches, they also believed that legal standards for accusing and trying them had been too lax. Some people also believed in newly proposed scientific views of the world that questioned the Devil's active intervention in human affairs. Thus, a sense of fairness, along with doubts about Satan's power, won out over the fear of the Devil's subversion of society by means of witchcraft.

The Fate of Spain and the Flourishing of the Netherlands

⬇ What were Philip II's successes and failures?
⬇ What explains the success of the Dutch economy?

In 1550, Spain, with its silver and empire, was the most powerful state in Europe. Philip II dominated international affairs, making war on Muslims and attempting to eliminate Protestantism throughout his lands. Philip also sought to defend the western Mediterranean from the Ottomans while making war on his own Moriscos and laying the grounds for their expulsion from the Iberian Peninsula. His greatest failure came in the Netherlands, where his attempt to crush Protestantism provoked a rebellion during which the northern provinces declared their independence. These provinces, now organized as the Dutch Republic, soon dominated the European economy.

Philip II

In 1556, Philip II succeeded his father, Charles V, as head of the **Habsburg** dynasty. Despite Charles's grant of the Holy Roman emperorship to his younger brother, Ferdinand I, Philip ruled over a vast assembly of territories: Castile, Aragon, and Granada in Spain; the Netherlands; Franche-Comté on the Rhine; Naples, Sicily, and Milan on the Italian peninsula; Spanish America; and the Philippine Islands (named after him) in East Asia. His global empire was the wonder of the world, and he was the most powerful ruler of his age.

Philip used marriage to increase his political power. His short-lived first wife, Mary of Portugal, allied him with the other great imperial power of his time, while his second wife, Mary Tudor of England,

Habsburgs   Dynastic family originating in Austria that provided many rulers there and in the Netherlands, Spain, and the Holy Roman Empire.

This portrait of Philip II by Sanchez Coello (1583) shows the king in the somber dress favored at the Spanish court. His commitment to Roman Catholicism is symbolized by the rosary he holds. Contrast this style of royal portrait with the one of his father, Charles V, in Chapter 13. *(Museo del Prado, Madrid)*

offered an English and Catholic alliance. When this Mary died childless in 1558 and was succeeded by her Protestant half sister, Elizabeth I, Philip wed Elizabeth Valois of France to cement relations with that kingdom. On her death, he married a cousin, Ann of Austria, who bore him his son and heir, Philip III.

By the time Philip became king, Protestantism was challenging the Catholic Church throughout central and northern Europe, and Philip undertook its defense, using both military and diplomatic means. He also continued Christian Spain's attack on the Muslim world, now dominated in the west by the **Ottoman Turks.** In Spain, he adopted the title of His Most Catholic Majesty and supported Teresa of Ávila's reform of the Carmelites while collecting manuscripts of her religious writings for his library. He also built a residence, just outside Madrid, the new Spanish capital. Called the **Escorial,** it housed both the royal palace and a monastery where Philip frequently

prayed and meditated with the monks. His most important advisers were the priests who heard his confessions and the theologians he kept at his side.

In appearance, Philip hardly looked like the self-appointed leader of the Catholic world. Short and soft-spoken, he presided over a somber court and rarely left the area around Madrid, since he thought that "traveling about one's kingdom is neither useful nor decent." In this he unwisely rejected the policy of his predecessors, whose frequent travels throughout their lands kept them in touch with their subjects. Cautious by nature, he kept tight personal control over government, making every important policy decision and spending hours alone in his office pouring over the mountains of memoranda that had to be prepared for his approval. Before his death, Charles V had urged Philip to fight heresy and to hold onto the lands God had given him. Philip followed this advice. The money he amassed through taxes and borrowing was spent in pursuit of these aims.

The Spanish War Against Islam

In the early sixteenth century, the Ottoman Turks continued to push into Christian territory. Hungary fell in 1521, and in 1529 a Turkish army laid siege, unsuccessfully, to Vienna. When the Ottomans conquered Christian peoples in the Balkans, they organized them as a **millet,** or non-Muslim subject people. Millet Christians had to pay special taxes and accept that some of their boys would be recruited into the army as **janissaries.** But they were allowed to practice their religion, and conversion to Islam was discouraged because the taxes Christians paid were an important source of state revenue. Nevertheless, many Christians did convert to improve their position in society. The Christian millet was dominated by Greeks in Constantinople, headed by the Orthodox patriarch there. Jews under the Ottomans were not organized into a millet but were encouraged to immigrate to Turkish lands when western Christian states expelled them.

Ottoman Turks   Muslims who captured Constantinople in 1453, ending the Byzantine Empire and founding the Ottoman Empire.

Escorial   Philip II's palace and monastery complex outside of Madrid.

millet   Legally defined community for non-Muslims living within the Ottoman Empire.

janissaries   Ottoman infantry composed mainly of Christian boys either captured or given in tribute to the sultan to be raised as Muslim soldiers.

The Turks also established contact with the **Moriscos.** Following Ferdinand and Isabella's conquest of Granada in 1492, its Muslim population, now called Moriscos, had been forced to convert to Christianity. Then Christians seized their lands and sought to stamp out their culture along with their religion. Speaking Arabic and bathing on Fridays, along with traditional dancing and eating couscous, were forbidden as signs of heresy. Faced with this repression, the Moriscos rose up in 1569. The revolt lasted two years and involved thirty thousand rebels joined by four thousand Turks and North Africans. Each side outdid the other in cruelty, since each believed that its enemy was God's enemy. The revolt was put down in 1571, but hatred remained on both sides. Finally, in 1609, Philip's son, Philip III, ordered all three hundred thousand Moriscos expelled from Spain. Many went to North Africa, while some went to northern Greece and Constantinople. The expulsion of the Moriscos was the last step in the dismantling of the cultural and religious diversity that had characterized medieval Spain. Some Spaniards hailed the expulsion as a purification of the land, but others, like the great novelist **Miguel de Cervantes** condemned it. In *Don Quixote,* Ricote, an expelled Morisco, laments, "Wherever we are, we weep for Spain, because we were born there and it is our native land."

In 1571, the last year of the Morisco revolt, Philip destroyed the Turkish navy at **Lepanto** off the coast of Greece; 195 ships in the Turkish fleet of 230 were captured or sunk, thirty thousand Turks were killed or wounded, and three thousand were taken prisoner. Although the Turks assembled another fleet in 1572 and continued to harass the coasts of Italy and Sicily, their dominance of the Mediterranean had been weakened. Then, in 1580, Philip became ruler of Portugal and its empire when the Portuguese king disappeared on a crusade in Morocco against the Muslims. Philip was now at the height of his power.

The Revolt in the Netherlands

Even as Spanish might awed Europe, Protestant forces in England and the Netherlands were rising to challenge it. Protestantism had not spread to Spain, but it had to the Netherlands, the Habsburgs' richest territory. Charles V had tried without success to eliminate it there, and Philip tried as well, with even worse results. Philip viewed his Protestant subjects as damnable heretics, but at first he recognized that their growing numbers required a political solution. Therefore, in 1566, on the advice of his court theologians, he granted religious **toleration** to the Protestants. Shortly thereafter, militant Calvinists went on a rampage across the country, destroying Catholic churches and religious images. Philip now decided on a military solution.

In 1567, a Spanish army marched north to subdue the Protestants. Its commander, the duke of Alba, then tried and executed more than a thousand people. To pay for his army, Alba also imposed a tax on the Netherlanders. Both Protestants and Catholics condemned it and rebelled when it was not withdrawn. Then, in 1572, Calvinist exiles in England returned home and joined the rebellion, seizing the country's northern provinces and electing **William of Orange** as their leader. The general rebellion in the Netherlands forced Philip to recall Alba in 1573.

In 1575, Philip declared a bankruptcy that delayed pay for his troops in the Netherlands. In response, his army mutinied and sacked Antwerp, destroying property and leaving eight thousand dead. This "Spanish Fury" signaled the end of Antwerp as Europe's leading commercial hub. Finally, in 1579, Philip's new military governor was able to consolidate Spain's rule in the southern provinces, thereafter known as the Spanish Netherlands. But the northern provinces were lost when rebels there forced the Spanish army to retreat by opening the dikes that kept the sea out, flooding large parts of the country. Having declared their independence from Spain, the northern provinces reconstituted themselves as the **United Provinces,** or **Dutch Republic.**

Queen Elizabeth I of England had aided the Dutch Protestants, and Philip decided to attack her. In 1588, he sent the **Spanish Armada**—130 ships and thirty thousand men—to join with his loyal forces in the Spanish Netherlands and then conquer the island kingdom. The Spanish met a slightly larger and much faster English fleet in the English Channel, where

Moriscos   Muslims in Spain who were forced to convert to Christianity or leave.

Miguel de Cervantes   (1547–1616) Spanish writer and critic of Philip II who wrote *Don Quixote.*

Lepanto   Naval battle won by Spain over the Ottomans in October 1571.

toleration   Recognition of the right to hold dissenting beliefs.

William of Orange   (1533–1584) Calvinist nobleman, also known as William the Silent, who led the Protestant rebellion against the Spanish in the Netherlands.

United Provinces/Dutch Republic   Northern Netherlands provinces that successfully threw off Spanish rule.

Spanish Armada   Unsuccessful armed fleet sent by Philip II in 1588 to conquer England.

MAP 15.1 **The Netherlands** When the Twelve Years' Truce was signed in 1609, the seven northern provinces of the Netherlands , along with parts of the Duchy of Brabant and the County of Flanders, were put under Dutch control. Spain continued to control the remaining southern provinces.

stormy weather and superior English cannon fire broke up the Armada. Only half the Spanish ships returned to their ports. The defeat was the beginning of Spain's decline. The failure to stamp out Protestantism in the Netherlands, followed by the loss of the northern provinces, was a bitter blow to Philip, who grieved that he had betrayed his father's trust.

The Dutch Miracle

It would take decades for Spain to acknowledge Dutch independence, but from the 1590s on, the breakaway provinces were free from serious invasion. Distracted by other wars, Spain was never able to conquer the north. Finally, in 1609, the Spanish signed the Twelve Years' Truce with the rebels. The Dutch Republic was founded by Calvinists who sought to reform church and state. But William of Orange and his successors feared that the rebellion's success would be jeopardized if the Catholics of the north, who made up a third of the population, were alienated. So a policy of partial toleration was instituted. Calvinism was recognized as the state religion, but the church was not allowed to control state policy. Although Catholics were forbidden to worship publicly, they were allowed unofficially to open private chapels. Anabaptists, Lutherans, and Jews also had their places of worship. None of these communities really welcomed the others; each tended to mix socially and marry only with its own kind. But a grudging live-and-let-live attitude prevailed in the country that was far different from the atmosphere in Philip II's Spain.

Although Calvinist church members were a minority of the Dutch population, Calvinist values were widely shared. Chief among them was the idea of the **calling.** Calvin had rejected Catholic practices such as renouncing the sinful world by joining religious orders or giving one's wealth to the church or the poor. Like Luther, he believed these acts were useless for salvation. Instead, he urged people to treat their ordinary work as a divine calling through which they could serve God with diligence and to avoid sinful idleness, luxury, and waste. When giving this advice, Calvin did not have a particular economic agenda in mind, but his ideal of a sober and serious attitude toward one's calling in the world encouraged attentive, thrifty behavior among the merchants, manufacturers, and artisans who heeded it. This attitude was one of the factors behind the Dutch economic miracle of the late sixteenth century.

The revolt against Spain hurt the economy of the southern Netherlands and hastened the decline of Antwerp. But while the economy faltered in the south, it boomed in the north. Unlike most of Europe, which experienced hard times after 1550, the Dutch Republic flourished. As both population and workers' wages rose, the Dutch economy became the wonder of the age. Its success rested on an adequate grain supply from Poland that prevented the food shortages plaguing other parts of Europe. With this staple assured, Dutch farmers were free to specialize in other foodstuffs: butter, cheese, hops for beer, and livestock for meat. In addition, the North Sea provided catches of nutritious herring. Half the labor force was engaged in agriculture, the rest in a variety of industries. There was a need for labor, and workers' wages rose as a consequence. Men worked on large reclamation projects as coastal land was pumped dry with windmills

calling Calvinist belief that ordinary work was a means for serving God.

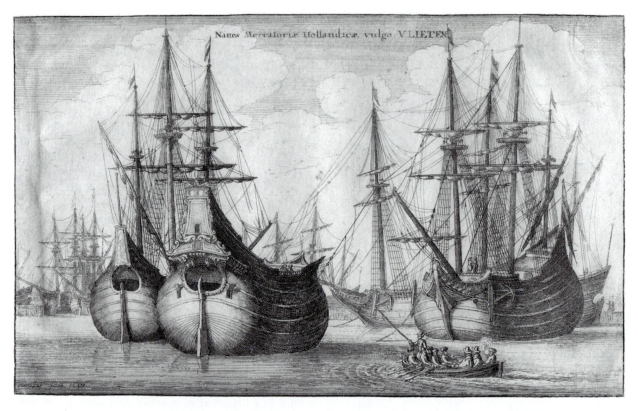

This engraving from 1647 shows fluteships in a Dutch harbor. The fluteship's deck is narrower than the bulging hull below it, which will be filled with the goods shipped in what the Dutch called the "mother trade" between Dutch ports and Baltic ports in the east. *(Courtesy, Stichting Atlas van Stolk [Historisch Museum Het Schielandhuis, The Netherlands])*

for agricultural use. Dutch cities grew and with them a demand for servants, carpenters, masons, and other urban workers. High literacy rates and lax censorship created a demand for books, news sheets, and pamphlets offering a wide range of opinions on often-controversial subjects like religion. These, in turn, called for printers and engravers. Shipyards employed others, while the ships they built needed crews. In fact, ships and shipping did the most to stimulate the economy.

After 1550, the Dutch became the best shipbuilders in Europe. They also created an international trading network and used their ships to move their goods. The success of Dutch shipbuilding and trade rested on the **fluteship,** a large-hulled boat with a shallow draft. Fluteships carried salt, herring, and cloth east to Poland and other Baltic ports and brought back grain and timber. Some of the imports were used locally, while the rest were sold abroad. Interestingly, Spain was one of the Dutch Republic's best customers. Although at war with the rebels for much of the time, Spain could not do without Dutch-shipped timber for its navy and grain for its food-hungry territories in Italy. So the Spanish swallowed their principles and traded.

The Dutch also entered the East Asian trade. In 1602, the government licensed the United East India Company to set up trading posts from Persia to Japan. Because Portugal was ruled by Spain after 1580, the Dutch aimed to reduce Spanish power by supplanting Portuguese traders in Asia. After the Portuguese were driven out, the company dominated the spice trade with Europe. It also dominated the inter-Asian trade, picking up cotton cloth in India and trading it elsewhere for goods like porcelain and silk that were then sold in Europe. After the Japanese government began persecuting Japanese Christian converts and shut off contact with the outside world, the Dutch

fluteship Merchant ship with an enlarged cargo hold and shallow draft used in Dutch trade with eastern Europe.

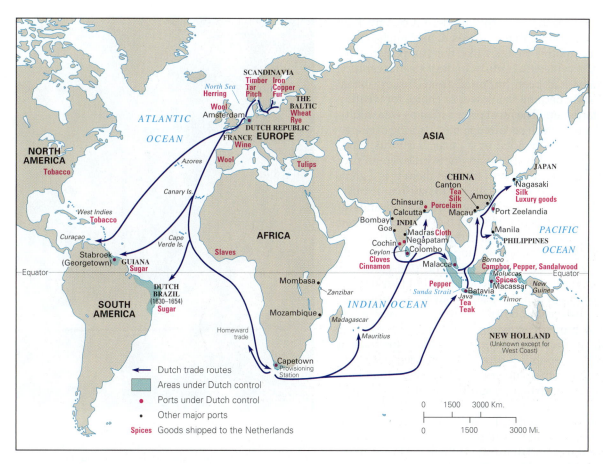

MAP 15.2 **Dutch Commerce in the Seventeenth Century** By the seventeenth century the Dutch had developed a complex global trading network. They took over Europe's East Asia trade from the Portuguese, dominated the European seaborne trade routes, traded with their New World colonies, and became the major trading partner with the Portuguese in Brazil.

alone were allowed a trading post there. In 1621, the Dutch government also chartered the Dutch West India Company, which set up posts in Curaçao on the Caribbean and Surinam on the South American coast. Soon the Dutch were trading with Brazil, exporting European goods to the colony and importing African slaves in return for sugar. Dutch settlers also founded the colony of New Amsterdam on Manhattan Island at the mouth of the Hudson River.

Dutch Civilization

Science flourished in the Dutch Republic, where scientific experimenters tried to develop practical devices that would aid people in their worldly callings. The Dutch scientist **Anton van Leeuwenhoek,** who perfected the magnifying lenses of the microscope, was the first to describe the world of microorganisms, drawing the protozoa he found in rainwater, the bac-

teria in the human mouth, and spermatozoa. As one scientist put it, the microscope opened a world "in which you will find wonder heaped upon wonder, and will be amazed at the Wisdom of God manifest in a most minute matter."

The hub of Dutch life was **Amsterdam** in the province of Holland. By the early seventeenth century, Amsterdam had replaced Antwerp as Europe's chief commercial and banking center. Because the republic's commercial activity spread across Europe and the world, involving people in complex, long-distance economic activity, the Dutch can be seen as

Anton van Leeuwenhoek   (1632–1723) Dutch scientist who perfected the microscope to see and describe the world of microorganisms.

Amsterdam   Capital of the Dutch province of Holland and commercial center of the Dutch Republic.

the creators of the first truly modern economy. Like modern economies that followed it, the Dutch experienced speculative frenzies like the "tulip mania" of the early seventeenth century. In the sixteenth century, tulip bulbs had been imported from Turkey, where they quickly became the flower of choice for wealthy Dutch gardeners. The most prized blooms were multicolored ones, which occurred in the offspring of single-colored bulbs if invaded by a particular virus. Since no one knew in advance if any new bulb would produce multicolored flowers, trade in them was a gamble. In the mid-1630s, a speculative frenzy in tulip bulbs swept across the United Provinces as thousands of people bought lots of bulbs that had not yet flowered in hopes of selling them at a profit to eager buyers. Thousands were risked in hopes of hitting on the most prized blooms. Then, suddenly, the craze collapsed, and those unlucky enough to hold unsold lots of bulbs suffered huge losses. But the complicated trade in these commodity "futures" was to be a feature of all modern economies.

More lasting was the rise in Dutch purchasing power. The republic's prosperity allowed people to spend more of their income on things other than food and shelter. In particular, middle-class Dutch families spent disposable income on furnishing their homes; Chinese porcelains and Turkish carpets became standard decorative items. But no item was more popular than paintings, and demand for them led to a remarkable flowering of Dutch art in the seventeenth century. Since Calvinists refused to decorate their churches with images of Christ and the saints, considering them idolatrous, the home became the setting for works of art. The paintings of **Jan Vermeer,** small in size, were made for household walls; they often depict household scenes that radiate with light and domestic peacefulness. More versatile was **Rembrandt van Rijn,** an artistic whirlwind who painted, drew, and etched throughout his long career. Rembrandt painted the great merchants of his generation along with ordinary people while also undertaking commissions for paintings of town councils and other public bodies that hung them in guild offices and town halls. He also painted religious scenes for purchasers who were less reluctant than the Calvinists to accept sacred art. In all his work, he was a master in depicting the contrasts of shade and light.

The art that hung in people's homes often drew its themes from domestic life, but it was never simply a reproduction of that life. It was also filled with symbols and associations that pointed to the complexity of Dutch civilization in its "Golden Age." Take, for instance, the Flemish artist Clara Peeters' 24 by 19.5

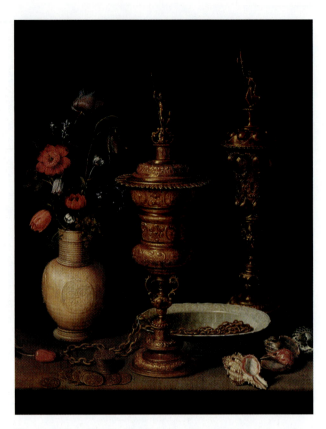

Women artists like the Flemish Clara Peeters were unusual. Peeters painted her tiny reflection on the goblet to the right. Dutch trade and wealth, the shortness of life and the certainty of death, the wonders of creation, and the wonders of little things—all are conjured up in her painting. *(Staatliche Kunsthalle Karlsruhe)*

inch *Still Life with Golden Goblets and Collectibles* (1612), This small picture is remarkable for the precision with which even the smallest details are painted, calling to mind the wondrous world that van Leeuwenhoek revealed. The bouquet contains a tulip and resonates with the tulip mania that would sweep over the Dutch Republic in 1637, as well as the beauty of God's creation and the fragility of life, for the flowers' petals will soon drop and dry up. The coins and the Chinese bowl point to Dutch commercial activity and reach, as do the shells, for they come from the

Jan Vermeer (ca.1632—1675) Dutch painter of peaceful household scenes that radiate with light.

Rembrandt van Rijn (1606–1669) Greatest Dutch painter of the seventeenth century; also a skilled printmaker.

François Dubois' painting of the Saint Bartholomew's Day Massacre, August 24, 1572, graphically depicts the chaos of this event. Note the killings, the corpses, the raised swords and clubs, the blood on the ground, and the men on horseback. The barking dog, at center left, seems to give voice to the violence. *(Musée Cantonal des Beaux-Arts de Lausanne, Switzerland/The Art Archive)*

non-European waters into which the Dutch sailed. And, like the flower, the shells call to mind the beauty of creation.

Political Contests and More Religious Wars

↓ What explains the violence of Europe's political contests and religious wars?

↓ What were the outcomes of the wars?

In 1562, France was plunged into religious warfare between Catholics and Protestants that lasted for nearly seventy years. In the end, the Protestants were granted limited religious toleration, but their attempts to create their own semi-independent political communities within France failed. The Holy Roman Empire also experienced a religious war. The German war lasted fewer years than the war in France, but it brought non-German states into the fighting, and its destruction was far greater. The peace settlement ending the war granted religious toleration to Calvinists, Lutherans, and Catholics and reduced the emperor's power. Like the French, the Germans had to learn to live with a new religious pluralism. The conflict also accelerated Spain's decline and France's rise as the most powerful state in Europe.

France's Wars of Religion

When Henry II died in 1559, he left his fourteen-year-old son Francis II to succeed him. In the confusion following Henry's death, the powerful **Guise family,** utterly committed to the extermination of Protestantism, seized control of the government. For the next thirty years, as three of Henry's young sons ruled France in succession, plots and fighting broke out between the Catholic Guises and the Protestant Huguenots. In 1572, a Catholic attack on the Huguenots that began in Paris on Saint Bartholomew's Day—thus known as the **Saint Bartholomew's Day Massacre**—spread to the provinces. Some five thousand people died as violence reached extraordinary levels—heads, hands, and genitals were cut off; pregnant women were stabbed in the stomach; and bodies were burned. The massacres put an end to the growth of Protestantism in France. The brutality of religious conflict demonstrated that both sides believed a fundamental issue was at stake—the belief that all members of a community had to share a common religious commitment for the community to function properly. In early modern Europe, religion was more a matter of community solidarity than of individual belief. Therefore, all religious dissent had to be stamped out to restore communal unity and win God's favor, especially since the Second Coming and Last Judgment were believed to be near at hand. Thus, Huguenots and Catholics saw each other not simply as different, but as dangerous polluters of the community. Killing as a rite of purification was not enough; the very bodies of the enemy had to be degraded.

In 1589, the last of Henry II's sons, Henry III, died, assassinated by a fanatical Catholic monk. Since Henry III had no children, the Crown passed to a cousin, **Henry IV of Navarre,** a Huguenot. Henry was eager to end the fighting, but he faced a dilemma. The law of royal succession made him king, but his coronation oath would require him to attack non-Catholic heretics. In 1593, Henry resolved the issue by converting to Catholicism, supposedly saying that "Paris is well worth a Mass." In 1595, when the pope absolved Henry of his Huguenot errors, Henry was able to win over all but the die-hard Catholics. He reassured the Huguenots by issuing the **Edict of Nantes,** granting official toleration, in 1598. This edict brought an uneasy religious peace to France, but at a high price to community unity. The Huguenots were permitted to worship undisturbed, and they were also granted some two hundred fortified towns, along with troops to defend them. These towns were effectively independent from royal control and became a Huguenot state within the state. To rally support for the edict, Henry showered powerful Catholic and Huguenot nobles with high government positions and large pensions. He also insisted that the king, who was the source of all law and order, should be obeyed regardless of his religion. Henry's emphasis on the importance of law and order vested in the king's authority became one of the basic principles of **absolutism,** which guided French kings' rule for the next two centuries.

The Resurgent French Monarchy

At the grass-roots level, Henry IV built on an expansion of government begun by his predecessors, who had sold administrative offices to middle-class lawyers and then forced them to loan the government money. This strategy raised additional revenue and built loyalty, as the new officeholders had a compelling reason to see that the monarchy remained strong. Henry IV used this expanded administrative force to consolidate royal power and initiated tax reform to erase the royal debt and build up a treasury surplus.

Henry's chief minister, the Huguenot duke of Sully, lowered direct taxes while raising indirect ones. Since the direct tax of the *taille* took one large bite out of incomes while indirect taxes on commodities nibbled slowly away at them, the pain of taxation was obscured. Most important, Sully imposed the annual *paulette* tax on all officials who had bought their offices. Because their numbers were now so large, *paulette* payments raised revenues that eventually rivaled the *taille* as the chief source of royal income.

Although Henry IV won many Huguenots and Catholics over to his policies of religious toleration and administrative consolidation, in 1610 he was stabbed to death by a deranged ex-monk obsessed with the

Guise family Powerful Catholic nobility committed to eliminating Protestantism in France during the French religious wars of 1559–1588.

Saint Bartholomew's Day Massacre 1572 Catholic massacre of Protestants in Paris and throughout France that ended the growth of Protestantism in the kingdom.

Henry IV of Navarre (r. 1589–1610) Protestant king of Navarre who became king of France, converted to Catholicism, and started to end the religious wars.

Edict of Nantes Decree issued by Henry IV in 1598 that allowed the Huguenots to practice their religion and gave them two hundred fortified towns,

absolutism Doctrine that a king was the sole source of all law in his realm.

continuing presence of heretics in the kingdom. Henry's heir was his nine-year-old son, **Louis XIII,** who, once king in his own right, resumed war against the Huguenots. In 1629, he issued the **Peace of Alès,** which dismantled the Huguenots' fortified towns and ended France's Wars of Religion. But the religious toleration granted the Huguenots in 1598 was reaffirmed.

The Habsburg War Against Islam

Charles V had put his younger brother Ferdinand in charge of the Holy Roman Empire before his abdication in 1556. Thirty years earlier, Ferdinand had also been elected king of Hungary and Bohemia after the previous king died fighting the Ottoman Turks. While Ferdinand had full control of Austria and Bohemia, the Turks conquered most of Hungary, leaving only the northern part in Habsburg hands. Even that was threatened when the Turks, marching up the Danube River, tried in 1529 and again in 1532 to seize all of Hungary and the city of Vienna in Austria. For Ferdinand, a devout Catholic, the Turks posed a greater threat than the Protestants.

Thus, during Ferdinand's reign, and that of his son Maximilian II (r. 1564–1576), various kinds of Protestants increased their followings in all Habsburg lands. Lutherans predominated in Austria, while Lutherans and Calvinists flourished in Bohemia, and Calvinists and **Unitarians** gained converts in Habsburg Hungary. "In affairs of religion everyone does as he pleases," one Catholic complained. After Maximilian died in 1576, effective Habsburg rule declined, as a contest between his two sons encouraged the great nobles who controlled the representative assemblies, or **diets,** to seek increased political independence. Their model for good government was **Poland-Lithuania,** where the nobility elected the king and had the right to rebel against him if he violated his coronation oath. In the Polish Diet, each noble had the right to veto a measure and thus "explode" the diet. They were also free to govern their serfs without royal interference and to choose between Catholicism and some form of Protestantism. When new war with the Turks broke out in 1593, the nobility in the Habsburg lands demanded more religious freedom and greater local control of government in return for funds for the war.

The Thirty Years' War

As Protestantism grew in Habsburg lands, the Catholics launched a counteroffensive. As early as the 1590s, Jesuits from Italy rallied Catholic communities, which soon established a militant anti-Protestant movement. Catholics found their leader in the new emperor, **Ferdinand II,** a fervent Catholic who prayed privately every morning for an hour before dressing and attended two morning Masses, during which he frequently knelt to kiss the ground five times in honor of Christ's five wounds on the cross. His determination to put an end to Protestantism launched the **Thirty Years' War,** the most devastating conflict of the seventeenth century. At first confined to Bohemia, it soon engulfed the Holy Roman Empire and drew in many European states as it went through Bohemian, Danish, Swedish, and French phases.

In 1617, after he was elected king of Bohemia, Ferdinand II ordered Protestant churches closed in two Bohemian towns. Enraged Protestants confronted two of Ferdinand's officials in Prague, the capital of the kingdom, and threw them out of an upper-story window. Surprisingly, they survived. Catholics claimed they had been wafted gently to earth on angels' wings, while Protestants protested that a pile of dung had broken their fall. This "defenestration of Prague" prompted a Bohemian rebellion, which Ferdinand subdued with help from the Spanish Habsburgs. Ferdinand seized rebel lands and gave them to Habsburg supporters. Believing that religious dissent polluted society and offended God, he banned Protestant worship, ordering Protestants to convert or leave. In 1627, a subdued Bohemian Diet declared that the Crown was no longer elective, but rather hereditary in the Habsburg family. The abolition of elective monarchy marked the high point in Ferdinand's reconquest of Bohemia.

Louis XIII   (r. 1610–1643) King of France who made war on the Huguenots and took France into the Thirty Years' War to weaken France's political rival, Spain.

Peace of Alès   Treaty in 1629 that ended France's religious wars, allowed Huguenots freedom of worship, but took away their fortified towns.

Unitarians   Christians who denied the traditional doctrine of the Trinity.

diets   In the Holy Roman Empire under Habsburg rule, representative assemblies dominated by the great nobility that sought increased control of government.

Poland-Lithuania   Kingdom formed in 1569 from two previously independent states; included modern Poland, the Baltic states, Belarus, and most of Ukraine.

Ferdinand II   (r. 1619–1637) Habsburg emperor who reestablished Catholicism in Bohemia and Austria but failed to do so in the empire as a whole.

Thirty Years' War   General war, 1618–1648, between German Protestant princes and their foreign allies against the Habsburgs, who were allied with Catholic princes.

A la fin ces Voleurs infames et perdus ,
Comme fruits malheureux a cet arbre pendus

Monstrent bien que le crime (horrible et noire engeance)
Est luy mesme instrument de honte et de vengeance ,

Et que cest le Destin des hommes vicieux
Desprouuer tost ou tard la iustice des Cieux . 2]

Thieving soldiers are executed in this etching from Jacques Callot's *Miseries of War.* A priest blesses the men as they are led up a ladder to be hung. A caption describes the executed as "infamous lost souls . . . hung like unhappy fruit." *(Erich Lessing/Art Resource, NY)*

The Habsburg victory in Bohemia had repercussions throughout Europe. The Spanish branch of the family used it to seize the Palatinate, a state on the Rhine River, and thereby expand its control of the "Spanish Road" that led north from Habsburg, Italy, to the Spanish Netherlands. Soon the king of Denmark entered the war as leader of the Protestants. But he was defeated and driven out of the empire in 1629. Victorious, Ferdinand II supposedly reaffirmed the 1555 Peace of Augsburg but in reality sought to strengthen Catholicism, not only in Habsburg lands but throughout the Empire. At this point, the Swedish phase of the war began, when the Lutheran king of Sweden, **Gustavus II Adolphus,** assumed leadership of the Protestant cause.

Gustavus Adolphus was a seasoned warrior, having already fought the Danes, the Russians, and the Poles. His chief concern was to expand Swedish power in the Baltic, as he feared that a Catholic Habsburg victory in Germany would threaten his interests. But his death in battle in 1632 spread confusion. When Ferdinand, realizing he would never be able to eradicate Protestantism, offered toleration for Lutherans, the war entered its French phase.

Although Louis XIII and his chief minister, **Cardinal Richelieu,** were devout Catholics, they feared that Ferdinand's reconciliation with the Protestants would increase the power of France's long-standing Habsburg enemy. They, therefore, entered the war, and for the next eleven years, French and Swedish

troops continued to fight the Habsburgs. Almost all the fighting was done on German soil, and the devastation was terrible. The Thirty Years' War made the region's economic decline immeasurably worse. Overall, the population of the empire fell between 15 and 20 percent as the warring armies disrupted agriculture, sacked villages and cities, and spread disease among the civilian population. In areas of the worst fighting, such as Bohemia and the southern Baltic coast, population declined by 50 percent as people died or fled. Cities fell into debt because of the huge bribes they paid the warring armies, whether friend or foe, in hopes of averting pillaging by the troops.

The Peace of Westphalia

The war finally came to an end in 1648 with the **Peace of Westphalia.** It amended the 1555 Peace of Augsburg to allow rulers to choose Catholicism, Calvinism, or

Gustavus II Adolphus (r. 1594–1632) King of Sweden who led Protestant forces against the Habsburgs until his death in battle in 1632.

Cardinal Richelieu (1585–1642) Louis XIII's chief minister, who persuaded Louis to enter the Thirty Years' War against Ferdinand II.

Peace of Westphalia Peace in 1648 ending the Thirty Years' War, allowing states in the Holy Roman Empire to establish their own foreign policies and state religion.

Voice

Simplicius Simplicissimus Encounters Some "Merry Cavalrymen"

Jacques Callot was not alone in commenting on seventeenth-century warfare. In 1669, a German innkeeper, Johann von Grimmelshausen, who had fought as a soldier in the Thirty Years' War, published Simplicius Simplicissimus *(Simplest of Simpletons), a tale that mixes humor and horror in equal measure. It went through three editions in 1669 alone. In the excerpt that follows, young Simplicius/ The Simpleton, while working as a shepherd for his father, meets a band of caval-rymen and accompanies them to his home. Here he tells us what happened next.*

➡ **Why does the author use these remarks to set up what follows?**

➡ **What effect in the reader does the author try to create when he mixes his account of pillaging with humor?**

➡ **Why does Grimmelshausen order the details of the pil-laging in the way he does?**

➡ **What is the point of this sentence?**

➡ **Thinking back on this account, why would Grim-melshausen describe the destruction of a clearly pros-perous, well-supplied peasant household?**

➡ Though I hadn't intended to take the peace-loving reader into my father's home and farm along with these merry cavalrymen, the orderly progress of my tale requires me to make known to posterity the sort of abysmal and unheard-of cruelties occasionally perpetrated in our German war, and to testify by my own example that all these evils were necessarily required for our own good by the kindness of our Lord. For, my dear reader, who would have told me that there is a God in heaven if the warriors hadn't destroyed my [father's] house. . . .

➡ The first thing these horsemen did in the nice black rooms of the house was to put in their horses. Then everyone took up a special job, a job having to do with death and destruction. Although some began butchering, heating water, and render-ing lard, as if to prepare for a banquet, others raced through the house, ransacking upstairs and down. . . . Still others bundled up big bags of cloth, household goods, and clothes, as if they wanted to hold a rummage sale somewhere. What they did not intend to take along they broke up and spoiled. Some ran their swords into the hay and straw, as if there hadn't been hogs enough to stick. . . . Some shook the feathers out of beds and put bacon slabs, hams, and other stuff in the ticking, as if they might sleep better on these. ➡ They flattened out copper and pewter dishes and baled the ruined goods. They burned up bedsteads, tables, chairs, and benches, though there were yards and yards of dry firewood outside the kitchen. Jars and crocks, pots and casseroles, all were broken, either because they preferred their meat broiled or because they thought they'd eat only one meal with us. In the barn, the hired girl was handled so roughly that she was unable to walk away, I am ashamed to report. They stretched the hired man out flat on the ground, stuck a wooden wedge in his mouth to keep it open, and emptied a milk bucket full of stinking manure drippings down his throat; they called it a Swedish cocktail. He didn't relish it and made a very wry face. By this means they forced him to take a raiding party to some other place where they carried off men and cattle and brought them to our farm. . . . I can't say much about the captured wives, hired girls, and daughters be-cause the soldiers wouldn't let me watch their doings. But I do remember hearing pitiful screams from various dark corners and I guess that my mother and our Ursula had it no better than the rest. ➡ Amid all this horror I was busy turning a roasting split and didn't worry about anything, for I didn't know the meaning of it. ➡ In the afternoon I helped water the horses and that way got to see our hired girl in the barn. She looked wondrously messed up and at first I didn't recognize her. In a sickly voice she said, "Boy, get out of this place, or the soldiers will take you with them."

Source: The Adventures of Simplicius Simplicissimus by Hans Jacob Christoffel van Grimmelshausen. A modern translation with an introduction by George Schultz-Behrend, second revised edition. Rochester, New York: Camden House, 1993. Reprinted with permission.

Lutheranism as their state religion. Thus, Ferdinand II's dream of reestablishing Catholic dominance in the empire died forever. Like the Peace of Alès in France almost twenty years earlier, the Peace of Westphalia ratified a grudging recognition that the state's religious unity had been shattered and that new ways of forming community and community identity would have to be found.

Important political changes also occurred. The empire's boundaries were altered: the Swiss Confederation and the Dutch Republic were now placed outside the empire and recognized as independent states. Within the empire, states were granted the right to develop their own foreign policies without the emperor's approval. Both France and Sweden took imperial territory. Sweden gained control of the southern Baltic shore, while France received three important bishoprics on its eastern frontier.

Although France ended its war in Germany in 1648, war against the Habsburgs continued, with fighting between France and Spain along the borders of the Spanish Netherlands and the Pyrenees Mountains. In 1659, the two countries signed the **Treaty of the Pyrenees.** France extended its rule along the eastern Pyrenees and took important cities in the Spanish Netherlands. To celebrate the peace, the king of Spain agreed to the marriage of his eldest daughter, Anne, to the young king of France, Louis XIV, who had succeeded Louis XIII in 1643. Spain, exhausted by decades of warfare, never regained the position it held under Philip II. France was now the most powerful state in Europe.

Europeans were to fight many more wars after the Treaty of Westphalia, but religious motivations for conflict were never again as strong as they had been in the century before 1648. Now, states formed diplomatic and military alliances to advance their political and economic agendas while curbing those of their rivals, thereby creating an unstable and ever-shifting **balance of power** that prevented any one state from overwhelming the others.

Reformation and Revolution in the British Isles

↓ How did the expectations of the English people change, or remain the same, from 1558 to 1660?

↓ What were the relations among the English, Scots, and Irish in this period?

England experienced a golden age during the reign of Elizabeth I, the last Tudor monarch. But during the seventeenth century, the British Isles experienced religious wars when different Protestant groups fought to control state churches. Like their counterparts on the continent, Protestant Scots and English believed that their communities should be united by a single church. Gradually, however, a party formed that called for toleration of different forms of Protestantism, but not of Catholicism. In Ireland, where Catholics predominated, English and Scots prejudice led to a brutal conquest of the island that established Protestant control. Conflict over religion also involved a struggle between the English monarch and Parliament for control of policy, which led to revolution in England, the execution of the king, and the establishment of a republic. In 1660, the republic came to an end and the monarchy was restored.

Elizabeth I

Elizabeth I was one of England's ablest and most popular rulers. At five feet ten inches, she was exceptionally tall for her time, and her flaming red hair, along with her trim, athletic body, caught everyone's attention. Elizabeth was a shrewd ruler who played on her womanhood, challenging contemporary views about women's weakness with her own force of will and political skill while instilling fear in anyone who challenged her. She was exceptionally well educated, speaking French, German, and Italian as well as reading Latin and Greek with ease. When Philip II, anxious to continue his English alliance, proposed marriage, the "virgin queen" turned him down, as she did everyone else, saying, "I am wedded to England." Her subjects hailed her as Good Queen Bess.

In addition to promoting a moderate form of Protestantism in England, Elizabeth faced two problems—the power of Spain and opposition in Ireland. Philip II's attempt to assert strong Spanish and Catholic control over the Netherlands threatened English economic interests there, since the Netherlands had long been the main market for English wool exports. Thus, in 1585, Elizabeth sent an army to aid the Dutch rebels against Philip. The next year, she sanctioned Sir Francis Drake's raids on Spanish colonial shipping. The English now identified themselves as pro-Protestant, anti-Catholic, and anti-Spanish. Thus religious, economic, and political issues deepened the rift between Spain and England, thereby ending the medieval al-

Treaty of the Pyrenees Treaty in 1659 ending the wars between France and Spain and leaving France the most powerful state in Europe.

balance of power Long-time European diplomatic aim for a distribution of power among several states that would prevent the dominance of any one state.

liance between the two countries that had led to the marriage of Catherine of Aragon to Henry VIII.

Rivalry with Spain also influenced developments in Ireland. Like her father and grandfather, Elizabeth was determined to strengthen English control of the island. But her attempts were met with a local rebellion led by Catholics, who received Spanish help, including the failed Spanish Armada of 1588. In the end, Elizabeth triumphed and transferred vast tracts of Irish land to loyal English Protestants, thus consolidating the conquest of the kingdom.

Elizabeth's England saw a flowering of literature, known as the **English Renaissance. William Shakespeare** wrote many of his plays during her reign, performing them at court and in his own theater, the Globe. Shakespeare's contemporary, **Christopher Marlowe,** wrote equally popular plays, including *The Jew of Malta,* which explored themes Shakespeare developed in *The Merchant of Venice,* and *The Massacre at Paris,* about the Saint Bartholomew's Day slaughter during France's religious wars. Marlowe's greatest play is *Doctor Faustus,* about a man who sells his soul to the Devil in return for power and knowledge.

Poetry also flourished in Elizabeth's reign. **Edmund Spenser** continued the tradition of epic poetry that stretched back to Dante Alighieri, Virgil, and Homer in his *Fairie Queene,* an elaborate allegory celebrating Protestant England's struggle with Catholicism and Spain. Spenser's friend and fellow poet **Sir Walter Raleigh** also extolled Elizabeth and Protestant England in verse. Both Raleigh and Spenser actively pursued politics. As a young man at court, Raleigh became a favorite of the queen, who commissioned him to attack Spanish shipping. In 1587 he founded a short-lived colony on Roanoke Island off present-day North Carolina, and in 1595 he led the first English expedition into South America, sailing up the Orinoco River in search of a fabled kingdom ruled by El Dorado, a man covered in gold. No gold was found, but his account of the expedition established him as a master of the literature of discovery and exploration. When Elizabeth began her conquest of Ireland, both Raleigh and Spenser joined her forces and were rewarded with estates confiscated from the rebels.

Elizabeth's refusal to marry was based more on political calculation than on personal preference; she feared the challenges to her power and independence that submission to a husband might bring. As the years passed, however, the problem of succession became acute since her heir was her cousin, **Mary Stuart, Queen of Scots,** the Catholic widow of King Francis II of France and a relative of the Guises. After Francis's death, Mary had returned to Scotland, where she married a Scots nobleman and had a son,

James. Mary's religion also caused problems in newly Calvinist Scotland, and in 1568 she fled to England after nobles deposed her and seized James. Elizabeth promptly imprisoned Mary because her Catholicism made her a magnet for those who favored the old church. Rumors of Catholic plots swirled around Mary for years. In 1587, when the rumors seemed to stick, Elizabeth had her beheaded.

The Early Stuart Monarchs

In 1603, Mary Stuart's son, **James VI** of Scotland, succeeded the virgin queen as **James I** of England and Ireland, and, for the first time, the separate kingdoms of Scotland and England were ruled by the same person. James had an excellent mind and published ten works, including a *Counterblast to Tobacco* that denounced smoking as "loathsome to the eye, hateful to the nose, harmful to the brain, [and] dangerous to the lungs." His greatest literary achievement was to sponsor a new translation of the Christian Bible for use in the Anglican Church. Published in 1611 and known as the **King James Version,** it has shaped the English language down to the present.

Two issues dominated James's reign and that of his son, **Charles I:** religion and relations between king and Parliament. Henry VIII and Elizabeth had used Parliament to implement the English Reformation, thereby

English Renaissance   Flowering of English literature during Elizabeth I's reign.

William Shakespeare   (1564–1616) England's greatest playwright, author of *The Merchant of Venice, The Tempest, Othello,* and many other plays and poems.

Christopher Marlowe   (ca.1564–1593) Playwright in Elizabeth I's reign, author of the play *Doctor Faustus* and a contemporary of William Shakespeare.

Edmund Spenser   (1553–1599) Poet and author of the epic poem *The Fairie Queene.*

Sir Walter Raleigh   (ca.1554–1618) Privateer, explorer, poet, and favorite of Elizabeth I.

Mary Stuart, Queen of Scots   (r. 1542–1587) Cousin of Elizabeth I and heir to the English throne whose Catholicism led to her execution.

James VI/James I   (r. 1567/1603–1625) Son of Mary, Queen of Scots, king who ruled in Scotland as James VI from 1567 and in England and Ireland as James I from 1603.

King James Version of the Bible   Translation of the Bible sponsored by King James I for use in the Church of England and published in 1611.

Charles I   (r. 1625–1649) King of England, Ireland, and Scotland who was beheaded by order of Parliament in 1649.

giving it a permanent place in the country's political life. But the exact nature of Parliament's authority was disputed. Both James and Charles believed that God appointed kings to rule and that they were accountable to Him alone. But they also knew that Parliament had a traditional right to raise taxes. For its part, Parliament believed the king could formulate state policy, but it claimed the right to criticize policy. James rejected this right. Parliament, he said, was no place "for every rash and hair-brained fellow to propose new laws of his own invention." At stake in these conflicts was a fundamental political issue: Should Parliament simply express opinions, or should it have a voice in policymaking? Traditions of strong kingship, stretching back to the Middle Ages, favored the king, but Parliament's power to grant or withhold taxes enabled it to assess the policies its taxes would finance. James and Charles leaned toward royal absolutism, while Parliament favored a theory of limited royal rule.

Religion regularly divided king and Parliament. Like Elizabeth, James was a moderate Protestant, but he was married to a Catholic. His moderation and his wife raised suspicions among the **Puritans,** Calvinists who thought that the Anglican Church was not completely reformed. Puritans wanted no bishops, no church ceremony, more sermons, policing of people's behavior, and an effective Protestant foreign policy. Their suspicions of James were overcome in 1605 when the government discovered a Catholic plot to blow up the king, along with Parliament. Thereafter, James followed Elizabeth in treating English Catholics as traitors.

Anti-Catholicism also shaped English policy in Ireland. In 1597, another rebellion broke out in **Ulster,** in the northeastern part of the island. It ended just as the plot to blow up the king and Parliament was discovered. In the anti-Catholic backlash, the lands of the rebel Catholic leaders were confiscated and given to English owners, who then colonized them with some one hundred thousand Scottish Protestants. The Catholic Irish, viewed as "savages," were driven onto marginal lands. Later, habits learned in Ireland were transferred to North America, where settlers drove Indian "savages" off the lands they then farmed. Ulster was England's first successful colony.

In North America, the Virginia Colony boomed when tobacco was grown for export. James I may have hated the "pernicious weed," but his subjects loved it and Virginia's economic success was assured. Beginning in the 1620s, other colonies were founded, this time by religious dissidents upset with the monarchy's support of Anglicanism and persecution of Catholics. The Pilgrims, Protestant Separatists who, like the Anabaptists, believed that the church should

be a voluntary association, founded Plymouth Colony in 1620. In 1629, Puritans founded the Massachusetts Bay Colony, while English Catholics emigrated to Maryland in the 1630s. Unlike the colonies of Spain and Portugal, the English settlements were not directly sponsored by the state. Instead, they began as commercial ventures, like the Virginia Colony, or as religious havens.

James died in 1625, and his son became king as Charles I. Like his father, Charles had an unshakeable belief in his right to rule as he pleased. He also shared his father's views about Parliament. Between 1625 and 1629, the king clashed with parliamentary leaders who criticized his policies and refused to grant him money for his wars against Spain and in support of the Huguenots, questioning the success of his campaigns and criticizing the men in charge of them. Finally, in 1630, Charles decided to govern without Parliament and did not convene it for ten years.

Charles ruled well enough on his own for most of the 1630s. One policy, however, provoked growing opposition—reform of the Anglican Church. In 1633, the king appointed **William Laud** archbishop of Canterbury; Laud introduced new church ceremonies and ordered the clergy to adhere strictly to Elizabeth's 1559 Book of Common Prayer. The Puritans were outraged, seeing Laud's program as an attempt to reintroduce Catholic practices. Some of them left for North America, where they joined their fellow Puritans in Massachusetts. Others waited for a chance to turn on Laud. Laud's position was further weakened when he stated that the clergy alone, not the local laity, would control church affairs. He also ordered the restoration of church lands that the laity had taken over. These policies angered a large group of landowners with seats in Parliament, who now had economic and political reasons, as well as religious ones, for opposing the king and his archbishop.

Charles and Laud were not content to revamp the Church of England. In 1637, the king imposed the Book of Common Prayer, along with bishops, on the Presbyterian Church of Scotland. In response, in 1639, the

---

Puritans Calvinists who wanted to eliminate bishops and favored more sermons, policing of people's behavior, and a strong Protestant foreign policy.

Ulster Northeastern part of Ireland colonized by Scots and English Protestants after England's defeat of the local Catholics.

William Laud (1573–1645) Archbishop of Canterbury who enforced Charles I's unpopular religious policies through royal courts.

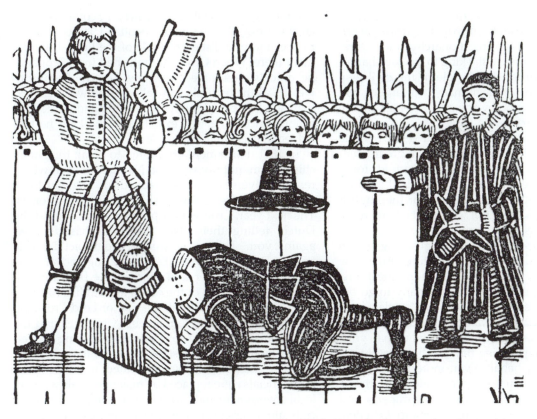

In this woodcut print of the execution of Charles I, the blindfolded king, his hat set to the side, puts his neck on the chopping block and waits for the executioner's ax. An Anglican clergyman prays while armed guards and a crowd look on. *(Hulton Archive/Getty Images)*

Scots rebelled. Charles, now at war with his Scottish subjects, needed funds for an army. In 1640, he resummoned the English Parliament and demanded money from it.

Civil War, Revolution, and the Commonwealth

The new **Long Parliament** was filled with men angry at Laud and the king. It passed a bill stating that the king could not dissolve Parliament without its own permission (which Charles signed, probably inadvertently). Parliament removed Archbishop Laud and sent him to prison. It also passed an act requiring the king to call Parliament into session on a regular basis. In 1641, Charles was forced to sign a treaty with the Scots that gave the Scottish parliament a role in the appointment of royal ministers and conceded the Scottish parliament's right to oversee policy. The English Parliament promptly demanded the same concessions, and when Charles refused, it proposed a bill abolish-

ing bishops in the Church of England. At this point, another Catholic rebellion broke out in Ireland, and several thousand Protestants were massacred in Ulster. In 1642, Charles demanded money from Parliament for an army to subdue the Irish. When Parliament refused and started to form its own army, Charles declared war on Parliament.

England had now fallen into civil war. For the next seven years, the king and his supporters fought Parliament's army. Troops of both sides damaged crops and disrupted trade, while cold temperatures ruined the harvests of the late 1640s. By war's end, popular rebellions against both sides had broken out in various parts of the country.

In 1643, Parliament reorganized the Church of England along Presbyterian lines and then executed Laud. In 1645, Charles, finally defeated in battle,

Long Parliament   English Parliament that sat from 1640 until 1660.

surrendered to the Scots, who turned him over to the English Parliament in 1647. In 1648, the army purged Parliament of those favoring monarchy, and the remaining members brought the king to trial on charges of treason and murder for his role in the civil war. Charles denied the court's legitimacy, proclaiming that "the king cannot be tried by any superior jurisdiction on earth." But Charles was convicted and publicly beheaded in London on January 30, 1649. When the executioner's ax fell on his neck, a huge groan went up from the crowd surrounding the scaffold, for it was a momentous event. Never before had an English court of law removed a monarch or the English people killed their king. Civil war had become revolution. England was now a republic.

Even as the civil war raged, the English engaged in an unprecedented debate over the nature of the state and the role of ordinary people in political life. Charles's growing unpopularity led many to go beyond older arguments about the king's relation to Parliament. The Levellers wanted to establish a democratic republic in England and allow all men to vote. Women activists supporting the Levellers petitioned Parliament on their behalf. Even more radical were the Diggers. Responding to economic hard times, they rejected the institution of private property and supported a form of communal ownership. Levellers and Diggers were always in a minority, but the very fact that they gave public voice to their ideas for reform stimulated popular thought about the nature of England's social order and raised questions about the political and economic identities of English men and women.

Oliver Cromwell

One of Parliament's generals in favor of Charles's execution was **Oliver Cromwell.** In 1649, Cromwell led an army to put down the rebellion in Ireland, where disruptions from fighting and crop failures had produced widespread famine; the Irish population fell by almost 40 percent. Cromwell's invasion delivered the final blows. His army massacred thousands, 80 percent of agricultural land was transferred to the Protestant minority, Catholicism was outlawed, and twelve thousand rebels were deported as penal slaves to Barbados and other English colonies in the West Indies. For the next two hundred years, English Protestant control of Ireland was assured.

With Ireland subdued, Cromwell turned to Scotland. Despite their differences with Charles I, most Scots favored the continuation of monarchy. After the king's execution, **Charles II,** Charles I's elder son, was summoned from exile and crowned Scottish king in 1650. Cromwell then invaded Scotland, forced Charles to flee, and established the rule of the English Parliament there. When Cromwell returned from Scotland, he quickly dominated the new English **Commonwealth,** as the republic was called. Cromwell believed that God had called him to leadership and guided his actions. In this he was exactly like the king he had helped to execute.

In 1651, Parliament attempted to break the Dutch shipping monopoly with the **Navigation Act,** which required overseas goods destined for England to be carried in English ships or ships of English colonies. The next year, Cromwell supported a war against the Dutch, telling them that "the Lord has declared against you." The war was short, and the act did little to limit Dutch trade, but it signaled England's rise as a commercial power and marked the beginning of government control of the emerging English Empire.

In 1653, Cromwell took the title of Lord Protector. Parliament continued to meet, but Cromwell and the army actually ruled. In 1655, after suppressing a royalist rebellion, Cromwell established a military dictatorship. Press censorship was instituted, and traditional local officials were replaced by major generals who ran local government and carried out a moral reform of society along strict Calvinist lines. Although Cromwell ruled as a Calvinist-inspired dictator, he abolished the requirement that everyone attend Calvinist church services, proclaiming, "I meddle not with any man's conscience." He did, however, ban Anglican and Catholic services for political reasons. By the 1650s, growing numbers of Protestants shared Cromwell's embrace of limited toleration.

Cromwell was offered a crown by some followers who wanted him to become King Oliver. He refused it. When he died in 1658, his son Richard became the new lord protector. Richard, however, did not have his father's political skills and soon retired to his country estates. His departure left England leaderless. Once

Oliver Cromwell   (1599–1658) General on Parliament's side in English civil war who eventually established a military dictatorship in England.

Charles II   (r. 1650/1660–1685) Son of Charles I, crowned king of Scotland in 1650 but ruled there only after 1660, when he was crowned king of England as well.

Commonwealth   Name of the English republic from 1649 to 1660.

Navigation Act   (1651) Parliamentary act requiring overseas goods destined for England to be carried in English ships or ships of English colonies.

again, a general stepped in; George Monck marched his army on London and negotiated the return of King Charles II, along with the House of Lords, the Church of England, and all its bishops. Oliver Cromwell's corpse was dug up and publicly hanged.

In 1660, it seemed that England's troubles had come full circle. Anglican monarchists viewed the post-1660 regime as a simple "restoration" of older ways. But in the wake of the Anglican Church being outlawed, a king executed, and a republic created, the merits of absolutist monarchy and limited constitutional government had been debated. There had been calls for democracy, communal ownership of property, and religious toleration. The debates and the conflicts unleashed during the civil war and revolution would shape the future of the English-speaking world.

Christian Reform, Religious Wars, and the Jews

> ↓ How did Europe's Jews define themselves as a community in the larger Christian world?
> ↓ What explains the rise and fall of Sabbatai Sevi?

The expulsion of Jews from Spain and Portugal destroyed Europe's largest Jewish community. In the early sixteenth century, Italy alone in western Europe had a significant Jewish population. In eastern Europe, Poland also admitted large numbers of Jews. Then, after 1550, Jews returned to western Europe when the Dutch Republic, Bohemia, France, and England once again admitted them. But the rising religious passions of the Christian reformations led to an upsurge of anti-Jewish attacks, including devastating massacres in eastern Poland. Like some Christians, Jews believed that the troubles they experienced were signs of the world's end. In 1665, thousands of them looked to a young Jew from Smyrna in Ottoman Turkey, Sabbatai Sevi, who proclaimed that he was the long-awaited Jewish Messiah.

Jews in Poland and Western Europe

Following their expulsion from England and France in the late Middle Ages, western European Jews were permitted to settle in Poland-Lithuania, where the Black Death had reduced the number of people on the agricultural estates of the king and the nobility. Soon Jews were working the land as peasants, supplying local needs as craftsmen, and serving as estate managers. Jews prospered with the growth of grain and timber exports to the west, acting as agents in organizing this trade. They also played an important role as moneylenders. By the end of the seventeenth century, Polish Jews numbered some 450,000, or about 4.5 percent of Poland's population and 75 percent of Jews worldwide.

Whether they lived in towns or the countryside, Jews were governed by local councils made up of prominent community members, who often dressed and acted like non-Jews. Like the Christian population, Jewish communities were hierarchically organized. At the top were a few rich and socially prominent people as well as rabbis and Talmudic scholars. Below them were craftsmen, peddlers, and shopkeepers. Lower still were the poor. Most Polish Jews were separated from the larger Christian population not only by religion but also by culture. Like the Arabic-speaking Moriscos of Spain, they spoke their own distinctive language, **Yiddish.** Aware of their minority position, the Jews worked hard to maintain a strong sense of community solidarity that fostered a distinctive Jewish identity. At times, however, internal tensions threatened to fracture the community, as when rich Jews adopted non-Jewish ways or well-to-do moneylenders seized land and other collateral from fellow Jews who defaulted on loans.

Beginning in the mid-sixteenth century, Jews started to return to western Europe. The largest Jewish community in the west, Rome excepted, was in Bohemia, where the Habsburgs encouraged Jewish settlement and used Jews as bankers and moneylenders. Bohemian nobles also courted Jews, who served as estate managers like their counterparts in Poland. Even Emperor Ferdinand II welcomed them, despite his determination to eliminate dissident Protestants. In his eyes, heretics were a greater danger to the Christian community than unbelievers. Throughout the Thirty Years' War, both the Habsburgs and the Swedes turned to the Bohemian Jews for the funds they needed to continue fighting.

The Dutch Republic also welcomed Jews. Both **Ashkenazim,** from Poland and Germany, and **Sephardim,** from Spain and Portugal, congregated in Amsterdam. Overall, some eighteen thousand Jews settled in the

Yiddish German dialect spoken by the Ashkenazim, derived from German and Hebrew and written in Hebrew characters.

Ashkenazim Jews of Europe who settled mainly in the Holy Roman Empire, Poland, Lithuania, and other eastern regions.

Sephardim Jews from the Iberian Peninsula.

Dutch Republic. Although this community was smaller than the ones in Poland and Bohemia, it played a crucial role in the booming Dutch economy. Its original members were Sephardim who had economic ties to merchants in the Iberian Peninsula, the Spanish Empire, and Brazil. The Dutch West India Company exploited these contacts to develop trade with Spain and to push into the profitable trade with the New World. Some four thousand Portuguese Jews eventually settled in the Dutch colonies.

France and England also permitted new Jewish settlements. French kings permitted expelled Portuguese Jews to settle in some cities as part of their struggle with Habsburg Spain. In England, Oliver Cromwell fostered a growing Jewish community in London. Like many Protestants, Cromwell believed that the conversion of the Jews to Christianity, along with the destruction of the Antichrist (that is, the pope), would usher in the Second Coming of Christ. He, therefore, welcomed the visit of an Amsterdam rabbi who came to London seeking formal recognition of a Jewish community there. The rabbi also had a religious agenda; for him, Jews had to settle in all parts of the world as a prelude to the coming of the Jewish Messiah. Although formal recognition of an English Jewish community was not forthcoming, as merchants and clergy resisted, Jews were allowed unofficially to settle in London and engage in trade.

War in Poland

In 1648, the year of the Peace of Westphalia, war broke out in Poland-Lithuania when **Cossacks,** warriors protecting lands bordering on Muslim territory, rebelled in Ukraine. The rebellion was provoked in part by a decision to reduce the number of Cossacks in the Polish army and in part by religious clashes—the Polish Cossacks were Russian Orthodox, while the kings of Poland were Roman Catholics. Catholic-Orthodox tensions were particularly high in the seventeenth century after the **Union of Brest-Litovsk,** which united bishops in Polish Ukraine with the Roman Catholic Church, despite Orthodox Christian opposition.

The Cossack revolt of 1648 inaugurated nineteen years of warfare. Like the Thirty Years' War, it started as a local dispute but was soon internationalized when both Sweden and Russia joined in. In 1655, Sweden, fresh from territorial gains during the Thirty Years' War, hoped to amass more lands on the Baltic's southern shore. The Russian **tsar** also used the war for territorial gain. The Swedes withdrew in 1660 after receiving territory from the king of Denmark, with

whom they were also at war. The Russians signed a peace treaty in 1667 that gave them the eastern half of Ukraine.

The devastation caused by two decades of warfare was immense. The Polish economy was disrupted, and food shortages occurred, followed by periods of famine. Predictably, armies of all sides spread disease, and epidemics ravaged a population already weakened by disruptions in the food supply. At the beginning of the war, the Cossacks slaughtered Catholics, Jews, and signers of the Union of Brest-Litovsk indiscriminately. These atrocities rivaled Ivan the Terrible's mass executions and matched the worst incidents during the French Wars of Religion. Like the French slaughters, those in Poland were intended to ritually degrade the bodies of a socially polluting enemy. Eventually, all warring sides committed atrocities, and all Poles were victims of them, but Polish Jews suffered disproportionately. The lucky ones fled to Jewish communities in western Europe. Others fled south into Muslim lands, where they were enslaved and then sold in Constantinople. In all, some forty to fifty thousand Jews, a quarter of Poland's Jewish population, perished in the war.

Sabbatai Sevi

In some Jewish circles, 1648 was widely held to be the year in which the Jewish Messiah would appear to gather the exiled children of the Covenant, lead them into the land of Israel, and rebuild the Temple in Jerusalem. The greeting "Next year in Jerusalem!" gave voice to this longing for restoration, which grew more intense after the expulsions from Spain and Portugal and the slaughters in Poland. But the Messiah did not appear. Then, in 1665, a twenty-nine-year-old Jew, **Sabbatai Sevi,** proclaimed that he was the Messiah.

Sevi grew up in Izmir, a commercial center on the western coast of Turkey. From an early age, he excelled in Jewish religious studies and was eventually ordained a rabbi. Before Sevi claimed to be the Mes-

Cossacks Warriors organized locally to protect frontier lands bordering on Muslim territory; also used by Polish kings and Russian tsars as fighting forces.

Union of Brest-Litvosk Agreement in 1596 uniting Orthodox bishops in Polish Ukraine with the Roman Catholic Church.

tsar (in Russian, "Caesar") Title of the rulers of Russia.

Sabbatai Sevi (1626–1676) Jew from Izmir of Sephardic ancestry who proclaimed he was the Messiah.

In the upper part of this engraving, Sabbatai Sevi is enthroned as the Messiah. The Hebrew inscription above his head reads "The Crown of Sabbatai." Below him is an inscription from the prophet Jeremiah, "I will cause to sprout for David the root of righteousness." In the bottom panel the tribes of Israel study Torah under the Messiah's guidance. *(From Freely, John, The Lost Messiah: In Search of Sabbatai Sevi [London: Viking Press, 2001]. Reproduced with permission.)*

siah, he had wandered around the Ottoman Empire from Greece to Egypt. He experienced dramatic shifts in his mental state, ranging from deep depression to frenzied exaltation. He also fell into religious ecstasies that some believed revealed his Messianic status. Although it has been speculated Sevi suffered from bipolar disorder, there were also historical reasons for Sevi's intense spiritual experiences, for they were at the heart of the Jewish mystical tradition centered on the **kabbala** that Spanish Jews had developed during the late Middle Ages.

In 1665, after his return to Izmir, Sevi openly proclaimed that he was the Messiah and started to gather followers. He dressed in royal robes and ordered changes in Jewish worship, turning fast days into feasts and altering synagogue services as signs of the dawning End Time of Jewish restoration. In the past,

other men had claimed to be the Messiah, but none attracted the following that Sevi gained. News of him spread quickly along trade routes. Soon Jews in the Ottoman Empire and Europe were performing the penitential acts prescribed for the time of the Messiah's arrival and saying prayers for Sevi in their worship. People said that Sevi was about to seize the sultan's crown or that he performed miraculous cures. In their own way, these proclamations were like contemporary Christians' belief in the Second Coming.

kabbala   (from Hebrew, "tradition") Field of Jewish mysticism dating to the twelfth century but of greater interest in the sixteenth century.

Both Jews and Christians shared a hope for a decisive divine event that would right all wrongs and usher in a golden age of peace and prosperity. The economic hard times after 1550, along with a seemingly endless cycle of war, slaughter, and religious conflict, heightened these expectations in both communities.

In 1666, Sevi set out for Constantinople. Before he arrived, the Turks arrested him for disturbing the peace and jailed him. His followers were allowed to visit, and he continued to act as the Messiah and even signed his letters, "I am your God Sabbatai Sevi." In September, Sevi was brought before the sultan and threatened with execution. He then converted to Islam, and the sultan named him Mehmet Efendi, gave him a pension, and appointed him a doorkeeper in the royal palace. He died ten years later.

As news of Sevi's **apostasy** spread, shocked congregations throughout the Ottoman Empire and Europe erased his name from their records. From the beginning, many Jews had doubted Sevi's claims and had been appalled at his self-deification. A few, however, continued to believe that Sevi was the Messiah. His conversion was part of his Messianic strategy, they thought, by which he burrowed like a worm into Islam with the aim of destroying it from the inside out. Some of his followers also converted to Islam and established communities that lasted into the twentieth century.

The furor over Sabbatai Sevi marked a turning point in Jewish history. Following his apostasy, any claim of Messiahship was severely scrutinized. Forms of Judaism that emphasized present faithfulness to the Law and focused less on the mystery of the Messiah's future appearance gained ground. Nevertheless, the kabbalistic traditions that had inspired Sevi continued to serve as a rich matrix for future mystical movements within Judaism.

> **apostasy**   Act of renouncing one's religious beliefs.

Summary

Review Questions

↑ How did political and religious issues shape the nature of warfare?

↑ How did the meaning of community change during a century of conflict?

↑ How did religious conflict affect the states of Europe?

After 1550, the European economy turned downward. A price revolution aggravated an economic crisis brought on by overpopulation. Hard times produced widespread anxiety, which in turn led to social unrest, fears that the world was coming to an end, and panic about witches. For the next century, religious strife tore Europe apart.

In Spain, Philip II undertook aggressive campaigns against Muslims and Protestants. He defeated his Morisco subjects in Spain and fought the Turks at sea. He also opposed the Protestant movement in England and fought his own Protestant subjects in the Netherlands. When he died in 1598, Protestantism had survived, and Spain's military might was in decline. The Netherlands were split in half, and the economically prosperous Protestant provinces of the north were virtually independent from Spanish rule. England under Elizabeth I was Protestant and prepared to challenge Spain on the seas and in the New World. Henry IV of France had granted religious toleration, along with a good deal of political autonomy, to the Huguenots, but he had also strengthened the French monarchy.

Warfare continued throughout the first half of the seventeenth century. Europeans believed that religious unity was essential for the well-being of the community, but renewed warfare failed to reestablish the unity lost in the sixteenth century. Louis XIII defeated the Huguenots and stripped them of their political autonomy, although they still had the right to worship. In Germany, the Thirty Years' War failed to curb Protestantism in the Holy Roman Empire, where the emperor's power was greatly weakened. When the war ended, German princes now had a third religious option for their states, Calvinism, in addition to the Lutheranism and Catholicism allowed in 1555. In England, Anglicans and Puritans fought each other in a civil war that ended in the execution of Charles I, the dismantling of the Anglican Church, and the establishment of a commonwealth. In 1660, monarchy and Anglicanism were restored when the republican experiment of the 1650s crumbled following Oliver Cromwell's death. All English Protestants agreed that the Catholic Irish must be conquered. The creation of the Ulster colony and Cromwell's campaign in Ireland established England's dominance of the island. By 1660, it was clear that the religious unity of western and central Europe was shattered, despite fierce attempts on all sides to preserve it.

Europe's Jews were allowed once again to settle in the west, where some benefited from the global trading networks established in the sixteenth century. But Jews were still often despised and sometimes suffered catastrophic losses, like the ones occurring in Poland after the Cossack rebellion of 1648. Some Jews, like some Christians, hoped for divine deliverance from the troubled times. But the rapid rise and shocking betrayal of the self-proclaimed Messiah

Sabbatai Sevi turned many Jews away from a belief that their deliverance was at hand. Like the Christians, they now lived in a religiously fractured world.

← Thinking Back, Thinking Ahead →

Once the principle of religious toleration was accepted, what changes would people eventually make in their understanding of religious and political allegiances?

ECHO

War Stories

This chapter opens and ends with a war story. War stories have been told in the western world for thousands of years. Some early ones are found in Homer's *Iliad* and the monuments of Egyptian pharaohs. From the beginning, war stories have been told with words and images. Homer wrote his stories in verse, while the pharaohs had workers carve battle scenes on the walls of their mortuary temples. Homer's warriors lose battles and die in them. In his temple, the pharaoh never loses.

Over the last hundred and fifty years, war stories in ever-greater numbers have circulated more and more quickly during conflicts. In the nineteenth century, American reporters wrote stories about the great battles of the Civil War, and Mathew Brady, following in Jacques Callot's footsteps, took shockingly graphic photographs of battlefield carnage. In World War I and World War II, carefully edited film footage of battle was shown weekly in newsreels to the civilian population in movie theaters. During the Vietnam War, reporters using portable video cameras shot fighting scenes that were shown every night on network television news. Never had scenes of war been seen so often by so many people. Their graphic detail alarmed some, who thought that the news broadcasts weakened the country's resolve to fight the war. During the 1991 Gulf War television cameras and news reporters were not allowed on the battlefield. In 2003, during the war in Iraq, the Department of Defense allowed some reporters and cameramen to be "embedded" with troops entering Iraq. But it also banned television coverage of flag-draped coffins from Iraq arriving at Andrews Air Force Base. Shortly thereafter, the president of the United States flew onto a navy aircraft carrier to be televised in front of a banner announcing "Mission accomplished!" Then pictures of torture at Abu Ghraib Prison in Baghdad appeared on the Internet.

Governments know the power of images in time of war and therefore try to control what people see. But some images seem always to get beyond their control. On the other hand, there is always the suspicion that images have been doctored to make a point. What lies just beyond the camera's frame? Has something been airbrushed out or pasted in? Digital photography, which does away with the fixed film image, makes these questions even more important and faith in the truth of pictures even more risky.

Suggested Readings

Cameron, Euan, ed. *Early Modern Europe: An Oxford History.* New York: Oxford University Press, 2001. A recent general account.

Davies, Norman. *The Isles: A History.* New York: Oxford University Press, 2001. The history of all the British Isles.

Edwards, John. *The Jews in Christian Europe, 1400–1700.* New York: Routledge, 1988. A good general account.

Freely, John. *The Lost Messiah: The Search for the Mystical Rabbi Sabbatai Sevi.* Woodstock, N.Y.: Overlook Press, 2001. The most recent account of Sevi's life and career.

Kamen, Henry. *Spain, 1469–1714: A Society of Conflict.* New York: Longman, 1983. A good study of Philip II.

Schama, Simon. *The Embarrassment of Riches: An Interpretation of Dutch Culture in the Golden Age.* New York: Random House/Vintage Books, 1997. An excellent examination of the formation of Dutch identity in the seventeenth century.

Watts, Sheldon J. *A Social History of Western Europe, 1450–1720.* London: Hutchinson University Library for Africa, 1984. An older account with a great deal of information.

Websites

Sections and links to readings on many of the topics discussed in this chapter, **Internet Modern History Sourcebook,** at www.fordham.edu/halsall/mod/modsbook03.html

On the history of Jews in early modern Europe, **Internet Jewish History Sourcebook,** at http://www.fordham.edu/halsall/jewish/jewishsbook.html

Information on artists and their work in the seventeenth century, **Web Gallery of Art,** at http://www.wga.hu/frames-e.html?/welcome.html

State Building and the European State System, 1648–1789

16

1500 B.C.E.	1000 B.C.E.	500 B.C.E.	1 B.C.E./1 C.E.

1640
Frederick William becomes elector of Brandenburg

1657
Leopold I becomes Holy Roman emperor

1660
Monarchy is restored in the British Isles

1661
French King Louis XIV becomes his own prime minister

1682
Peter the Great becomes tsar

1688
Glorious Revolution begins

1640	1650	1660	1670	1680	1690	1700	1710

Europe in 1715

In 1715, when Louis XIV died, France was still the dominant power in Europe. But other centers of power—the Austrian Habsburg lands, Great Britain, Russia, and a small newcomer, Prussia—were prepared to challenge France. After 1715, how did the ambitions of all these states affect the goal of maintaining a European wide balance of power?

Austrian Hapsburg lands
Prussian lands
Swedish lands
Boundary of Holy Roman Empire
Major battle

SWEDEN

NORWAY
Oslo

St. Petersburg
INGRIA

ESTONIA
Moscow

KINGDOM
OF
DENMARK

LIVONIA

RUSSIAN
EMPIRE

SCOTLAND
Edinburgh

North
Sea

LITHUANIA

GREAT BRITAIN

Baltic
Sea

Dublin
IRELAND

DENMARK

EAST
PRUSSIA

ENGLAND
London

UNITED
PROVINCES
Utrecht

BRANDENBURG-PRUSSIA
Berlin

POLAND
Warsaw

Kiev

SAXONY

SILESIA

ATLANTIC
OCEAN

HOLY ROMAN EMPIRE
PALATINATE

BOHEMIA

Poltava
1709

Versailles Paris
LORRAINE
Strasbourg

AUSTRIA

FRANCE

BAVARIA

Vienna

Danube

SWITZERLAND

Buda Pest

HUNGARY

Toulouse

SAVOY

Venice
MILAN
REPUBLIC OF VENICE

Black
Sea

GENOA

Marseilles

TUSCANY
PAPAL
STATES

Adriatic
Sea

PORTUGAL

SPAIN

CATALONIA

Corsica
(Genoa)

MONTENEGRO

Rome

Constantinople

Lisbon

Madrid

Minorca
(Gr. Br.)

SARDINIA

KINGDOM
OF
NAPLES

Naples

Corfu
(Rep. of Venice)

OTTOMAN

Balearic Is.

GIBRALTAR
(Gr. Br.)

Mediterranean

SICILY
(Savoy)

MOREA
(Rep. of Venice)

EMPIRE

MOROCCO

ALGERIA

Sea

TUNIS

0   200   400 Km.
0   200   400 Mi.

TRIPOLI

OTTOMAN EMPIRE

500 C.E.   1000 C.E.   1500 C.E.   2000 C.E.

1740
Frederick the Great
becomes king of Prussia

1756
Seven Years' War begins

War of the Austrian
Succession begins

1763
Seven Years' War ends

1720   1730   1740   1750   1760   1770   1780   1790

Choice

Louis XIV

Louis XIV of France embodied the ideal of the vigorous, state-building monarch. Throughout his long reign, he dominated European diplomacy and warfare, and his glittering court established standards of grandeur that other monarchs tried to imitate. As a young man, he seemed more interested in the pleasures of the court than in politics. In fact, however, he emerged as one of Europe's ablest and most disciplined rulers following the death of his prime minister, Cardinal Mazarin. (Château de Versailles/Laurie Platt Winfrey, Inc.)

Louis XIV Decides to Rule France on His Own

On March 9, 1661, France's prime minister, Cardinal Jules Mazarin, wracked by gout, kidney stones, and fluid in his chest cavity, died. When news of Mazarin's death was announced, the royal court was abuzz with rumors about who would be next in line for the position. Within hours of Mazarin's death, King Louis XIV made his choice: himself. Standing before the highest officials in the kingdom he announced: "Up to this moment I have been pleased to entrust the government of my affairs to the late Cardinal. It is now time that I govern them myself. [Monsieur the Chancellor], you will assist me with your counsels when I ask for them. I request and order you to seal no orders except by my command. And you, . . . my secretaries of state, I order you not to sign anything, not even a passport . . . without my command."

Courtiers were astonished by Louis' announcement. The twenty-three-year-old seemed more interested in dancing the role of the god Apollo in court ballets and engaging in sexual escapades with young ladies-in-waiting than sitting at his desk and shuffling through reports on wool weaving in this province or sheep farming in that one. Besides, Louis' announcement that he would rule by himself broke with family tradition. Both his father and grandfather had relied on strong prime ministers to help them with the affairs of state, and since 1643, Cardinal Mazarin had guided France skillfully through the last years of the Thirty Years' War. In the 1640s, France seethed with unrest as taxes rose to pay for the war and great nobles rebelled against Mazarin's policies. There was fearful talk that France—like England—would slip into a civil war. Would monarchy be attacked in France? Would the French king be executed like Charles I? Would the French Calvinists, tolerated but no longer politically independent, rise up like the Puritans and declare a republic? Mazarin had played on these fears of chaos and bloodshed in order to keep the monarchy safe.

By 1653, calm was restored, and the fourteen-year-old Louis XIV's throne was secure. Louis believed that Mazarin had saved the monarchy, and his devotion to his prime minister knew no bounds. For the rest of his life, Mazarin continued to advise the king on policy and even chose his companions, dismissing young men he thought unfit for association with Louis. Mazarin also amassed the largest personal fortune ever known under the monarchy. On his deathbed, he gave it to the king.

Given Mazarin's role in guiding the French monarchy through tumultuous times and the seeming frivolity of the young Louis, it is no wonder that courtiers looked askance at the young king's surprising decision to rule on his own. In the end, however, Louis fooled them all. For the next fifty-four years, until his death in 1715, he refused to appoint a prime minister and directed the affairs of state himself. The discipline, endurance, and stamina this "bureaucrat king" showed in running the government became legendary. Both the successes and the failures of his very long reign rested on his determination to control all the affairs of state.

Introduction

Louis XIV was one of the most successful rulers in the years after the Peace of Westphalia and the very embodiment of absolutism—a style of monarchy that spread across Europe in the seventeenth and eighteenth centuries. Royal absolutism was a way to build the power and effectiveness of the central state. A century of religious warfare had taught Louis and other absolutist rulers that only a strong central government, coupled with a policy of either tolerating or crushing religious dissent, could bring political stability.

Although wars continued to be fought after 1648, religiously motivated warfare declined. Increasingly, the roots of conflict focused on issues of territorial expansion, power, and prestige. By the mid-eighteenth century, European warfare had also taken on global dimensions as states fought each other for control of overseas empires. To meet the challenges of European and global warfare, rulers increased the size of their armies and brought them under tight state control. Absolute monarchs saw war as a means to enlarge their territories and, simultaneously, to deny the territorial ambitions of other states. In their eyes, Europe, and then the world, was like a chessboard on which each state's diplomatic and military moves were met with countermoves from other states. But war and territorial gains were expensive, and throughout the century after the Peace of Westphalia, states increased taxes, tried to collect them more efficiently, and sought to improve their economies to increase their tax base.

All over Europe, the needs of almost continual warfare drove expansion in state administration and improvements in financial and judicial bureaucracies. State authority aimed to direct economies and to reach more aspects of people's lives. Key to these expansions was the creation of officials accountable to the Crown. In western Europe, loyal middle-class people were recruited into these bureaucracies, while in eastern Europe, monarchs drew their officials from the ranks of the lesser nobility. The goodwill of the public in general was also essential, as was the allegiance of the nobles in particular, since they constituted the political and social elite. Some states also tried to increase services to their subjects, such as infrastructure improvement and better policing of town and country.

On the European continent, states tended to develop along the absolutist model pioneered by Louis XIV in France. In Britain, however, the rebellion and revolution of the mid-seventeenth century ended the absolutist ambitions of the early Stuart kings. After 1660, their successors ruled with Parliament in a constitutionally limited monarchy. The joint rule of king and Parliament ensured a high degree of political stability and proved important to Britain's success in empire building, trade, and manufacturing. In some parts of Europe, warfare and state building fostered a strong sense of national identity as people embraced the policy perspectives of their rulers and defined themselves as the opposite of their enemies. In other European states, however, the religious and ethnic roots of collective identity were so strong that a common sense of community centered on the state failed to emerge.

Absolutism in France, 1648–1740

↓ What were the characteristic features of French royal absolutism?

↓ What were the outcomes of the French monarchy's attempts to strengthen the state?

Louis XIV of France dominated Europe in the second half of the seventeenth century. After assuming personal rule (see Choice), he launched wars that added to France's territory. He also continued the policy of stamping out Protestantism in his kingdom, tarnishing his image in Protestant Europe. Eventually continual warfare drained his treasury and forced him to reorganize the French state. His successor built on Louis' successes, expanding state activity in several new directions. But France was also rocked by a new religious crisis, which pitted the state against a dissident Catholic movement.

The Sun King at Versailles

Since 1500, Europe's royal courts had grown in size. In the 1520s, the French court had just over five hundred members. **Louis XIV**'s court had ten thousand, half of them nobles. For the nobles, closeness to the king brought honor, appointments in the royal army, and pensions. Since nobles had a prickly sense of self-worth, a tradition of military service, and extravagant lifestyles that strained their purses, Louis' attentions were highly prized. Thus nobles flocked to the king's court, and, as he established a working relationship with this powerful elite, Louis was also able to keep his eye on them.

At court, the entire day focused attention on the king. From his rising to his bedtime, great nobles

Louis XIV (r. 1638–1715) King of France and the most powerful ruler in Europe during the second half of the seventeenth century.

Chronology

1640	Frederick William becomes elector of Brandenburg
1657	Leopold I becomes Holy Roman emperor
1660	Charles II is restored as king of England, Ireland, and Scotland
1661	Louis XIV becomes his own prime minister
1672–1679	Dutch War between Louis XIV and the Dutch Republic
1682	Peter I the Great becomes tsar
1685	Louis XIV revokes Edict of Nantes
1688–1689	Glorious Revolution dethrones James II
1700–1721	Great Northern War between Russia and Sweden
1701–1713	War of the Spanish Succession between Louis XIV and most of Europe
1702	Anne becomes queen of England, Ireland, and Scotland
1707	England and Scotland unite to form the kingdom of Great Britain
1711	Charles VI becomes Holy Roman emperor
1713	Pope condemns the Jansenists
1713	Spain grants Britain the *asiento*
1714	George I of Hanover becomes king of Great Britain
1715	Louis XV becomes king of France
1727	George II becomes king of Great Britain
1740–1748	War of the Austrian Succession ends in a draw
1756–1763	Seven Years' War leads to British and Prussian victories
1762	Catherine II the Great becomes empress of Russia
1772	First partition of Poland
1780	Joseph II becomes ruler of the Habsburg lands
1780s	Joseph II abolishes serfdom in the Habsburg lands
1790s	Leopold II reestablishes serfdom in the Habsburg lands

attended him. At midday, Louis ate alone while courtiers stood and watched. The dinner table etiquette was so complicated that it took three men seven minutes to give the king a glass of wine. When Louis went to Mass, he sat in a balcony, looking down at the altar, while the court, turning their backs on the priest, sat looking at Louis. This distinctive arrangement emphasized the king's pivotal position between God and France. Louis believed that he ruled by **divine right** because God had decreed monarchy to be the correct form for France's government and had called Louis to the throne as the eldest legitimately born son of his father. The elaborate court rituals also proclaimed that Louis, as an absolute monarch, was the only real political player in France. He alone made policy and laid down the law. He was also the only person who unified the different regions and peoples of France, since he alone ruled over them all.

Louis was also the perfect gentleman, famous for his politeness and beautiful manners. Courtiers commented that they rarely saw him lose his temper. If someone misbehaved, a simple look or short comment was enough to convey his displeasure. Like court etiquette, the king's gentlemanly behavior had a political purpose, since it reinforced a new trend in noble society that emphasized polite speech and good manners as necessary qualities for the highborn and powerful. Encouraged by noblewomen in Paris, who presided over **salons** in which this conduct was

divine right   Theory that kings were called by God to rule and that opposition to the king was therefore opposition to God.

salons   Meetings in great Parisian homes presided over by well-born women who set the style for discussions of literature, science, and other matters of current interest.

This aerial view of Versailles shows the palace as it appeared toward the end of Louis XIV's reign. Its grandeur is apparent. At the top, the town's boulevards converge on the palace front. The rear façade looks out over the palace's large gardens and park. Louis' personal rooms were located in the center of the central wing to emphasize that everything at Versailles was centered on the king. *(Yann Arthus-Bertrand/Altitude)*

required, the new emphasis on manners disciplined the often violent and crude behavior of nobles.

The setting for Louis' court was **Versailles,** originally a hunting lodge for Louis XIII. Throughout his reign, the king worked to turn his father's modest building into Europe's most magnificent palace. He laid out acres of grounds decorated with lavish fountains. Louis adopted the sun god Apollo as Versailles' symbol and symbolically identified himself with Apollo as the "Sun King," spreading radiance on his lands and subjects. At Versailles, an entire town sprang up to meet the needs of courtiers and their thousands of servants. The palace itself was the centerpiece in a carefully orchestrated propaganda campaign designed to celebrate the king's *gloire*—that is, his glory or renown—in architecture, painting, sculpture, and other artistic media. Above all, Louis' *gloire*

rose when he led his troops into battle and fought other kings for territory, honor, and prestige.

Forty Years of Warfare

The early years of Louis' reign were marked by peace at home and victory abroad. But after 1668, the king, increasingly worried about the weakness of France's eastern border, launched a series of wars. The greatest of these campaigns was the **Dutch War.** Resenting

Versailles   Louis XIV's palace near Paris begun in the 1660s and housing the king after1683.

Dutch War   France's 1672–1678 invasion of the Netherlands aimed at breaking Dutch control of international trade and shipping.

Voice Voice Voice Voice

Louis XIV Advises His Son

In 1666, Louis XIV assembled a team of collaborators to help him write his memoirs, which were intended for his young son, another Louis, when he became king. Such memoirs were common in early modern Europe. Charles V had written one for Philip II, and Cardinal Richelieu had composed one for Louis XIII. Although Louis' son died before the king and, therefore, could never follow his father's advice, the Memoirs *reveal the preoccupations and principles of Louis XIV some five years after he became his own prime minister.*

→ *What do these remarks say about Louis' understanding of his relationship with his subjects?*

→ *Why would Louis argue that the happiness and tranquility of France depended on the union of authority in the king?*

→ *What do these remarks tell you about the king's personality?*

→ My son, many very important considerations caused me to resolve to leave you, at the cost of much labor in the midst of my most important duties, these memoirs of my reign and principal acts. . . . I even hoped that in this way I might be the most valuable person in the world to you and consequently to my subjects. For no one with more talent and experience has ever reigned in France, and I do not hesitate to say to you that the higher one's position, the more it has qualities that no one may perceive or understand without occupying it . . .

→ For it is generally agreed that nothing preserves the happiness and tranquility of the provinces with greater certainty than the perfect union of all authority in the person of the sovereign. → The slightest division of authority always produces the greatest misfortunes, and whether the alienated portion falls into the hands of individuals or groups, it cannot remain there except in a state of violence . . .

→ *Why would the king be concerned that a division of political authority would lead to the "greatest misfortunes"?*

→ As for the work of [governing], my son, . . . I imposed upon myself the rule to labor twice daily. I cannot tell you what benefit I received immediately after making this resolution. I felt elevated in spirit and courage, a changed man, discovering in myself unknown resources and joyfully reproaching myself for having ignored them for so long. . . . I now seemed to be king and born to be so. As for those who were to assist me in my work, I resolved above all else not to appoint a first minister. . . . For in order to unite in myself all sovereign authority, I resolved after I had chosen my ministers to call upon them when they least expected it, even though their duties might involve details to which my role and dignity would not ordinarily allow me to stoop, so as to convince them that I would follow the same procedure regarding other matters at any time. The knowledge that resulted from this small step, which I took but rarely and more for diversion than because of any principle, instructed me gradually without effort regarding a thousand things that were of value in making general decisions. . . .

→ Kings are often obliged to do things contrary to their inclinations and good nature. They should enjoy giving pleasure, but they must frequently punish and ruin persons whose good they naturally desire. The interest of the state should take precedence. One should counter one's inclinations and not place oneself

→ *How did Louis' concern to promote the interest of the state shape his behavior toward others?*

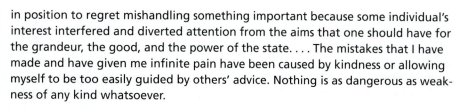

in position to regret mishandling something important because some individual's interest interfered and diverted attention from the aims that one should have for the grandeur, the good, and the power of the state. . . . The mistakes that I have made and have given me infinite pain have been caused by kindness or allowing myself to be too easily guided by others' advice. Nothing is as dangerous as weakness of any kind whatsoever.

Source: From *Louis XIV* by John B. Wolf. Copyright © 1968 by W. W. Norton & Company, Inc. Used by permission of W. W. Norton & Company, Inc.

the "maggots" who dominated European trade and shipping, in 1672 Louis ordered his generals to invade. In response, the Dutch **stadholder, William,** broke the dikes that protected his low-lying country and flooded it, as the government had against the Spanish in 1579. The strategy obviously caused much hardship for the Dutch, but it also bogged down the French. In the end, neither side could defeat the other, and a peace was signed in 1679. The chief consequence of the war was to alienate William, who was now dedicated to the defeat of France.

To further challenge Dutch economic predominance, Louis' financial minister, **Jean-Baptiste Colbert,** developed a strategy for increasing France's national wealth. Known as **mercantilism,** it regulated economic policy for France's benefit. Consumers were encouraged to "buy French," and the state supported porcelain manufacturers capable of competing with imports from Asia. Monopolies were given to trading companies that would challenge the Dutch in overseas markets. Finally, French colonies were encouraged to grow. The population of Canada, known for its exports of furs and fish, rose from three thousand to twenty-five thousand, and the French founded settlements on the Gulf of Mexico at Mobile and New Orleans. These colonies secured the French in the North American heartland watered by the Mississippi and Ohio Rivers. **Saint-Domingue** and other colonies in the Caribbean specialized in cash crops, first tobacco and then sugar. Colbert's mercantilism established a new goal for the monarchy—the development of a national economic policy.

The mid-1680s brought a downturn in Louis' fortunes. In 1683, Louis refused to declare war on the Turks when they besieged Vienna. His decision was in line with France's traditional anti-Habsburg policy, but his refusal to help a Christian state attacked by Muslims scandalized many Europeans. Then, in 1689, Louis again went to war on France's eastern frontier, this time against Austria, a war that was quickly joined by the Dutch. The **War of the League of Augsburg** lasted until 1697. Louis, who had the largest army in Europe, strengthened the eastern frontier by conquering the province of Alsace and the

city of Strasbourg. But his finances were exhausted. In 1693, crop failures, caused by a drop in average yearly temperatures during the Little Ice Age, led to a terrible famine in which over a million people perished from hunger and disease.

Then an even greater political crisis loomed—the succession to the Spanish throne. Spain was ruled by Charles II, who was childless and feeble-minded. On his death, the vast Spanish possessions would have to pass either to the Austrian Habsburgs or to the French Bourbons, since both had claims to the crown. Although on his death in 1701 Charles had willed his lands to the Bourbons (Louis XIV's grandson, Philip), the Austrian Habsburgs disputed the will and went to war. This **War of the Spanish Succession** was the most devastating one Louis ever fought. It further shattered his finances, while a crop failure in 1709 was followed by the coldest winter of the century, leaving thousands frozen to death in their homes or on the roads. At war's end, Philip remained king of Spain and its empire, but the **Treaty of Utrecht** stipulated

stadholder   Chief executive in the Dutch Republic.

William   Stadtholder of the Dutch Republic (1672–1702) who later became king of England as William III (r. 1689–1702).

Jean-Baptiste Colbert   (1619–1683) Louis XIV's financial minister who implemented French mercantilist policies.

mercantilism   State-initiated economic policy encouraging exports, discouraging imports, and stimulating domestic industries.

Saint-Domingue   Sugar-producing French island colony in the Caribbean.

War of the League of Augsburg   (1689–1697) First of Louis XIV's two great wars fought against Austria, England, and the Dutch Republic.

War of the Spanish Succession   (1701–1713) Louis XIV's last great war, with France and Spain allied against the Austrians, Dutch, and English.

Treaty of Utrecht   Treaty signed in 1713 between France and the states fighting France that ended the War of the Spanish Succession.

that France and Spain could not be united as a single state. The Austrians received northern and southern Italy, along with the Spanish (now the Austrian) Netherlands.

Louis' many wars had increased the size of France by 12 percent and strengthened its eastern borders, now protected with state-of-the-art fortifications. But they had left a bitter legacy. In 1713, France was virtually bankrupt and the economy in a shambles. Moreover, other Europeans states, especially the Dutch Republic and Britain, feared that the Sun King was trying to upset the balance of power, which aimed to prevent any one state from establishing permanent military dominance in Europe.

A Unified French State

Within France, however, the wars had a unifying effect. Continuous warfare after 1688 had led Louis to search desperately for new revenue, and he sold waves of new offices. Then, in 1695, he took the unprecedented step of imposing a tax, the **capitation,** on all his subjects without exception. To supervise the collection of these taxes, Louis relied on his **intendants,** chief local royal administrators appointed on the basis of their ability and loyalty to the Crown. The intendants also gathered information about local conditions for the central government, and their reports allowed the king and his ministers to be better informed about the state of the economy. The result was better policymaking.

Thus, in his later years Louis was able to transform the French state. He reduced the power of the royal courts, known as **parlements,** which were now forbidden to criticize royal edicts. But their members were guaranteed their right to hold office and encouraged to enforce the law. As royal administration became more efficient, relations between the king and his subjects improved. Well-run parlements appealed to the king's subjects, who increasingly used them instead of church or landlords' courts, believing that they offered fairer rulings. Although taxation was still resented, the better-organized collection of taxes, along with a continuing shift to indirect taxation on items like paper and tobacco, took some of the sting out of payment. Even the royal armies were appreciated. During the religious wars earlier in the century, royal troops had been hated because of their violence and unruliness, but Louis' army, though huge, was well disciplined. His troops were now seen as protectors, welcomed by civilians and local vendors who supplied their needs. Under Louis, the French government functioned more fairly and efficiently.

The unity of France was important to Louis. As a child, he twice had to flee Paris for his safety, during a noble revolt against royal rule known as the **Fronde.** When he assumed personal rule of France, he was determined to prevent a similar rebellion. His policy of coaxing the most powerful nobles to his court with promises of honors, careers, and money was designed to tie them closely to the fortunes of the Crown.

Louis also sought to secure religious unity in France, believing the kingdom should have "one king, one law, one faith." In Louis' mind, the French Huguenots were potentially rebellious, so in 1685 he revoked the Edict of Nantes, thereby ending the limited religious toleration Louis' grandfather had granted. Huguenots who failed to convert to Catholicism were forced to flee. Around three hundred thousand, many of them middle-class merchants, left for the Dutch Republic, England, and America, spreading tales of the king's brutality. The Huguenot exodus cost France dearly, since it deprived the kingdom of a commercially skilled group just as the Anglo-French struggle for global commerce was beginning. Those still in France were subject to the quartering of troops in their houses, while in the mountainous south, where many Protestant peasants lived, royal troops burned hundreds of villages. In retaliation, peasants carried on a **guerrilla war** against the royal army. In Protestant Europe, news of the army's atrocities, coupled with exiles' grim accounts, produced a new image of Louis. The glorious Sun King was now a vicious tyrant. In France, however, most Catholics supported the king's policy. Louis' campaign against the Huguenots resulted not only from a belief that France should be religiously unified but also from fear that the Huguenots were secretly republicans, a charge that bedeviled them after English Calvinists declared a commonwealth in 1649.

Louis also quarreled with the pope by supporting

capitation   Royal tax imposed on all French subjects in 1695 that introduced the idea of taxation of all people in defense of the state.

intendants   In the second half of Louis XIV's reign, the most important local royal administrators, appointed by the king.

parlements   France's highest royal courts, which enforced the king's edicts.

Fronde   (1648–1653) Rebellion of the French nobles against Cardinal Mazarin and the regent, Queen Anne, during Louis' early years as king.

guerrilla war   An undeclared, irregularly fought war.

the French clergy's adoption of the **Four Gallican Articles,** which proclaimed that church councils were superior to the pope and that the pope could not alter the way the French church was governed. The attack on the Huguenots was designed in part to heal the rupture with the pope. Relations with the papacy were further improved when Louis supported the pope's condemnation of the **Jansenists,** austere Catholics whose notions about human sinfulness struck some Catholics as too close to the views of John Calvin.

During the famine of 1709, Louis took the unprecedented step of issuing a letter directly asking his subjects for help. This appeal went against the principles of absolutism, in which the king was the only political player, but it was well received. As a result, king and subjects bonded in an effort to meet the crisis, and a new sense of collective identity was forged. Now people started to think of themselves as part of a unified nation facing a common task. Louis XIV's regulation of religious affairs, his control of the French nobility, his efficient royal administration of tax and economic policies, and his establishment of better working relations with his subjects all promoted a growing sense of national unity, exemplifying French royal absolutism in action.

Yet in 1715, seventy-seven years old and dying, Louis reflected on his failings. He told his five-year-old great-grandson and heir, **Louis XV,** "Try to remain at peace with your neighbors. I loved war too much. Do not follow me in that or in overspending."

Louis XV

After 1715, France avoided prolonged warfare. Capitalizing on peaceful times and a smoothly functioning state administration, Louis XV continued his great-grandfather's absolutist policy of expanding the state's activity in new directions. One was policing. Traditionally, cities maintained rudimentary police forces, and the army was the real maintainer of public order. Under Louis XV, the army's policing role declined, and professional police forces were created. Paris saw the first changes. Its police force, which numbered 193 in 1700, grew to 725 by 1760. In the rest of the kingdom, about 3,000 men functioned as police. These forces were spread thinly over a population of 24 million, but they represented the beginning of a modern, professional police network.

Another area of activity concerned poor relief. Increasingly, the state assumed care of poor children and the elderly, who were housed, clothed, and fed in urban "hospitals." Life in the hospitals was strict; attendance at morning and evening prayers was oblig-

atory, and the able-bodied were forced to work. Some historians argue that the new state program aimed to isolate the socially undesirable from society at large, while others see it as the beginning of a modern state-sponsored welfare system.

In religious policy, however, Louis XV struggled, as the problem of the Jansenists remained. While his government continued its predecessor's condemnation of the Jansenists, the Parlement of Paris, following the Four Gallican Articles, declared that the pope was illegally intruding into the French church's affairs. The conflict was intense because in 1715 the Duke of Orléans, the regent for the new child king, had once again permitted the parlements to criticize royal policy. By 1730, the Parlement of Paris was openly defying Louis on the Jansenist issue and challenging the absolutist principle that the king alone made law. Neither side could silence the other, and it now seemed that Louis XV could no longer keep religious peace in the kingdom. Despite this failure, however, absolutism in France had brought the state into new areas of people's lives and made the state more demanding, as well as more responsive, than ever before.

The Austrian Habsburgs, 1648–1740

↓ How was the Austrian Habsburg form of absolutist kingship similar to and different from French royal absolutism?

↓ What factors delayed the implementation of state building in the Habsburg lands before 1740?

The Habsburg emperor Leopold, a lifelong rival of Louis XIV, successfully contained France's bid for dominance in European affairs, thus maintaining the balance of power. His reign, too, was marked by warfare. Positioned between the French in the west and the Turks in the east, Leopold often had to fight both at the same time. But unlike France, warfare in the Habsburg lands did not accelerate a drive for unity in

Four Gallican Articles   Decrees of 1681 proclaiming church councils superior to the pope and denying Rome's power to alter internal rules governing the French church.

Jansenists   Austere Catholic reformers who were accused of holding views about human sin similar to the Protestant John Calvin and were condemned by the pope.

Louis XV   (r. 1715–1774) Louis XIV's five-year-old great-grandson who became king on Louis XIV's death.

In this engraving by Caspar Luyken, Emperor Leopold I is shown in the Spanish style dress worn at his court, far more somber than the fashions favored at Versailles. Leopold looks out at the viewer with piercing eyes. The elongated lower jaw, characteristic of the Habsburgs, is also apparent. *(Austrian National Library, Vienna)*

the state, and Austria was not remodeled along absolutist lines. Its reach was simply too great and its population too diverse—particularly after the reconquest of Hungary—to permit the perfect alignment of the king and the law that had been Louis XIV's aim.

Leopold I

In 1657, on the death of his elder brother from smallpox, the seventeen-year-old **Leopold I** unexpectedly became Holy Roman emperor and head of the Austrian Habsburgs. He had been destined for a career in the church, and at first he did not play the role of monarch very well. Throughout his life he remained deeply religious. He married three times and had sixteen sons and daughters, only five of whom outlived him. He was also withdrawn and bookish as well as an accomplished musician who composed many pieces performed at his court in Vienna.

Like most rulers of his day, Leopold was aware of the political implications of Louis XIV's Versailles and set out to rival him by building his own palace, **Schönbrunn,** on the outskirts of Vienna. Plans to convert the building, which like Versailles had been a hunting lodge, were drawn up during his reign. They included an imposing residence of four hundred rooms as well as gardens and fountains in the manner of Versailles. But there were differences. Versailles was situated on high ground, so the gardens sloped down

> **Leopold I** (r. 1657–1705) Head of the Austrian Habsburgs, emperor, ruler in Austria, king of Bohemia, and king of Hungary, which he reconquered from the Turks.
>
> **Schönbrunn** (in German, "beautiful spring") Leopold I's palace on Vienna's outskirts, built on the model of Versailles.

from the palace, creating long vistas. Schönbrunn sat at the bottom of a hill. This allowed designers to sweep the gardens upward and to incorporate cascading water into their plans. The effect was different from Versailles, but equally impressive.

The Turkish Siege of Vienna and the Reconquest of Hungary

In 1683, a Turkish army, under the leadership of the Ottoman **grand vizier,** Kara Mustafa, marched up the Danube River and besieged Vienna. Once again, Europe shuddered at the threat of Muslim conquests. Leopold, forced to flee the city, tried to rally support from Christian princes. Many responded, though not Louis XIV, for whom dynastic rivalry was more important than Christian solidarity. In September, after a savage two-month siege of the city, a united force, which had received the pope's blessing, defeated the Turks, and Kara Mustafa fled south. The grand vizier blamed everyone but himself for his failure, executing subordinates as he made his way to winter quarters in Belgrade. There, on Christmas Day, he received a silk scarf signaling the sultan's displeasure. He was strangled on the spot and his head then shipped to Constantinople, to be presented to the sultan on a silver platter.

These dramatic events opened the way for the Habsburgs' reconquest of Hungary. By 1687, Leopold was master of most of the kingdom and the semi-independent principality of Transylvania. Summoning the Hungarian Diet, he convinced the deputies to decree that the Crown was no longer elective but hereditary in the male line of the Habsburg family. The Hungarians also renounced their traditional right of rebellion against a ruler they thought had violated the kingdom's customary laws. Despite these concessions, Leopold did not trust the Hungarians. Earlier in his reign, some of their great nobles had rebelled against him, while others were Protestants. Hungarians were also culturally distinct, dressing in local costumes and speaking their own language—Magyar.

Turkish occupation and the war of reconquest had devastated the Hungarian countryside, and vast stretches of farmland lay unoccupied. To restore agriculture, and also to neutralize possible Hungarian rebellions, Leopold encouraged Serb, Bohemian, and German peasants to resettle the lands, promising them limited freedom from royal taxes and the obligations of serfdom. This resettlement complicated the religious situation in Hungary, where, for a century, Hungarians had been split over religion; along with Catholics, there were Calvinists, Lutherans, Unitari-

ans, Eastern Orthodox, and Muslims. The resettlement also reduced the proportion of Hungarians. In 1526, they had constituted 85 percent of the kingdom's population; by 1700, they made up only 40 percent.

Peace in Europe during the 1680s had freed Leopold to concentrate on Hungary. When the War of the League of Augsburg with France broke out in 1689, he was forced to turn west once again. Then, with Habsburg troop strength reduced in the east, the Turks attempted to retake Hungary, only to be defeated again in 1690. This time a new grand vizier lay among the battlefield dead. Finally, just as war in the west was ending, in 1697 Leopold scored another smashing victory. At **Zenta,** the vizier and thirty thousand men were slaughtered before the sultan's eyes, for this time the sultan himself had accompanied the Turkish army into Hungary. The Habsburg commander ripped the great seal of the Ottoman Empire from the dead vizier's neck and sent it back to Vienna. In 1699, the **Treaty of Carlowitz** confirmed the Habsburg conquests. Although the Ottomans had lost Hungary, they continued to hold the Balkans and challenged the Russians in the northern Black Sea region.

During the War of the Spanish Succession, more trouble flared up in the east, this time a rebellion led by a Transylvanian prince, **Francis II Rákóczi.** Rákóczi typified the touchy Hungarian noble resentful of Leopold's preference for Germans. His father, mother, and stepfather had all led rebellions against the Habsburgs, and he was determined to guarantee Hungary's traditional rights. By 1711, however, he had been defeated, as the Habsburgs were now able to rely on the enlarged non-Hungarian population of the kingdom for support. War and plague devastated the kingdom during the rebellion; almost a half million people perished. Rákóczi eventually sought protection from the sultan and died in exile in Turkey. The **Peace of Szatmár** (1711) united Hungary to the Habsburg lands through a common ruler.

---

grand vizier   Chief minister of the Ottoman sultan.

Zenta   Battle in 1697 in which the Habsburgs defeated the Turks and reconfirmed Habsburg conquests in Hungary.

Treaty of Carlowitz   Treaty of 1699 between the Austrian Habsburgs and the Ottoman Turks confirming the Habsburg reconquest of Hungary.

Francis II Rákóczi   (1676–1735) Prince of Transylvania who led the last major rebellion against the Habsburgs in Hungary.

Peace of Szatmár   Treaty of 1711 uniting Hungary to the other Habsburg possessions through a common ruler.

The Habsburg Monarchy

The Habsburgs ruled over lands that were far more socially polarized than Louis XIV's France. At the top were the **magnates,** who were often fabulously rich. Visitors to the magnate Esterházys in Hungary could travel for days before they reached the end of their lands, passing through entire towns that were under the family's exclusive control. Magnate families were few in number, but their cooperation with the Habsburgs was essential for the smooth functioning of the government, and they dominated Habsburg administration at the central and local level. Unlike in France, there were few independent cities and towns in the Habsburg lands. The vast majority of people, tied to the land as **serfs,** lived in the countryside.

Serfdom had expanded in the sixteenth and seventeenth centuries as eastern European landlords, all of whom were noble, successfully bound peasants to the soil as a labor force producing grain and timber for the western European market. During the dislocations of the Thirty Years' War, they also bound them to the soil to prevent them from fleeing to more peaceful areas. Landlords used their serfs to work their estates without compensation. Leopold tried to reduce uncompensated work to three days a week, but his success was limited because direct control of serfs lay with the landlord class, not the Habsburgs. Thus, Leopold's policy had to accommodate noble self-interest before it could become effective. Because Leopold's direct rule over the mass of his subjects was very limited, he never established the kind of centralized, intrusive state that Louis XIV and Louis XV created. The Habsburg state was also characterized by a high degree of ethnic and religious diversity, particularly in Hungary. Habsburg rulers manipulated these groups to their own ends, with the result of enhancing the sense of difference between communities. Unlike in France, no sense of common identity emerged that spanned all the people of the Habsburg hereditary lands.

Leopold died in 1705, leaving two sons, Joseph I (r. 1705–1711) and Charles VI (r. 1711–1740), to rule. When Joseph died during the War of the Spanish Succession, Charles, as the sole surviving Austrian *and* Spanish Habsburg male, was poised to inherit the Austrian territories along with Spain and its lands in the Netherlands, Italy, and America, thus reconstituting Charles V's empire. This was too much for the other European states, which feared that an Austrian Habsburg succession in Spain would upset the European balance of power. They, therefore, supported the division of lands between Habsburgs and Bourbons that was written into the Treaty of Utrecht ending the War of the Spanish Succession.

Warfare did not lead Charles to reform the Habsburg state, as it did in France. Instead, during his twenty-nine-year reign, he devoted his mediocre talents to two basic policies: making sure that his brother's daughters did not succeed him and that his own daughter did. The matter was complicated. The emperor had always been male, so Charles's daughter, **Maria Theresa,** could not follow him in that office. But she could succeed him as ruler of the family's hereditary lands. To this end, Charles coaxed the magnates into recognizing her succession and then sought guarantees from the other European rulers that they, too, would recognize it. When Charles died in 1740, his careful plans exploded. In the **War of the Austrian Succession,** another new ruler, **Frederick II** of Prussia, attacked Maria Theresa during the opening phase of the two world wars that convulsed Europe in the mid-eighteenth century. The new war showed just how weak the Habsburgs had become.

The Rise of Prussia, 1640–1740

> ↓ What factors accounted for Prussia's rise in power?
> ↓ What role did the army play in forging a collective Prussian identity?

North of the Habsburg lands, another state emerged out of the chaos of the Thirty Years' War—Prussia. Prussia was a poor country, lacking the human and material resources of France and the Habsburg lands. But its rulers wanted it to become a major European power. To this end, they consolidated the state's territories, strengthened the state administration, raised revenue, and above all enlarged the army. These am-

magnates   Politically powerful nobles in the Habsburg lands who owned vast agricultural estates worked by serfs.

serfs   Peasants bound to the land who owed payments and labor service to their landlord.

Maria Theresa   (r. 1740–1780) Daughter of Charles VI and ruler of the Habsburgs' hereditary lands whose husband was elected Holy Roman emperor.

War of the Austrian Succession   (1740–1748) Mid-eighteenth century world war, fought on land and sea in Europe, the Americas, and India.

Frederick II   (r. 1740–1786) King of Prussia during the War of the Austrian Succession and the Seven Years' War.

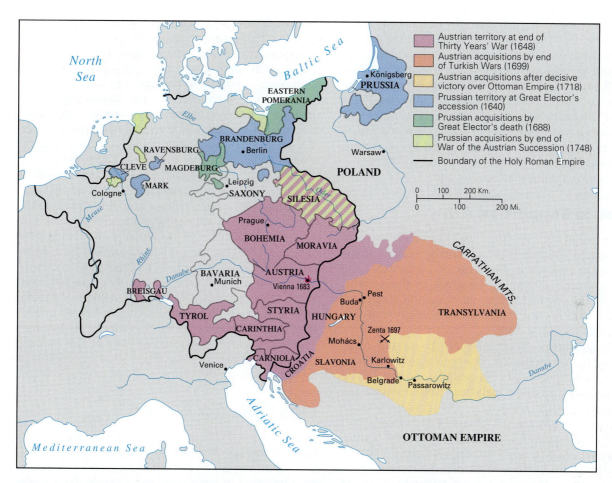

MAP 16.1   **The Growth of Austria and Prussia to 1748** Both Austria and Brandenburg-Prussia were expanding in the first half of the eighteenth century. The Austrians continued adding territories in their southeast, but in the north lost Silesia to Brandenburg-Prussia. Prussian lands were still scattered; by 1772 however, Brandenburg would be joined to Prussia in the First Partition of Poland under Frederick the Great.

bitious plans meant that the state had to mobilize the country's limited resources to a unique degree.

Territorial Consolidation

In 1640, a twenty-year-old, **Frederick William von Hohenzollern,** known as the Great Elector, became ruler of Brandenburg and a string of other territories that stretched across northern Germany from the Rhineland to the Polish border. In the west, little Cleves and Mark owed him allegiance; in the center were Brandenburg and its capital, Berlin, where he ruled as margrave; to the east was the duchy of Prussia, which he held as a vassal of the king of Poland. These Hohenzollern lands were separated by territories belonging to other rulers, and each had its own jealously guarded political traditions. Because Frederick William was

one of eight German princes entitled to elect the Holy Roman emperor, he had an important place in imperial politics. But his own lands were weak. Those in the center had been devastated during the Thirty Years' War, and some were still under foreign occupation. Overall, the population of his lands had fallen by 50 percent since 1618. But the Peace of Westphalia allowed Frederick William to reestablish princely authority in his territories.

In 1655, when Sweden went to war against Poland in hopes of gaining territory on the southern shore of the Baltic Sea, Frederick William faced his first test

Frederick William von Hohenzollern (r. 1640–1688)
Known as the Great Elector, ruler who started to create the modern state of Prussia.

since the Peace of Westphalia in the treacherous game of warfare and diplomacy that was the norm among European states. At first, he proclaimed his neutrality. When the Swedes suffered temporary losses, he allied with them on condition that they recognize the independence of Prussia from Poland. When the Poles started to lose, he joined them, again demanding that they abandon any claim to the duchy. At war's end in 1660, he was master of an independent Prussia. Now the Hohenzollern lands were scattered from the Rhineland to the Russian border.

Taxes to Support an Army

For the rest of his reign, the Great Elector set two policy goals: to build up his army and to reorganize his finances to pay for it. Between 1653 and 1688, the army grew from eighteen hundred to thirty thousand. As the one institution established in all territories from east to west, it became the primary unifying force in the elector's state.

A bigger army called for more taxes, and more taxes led to a confrontation between Frederick William and his diets, local political assemblies dominated by the nobility. Like their Habsburg counterparts, the Hohenzollern diets had traditionally granted taxes to the ruler. The elector had obtained a six-year grant from the Diet of Brandenburg in 1653 that he continued to collect on his own authority during the war of 1655–1660. Also in 1653, he proposed supplementing the grant with a general **excise tax,** taking his cue from the French, who had lowered direct taxes while raising indirect ones. When the local nobility objected that the excise violated their traditional rights of tax exemption, the elector asked only towns to pay it. This solution created two tax systems. The countryside, dominated by nobles, paid a land tax, while towns adopted the excise tax. In creating this twofold system in Brandenburg, the elector split the united opposition of urban and rural taxpayers to new taxes. When Prussia balked at taxes, Frederick William introduced the two-tiered system there with the same results. Shorn of their taxing power, the diets withered away, and, as in France, political power was increasingly consolidated in the hands of the ruler and his government.

Frederick William had another source of revenue from his own domain. All European rulers had these private income streams, but the Hohenzollerns were blessed by very large family landholdings, constituting about one-third of their country's agricultural land and worked by 30 percent of the country's serfs. Under the leadership of an efficient administrator, Dodo zu Knyphausen, these domain lands produced ever-larger amounts for the elector's treasury.

In addition to imposing his right to tax and reorganizing his domain revenues, the elector encouraged economic growth along mercantilist lines by increasing exports and introducing new manufacturing centers. As a youth, he had spent time in the Dutch Republic and seen firsthand the thriving economic life there. After 1685, he welcomed some twenty thousand exiled Huguenots. These French artisans, merchants, and manufacturers played a vital role in the economic recovery after the Thirty Years' War.

During his reign, Frederick William had united his far-flung lands into a single state, imposed his right to tax them on a regular basis, and reinvigorated the economy. His growing army made him the most important military figure in Germany after the Habsburgs. In 1688, the elector was succeeded by his son, Frederick, who ruled until 1713. Frederick spent most of his time in Berlin, presiding over a lavish court in the style of Louis XIV. His one major accomplishment was to adopt the title of King in Prussia in 1701 after obtaining Leopold I's recognition with promises of military aid in the looming War of the Spanish Succession. The title gave Frederick the standing he thought appropriate for his state's new power.

King Frederick William I

In 1713, King Frederick was succeeded by his son, King **Frederick William I.** Although Prussia was Lutheran, Frederick William was a strict Calvinist who believed in the absolutist principle that he was responsible to God alone for his rule. His subjects were to obey him without question. The king hated all elegance and refinement and spent most of his free time with his military men, smoking and getting completely drunk. These "tobacco evenings" sometimes ended with a participant being set on fire, a great joke in the king's eyes. Frederick William also stalked the streets of Berlin, roaring at his subjects, beating them with his cane, and leaving them with broken noses and teeth. The king was obsessed with tall men and scoured the kingdom for fit specimens to fill the ranks of his personal guard. If necessary, he

excise tax   Indirect tax imposed on consumer items and collected at the moment of sale. **Frederick William I** (r. 1713–1740) King of Prussia who further centralized the state administration and continued to build up the army.

Frederick William I   (r. 1713–1740) King of who Prussia who further centralized the state administration and continued to build up the army.

resorted to kidnapping. Frederick William was a strange, violent, and crude man, but he was also a very successful ruler.

Like his grandfather, the Great Elector, Fredrick William I pursued the twin policies of strengthening the royal administration while enlarging the army. The excise tax was expanded to new commodities, and the land tax was imposed directly on the nobility in East Prussia, as the old duchy was now called. Income from the royal domain was further increased through yet more efficient management. Town councils were abolished and new royal officials put in their place. A new administrative body called the **General Directory** was created in 1723 that brought together all officials involved in collecting taxes and revenues from the royal domain and supervising the overall economy of the kingdom. The directory improved administrative centralization and efficiency.

The king stood at the apex of this new administrative system. Unlike his predecessors, Frederick William I did not consult regularly with his top officials because he had a low opinion of the men who worked for him, criticizing them for laziness and greed and paying them poorly. Instead, he worked in private, receiving reports and then secretly making decisions that were transmitted in writing to his officials. His was a system of personal absolutism unknown even in Louis XIV's France, where the king always consulted with a handful of trusted advisers.

The king's government produced what Frederick William I wanted above all else—an enlarged army. At his death in 1740, the Prussian army had eighty thousand men, making it the fourth largest in Europe. Command of the troops was given to the Prussian nobility, who also served in the civil administration. The king thus bound the nobility to his government and created a tradition of loyal state service among his nobles that was to last into the twentieth century. He also guaranteed the nobility's economic preeminence by recognizing their rights as landlords to control the serfs on their estates.

The military had always been the one institution common to all the Hohenzollern lands, and the state's financial administration was geared to its maintenance. The military budget was met with tax and domain revenues, not with borrowing, as in other states. As he enlarged the army, Frederick William drafted more and more of his own subjects. All parts of the kingdom were required to present men, mainly peasants, for service. To lower costs, the soldiers were quartered in civilian homes, where they paid for their food and lodging and thereby stimulated the local economy. Because the rank and file of the growing army was made up of Prussians who lived among the civilian

population, historians have described eighteenth-century Prussia as a "barracks state."

When Frederick William died in 1740, he was succeeded by his son, Frederick II. Frederick was everything his father was not—refined, an accomplished flute player and composer, and a lover of philosophical discussion. He and his father had not gotten along. Relations between ruling monarchs and their successors were often stormy because the next in line attracted those who were out of favor in the current reign. But Frederick William I's treatment of his son was particularly violent. At one point, having beaten Frederick bloody with his cane, he put him in solitary confinement and forced him to witness the beheading of his closest friend on largely falsified charges.

Frederick William I had doubled the size of his army, but he was reluctant to use it in war. Frederick II's first act as king was to attack Charles VI's successor, Maria Theresa, seizing Silesia, her richest territory, and thereby starting the War of the Austrian Succession, the first of two world wars that engulfed the major European states in the mid-eighteenth century.

Russia and Europe, 1682–1796

↓ How were the state-building efforts of Russia's rulers similar to or different from the reform programs of European rulers farther to the west?

↓ How were Russian rulers' relations with their nobility similar to and different from relations between monarchs and nobles farther to the west?

Beginning in 1700, Russia began to realize Tsar Ivan the Terrible's dream of turning westward to expand its territory. In addition, rulers restructured Russia's state and church, along with its economy and society, along western lines. By the end of the eighteenth century, Russia was a major player in European politics.

Peter the Great and Westernization

Following Ivan the Terrible's death in 1584, Russia sank into a thirty-year period of political instability during which aristocratic factions fought for control of the state. In 1613, stability was restored when the first **Romanov** tsar, Michael, ascended the throne. At

General Directory Prussian central administrative agency created in 1723.
Romanovs Family that ruled Russia from 1613 to 1917.

the end of the century, another Romanov, **Peter I the Great,** transformed Russia into a major European power. Peter was six feet seven inches tall and powerfully built. His huge size had a personality to match—restless, energetic, and always on the move. Peter was ten when he became tsar in 1682. He shared rule with a half brother, Ivan V, until Ivan's death in 1696 and then ruled alone. The young tsar was fascinated by technology. In 1697, he traveled to western Europe under an assumed name, which fooled no one. Settling in the Dutch Republic, he spent hours visiting sawmills, cloth manufacturers, botanical gardens, and museums. He listened to lectures on anatomy and met with local architects. But, above all, he visited Dutch shipyards to learn about shipbuilding, and then, having bought his own tools, he worked alongside Dutch shipbuilders. On a visit to England, he went to Anglican church services, attended a Quaker meeting, went to the theater, and visited Parliament, which did not impress him. And, again, he studied ships.

Peter worked for the rest of his life to apply what he had learned in the west to Russia. He began with fashion. Immediately on his return to Moscow, he forbade men to grow beards, the traditional sign of manhood in this Orthodox Christian country, and personally cut them off his courtiers. Traditionalists were horrified and protested that their hairless faces made them look like Protestants, Poles, or monkeys. His court was then ordered to dress in western clothes and to meet in "assemblies," where men and women together conversed and engaged in other polite pastimes. This mingling of men and women overturned traditions decreeing the separation of women in special quarters.

In 1700, the tsar began a two-decade struggle with Sweden, the greatest power in northeastern Europe, for control of the Baltic Sea. Since the sixteenth century, tsars had believed that Russian access to the Baltic, the central sea link between eastern and western Europe, was essential if Russia hoped to be a major European power. Peter acted on this belief in the **Great Northern War,** which marked a turning point in Russian history.

After early Russian victories on the Baltic, Peter took the examples of Louis XIV and Leopold I further by building not a palace but a city, **St. Petersburg,** founded in 1703 on swampy coastal land seized from the Swedes at the mouth of the Neva River. The new city proclaimed his success in securing a Baltic port. In 1712, Peter made St. Petersburg the new capital of Russia, and the next year the court and state administration moved there from Moscow. Peter also forced skilled craftsmen to settle there with their families. When they resisted or attempted to flee, the army brought them back in chains and branded them to make flight more difficult. In 1718, well-to-do landowners were required to build a house there and spend some of the year in the city. St. Petersburg was designed using western principles of urban planning, and western architects constructed its beautiful classical buildings.

Peter knew that continuing military success in the war with Sweden depended on an unprecedented refashioning of Russia's fighting forces and tax structure. He therefore reorganized his army along western lines, ordering a draft for soldiers and introducing up-to-date western drill and weapons. By 1715, he had an army of 215,000, supplemented by 100,000 Cossacks, locally organized warrior bands used by tsars as fighting forces. Peter also built a Baltic navy from scratch. To pay for this huge military mobilization, he imposed new taxes on everything from beehives to beards to baths. He abolished the old household tax and imposed a new head tax that all unprivileged people had to pay at higher rates than the old one. Overall, taxes skyrocketed during Peter's reign, as they had in France during the Thirty Years' War. To improve his tax base, Peter inaugurated a mercantilist stimulation of the Russian economy by encouraging exports, discouraging imports, and sponsoring new industries in metallurgy, mining, and textiles.

The decisive battle in the Great Northern War came in 1709 at **Poltava,** where Peter destroyed the Swedish army. Nine thousand Swedes lay dead on the battlefield, and sixteen thousand more surrendered a few days later. The Swedish king, Charles XII, who commanded the army, fled into Turkish territory. Although the war lasted another twelve years, the Swedes never recovered from the disaster at Poltava. At the end of the Great Northern War, in 1721, during a solemn ceremony in St. Petersburg, Peter was proclaimed emperor of Russia, a title taken from Rome that was to supplant the traditional one of tsar.

Peter I the Great   (r. 1682–1725) Greatest Romanov tsar who westernized Russia and made the country a major European power.

Great Northern War   (1700–1721) War between Russia and Sweden that resulted in Russian dominance of the Baltic.

St. Petersburg   City founded by Peter the Great in 1703, which became the Russian capital in 1712.

Poltava   Decisive battle of the Great Northern War in 1709 in which Peter the Great defeated Charles XII of Sweden.

A young Peter is shown in this painting in the workman's clothes he often wore during his tour of western Europe. His dress and demeanor are nothing like the elegance and majesty typical of royal portraits of the eighteenth century. Would his attitude and appearance have made him more, or less, popular with his subjects? (*Collection, Countess Bobrinskoy/ Michael Holford*)

Peter also continued to restructure Russian society. Traditionally, Russians thought of their society as a three-tiered hierarchy. At the base were the millions of serfs who toiled for their landlords. Serfs, who constituted more than half of the Russian population, were under the complete control of their landlord, needing his permission to marry or leave his estate. They also had to work for him without pay, often as many as six days a week. In their lack of freedom of choice, they resembled the African slaves laboring in the fields in the Americas more than the European peasants farther to the west. The landlords in turn worked for the emperor. Peter intensified this traditional pattern, first by demanding more in taxes and military service from the serfs and then by requiring the landlord class to serve for life in either the military or the civilian administration. Candidates for state service had to start at the bottom of their service branch and then work to the top on the basis of personal merit. Peter applied the test of merit to himself when he rose through the ranks of the army and the navy. This sys-

tem was codified in the **Table of Ranks.** Administrators received noble status as they moved up. Peter's reform of his civil and military administration was one of the first attempts in modern European history to overturn the idea that nobles had a right to govern in favor of the notion that government should be in the hands of a civil service staffed by experts whose advancement depended on their performance. To train experts for state service, Peter established engineering, artillery, and medical schools, a school of mathematics and navigation, and a naval academy. In 1725, he established an Academy of Sciences that quickly gained an international reputation for excellence. Peter's insistence on able and expert administrators was central to his program of state building.

Peter loved alcohol, coarse language, and even coarser practical jokes. Throughout most of his reign, he presided over a "Most Drunken Council" that engaged in monumental drinking bouts while mocking Catholic, but not Orthodox, church ceremonies. His practical joking was often violent, as when he forced food down the throat of a courtier, who collapsed in a fit of coughing with blood running from his nose and mouth. Peter's violence matched that of Frederick William I of Prussia and contrasted sharply with the refined manners promoted at the court of Louis XIV and the piety of Leopold I.

Peter's most radical reform was to abolish the office of **patriarch** in the Russian Orthodox Church. In the Orthodox world, patriarchs were bishops with great prestige and influence. The patriarch of Moscow, who had received the title in 1589, had served as a counterweight to tsars and a check on their power. By Peter's time, however, the patriarchate had been weakened by a schism in the church when the **Old Believers** rejected his authority and denounced him as the Antichrist. The patriarch had tried to reform church practice, and although Russian church councils and the other patriarchs approved the reforms, Old Believers rejected them because they had not been used traditionally in "Holy Russia." Moreover, people unhappy about Peter's policy of cultural westerniza-

Table of Ranks   Decree by Peter the Great in 1722 that restructured civil and military administration into a system of advancement based on merit.

patriarch   Title of the most important bishops in the Eastern Orthodox Church.

Old Believers   Orthodox Christians who rejected the Russian patriarch's attempt to alter church ceremony.

tion looked to the patriarch for support of traditional ways. Peter never openly attacked Orthodoxy, but his own theological beliefs were heavily influenced by Lutheranism. In 1721, he abolished the patriarchate and replaced it with a **Holy Synod,** which embodied his Lutheran leanings, since it reduced the church to a simple department of the state.

Peter's plans for the remaking of Russia were far reaching, and many of them looked better on paper than they worked in reality. But his reforms brought a new centralization and rationality to government while demanding more from all Russians and advancing the country as a major European power. Thus, he set Russia on a new course.

Catherine the Great and Russian Expansion

From 1725 to 1762, Russia was allied with Austria against France, the traditional ally of the Poles, the Swedes, and the Turks, all enemies of Russia. The Austrian alliance implemented Peter's policy of bringing Russia directly into the European system of international politics and diplomacy. Domestically, one far-reaching change took place: in 1762, the landlord class was freed from Peter's compulsory state service obligation. From then on, landlords served voluntarily; many did so, since service brought prestige, influence, and wealth.

In 1762, Peter III, Peter I's grandson, became emperor. Peter III was violent, crude, and dimwitted. Raised in Germany, where his Romanov mother had married a duke, Peter feared Russians and loved Germans, thereby alienating many at court. In religion, he also leaned toward Lutheranism and ordered icons removed from Russian churches while demanding that Orthodox clergy dress like Lutheran pastors. No one dared to implement these decrees. Peter was married to Sophie, a princess from a minor German state. Six months after Peter's accession, Sophie plotted with powerful courtiers, one of whom was her lover, to depose Peter in a palace **coup d'état.** He was soon murdered, and the conspirators proclaimed Sophie his successor. For the next thirty-four years, she ruled Russia as **Catherine II the Great.**

Catherine's first major decision was to continue Peter III's seizure of all ecclesiastical lands, thereby further reducing the church's independence from the state. She then granted large tracts of state land and their peasants to her favorites. This action increased the number of serfs because state peasants were reduced to serfdom when their lands passed into private hands. Catherine also continued her predecessors' policies of

For her portrait (c. 1765), Catherine II the Great is dressed in shiny splendor. On her head is the Romanov crown, and in her hands are an orb and scepter, emblems of royal and imperial rule. She gazes straight out at the viewer with a kindly expression, perhaps to convey an image of her womanly concern for her subjects. *(The Granger Collection, New York)*

exempting the landlord class from compulsory state service and freeing them from taxation while forbidding serfs on their lands from directly petitioning the empress for redress of grievances.

Like Peter the Great, Catherine dramatically expanded Russia's borders. In 1772, she joined Prussia

Holy Synod Council of clergy established by Peter the Great in 1721 that made the church a department of the state.

coup d'état (in French, "blow of state") Abrupt overthrow of a government by a small group of conspirators.

Catherine II the Great (r. 1762–1796) German princess who, as Russian empress, was one of Russia's most powerful rulers.

M A P   1 6 . 2   The Partition of Poland and the Expansion of Russia Prussia, Russia, and Austria all benefited from the partitions of Poland. By incorporating the part of Poland that had previously separated them, Prussia and Brandenburg were finally united. But Prussian lands further to the west were still separated from those in the east by other states. Russia continued its westward expansion taking present-day Belarus, Lithuania, and Ukraine. Austria took part of southwestern Poland and Galicia, the lands closest to its eastern border.

and Austria, which were also looking to expand their territories, in the first **partition of Poland.** In the 1760s, Prussia and Russia had instigated a civil war in Poland by demanding full toleration for its Protestant and Orthodox inhabitants. Claiming that they were putting an end to that civil war, Austria, Prussia, and Russia proceeded to divide up sections of Poland among themselves. Two more partitions took place in 1792 and 1795, bringing an end to an independent Poland.

> **partitions of Poland** Divisions of Poland carried out by Austria, Prussia, and Russia in 1772, 1792, and 1795, leading to the end of an independent Polish state.

Catherine also fought two wars with the Turks. In 1792, when the second war ended, Russia seized the north shore of the Black Sea and the Crimean peninsula along with the northern Caucasus. These conquests, along with the partitions of Poland, rivaled Peter the Great's advances in the Baltic region and established the modern western boundaries of Russia. Catherine encouraged colonization in the lands of the south by urging Russian landlords to move there with their serfs and sponsoring German immigrants in the region. At the end of Catherine's reign, the Russian Empire contained dozens of different ethnic and religious communities, 50 percent of whom were Russian. Thus, cultural diversity in the Russian Empire rivaled that of the Habsburg lands and similarly retarded the development of a common identity among the peoples ruled by the empress in St. Petersburg.

The Pugachev Rebellion and Russian Society

In 1773, during the Turkish war, a massive rebellion against the empress broke out in the south. It was led by a Cossack, **Emelian Pugachev,** who claimed to be Peter III. Popular revolts led by men pretending to be long-lost tsars were a feature of early modern Russia's political life. So were Cossack frontier rebellions. What made Pugachev's revolt distinctive was its size and its social composition. Thousands rose with him, including many serfs. In 1774, when the Turkish war ended, Catherine was free to turn her professionally trained army against the insurgents, who were no match for the imperial troops, and the revolt fell apart. Pugachev was taken to Moscow in a cage and then executed. Although the revolt failed, it was a sign of a deep social crisis in Russia. The elimination of compulsory state service for the landlord class had undercut the traditional structure of the Russian community, in which landlords toiled for the state while their serfs toiled for them. When the landlords were freed of their obligations, many peasants believed they should be free as well. When they were not freed, alienation and anger exploded into revolt. Those who followed Pugachev demanded an end to serfdom, taxation, and the military draft. In 1775, Catherine clamped down. She imposed administrative centralization by reorganizing Russia into fifty provinces and putting the landlords in charge of local government, where they had enough force to control peasant protest.

Under Peter I and Catherine II, Russia emerged as a first-rate European military and diplomatic power.

Coercion from above was crucial in this transformation. Modernization and westernization also increased privileges for the landowning class and reduced the condition of the peasant population, which (serfs and free peasants together) constituted more than 90 percent of Russia's inhabitants. The gulf between the landowning elite and the mass of inhabitants was as great as, if not greater than, any in Europe.

The English Constitutional Monarchy, 1660–1740

⬇ How did religion continue to play a role in English politics?

⬇ In what ways did political development in England differ from that in the absolutist regimes on the continent?

In 1660, after eleven years of civil war, religious controversy, republican government, and Oliver Cromwell's dictatorship, monarchy was restored in the British Isles when Charles I's son, already crowned king of Scotland, was crowned king of England and Ireland. Restoration, however, did not bring either political or religious peace. For the next seventy years, the British Isles were torn apart by conflicts pitting king against Parliament. Religious divisions also persisted, as restored Anglicans refused all compromise with the Puritans. When the Catholic king James II seemed to have established a permanent Catholic dynasty, he was overthrown, and his Protestant daughter Mary II, along with her husband, the Dutch stadholder William III, were crowned with Parliament's blessing. But Mary and then her successor, Anne, died without heirs, and Parliament again determined who would rule when it chose a German Protestant prince, George I. In this turbulent period, as Parliament made and unmade monarchs, its power grew. Political stability was achieved in the early eighteenth century, when Crown and Parliament started to cooperate in governing the country.

The Restoration of Charles II

The restoration to the throne of **Charles II** in 1660 sparked a repudiation of Oliver Cromwell's Calvinist moral reform of society. The king led the way. Charles

Emelian Pugachev (1742?–1775) Cossack who claimed to be Peter III and led an unsuccessful rebellion of thousands of serfs against Catherine the Great.

Charles II (r. 1660–1685) Elder son of Charles I who became king of England, Scotland, and Ireland.

was a charming, witty man with a taste for good living and an eye for women. A string of mistresses, along with packs of spaniels, shared his bed. "God will not damn a man for taking a little unregular pleasure along the way," he once quipped. In pursuit of pleasure, Charles reopened London theaters and canceled the traditional prohibition against women playing female roles. Now people could revel in worldly comedies like *Love in a Wood* or *The Gentleman Dancing-Master*.

Underneath the glitter of **Restoration** society, the long-standing political conflict between king and Parliament continued to shape events. Like his predecessors, Charles could conduct foreign policy on his own and choose his ministers. He could also call Parliament into session and dismiss it, veto its legislation, and override any parliamentary law by suspending it or dispensing people from its provisions. For its part, Parliament could impeach royal ministers. It also controlled state finances through its right to raise taxes. In sum, both sides had formidable powers, and neither could gain a permanent advantage over the other. This situation contrasted to the absolutist monarchies on the continent, where power was increasingly concentrated in the hands of the king.

The issue that provoked the greatest political fights was religion. Although Charles II was officially Anglican, he favored some form of religious toleration in England. But the Parliament elected in 1661 was determined to promote Anglicanism alone and force conformity to the Book of Common Prayer. Therefore, it enacted the **Clarendon Code,** which required all clergymen to swear an oath supporting Anglican theology and prohibited non-Anglican Protestants from worshiping in public. About 10 percent of the clergy refused to accept it and turned their backs on Anglicanism. These clergymen and their supporters, known as **dissenters,** supported the king's more tolerant attitude. Most Anglicans suspected that the king's policy of religious toleration was shaped by loyalty to his Catholic family—his mother, wife, and younger brother, James, Duke of York, were all Roman Catholics.

These suspicions deepened when Charles allied with his cousin, Louis XIV, in the Dutch War of 1672. In fact, Charles and Louis had signed a secret treaty in 1670 in which Louis granted Charles a subsidy to free him from Parliament's control of the purse. In return, the king promised to convert to Roman Catholicism when the time was ripe. Always politically astute, Charles postponed his conversion until he was on his deathbed.

The problem of Catholic members of the royal family became especially acute in the 1670s. Although

Charles fathered at least seventeen illegitimate children by his many mistresses, he had no legitimate heir to succeed him, so his brother James would be the next king if the rule of strict hereditary succession was applied. The prospect of a Catholic king created a rift among the Anglican elite, which controlled Parliament and ran local government, since Anglicans hated Catholics as well as dissenters. Soon two parties, the **Tories** and the **Whigs,** fought each other over the issue of succession. Tories supported the Duke of York's right to the crown, even if this meant that Protestant England would have a Catholic king, because they believed that hereditary monarchy was divinely instituted and that opposition to it was a sin. Whigs wanted a Protestant monarch at all costs. Following the argument of the English philosopher **John Locke,** they believed in the contractual theory of government. The English monarchy was based on a contract between the ruler and his subjects, represented in Parliament, which could be broken for good reason. As battles between the two parties raged, a new politically active press emerged under the relatively moderate censorship regime of the restored monarchy. Press and parties encouraged the English publicly to discuss politics and take sides on issues in ways that were inconceivable under the absolutist monarchies on the continent.

James II

In 1685, when Charles II died, the principle of hereditary succession won out, and the Duke of York became **James II.** James kept up some Anglican appearances,

> **Restoration**   Name given to the period 1660–1689 in which the restored Stuart kings Charles II and James II ruled.
>
> **Clarendon Code**   Law of 1661 requiring clergy and officeholders to swear allegiance to the Anglican Church and banning non-Anglican Protestants' public worship.
>
> **dissenters**   Non-Anglican Protestants.
>
> **Tories**   Supporters of strict hereditary succession to the crown.
>
> **Whigs**   People who believed in the necessity of a Protestant monarch, even if this meant that the rule of strict heredity would have to be violated.
>
> **John Locke**   (1632–1704) Political philosopher who argued that legitimate government rested on a contract between rulers and subjects.
>
> **James II**   (r. 1685–1689) King of England who was removed from the throne by Parliament.

being crowned in public according to the Anglican rite after being crowned in private according to the Catholic one. When one of Charles II's illegitimate sons, the Protestant Duke of Monmouth, rebelled against his uncle, the duke was taken prisoner and executed. At first, many Tories and Whigs could accept James because his heirs were his two Protestant daughters, Mary and Anne, the children of his first marriage. Although James had remarried, none of the ten children by his second marriage had survived past infancy.

Like his brother, James promoted religious toleration of both dissenters and Catholics, granting them the right to worship in public and using his power of exempting people from the law to override a provision in the Clarendon Code forbidding non-Anglicans from serving in high civil and military office. This action infuriated the Anglicans, who saw the king's actions as a backdoor way of promoting Catholicism. When Anglican bishops objected, James resurrected King Charles I's hated church courts, and purged Anglican opponents from local government office, replacing them with Catholics and dissenters.

In 1688, England was rocked by news that James's wife had given birth to an eleventh child, a baby boy who would rule as James III. Outraged Protestants tried to argue that the queen had faked a pregnancy and that the baby had been smuggled into the palace in a bed-warming pan. Tories and Whigs alike were horrified at the prospect of a perpetual Catholic monarchy and furious with James's high-handed exempting of the law in favor of non-Anglicans. Joining forces, they asked the stadholder William, the husband of James's daughter Mary, to come to England in defense of Protestantism. When William landed, James panicked. Unable to sleep and suffering from endless nosebleeds, he led an army against William but failed to find him because his generals had no maps. After sending wife and baby out of the country, James fled to France.

The Glorious Revolution

When Parliament reconvened in 1689, it determined who would rule, proclaiming that in leaving the country James had abdicated and then offering the crown to Mary, his daughter, who accepted on condition that William rule jointly with her. Parliament then passed the **Bill of Rights,** which upheld the Whig view that monarchs ruled not by hereditary right but by right of a contract with their subjects. It overturned James II's suspension of parliamentary law, stating that "the pretended power of suspending

the laws or the execution of laws by regal authority without consent of Parliament is illegal." It also undercut royal power by denying the king the right to raise an army on his own, saying that "raising and keeping a standing army within this kingdom in time of peace without the consent of Parliament [is] contrary to law." This bill also guaranteed subjects' right to petition the government as well as to a jury trial, along with freedom from "cruel and unusual punishments," excessive bail, and excessive court fines. It did not, however, guarantee the right of all subjects to vote for members of Parliament's **House of Commons.** Voting for this lower house, made up of non-nobles, was still limited to a relatively small number of property-owning adult males. Candidates for the Commons also had to meet substantial property qualifications.

In support of Protestantism, Parliament also repealed the most oppressive portions of the Clarendon Code in the **Toleration Act** (1689), which granted religious toleration to all dissenters except Unitarians, people who did not believe in the doctrine of the Trinity. Dissenters, however, were still subject to a law that required all officeholders to take Holy Communion in an Anglican Church. Some dissenters evaded the law by taking Anglican Communion once a year and then going to their chapels for the next twelve months. This "occasional conformity" infuriated Anglicans. Overall, the Bill of Rights and the amendments to the Clarendon Code implemented the contract theory of government by strengthening Parliament while providing subjects of the Crown with a wide range of rights that were spelled out in detail and had the force of law.

Large-scale landowners controlled Parliament. After 1689, these people also enjoyed control of local government in the countryside with little interference from the king. This situation contrasted with the absolutist monarchies on the continent, where royal control of local affairs was implemented. William knew that his predecessor's dismissal of Anglican landlords from local office in favor of Catholics and dissenters had contributed to his overthrow and did not intend to provoke these powerful people again.

Bill of Rights Parliamentary act passed in 1689 stipulating the basic rights of English subjects; based on the contract theory of government.

House of Commons Lower elected house of Parliament made up non-noble men (commoners); nobles sit in the upper house, the House of Lords.

Toleration Act Parliamentary act of 1689 granting religious toleration to all Protestants except Unitarians, and also excepting Catholics.

In this painting of the House of Commons by Karl Anton Hickel, the Speaker of the House sits with his hat on at the center behind secretaries. The MPs (Members of Parliament) flank him on either side. The man standing is the king's first minister, William Pitt the Younger, who is addressing the House. *(National Portrait Gallery, London)*

In 1701, royal judges were given life tenure, subject only to impeachment and removal from office by Parliament. This reform, which created an independent judiciary, was intended to strengthen the **rule of law** called for in the Bill of Rights. William accepted these reforms from below and thereby acknowledged that he ruled by right of contract with his subjects. He had come to England as part of his grand strategy to defeat Louis XIV. As king he could take England into the War of the League of Augsburg on the Dutch side. Mary reluctantly accepted the crown, believing that she was sinning against her father, who led a French landing in Ireland to reclaim the monarchy. When William defeated James, James fled once again to France, where he died in 1701. The changes brought about in 1689 spelled the end of royal absolutism in the British Isles and laid the foundations for a **constitutional monarchy** in which the monarch and Parliament ruled as partners following the principles of the rule of law.

The reign of William and Mary inaugurated twenty-five years of war against France. Whigs supported William's pursuit of Louis XIV, while Tories grum-

> **rule of law**   Principle that law has a higher authority than rulers, governments, and officials; rulers must obey the laws.
>
> **constitutional monarchy**   Form of government in which the monarch and legislature rule as partners following the principles of the rule of law.

bled about rising land taxes. The two parties fiercely contested elections to seats in the House of Commons. In principle, Parliament controlled taxation and the Crown controlled foreign policy. But ongoing warfare forced the two sides to work together, since William had to explain his policies to Parliament if he hoped to get the money he needed.

Mary died childless in 1694, and when William died in 1702, the crown passed to James II's younger Protestant daughter, Anne. Anne had had nineteen children, all of whom were stillborn or died in infancy. She believed this calamity was God's judgment on her father's removal from the throne. As Anne had no heirs, Parliament determined who would rule when Anne died. In 1701, fifty-seven Catholic Stuarts were passed over in favor of a Protestant granddaughter of James I, Sophia, of the German state of Hanover. In 1707, Scotland, still an independent kingdom ruled by the English monarch, but suffering from an economic depression and a financial collapse, agreed to accept the **Act of Union** with England to create a united Great Britain ruled over by a Protestant monarch. In 1714, when Anne died, Sophia's son George became king. Later generations in England referred to the events of 1688 and 1689 as the **Glorious Revolution,** which kept the state Protestant while advancing the power of Parliament and repudiating absolutist and divine right theories of kingship.

The Georges from Germany

George I was already middle aged when he became king of Great Britain in 1714. He spoke no English and had to communicate with his ministers in French. He also spent half his time in Hanover. The Great Britain he presided over had emerged victorious from the wars against Louis XIV, and his right to be British throne had been recognized by the Treaty of Utrecht ending the War of the Spanish Succession in 1713. The treaty had also awarded Britain Gibraltar, Hudson's Bay, Nova Scotia, Newfoundland, and the *asiento,* which gave the British the exclusive right to import African slaves into Spanish America. In addition to the *asiento,* Britain was allowed limited rights of trade with the Spanish colonies. These concessions spurred development of the British navy and the establishment of trading posts that were vital to the kingdom's growing colonial empire. The territorial grants in North America intensified the contest between France and Britain for control of Canada.

Recognition of George as king provoked James II's baby boy, now grown up, to lead an uprising in Scotland to regain the crown. It failed, but when a number of Tories expressed sympathy for the **pretender,** the Whigs accused them of treason. This charge, coupled with George's clear preference for the Whigs, turned the Tories into a minority party for the next forty-five years. The leader of the triumphant Whigs was **Sir Robert Walpole,** a rich landowner and country gentleman. Walpole, unlike his ministerial predecessors, refused the king's offer to ennoble him and give him a seat in the House of Lords, the upper house of Parliament. Walpole preferred to stay in the Commons because he believed he could be more effective there in creating majorities to support royal policies. His skill in winning over both the king and Parliament contributed to the smooth running of the central government, while his decision to remain in the Commons added to the power of that house. Walpole also tried to calm the partisan passions that had agitated the country since 1660. He emphasized good manners in politics and signaled his willingness to accept moderate Tories into his political coalitions. Thus, in his own way, he agreed with Louis XIV that politeness had its political uses. Under Walpole, Britain enjoyed a period of political stability that contrasted sharply with the turmoil preceding George I's reign.

At the same time, a new sense of collective British identity was forming. Britons enjoyed the rights guaranteed in 1689 and were thereby "free-born," in opposition to what they thought were the "slavish" Catholic peoples of France or Spain. This new sense of identity was given voice in the poem "Rule, Britannia," set to music in 1740: "Rule, Britannia! Britannia, rule the waves / Britons never never never shall be slaves." After their union with England, Scots could also identify with this sense of national unity, especially since they profited increasingly from British overseas and colonial trade. The Catholic Irish, however, conquered and impoverished, were excluded from the community of the "free-born."

Act of Union   Parliamentary act of 1707 uniting Scotland and England in the one kingdom of Great Britain.

Glorious Revolution   (1688–1689) Name given to the events leading to the dethronement of James II and the rule of William and Mary.

George I   (r. 1714–1727) Elector of Hanover who became king of Great Britain.

asiento   Monopoly on the importation of African slaves into Spanish America granted to English merchants by Spain in 1713.

pretender   Claimant to a throne.

Sir Robert Walpole   (1676–1745) Leader of the Whigs and the most important minister in England from 1721 to 1742.

When George I died in 1727, Walpole survived the change of reign and continued to serve George II. Throughout his career he promoted a policy of peace with the rest of Europe and used this time to consolidate the religious and political gains of the Glorious Revolution. When he left office in 1742, the principle of mixed monarchy, in which a constitutionally sanctioned Protestant king ruled jointly with Parliament, had become the cornerstone of British political life. Finally, the defeat of James II in Ireland in 1689, along with the union of Scotland and England in 1707, consolidated English dominance.

Two World Wars, 1740–1763

↓ How did the competitive European state system effect the conduct of war?

↓ What were the outcomes of the two world wars for the states that fought in them?

In the middle of the eighteenth century, all the major states of Europe were drawn into two great wars. Warfare, a permanent feature of relations between states in early modern Europe, often ended in stalemate, but the midcentury wars fundamentally altered European power relations. Because they were also fought in the overseas empires of Britain, France, and Spain, they had long-lasting consequences for peoples in the Western Hemisphere and Asia.

The Wars

In 1740, Frederick II of Prussia attacked Maria Theresa of Austria, beginning the War of the Austrian Succession. The rulers of Bavaria and Saxony challenged Maria Theresa's right to rule on the grounds that they were more legitimate heirs to Charles VI than she. Frederick, however, accepted the legitimacy of her succession. What he wanted was Silesia, the richest of Austria's territories. Taking advantage of challenges to Maria Theresa's right of succession, he claimed that Silesia rightfully belonged to Prussia and then seized the province. Britain had been at war with Spain since 1739 over the trading rights conceded to it at the end of the War of the Spanish Succession. In 1740, Britain joined Austria to fight Prussia, renewing the British-Austrian alliance that had been forged in the wars against Louis XIV. The British also attacked the French in North America and India. France, in turn, stood by its traditional ally, Prussia, in order to check Austrian power. In 1748, at war's end, Prussia emerged victorious, keeping Silesia. The war between Britain and France ended indecisively.

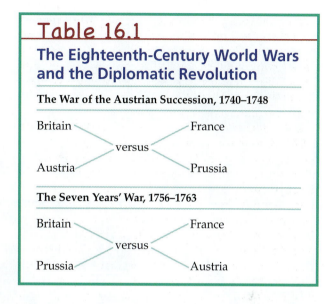

Table 16.1

The Eighteenth-Century World Wars and the Diplomatic Revolution

The War of the Austrian Succession, 1740–1748

Britain   France

         versus

Austria   Prussia

The Seven Years' War, 1756–1763

Britain   France

         versus

Prussia   Austria

War broke out again in 1756 between Austria and Prussia over Silesia, this time with Russia allied with Austria against Prussia. Since 1754, France and Britain had again been at war in North America along the western frontier of the British colonies there. In 1756, they continued the fight in Europe and India during the **Seven Years' War.** Because Austria had recently concluded an alliance with France, Britain also switched sides and joined with Prussia against the two in the **diplomatic revolution.** The war ended in 1763. The complicated alliances in these two wars are summarized in Table 16.1.

Eighteenth-Century Warfare

The complex, ever-shifting alliances and counteralliances that characterized the world wars of the mid-eighteenth century were typical of the culture of war in early modern Europe. War was accepted as an inevitable and ongoing feature of the relations between European states. Rulers did little to counteract this idea; the old ideal of the king as head of the warrior band was too deeply embedded in European tradition.

The growth of large professional armies in the hundred years between 1650 and 1750 reinforced the idea of the inevitability of ongoing warfare. The profes-

Seven Years' War (1756–1763) World war fought in Europe, North America, and India.

diplomatic revolution Shift in alliances between European states that preceded the Seven Years' War.

In this engraving from a Prussian army manual of 1726 a drill master supervises the marching and field maneuvers for which the Prussian army was famous. Soldiers who fail to follow his commands will have to mount the donkey punishment device shown on the left. By emphasizing the stark simplicity of the surrounding buildings, the engraver reinforces the precision and orderliness of the troops at drill. *(Bildarchiv Preussischer Kulturbesitz/Art Resource, NY)*

sional standing army, pioneered by Louis XIV, became a standard feature in eighteenth-century states. The one exception was Britain, which preferred to keep its army small while offering financial aid to its continental allies' forces. Armies were now better provisioned and disciplined than they had been during the period of religious warfare and were, therefore, less of a danger to the civilian population. Although troops were sometimes quartered in civilians' homes and taxes were imposed for the armies' upkeep, the fear of military pillaging lessened.

A science of warfare also emerged, taking several forms. One was an interest in military engineering. In France, Sébastien le Prestre de Vauban improved the architecture of fortresses and supervised their construction along France's northern and eastern frontiers. The idea that impregnable fortresses could protect France from its enemies was to shape French military planning into the twentieth century. Military scientists also produced new drill manuals for soldiers, specifying a series of increasingly complicated battlefield maneuvers, including the Prussian "goose step," which kept soldiers in a straight line. Not surprisingly, Frederick William I was a pioneer in this field, earning him the nickname "the royal drill sergeant." Soon, other armies were training their troops in similar ways. Army officers, almost always drawn from the nobility, received instruction in drill and battlefield tactics in new military academies and then applied them to the common soldiers under their command.

Eighteenth-century statesmen used warfare to enforce the doctrine of the balance of power, based on the assumption that Europe's international system functioned best when power was evenly distributed among states, thereby preventing any one of them from achieving dominance over the others. Thus, the coalitions against Louis XIV were explained as restoring the balance that the Sun King's aggressive military activity had threatened. Of course, agreement on the balance rested on the agreement of all the interested players. And that was where the problems began.

Since one player's "balance" was often another's "domination," European states were thrown into a never-ending defensive and offensive scramble. Religious division played a smaller role in the wars of midcentury than it had a century earlier. Now issues of territory, power, and prestige were central.

Winners and Losers

When war ended in 1763, there were clear winners and losers. In central Europe, Frederick II was a winner; Silesia was never returned to Austria. But the wars put huge strains on Prussia's finances and military, and at times it looked as if the kingdom would be defeated. In 1762, Frederick was saved when the pro-German emperor Peter III broke Russia's alliance with Austria and signed a peace with Prussia. This was the most consequential act of his short reign. After 1763, Prussia rested. "Old Fritz," as his subjects called the king, lost his taste for wars of conquest. Now he preferred more

In this painting by R. Warthmülle, Frederick II of Prussia inspects a potato field. Potatoes grew well in the sandy soils of Frederick's lands, and he promoted the cultivation of this New World vegetable for its high nutritional value and abundant yield. Well-fed Prussians, he knew, would live to pay taxes and serve in the army. *(Private Collection, Hamburg/akg-images)*

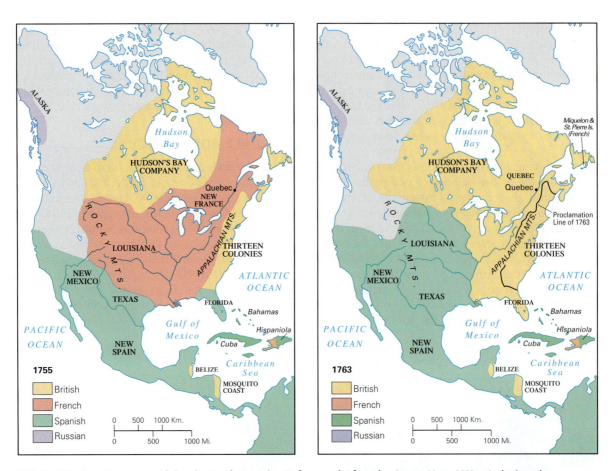

MAP 16.3   **European Claims in North America Before and After the Seven Years' War** In losing the Seven Years' War, France lost its continental North American empire. New France went to Britain, and Louisiana went to Spain. France retained only Newfoundland and its island colonies in the Caribbean.

peaceful means for gaining territory, such as joining with Austria and Russia in 1772 to partition Poland and finally link Prussia with Brandenburg.

Austria was a loser. Before 1740, the Habsburgs had not followed Prussia and Russia in reforming state finances, strengthening the central administration, and updating the army. The shock of Silesia's loss galvanized Maria Theresa into a frenzy of state building. She began with the army, founding a military academy, introducing advanced drill and maneuvering techniques, and expanding the government's ability to house and supply its troops. To pay for reform, she overhauled the state's tax structure. Beginning in 1748, she coaxed the diets of Bohemia and Austria to grant taxes for ten years. In effect, this action made state taxation permanent, and the power of the magnates in the diets to control state finances waned, just

as it had in Prussia under the Great Elector. To increase government efficiency, she founded a school to train state administrators. In 1761, she decreed that her state council, staffed by experts, could make policy decisions that were binding on her and the state administration. She, therefore, repudiated the king-centered decision making that Louis XIV and Frederick William I of Prussia had developed.

In 1756, when the Seven Years' War began, Maria Theresa's reforms were put to the test and failed. With Silesia still in Frederick's hands at war's end, Austria initiated more reforms, primarily to increase revenue to pay for a better army. This time, however, Maria Theresa tackled the problem by focusing on the economic improvement of the mass of her subjects, the serfs. Like Leopold I, she tried to reduce serfs' uncompensated work for their landlords, de-

Some official portraits of Maria Theresa show her with her husband and children, emphasizing her role as wife and mother. This one, by Martin Meyhens (c. 1743). shows her in military dress as commander of the Austrian army. *(Erich Lessing/Art Resource, NY)*

creeing that the traditional minimum of three days a week would now be the maximum. Reform of serfs' lives pitted Maria Theresa against the interests of the landlord class, but she made headway, especially in Austria and Bohemia, when serfs took matters into their own hands by going on rent strikes and fomenting local rebellions against landlord demands.

Maria Theresa also imposed new taxes on the Catholic Church. Although she was a pious Roman Catholic who hated heresy, she believed that the church should assume a greater part of the expenses needed to defend the state against competitors. The clergy were taxed without the pope's permission, and the church was forbidden to acquire new land that would be tax-free.

Defense of the Habsburg lands against enemies went hand in hand with attacks on weaker states, as the Polish partition of 1772 shows. Maria Theresa had moral scruples about the partition, but fear of continuing vulnerability in the competitive international system overcame her qualms. Frederick II of Prussia remarked unkindly, "The more she weeps, the more she takes."

Maria Theresa died in 1780 and was succeeded by her son, **Joseph II,** who was also determined to strengthen Austria against Prussia. But as his foreign policy never resulted in clear victories, he pushed domestic reforms in a more radical direction. In the 1780s he abolished serfdom. Then, in 1789, using new property tax rolls, he abolished the rents and uncompensated work obligations peasants owed their landlords, replacing them with a single cash payment. He also imposed state taxes on the ex-serfs. Traditional procedures had denied the state direct jurisdiction over peasants; the state had to work through the noble landlord class. But Joseph's reforms asserted direct state control. Peasants were to keep 70 percent of their income, the rest going in payments to the landlord and the state. Predictably, landlords resisted his radical restructuring of political and social relations, but peasants rose up in support of the reforms. The result was widespread rebellion when Joseph died in 1790. His brother, who succeeded him as Leopold II, restored order by making concessions to the landlords. He reinstituted serfdom and landlords' control of peasants. Serfdom was not permanently abolished until 1848.

Austria's defeat in war led to radical social reforms intended to increase peasant prosperity, which in turn would allow for higher taxes and more money for the army. Thus, the dynamics of Europe's fiercely competitive international system fundamentally shaped the course of Austrian state building over the second half of the eighteenth century.

Although Britain and France fought each other in Europe alongside their respective allies, their real contest was overseas in North America and India. In 1763, at the end of the Seven Years' War, Britain was the undisputed winner. British victories drove the French off the North American mainland. Britain also secured its predominant place in India. But the victory in North America created problems of its own that led directly to the American Revolution and indirectly to revolution in France.

Joseph II (r. 1780–1790) Holy Roman emperor and head of the Austrian Habsburg lands who tried to strengthen his realm through radical reform of its social structure.

Summary

Review Questions

↑ How did governments try to establish good working relations with the people?

↑ What effect did state building have on the various religious communities of Europe?

↑ What factors worked to develop or retard a collective sense of national identity?

After 1648, Europe's rulers engaged in vigorous state building. In France, Louis XIV pressed change from above based on the principle of royal absolutism, as did rulers in Prussia, Russia, and, eventually, Austria. In the British Isles, absolutism gave way to limited constitutional monarchy after the Glorious Revolution, but William III's wars against Louis XIV increased the effectiveness of the central government in Britain while strengthening Parliament's role in policymaking and administration. In all cases, the frequent warfare fostered by the competitive European state system was the prime incentive for strengthening the state.

Successful state building involved establishing good working relations between rulers and elite groups. In France and Prussia, nobles' political independence was curbed while their social preeminence was confirmed with honors and opportunities for state service. In England, after the failure of royal absolutism in 1689, the monarch had to cooperate with the landowning classes who controlled Parliament as well as local government. In Russia, rulers after Peter the Great wooed the landlord class by canceling compulsory state service but confirming landlords' rights over the serfs on their estates. Failure to establish working relations with the elite could lead to rebellion, as it did in Austria when Joseph II antagonized the nobility with his attacks on serfdom.

Joseph's abolition of serfdom was motivated in part by a desire to use state power to improve the lives of ordinary people, and the serfs responded by cooperating in the updating of property rolls and rising in support of reform when nobles resisted change. In France, Louis XIV's reforms also had the same effect; control of the army eased fears of violence and looting, and efficient and fair royal courts encouraged confidence. Louis XV's reforms of police forces and poor relief offered new services to his subjects. But when ordinary people's needs were overlooked by rulers, revolt could follow, as Pugachev's rebellion in Russia shows.

After 1648, religious commitments continued to shape identity and sometimes led to conflicts. Although Protestants throughout Europe denounced Louis XIV's revocation of the Edict of Nantes, the French Catholic population supported it. In England and Scotland, attacks on Catholics had widespread popular support. The Old Believers in Russia refused any cooperation with the state-supported Russian Orthodox Church. In France, Huguenots who refused conversion to Catholicism were also brutally dealt with. In general, however, the trend after 1648 was toward limited toleration of religious dissenters. In addition, forms of collective identity shifted from religion toward the national community. Wars between Britain and France produced a surge of patriotism in each country. While religious difference contributed to the stereotyping of the enemy, more state-centered issues, such as control of colonies or prosperity in trade, also whipped up patriotic fervor.

← **Thinking Back, Thinking Ahead** →

How were the European states of the eighteenth century similar to and different from the states of previous centuries?

ECHO ECHO ECHO ECHO ECHO

Palaces

The word *palace* derives from the name for the hill in Rome, the Palatium, where the Emperor Augustus resided. In the Middle Ages, *palatium* ("palace") referred to the temporary lodgings of kings on the move. It was also used for a monastery's guesthouse for royalty. Charlemagne's residence at Aachen was a palace of sorts. At Fontainebleau, Francis I of France built a palace blending Italian Renaissance architectural principles with traditional French design. In the late sixteenth century, Philip II of Spain built the Escorial, a grand palace-monastery complex outside Madrid. In the late seventeenth century, Louis XIV's Versailles outdid them all and set the standard for later palaces throughout Europe.

In the eighteenth century, Frederick II, following Leopold I's Schönbrunn, built a palace at Potsdam to show that Prussia also knew how to keep up with the Bourbons. The British monarchs lagged behind these palace makers. In 1762, George III bought the run-down townhouse of the Duke of Buckingham for his wife. It was only in the nineteenth and twentieth centuries that remodeling made it into the Buckingham Palace of today. British monarchs from Queen Victoria on have lived there.

Although Versailles was Europe's grandest palace, it was not very clean. Men used areas under stairways as urinals, and contemporaries remarked on the stench when they climbed the stairs. Interestingly, Versailles was open to the public. All a man needed to stroll the gardens and walk through the public rooms was a hat, gloves, and sword. If you forgot yours or did not own them, they could be rented at the gate. Visitors could also watch the king eat at midday; they got in line and filed through the far end of the room. Easy public access to the ruler's residence contrasts with the strict security that now surrounds almost all political leaders.

Today, most government heads do not live in palaces. The president of the United States lives in the White House, not the White Palace. The prime minister of Britain lives at 10 Downing Street. One exception is the president of France, who lives in Paris in the Élysée Palace, decorated in the style of Louis XIV and Louis XV. By the twenty-first century, many old palaces had undergone democratization. The Louvre Palace in Paris, the Winter Palace in St. Petersburg, and even Versailles have been turned into public monuments or museums. You can stroll through them for the price of a ticket.

Suggested Readings

Collins, James B. *The State in Early Modern France.* New York: Cambridge University Press, 2001. A good introduction to state building.

Gagliardo, John. *Germany Under the Old Regime, 1600–1790.* New York: Longman, 1991. A good general account.

Ingrao, Charles. *The Habsburg Monarchy, 1618–1715.* 2nd ed. New York: Cambridge University Press, 2000. A history of state building in the Habsburg lands.

Riasanovsky, Nicholas V., and Mark Steinberg. *A History of Russia.* 7th ed. New York: Oxford University Press, 2005. The standard account in English.

Smith, Lacey Baldwin. *This Realm of England, 1399–1688.* 8th ed. Boston: Houghton Mifflin Company, 2001. A standard account.

Spielman, John P. *Leopold I of Austria.* London: Thames and Hudson, 1977. A good biography.

Willcox, William B., and Walter L. Arnstein. *The Age of Aristocracy, 1688–1830.* 8th ed. Boston: Houghton Mifflin Company, 2001. A standard account of British history after the Glorious Revolution.

Websites

On early modern absolutism, **Structures of Politics–Absolutism,** at www.fordham.edu/halsall/mod/modsbook1.html#Structures%20of%20Politics%20-%20Absolutism

On politics in the Dutch Republic and the British Isles, **England, Holland, and America—Alternative Polities and Economies,** at www.fordham.edu/halsall/mod/modsbook1.html#England,%20Holland,%20and%20America

On early modern Russia, **Romanov Dynasty,** at www.mnsu.edu/museum/historyrussia/romanov.html

CHAPTER 17

The Scientific Revolution and the Enlightenment, 1550–1790

CHAPTER OUTLINE

1500 B.C.E.	1000 B.C.E.	500 B.C.E.	1 B.C.E./1 C.E.

1543
Copernicus, *On the Revolution of the Heavenly Bodies*

1637
Descartes,
The Discourse on Method

1540	1560	1580	1600	1620	1640	1660

Europe During the Scientific Revolution and the Enlightenment

This map shows that most scientific and Enlightenment centers were in the cities of western and central Europe. What factors explain this geographical spread? Why do you think intellectual life was focused in cities?

Legend:
- 🏰 Major university
- 📘 Scientific society
- **S** Salon
- ☕ Tea/coffee house
- — Boundary of Holy Roman Empire

KINGDOM OF SWEDEN
- Oslo
- Stockholm
- St. Petersburg — Catherine II

KINGDOM OF DENMARK AND NORWAY
- Copenhagen
- Brahe

RUSSIAN EMPIRE
- Moscow

GREAT BRITAIN
- Edinburgh
- Dublin
- Oxford
- Cambridge
- London

Bacon, Harvey, Hobbes, Boyle, Locke, Behn, Newton, Pope, Lady Montagu, Wollstonecraft, Cook

North Sea

UNITED STATES OF AMERICA
- Franklin
- Jefferson

DUTCH REPUBLIC
- Amsterdam
- Leiden
- Vesalius, van Leeuwenhoek

PRUSSIA
- Königsberg — Copernicus, Kant

POLAND
- Warsaw

ATLANTIC OCEAN

Descartes, Pascal, Baron de Montesquieu, Voltaire, Châtelet, La Mettrie, Abbé Raynal, Diderot, Vigeé-Lebrun

FRANCE
- Paris **S**
- Göttingen
- Kepler, Mendelssohn, Frederick II
- Berlin **S**
- Heidelberg
- Prague 📘
- Tübingen

AUSTRIA
- Vienna ☕ — Rudolph II, Mozart

SWITZERLAND
- Freiburg
- Bern
- Geneva
- Rousseau
- Lyons

HUNGARY
- Budapest

AUSTRIAN NETHERLANDS

- Toulouse
- Montpellier
- Genoa
- Venice
- Padua
- Bologna 📘

REPUBLIC OF VENICE

Gallileo, Cosimo II — Florence

PORTUGAL
- Lisbon

SPAIN
- Salamanca
- Madrid

PAPAL STATES
- Rome

KINGDOM OF THE TWO SICILIES
- Naples

OTTOMAN EMPIRE
- Constantinople

Black Sea

Mediterranean Sea

0   200   400 Km.
0   200   400 Mi.

| 500 C.E. | 1000 C.E. | 1500 C.E. | 2000 C.E. |

1687 Newton, *Mathematical Principles of Natural Philosophy*

1690 Locke, *An Essay Concerning Human Understanding*

1733 Voltaire, *Philosophical Letters on the English*

1748 Montesquieu, *The Spirit of the Laws*

1751 Diderot, *Encyclopédie*, volume 1

1776 American Declaration of Independence

1784 Kant, *What Is Enlightenment?*

| 1680 | 1700 | 1720 | 1740 | 1760 | 1780 | 1800 |

Choice

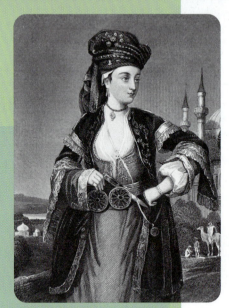

Lady Mary Wortley Montague

Lady Mary Wortley Montagu, an aristocrat, moved in England's literary circles as well, publishing poems and pamphlets anonymously. Her letters to friends and family were eventually collected and published, since letter writing was considered an art form in her day. She was also the wife of the British ambassador to the Ottoman Turkish sultan's court in Constantinople. In 1718, she witnessed the Turkish practice of inoculating people against the deadly disease of smallpox. (Boston Athenaeum)

Lady Mary Wortley Montagu Introduces Smallpox Inoculation in England

In March 1718, an aged Greek woman, her hands shaking, reached for the arms of the six-year-old son of the British ambassador to the sultan's court in Constantinople. After opening veins in the boy's arms with a blunt, rusty needle, she smeared pus into the cuts. The pus, carried in a nutshell, had come from a victim of smallpox. The old woman then bound up the wounds with more nutshells. A day later, the boy's arms began to swell, and on the third day bright spots appeared on his face and quickly turned into a hundred pustules. For a week he lay in bed with a fever. Then the pustules subsided, the fever fell, and the boy was well. He had survived a mild case of smallpox and would not get the disease again.

The boy's mother had supervised this "engrafting," as the procedure was then called. Lady Mary Wortley Montagu had seen it performed and had written home that Turks and Greeks in the sultan's lands often held engrafting parties, at which ten or fifteen people were infected with "the best sort of smallpox." Some Greeks liked to have the cuts made on their foreheads, arms, and chest to make the sign of the cross. For the Protestant Lady Mary, this was pure superstition; she preferred cuts in hidden places so that the scars they caused would not be seen. After contracting a mild form of the disease, almost everyone survived in complete health. Impressed with the procedure's success, Lady Mary decided on engrafting for her son to protect him from the death or disfigurement that smallpox so often brought.

Lady Mary knew, personally, the ravages of smallpox. In 1713, a beloved brother had died from the disease. Three years later, she contracted it. Luckily, she lived, but she lost her eyelashes and had deep pits on her face from scars the pustules had left. When her son survived his inoculation unblemished, Lady Mary became a strong advocate for the procedure. After her return to England in 1718, she encouraged friends and family to undergo inoculation and set the example again by having her infant daughter engrafted. As an aristocrat, she moved in Britain's highest social and political circles, and in 1721 the Princess of Wales joined her cause. At the princess's command, six volunteers were recruited at London's notorious Newgate Prison, and promised freedom if they survived. Physicians, surgeons, and members of the Royal Society, England's leading scientific institute, witnessed the engrafting, which was successful. The princess then ordered more experiments on London orphans. When they, too, were successful, she had two of her own daughters inoculated. Members of the royal court then began to inoculate themselves and their children. However, when two of them died, a huge controversy erupted over the wisdom of the procedure.

Some Anglican clergymen attacked inoculation on the grounds that it was contrary to God's will. But six Puritan clergy from Boston wrote that they found nothing theologically offensive in the treatment. Physicians attacked it on all fronts: inoculation's protective power was not satisfactorily demonstrated; the disease might be spread through it; the procedure was the work of amateurs who should leave such matters to the medical professionals. Worst of all, not only was it foreign, it was Turkish! As one doctor fumed, inoculation was the work of "*Ignorant Women* amongst an illiterate and unthinking People."

Faced with these attacks, Lady Mary wrote a scathing article in which she accused physicians of opposing the procedure out of greed and snobbery. Here she made public the speculation she had stated privately in a letter to her sister—whether doctors would be willing "to destroy such a considerable branch of their revenue for the good of mankind." The article, printed in a leading London newspaper, was published anonymously, for Lady Mary did not believe that a person of high breeding, like herself, should write for the public. Nevertheless, her campaign "for the good of mankind" continued to flourish. The practice of inoculation spread, and improvements, such as using cowpox, a milder variant of smallpox, made it safer.

In the nineteenth and twentieth centuries, wide use of vaccine essentially eradicated smallpox, a lethal disease that had long ravaged human populations. Therefore, routine vaccination is no longer necessary today for prevention.

Introduction

Lady Mary was caught up in many of the intellectual currents of the seventeenth and eighteenth centuries. Her interest in medicine and her attention to observation and experimentation were part of a general shift in scientific theory and method that had begun in the sixteenth century. This Scientific Revolution, which first occurred in astronomy, physics, and anatomy, had fundamentally altered people's view of the universe and led to the development of a scientific method that relied more on human reason to arrive at truth and less on the authority of ancient authors and sacred scripture. Now a new intellectual figure, the scientific expert, began to challenge the views of traditional theologians and those who believed that the best human knowledge was found in the works of ancient Greeks and Romans.

The New Science also inspired attempts to apply scientific methods to other fields of inquiry in an intellectual movement known as the Enlightenment. Relying on the scientific method's use of human reason to arrive at truth, the Enlightenment created the modern social sciences. Traditional Christianity also came under scrutiny; Lady Mary's scorn for religious "superstition" was shared by many supporters of the Enlightenment, who thought that religion should be based on observation of the natural world and the exercise of human reason. Some abandoned traditional Christianity altogether. As a result, the Christian worldview that had dominated European thought for more than a thousand years now competed with non-Christian and even nonreligious alternatives.

The principles of both the New Science and the Enlightenment were spread through new communication networks. Scientific societies, polite salon gatherings, coffeehouses, Masonic lodges, and debating clubs, for all their differences, created environments for discussion of the ideas and methods of both movements. Discussion also filled the pages of a growing number of books, newspapers, and pamphlets, as writers and publishers produced a wide variety of reading material for increasing numbers of literate Europeans. As more and more people engaged in public discussion of current affairs, a new intellectual and political force arose—public opinion—that could determine an author's success or failure and even sway the policies of kings.

When Lady Mary entered the debate over inoculation, she acted as a woman defending a Turkish medical practice carried out by other women. Debate was a central feature of both the Scientific Revolution and the Enlightenment. Women participated in these debates, and soon their increasing presence in European intellectual life led to a debate over issues of gender equality and the relations between men and women. Growth in commerce and the establishment of overseas colonies around the world also provoked debate about Europe's place in the larger world. By the end of the century, debate also centered on a central feature of commerce and colonization—the institution of slavery. In these debates, as in religion, Christian ideas had to compete with approaches that paid more attention to nature, climate, and biology than to traditional theology.

Chronology

1543	Copernicus publishes *On the Revolution of the Heavenly Bodies*
1637	Descartes publishes *The Discourse on Method*
1651	Hobbes publishes *Leviathan*
1687	Newton publishes *Mathematical Principles of Natural Philosophy*
1688	Behn publishes *Oroonoko*
1690	Locke publishes *An Essay Concerning Human Understanding* and *Two Treatises on Government*
1717	First Masonic lodge opens in London
1718	Lady Mary Wortley Montagu introduces smallpox inoculation in England
1733	Voltaire publishes *Philosophical Letters on the English*
1746	La Mettrie publishes *Man the Machine*
1748	Montesquieu publishes *The Spirit of the Laws*
1751	First volume of Diderot's *Encyclopédie* is published
1761	Voltaire takes up the case of Jean Calas; Rousseau publishes *The New Heloise*
1762	Rousseau publishes *The Social Contract* and *Emile*
1770	Raynal publishes *The Philosophical History of the Two Indies*
1772	Diderot publishes *The Supplement to the Voyage of Bougainville*
1775	Pierre Roussel publishes *The Physical and Moral Makeup of Women*
1776	Declaration of Independence states independence of American colonies from England
1778	Voltaire returns in triumph to Paris
1781	Thomas Jefferson publishes *Notes on the State of Virginia*
1784	Emmanuel Kant publishes *What Is Enlightenment?*
1789	Olaudah Equiano publishes his *Life*
1791	Mozart's opera *The Magic Flute* is performed in Vienna

A Revolution in Astronomy

↓ What were the central features of the new scientific method?

↓ What factors explain the rise of the New Science?

The religious crises that shook Europe in the sixteenth and seventeenth centuries were accompanied by an intellectual crisis. Beginning as a new theory of the universe that placed the sun, not the earth, at its center, it grew into a questioning of the traditional sources of authority guiding European thought about the natural world—ancient authors, and Christian scripture. Gradually, as the new view of the universe gained acceptance, new sources of authority based on close observation of natural phenomena and the use of independent human reasoning were embraced. These changes are usually described as the Scientific Revolution.

Ancient and Medieval Astronomy

Following the translation of classical works in the twelfth century, Europeans' views of the universe had been shaped by two ancient Greek authorities: the philosopher Aristotle and the astronomer Ptolemy. For centuries, medieval universities had synthesized their teaching with Christian theology to describe how the universe worked. In this system, the earth was at the center, created by God to be fixed and unmoving. But in terms of worth, earth was the lowest element in the cosmic scheme. It was the place of decay; as one philosopher put it, our world was "the worst, the lowest, most lifeless part of the universe, the bottom story of the house." It was only in this region, which stretched upward to the moon, that change took place. Here night turned to day; plants sprouted, bloomed, and died; and human beings moved from cradle to grave. The innate nature of objects determined some of the movement in this region. Thus acorns grew into oaks and kittens into cats because both strove to realize their potential and reach their goal as mature organisms. The same striving toward their goals also characterized nonliving things; fire leapt upward because its proper place was in the heights, while a rock thrown in the air fell because its place was on the earth. Essentially, objects were urged along by their inner natures to come to rest in their rightful place. Rest was the natural state of being for objects; it was only motion that had to be explained. In the case of human beings, God's decrees determined the movement of their lives; they hurtled toward death and decay because of their sinful rebellion against God until Christ redeemed them and they found their place of rest in Heaven.

Above the moon, a radically different part of the universe reigned. In these regions there was no change or decay. The sun and the planets, made of a uniquely pure and perfect substance, moved endlessly in circles (the noblest form of motion, as Plato had taught). Above them were the fixed stars, which also moved in a circle, propelled by the angels. As all these bodies moved, they created a wondrous music, the harmony of the spheres. Beyond the stars the universe ended, and the mysterious realm of God's Heaven began.

This picture of the natural world seemed to work because it was confirmed in multiple ways. First, it corresponded with common sense (sun, moon, and planets *did* move across the sky.) Common sense was in turn reinforced by prediction. Ptolemy had shown that it was possible to calculate the trajectories of the planets in advance, and astronomers in the centuries after him had confirmed and refined his calculations. Finally, this view corresponded with what were taken as the revealed truths of Christian scripture.

A New View of the Universe

In the sixteenth century, a new view of the universe challenged the traditional one. As it spread, an intellectual crisis developed, rivaling the crises in faith and certainty created by the Protestant Reformation, the Wars of Religion, and the discovery of the New World—an entire hemisphere with previously unknown plants, animals, and human beings.

The challenge began with a Polish clergyman in East Prussia, **Nicholas Copernicus.** Seeking to improve Ptolemy's predictions of planetary movement by making them simpler, Copernicus started with the assumption that earth and the planets moved about the sun. His *On the Revolutions of the Heavenly Bodies,* published in 1543, was quickly denounced by both

In an engraving from Johannes Hevelius' *Selenographia* (1647), an astronomer, perhaps Hevelius himself, looks at the heavens through a telescope. After Galileo's pioneering efforts, observatories sprang up all over Europe. Hevelius' observatory, on the roof of his house in Danzig, was one of the best. (*The Syndics of the Cambridge University Library*)

Protestants and Catholics. Nevertheless, Copernicus caught the attention of some astronomers, who began building on his work.

One of the first was a Dane, **Tycho Brahe,** who spent years producing the best logs of planetary movement yet compiled. He also described in detail a new star that appeared in 1572 and, thereby, disturbed the traditional view that the universe above the moon was changeless. But Brahe held the traditional view that the earth was the unmoving center of the universe; for him, the planets moved around the sun, but

Nicholas Copernicus (1473–1543) Polish astronomer who posited a sun-centered universe in which earth and the other planets move around the sun.

Tycho Brahe (1546–1601) Danish astronomer who partly confirmed Copernicus's theory of a sun-centered universe.

Sir Isaac Newton was sixty-years-old when this portrait was painted by Sir Godfrey Kneller in 1702. He had published his *Mathematical Principles* some fifteen years earlier and was at the height of his fame. *(By courtesy of the National Portrait Gallery, London)*

the sun moved around the earth. Brahe's work was continued by his pupil, **Johannes Kepler,** who used Brahe's calculations to argue that the planets moved in elliptical, not circular, orbits around the sun and that the speed of their movement varied. Both points also challenged older ideas about the unchanging nature of the upper universe.

Galileo Galilei, a professor of mathematics from Florence, continued the work of Copernicus, Brahe, and Kepler. While these men had viewed the heavens with the naked eye, Galileo used the newly invented telescope to see craters and other "imperfections" on the moon and describe sunspots for the first time. He also confirmed Copernicus's theory that the planets and the sun rotated on their own axes and posited that earth did the same. These phenomena further undermined traditional ideas. Galileo also conducted carefully controlled experiments on earthly bodies, rolling metal balls down slopes of varying degrees. He argued that material bodies were naturally in motion, thereby questioning the older idea that they moved only when

they were displaced from their homes and rested once they arrived there. A brilliant writer, Galileo knew how to present his findings to a broad public. Despite his cordial relations with Pope Urban VIII, Galileo eventually caught the eye of the Roman Inquisition, which ordered him to stop arguing in favor of the sun-centered universe and placed him under house arrest.

The Inquisition's condemnation of Galileo virtually guaranteed that sympathetic Protestants would take up his cause. The greatest of them was the Englishman **Sir Isaac Newton.** In his *Mathematical Principles of Natural Philosophy* (1687), Newton brought together the work of Copernicus, Brahe, Kepler, and Galileo to present a complete picture of the universe. Planets, rotating on their axes, traveled around the sun in elliptical orbit. Their orbits and the variations in their speed were controlled by gravity, a force of mutual attraction that kept the planets from flying off into space. Gravity also explained the behavior of bodies on earth, as described by Galileo. Beyond the solar system, the universe stretched out infinitely. Newton presented his picture mathematically. Although only a handful of his contemporaries understood his advanced equations, his ability to knit the work of his predecessors into an all-encompassing description of the universe proved compelling and established the modern science of physics.

Models of Scientific Knowledge

Just as important as the new view of the universe were the methods developed for proposing it. Taken together, they radically altered traditional European views of how human beings know anything. **Sir Francis Bacon,** lord chancellor of England under James I, was an early advocate of an approach to knowledge grounded in careful observation and experimentation. For him, the source of authority for knowledge about the natural world was found in that world itself, not in the writings of Greeks or Romans. He was, there-

Johannes Kepler   (1571–1630) German student of Brahe who argued that the planets moved in elliptical orbits around the sun.

Galileo Galilei   (1564–1642) Italian astronomer who first used the telescope to view the heavens and argued in favor of the Copernican system.

Sir Isaac Newton   (1642–1727) English mathematician and philosopher who established the modern science of physics.

Sir Francis Bacon   (1561–1626) English defender of the New Science who endorsed the inductive method of inquiry.

fore, an early defender of a purely **inductive method** of reasoning, which based general statements on observation of phenomena as the only proper way to gain knowledge.

Just as influential was a French mathematician and the inventor of analytic geometry, **René Descartes.** Descartes was deeply affected by the intellectual crisis the Protestant-Catholic split had created in western Christendom. The constant attacks of each side against the other had led to massive intellectual confusion. Some maintained that since no human opinion could ever be shown to be definitively true, one had to take a leap of faith and submit to the authority of the church and its teachings. Others embraced a thoroughgoing skepticism about the truth of any human argument. Descartes began by examining himself.

Self-examination was something Christians had practiced for centuries, but Descartes struck off in a new direction. He decided that he would submit every statement he had heard about humans and their world to radical doubt. If there was any reason, no matter how small, to doubt it, he would treat it as worthless. Statement after statement was tossed aside until, finally, Descartes came upon something that, try as he would, he simply could not doubt: "I think." This undoubted truth became his principle of knowledge. From it he drew another equally firm conclusion: "Therefore I am." I exist as a thinker—that was the starting place for knowledge. Descartes then went on to reconstruct the world, moving from previously established points to new ones that followed logically from them. This **deductive method,** modeled on geometry, lay behind his *Discourse on Method* (1637).

In arriving at reliable knowledge, Descartes departed from Bacon. Instead of looking out at the natural world, he looked inside himself and found an authoritative source for all knowledge—the principle of autonomous, or independent, human reason. Human reason had always played an important role in traditional Christian views about the sources for human knowledge; the medieval Scholastic movement had placed a premium on logically presented argument. But in the older view, reason was also supplemented by divine revelation, which corrected or completed what human beings could think on their own. For Descartes, human reason stood alone as a reliable source for human knowledge.

Newton combined Bacon's and Descartes' methods to argue that any statement about the natural world had to pass two tests. First, it had to correspond to what was found by observation and experimentation. Second, it had to fit logically with all else that was known about the phenomenon being investigated. He thus combined inductive and deductive

methods to arrive at knowledge about the world and thereby laid the foundations for the modern **scientific method.** Newton's method impressed people as much as his description of the universe. His mighty mind had swept heaven and earth, revealing for the first time how the universe worked. As the English poet **Alexander Pope** exclaimed:

> *Nature and Nature's laws lay hid in Night:*
> *God said, Let Newton be! and all was light.*

Why Change Occurred

Many factors contributed to the new view of the universe. One stemmed from Renaissance humanists' rediscovery of ancient authors, including Plato. In the medieval west, Aristotle had reigned supreme. With the recovery of other ancient works, it became clear that Aristotle's theories had been contested in their own times and could be challenged again by new approaches to nature.

Another factor concerned the people engaged in the study of nature. Traditionally, philosophers pursued natural studies in a university setting. Much of the new work, however, was done by mathematicians working outside the universities. Copernicus, Kepler, and Descartes worked on their own or sought support from princely patrons.

Mathematicians' prestige rose when they were called on to help with land reclamation and canal building in places like the Dutch Republic or land surveys for taxation purposes in states trying to raise more revenue. Applying mathematics to solve specific problems was also in tune with humanist emphasis on useful knowledge.

Usefulness also lay at the heart of another tradition contributing to the New Science, that of craftsmen. As

inductive method   Method starting with observation of phenomena and then making general statements about them based on the observations.

René Descartes   (1596–1650) French philosopher who argued for the principle of autonomous human reason as the basis for human knowledge.

deductive method   The process of drawing logically coherent conclusions from self-evident first principles.

scientific method   Newton's combination of the inductive and deductive methods to establish a twofold method for scientific inquiry.

Alexander Pope   (1688–1744) English poet and literary critic who championed Newtonian physics and the Enlightenment's emphasis on the study of human beings.

sailors ventured out into the Atlantic, the need for precise astrolabes and quadrants to measure their positions had enhanced the work of those who produced these instruments and improved them through experimentation. Thinkers such as Galileo employed craft traditions of experimentation using metal balls, telescopes, and other devices to examine natural phenomena more precisely. They then wedded observation and experimentation to mathematics.

Another intellectual pursuit fostering experimentation was **alchemy.** Alchemists believed that nature contained hidden powers that influenced how the world worked and that these powers might be revealed through careful observation of and experimentation with chemical and other natural processes. Isaac Newton, for example, was an accomplished alchemist, and his experiments in a little shed outside his rooms at the University of Cambridge contributed to his endorsement of the inductive method in physics. In addition, his theory of gravity was influenced by the belief that hidden forces determined how the universe functioned.

Developments in anatomy also fostered increased attention to observation and experimentation. **Andreas Vesalius,** a Flemish professor at the University of Padua in Italy, broke with medieval tradition by conducting his own dissections of corpses during his lectures. Previously, anatomists had lectured from ancient authorities on what dissections would reveal but left the actual cutting to surgeons, who were considered inferior to professors. Vesalius's dissections, which students loved, revealed that Galen, the greatest ancient medical authority, was incorrect when he stated that the interior wall of the heart separating the ventricles was perforated, allowing for the circulation of the blood. That the heart wall was solid now required a whole new theory of blood circulation. An English student at Padua, **William Harvey,** worked one out in 1628 after examining animals slaughtered for their meat. Harvey combined Vesalius's insistence on direct observation with the craft traditions of butchers to develop his theory and thereby laid the foundation for modern physiology.

Defenders of the New Science argued that it stood in sharp opposition to the rigid, unalterable medieval version. In fact, however, the relationship was more complex. For example, both the old and new science insisted on the importance of a logical presentation of an argument. Medieval science had also raised issues like the nature of the terrestrial and celestial realms that preoccupied the New Scientists, and medieval terminology continued in use. But as the **Scientific Revolution** progressed, the criteria for making arguments shifted. Scientists who relied more on mathe-

matics, craft traditions, and careful experimentation were developing a new view of the universe as a place full of motion, with much still to be discovered, a view in stark contrast to the unchanging and unchangeable world of Aristotle, Ptolemy, or the Bible.

The Impact of the New Science

> ↓ Who participated in the Scientific Revolution and how did the participants characterize themselves?
> ↓ What was the impact of the New Science on theology and political theory?

Those practicing the New Science were from many regions of Europe. Their findings were spread by means of a new institution, the scientific society, made up of well-to-do men who thought of themselves as a new type of educated person, the modern man of science. The societies developed procedures for presenting and verifying scientific experiments. They also provided guidelines for reproducing them and published new information for the interested public. As new views of the universe spread, along with the new scientific method and the principle of autonomous human reason, traditional European religious and political thought expanded in new ways.

Scientific Networks

The first scientific societies developed in princely courts. In Prague, the emperor Rudolf II (r. 1576–1612) established one of the first. Rudolph was a moody, reclusive man who fought with his brother for control of the Habsburg Empire, but he was also interested in artistic and scientific developments and joined with the king of Denmark to support Tycho Brahe's work. In Florence, Cosimo II not only patronized artists such as the French printmaker Jacques Callot but also supported Galileo and encouraged scientific discus-

alchemy   Discipline practiced in the Middle Ages that searched for the hidden relations between natural phenomena.

Andreas Vesalius   (1514–1564) Flemish physician who dissected human corpses and corrected some ancient statements about human anatomy.

William Harvey   (1578–1657) English physician who described the circulation of blood in the human body.

Scientific Revolution   Name given to the new views of the natural world and the new methods for obtaining them that began in the sixteenth century.

sion. In England, Bacon called for a research institute whose members would be royal employees collecting information to enhance state power. In fact, no such institute was created. Scientists' connections with the state were therefore looser than Bacon had hoped. Although Charles II of England and Louis XIV of France granted charters to the Royal Society of London and the French Royal Academy of Sciences, respectively, scientists generally worked free of direct royal control.

Membership in scientific organizations was overwhelmingly male. That men interested in science had to have a formal education further limited membership to the economically well-off. Members met to discuss issues of method and to learn what experiments others in the organization had performed. Some societies followed the lead of the English Royal Society and published reports of scientific findings.

Demonstrations of observable physical phenomena played an important role in scientific meetings. The correctness and accuracy of observations could be confirmed when many members agreed on them. During meetings, orderly procedures and polite behavior were insisted on. In addition, gentlemanly codes of honor and honesty helped to guarantee that the experimenters could be taken at their word. In printed presentations of experiments, detailed descriptions of equipment, procedures, and results were given so that readers could feel that they, too, had been present when the experiment took place. Detailed description also made possible the reproduction of the experiment.

Members of scientific societies believed they were a new class of people called to interpret the book of nature. Robert Boyle, a founder of the Royal Society of London who made important contributions to the study of air pressure and chemistry, called its members "priests of nature," because they revealed God's work through experimentation and observation. Boyle was a deeply religious man. He believed that men performing experiments must be modest and unassuming, in contrast to university debates, which had traditionally been conducted in public with lots of verbal fireworks. Personal ambition, prejudice, and passion had no place in proper scientific work. From these ideas emerged the modern concept of scientific objectivity.

Science and Religion

Newton's theory bound earth to the heavens, describing both as operating under laws that made motion as natural as rest. In his view, the universe seemed to function like a machine or a huge self-regulating clock. After being wound up, clocks ticked away in orderly fashion, following the laws governing their construction. The universe, he proposed, operated in the same way. In addition, Descartes and others argued that everything in the universe was made up of tiny particles that moved mechanically by universal laws of attraction and repulsion. Rocks, plants, animals, and human beings were like the planets—matter in motion. So it now seemed that there was a man-machine as well as a universe-machine. If all this was true, where did God fit in? For a few, the answer was clear: he didn't. For the great majority, however, there was definitely a place for God in the new order.

Clocks required a clockmaker, and, by analogy, the universe required a universe maker. This widely held belief was reinforced by the argument from design. Newton's wonderfully regulated universe could not have come into being without a designer. The microscope, perfected by the Dutch lensmaker Anton van Leeuwenhoek, was also important in this regard, since it revealed previously unknown worlds, small in size but intricate in detail, that also pointed to a divine designer.

Descartes' view that all bodies, including human ones, were simply matter in motion struck many as atheistic. But Descartes, a Catholic, believed in the Christian God. He argued that humans were unique. Not only did they have bodies made of matter, which were governed by the laws of attraction and repulsion; they also had minds, which were nonmaterial. God endowed human minds with the ability to reason, and Descartes reasoned his way to God's existence. For example, he argued that humans were finite beings who yet had a clear and distinct idea of God as an infinite being. Since the idea of an infinite being cannot be conceived by a finite one, it must be an innate idea given to humans by God himself. Arguments like these were meant to preserve the basic features of traditional Christian theology while relying solely on the principle of autonomous human reason for arriving at them.

Royal Society   One of the earliest scientific academies, founded in London in 1660.

Robert Boyle   (1627–1691) Founder of the Royal Society who advanced understanding of air pressure and chemistry.

argument from design   Widely held belief in the seventeenth century that the complex and beautiful design of nature was proof of a divine designer's existence.

atheism   Belief that there is no God.

innate ideas   Ideas about God, the human mind, or anything else that seem to be a primary part of human mental equipment.

If the universe was like a huge clock, did God wind it up at the beginning and then allow it to run on its own? Some of Descartes' arguments seemed to imply this belief, while others made room for ongoing divine intervention. Newton also insisted on God's regular activity in keeping the universe running and denounced the idea of a "dwarf-god" who did nothing more than set the world machine in motion.

For the New Scientists of the seventeenth century, the universe was not only a great machine; it was also the book of nature. Like the book of scripture, it could be consulted for knowledge of the Christian God. Protestants argued that the book of nature could be enlisted in the battle against Catholic error. A universe operating in a regular way under natural laws had no place for Catholics' superstitious beliefs in miracles performed by saints. Lady Mary Wortley Montagu's dismissal of smallpox inoculation in the form of the cross fitted into this rejection of "superstition" (see Choice). The Catholic Galileo argued that knowledge of nature led to a proper interpretation of scripture. Biblical references to the sun's motion around the earth should not be taken literally; they were simply God's concession to "the shallow minds of the common people."

One mathematician and scientist, **Blaise Pascal,** took issue with the heavy reliance on observation and reason as the best guides for religious thought. Pascal was a devout Jansenist who worried that Descartes' emphasis on autonomous human reason and innate ideas improperly downplayed the traditional Christian emphasis on revelation as a source of religious knowledge. Pascal gave reason and observation their proper place in the construction of human knowledge: although humans were mere specks in an infinite universe, and frail as reeds tossed about in the wind, they were thinking reeds. But Pascal introduced another source of knowledge: "heart." Heart drew on intuition, allowing a deeper view into the human condition than either reason or observation. "Heart has its reasons that Reason does not know," Pascal explained. For him, the human condition was characterized by both wretchedness and grandeur. Human wretchedness manifested itself in people's selfish, passion-driven, sin-filled lives as they hurtled toward the abyss of death. Grandeur manifested itself in the deep self-awareness of that wretchedness that "heart" opened up. Life as it is is not life as God originally meant it to be. Pascal died before he could present his ideas in a defense of traditional Christianity, but his notes have survived in his *Pensées* (*Thoughts),* one of the great philosophical and religious statements of the seventeenth century and published in various editions since 1670.

Pascal was one of many seventeenth-century scientists whose beliefs were shot through with traditional Christian values and concerns. Bacon believed that the accumulation of natural knowledge would prepare for Christ's return to earth, while Newton believed that human mastery of nature was a step in restoring the human race to Paradise, where Adam was master of the world before he fell into sin.

Science and the State

On April 2, 1662, Jacques-Bénigne Bossuet, a bishop in the Catholic Church, preached a sermon "On the Duties of Kings" before Louis XIV in which he celebrated the theory of absolute monarchy. "You are gods," he said to Louis. "You are all sons of the Most High." These flattering words came from Psalm 82. Bossuet then went on to describe how the king ruled without any human check on his power. Each point was justified by an appropriate quotation from Christian scripture. Basing politics on the Bible had been practiced since the days of the first Christian emperors of fourth-century Rome. Bossuet was, therefore, the heir to centuries of European political thought. At the same time, however, justifications for absolutism based on the New Science were also being proposed. Descartes' endorsement of the sun-centered universe, for example, was adopted as a model for Louis XIV's monarchy. Just as the planets orbited around the sun, so French subjects should be obedient to the Sun King.

The Englishman **Thomas Hobbes** also drew on scientific thought to argue for absolutism. Hobbes had lived through the turmoil of the English civil war and Commonwealth and had accepted Descartes' idea that human beings were matter in motion. Combining his experience of political instability and violence with his mechanical view of human beings, he argued in *Leviathan* (1651) that people, if left to themselves, would simply attack each other. The prepolitical, or natural, state was "every man against every man," because each human piece of matter in motion would try to fulfill its desires at the expense of the others. "Man is a wolf to his fellow man," he concluded, and all life "nasty, brutish, and short." The solution was to submit to an ironclad authority, a "mortal God," who would rule over everyone and force obedience to

Blaise Pascal   (1623–1662) Scientist and defender of traditional Christianity who stated that "heart" could lead one to the deepest religious truths.

Thomas Hobbes   (1588–1679) English political theorist who tried to defend absolutism on scientific grounds.

laws that restrained the aggressive impulses in people. Hobbes's defense of absolutism differed from traditional ones by not being based on the ruler's divine right to rule. He believed that the people created the absolute ruler (who might be a king or a parliament) to end the self-defeating violence of prepolitical society. Absolutism was, therefore, based on a contract between ruler and ruled, not on God's will.

Another Englishman, **John Locke,** also argued that government rested on a contract between ruler and ruled. But he drew quite different conclusions from this premise. Locke was an opponent of absolutism and had fled to Holland when James II became king in 1685. Returning to England with William and Mary, he published *Two Treatises on Government* (1690), in which he justified the Glorious Revolution. Locke had a more optimistic view of human nature than Hobbes. He believed that people could curb their aggressive impulses without coercion from an absolutist government. People entered into a political contract voluntarily and could withdraw from it when it no longer suited their purposes. The chief purpose of government was to protect private property rights. Locke's notions of contractual government and rights of private property supported the overthrow of James II, the repudiation of absolutism, and landowners' control of Parliament under a constitutional monarchy. His thought also had an impact on the American revolutionaries of the eighteenth century.

Although Hobbes and Locke had different views of human nature and endorsed different kinds of states, both tried to construct their politics on the basis of experience and reason rather than tradition and scripture. Their work represents some of the first attempts to construct a "political science."

The Nature of History

Growing enthusiasm for the New Science also provoked a sharp argument over the nature of human history. Traditional seventeenth-century understandings of history were pessimistic. Some stated that history was the sad story of decline and decay from an original high point, sometimes identified as the Garden of Eden and sometimes as Greek and Roman culture. In either case, humanity's passage through time was simply a slide downhill from an earlier golden age. A less dismal view presented history in cyclical terms. Humanity passed through high stages and then slid into decay until, once again, it started to ascend to a high point that, in turn, would provoke another period of decline. Thus, in a Protestant version of the cyclical theory, the high point of Christianity's first days was followed by a decline as Catholicism spread,

until Martin Luther's or John Calvin's day, when Protestantism returned Christianity to its original purity and a high point was once again reached. Traditionalists sometimes argued that the natural world was subject to decay as well; plants and animals, along with people, had degenerated over time. People who held these traditional views of natural and human history were called Ancients.

Beginning in the late seventeenth century, a new view of history gained ground, held by people dubbed Moderns. Inspired by the New Science, the Moderns argued against a decay over time of the natural world, citing the timeless, universal laws that Newton had discovered. Moderns also optimistically argued that human history was the story of intellectual progress. Although ancient Greek and Roman poets and playwrights were as good as contemporary ones, ancient scientists had been surpassed. Progress pointed to the overall superiority of Moderns. The battle between Ancients and Moderns continued on into the eighteenth century.

The Enlightenment

↓ How did the Enlightenment employ the methods of the New Science?

↓ What were the major items on the Enlightenment's agenda for reform?

Isaac Newton was the inspiration for a new European intellectual movement that emerged in the last years of the seventeenth century. People who joined it described themselves as enlightened, because they had embraced Newton's view of the universe along with his scientific method. Historians have adopted the term for the movement itself. The Enlightenment was the most energetic current in European thought during the eighteenth century.

The Early Enlightenment

England, the home of Isaac Newton, was one center for the early **Enlightenment.** The power of Newton's scientific method inspired his fellow countryman,

John Locke (1632–1704) English political theorist who argued, like Hobbes, that government rested on a contract between ruler and ruled.

Enlightenment European intellectual movement of the eighteenth century using the scientific method of the New Science.

John Locke, to apply it to a new field of study, the human mind. In 1690, Locke published *An Essay Concerning Human Understanding,* in which he took issue with Descartes' belief that God had planted some innate ideas in the mind. Instead, Locke argued, our minds at birth are like "white paper, void of all characters, without any ideas." Ideas arise only through experience of the world around us. And that experience comes through our senses of sight, hearing, taste, touch, and smell.

Locke's *Essay* was one of the foundational documents of the Enlightenment. It showed how Newton's scientific method could be used to establish a new science, that of the human mind, and thereby laid the foundations for the modern discipline of psychology. At the same time, it ratified a central tenet of the scientific method—reasoning on the basis of experience and observation. The *Essay* also had one profound implication. Sense knowledge can come only from the physical, material world, since it alone is capable of registering on the senses. That meant that human beings could not directly know the immaterial or supernatural world, even if it exists. Thus, the *Essay,* repudiating the notion of innate ideas and limiting human knowledge to sense impressions, cast serious doubt on the reality of divine revelation as an authority for guiding people's lives. Messages from the supernatural beyond seemed less and less likely in Locke's world.

Locke's interest in the mind testifies to a central concern of the Enlightenment: the study of human beings. In the sixteenth century, when the western Christian world split into two warring camps—Catholic and Protestant—the problem of God was a central intellectual issue. The Scientific Revolution brought the study of nature to the fore. In the Enlightenment, attention shifted once again. As Alexander Pope put it:

> Know then thyself, presume not God to scan;
> The Proper study of Mankind is Man.

Another center of the Enlightenment was France, where the **Baron de Montesquieu** took the study of humans in a different direction. A nobleman and a lawyer, Montesquieu sat in the French Parlement of Bordeaux. He made his literary debut in 1721 with *The Persian Letters,* a witty critique of French society supposedly written by Persian tourists. In 1748, he published one of the great works of the Enlightenment, *The Spirit of the Laws.* Unlike Locke, who had studied the individual human mind, Montesquieu focused on human beings as a group. Assuming that there was a universal human nature, he then sought the causes for the great variety of human political arrangements—monarchies, republics, despotic states—and found them in environmental factors. A comparative analy-

sis led him to argue that climate and geography played an important role in shaping the features of any given society. He concluded that a society's traditions concerning religion, government, and economic activity also contributed to its distinctive shape, or "spirit."

Montesquieu argued that good government in France depended on the nobility, seated in institutions like the parlements, which put restraints on both the monarchy and the common people. He also greatly admired the constitutional monarchy of Britain. Montesquieu's interest in the role of natural and historical factors in shaping a society laid the foundations for the modern discipline of sociology.

Voltaire

If any person embodied the Enlightenment, it was the French philosopher and author **Voltaire.** The son of a middle-class Parisian lawyer, Voltaire attended the prestigious Jesuit school of Louis-le-Grand. He then defied his father, who wanted him to enter the law, by deciding to make his living as a writer. In 1718, his first play, *Oedipus,* which recounted the Greek legend of the king who killed his father and slept with his mother, ran on the Paris stage for an unprecedented forty-five nights. This success established the young man as France's foremost author of tragedies. A few years later, he published an epic poem on the reign of Henry IV of France, the *Henriade,* his most popular work.

In late 1725, a quarrel with a descendant of one of France's greatest noble families landed Voltaire in the **Bastille,** a notorious royal prison. He was released in 1726, on the condition that he go into exile in England. He did, and his exile set him on the path that made him France's greatest **philosophe,** the name French supporters of Enlightenment gave themselves.

Voltaire stayed in England until 1729, becoming familiar with Newton's and Locke's writings and learning about the English form of monarchical and parliamentary government. In 1733, he published *Philosophical Letters on the English,* a seemingly inno-

---

Baron de Montesquieu   (1689–1755) One of the founders of the modern discipline of sociology and author of *The Spirit of the Laws.*

Voltaire   (1694–1778) Social critic, attacker of Christianity, defender of the principle of autonomous human reason, and author of *Candide.*

Bastille   Medieval fortress in Paris serving as a royal prison.

philosophes   (in French, "philosophers") Name French supporters of Enlightenment ideas gave themselves.

In this contemporary portrait, Voltaire is fashionably dressed and wears a wig. His eyes have moved slightly to his right so he can look directly at the viewer as if in conversation, a pose that would have pleased this master of salon culture. *(Mary Evans Picture Library/The Image Works)*

cent account of English politics, religion, and society that was, in fact, a scathing denunciation of contemporary France. The issues Voltaire raised in the *Letters* formed the basis for his subsequent career as a reformer. The subversive tone of the book was not lost on the French authorities, who ordered it burned in public by the royal executioner and issued a warrant for Voltaire's arrest. Fleeing Paris with his new mistress, **Emilie du Chatelet,** he took up residence near the French border in case a quick getaway was needed. Mme. du Chatelet, an accomplished physicist and mathematician, helped Voltaire deepen his understanding of Newton. In 1738, he published *Elements of Newton's Philosophy,* which helped to establish Newton's reputation in France.

Voltaire was also interested in the improvement of French society. He sought reform of the criminal justice system, especially an end to the use of torture. In 1761, he heard of the perfect case to make his points. In the southern French town of Toulouse, a young Huguenot, Marc-Antoine Calas, was found hanged in his father's

shop. It was rumored that Calas was about to convert to Catholicism. Although his family claimed that Calas had committed suicide, the Parlement of Toulouse, dominated by Catholics, charged his father, Jean, with murdering him to prevent his conversion. The elder Calas was found guilty and then subjected to excruciating torture to get him to confess to his crime before his execution. The elder Calas refused, even when his bones were broken, and he was finally strangled to death. Was the father guilty or not? If he was, for Voltaire he demonstrated Protestant fanaticism; if not, the court demonstrated Catholic fanaticism. Either way, the case demonstrated the barbarity of judicially sanctioned torture. Voltaire turned the **Calas affair** into a European scandal that widely discredited the use of torture in criminal proceedings.

The affair also gave Voltaire the opportunity to attack traditional Christianity, whether Protestant or Catholic. For years he had rejected Christian teaching. Now he openly subjected Christianity to withering ridicule and began closing his letters with the phrase "Stamp out the infamous thing," by which he meant the churches, their ministers and priests, and their teachings. The Jesuits, in particular, came under heavy attack, perhaps because, as Voltaire told Alexander Pope, they had sexually molested him while he was a student at Louis-le-Grand. Although most supporters of the Enlightenment remained Christians, Voltaire's public, passionate attack on Christianity marked a turning point in the religious history of Europe.

Voltaire's campaign to improve human society was waged despite his sense of the limits of reform. When a huge earthquake destroyed the city of Lisbon in Portugal, he published his most famous work, *Candide, or Optimism,* which ridiculed the German philosopher Gottfried Wilhelm Leibnitz and the English poet Alexander Pope, who argued that we live in the best of all possible worlds. Nevertheless, Voltaire endorsed a limited optimism. As Candide says at the end of the novel, "We must cultivate our gardens," by which Voltaire meant that despite calamities like the Lisbon earthquake, which are beyond any human control, some things can and should be changed. Voltaire also carried on a huge correspondence, exchanging letters with his fellow philosophes, and also with Catherine

Emilie du Chatelet (1706–1749) Voltaire's mistress and intellectual companion who was an expert in Newtonian physics and mathematics.

Calas affair Trial, torture, and execution of Jean Calas, who was accused of killing his Huguenot son to prevent his conversion to Catholicism.

Voice Voice eVoiceVoice

Voltaire Attacks Christianity

Voltaire wanted to present the ideas of the Enlightenment to a large reading public. He therefore polished a literary style that sparkled with wit and was laced with biting satire and moral outrage. The two pieces presented below illustrate Voltaire's attack on traditional Christianity, "the infamous thing." They were published anonymously, without the approval of the French royal censors, and represent the Enlightenment attack on Christianity in its most radical form. They offended many traditionalists, who dismissed Voltaire as a "filthy little atheist," but they expressed views that many people repeated in the years after Voltaire published his attack.

On the Trinity

Here is an incomprehensible question which for over sixteen hundred years has exercised curiosity, sophistical subtlety, bitterness, the spirit of cabal, the rage to dominate, the rage to persecute, blind and bloodthirsty fanaticism, barbaric credulity, and which has produced more horrors than the ambition of princes, which indeed has produced enough.

➔ Is Jesus Word? If he is Word, did he emanate from God, is he co-eternal and consubstantial with him, or is he of a similar substance? Is he distinct from him or not? Is he created or engendered? Can he engender in turn? Has he paternity, or productive virtue without paternity? Is the holy ghost created or engendered or produced? Does he proceed from the father, or from the son, or from both? Can he engender, can he produce? Is his hypostasis consubstantial with the hypostasis of the father and the son? And why, having precisely the same nature, the same essence as the father and the son, can he not do the same things as these two persons who are himself?

I certainly do not understand any of this; nobody has ever understood any of this, and this is the reason for which people have slaughtered one another.

The Story of the Banishing of the Jesuits from China

Brother Rigolet: ➔ Our God was born in a stable, seventeen hundred and twenty-three years ago, between an ox and an ass. . . . [His mother] was not a woman, but a girl. It is true that she was married, and that she had two other children, named James as the old gospels say, but she was a virgin none the less.

The Emperor: What! She was a virgin and she had children!

Brother Rigolet: To be sure. This is the nub of the story: it was God who gave this girl a child.

The Emperor: I don't understand you. You have just told me that she was the mother of God. So God slept with his mother in order to be born of her?

Brother Rigolet: You've got it Your Sacred Majesty; grace was already in operation. You've got it I say; God changed himself into a pigeon to give a child to a carpenter's wife, and that child was God himself.

The Emperor: But then we have two Gods to take into account: a carpenter and a pigeon.

➔ How does Voltaire turn the technical theological terms he uses here against the doctrine of the Trinity?

➔ Why would Voltaire choose to mock the Jesuits in this little dialogue?

Brother Rigolet: ➡ Without a doubt, Sire; but there is also a third, who is the father of these two, and whom we always paint with a majestic beard: it was this God who ordered the pigeon to give a child to the carpenter's wife, from whom the God-carpenter was born; but at the bottom these three make only one. The father had engendered the son before he was in the world, the son was then engendered by the pigeon, and the pigeon proceeds from the father and the son. Now you see that the pigeon who proceeds, the carpenter who is born of the pigeon, and the father who has engendered the son of the pigeon, can only be a single God; and that a man who doesn't believe this story should be burned in this world and the other.

The Emperor: That is as clear as day.

➡ How does Voltaire develop this story for comic effect?

Source: Extract from Peter Gay, *Voltaire's Politics: The Poet as Realist* (New Haven, CT: Yale University Press, 1959), pp. 246–247. Reprinted by Yale University Press.

II of Russia and Frederick II of Prussia, who invited him to his court outside Berlin. No European writer since Erasmus in the sixteenth century was as well connected as Voltaire.

In early 1778, Voltaire, now eighty-three, returned in triumph to Paris. The city's most prestigious theatrical company, the Comédie-Française, performed his tragedy *Irene* and placed his statue in their theater, the only living author to be so honored. At his death, in May of that year, he was arguably the most famous man in Europe. The modern edition of his works fills more than 135 volumes.

Enlightenment Religion

Although Voltaire declared war on Christianity, he was no atheist. He embraced **deism,** a rational religion based solely on the observation of nature. Deism drew on Locke's sense-based psychology, the argument from design, and Newton's clocklike universe. As a religious movement, it denied Christian doctrines of the Trinity, the divinity of Jesus, and the divine authority of the Bible. Most deists also rejected Newton's notion that God intervenes in the universe to keep it going. Deists emphasized the need for humane treatment of human beings, supporting the campaign against judicial torture.

For Voltaire and other deists, like Benjamin Franklin and Thomas Jefferson, deism and religious toleration went hand in hand. Since traditional religion, whether Jewish or Christian, was based on fraud and foolishness, it could never be legitimately defended by attacking those who rejected it. Even acceptable religious belief, like deism, was a matter of individual conscience over which no state or church authority ought to have jurisdiction. Voltaire's pursuit of these points in the Calas affair met with growing sympathy, and,

in 1787, on the eve of revolution in France, Louis XVI signed an edict granting limited religious toleration to the Huguenots. Deist-inspired calls for religious toleration also spread in Britain's North American colonies. After gaining independence, the new United States proclaimed religious toleration in its own Bill of Rights (1791).

In addition to battling traditional Christians, Voltaire also denounced atheists. On this score, however, he was fighting a losing battle. By the mid-eighteenth century, more and more philosophes believed that the existence of God could never be proved by an argument from design or demonstrated as necessary for explaining the world and human beings. The **materialism** of Descartes, stripped of its Christian beliefs, could account for everything. The universe simply was, and humans were wholly material beings without souls or immaterial minds. At death, they ceased to exist. In 1746, a French physician, **Julien Offroy de La Mettrie,** argued these points in *Man the Machine.* His work caused a scandal in conservative circles, but, undaunted, he followed it up in 1749 with *Man the Plant.* La Mettrie also preached a gospel of pure physical pleasure, which made him doubly scandalous. In 1751, when he died after gorging himself on pheasant pâté, his enemies said the punishment fitted the crime.

deism   Religious belief that rejected traditional Christian teachings and tried to base its theology on scientific method.

materialism   Argument that material things alone exist, therefore denying the existence of a soul or of an immaterial world.

Julien Offroy de La Mettrie   (1709–1751) French author of the materialist and atheistic works *Man the Machine* and *Man the Plant.*

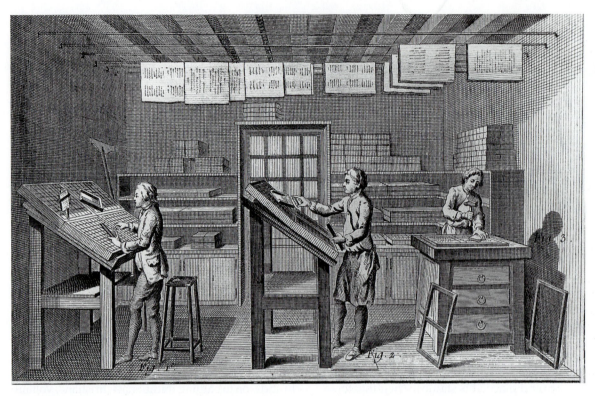

This engraving of a craft process from Diderot's *Encyclopédie* shows a printer's shop. From left to right men set type for a page, arrange lines, and lock the type in place. The type will print four pages at once. Previously printed pages are drying on lines above workmen's heads; when dry, they will be folded to arrange the pages in proper sequence. Diderot's emphasis on craft and manufacturing processes reminded readers of their importance and gave them a new dignity. *(Division of Rare & Manuscript Collections, Cornell University Library)*

Some Jewish thinkers were also caught up in the debates over revealed versus natural religion and atheism. One of the most important was the German Jew **Moses Mendelssohn.** Mendelssohn argued for a Judaism stripped of miracles and other supernatural phenomena. Its basic truths could be proved by reason. He also rejected the idea of Jewish uniqueness, denying that the Jews were a chosen people. But he asserted that, in the larger Christian world, they were an oppressed people, and he worked tirelessly to end discriminatory legislation against them. He also urged Jews to be more open to the larger European culture. They should stop using Yiddish as a literary language and follow his example of writing in German. They should also stop persecuting Jewish sects, like the followers of the seventeenth-century self-proclaimed Messiah Sabbatai Sevi. If Jews demanded toleration from Christians, they should grant it themselves. Mendelssohn shocked many Jewish traditionalists, but his views appealed to others and were to be influential in the nineteenth century.

Diderot and the *Encyclopédie*

While Voltaire was crusading against Christians and atheists, some of his fellow philosophes were embarking on a highly successful publishing venture. In 1751, the first volume of the *Encyclopédie* appeared. Under the editorial leadership of **Denis Diderot,** sixteen more volumes followed over the next twenty-

Moses Mendelssohn (1729–1786) German Jew who said that Judaism's basic beliefs were rationally provable and who worked to end discrimination against Jews.

Encyclopédie Multivolume work with contributions from philosophes throughout Europe that summed up the philosophy of the Enlightenment.

Denis Diderot (1713–1784) French writer and editor of the *Encyclopédie.*

one years. The *Encyclopédie* was a huge commercial success, making millions for its publishers. Diderot wished to present current knowledge on all subjects in a single multivolume reference work. He also wanted to show how all knowledge was interconnected and that the key to it rested on observation, experiment, and autonomous reason. Throughout the *Encyclopédie,* Diderot drew on the works of Bacon, Descartes, Locke, and Newton. He also got major Enlightenment writers, such as Montesquieu and Voltaire, to contribute articles. In addition to standard articles on religious, philosophical, scientific, and artistic subjects, the *Encyclopédie* also had groundbreaking contributions on craft and manufacturing processes such as brassmaking, printing, tapestry weaving, and fishing with nets. Inclusion of these articles testified to the importance that craft traditions had played in the emergence of the Scientific Revolution. They also met Diderot's insistence that the *Encyclopédie* should be useful. Usefulness also lay behind articles like "Asparagus," which not only described the plant and its cultivation but gave five recipes as well.

Diderot had to work under conditions of government press censorship, which was always on the lookout for unorthodox political or religious ideas and often forced him to make controversial points in subtle ways. One device he and his associates perfected for sneaking in inflammatory material was a system of clever cross-referencing. For example, in the article on "France," when Louis XIV's revocation of the Edict of Nantes was described, a cross reference to "Toleration" was given. If Voltaire was the one man who best embodied the ideals of Enlightenment, the *Encyclopédie* was the one work that summed them up.

The Late Enlightenment

As editor of the *Encyclopédie,* Diderot had to be discreet in voicing his own opinions, but his works make clear that he, too, had embraced materialism and atheism. The leading philosophe of the late Enlightenment, however, did not. He was **Jean-Jacques Rousseau,** the son of a Genevan watchmaker. Rousseau was a Calvinist who converted to Catholicism and then embraced deism. His *Profession of Faith of a Savoyard Vicar,* an emotional defense of deism, won Voltaire's praise.

Rousseau was touchy, paranoid, and blunt. In the 1750s, he attacked the refined world of the philosophes and their aristocratic patrons. Rejecting the Christian idea of original sin, Rousseau believed that human beings were good by nature but that civilization had

In this etching Jean-Jacques Rousseau is depicted as a "man of nature" who rejected the refined world of the salons. Leaning against a tree and holding a bunch of wildflowers, he contemplates the beauty of the natural world, which his deist God had created. *(The Granger Collection, New York)*

corrupted them because it encouraged injustice and inequality. His attacks alienated Voltaire, Diderot, and others who believed that civilization was a sign of human progress, not degeneration. Voltaire said he thought Rousseau wanted him to walk around on all fours. In fact, however, Rousseau did not want to abolish civilization; he wanted to reform it.

In 1762 Rousseau published *The Social Contract,* which advocated a democratic society and pioneered modern democratic theory. This work set him apart from other philosophes. For all their radicalism, Vol-

Jean-Jacques Rousseau (1712–1778) Genevan Swiss social critic, philosophe, and novelist who pioneered modern democratic theory in his *Social Contract.*

taire and Diderot were part of the eighteenth-century literary establishment. Like the gentlemen who gathered in the scientific societies of the seventeenth century, they criticized society but did not want to overturn it. In contrast, Rousseau wanted fundamental change. He argued that the good society is one in which all members voluntarily give up their individual rights and submit to what he called the general will. Usually, the general will amounted to the will of the community's majority, although Rousseau was careful to say that sometimes it did not. This point has confused some of his readers. What Rousseau really wanted was a community in which people participated in politics and acted openly for the true good of all the community's members. This ideal has served as a benchmark for democratic societies ever since.

Rousseau's hunger for openness in human relations prompted him to write his *Confessions*. Published in 1781, three years after his death, the *Confessions* recounted in detail many of the most private facts of his life, among them acts of theft, sex with a sailor, and the abandonment of a child he had fathered. While some were shocked by these revelations, Rousseau's real intent was to demonstrate that he was a man who hid nothing but presented himself fully to other human beings. If all people were as open, society could be fundamentally transformed.

Rousseau's radicalism and rejection of refined aristocratic society was also endorsed by a host of pamphleteers and writers for hire who never made it into Voltaire's or Diderot's elite publishing circles. These people produced political criticism that mixed opposition to government policies with pornographic accounts of the degenerate lives of kings, queens, and nobility. Although these works had roots in earlier traditions of satire and slander, their volume and intensity increased in the late eighteenth century, especially in France after its defeat in the Seven Years' War. Overall, they undermined the legitimacy of traditional government as much as Rousseau's democratic criticisms did.

Other parts of Europe were less receptive to the radicalism that swept over France after 1750. In Prussia, **Immanuel Kant** summed up the philosophes' program in *What Is Enlightenment?* (1784): "Dare to know. . . . Have the courage to use your own understanding is . . . the motto of enlightenment." Kant, however, never advocated democracy or any real social or political reform. People were free to use their minds to seek the truth but, according to Kant, should submit to the current political, social, and economic orders in which they found themselves.

Society and the Enlightenment

> ↓ What impact did developments in publishing and reading habits have on European intellectual life?
> ↓ What additional trends promoted the Enlightenment?

Just as scientific societies helped to spread Newtonian physics, so new institutions served to popularize the Enlightenment. Publishers expanded the types of books they produced from religious works to new literary forms like the novel. Newspapers also became increasingly available to readers. This wider array of reading materials, which encouraged readers to digest the news of the day or enter into the world of the novel, offered new ways of thinking about human experience. The Enlightenment's insistence on rational discussion of topics spread through society as new opportunities opened for comment on current affairs in coffeehouses, salons, and Masonic lodges. Critical discussion of issues also spilled over into the political realm as ordinary people commented on rulers' policies and required rulers to justify their actions before a new political force, public opinion.

The New World of Reading

The invention of the printing press in the mid-fifteenth century, along with the Protestant Reformation and Catholic reforms of the sixteenth, ushered in a new era in the history of European book reading. Both Protestants and Catholics used print to attack their opponents and to present their co-religionists with catechisms and prayer books. Most of this popular literature was written in the languages spoken by the people rather than Latin, which was still the official language of learning. In Protestant countries, translations of the Bible also multiplied. Prayer books, catechisms, and Bibles were read reverently and reread many times; Bible study required returning to passages over and over again, while prayers for the morning and evening were repeated daily. Habits of devout, repetitive reading, a reading style intimately linked to Christian belief, were predominant among literate people in the sixteenth and seventeenth centuries as religious publications multiplied.

In the eighteenth century, both the types of litera-

Immanuel Kant (1724–1804) Leading German philosophe of the late Enlightenment.

In Pierre-Antoine Baudoin's *Reading,* the woman reads in private. Note how the screen behind her would prevent anyone coming through the door to see directly into the room. Her book, a novel, has fallen from her left hand as she swoons over it, thinking of the scene she has just read. *(P.A. Baudoin, La Lecture. Les Arts Decoratifs, Musée des Arts decoratifs, Paris. Photo Laurent Sully Jaulmes. All rights reserved.)*

ture available to people and styles of reading changed. Throughout the century, religious publications declined dramatically, and **novels,** a new literary type, rose to first place. Novels were particularly popular with women, who were now more likely to read than they had been earlier. Women like the Englishwoman **Aphra Behn** also figured prominently as authors of novels. Although some people seemed to have read and reread novels many times, and thereby used the same technique for reading them as for Bibles or prayer books, most readers read the latest bestseller only once, then turned to something else.

In addition to novels, newspapers and political pamphlets became increasingly available in the eighteenth century, especially in Britain and the Dutch Republic, where censorship laws were relaxed or abolished. Reading newspapers had often been a collective activity in which one person read aloud to a group, but increasingly newspapers were read privately and silently, like novels, and passed along un-

til the next day's newspaper was available. As the variety of reading material expanded, it is likely that Europeans received more information about the world and, often lost in the contents of the page in front of them, had a wider range of imaginative reading experiences than people had ever had before. One of the clearest signs of Europeans' expanding reading habits was the spread of **lending libraries,** which al-

novel   Literary form of prose fiction that was popular in the eighteenth century and sometimes used to promote social criticism and programs for reform.

Aphra Behn   (1640–1689) English novelist who pioneered the form and made a financial success of writing.

lending libraries   Institutions allowing readers to borrow books from their shelves and then return them, thus avoiding the need to buy them.

In this London coffee-house, as the elegantly dressed owner looks on, a waiter pours coffee for the well-to-do men sitting at tables. They are reading and conversing and may be transacting business. Note the coffee pots being kept warm in front of the fire. (© *Michael Holford*)

lowed anyone who joined to check books out to read where they wished and thus eliminated the cost of purchasing them.

The nature of writing and publishing changed with new reading habits. Formerly, writers had either worked as economically self-sufficient gentlemen or had sought commissions from wealthy patrons. In the eighteenth century, some, like Lady Mary Wortley Montagu, thought that the profession of author was beneath the well-born, but others, like Voltaire and Diderot, were eager to make a living from writing. Few became as rich or famous as they, but many managed to survive on wages paid for their work.

Those wages came from publishers. Publishing became big business in the eighteenth century. Publishing houses often specialized in certain types of literature. Some produced cheap editions of fairy tales or almanacs, which peddlers carried in their packs throughout town and countryside. Others, especially in the Dutch Republic, concentrated on controversial works that might be censored in other countries; Diderot, for example, used a publisher in the Netherlands for the *Encyclopédie*. Many of these works were then smuggled into places like France, where censors were sometimes bribed to look the other way when the books went on sale. Authors also tried to evade censors when they wrote something particularly scan-

dalous; Voltaire was fond of blaming his literary rivals for his anti-Christian works.

Publishers stayed in business by both meeting and shaping readers' demands and tastes. When a particular type of novel sold, they urged other writers to produce similar works. This worked well for Rousseau, whose *The New Heloise*, a runaway bestseller in 1761, fed a growing late-eighteenth-century taste for novels describing domestic settings that were full of romance, heartbreak, and feeling. His *Emile* (1762), a novel that advocated a "natural" course for children's education based on direct observation and experience at the various stages of a child's development, also sold well. In fact, during his life, Rousseau was better known for these novels than for *The Social Contract*.

Increasing numbers of Europeans could afford books and newspapers, or lending library fees, in part because their disposable incomes rose as Europe entered a new period of prosperity in the early eighteenth century. Moreover, printed material was viewed less as an avenue to God or a source for spiritual improvement than as a means to worldly information and pleasure. The new world of reading, writing, and publishing constituted a major shift in the intellectual activities of Europeans that the philosophes put to good use for popularizing their ideas and advocating programs of reform. Reading still remained, however, a practice that only a minority of Europeans engaged in, and the ideas of the philosophes were embraced by only a part of this reading public.

Enlightenment Sociability

Along with new types of literature and changing styles of reading, new institutions sprang up in which people could discuss what they read and put into practice the central method of the Enlightenment—thought based on autonomous human reason. Chief among them were coffee and tea houses. Europeans' consumption of coffee and tea rose significantly during the eighteenth century as a result of expanded colonial trade and an improving European economy. While both beverages were drunk at home, many people, especially men, liked to take them in cafés where there were newspapers and pamphlets to read, opportunities to buy and sell stocks in joint-stock companies, and people to talk to. The coffeehouse phenomenon had begun in Restoration London when Whigs took tea or coffee and discussed politics at Old Slaughter's, while the Tories gathered at the Cocoa Tree. Coffeehouses then sprouted up in Paris, Vienna, and other major European cities. The atmosphere in them was informal; one dropped in and left at will. Originally patronized by the rich and fashionable, coffeehouses became more socially inclusive over the century. Men of different backgrounds who would normally be separated on more formal occasions mixed easily with one another in the coffeehouse atmosphere. And always, politics and other current events were discussed. Because coffee is a stimulant, animated discussion was the rule. Unlike taverns, however, where drinking often led to brawling, coffeehouse conversation was supposed to be orderly and polite, even if heated.

Conversation was also the rule in salons. Invented in Paris during the seventeenth century, the **salon** became a central Enlightenment institution for the educated and well-born. Women like Madame du Deffand, the wife of a rich Parisian financier, presided over salons that met in their homes on specified days and discussed topics that the hostess announced. The hostess also set rules for conversation that prohibited shouting, swearing, and name calling. Guests were to converse politely, intelligently, and amusingly about the scientific, artistic, or political matters assigned for discussion. Anyone able to do this would be admitted. Thus, men and women, nobles and commoners, joined in. Although the hostess was usually rich and often noble, salons, like coffeehouses, were relatively informal institutions in which an ability to converse well counted more than wealth or social background.

Even religious differences were overlooked in salons, especially in Berlin, where Jewish hostesses brought together Jews and Christians.

Masonic lodges also offered a new form of social interaction in which religious or class differences played a minor role. Guilds of masons who laid brick or stone had existed since the Middle Ages, but modern **Freemasonry** began in London in 1717, when a group of middle-class men formed a club in which Newton's science and other issues of current interest were discussed. By the 1720s, 75 percent of the London lodge members also belonged to the Royal Society. Although Masonic lodges modified old rituals from the medieval guilds when they initiated new members, their main purpose was to create an environment like that of the salons, in which polite conversation on issues could occur. Masonic lodges spread throughout Europe in both Catholic and Protestant countries, despite the pope's condemnation of the movement in 1738 on the grounds that it advocated anti-Catholic ideas. Like the salons, the lodges downplayed the social and economic differences of their membership. Brotherhood in the lodge made all members equal. These Masonic ideals were articulated in one of the century's great operas, *The Magic Flute*, written by **Wolfgang Amadeus Mozart** and performed in the last year of the composer's life. Mozart made a point of stressing Masonic ideals of human equality. At one point, when a priest exclaims that the hero is a prince, the high priest corrects him: "More than that! He is a man!"

The Enlightenment and Politics

The rational discussion taking place in new social settings also extended to politics, taking different forms in eastern and western Europe. In Scandinavia, Germany, and Russia, Enlightenment rationalism melded with an older political tradition, **cameralism.** Devel-

salon Meeting place where current ideas are discussed, in the eighteenth century presided over by a woman.

Freemasonry Social and intellectual movement that originated in England during the eighteenth century and spread across Europe.

Wolfgang Amadeus Mozart (1756–1791) Composer of symphonies, operas, and many other works who perfected the classical style in music.

cameralism Eastern European tradition of political thought emphasizing rational government policymaking that melded with Enlightenment principles.

oping in the seventeenth century, cameralism aimed at increasing a state's wealth through direct management of people and resources. Government should intervene in people's lives to make them better fed, better housed, and better behaved so that they could become more productive. Cameralism also emphasized the need for a rational assessment of a state's strengths, weaknesses, and needs as the basis for good government policy. The state itself was compared to a machine. When properly managed it could regulate society in the interests of increasing its wealth.

Cameralism was taught in eastern European universities to candidates for posts in the state bureaucracy. At the head of the bureaucracy was the ruler, whose job was to see that the machine of government ran smoothly and produced good results. Thus, kings were viewed more as supreme political managers than God-appointed rulers endowed with the sacred authority to govern. Many of the policies of Frederick William I and Frederick II of Prussia, as well as Peter the Great of Russia, were inspired by cameralist principles. Cameralism's emphasis on rational assessment of political needs, along with its conception of government as a well-run machine improving people's lives, fitted into many Enlightenment principles.

In western Europe, greater discussion of politics by ordinary people gave rise to increased popular participation in politics. In Britain, the political turmoil of the seventeenth century, which led to constitutional monarchy and a permanent role for Parliament in shaping government policy, fostered ordinary people's discussion of political affairs. Elections to the House of Commons also stimulated political debate, and, occasionally, commoners with widespread popular support could force the king to accept them as government ministers. In 1757, George II thus accepted **William Pitt the Elder,** though he despised Pitt's insistence that Britain's imperial interests were more important than Hanover's, the German principality from which the king and his father had come. It was Pitt who later masterminded the British victories in the Seven Years' War.

For its part, Parliament tried to shield its debates from the public by forbidding publication of its proceedings. But intense interest in the kingdom's politics, along with the growth of the press, forced Parliament to back down in the early 1770s. With parliamentary proceedings now publicly distributed, popular discussion of politics intensified.

Similar developments also occurred in France. There the monarchy still clung to its absolutist principles, which proclaimed that there was only one political player in the realm, the king. Everyone else was supposed to be a mere spectator watching royal politics from the sidelines. While court etiquette at Versailles and official press accounts of the king's daily activities reinforced this view, it proved increasingly difficult to maintain. Prolonged conflicts between the French king and the parlements over Jansenism, during which the parlements published their grievances, made it clear that others beside the king claimed a political role. The growth of the newspaper press and the rise of rational discussion in new social settings also encouraged the king's subjects to become actively engaged in discussion of policies and events.

In both England and France, therefore, public opinion played a growing role in politics. Its advent constituted a major shift in European political life. Monarchs who had previously argued that they ruled by divine grace and operated in a political world, whose rules could not be understood by the mass of their subjects, now had to contend with a growing chorus of voices commenting on and even criticizing what they did. Although criticism of rulers could lead to charges of treason, it also forced governments to become more open in explaining and justifying their policies. As states made increasing demands on their subjects, rulers were increasingly expected to account for their actions.

Enlightenment Debates

↓ How did ideas about Europe's place in the world change during the Enlightenment?

↓ How did Enlightenment thinkers confront ideas about difference among human beings?

Discussion and debate were at the heart of Enlightenment intellectual life. Debating clubs, where men and women could hear opposing views on subjects of current concern, often addressed the degree of likeness and difference in the human community. The philosophes believed in universal natural laws and a universal human nature. At the same time, they lived in a world where difference separated some people from others and thereby challenged universalism. Debates on human likeness and difference, which raged throughout the eighteenth century, focused especially on three issues: the relation between Europeans and non-Europeans; the institution of slavery; and the relation between men and women.

William Pitt the Elder   (1708–1778) British minister during the Seven Years' War.

This painting of a New Zealand warrior was made by Sydney Parkinson who accompanied James Cook on his first voyage to the South Pacific. It would seem both familiar and odd to Europeans. Their warriors often wore plumes on their hats, but a cape of fluffy flax and dog skins would never be seen on Europe's battlefields. *(Plate XV, "A New Zealand Warrior in His Proper Dress, & Completely Armed, According to Their Manner," from Sydney Parkinson,* Journal of a Voyage to the South Seas. *Department of Special Collections, Charles E. Young Research Library, UCLA)*

Europeans and Non-Europeans

As early as the 1540s, the debate over the humanity of non-European people had pitted Bartolomé de Las Casas against Juan Guinés de Sepúlveda. Las Casas argued that New World Indians were fully human, while Sepúlveda said they were not. In the sixteenth century, Europeans thought of their culture primarily in religious terms; they lived in Christendom, while others were either infidels (Jews and Muslims) or pagans (everyone else). During the Enlightenment, as the debate continued, the terms in which it was conducted started to change. Under the influence of the New Science, natural factors like geology and climate, rather than the traditional religious categories of Christian and non-Christian, were used increasingly to explain diversity in the human community and to shape separate collective identities.

Debate centered on two sets of people: those in the New World and those in the South Pacific. In 1770, a French priest and philosophe, the **Abbé Raynal,** published *The Philosophical History of the Two Indies,* which quickly became a runaway bestseller. Raynal argued, like Sepúlveda, that the Indian natives of the Western Hemisphere were inferior human beings. But Raynal went further, arguing that the natural world in America was as degenerate as the human one. America, he wrote, had been formed later than Europe, rising from the sea in the recent past. This explained why the climate was damp and cold, making New England, which was on the same latitude as Spain, so snowy in winter. This chilly, watery New World produced plants and animals that were puny compared to their counterparts in Europe. Going even further, Raynal stated that Europeans who migrated to North America soon degenerated. Thus, America's geological history produced a climate that was inhospitable to all forms of life.

Raynal's attack provoked a sharp response from the North Americans. In 1781, **Thomas Jefferson** published his *Notes on the State of Virginia,* a spirited refutation of Raynal's work. Was Raynal correct when he wrote that Virginia's Indian men were less manly than Europeans because they had no facial hair? No. The Indians simply chose to pluck out their beards, and such warlike men could not be considered unmanly. Did the New World produce puny animals? No. Look at the newly discovered bones of a huge American elephant, the **mammoth.** Were Americans of European origin degenerate descendants of their ancestors across the ocean? No. Look at **Benjamin Franklin.**

Franklin was Raynal's cleverest opponent. When the Continental Congress sent him to France in 1776 to seek French aid for the American Revolution, he made a point of refuting Raynal at every turn. Franklin's ear-

Abbé Raynal (1713–1796) French priest (*abbé*) and philosophe who argued that the natural world of the Americas was as inferior as its Indian inhabitants.

Thomas Jefferson (1743–1826) American revolutionary and author of the Declaration of Independence who refuted charges of the New World's inferiority to Europe.

mammoths Extinct American elephants of great size whose bones were found in the eighteenth century.

Benjamin Franklin (1706–1790) American revolutionary, diplomat, and scientist who refuted Raynal's claims of American inferiority.

lier experiments with electricity made him the ideal man of science, someone who, like Newton, revealed the workings of nature. His invention of the lightning rod made him the philosophe who worked for the betterment of humanity. At Versailles, Franklin shunned the silks and lace fashionable men favored and dressed in plain brown, presenting himself as a simple American who was, nevertheless, the intellectual equal of any European. The French court was charmed. Franklin was a natural but noble man who showed no trace of deformity. One evening, he and other Americans found themselves at a dinner party with Raynal. When the theory of American degeneracy came up, Franklin asked all the Americans at the table to stand, and then all the Frenchmen. The Americans towered over the French, and especially over Raynal, whom Franklin dismissed as a "mere shrimp." Soon afterward, Raynal retracted his unflattering picture of America. Franklin triumphed again in 1777, when France signed an alliance with the Americans in their war for independence from Britain.

Debate about non-Europeans also focused on the peoples of the South Pacific. In the 1770s, an Englishman, **James Cook,** and a Frenchman, **Louis-Antoine de Bougainville,** led scientific voyages through the region and published accounts of their expeditions, feeding French and British thirst for travel literature. The South Pacific was a new frontier for Europeans, and these accounts sparked interest in the local peoples. Diderot wrote a fictional *Supplement to the Voyage of Bougainville* (1772) in which he used Bougainville's account of Tahitians' free and open sexual activity to attack traditional Christian sexual morality as cruel and unnatural.

Raynal's denunciation of a degenerate America and Diderot's titillating account of the Tahitians' erotic freedom were part of a sustained discussion of European civilization and Europe's proper place in the larger world. One central issue was the nature of civilization itself. Many Europeans continued to think in **Eurocentric** terms and to assert the superiority of their way of life, and most philosophes encouraged this view. Kant declared that the spread of Enlightenment and of reliance on autonomous human reason was a sign that Europeans, after centuries of immaturity, had finally reached adulthood. Voltaire celebrated the refined world of salon conversation, seeing it as a sign of a truly civilized world. But Rousseau attacked civilization as a corrupter of humanity's original goodness and purity. Pointing to the tea and coffee drunk in Enlightenment salons, he claimed that overseas trade and colonies promoted an improper love of luxury and harmed other peoples. Raynal also had his doubts. His depiction of America as an alien and hostile place that Europeans should have avoided arose in part from his belief that colonization had harmed **indigenous people,** as indeed it had. Following their first encounters with Europeans, the native populations of the Americas declined by 90 percent, largely as the result of epidemic diseases that swept through their communities, a demographic catastrophe unparalleled in human history. Diderot's Tahitians also suffered from European intrusion into their world. In the *Supplement,* a Tahitian complains to Bougainville that "the idea of crime and the fear of disease entered among us only with you." Diderot rejected Rousseau's attack on all civilization but agreed that European colonization had introduced corruption and inequality to other peoples.

As philosophes like Rousseau, Raynal, and Diderot debated the nature of non-European peoples and the worth of commerce and colonies, they increasingly sought nonreligious explanations for differences among human beings and tried to articulate a sense of European identity in non-Eurocentric terms. Europe was simply one human community among many others in the world and could make no valid claims for superiority on religious, cultural, or commercial grounds.

Slavery

"We hold these truths to be self-evident: That all men are created equal; that they are endowed by their Creator with certain inalienable rights; that among these are life, liberty, and the pursuit of happiness." These words in one of the Enlightenment's most famous documents, the **Declaration of Independence** (1776), were written by Thomas Jefferson and proclaimed the philosophes' belief in universal **human rights.**

James Cook (1728–1779) Head of three British Royal Society–financed expeditions into the South Pacific.

Louis-Antoine de Bougainville (1729–1811) French explorer in the South Pacific who gave his name to the bougainvillea, a flowering vine he discovered there.

Eurocentric Idea that Europe and European culture are either superior to or more important than the lands and cultures of other peoples.

indigenous people Original inhabitants of a region, or "natives."

Declaration of Independence Document justifying separation of American colonies from Britain in 1776 and defending the theory of self-government.

human rights Rights given to all human beings by God or the natural order and that neither the state nor society may take away.

But Jefferson was a Virginia plantation owner who never freed his slaves. This contradiction lay at the heart of Enlightenment debates over slavery.

By the eighteenth century, trade in slaves from sub-Saharan Africa had gone on for more than a thousand years. During the Middle Ages, Arab traders had brought millions of them into the Islamic world. Beginning in the fourteenth century, the Portuguese brought African slaves to the Atlantic islands. Later Spanish, English, French, and Dutch traders transported Africans to Europe's colonies in the Western Hemisphere, where they worked the plantations that produced the coffee that Europeans drank in their coffeehouses and the sugar that sweetened their tea. By the end of the eighteenth century, 11 million slaves had been forcibly taken to the Americas to labor for the 2 million Europeans who had migrated there. As demand for slave-produced commodities rose, the slave trade rose also, justified again and again with traditional arguments about biblical passages accepting the practice and the subhuman nature of Africans.

The philosophes' attitude toward slavery was mixed. Both Hobbes and Locke endorsed the practice. Although Voltaire had attacked slavery in *Candide,* he came, reluctantly, to accept it as a fact of human life. Montesquieu argued against it, claiming that it undermined a society's moral well-being by oppressing the slaves while giving slave owners too much power. On the other hand, supporters of slavery could point to Montesquieu's argument that the hot, humid climate of the tropics had conditioned the people who lived there to resist work unless forced to do it.

Moral objections had been raised against slavery since the late seventeenth century. In England, several Protestant groups called for its abolition. For example, **Quakers,** who believed that God's "inner light" shone in every human being's heart, argued that the taking of slaves was simply kidnapping and should be stopped, while Quakers in America who owned slaves were urged to free them. Some Anglicans also condemned the trade, arguing that slavery was incompatible with Jesus's gospel of love, despite scriptural passages that sanctioned it. Thus, both Christian and Enlightenment arguments could be made for or against slavery. Over the course of the eighteenth century, however, the balance tipped toward the antislavery position.

Novelists, poets, and playwrights played a crucial role in this development. Writers of fiction took the lead in arousing sympathy for slaves and an imaginative understanding of the conditions in which they lived. One of the first was Aphra Behn. Her novel *Oroonoko,* published in 1688, described the enslavement of an African prince and his beautiful love, Imoinda. Prince Oroonoko is a physically handsome

and morally upright man with an unquenchable love for freedom, while Imoinda displays all the womanly virtues. Showing her readers that Oroonoko and Imoinda possessed the physical traits and moral qualities that Europeans admired, Behn wanted to evoke admiration for them and outrage over their enslavement. Her novel was eventually turned into a play, and its themes were repeated in a growing body of antislavery literature.

Works like *Oroonoko* and later narratives by slaves who escaped to tell their story drew readers into a world in which slaves were upright and blameless human beings who had suffered terrible cruelty and injustice. The effect was to cut through centuries of dehumanizing stereotypes and indifferent or hostile theological traditions. By the late 1780s, both the London Committee for the Abolition of the Slave Trade and the French Society of the Friends of the Blacks were campaigning tirelessly for an end to the slave trade and the abolition of slavery. Although both the trade and slavery itself ended only gradually, the antislavery momentum would not, from this point, be reversed.

Men and Women

The problem of difference and likeness in human beings, which shaped the debate on slavery, was also addressed in debates over the nature and roles of men and women. Women participated actively in the Enlightenment. Those who, like Madame du Deffand, presided over Europe's salons were arbiters of intellectual discussion. Those who, like Aphra Behn, joined men as professional writers became respectable public figures. Women also wrote some of the pamphlets that increasingly shaped public opinion, while others, like Mme. du Chatelet, contributed to the spread of Newtonian science. In the arts, France's most sought-after society painter was a woman, **Elisabeth Vigée-Lebrun.** Women's new social, intellectual, and professional activities raised the issue of similarity and difference between men and women and the proper relations between them.

To Descartes and Locke, it seemed self-evident that men and women not only possessed a common human nature but were intellectual equals. Descartes had

Quakers An English Protestant sect that rejected ceremony and an ordained ministry, relying instead on a mystical "inner light" to guide conscience.
Elisabeth Vigée-Lebrun (1755–1842) French society painter.

coupled his arguments about the power of autonomous human reason with a discussion of the mind's relation to the body. He argued that the two were radically different; humans' bodies were wholly material and were subject to the laws of matter in motion. The mind, however, was nonmaterial. This Cartesian dualism made one thing perfectly clear: mind was not shaped by the body it went with, whether male or female. It floated free in a nonmaterial and, therefore, sexless world. Locke's picture of the human mind pointed to similar conclusions. If the mind was like a blank sheet of paper, there seemed no good reason to argue for different male and female minds, since both were subject to the same stimulus from sense experience.

Many philosophes accepted the implications of Locke's and Descartes' arguments. Diderot did not think that men and women were all that different and agreed with Montesquieu that a woman's sexually based role as a mother was only one part of her life, not its defining characteristic. Voltaire rejected the idea of distinct male and female minds; men and women were intellectual equals, as his collaborator, Mme. du Chatelet, demonstrated.

Acceptance of intellectual equality between men and women, however, did not prevent many philosophes from assigning them separate social roles. Rejecting the traditional idea that men had to rule women because women were prone to irrational and unruly behavior, the philosophes now argued that women should enforce the rules of civilization in society and thereby tame *men's* unruly behavior. The salon hostess performed this task and did so in women's traditional sphere, the household, while other women performed it as mothers who educated their children in proper behavior.

Some philosophes rejected outright the idea of gender equality. Chief among them was Rousseau. Resurrecting old ideas about women's inferiority, Rousseau argued that women were irrational. Above all, they should play no public role in society as salon hostesses or commentators in the realm of public opinion. Their actual roles in this regard were simply another symptom of civilization's corrupting effect. Women belonged at home, breast-feeding their children and obeying their husbands. As creatures of feeling, they played a central role in training children. Men alone, however, should carry on rational discussion and engage in politics.

A growing body of medical literature seemed to support Rousseau's denial of women's equality to men and their banishment from public life. Works by physicians, such as Pierre Roussel's *The Physical and Moral Makeup of Women* (1775), offered a new view of male and female difference that in good Enlightenment fashion claimed to be based on scientific observation. Rejecting the traditional view that women were simply incomplete men, Roussel and others argued that women were completely different from them. For example, their nervous system, which included smaller brains, made it impossible for them to develop men's rational capacities. Their job was to nurture their babies and their husbands.

Rousseau and the medical men found their opponent in Mary Wollstonecraft, the author of *A Vindication of the Rights of Woman* (1792) and the ablest defender of women's equality. Wollstonecraft pointed out the basic paradox of their views on women. These men attacked the despotism of kings and rejected the institution of slavery but endorsed the subordination of some human beings to others on the basis of gender. Wollstonecraft believed with Rousseau that women as mothers should take charge of the moral and emotional education of their children, but she denied that they were inferior to men. If defects existed, she pointed out, they came from the inadequate education women received in a world where the best teaching was available only to men. Wollstonecraft argued that if women were educated with men on an equal basis, their seeming deficiencies would disappear.

In the Enlightenment, ideas about a universal human nature and gender-neutral minds mixed ambiguously with older ideas about women's inferiority and their proper place in the private, domestic sphere. But the debate among people like Rousseau, Roussel, and Wollstonecraft was conducted in increasingly nonreligious terms. Despite their differences, all sides looked less to Christian scripture and traditional church teaching on gender issues and turned instead to biology, psychology, and an examination of social conventions to demonstrate their respective positions.

Cartesian dualism Descartes' idea of the radical difference between material human bodies and nonmaterial human minds.

Mary Wollstonecraft (1759–1797) English writer and feminist who rejected the idea that women were physically and mentally inferior to men.

Summary

Review Questions

⬆ What were the basic differences between traditional Christianity and the New Science on views of God, the natural world, and the human world?

⬆ How did the Enlightenment draw on and expand the method and findings of the Scientific Revolution?

⬆ How did Enlightenment debates reshape Europeans' sense of identity?

The Scientific Revolution changed European views of earth in fundamental ways. No longer were humans at the center of things; now they spun around the sun in an infinite universe. "These vast spaces terrify me," Pascal lamented in his *Pensées (Thoughts).* Many others, however, were excited by the new understanding of the universe. It rested on a scientific method that relied on autonomous human reason and careful observation to demonstrate that it was true, thereby advancing knowledge far beyond anything achieved in the ancient world. So great was the prestige of the New Science that its method was quickly applied to other fields of learning in hopes of turning them into sciences as well.

The application of scientific method to an ever-expanding set of problems was at the heart of the intellectual movement known as the Enlightenment. The philosophes employed autonomous human reason and careful observation to establish the modern disciplines of political science, psychology, and sociology. At the same time, they subjected traditional Christian views on politics, human beings, and human society to systematic criticism. Above all, traditional Christian theology was scrutinized and often rejected, wholly or in part.

The Enlightenment promoted the principle of rational discussion in a variety of ways. Discussion and debate were put into practice firsthand in salons, coffeehouses, Masonic lodges, and debating clubs, where people met as equal intellectual partners regardless of their social backgrounds. As more and more people gathered in these new institutions, the habit of collective discussion of and participation in matters of current interest spread. The growing numbers of books, newspapers, and pamphlets also aided this sense of participation in current affairs as readers learned of debate and discussion going on in other parts of Europe. Although gossip and misinformation jostled uncomfortably with accurate information in this new world of talk and print, participation gradually turned people into a public whose opinions mattered. The growing activity of an engaged public would soon manifest itself in demands for more popular participation in political life, a fact that states recognized when they began appealing to public opinion for support of their policies.

Although rational discussion was central to both the New Science and the Enlightenment, it did not always resolve problems to everyone's satisfaction, as ongoing debates over Europe's place in the world, the nature of non-European peoples, the acceptability of slavery, and issues of gender equality demonstrated. That these debates were conducted in increasingly nonreligious terms indicates a profound shift in western culture and an erosion of Christianity's dominance in Europe's intellectual life.

← Thinking Back, Thinking Ahead →

To what degree do the scientific method of the New Science and the values and agendas of the Enlightenment still shape western people in the twenty-first century?

ECHO ECHO ECHO ECHO ECHO ECHO

Coffeehouses

Coffeehouses were a central Enlightenment institution. They soon came to specialize in certain areas of discussion and information, some offering commercial or political news and others concentrating on reviews of recent plays, poems, and books. Still others were simply places where you could be seen. The famous British insurance company Lloyd's of London began in a coffeehouse. Also in London, by the end of the eighteenth century, some coffeehouses had begun to charge dues for membership, gradually becoming private clubs.

On the continent, public coffeehouses also underwent change. By the late nineteenth century, they were no longer meeting places for men only; whole families would now go to them for coffee and sweets. One of the grandest nineteenth-century coffeehouses was the Café Sacher in Vienna, which offered patrons slices of its famous sacher torte, a chocolate cake with chocolate icing and an apricot filling, topped with whipped cream. In the twentieth century, two Paris coffeehouses, Les Deux Magots and its rival next door, the Café de Flore, became meeting places for famous writers such as the American Ernest Hemingway, the French philosopher Jean-Paul Sartre, and the French feminist Simone de Beauvoir. People still throng their sidewalk tables, trying to recapture something of the earlier intellectual atmosphere.

Today coffeehouses have been rediscovered and are booming throughout the world. Starbucks, which started in Seattle, can now be found across the United States as well as in London and Hong Kong. Independent owners challenge the large franchise chains, and some advertise particular specialties—organic coffee, or fair-trade coffee, or coffee in a Christian atmosphere. Recently, the English magazine *The Economist* suggested that the Internet was a new version of the coffeehouse, serving as a virtual meeting place for the exchange of information, opinion, and gossip. Since the Internet is available in Internet cafés, the old coffeehouse and the virtual one sometimes occupy the same space.

Suggested Readings

Black, Jeremy, and Roy Porter, eds. *The Penguin Dictionary of Eighteenth-Century History.* New York: Penguin, 2001. A useful one-volume handbook.

Gay, Peter. *The Enlightenment: An Interpretation.* 2 vols. New York: Knopf, 1966–1969. A classic interpretation written in a very engaging style.

Henry, John. *The Scientific Revolution and the Origins of Modern Science.* 2nd ed. New York: Palgrave, 2002. A recent introductory account.

Jacob, Margaret C. *The Cultural Meaning of the Scientific Revolution.* New York: Knopf, 1988. An account placing the Scientific Revolution in its larger European cultural context.

_____. *The Enlightenment: A Brief History with Documents.* Boston: Bedford/St. Martin's, 2001. A recent introduction.

Shapin, Steven. *The Scientific Revolution.* Chicago: University of Chicago Press, 1996. An excellent recent analysis.

Voltaire, *Candide.* Edited by Daniel Gordon. Boston: Bedford/St. Martin's, 1999. A recent edition of Voltaire's best-known novel.

Websites

A useful site for the New Science , **Scientific Revolution,** at http://web.clas.ufl.edu/users/rhatch/pages/03-Sci-Rev/SCI-REV-Home

Another site for the New Science, **Scientific Revolution,** at www.fordham.edu/halsall/mod/modsbook09.html

A site for the philosophes, **Enlightenment,** at www.fordham.edu/halsall/mod/modsbook10.html

Index